The Complete Website Upgrade & Maintenance Guide

The Complete Website
Upgrade & Maintenance Guide

Lisa Schmeiser

SYBEX®

San Francisco • Paris • Düsseldorf •Soest

Associate Publisher: Amy Romanoff
Contracts and Licensing Manager: Kristine O'Callaghan
Acquisitions & Developmental Editors: Suzanne Rotondo,
Maureen Adams, Cheryl Applewood
Editors: Davina Baum, Brenda Frink
Technical Editor: B.K. DeLong
Book Designer: Kris Warrenburg Design
Graphic Illustrator: Tony Jonick
Electronic Publishing Specialist: Maureen Forys, Happenstance Type-O-Rama
Production Coordinators: Rebecca Rider, Shannon Murphy
Indexer: Ted Laux
Companion CD: Ginger Warner
Cover Designer: Design Site
Cover Illustrator/Photographer: David Gaz

To Anna R. Schmeiser and Bernadine Nielsen

ACKNOWLEDGMENTS

When I first told my housemates I was about to write a book, and I rattled off how long it was supposed to be, they were both silent. Then, one asked, "Ummm. Is it a picture book?" So it is only appropriate to acknowledge Ian Connolly and Sasha Pave, both of whom tolerated six months of me using the living room as my office away from the office.

I would also like to thank the following people in no particular order:

Elliott Gordon, who possesses both a fabulous sense of humor and a fierce sense of loyalty. David L. Wilson, who kept me from going insane as I was proposing the book. Linda Cicero, Liz Chapin, Todd Elliott, and T[dot]Jay Fowler have all been wonderfully understanding bosses and colleagues, and they're responsible for any intelligent recommendations I made in the book. Thanks also to Monte Goodee for his continued humor and superlative sysadmin skills, both of which he shared freely. My coworkers at Studio Verso, and my ex-colleagues from Wired Digital also deserve a big thank you.

Cliff Maier has been patiently helping me with my scripting questions since 1995, and his friendship is truly appreciated.

Dale Macmurdy, Matt Barnes, Katherine Groeninger, Lynne Cooke, Amelia Deloach, and Michael and Molly Klein are all valuable friends who helped me keep whatever shredded sanity I have left. Jenn Sweigart, who has ten years' worth of mutual sanity check experience behind her, repeatedly demonstrated her ESP abilities by sending cards and e-mail just when I needed a lift.

Philip Michaels has been the most pleasant surprise I've encountered during the writing of this book.

My parents, Raymond and Anna Schmeiser, have been wonderful word-of-mouth marketers for all of my writing, and their unwavering support is most appreciated, as is my brother's offbeat brand of sympathy—the homespun wisdom, "When life hands you lemons, throw them at the doctor."

David L. Rogelberg is Super Agent, and I owe my introduction to David to Steve Weiss.

B.K. DeLong did a heroic job checking the technical accuracy of the book, and Ann Navarro lent her eagle eye at the end of the project.

And then there are the wonderful people at Sybex who midwifed this project: Suzanne Rotondo acted as the initial editor and advocate for this project, and did an extraordinary job. Brenda Frink brought some key editorial refocusing in the midst of the project, and Davina Baum stepped in with a clear editing eye and a much-needed morale lift at the end. Maureen Adams steered the entire project with patience, as did Amy Romanoff and Cheryl Applewood. Other Sybexians provided crucial behind-the-scenes support: Rebecca Rider, Shannon Murphy, Maureen Forys, Heather O'Connor, Tony Jonick, Ginger Warner, and Dann McDorman.

CONTENTS AT A GLANCE

Part IV: **Exploring the Cutting Edge**

Appendices

TABLE OF CONTENTS

PART III   Moving from Static to Dynamic Website Production

11   Applying the Document Object Model (DOM) to Your Site   **387**

12   Moving Data between You and a User: Forms   **419**

Appendices

INTRODUCTION

I decided to write this book because I'm really lazy.

No, really. I've been slinging code for various websites for about five years, and the one thing that stands out in my mind, above the sea of CGI scripts and DHTML and W3C specs, is that I end up doing a lot of work over and over and *over*. And as much as I love Web development, I don't love it enough to cheerfully submit to repetitive tasks.

Let's face it: Building a site from scratch can be rewarding. Changing the copyright date on 200 discrete pages is tedious and eye-crossing, to say the least; rebuilding all 200 pages is an exercise in masochism. Clearly, it's in your best interest to make your job more rewarding and less repetitive.

How? *Get lazy.* Don't look at your website as "just 20 pages" to toss up over the course of a week. Look at it as a long-running project, a testament to your skill and foresight. Look at it as a challenge, to build something that you can expand the scope of with no effort at all. Most importantly, look at your website as something where the working mantra should be, "Work smarter, not harder."

That's where this book comes in. Now that the Web development industry is a few years old, some of us sitting in the code trenches have found sound strategies for building sites that can be maintained with little effort, or renovated with relative ease. This book passes on what I've learned from my mistakes, so you don't have to repeat them.

Most importantly, this book focuses on how to improve the site you've already got, instead of suggesting that you build your site from scratch.

Why You Should Buy This Book

A lot of Web development articles and books assume that you have some sort of control over the site—from when it should be built to how it should be structured to how it should be designed. This book assumes nothing of the sort. Instead, I figure you've probably inherited a site from someone else, and your job is to perform miracles on an already existing nest of files.

This book is an extended cheatsheet for all those miracles you have to pull off. You'll find something in it for you if you do any of the following:

- Plan a site's structure, information architecture, or predicted growth

- Implement or report on advertising and commerce on a website

- Maintain large-scale sites

- Create or maintain portable sites for clients

- Build and maintain websites in "nonwired" settings

- Wear the hats of designer, programmer, and producer on one site

- Inherit a site—with no documentation—from a long-departed predecessor

How This Book Is Organized

The book is divided into four separate parts:

Part I, "Getting Started," is a crash course in thinking ahead. You'll find five chapters chock-full of the strategies and questions Web developers should have firmly in hand before beginning any type of Web work. From determining your site's reason for being, to deciding whether or not to build your own tools, to setting up your own servers and backend—this section is the groundwork for the philosophy I try to maintain through the book.

Part II, "Building on the Foundation," covers all of the skills that contribute to a strong technical base for any site. If Part I is the brainwork that goes into overhauling a site, Part II is the work you'll do to ensure smooth coasting later. Hey—being lazy takes some initial effort. Here, you'll find the smartest ways to create lightweight, effective, and usable designs, and you'll be given a technical toolbox for your own site tune-ups. The section ends with a case study where I walk you through three iterations of a site, from inception to fully tricked-out leading-edge code.

Part III, "Moving from Static to Dynamic Website Production," takes those technical and cognitive skills from the first two sections, and demonstrates how to use them to nudge your site from a series of static pages to a collection of dynamically-generated pages that can maximize your site content with minimal additional production. I'll cover the shift in site building strategies from "flat" documents to script-controlled objects, give you a primer on using scripting to template your own site production, and deal with some issues that tend to raise their head during a site's adolescence: advertising and universal accessibility. I'll close out this part by looking at two more case studies, again following the path of a site from inception to of-the-moment code iterations.

Finally, in the last part, "Exploring the Cutting Edge," I'll look at the likely directions in which you'll be expending future upgrade and maintenance efforts. This part will cover the organizational changes XML will wreak in site structure and page markup and the likely technical trends in daily website work like version control systems and streaming multimedia markup languages. I'll also be looking at the burgeoning field of intranets and extranets, and how Web technologies are the new killer app in the workplace. I'll wrap up the part with a final case study—one that uses newer technologies to work around a sudden change in workflow requirements.

Fortunately, you don't have to read these sections sequentially to find what you want. Just skip to the chapter covering what you are most interested in and what is most relevant to you and your work.

A Deeper Look: The Case Studies

One of my biggest kvetches with learning new technologies is that frequently I don't have a chance to assess how they affect my site as I'm reading through the spec, the tutorial, or an article. I decided that the source code in the book would all demonstrate how some elements can change over time while some elements can be recycled.

There are three case study chapters in the book, and four websites that were built. Each website case study has the following:

Building criteria   Each study starts off with a different premise: a contractor building a portable site for a client, a lone intern building a site for an under-funded organization, two hopeful start-up employees building a saleable product, and an editorial/design duo producing a magazine online.

Conditions for change   Each site is compelled to redesign and relaunch for reasons as ordinary as boredom or as market-driven as identifying a new niche. Each study looks at how these reasons drive technical decisions.

Complete scripts and HTML   In addition to explanatory excerpts and how-tos, you'll be able to see all the code from each site, or download the site from the CD-ROM.

An emphasis on laziness   I'm a big fan of recycling—everything from the myriad cases of diet soda I drank writing this, to the code I wrote as I sucked down yet another 12 ounces of caffeine. All the sites are designed to show you how easy it is to build a recyclable site during redesigns.

What's on the CD

Added bonus! That's right: with this book comes a CD-ROM chock full of fantastic products, including:

- Adobe After Effects and Premier
- Allaire HomeSite
- The Apache server
- Boutell MapEdit
- Equilibrium DeBabelizer
- Macromedia Dreamweaver
- Nico Mak WinZip
- Ulead GIF Animator

These are all products that I've found indispensable in my Web travels; check them out to see how they can help you.

In addition to these, you'll find all the source code from the book, including the case studies. This way, you'll be able to muck around in the files I've written about and get a hands-on look at the stuff on the printed page. So you'll see numerous sections of code that have headings.

I_am_code.html

```
<!--I can be any sort of code, and I am found on the companion CD-ROM-->
```

They can be found on the CD in their appropriate chapter folder, with their assigned name.

One Last Word

Being lazy doesn't excuse doing a poor job. Being lazy in the context of Web development is finding a best practice in a highly fluid field.

One of the things that keeps me perpetually enamored of Web design is how it makes you stretch your brain creatively to come up with elegant solutions for complex problems. I hope this book inspires you to come up with some elegant and efficient laziness of your own.

I'd love to hear how this book works for you. Don't hesitate to visit me online at http://www.schmeiser.com/, or e-mail me at lisa@schmeiser.com.

And now, go forth and upgrade.

PART I

Getting Started

CHAPTER
ONE

Building a Smarter Website through Upgrade and Maintenance

- The importance of planning

- Avoiding trouble via maintenance

- Understanding upgrading

- Leaping obstacles

The central problem in most website development processes is that everybody believes the site will be done once it is launched. This is a mistake. Websites are never done, they're only launched. Unlike books, which appear in a fixed physical medium, or broadcast, which is only shown once, websites can persist indefinitely but the tools used to make them can degrade over time. Maintaining a website is inevitable. If you go into your job *expecting* to maintain and upgrade, not only will you be better equipped to deal with problems as they arise, you'll also be in the position to make suggestions that guide the site over time; this can make your life as a site developer/manager a lot less stressful and more interesting.

The good news is that websites combine the best features of print media and software products. They provide content within a functional interface, creating a tool for the user to learn or be entertained. For the user, websites combine the functionality of a software tool with the permanence of print media. Websites are like print media in providing a lot of rich, readable content quickly. You can return to specific pages again and again, which echoes the permanence of a book. Websites are like software in that some websites act as tools, proving users with a way to search for specific information or calculate data. For the website designer, websites do combine the quick deadlines you find in print media with the line-by-line code you find in software development.

The bad news is that websites also combine the worst of print media and software products. Like print media, Web development has tight deadlines. Like software development, Web development is fraught with bugs. There is often an unfortunate split in developers' workloads: they spend half their time fixing code that is broken and the other half producing code that may break later. Websites' compressed schedules makes it difficult for project managers to build in software's traditional development steps, especially user testing and quality assurance.

Because most websites are launched, or continuously produced, in a relatively short time period, there's a lot that can go wrong: A link-checking script guaranteed to find all the dead links on a site can choke on the odd syntax you used to generate URLs. Cleaning up seemingly redundant directories can lead to the sudden disappearance of your navigation bar on a third of the site. The incredibly well-researched link list you posted a year ago can produce more 404s than live links. (A 404 is a server error message that tells the user the file they wanted to display in the browser no longer exists.)

It's tempting to chuck the whole site and start again. Don't do it. You'll only be buying into the common myth that mistakes on websites are easily fixed by creating a new website. And, you won't have addressed the central problem in website development: By definition, websites are constantly evolving, so you need to build a solid foundation to prevent excessive future work. The time you spend hashing out the information architecture in a site, or settling a technical policy, will save you the time and effort of re-creating the site from scratch.

Myth #1: It Is Better to Toss Than to Fix

There is a myth about websites that needs to be dispelled before we go any further: It's easier to create a new website when you run into problems than it is to fix the old one.

Not true.

For one thing, not all website problems are related to old or faulty technology, so you may be repeating organizational or content problems.

Second, no website is ever going to be finished. Newer and better technology debuts on the market all the time. As a website developer, you have a professional interest in making sure you are using the best tools to do your job. You do have the option of using the latest tools to rebuild your site every year, but why bother doing boring, repetitive, detail-oriented work in trying to transfer all the old content to a shiny new format? Why not just build a product that performs well and only needs slight fine-tuning?

Don't look at website maintenance or upgrade work as a criticism of the original site. All sites need attention, all the time. If you plan for this, you can prevent having to rebuild your site over and over.

How to Plan Ahead When Everything Changes So Quickly

Planning ahead is obviously going to save you some last-minute panic, but it can be extremely difficult. Many Web developers and project managers don't have a lot of time to meet their deadlines, so it can be difficult to try and set aside time to plan things in excruciating detail before writing code. Subsequently, there is the temptation to skip over planning ahead, and move on to writing code that responds to a specific request.

Myth #2: It's Better to Plan *While* You're Working, Not Before

When you're on a really tight deadline, the temptation to begin coding immediately is very strong. This is understandable: As HTML grows more complex and the number of browser-computer combinations grows more varied, Web developers are discovering more bugs in their beta products than ever before.

However, if you plan ahead, you might save yourself several rounds of bug testing. Your team members and you will also have a better idea of what the finished site is supposed to do and what browsers and computers the site performs best under.

Even if you only spend an hour establishing your goals for this round of site development and how you plan to accomplish those goals, it's better than not planning at all.

Since so few websites are planned ahead, most production is done as a reaction to an established problem. You want to avoid that treadmill and start developing your site so you can anticipate problems.

So how do you move from a purely reactionary state of development to a state of planned chaos? The key is *not* in planning *every* element of your site but in planning ahead with regard to only what's going to affect you the most.

Plan your site maintenance relative to what you can reasonably do to prevent future errors. This may mean checking every page on your site any time the ad serving system pushes out new data; it may mean running searches on your site's search engine and checking all the results to see what dead links there are in your search database or on your site.

You should also perform your site upgrades relative to the effort they will require. You need to balance the results of the upgrade against the effort it will require to implement and against any extra work you will have to do to integrate it into the site. Remember: Every upgrade eventually evolves into a site element to be maintained.

Maintaining Your Website

You maintain your website for the same reason you maintain your automobile—you want it to perform well. A website should load quickly, all of the parts (text, graphics, hyperlinks, and applets) should work when requested, and the user should be able to perform tasks without interference.

Maintaining a site will help you to spot trouble before it blindsides you. If you notice that the site map is not being updated to reflect the additions you've made over a week, you can take short-term and long-term steps to correct the problem:

- In the short term, fix the site map so it reflects the latest content. Incorporate a site map check into your daily routine.

- In the longer term, find out what the process is for updating the site map and identify the steps that need to be taken to ensure that this updating continues.

Maintaining a website also makes the eventual and inevitable upgrades less difficult. As you maintain a site over time, you'll build a solid quality control process, so it will be easier to do massive search-and-replace revision to the files because you will already know where any exceptions are. You'll also be less likely to discover coding errors during upgrades because you'll already have fixed them. Finally, you may find that the document and site structure are solid enough to be left intact, and the scope of the upgrade may be reduced.

Site maintenance allows you to expend a little effort intermittently so you don't have to deal with an enormous workload over a long period. Setting up and integrating a new way to serve navigation bars can be a project done in increments. The results enhance the performance of the site for the user and clean up the backend for you. The process requires less intensive work than reorganizing and redesigning the site because nobody knows how to navigate from section to section.

A final benefit to regularly maintaining a website is a human resources benefit. When you maintain a website, you have a list of identified site production tasks and a history of work over the lifespan of the site. These two items can provide critical background for new employees, and thus allow them to work more effectively and quickly.

What Does Performing Maintenance Entail?

What exactly comprises "maintaining" a website? Some people define it as adding new content. Others tie it closely to quality assurance measures; for instance, a production editor may do site maintenance by checking all just-published material on the live site against the same material on the staging server to make sure the correct files are live.

Maintenance does not have to be tedious. It can be an exercise in detective work, especially if you're dealing with a very large or very old website. It can be a way to reacquaint yourself with the content on your site, especially if you have to check it. Or, it can be a way to set up and enforce standards.

Website maintenance is going to be extremely detail oriented, which is the flip side to detective work. The problems are fascinating, but the troubleshooting process involves a lot of close attention. You will need to check the consistency of your code on the backend; this sort of syntactical consistency will allow you to write scripts that maintain or upgrade your code for you later. You will need to check the consistency of code standards across your site. For example, early browsers didn't support width or height attributes for any image tags; later browsers do, and it makes a difference in the speed with which an image is rendered. Check your tags and code chunks to make sure they comply with a uniform level of HTML standards.

You'll also need to check the backend of your site. If you are running scripts to upgrade or maintain old files, check for the backup copies of the files altered, or for invisible pre-live copies in old files, or for duplicate files. Try to make your directories as lightweight as possible. This way, when you do have to do detective work, there's less material to review.

The strategies above are only a few ways to approach maintaining your site. The principles upon which you should base your own maintenance routines are code performance, code details, interface details, and overall site quality assurance.

How Do You Know When It's Time to Maintain a Website?

Unless you're a member of the small and annoying statistical minority that never procrastinates, you're probably used to doing a lot of your work, including website maintenance, at the last minute. Typical website maintenance consists of:

1. Discovering the problem
2. Investigating the scope of the problem
3. Fixing the problem

In other words, maintenance is not internally driven. Most site developers are too busy fixing the problems they know about to go looking for more. If a page is faulty, you can change it whenever you want. That means, by extension, that you can change it only when you have to.

Lose this type of cause-and-effect thinking. It's one of the reasons that a compact site turns into a sprawl of unrelated files or ends up with three different types of layout, design, and navigation. It's also why a lot of sites have given up on organizing their older content and thus lose a lot of opportunities to crosslink old and new content or fully exploit the depth of their content.

Performing a Maintenance Check

The real question is, how do you know when to perform a maintenance check on your site? The most immediate indication that it's time to run a check is when you do a breakdown of your or your developers' workdays and you realize that you're spending more time fixing things that are broken than you do developing new material.

If this is the case, put out the latest fire, then try to find trends in the types of errors you're fixing. Can they be linked to content published during a particular product launch? Are they unrelated functional errors but all linked to a particular time of content creation or revision? If you can find a pattern, you're lucky. You can begin basing a regular maintenance routine on the characteristic causing most of the breaks and move out from there.

Other ways to decide may be based on your website development scheme. If you're planning on adding new content to an already-constructed site, you have a perfect opportunity to examine both the process you use to add the new pages and the effect the new material has on the already-existing site. You'll need to see whether or not the new material affects the existing site in any way. If you publish frequently, you may want to take time to focus on known troublespots in your publishing routine as a preventive effort. For example, if you notice that the press releases you've been adding to your site are not being added to the site's archive or search engine, you'll need to see how you can automatically update the archive and search engine, and you'll need to build those technical steps into your production routine.

There are no hard-and-fast criteria for deciding when to do maintenance on your site; you can best decide that based on when you publish and what problems are cropping up with your current site.

What You Should Maintain Regularly

No website is going to remain frozen in time after you push it live to the public. There are elements of every page, across the site, that you will need to maintain to ensure that your site is performing well:

- The first item on your maintenance list is the performance of every page on your site. If you update the site frequently, you need to make a habit of checking all of the new content as it is posted live. Check to make sure that all of the hyperlinks work, that the formatting is correct, and that the new content does not cut off or eliminate the user's access to older content. The goals here are twofold: You want to make sure that your new content is correct once it's pushed live, and you want to make sure the new content does not affect how your users navigate through the site.

- You should always maintain any navigation devices you have on your pages. This includes the navigation bar and more specific intrapage navigation. For example, suppose you've produced a number of stories that hyperlink back to old stories. You'll need to periodically check to ensure that those hyperlink destinations within the site are still accurate. You'll also need to note what files reference links within the site—if you decide to reorganize the site, you want to be sure that none of the content is adversely affected.

- Be sure to check and maintain legal notices and points of contact. Copyright notices should be sitewide and should be updated to reflect the most current year. There should be reliable, working addresses listed on your site for users.

- You will also want to perform backend maintenance, which can include checking file and directory structures to ensure that old or unused code and graphics aren't getting copied to new directories; checking that the file paths for all scripts, graphics, and other files are consistent; and checking the total file size of pages as they load; or reformatting old code to meet the same standards as your current content.

NOTE For example, you might decide that your navigation bars need backend maintenance: If you recently decided to use a server-side include (a discrete chunk of code that can be called by several pages and formatted as HTML) to format your navigation bars, you might decide to go back to the older site pages and retrofit the new code so all the pages have the same level of performance.

- You will also need to undertake large-scale maintenance projects. When a new browser version or HTML standard debuts on the market, you will need to test your site to see if it still performs well on the new software. You'll also need to diagnose and repair any problems you notice with the site's appearance and performance over various browser versions.

Maintaining a website is a lot like maintaining an automobile. There are small, low-effort tasks that you'll perform frequently and large, intensive tasks you'll perform intermittently.

How Do You Decide *What* to Maintain?

Start by assessing the importance of the repairs you're making relative to the site as a whole. If you're sinking time into fixing the linking scheme on your search engine results, how integral is the search engine to the rest of your site? How frequently is it used? Does checking and tweaking the code regularly take the same amount of time and effort as a one-time fix upon breaking?

You may also want to weigh the effort made to maintain code against the effort it would take to completely replace it.

For example, back in 1995, the hottest way to create pages that responded to user queries was to use a scripting technology called CGI scripting. CGI stands for *common gateway interface*—every server has a CGI that lets it talk to the user's browser. In order to create pages on the fly, the server read a bunch of a variables from the browser, ran those variables through a script designed to handle CGI variables, then spit out a page based on those variables.

If you look at any search engine URL, you'll usually see something like `http://search .yahoo.com/bin/search?p=verso%2c+web+design`. The stuff after the ? is composed of different variables. While building pages on variables is great for direct question-and-answer transactions, it's not a smart way to build persistent, printable URLs for your site.

So why did developers use CGI scripts to build pages? They did it because they can use those variables to control the color scheme of a page, the ads a user sees on a page, even the links the user will see if they hit the forward or back buttons. But most of these things can now be accomplished by using different, less server-intensive technologies. I'll discuss those strategies in subsequent sections of the book.

Upgrading Your Website

Sometimes, performing measures to maintain code is more trouble than simply rewriting the code to perform more functions in fewer lines. If you discover that the website's maintenance routines all lead to elaborately coded work-arounds, it's time to cease doing maintenance on a site and start upgrading.

What Does Performing Upgrades Entail?

There are three main kinds of upgrades you can perform:

- The first type of upgrade is a backend upgrade. This type of upgrade makes the files and code behind the site much more efficient. The goals are to make production run more smoothly, to decrease any chance of redundant site elements, and to streamline the countless files living on the server.

- Another type of upgrade may focus on the HTML and scripts that compose the site. You may want to rewrite your pages so the parts are easily broken down into separate, easily templated parts. You may want to rework your HTML so it's compliant with the latest HTML specification. Or, you may want to write HTML that guarantees that the site looks similar across a wide variety of different browsers and platforms.

- Still another type of site upgrade entails completely changing the look and feel of your site. You may focus exclusively on the graphics, color scheme, and layout that comprise your site.

The primary difference between site maintenance and site upgrade is that site maintenance seeks to optimize and sustain an existing website product, and a site upgrade seeks to change an integral site element in order to dramatically improve the overall quality of the site. An upgrade is a step above and beyond site maintenance.

NOTE   Site upgrades should be done less frequently than site maintenance; once you've developed an effective maintenance schedule, upgrades should be done only to retain or improve a competitive edge or to improve overall site performance. Think of your website upgrades as intelligent, controlled development, meant to contribute to the never-finished website.

How Do You Know When It's Time to Upgrade a Website?

There are a few clear signs that will tell you when it's time to upgrade your site. The most obvious externally driven sign is that your primary competitor just overhauled theirs and it out-performs yours. However, most upgrade signs are internal. They include:

- Aggregating enough content to reorganize the site's content structure

- Deciding to adopt a new HTML standard or backend technology

- Adding a new content area to your site

- Adding a new type of user-based functionality, like a search engine or customizable front door

- Realizing that the code you're using to maintain a site is so convoluted that it makes sense just to scrap it and start over

Note that the key word in this section is "upgrade," not "rewrite." You want to be able to do your new development within the framework of the existing site. You want to be able to exploit old code and content as much as possible. You also want to be able to implement the upgrades in controlled stages, so you can ensure that each new chunk of code helps the site more than it hurts the site.

Upgrade should be synonymous with *improvement*. It should not mean the creation of a new site—that's a different process, and you're probably already fluent in how to do that. Upgrading a site is modifying the site you already have. It may mean redoing the look and feel of the interface, integrating a database system to track your advertising delivery, or modifying your archive to automatically update after every publishing period.

In other words, it's time to upgrade when you're not satisfied with the way your current website looks or operates. Remember, a website is never finished.

Obstacles to Implementing Maintenance or Initiating Development

There are a number of obstacles standing between you and a regular site maintenance regime. Time, money, personnel, and organizational support can all conspire against your efforts to keep your website fresh and fast-performing. Of these four obstacles, personnel shortage and organizational support are the most prohibitive.

Personnel Shortages

In many nontechnical organizations, there is one designated "Webbie." That person must act as designer, developer, and sysadmin for a site, which makes an impressive workload. In addition, the sprawling, constant nature of website development and the frequent changes in site development standards and tools make keeping up with the industry while keeping up with work challenging.

Another personnel shortage may be due to having contracted the website out to a third party. Unless specified in the business agreement, the outside developers' responsibility ends when they drop the final code; what to add to the site and how to add it are left to the in-house staff.

Third-party development can also cause a kind of personnel shortage that affects how you upgrade your site. If a very small group of people understand the logic or pressures that drove the development of the first site, you either need to retain those same people or find someone who can puzzle out the development rationale before you begin rewriting code. This is a good argument for building maintenance and documentation into a contractor's work agreement.

TIP   If you're a contractor, offering to do future maintenance should be a strong selling point for your services, as it will guarantee the longevity of your work. It is much less time consuming to fine-tune an existing site when all of the team members assigned to it are already familiar with the information architecture and the nuts and bolts used to assemble the site.

Another personnel obstacle hindering maintenance or upgrades is a lack of prior knowledge, especially if you did inherit the site from people who are no longer around. Everyone has their personal set of reasons governing their development decisions: One person may be a strict HTML purist who cares very deeply about the structural integrity; another may argue that the site's client-end appearance is much more important than the orderliness of the code on the backend. There may be idiosyncratic kludges that correspond to no-longer-existing standards, software, or organizational policies. Unless everything is very well documented, it's hard to tell. Given that most development is done with an extremely rapid turnaround, the odds are against complete documentation on every site component.

Another personnel obstacle hindering site maintenance or upgrading is a lack of consistency in development processes. This is usually more of a problem on sites that have several discrete areas, especially if each new area was added over time. But it may also be a problem on smaller-scale sites, or sites maintained by one person: as you need to add new content, redesign the interface, or fix a bug in the code, you do so with the latest and greatest code, but you don't ramp up the rest of your code to correspond to your standards. Or, the types of content each individual section in your site offers all differ dramatically, so the production method is optimized to produce the content, rather than try to fit the content into a pre-established site development process.

All of these obstacles are quite understandable, and none are entirely avoidable. You can try to lessen the severity of each by evaluating whether consistency or efficiency of process is more important. You may still be able to set standards within several highly individual processes, without losing the characteristics that make each separate development process the best possible for its site. When you note how a site is produced or what the reasons were for producing it a certain way, add data and a contact name for each revision or addition.

Organizational Support

Ultimately, there are two groups involved in website development: those who think of a site and its features and those who build that site. Sometimes they're the same person; more often they're not. As website development is integrated into more traditional workplaces, or Web-driven companies hunker down and start getting down to the business of making money, a Web developer who used to work without a lot of direct supervision may find themselves being managed by someone who doesn't have the same Webbie background. Unfortunately, the rapid development pace that characterizes the Web leaves ample opportunity for either a manager or a developer to cause a Dilbert-like situation where managers and developers just don't speak the same language.

It may not be entirely reasonable to expect a programmer and a project manager to speak the same language. Each performs very different functions at work, and it's safe to say each has a different set of skills that led them to the job they hold. However, project managers and developers usually end up working together. So try to make the best of the situation.

Agree on your project goals early on, and touch base often to make sure those goals haven't changed unbeknownst to one party or the other. Do not hesitate to speak up and tell the other party what you need. It may be a brutal process at first, but it will prevent a lot of late-night-deadline resentment, delays on the project, or crash-and-burn failures. If neither one of you is open to hearing what the other side has to say, step back and reconsider.

If You're a Developer

If you're a developer, you may think you were hired to build websites. In reality, you have two jobs:

- First, you have to find the best way to build the site.

- Second, you have to find a good way to communicate how you do your job to management.

You frequently don't have the same vocabulary as your boss. Remember to define highly specific technical jargon in approachable terms. Telling your boss there's a permissions breach in the CGI directory may not have the same impact as saying that the search engine script is causing a security leak. When you have a problem, it's not enough just to say, "I have a problem." You also need to explain why it's a problem and how it came to be a problem. Although you may have a great grasp of the technical glitches that lead to website errors, you'll need to reconstruct them for your bosses so they can begin to get a well-rounded picture of what you do on the job and how they can improve your circumstances so you can do a better job.

The most important thing you can do for your managers is develop a common vocabulary. Make sure you and your manager both understand the technical definitions you take for granted and be sure to reiterate those definitions until your manager starts using them with ease.

TIP   No one in management is out to get you. They have to answer to a higher power than you: a vice president or regional suit who may be even further removed from the coding trenches than they are.

Remember that your managers just want to get a good job done on time. You may need to make a special effort to communicate what sort of resources and effort it will take to deliver what they want, when they want it. Make that effort early on, and you probably won't have to reiterate with profanity later on.

Be flexible; you don't know when you're going to find yourself writing regular expressions on Sunday night to get the job done or being tapped to head a new project thanks to your diligence in your last coding gig.

If You're a Manager

If you're a manager, you speak a different vocabulary than many Web developers. While you may have to devote a lot of your time to learning more acronyms than you thought possible, the payback will be the start of a common vocabulary. You can use this vocabulary to begin to get a more well-balanced picture of what your team can do and what they need you to do for them.

In return, share some of your vocabulary with your developers. They need to know what you mean by "deadline," "delivery," and "benchmark." They also need to understand the organizational context of the deadlines and goals you're requesting. A 60-page site overhaul requested with a two-day turnaround seems like the request of a clinically insane boss; a 60-page site overhaul with a two-day turnaround because the CEO will be using the site in her annual address to the Board of Directors lends context to the request.

TIP

The developers don't secretly meet and plot to sabotage your career. Nor do they throw around all of those acronyms to try and confuse you. You usually focus on what a project is; they focus on how to get it done, and those acronyms are part of the toolbox they'll use to do the job.

They're in a position to assess how well they'll be able to do their job under the current circumstances and how much better they could do their job if their circumstances improved. Offer them a chance to share what they know. And remember that the Web is a very new industry. Most of the workers are new at development in this constantly-shifting medium.

Summary

No website is ever done; it just requires more or different work. This chapter outlined some of the questions you should be asking yourself if you want to maintain your website without losing your mind. There are two alternatives to rebuilding your site from the ground up: maintaining the current site or upgrading it a piece at a time. You should be able to detect when one or the other is appropriate and begin overhauling your work processes to incorporate maintenance or upgrades.

The next chapter outlines some of the questions you should answer before you begin to do any further work on your website. These questions will help you define what you want to do with your already-existing site and how you should go about doing it.

CHAPTER
TWO

Asking the Right Questions about Website Development

- Considering the idea questions

- Considering the implementation questions

- Considering the technology questions

Website building is not like barn raising. For one thing, it frequently takes longer than a day; for another, websites, unlike barns, are never finished products. You've been charged with maintaining or upgrading a product. You need to find a way to combine the corporate-mission speak with the code and produce something at the end of a URL that is usable, compelling, and compliant with the reason you're doing all this work in the first place.

This chapter showcases questions any site developer should be asking themselves and should have answered before typing the first set of HTML tags. The questions are divided into three catagories: idea, implementation, and technology. Idea questions exist to help you get a firm grasp on why you're building your website; implementation questions exist to help you figure out how you're going to do it. Technology questions nail the issue down even further, by providing concrete solutions.

A final word about these questions: it helps if you ask them in a large group. Asking yourself is not going to be as eye-opening or insightful an experience as asking a varied audience. Don't hesitate to bring everyone into this process: What your marketing people perceive as the target audience might come as a surprise to your editorial staff; what user experience your designers envision might be well beyond the limits of Moore's Law.

NOTE Coined by Intel co-founder Gordon Moore, his namesake law states: The speed of a computer microprocessor will double every 18 months. Remarkably, the prediction was made 30 years ago, and has remained mostly true. Moore's Law is often used to illustrate the ever-accelerating pace of high-tech development.

Bringing team members from every different area only seems like you're asking for trouble. In the end, you'll all have a much better, much more well-rounded idea of what you all want to do for the user, how you all can assist each other in reaching your goals, and what is possible for you to deliver.

And now, on to the questions.

The Idea Questions

The questions listed below are meant to help you wrap your brain around every possible reason you're building your website. If you answer them all up front, the answers can act as a mission statement that takes you through several rounds of revision.

Why Is My Organization Maintaining or Upgrading a Website?

The initial purpose for developing a website is moot: Everyone has one, and they have one either because they wanted to colonize a new medium, or because everyone else had a website and they didn't want to feel left out. The question for today is: why bother with the website you have?

Websites cost money. They require people, server space, bandwidth, and constant maintenance. Websites are a hybrid between time-driven media like broadcast, and performance-driven tools like software. Subsequently, websites frequently combine the worst characteristics of both software and media: short deadlines, performance based on user interaction, and no fixed finishing point.

This doesn't mean you should pitch the website and return to life pre-WWW. This means that you should understand that websites aren't effortless. They suck up both time and money. Websites can also be incredibly rewarding: they can raise brand-name awareness, act as a public gateway for mail-order businesses, or provide a creative or informative space for writers, programmers, and artists. Your job is to identify what you want out of your website so you can get the maximum product for your time and money.

If your organization is making a decision to maintain a website, it's because the website is necessary to some facet of the business your organization does. Figure out what that facet is, and how this iteration of the website can further assist or improve this facet.

What Is the Purpose of My Site: To Inform, to Teach, to Guide, or to Act as a Resource?

On a very fundamental level, every website is about information. The difference between each website is the level of that information relative to the audience's knowledge level, and the way that the information is presented to the audience. Sometimes, you're building your website as a way of contributing information to a pool already started by your peers; sometimes, you're building a site to instruct an audience that may not be as well-versed in a topic as you.

For example, there is a difference in purpose between the W3C (http://www.w3c.org/) and HotWired's Webmonkey channel (http://www.hotwired.com/webmonkey/). The Webmonkey site is developed as a resource for Web developers who are assessing new technologies and learning how to use them for their sites. The W3C site is a resource for the people who are writing and creating the new

technologies that the Webmonkey site will later write about. Both sites deal with
Web development, but one chooses to play an explanatory role and the other
chooses to play a reference role. You can see just how different these two sites are: in
Figure 2.1, Webmonkey sets up its information as a series of topics that the reader
may be interested in, and in Figure 2.2, the W3C lists its information as a series of
organized topics, much like a card catalog.

FIGURE 2.1:

The Webmonkey front door

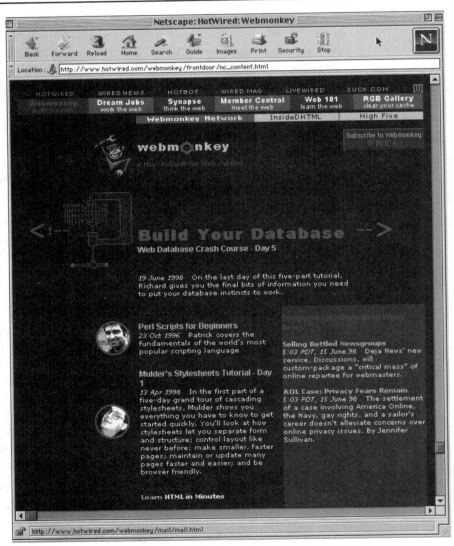

FIGURE 2.2:

The W3C front door

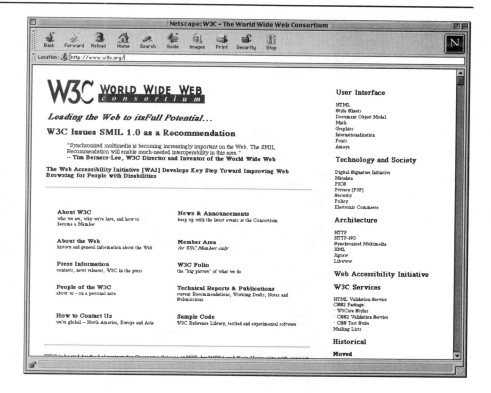

Your site also has information to offer. There are four typical ways in which that information is going to reach the reader:

- Data the reader will apply to a project independent from the website

- Information the reader will learn as a result of having visited the website

- Instructions to be followed to complete a specific task

- A reference resource to handle further acquisition and application of information

The following sections will breakdown each of these four roles that websites play.

Websites That Inform

Readers visit informative sites to augment an already-existing knowledge base. They want unique data, couched in the context and vocabulary of a field they already know about. Websites housing the academic or trade journals for specific disciplines are informative sites. They presuppose both prior interest and prior knowledge of the field that the site explores. Informing sites aren't the exclusive province of academia or professional disciplines. News sites are also informing sites, since they base their content on a reader's already-existing interest, and their content broadens what the reader knows about their already-existing world.

Figure 2.3 illustrates the informative website CNet. This website fits in the "websites that inform" category because it shows news specific to an industry, in this case, the computer industry.

FIGURE 2.3:

The CNet front page at http://www.cnet.com (October 29, 1998)

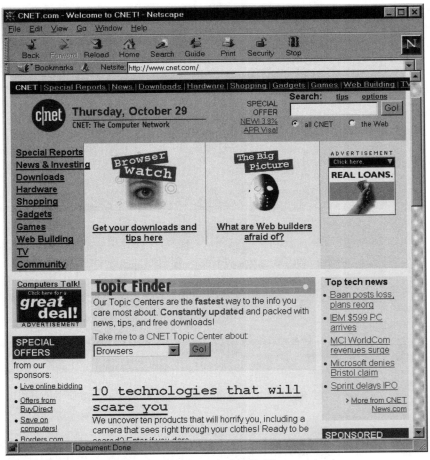

Reprinted with permission from CNET, Inc. Copyrght ©1995–98 www.cnet.com

Websites That Teach

Readers visit teaching sites to gather information about something, in a purely abstract context. These are the types of websites that provide information in a structured setting, but don't provide specific instructions for how to accomplish a task.

Figure 2.4 illustrates a classic teaching website: the college course site. This page belongs the to Miami University Tropical Marine Ecology class website (`http://jrscience.wcp.muohio.edu/html/TropEcolSyl.html`) and includes a weekly syllabus, links to reading and reference materials, and ample feedback areas.

FIGURE 2.4:

The front page of the Miami University Tropical Marine Ecology class website

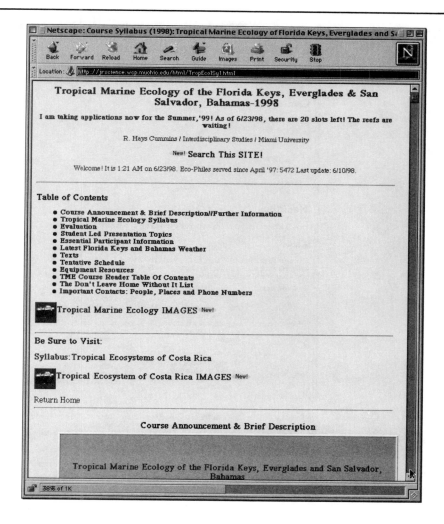

Websites That Guide

Websites that guide are task-oriented. Readers visit these sites to get step-by-step instructions on how to accomplish a given task.

Figure 2.5 shows a website that walks readers through how to tie different types of ties: The Necktie Repository at `http://fly.hiwaay.net/~jimes/necktie/`.

FIGURE 2.5:

The front page of the Necktie Repository, with links to diagrams on different tie-tying methods

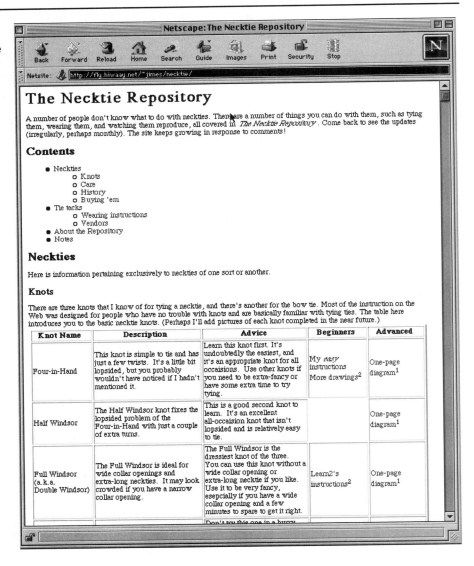

Websites That Are Reference Materials

The strength of a reference site isn't its data. It's how the data is presented to the user. A reference site offers a way to organize data that allows the reader a way to find a specific item, or to find a specific pointer to another, informing resource. Website directories, when done right, are references. Figure 2.6 shows a typical reference site: the Infomedical medical dictionary.

Bear in mind a site can fulfill more than one informational strategy. For example, if you run a software company, you can provide both instructional materials and guides on your site. A scientific association might have both reference materials and informative materials. It's okay to mix and match different information strategies— just be sure you can clearly identify the strategies you have.

What Will My Site Offer That a Product Based in Another Medium Wouldn't?

How is your website going to be different from your marketing material, your print publication, or your shrink-wrapped software product? Some corporate sites are referred to as *brochureware*: Each page is the same type of copy you'd get if you ordered a press kit. Other sites are called *shovelware* because they offer the exact same content as their print counterpart.

There is a place for brochureware and shovelware, but does a site devoted to repurposing existing content really need a lot of time or effort for upgrades? And if you're posting a website full of shovelware just to promote another product, how much independent identity do you want that product to have?

In other words: Is it a more effective use of your time to extend an existing product via the website or to simply mirror the product?

NOTE   Throughout the book I refer to websites as *products* because you need to think of your website as being the result of systemic, professional work. In any other business—software publishing, print media, shoemaking—the fruits of your work are considered the product you have for sale. Your website sells your skills and your organization. Therefore, it's a product.

FIGURE 2.6:

The Infomedical medical dictionary at `http://home.ipoline.com/~guoli/med/0head1.htm` organizes its information alphabetically, in parallel with a written counterpart.

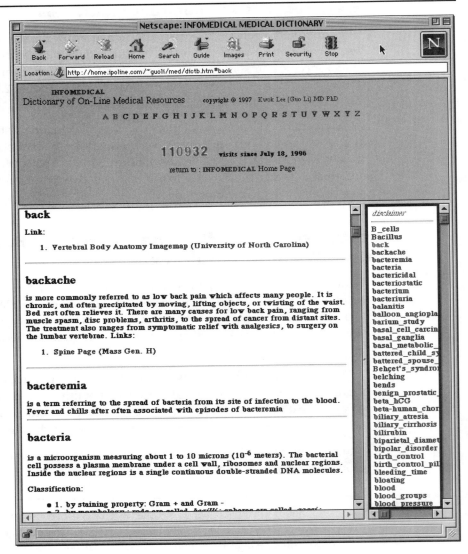

What Would I Like to See as My Ideal Product?

Toss out the marketing considerations, the sales numbers, and the human resources considerations for a minute, and think of what your ideal product looks like on the screen. What sort of information and services does it offer to your readers? When a user clicks on a choice in the navigation bar, what happens? How does it look? And how is that executed on the backend?

This backend question isn't one that everyone needs to answer, just the people whose job it is to take the design, interface, and editorial goals, and make them work. When you identify what you want the site to do for the user, be sure to include your technical staff to find out what you want the site to do on the server side. You'd be amazed what people want in a site, from floating toolbars to self-archiving content. Because it's doubtful one person will be able to think of everything from the front to the backend of the site, bring in every department that will be working on the site and ask them to describe what they want to build.

Clearly articulating the goals that every department would like to achieve under ideal conditions does three things that will help the total project. First, it forces you to examine and clearly articulate exactly what you want to do. With any luck, you can move from vague statements like "We want to provide an immersive multimedia experience" to clearly articulated action statements like "We want to build an informative website about commercial protein structures." Second, it provides a total picture of what everybody wants. This total picture will allow you to buckle and down and figure out exactly what everyone is capable of delivering. Third, it will provide a roadmap to future website development.

What Is the Minimum Acceptable Standard I Can Get Away With?

This is where the reality check comes in. It's one thing to aim for a total immersive multimedia experience; it's another to try building it using your company's current resources. It's one thing to ask everyone what they'd like to see happen in this round of website development; it's another to try and make everyone happy. The truth is, you will not be able to make everyone happy. You will be able to try to incorporate related ideals into a real-life project. That's the best you can do, and you'll do that assuming you have the time and resources to meet those goals.

This question doesn't exist to negate the "ideal product" question. It exists to put parameters on what people want and to begin hashing out what can realistically be done. Ask yourself this question as a way to evaluate the types of resources you can readily devote to the project and to assess what extra resources you'll need to acquire.

A few paragraphs prior, I argued for letting the technical folks in on the site brainstorming. This allows both the techies and the management types to understand what the other party wants. Now it's time to figure out if either side can get anything they want: is it possible to do what the marketing or editorial people want? If it's not, why not? Is it a lack of skilled workers, a lack of raw computing resources, or just a request that defies the laws of physics and the capabilities of any existing product or person?

Why isn't it possible to meet some people's ideal goals? Are the goals unreasonable in terms of the time and resources they'll take to be fulfilled? Is the amount of effort to meet the goal disproportionately high compared to the end result? Does the goal stick out as completely incongruous in the context of the rest of the goals you brainstormed?

And even if some of the ideal goals move from the realm of the ideal to the realm of the possible, will they have to be scaled back or altered to fit into a bigger project picture? If these goals are scaled back or altered, does that make them moot?

Once you've subjected all of the stated ideals to a reality check and taken account of the surviving ideals, do it again. Keep triaging your best-case scenarios until you have an idea of what the minimum acceptable standard is. This is your baseline from which to work; you'll build subsequent project goals on top of it.

Am I Upgrading My Site Because I Think It Will Result in a Better Product or Because an External Force Told Me It Was Time?

Typically, there are two different reasons to maintain or upgrade a site: the people who work on the site feel that the extra effort will result in a better project, or people who work with the site see a need for the site to respond to or challenge market conditions. Neither reason is better or worse: they're just different. Identifying whether the push for website work is internal or external will help you better focus your efforts on what needs to be done to meet the specific request.

For example, if your production head decides to revise the site in order to more closely meet the standards for HTML 4.0, that's an internal impetus to improve the site. If your marketing manager pushes to add a commerce section to a news site because it will help the site maintain a competitive edge, that's an external impetus. In the case of the production head, the goals and challenges within the task are all centered around maintaining the finished product while improving its parts; in the case of the marketing manager, the goal is to introduce a new service within the finished site. Both tasks have distinctly different aims. Again, make sure you identify the aims that are directly related to helping you respond to the internal or external pressure you've identified.

Of course, you can take advantage of a big project to incorporate goals that are both internally and externally driven. Overhauling a news site to provide specialized "beats" is an externally driven task; migrating from static templates to database-driven content is an internally driven task. Both can be incorporated into a project plan for the same website relaunch.

What Sort of Content Boundaries Do I Have?

Hypertext and HTML are both the blessings and the bane of online development. Hyperlinking allows for a varied, information-rich reading experience and endless editorial revisions. HTML is both easy to use and easily modified, so it lends itself almost too well to endless rounds of revision. As a result, it's easy for different project team members to have one more good idea, and request one more small change before the website goes live or immediately after the website goes live.

You need to stop this practice. These last-minute editorial and stylistic revisions tack on more time and result in some hasty, last-minute kludges. They distract from the original project goals and they extend a project long beyond its natural life.

To avoid never-ending production schedules, you need to find a set of concrete goals for interface, content, and function. Make your goals as explicit as possible, and as complete as you can anticipate. Think about past experience: Did you once vow to knock out twenty new pages and then forget to make a navigation bar that addressed where these pages fit in the whole website? Use those experiences to anticipate those last-minute fixes, and incorporate both big goals and small tasks into a list of goals to be met in order to finish the project.

Draw up these milestones, then draw a line underneath them. Small fixes (typos, unclosed <P> tags) aside, these goals are static, and they constitute the finish line of the project. As the website construction/renovation gets bogged down in setbacks, or overwhelmed by new technologies, these goals are going to provide a important sense of closure for everyone on the project. Don't mess with them.

What Did I Learn about My Website Structure during the Last Round of Site Development?

Every time you made a mistake, someone has inevitably been on hand to say something like, "Well, at least it's an experience you can learn from." These people are really annoying. Fortunately, sometimes they're also right. If you're about to undertake a website renovation, or ready to plot a maintenance routine for your site, you're going to need to dredge up all those mistakes you made and figure out what you learned—or could learn—from them.

Resurrecting your messy past can provide helpful diagnostic tools for you. What skills did you have to learn last time? Did you budget time to learn them, learn them as you went, or miss a deadline while you hammered out the finer points of DHTML or object-oriented JavaScript? What technical tools did you need and not have last time? What new technologies and design trends were added to the project after you had begun working? Who pushed for adding them? Was there a good reason to add them, or was there just nobody who would say no?

The first website I developed professionally was for the communications office of a fairly active nonprofit corporation. This was in the summer of 1995, and I had just fallen in love with the table-plus-single-pixel-GIF method of page layout.

I had also forgotten that I was going to have to duplicate the layout for our rapidly-expanding press release section. After a few months, I had one wide, shallow, tangled backend.

As a result, I ended up reorganizing, relinking, and duplicating a lot of files to try and undo the previous damage without giving readers dead-end URLs. If I had only thought ahead and tried to extrapolate what the site would contain in a year, I would have been a little more conservative with my design and broken it down into templates that could easily be mixed and matched.

In a lot of cases, a project post-mortem from the last round of development is useful. However, these post-mortems are usually done immediately after the project is launched, and they frequently do not document the problems that crop up two months after relaunch. Nor are post-mortems done as frequently as they ought to be. The time after relaunching is usually filled with patching unforeseen errors and hammering out new daily production routines.

It's these observations that you need to recollect before leaping into a new project. Finding the post-launch trouble spots, resource shortages, or immediate fixes—and figuring out why they happened—will help you prevent repeating the same mistakes the next time.

Do I Know Whom I'm Building the Website for and What My User Is Like?

If you're getting ready to launch or relaunch a product, chances are high that you're responding to some sort of external impetus. You either want to retain your user base, or expand it. Before you can do that, you need to make sure that you have a clear idea of exactly whom you're trying to reach.

Do some market research. Take a look at your competitors and extrapolate who they've targeted as their audience. Take a survey of your own audience. Do a little reading to see what markets are growing and whether or not you can link these emerging audiences into the one you already have.

Which leads to the most important, and most basic, question: Do you know who your current audience is? Before you even begin to refine or modify your new site plan, you need to be able to say that you know, without a doubt, whom you already serve.

What Kind of Interaction Is There Going to Be between the User and Whatever It Is My Site Has to Offer?

Before you can begin to flesh out how your website is going to work, you need to be able to define what it is you want the site to do for the visitor. This question is best answered after you've determined who your audience is and what you want them to be.

For example, you've identified your core site audience as college-aged people interested in travel. From a survey you took, you know that they spend about 20 hours a week online, they have low-end browsers because they're accessing the site from a school computer lab, and they have limited incomes.

You now have facts that allow you to set both editorial and technical parameters. You know that your audience has no problem spending hours online, so you can structure your site to allow both at-a-glance information and lengthier searches for specific data. You also know that the means for delivering the information has to be able to be effective all the way down to 2.0 browser versions. These factors can help you structure both your site interface, your site backend, and the code that specifies the tasks the users will perform.

You also know that your audience is operating on a lot of free time and not a lot of money, so you can structure your features around budget travel, off-season bargains, extended trips, or flexible and unorthodox travel means like courier flights. You can bring in co-sponsors who are targeting the same market or advertisers looking to build brand loyalty early. The point is, you have an idea of what sort of content your readers are looking for and what priorities they have concerning travel.

Armed with the technical parameters and editorial mission of the site as they pertain to the reader, you can map out what routes you want your reader to take as they travel toward what they want.

In the hypothetical case I've set up so far, I've established that your site is a travel site frequented by college students with a lot of time but little money. You can structure your front page to appeal to what matters to them most—finding novel travel bargains—and clearly communicate that the whole point to the site is to cover every aspect of low-cost, fun travel from transit to lodging to site-seeing to food. Then, your designers and site builders can map out probably reader routes that let them get to their destinations.

Deciding early on what you want your readers to do and how they're going to do it is a crucial step in mapping out your site's future development. It also has a two-fold benefit: Your site is more usable and thus more attractive to your audience, and you have a clear-cut set of development goals. Those goals allow you to begin to plot how to apply the technologies you've chosen. They allow you to intelligently manage your resources and produce a quality website without causing major employee unrest.

The Implementation Questions

The following questions are meant to help you impose order and control on your website development process. Let's face it: Your site development will probably veer off into unanticipated questions, but if you have set definitive parameters on how you're doing Web development, you'll be able to curb how far away from your goal the unanticipated takes you. If the idea questions answer the uber-question, "Why am I building this website?" the implementation questions are meant to answer the uber-question, "How will I build this website?"

Why Am I the One Doing the Work?

If you're living in a Dilbert cartoon, the answer is, "Ummmm. I didn't duck fast enough?" But most of us are living in a slightly less dysfunctional world, and we probably have more articulate reasons for working on the website.

It's important to articulate why you're working on a website. Are you doing the work because you have experience upgrading websites? Are you doing the work because you've been maintaining the website and therefore know why everything is where it is? Or are you doing the work because you've inherited the site from someone who's left, and you were the only available option?

You need to have a clear sense of why you are the person who is working on this website. This will let you assess what prior experience and technical experience you bring to the project, and what skills you need to acquire or find someone to provide. Being able to realistically evaluate your skills early in the project is important. You'll be able to see what you need to learn. You can budget time for learning your new skills. This is highly advisable. You will need to actually learn these new skills and how to apply them. You will also need to learn how those skills fit within the larger project: what you'll be able to contribute to the team, how those skills affect the already-existing site, and how those skills will be incorporated into the new site.

Being able to acknowledge what sort of outside resources you need to find is even more important. Forcing yourself to stay up all night because you underestimated the amount of time it takes to learn Java is one thing; forcing your staff to do so because you didn't allot them enough time or because you're holding them up is another. You must be able to identify your strengths and your weaknesses and be sure each member of your staff does the same. Compile a list of what attributes the team has and a list of what skills and background the team needs in order to finish the job.

Once you have an idea what skills everyone has, and those skills can be measured against what skills you need to do the job, you can begin to figure out two important things:

1. Who needs to learn new skills.

2. Whether there's going to be enough time for your team to acquire the skills they need and complete the tasks under deadline.

Be realistic, both about learning curves and deadlines. Given the pace of new Web technologies and the likelihood that you'll be requested to incorporate something new and unanticipated into the total project, you're going to want to pad your schedule.

If you've gone through and assessed you and your coworkers' skills and discovered that there isn't enough time to learn everything needed for the project, you need to do one of two things: revise the project expectations, or hire someone with the skills. There is no one correct path, just a decision to be made: Which choice is better for the project?

Isn't it amazing how the question, "Why me?" can lead to resource assessment?

What Sort of Website Am I Starting Out With?

Sometimes, having a previous website to work with can be a good thing because you're building on a strong foundation. Sometimes, it can be a bad thing, because you have to undo or redo a lot of work. The question that this section poses allows you to assess whether you're dealing with a good thing or a bad thing.

But first, let's define *website*. What the product is supposed to be to the user has already been covered in the idea questions. For our purposes here, a website is the collection of code that makes up the structure and functions composing the finished product.

Are you lucky enough to have a site with a solid backend structure, one that is modular enough for you to move or remove sections without affecting every file on the site? Do you have files grouped in some coherent organization scheme? Are commonly used chunks of code centralized? If so you're fairly lucky. You have a solid, functional file foundation. If you looked at these questions and answered "no," you may want to factor in time to build a flexible, durable backend before you even begin to overhaul the site.

How have the site workers treated files as they get older? Do you have a clearly defined archiving system set up? Do you overwrite old files with new ones to maintain a persistent URL? Are you reading these questions and saying, "no" to them as panic wells up in the back of your mind?

There's time to panic later. Now, your job is to realistically assess the state of the project you've inherited. Figure out what assets you have, what disadvantages you have, and how each will affect the progress of the project on the table. Having a clear idea of your current site is the best favor you could do yourself before you begin to renovate the site.

How Much Time Can I Allot to the Website?

Realistically assessing the length of a website renovation or creation project is only half of the challenge. The other half is assessing how much time you'll be able to spend on the project. Before you even begin to work on the website, you need to determine if you're going to have (or be willing to spend) enough time to complete the deadlines necessary to finish the project.

NOTE
The purpose of this question isn't to make you feel bad about not being able to do everything within the deadline. It's to force you to realistically assess your ability to contribute to the project under its current time constraints and to be aware that you may have to bring in outside help, reassess your deadlines, or scale back the scope of your project. Conversely, you may find that you've got more time than you anticipated. In this case, congratulations. Don't reduce your deadlines, or resources, for completing the project: Having a cushion to deliver a good product is a lot more desirable than cramming at the last minute.

How many people will you have working on the site? If it's you and only you, I have good news and bad news. The good news is, you'll only have to figure out a time/task budget for one person, and you're in a really good place to assess how much time you can devote per task. The bad news is, you're going to have to do more by yourself.

If you're getting ready to launch a site maintenance/overhaul effort with a team, the initial job of determining time per task and then assigning tasks to individual team members is going to be more complex. You'll need to determine:

What skills does each team member have?   Does more than one person have the same set of skills? You will always want to make sure that you have a backup person for every single skill used to build the website. Otherwise, you're in deep trouble if someone gets sick, goes on vacation, or resigns. Have individual team members expressed a willingness to learn new skills that are crucial to the site project?

How much time does each person have to devote to the project?   Does that time include hours spent learning new technologies? When you're budgeting time, make sure you account for the time your team members are going to spend learning and experimenting with new software or development languages.

How much time do you anticipate per task if one person is performing a task?   How much time does the task take if you throw more bodies at it? Does learning time have to be built into the task, or is that something you expect each employee to pick up on her own? If everyone comes on to a project knowing every skill you could possibly need, you're blessed with extraordinary luck or an extraordinarily simple site. Be sure to budget time for your employees to nail new software packages and coding techniques.

How much time have you built in for integrating different people's work?   Having several people complete discrete tasks isn't terribly hard. The real challenge is integrating those finished chunks of code or content with each other.

How are you going to handle integration of discrete tasks?   Who is going to be responsible for identifying and implementing steps to make the disparate pieces mesh smoothly?

Have you budgeted time for work review?   Relying on other people to do work is part of good management, but so is checking work once it's done.

Have you budgeted a little extra time in case someone leaves or is reassigned to a different project?   Sometimes, companies handle their websites by having a group of people who do nothing but work on a specific site or property. Others draw their technical resources from a pool of workers who do Web work on top of their regular duties. You need to be able to assess how to make a project work both with and without its assigned staff.

Being able to realistically assess how deadlines and tasks are going to translate into work hours is smart management. It keeps your goals realistic and your employees from muttering about sweatshops as a manager walks out at six while they stay, coding to meet a deadline the manager set. You want to prevent that from happening. Resentful coders don't speak well of a manager's project-handling skills.

How Will I Handle People Leaving? What Redundancy Have I Built into the Production Process?

The questions sound horribly cynical, but given the fluidity of today's job market, both questions are very necessary. Independent contractors can part ways with their client. Web developers on loan from another department can be snapped back into their home office. Key developers or designers can get a more attractive offer from a competitor and leave.

You want to develop a project plan that provides all the participants with challenging and interesting work that taps their skill set, but you can't hinge the plan on the performance of one employee.

You can go one of two ways with this: Weigh responsibilities evenly so no one team member feels disgruntled and wants to leave, or arrange backup personnel for every specific discipline.

The first method—distributed work weight—is ultimately fair to employees. So long as everyone is working evenly hard, there's no room for resentment—or raging delusions of indispensability—to develop. Michael Bloomburg, CEO of the business-media business the Bloomburg Group, rotates his newscast anchors weekly so that none develops a brand-name following and greater power in building the product. His solution is a little drastic, but the background reasoning provides food for thought.

You probably don't want to be in a position where you or someone else is the ultimate indispensable employee on a project. Leaving is then disruptive and counterproductive. The alternate solution to retain the prize employee—dramatically increased salary or special treatment—only breeds resentment among remaining team members. You'll have a big backlash on your hands or possibly more employees threatening to leave as a negotiating tactic.

So distributing work weight and emphasizing to each team member that they perform an important function, is an equitable, management-safe solution. It is also extremely hard to implement in a Web-driven workplace. Projects tend to have rapid inceptions, fluid staffs, and highly inconsistent recruiting processes. It may simply be easier to sidestep studied egalitarianism and shift your priorities to a one-two-three strategy:

1. Find out who is going to do what on your project.

2. Decide who is going to act as an assistant or backup for each person on your team.

3. Try to keep everyone happy by giving them work that plays to their skills.

By assessing what you'll do in a worst-case scenario, and working with that plan tucked in the back of your head, you'll be able to move forward on your project.

What Do My Nonhuman Resources Look Like?

Yeah, yeah, they're 2 feet tall, 6 inches wide, and beige. Everyone knows what servers look like. The real questions here are: How many different technical resources do you have available, and how much room do you have for expansion?

Find out what kind of computers everyone on your development team is going to be using. Find out if every team member has the software to perform their job and if they have the means to handle code, text, or images from other team members. Does each team member have access to a testing area? To the central project file drop? To the live site? Not every employee needs access to the live site (in fact, few people do) but everyone needs to have a way to get to the project's central filespace without relying on floppy disks and the kindness of fellow employees.

Once you've determined what software and hardware your employees have, find out what they want and what they need. Bear in mind, these may be two very different things. On an ideal planet, every developer would get the Macintosh of their dreams, the PC of their dreams, a laptop for telecommuting, and a PDA for street cred. Since most Web development is done on this planet, you or your boss need to weigh what makes your developer delirious with joy against what will permit them to do their job without fuming.

It may be very necessary to shell out the money for the latest version of a software package to allow your development team to do what the interface designers have specified. It may be very necessary to buy a laptop to allow your QA team to do testing from home at midnight after everyone else is off the server. You should leave room in your budget for new acquisitions that improve the ability of your workers to do their jobs.

After you've tried to match employee to technical resource, take a look at the machines and server software that will push your site public. Do you have the machine capacity to handle a dramatically expanded site? What about a site that just migrated from a series of static files to a series of dynamically-produced files? Do you have adequate storage space for the site now? How about four years' worth of continuous site publishing? Can your server handle continuous CGI requests? Do you have the bandwidth to handle a lot of outgoing traffic? What about handling incoming traffic?

If you're not on the engineering or technical staff, find them now, buy them a cup of coffee, and ask them to answer these questions. You need to assess the state of the site resources, from storage to server speed to bandwidth, before you begin to develop new and improved site features.

What Did I Learn about the HTML and Scripting during My Last Round of Site Development?

Think in much broader terms than the specific skills you learned; try to detect trends. For example, I always notice that I don't separate out discrete page parts as soon as I should. I'll build an entire site and copy the conditional HTML for a color scheme on every page instead of separating the code and making it a virtual include. So I know that I should always build in a review step to see if I can optimize re-use of code. You may notice that you always write JavaScript that works beautifully on one browser but not the other. Or you may notice that all of your developers built a site that looks beautiful only on Macs because that's what they're using.

Find your weak spots in the development and production processes. Sometimes they're glaringly obvious. For example, if anyone who comes in on an AOL browser complains that they're seeing gibberish, obviously you need to work on developing a chunk of code that anticipates small market-share browsers and provides a legible alternative. If you notice instead that you get great Java apps from the engineering department on launch but no follow-up support, you'll want to factor in technical support as a development issue.

Just be sure not to pitch the stuff you do right because you're working on amending past mistakes. This question is meant to bring up the unexpected crises and forehead-smacking midnight discoveries that set back your last round of development. Be sure to determine what you did right last time or what positive lessons you learned and can apply to future projects.

How Much Daily Production Will I Have to Do after This Version of the Site Is Completed?

This question will be most easily answered if you have a clear idea of the site's purpose. Some informative sites are one-shot deals: trade show websites are built to inform prospective attendees what they can anticipate at a show and how to attend the show. After the show, their usefulness is limited. Therefore, it's a project with a large initial development and minimal maintenance. An instructional website also requires a lot of initial effort in development, with little follow-up maintenance; the most obvious exceptions would be if the process or idea being taught had been dramatically revised.

A news website or a resource website may require much more frequent maintenance, especially if the content is always updated, or expanding. Hypertext references require more work than most of their creators realize: Links move or expire frequently, growing resource lists call for increasingly specialized classification methods, and expanding content requires backend care to make sure the site's performance doesn't suffer. News sites require constant checking to ensure that the site's appearance hasn't changed for the worse with every addition; that the addition of new material has allowed older material to integrate naturally with already-existing content; that new material didn't permanently overwrite older material; the tools used to generate and update pages are all working correctly.

Development stops at launch; production never stops. Be sure to factor in time for daily or weekly maintenance and QA, as well as "service checks" to make sure the pristine site you pushed live a few months ago hasn't turned into a rat's nest of symbolic links, extra folders, and kludges. You can also use these service checks to correct small development errors, like typing **cellsapcing=0** on 50 files, or separating out the code specifying your color schemes.

NOTE   *Symbolic links* (or *symlinks*) are Unix constructs that allow you to create a virtual link to a file that may or may not exist. You can learn more about how symbolic links work by visiting Chapter 8.

How Much Backend Maintenance and Upgrading Am I Willing to Do?

If the whole point to your project is to overhaul your backend, you're already saying, "I'm spending a lot of time, thanks for asking." But treating backend overhaul as a discrete project isn't within the scope of this question.

Specifically, how much time are you willing to spend on a finished, launched product to make it work better? Are you going to be moving content from one set of files to an archive fileset on a regular basis? Are you going to integrate a new site-development technology like extended server-side includes into your production process? Have you thought about whether a new technology integration is only going to happen from initial launch forward, or whether you're going to apply it to old content too?

Deciding how consistently to apply new technology to a site is crucial. Equally important are documenting your decision, outlining the new technology, and describing how it differs from the old technology. If you find out that you don't know how it differs from your old technology, hold off on integrating the new fix until you figure out the answers. This will prevent unanticipated breakage.

You may also have to prune your file tree from time to time. Sites get large and unwieldy, and you may discover that pruning several special sections improves your storage space. You may also discover you've been copying a particular image and calling it from several different directories. Therefore, maintenance of your site might include trying to rewrite old pages to take advantage of common code chunks, or it might include pulling down old, rarely trafficked sites. Just one word of caution before you delete anything: Set up a symlink or redirect to your site's index or site map for users, just in case the 12 people who visited your special section decide to return.

Decide what maintenance goals you have toward maintaining your launch product or improving its backend performance. Allocate times and resources from there—just recognize that few sites are perfect on launch and almost all will require post-launch tuneups.

TIP

No matter how carefully you plan your site, you're going to have to spend the day after launching the site fixing all the things you didn't anticipate. On the last site relaunch I worked on, I spent four hours double-checking all the redirect links that took us off the site and on to another server. Remember: no matter how carefully you plan ahead, make allowances for mistakes you didn't anticipate.

How Do I Know When I'm Done?

Actually, very few websites are ever done. The immense flexibility of hypertext allows deadlines to be stretched; it has also taken the idea of a discrete project and pushed it into an ever-expanding body of work.

You, or the hired brain squad who thinks of all the work the developers get to do, should have already figured out when the front-end user experience is done. The editorial content and features should have a cutoff point, and that cutoff point should be rigorously enforced. The *real* question is, how do you know when you're done with the backend?

When you're working on a tight deadline schedule, sometimes the code that gets the job done on deadline isn't the same code that does the job elegantly. You may look at 50 pages of new content, five templates meant to generate 50 pages of content, or 50 text files meant to be spliced into five templates, and realize that the code repeats the same mistakes that caused the whole site revamp.

You need to define three different levels of development for the folks doing the code. The first level is what is not acceptable. This may include browser-extension-based code, HTML that doesn't degrade down a browser level or two, or a layout based on eight embedded tables and 80 single-pixel GIFs.

The next level is what is acceptable for site performance. This code needs to perform the task you want it to perform, it needs to do so without breaking on any browser or platform, and it needs to do so without breaking any of the site's other code. The final level is elegant code: this is code that you'd feel comfortable flashing on an overhead projector in front of your boss and saying, "I made this!" This code not only does the job, it does it with extra benefits, such as lower loading time, fewer server hits, or easier recycling across pages.

Clearly, you want elegant code across the site. But if you're under extreme deadlines, or you just lost a passel of coders to another project, you're going to have to decide what code is acceptable for a launched project.

Having clear performance benchmarks for the code you want to push live is important. It will prevent feature creep and excessive last-minute corrections that often come at the expense of testing.

The Technology Questions

The chaotic technical bazaars known as trade shows frequently showcase software that promises to do everything for your website, up to and including shepherding users to your site. If you're facing enormous sitewide maintenance or upgrade, it may be tempting to buy all the software solutions that you think you're going to need. But realistically, not only do you not have the budgetary resources to buy everything, but also you or the engineer on your project is going to have to read the software specs a little more carefully and realize that software and hardware hype frequently promises a little more than it delivers.

You have two issues to consider:

- How do you best assess what tools are going to help produce the site you want in the time frame you want?

- How are you going to keep your technical staff happy?

Those two goals are not mutually exclusive. This section will set forth the questions you need to ask, and the criteria you need to consider, before you buy into the latest greatest technologies. Please note that by "technology" I don't mean simple utility programs like Hoverbar, or basic technologies like WS-FTP or Fetch. I'm talking about tools that affect the way you generate content; the ways you store and handle text and images; the ways you create, combine, and call templates; and the ways you move a site from a collection of backend source code to a live page.

Should I Build the Tools I Need or Should I Buy Them?

Yes, there is a debate between building the tools you need to develop and maintain a site and buying an off-the-shelf package. The experience you have with building your own tools versus the experience of implementing someone else's tools is completely different.

There are four issues to keep in mind when making this decision:

Return on investment (ROI)   Will you get something in return for the time and money that you're sinking into the project, or will the entire development process provide nothing but a "learning experience" and several bulleted action items on someone's resume? You need to see if the tool is worth what you put into it, whether it be time, money, or both.

Support   When your company builds a tool and it breaks, you can walk over and fling yourself across the engineer's desk in a cry for help; calling the 800 number or budgeting another $5,000 in consultation fees for a third-party tool is a different experience.

Extensibility   Unless you've managed to find a tool that you can contort to meet the ever-changing needs of your site, it's going to be easier to persuade the engineer two rooms over to add a new text-parsing feature than it is to wait for either customization or upgrading the software.

Time   If you're a company with a specific mission to deliver content, do you have the time to build, test, and perfect a tool along with the usual Web development process? Off-the-shelf software has already been subjected to testing and requires little initial development effort from you.

The four factors I've listed above are only the overarching issues shaping the technology acquisition landscape for Web developers. The questions below will help you refine just what it is you want out of a technology, and whether or not it's time to add that technology to your site.

What Do I Want the Tool to Do?

You need to be as specific as you possibly can when deciding what you want the tool to do. "I want the tool to do _____." (Fill in your own blank.) You want the tool to do this on any platform. You want the tool to perform this task regardless of which human is entering the correct commands. You want the tool to work when you add new content, when you move directories, when you move physical locations.

A good tool should be like a good toothbrush. A toothbrush has a discrete function: scrubbing your teeth. It doesn't matter which hand you use to brush your teeth, which faucet you wet the toothbrush underneath, what time of day you use the toothbrush, or even who uses the toothbrush. It's a tool and it will scrub teeth regardless. You want your tool to work regardless of the conditions surrounding it.

A toothbrush doesn't double as a washcloth, a bath towel, or a facial cleanser. Each of those items is a discrete item performing a discrete task. Each tool in your array should also have a discrete function. Tools can work together to produce something larger than the sum of their parts, but they don't pinch-hit for each other.

Suppose, for example that you have an extra fancy toothbrush, called a toothbrush++, that doubles as your soap and your nail clippers. It's great at first, but when the soap function breaks, you can either sink money into a whole new toothbrush++ system, or you can try to fix the current soap function. In the meantime, you have no soap, so your entire bathroom routine is affected.

An alternate scenario: You have the toothbrush++, but you don't like the soap function's smell—in other words, the execution is incompatible with the way the rest of the routine is performed. Do you pay extra money to install a new soap function into your toothbrush++, or do you break down your tool into easily modified individual parts?

Website tool suites are frighteningly similar to bathroom products. Your goal should be to find the tools that do their job well and are easy to implement, integrate, and upgrade. If an individual tool breaks, you can easily isolate the problem and work around it without killing the rest of your site operations. Moreover, if you're building the tools, it's less costly to build one working tool and use that as your development base than it is to try and build the be-all-end-all tool.

Which brings me to my next belabored effort to extend the toothbrush metaphor: Do you really need more than one toothbrush? Sometimes, yes, you do. If you travel excessively, for example, or work really long hours, it doesn't hurt to have an extra toothbrush lying around. The same types of questions should be asked of website tools: Is there a conceivable circumstance where you'll need the tool but won't have access to it? Would it make sense to duplicate the tool on another server, just in case?

And finally, you want to avoid buying or building tools you really don't need. There is a big difference between how much you need soap, and how much you need an alpha-hydroxy eyelid nighttime cream. One does something solid: cuts the dirt and leaves you squeaky clean. The other appropriates a lot of jargon to push a product that may make you feel chic, but has little proven use. Some Web technologies are the equivalent of alpha-hydroxy eyelid nighttime cream. Sure, you're the first person on the block to try it, but if you don't thoroughly understand the technology or if it shows you no demonstrable difference after use, it's not worth the resources you'd invest in getting it.

So think function: What functions do you need fulfilled, and what tools would best fulfill those functions? You may discover that the tasks are already being completed by a tool that does its job admirably without any unnecessary frills. You may also discover that you need a new tool or two to fulfill some specific tasks. The point is, you now know to go looking for a specific tool that performs in general circumstances.

How Conversant Am I in New Technologies?

Information is power, but knowing how to apply information to a given situation makes you a demigod. In order to assess how well a new tool would fit into and improve your current website, you need to know enough about new technologies to be able to figure out how they work with your existing system.

But there is a flood of new products out there, and you don't have the time to read up on all of them. You have one of two choices: delegate the info-gathering to someone else (or many other people), or perform information triage. Making a narrowly focused search for information is often more effective than making a broad search and then processing the results. You'll be able to quickly discover if the technology you're learning about has a whole host of supporting data, or if it's suspiciously undocumented.

One way to perform information triage is to limit your input of new knowledge to new knowledge in only one area. This approach works best if you are working within a team environment. Each of the team members can tackle a specific facet of the development project and do a preliminary fact-finding run. The next step is crucial: Meet to share information and to ask each other how one person's adopted technology topic will affect another person's technology topic. A second fact-finding mission and recap may then be necessary.

If you're working on a one-person operation, you're going to need to approach your acquisition of new-tech literacy differently. Develop a stable of resources—tech news sites, newsgroup digests, or friends—and look to them to answer specific queries. A lot of sites run comparisons of different function-specific software or hardware. Run a search on these sites to see if the tool you want to adopt has been reviewed. Two good starting points are ZDNet (`www.zdnet.com`) and CNet (`www.cnet.com`): Both sites feature distinct news areas and consumer review areas.

Is the Tool Cross-Platform?

Finding out if a tool is cross-platform is important because you will never be able to accurately anticipate where the tool is being used:

- If you're a contractor, you may be developing on a different system than your client's.

- If you work for a large Web content company, chances are good that you have a very different job from the person who runs the server.

- If you're the lone Webslinger in a non-Web business, you may have to answer to an IT staff using different hardware than you.

Any tool that your site relies on for construction or live publication needs to work for both the developer and the site home. If you have to buy a software tool, make sure you purchase something that produces results that port well across platforms. If the tool doesn't do that, assess which next step will produce better results: finding a supplemental tool to maintain cross-platform porting, or finding a different tool that produces more flexible results.

Is the Tool Producing Reliable Results across Browsers?

Consistency in backend performance is one issue you need to resolve; another issue that your users will think important is how consistent your site is across different browsers. Subsequently, you need to be sure that the tools you're using produce reliably similar results across browsers.

For example, the nested-table kludge that tiles images perfectly in Internet Explorer won't work in Netscape unless the code has also been compacted with any extra spaces removed; can your tool account for those browser quirks?

Your tool should be able to work around existing browser bugs, not develop its own bugs when faced with different browsers. If you're relying on an off-the-shelf HTML editor, you need to test your pages extensively to see if they work correctly; if you're relying on a series of canned scripts to generate forms, you need to make sure those scripts degrade down and work across a wide variety of browsers.

If your tool claims only to do its job well under specific circumstances, think back to the toothbrush: A toothbrush performs the same task the same way regardless of the hand you use to brush or the faucet you've dunked the brush in. Your tools should be similarly impervious to their environment.

How Important Are Fancy Features and Where Am I Going to Draw the Line on Feature Creep?

Our metaphorical toothbrush comes in handy when discussing features. Some toothbrushes have specially angled handles, some have blue bristles alerting you to toothbrush replacements, still others are brushes attached to $100 sonic pulse transmitters. All of these toothbrushes still clean your teeth. You only have to decide which bonus features are vital to your toothbrushing task.

The same feature dilemma awaits you with website technologies. This dilemma is one of the few areas that amplifies the difference between building a tool and buying it.

When you build a tool (or when you contract engineers to build a tool for you), you have unusually close access to the developers. The temptation to add on an extra feature because it would be cool or because it would make up for the deficiencies of another tool is there. It's also a temptation a lot of manager-level people give in to. At the end of the development process, the simple and elegant tool you build is covered with extra features that may or may not affect its performance.

This just-one-more-thing phenomenon is known as *feature creep*. It can be the bane of your developers' existence. It can also be a selling point for third-party software.

When you are doing the research toward purchasing a new Web development tool, you'll find a lot of companies that market their tool thusly: "It lets you write HTML. But it does more: It color-codes tags for easy visibility! It provides coding at the click of a button so your developers don't have to type <B></B>! It has templates! It can search-and-replace strings of characters!"

The questions you need to ask yourself are:

- Do I need any of these extra features?

- Would they replace anything I am currently using?

- Would they make using the tool easier?

You need to know where to draw the line on tool features and what prompts you to draw that line. In the case of building a new tool, ask whether the feature is addressing a shortcoming in the tool function or whether it's going to enhance the already-adequate performance of the tool. Is the feature meant as a patch for yet another tool? That's one good reason not to include it: Your goal should be to keep all of your tools as discrete as possible. If a feature is going to make using the tool easier and therefore quicker, it's a strong argument for incorporating it into the tool. If a feature is going to make the tool more effective and powerful, it's another reason to look for it in any tool you build or buy.

If you're buying an off-the-shelf tool, you need to pay attention to the criteria determining those lines you've drawn. A frustrating truth among software or hardware shopping is that no one product is going to have all of the features you want; another is that two products will have all the features you want, plus six or seven separate features you don't. If you can assess what features you think will contribute the most to your work process, then weigh your purchasing choices relative to the most important features, you'll be ahead of the game. Extra features aren't necessarily bad, but if they're not going to significantly improve your work, why pay extra for them?

Finding the Perfect Advertising Tool

If you're looking for a software package that serves ads, do you need one that simply couples an ad banner with a specific location on your site, or do you need a tool that lets you schedule ads according to the time of day, domain of the user, or number of ad impressions promised to the client? You can settle that question by finding out the following:

- What conditions your ad reps sold the ads under. The more complex and specific the ad-serving conditions, the more sophisticated your tool needs to be.

- What conditions you anticipate in the future. Even if you're only doing simple banner exchange now, do you anticipate serving more specific ads in the future? Determine if you would sell the ads if you had the tool with which to serve them.

- How any tool permits you to enter an advertising buy. Would it be more work because the tool demanded more information, or less work because the tool fits right in with current production processes?

- If you want a tool that can be accessed through a browser. If you've got more than one person working on the ad tool, you may want one that can be accessed via a network by multiple users.

But first, you need to decide if these features are merely bonuses or if they are crucial for making ad serving easier for your site.

For example, if you're picking a tool to serve highly targeted ads to people visiting a hockey site, you'll want a tool that can target users by their region, for team-specific merchandise, or by the time of day they surf, for hockey game promotions.

Because you've set the primary criteria to be highly targeted ads, you'll be able to sort among the tools from there.

In this case, the advertising demands will probably drive the tool selection; production concerns are secondary. Once you have a clear picture of what to look for—in this case, a tool that lets you specify everything about an ad from its placement to the frequency of its appearance—you can narrow down your choices. (Is your interest is piqued by all this ad talk? See Chapter 16.)

Can I Get at the Source Code for the Tool?

Whether you build or buy, you need to be able to understand how the tool works. The ability to extend and modify Apache's server mods is one of the reasons the free serverware is so popular. Having access to the source code allows you to customize off-the-shelf software to better perform the task you purchased it for.

Tools and Training

The beauty of basic Web production is the ease with which even committed computerphobes can pick up and learn software tools to publish websites. However, as your site gets more complex and becomes more of a professional undertaking, you may want to get training in specific software packages and tools. The creators of some of the most popularly used tools, and further resources for classes in their tools, are listed below:

Adobe   Adobe's high-powered graphics software packages, Photoshop and Illustrator, probably create or modify most of the Web's images, and their Acrobat application was the Web's first attempt at making documents universally readable and tightly formatted. Adobe offers excellent backup—including a support database—on their website at `http://www.adobe.com`.

Macromedia   This company has contributed heavily to the "multimedia" part of Multimedia Gulch in San Francisco, CA. Applications like Shockwave, Dreamweaver, Flash, and Fireworks are *de rigeur* for cutting-edge Web developers or anyone who wants to move beyond basic `<B>` tags and GIFs. Their website offers online support, plus information about Macromedia training. Go to `http://www.macromedia.com`.

Netscape   After aggressively remodeling their site to better accomodate site developers, Netscape began targeting intranet and database geeks. They recently cosponsored a series of educational training sessions for integrating Netscape and Sybase database tools; keep visiting the development site at `http://developer.netscape.com` for more information and training support.

Sybase   Sybase's education programs offer Web developers a chance to enroll in classes or self-study and gain some hands-on database experience. For more information, go to `http://slc.sybase.com`.

Microsoft   The company provides training in most of its software packages, including the Windows NT server. There are both classes and extensive online support resources on their website. For more information, go to `http://www.microsoft.com/train_cert/`.

ZDU   Ziff Davis University offers classes on basic Web-building skills and advanced Web development. For more information on classes and curricula, go to `http://www.zdu.com`.

Access to source code allows you more control over the tool; it allows you to figure out why it works like it does, and whether or not you can improve it.

NOTE A notable drawback to off-the-shelf tools is that they're often developed using a proprietary development environment. In this case, you might want to see if the company offers training in the language or if it offers support for customizing the tool after purchase and installation.

Can I Modify or Extend the Tool's Functionality?

Sometimes the use for which you purchased a tool evolves into a related but markedly different use. In this case, the function of the tool may still be useful, but its total ability to do the job it was meant to has been reduced. In other words, the toothbrush you used as child doesn't brush a full-sized adult mouth.

In order to get your money's worth—either in the human resources and time you've sunk into developing a tool or in time and money you've sunk into purchasing and learning an off-the-shelf solution—you need to extend the function that the tool was meant to perform.

There are three different strategies for extending a tool's functionality:

- See if you can find an alternate way to use the tool.
- Write the new functionality into an existing tool.
- Buy an upgrade or replacement tool.

These three strategies are discussed in the following sections.

Finding Tool Alternatives

The first option requires the least code-rewriting: See if you can find a way to extend the tool's abilities within the already-existing tool. Remember all those features you agonized about purchasing or developing? It's time to see if they come in handy.

Writing New Functionality into an Existing Tool

Another strategy toward extending functionality of a tool is to write it into the existing tool. Assuming you have access to the source code, you will be able to write a module that alters the original task or replaces it with the related, new task.

An Example of Modifying a Tool's Functionality: Using BBEdit to Radically Rewrite Code

BBEdit is a Macintosh-platform HTML editor. BBEdit has a search-and-replace function that encompasses varying levels of technical proficiency. You can do simple searches, searches-and-replaces through a document, or searches and searches-and-replaces across an entire directory structure. This function works well in a limited capacity, but the interface is difficult to use, and you must have your replacement code written well ahead.

Fortunately, BBEdit also has a feature that allows you to write search-and-replace scripts using a combination of Unix-style commands executed within BBEdit. This scripting extension allows you to write far more flexible search-and-replace tasks than the simple substitutions that the search/replace window permits.

Consider, for example, an ad-serving database. Suppose a database was developed by a few engineers to record a few simple data about an ad: who the sponsor was, what the name of the ad banner was, what URL the banner led to, and when the ad was posted. But suppose the ad salespeople come back and request that the frequency that an ad would be served over time be added. In this case, the database gurus could add another table to the database, this one calculating the frequency of the ad appearance over the length of its run. The engineers have to draw on the existing tool function of storing the data about the beginning and end of the ad posting and use that data to perform a new function. They would, however, keep the frequency data separate from the other tables in the database so it could be lifted out if necessary.

Upgrading or Replacing Your Tool

A third and final strategy is to buy an upgrade or replacement tool if the existing tool simply doesn't perform the functions you want it to perform. This is probably the most extreme possibility as it doesn't maximize on your past work or current tool implementation. But if you're not able to extend the functionality of the tool yourself, or if you've assessed the time and effort it would take and decided the return on investment isn't worth it, buying a new tool may be the smartest long-term strategy.

Returning to our ad-serving database example: The database keeps track of basic data and performs simple distribution math. If the sales people come back and ask for ads triggered by certain browser variables or ads triggered by the appearance of particular users, the level of complexity of the task has jumped dramatically. It may not be worth the time and effort to develop, test, and roll out a modified ad database. Two other factors to consider are that the time taken to modify an existing tool may far exceed the deadline you have to incorporate the total functionality, and that an off-the-shelf solution may already exist.

So before you even begin to build or purchase a tool, determine how easy it would be to adapt the tool to a changing task and what sort of strategies you would be able to pursue if you had to adapt the tool.

Does the Tool Fit into an Already Existing Production Process?

The whole point to buying a Web development tool is to make the process of building or maintaining a website less difficult. If implementing the tool is going to require more work than proceeding with daily tasks without it, then there's no reason to get the tool.

Tools you've built yourself aren't exempt from criticism. If anything, there's even less of an excuse to develop a tool that's going to require a total production process overhaul. To do so would require even more of a human resources investment than you're making already. Why bother developing a tool that is going to create more work than it saves?

Any new technology or tool should fit into production intuitively. You and your development team should understand *why* there was a need for that tool, and *how* this met need will positively affect the rest of your work.

The only exception to the integration rule is this: If you find that your development process is nothing more than an elaborate and inefficient daisy-chain of tools, it may be time to reassess the process and rebuild it based on one or more of the most effective tools you've acquired.

How Does This Tool Fit into My Website's Overall Application Framework?

Smoothly integrating a tool into someone's production routine is important, but one of the larger-scale questions you should be asking is how well the tool fits into your overall development environment. You need to keep in mind that every step of website production affects every other step. If your designers are dropping vector-based illustrator files to your production managers, your production managers are going to have to be the ones who figure out how to translate those highly specific file types into more accessible HTML and the JPEG formats. If all of your code is done in BBEdit on a Mac, but you're serving your pages off a Unix box, you're going to have to build in a step to check the files for linebreaks and extra ^Ms that could disrupt a parsing string.

NOTE The extra characters show up courtesy of the way a file is formatted in one platform as opposed to another; keeping this information in mind may actually turn into a criterion for a software tool.

When you're selecting your tools for a specific production process, find out how they're going to affect other processes. Determine if those tools have features that can minimize the impact. For example, the developers using BBEdit can set their copy of the software to always save files in Unix line format; then, when they FTP the files to a Unix-based server, there's no worry that extra ^M characters will interrupt server calls or CGI variable strings.

If you're developing your tools for website production, do so not only in the current site framework but also in the projected site framework. For example, if you're writing a Web-based tool that lets editors mix and match page elements to create front doors for each content section, you need to consider not only the current file organization scheme but also possible file expansion. Keep the following in mind:

- Whether the editor's new page combinations will affect the ones that are already live.

- Whether a function needs to be built into the tool to move the old pages out of a live directory and where the old pages will go.

- How long the process will take and whether it's a cumulative process or a fresh process every time. For example, a cumulative page tool would produce all the possible elements and combinations an editor had to choose from; after a year or two of publishing, loading the tool would take longer than using it. If the tool were written with some stringent display parameters, it would be less of a system load, and it would be easier to use.

So before you buy or begin to write any tool, remember that your goal is to buy a tool that will fit into and grow with the site's application framework. You want a tool that will retain its ease of use over time, with relatively few modifications.

Figure 2.7 illustrates the flow of individual site pages through the site's development chain.

FIGURE 2.7:

A typical Web page development path

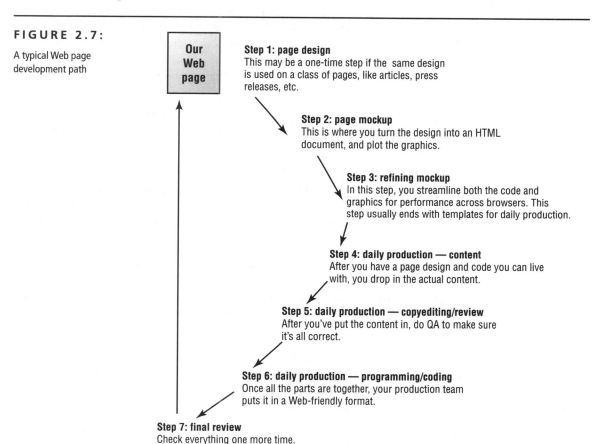

Our Web page

Step 1: page design
This may be a one-time step if the same design is used on a class of pages, like articles, press releases, etc.

Step 2: page mockup
This is where you turn the design into an HTML document, and plot the graphics.

Step 3: refining mockup
In this step, you streamline both the code and graphics for performance across browsers. This step usually ends with templates for daily production.

Step 4: daily production — content
After you have a page design and code you can live with, you drop in the actual content.

Step 5: daily production — copyediting/review
After you've put the content in, do QA to make sure it's all correct.

Step 6: daily production — programming/coding
Once all the parts are together, your production team puts it in a Web-friendly format.

Step 7: final review
Check everything one more time.

How Important Is Standard Technology to Me?

As I mentioned previously, one of the major drawbacks to off-the-shelf tools is that they're often built using proprietary languages. This can present problems if you're trying to integrate the results into a website that's meant to be standards-compliant. It's also a problem if you stake a large part of your site development on an emerging technology before other companies have had a chance to play with it and develop other, possibly better ways of accomplishing the same task.

WARNING Before you invest a significant amount of time or money in building or integrating a very new, nonstandard technology into your site, measure the benefits against the possible drawbacks. Is solving a very specific problem worth having to install five extra troubleshooting routes?

This warning isn't restricted to hardware or software: it also applies to development languages. One very good example of the consequences of nonstandard technology adoption is the emergence of the `<layer>` tag, a browser-specific tag Netscape introduced with its 4.0 browser.

A container tag that supported style sheet attributes and provided a handy object for JavaScript, `<layer>` was like the `<div>` tag, only nonstandard. Netscape built elaborate DHTML displays using `<layer>`s; JavaScript in Netscape allowed developers to write object-oriented code that manipulated the `<layer>` containers with seamless ease.

Unfortunately, if you viewed the same demos in anything other than Netscape 4.*x*, you missed the experience. Pages with `<div>` tags degraded a little more gracefully because `<div>` had been incorporated in the HTML standard since HTML 3.0. But anyone who had staked their cutting-edge development on the `<layer>` tag got burned.

The moral of the story is not that browser extensions are wrong—several of the now-standard tags in HTML started life as a browser-specific extension. The moral is that solving one problem—control of objects on a page by using `<layer>`s and JavaScript—caused many more problems.

If you're going to adopt a nonstandard technology because you honestly think it is the best solution, be prepared to have a backup plan.

The two contrasting screenshots shown in Figures 2.8 and 2.9 demonstrate what happens when a site doesn't consider adapting its pages to accommodate two different browsers. Figure 2.8 shows a page that relies on `<layer>` tags in Netscape, which supports layers; Figure 2.9 shows the page in Microsoft Internet Explorer, which does not.

FIGURE 2.8:

A simple layers-based
layout in a browser that
supports layers

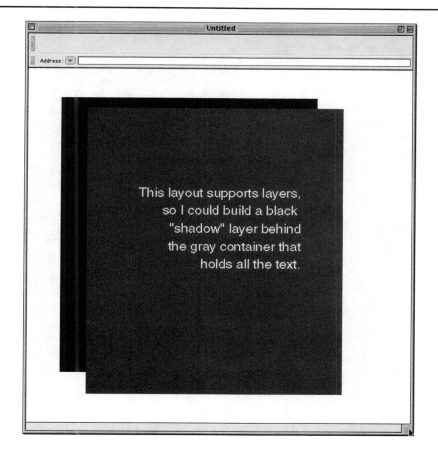

FIGURE 2.8:

A simple layers-based
layout in a browser that
supports layers

How Much Support Is This Tool Going to Have?

Support is another area where the difference between building a tool and buying
it is especially sharp.

Let's look at the support issues if you build the tools in-house. You enjoy access
to the developers as they're developing the tools, and you'll be able to ask a lot of
questions on initial installation. You'll know that the tool is developed to blend in
with your entire application environment.

FIGURE 2.9:

The same layout in a browser
that does not support layers

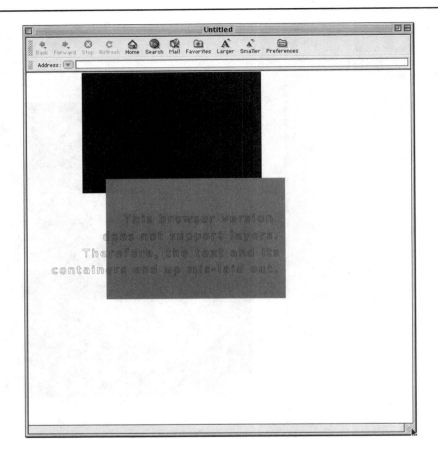

But how much support can you count on in the long run? The department that builds the tool may have done so as a temporary solution, or they may regard the tool as sufficiently flexible and self-explanatory. Or, they simply may not have the time and resources to support the tool after they develop it. Or—and this is a worst case scenario—the people who develop the tool may leave the company and nobody else will know how the tool was developed. In-house development is no guarantee of in-house support.

If you buy a tool from an established software company, you can typically trust that they will offer some type of support to their customers. Depending on the tool and the vendor, you may have e-mail or phone numbers for questioning. You may be able to access an application bug database, so you can see if other people using the tool have encountered the same bugs you did. You may even enjoy a certain number of hours of free consultation after installation.

However, not every software or hardware company is customer-service oriented, and there may not be a viable user community to turn to for support. Although a number of companies that produce Web-related products have made a noticeable effort to foster a product user/product developer community—most notably Macromedia (www.macromedia.com), Microsoft (www.microsoft.com), and Netscape (www.netscape.com)—many others simply push their product out to the public, then charge for customer support.

Figure 2.10 shows the front page of Macromedia's extensive developer support area.

FIGURE 2.10:

Macromedia's index page to its developer resources, located at http://www.macromedia.com/support/

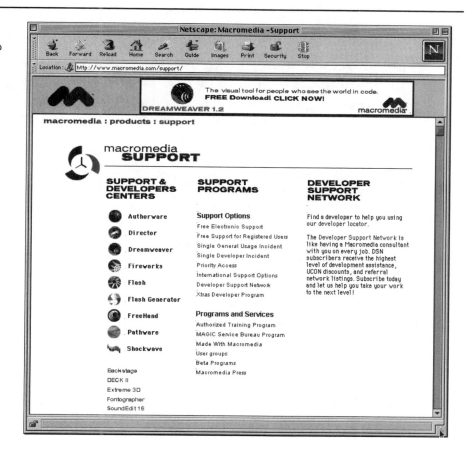

If you're going to buy a tool for Web development, be sure to estimate the cost for support. That cost doesn't just mean the specific hours of follow-up consultation you need after you've used up the initial hours of free consultation provided by the software company. It also means cost in time, cost in hiring a contractor savvy in that tool to come in and work with your site to implement it, and cost in human resources as you train an in-house person as the tool expert.

As you can see, neither building a tool nor buying one is clearly superior when it comes to customer support. Each method has its drawbacks.

When Applications Attack: Anatomy of a Home-Grown Application

In one of my previous jobs, my days and nights were occupied with detail-oriented production on a fairly large website. Because I also had to track the results of my work, I needed a set of production tools that would allow me more control than the handful of Perl scripts I was currently using for logging results.

The engineers at the website built a tool that was perfect for the production I was doing at that moment. The tool was easy to use, provided instant feedback so I could see what I had just done, and gave me an area to test my work. I was doing much more precise sitewide production.

Only one kicker: My boss was ready to move to another level of detail in reporting production. We could try to build a tool that anticipated my boss's demands (which, in all fairness, were market-driven), or we could buy a supported software package that already met my boss's demands and would be easily expandable.

We went with the software package. The tradeoff? We had to install separate Web servers just to support the software, and the nature of my old job changed dramatically. Instead of two engineers spending their time writing and supporting a home-grown tool, we had two engineers trying to maintain an outside piece of software, plus a hefty support bill whenever we needed to resuscitate the system.

The moral is sometimes, the best solution for your customers is going to cause a few headaches for your staff. In this case, the website continues to enjoy high traffic and revenue, so the organization has benefited, even as the human resources required to administer the tool continue to grow.

How Much Time and Money Is This Tool Worth?

When you're trying to decide whether to acquire a new tool, determine what impact the tool will have on your work by considering the following:

- Whether it will make doing your job easier in the short run

- Whether it will be the type of tool that you can build into your website production process over several different revisions

- Whether it will require a lot of extra work just to get it to work right

Once you've determined the value of the tool, figure out what you're willing to tolerate in order to acquire it. Be aware that developing your own software applications for your website requires a huge investment in labor hours, although the cost can be spread out over time. Buying a software package, on the other hand, has a large initial cost that amortizes over time.

Balance what you need the tool to do over the cost the tool will extract from you over time. You may decide that developing your own software allows you to write something highly specific for your site, and the modifications you can make over time will cost less in money and work than upgrading or switching software tools. You may decide to go for an off-the-shelf tool and modify your production process to take advantage of whatever the tool does best. So long as you understand the relationship of time and money to the tool you're getting in return, and you factor in those costs when planning the project, you'll be fine.

What Sort of Risks Am I Willing to Take and Absorb?

Being the first on the block to adopt a new technology can be exciting; it can also leave you high and dry if the code the technology is built on is declared nonstandard and the product becomes a small niche market. Even if you don't have nonstandardization to worry about, how likely is it that the company creating the new technology will be around as long as your website is? Can you rely on them for support?

The uncertainty that dogs the decision to adopt a new technology can be one of your most useful tools in diagnosing your website's relationship with new technologies. This relationship between site and technology varies from site to site. Factors that affect how different sites adopt new technologies may include purpose, functionality, and maintenance.

Purpose

How much of your site user experience will depend on you using a well-supported technology? How much of your audience would benefit from using an exciting but not yet standard technology?

Or, looking at the criteria from a production perspective: How much work would you have to re-do across the site if this new technology tanks? Is the work going to be worth the traffic or press you're hoping to get with adopting the new technology?

If the role that your site plays for your audience is dependent upon a specific technology, you need to base all of your new technology decisions on how well an experimental or new technology will serve you and your audience.

For example: if you bet all of your development resources against the possibility that Netscape's proprietary `<layer>` tag was going to become as widely supported as the standard `<div>` tag, you may have discovered that it was an expensive gamble, especially if your audience is not composed of early adopters.

Functionality

If you're providing a site explicitly devoted to providing good graphics resources, how much experimental effort are you going to put into adopting new sound technologies? If a new technology isn't directly related to the primary function of your site, you probably have more latitude to experiment because the technology isn't as directly integrated. You have more room to experiment when the results aren't going to be a direct reflection of how well your site performs. Conversely, when your site relies on a specific technology, it's in your best interest to make sure you can deliver under a wide variety of circumstances.

If you do rely on radio broadcasts as a part of your website experience, learning about different types of audio file formats and audio file delivery is crucial. Similarly, if your site's strength is its excellent graphics resources, you'll want to make sure you created and displayed your images to the best advantage.

Maintenance

If a nonstandard technology does not become standard but instead fades into niche market obscurity, are you going to stick with it, or do you have a Plan B? Before you adopt a new and risky technology, do you determine how much you're willing to invest in the technology on risk of failure?

Plenty of websites plan for success or for a whole new user experience using a combination of code and plug-ins that nobody's done before. Few plan on what to do if the technology is largely unsupported or if it disappears.

When a technology tanks, your users aren't the only ones who notice. Your production and engineering staffs are going to have to work late to mend the damage and to provide a palatable new solution. Make their job a little easier by fully thinking through the results of what happens if your new site tool breaks.

This section isn't meant to discourage anyone from experimenting with new multimedia formats, new content-serving systems, or new HTML standards. It's just pointing out that any untested technology carries a set of risks that can be costly for a website. Be sure you understand those risks and can accept the results before you embrace the newest, latest, greatest widget.

How Will the Tool Affect My Overall Production Deadlines?

One of the reasons everyone is talking about content delivery processes, dynamic page systems, and DHTML is that all three technologies promise to expand the roles information organization and presentation play in the user's website experience. All three technologies are good ideas with strong industry backing, and once adopted they will provide a valuable bridging point to progressively more polished and information-rich Web products.

But somebody has to do the dirty work of actually hacking these hot new technologies into a site created back in 1995. And while good website tools do one job well no matter the circumstances, great website tools do the job well despite the circumstances.

For example, content delivery processes present a production solution few can argue with: They separate page content from structure so people who write content can enter or edit content then hit a button to merge their new content with pre-written templates. The merged results are then pushed live. This way, production is not dependent on editorial meeting deadlines, and the editorial department doesn't have to get involved in the production process.

However, these systems may require a dramatic reworking of the way that the site's staff works. They may work best using a backend file scheme that is completely incompatible with the way that the developers have been working for three years. Or, they may impose technical limitations on the code or scripts used to build pages. A content delivery system also raises the question of how to integrate newly-generated content with archived content and whether or not the old archived content should be reworked to take advantage of the content delivery system.

One of these obstacles could hinder the intended effectiveness of a tool; several could hinder the productivity of your site. Then the tool is doing exactly the opposite of what you *meant* it to do: make work easier for the people producing your site.

TIP   If a tool makes a production process more complicated for you or your staff, you should invest in it only if the long-term benefits outweigh the short-term inconvenience and delayed deadlines.

Another factor to consider before integrating a new tool into an already-existing production process is whether the tool will simplify a task or make it more complicated. Sometimes, adding complexity is better: It may be the difference between copying and pasting the same HTML file into 50 different documents and taking the time to break out that file into a series of virtual includes or template parts to be assembled later. But other times, a tool can add unnecessary complications to a task. Before adopting a tool that promises to add extra steps to a task, ask what benefit adding those steps has and whether you're going to reap the benefit in the short run or the long run.

Does This Tool Permit Me to Reuse My Most Useful or Popular Code?

Any technology should make producing your site easier. A new server eases the file serving loads on existing servers and allows developers to have more space to build and test site content. The latest version of a powerful graphics program like Debabelizer will allow designers to skip a step when converting a vector-based illustration to a bitmapped graphic for later production.

The tools you use to organize, build, or distribute your content should allow your developers to work more efficiently. One of the most obvious—yet infrequently done—ways to do this is to find a way to break out and recycle the site's most popular code or scripts.

There are two very powerful arguments for finding a tool that will let you do this. First, you will only have to write once and test extensively, as opposed to writing and testing frequently. Second, your server will cache a recycled file, so if a user calls five different files each using a chunk of recycled code, it's less of a strain on the server.

Look for tools that prevent you from having to repeat work. Recycling code, which can work in concert with content-serving systems, is a good, basic step almost any site can take.

How Frequently Do I Plan On Reassessing My Website Toolbox?

No matter how many tools you have at your disposal, there's going to come a time when they fail to do the job you want them to. This may be because the website development process changes significantly, because your site grows too large for a tool to be efficient, or because you want to ramp your site up to the next level.

No matter the cause, your website toolbox is going to need reassessing on a regular basis. "Regular" is up for definition: If your site derives a lot of its identity or content from a grasp of up-and-coming technologies, you'll want to assess or incorporate new technologies on a regular basis. This means, of course, that your development processes need to account for frequent early adoption routines. If your site focuses instead on performing a very specific data process, you may want to restrict your toolbox maintenance to the technologies that refine the data process in your site.

Just remember: *Adopting a technology is not a one-time process.* You're going to have to evaluate its efficacy over time, and be prepared to replace it when it fails.

What's in My Website Toolbox

Assembling the tools you use to build websites is a great way to justify spending an afternoon surfing the Web, but it's also a long-range time saving device. Any time I get a new computer, the first thing I do is install the software tools I know I'll probably need to do my job. Here's what I include in my website toolbox:

A telnet application   Important because you may need to access files remotely, FTP things between different machines, or do live-site editing in Unix. If I'm on a PC, I simply type **run telnet** on my Windows 95 menu; for my Mac, I have NCSA Telnet.

A drop-and-drag FTP application   If you're trying to move entire directory structures from your desktop to a remote machine, using your mouse to drop folders is easy. I usually use Fetch if I'm on a Mac and CuteFTP on my PC.

Continued on next page

An HTML editor   Although I'm opposed to WYSIWYG editors on principle, I do think that these apps are good for quick viewing and editing of files you've already coded by hand. I can't say enough good things about BBEdit for the Mac, and HomeSite is one of my favorite PC applications. Both color-code tags for easy debugging, offer remote access via FTP, and let you view your results in a browser window without leaving the application.

Assorted graphics shareware   I'm not a designer, so most of my image applications are more focused on working with already-created applications instead of making original art. I also do most of my graphics work on a Mac, so the applications I use are GifBuilder, a nice little shareware app that lets you assemble or alter gif89as; GifTransparency, which lets you select a specific color and specify it to be transparent; and Jpeg Viewer, a great app for checking out what graphics look like and how big they are. For a PC, my friend Cliff recommends GIF Animator (available on the companion CD). If you want to create graphics, you're probably better off spending a small chunk of cash on a supported application like Photoshop or Corel's Photopaint. And if you feel like splurging, get Debabelizer; it's great for reducing pallette information and streamlining GIFs. Best of all, it lets you modify graphics in batches.

Multiple browsers   I always have the latest versions of both Microsoft Internet Explorer and Netscape Navigator on my computers. Space and operating system permitting, I also have a few old versions of Netscape installed too (my last PC had Netscapes 2–4). I would also recommend using Lynx on your telnet window to test your site.

Summary

None of these questions is meant to make your life more difficult. Maybe the immediate future is going to be unpleasant. But hashing out the answers to these questions and clearly articulating what you want from a site—and what resources you have to do it—is the project-planning equivalent of an ounce of prevention. Retroactive site repair is often more resource-intensive, time-consuming, and messy than doing the job right the first time.

Using different Web technologies to develop and publish your site should ultimately make your job easier and improve the quality of your site. Filtering out the tools that only complicate your site or production is the first step toward improving how you use technology to maintain or upgrade your site.

CHAPTER
THREE

Creating a Development Process for Your Site

- Adapting software development to Web development

- Performing triage

- Evaluating information

- Implementing changes

- Reevaluating your work

The editorial mission of your site has been hammered out, you've thought hard about the human resources and processes that will be required to translate the site from editorial mission to code, and you've managed to wade through some of the software purported to help you build your site.

What's next?

Primarily, pulling together all of your information and translating it into a four-step site development process. Typically, a *development process* is something associated with creating software products. Much has been written about the "software development cycle." Trees have gone on to an afterlife as a software manual ever since the first software developer realized that they were going to have to repeat the arduous process all over again, only faster. So why hasn't anyone written about the "Web development cycle?" The truth is it's a lot harder to treat Web development as a concrete process. The ideas of "product" and "deadline" are much different.

Benchmarks for Development

Conventional software development involves six well-defined steps attached to a very specific timeline, as illustrated in Figure 3.1:

1. **Conception.** In this step, developers think of the driving idea behind the software product. In other words, they identify an area for development and identify what, specifically, they would want to do. For example, if you looked at your PDA's calendar ability and thought, "Hmmm.... I need a utility that cross-references my schedule with my phone book and to-do list. Why don't I write one?," you'd be conceiving a software product.

2. **Design.** This is where developers plot how to actually execute their idea. This step involves planning all possible functions of the product, all worst-case scenarios, and how to write the code that will handle all these functions and scenarios.

3. **Implementation.** This step is where developers buckle down and write the code.

4. **Testing.** In this step, testers repeatedly hammer on the product to see what breaks it. The developers write code fixes. Then, there's another round of testing to see if the fixes caused anything else to break.

5. **Documentation.** This step involves the creation of two distinct products: documentation for users and documentation for developers. For users, you wrote down information so they can take advantage of all of the tool's features. For future developers, you make notes so they can decipher your code later.

6. **Release.** The product is made publicly available.

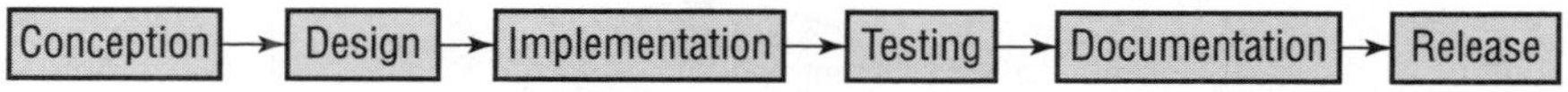

FIGURE 3.1:

Six benchmarks of software development processes

Conception → Design → Implementation → Testing → Documentation → Release

Not only are these steps (a.k.a. *benchmarks*) completed on a given date within the development period, but also once they are completed, they're not repeated. In other words, once the design is approved, it is frozen—no more revisions are made until the next version.

Contrast that with Web development. Designs may be temporarily frozen, but the concept of the product as a whole is rarely frozen. Pages are added, sections are redesigned, information within pages is changed *ex post facto*. In other words, the site is a fluid project, with no tangible end date.

Generally speaking, there isn't a concrete Web development cycle, unless you're referring to the treadmill that characterizes the develop-update-revise-repost loop many Web designers find themselves in. In addition to the maintenance work websites require, there are the added tasks of staying abreast of the latest Web trends, learning how to use new Web development tools, and overhauling the site to take advantage of the Web tools.

The learning and implementing tasks are often the most risk-intensive and time consuming. To paraphrase an old boss: There is no finish line. But there are ways to make sure you don't wear yourself out before you hit your stride as a Web developer.

The easiest way to do that is to recognize that Web development can be parsed into four fluid steps, rather than six well-defined steps. Those steps are:

1. Information triage

2. Evaluation

3. Implementation

4. Reevaluation

Figure 3.2 illustrates how the steps feed back into each other.

FIGURE 3.2:

The Web development cycle

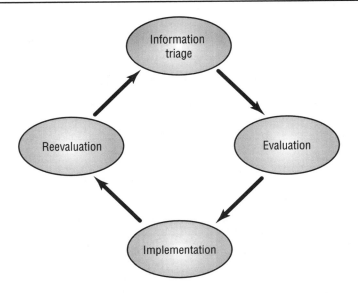

These are the steps you will be taking once you have a clear understanding of what the concept behind your site is. In Chapter 2, there are questions designed to help you narrow the focus of your site and get a clear idea of what goals you want to work toward. The remainder of this chapter will give you tools for taking the answers to those questions and applying them to the hands-on solutions you need to implement in order to build a site.

These four steps characterize the steps and work flow you need to anticipate when you begin to modify or upgrade your site. The beauty of this process is that it's really a cycle: You can step into it at any point and it will still work.

Before You Start: Developing a Concrete Concept

It is now possible to get a Web development job and not have to build a site from scratch. The majority of this book explores the steps and strategies you can take to make maintaining and upgrading an already existant website easier. But if you *are* developing a site from scratch, there is a crucial first step you need to take *before* you enter the Web development cycle: You need to develop the big idea behind your website. In this step, you meet to discuss the goals for your website project and the best way to carry out those goals on your site.

Continued on next page

Chapter 2 should help refine your website concept. A quick summary of what you need to determine includes:

- Who your target audience is
- Who your existing audience is
- What perceived reason you have to build the site
- What functions the site is going to perform
- How the site is going to perform these functions

Developing a concrete concept is more thoroughly outlined in Chapter 2. In many cases, the maintenance or upgrade is going to be driven by an already-existing reason. However, when you build a site from scratch, nailing down the concepts is the first item you should accomplish.

Information Triage

Anyone who works anywhere near a website is dealing with a deluge of information on a daily basis. Everything from hardware configurations to business strategies is profiled and reported across the Internet in the media. Given that there are more than 85 different technology news sources listed in Yahoo alone (and that's not even mentioning subcategories or news sites that are not yet listed), anyone trying to stay on top of the flood of information needs to develop a coping strategy.

The answer is *triage*. Develop a set of criteria for the news you receive and cull your news sources mercilessly. You will get more out of carefully digesting four or five different news sources and mailing lists than you will filtering ten to twenty different lists and sites.

This advice runs counter to the net ethos of "information wants to be free." But there's a big difference between data, information, and knowledge. Data is composed of raw facts or observations. Information is data applied to a particular context or idea. Knowledge is being able to apply information to a specific situation. Surfing 20 news sites allows you to digest a lot of data, but unless you have the time to develop a context for all of it, you're not going to be able to apply it when you need to.

So how do you filter out the sites and lists that comprise your current infodiet? There are a few criteria that you can use.

Determine the information relevance.   Checking an ActiveX site just to see what those wacky developers have done now is a good idea if you're working on embedded extensions like ActiveX controls for your website. If you're slinging text for a finance site, keeping up with that technology isn't going to be as beneficial. Ask yourself whether you've actually referenced any of the items you've read on that website. If the answer's no, banish it from your bookmark list.

The same rule goes toward e-mail lists. Subscribing to an e-mail list is a quick way to learn more about a field and its particulars. But if your mailing lists are flooding your inbox and you're not getting anything out of them, unsubscribe or filter the messages for once-a-week perusal. The quickest step toward eliminating data overload is to eliminate unnecessary data.

Develop an expiration date for relevant information.   Another step toward stemming the flood of data is to recognize that not every item of news has to be read this minute. Prioritize, and stick to those priorities. Realize that a lot of industry news sites are aiming to get a lot of hits, so they're going to update frequently to build a devoted following. Decide when you're going to check for information, do it, and then move on to the next item on your to-do list. Checking for the latest news should not take all morning.

Draw a distinction between news and research.   Be sure you understand the functional differences between news and research in Web development. Researching a topic allows you to gain a broad, deep background. Finding news on that same topic allows you to evaluate the new finding or explanation in context of the research you've done.

NOTE   Don't mistake news for research. Research forms the basis for your development skills. News allows you to assess how new market conditions, software, or standards will affect that skillbase you have. News and research have a symbiotic relationship: They're very different, but they each enhance the other's effectiveness.

Set topical parameters.   You can't know a lot about everything on the Web. You can, however, acquire and maintain a working knowledge of a few topics. Prioritize what you need to know, what you should know, and what you'd like to know. Work on a need-to-know basis, and add or subtract the other categories when time permits.

Use news digests whenever possible.   A lot of prominent news sites send out daily e-mails to tell their subscribers what new articles are on the site; still other e-mail lists do nothing but pull together related news items. Find a few that seem useful and subscribe. The advantage to these e-mails is that you don't have to go hunt for updated information, and the medium is noninvasive enough that you can put aside the e-mail when you're busy.

Swap information with your colleagues.   You and your colleagues are going to have slightly different interests and jobs. If you can give each other thumbnail reports on what's going on in your beat, you'll both benefit from it. Not only will you have acquired some easy-to-digest information, but presenting the information to your colleagues will have forced you to practice triage. And as we all know, practice makes perfect.

Evaluating Information

Stemming the flow of information is only one step in the cycle. Your next step is to evaluate all the information you have. This information includes:

- News of new technologies
- Answers to the questions asked in the previous chapter
- Individual observations from the last round of development

The purpose of evaluating information is to figure out how to apply everything you've learned to the current or next rounds of development. Evaluating information means coming up with a specific, topical focus and applying that focus to every item in your information collection. If the item doesn't fit within the topic, chuck it.

Your focus should allow you to sum up what you want to accomplish by building and maintaining a website, why you want to build a website as a means of accomplishing a goal, and how you want to execute the technical implementation of your website, without ambiguity.

Some of the factors to consider when trying to coming up with the focus of your evaluation are feasibility and time frame.

Feasibility   We all want to provide the ultimate rich media experience without clogging a 14.4 modem, but that's not always feasible. You need to decide how realistic the goals you should have set when you brainstormed your website are relative to the actual capabilities of a given technology as reported in an industry-specific news outlet. You also need to evaluate whether the performance goals you've envisioned for your site are achievable with the current iterations of Web-building tools, or if you're ahead of or behind your time.

Time frame   Some data is immediately applicable to the topical or functional focus of your website. Some data provides you with answers to long-standing site technology implementation problems.

Other data provides you with food for thought and an idea of where you want to go after the immediate revisions or repairs to the site have been done. Sift your information out by its usefulness over different lengths of time.

Ultimately, you want to be able to assemble enough information to make an informed decision about what you want to do, why it is the right thing to do, and how to do it correctly. The catch is to assemble enough and not too much. Too much information can distract or sidetrack. Remember, your site is never going to be done. Break down the information like you're breaking down the work, one step at a time.

Implementing Maintenance and Upgrades

Now that you've filtered your information through the evaluation filter and determined what's useful data and what's a glorified press release, it's time to apply some of that information. This step is known as implementation. The processes and skills that compose implementation are building a better backend, writing better HTML, determining when it's time to upgrade, migrating from a static website to a dynamic one, optimizing graphics and animation, using scripts, and building tools. You'll learn more about them throughout the rest of the book.

Building a better backend   Because a good website is code-intensive, you will want to spend the majority of your time modifying and streamlining your code. Therefore, it is in your best interest to organize your files so you can work as efficiently as possible. Your goals should be to eliminate redundancy whenever possible and to make the primary website functions correspond to modular code that can be replaced or modified without greatly affecting the rest of the site. Chapter 8 covers the backend.

Writing faster, cleaner, more flexible HTML   HTML has a threefold emphasis: It creates the structure for a document, it provides the tags to organize the content within a document, and it controls, or renders, the appearance of the content. The development emphasis for HTML is shifting from a rendering language to a structural language. This means that HTML is going to be used more for creating a structure in which information can be manipulated. In the coming chapters, you'll learn smart strategies for writing HTML that preserves your site's structural integrity across different browsers and platforms. You'll find ways to control the appearance of your site without sacrificing cross-browser compatibility and without wrecking the structural rules set up in the HTML specs. You'll also learn how to write HTML that nudges your site from a series of static pages to a collection of objects that can be manipulated to meet readers' needs.

WARNING   As the numbers of browsers, browser versions, and platforms all increase, the various combinations of the three will grow, and it will become more difficult to justify developing for only one platform.

Determining when it's time to upgrade   Gathering information and applying it to site development is not something you do only when you build the first version of a site. You should also notice if a new technology addresses an existing site production problem.

For example, you run a graphics-intensive site targeted toward people with high-end browsers and speedy Internet connections. Maintaining an accurate color palette for your images is difficult, thanks to compressed file formats and the wide range of gamma settings on different monitors.

Enter a new technology—the Portable Network Graphics (.png) format. You might read up on .png to see that it self-adjusts its gamma levels. Further research turns up two more related facts: It only works with plug-ins in Netscape 4.*x*, and 85 percent of your audience uses Netscape 4.*x*.

Therefore, you could assess whether or not this technology, which solves a longstanding content problem, is worth the measures you'll have to take to integrate it into your site, and whether your audience is technologically prepared.

Migrating from a static website to a dynamic data-driven one   Another critical decision involves shifting your website production paradigm from the one-page-at-a-time assembly method to the mix-and-match compartmentalized assembly method. This latter method allows you to reuse chunks of code across your site as efficiently as possible and lets you expand your site to meet an increasing flow of daily content.

Modular, data-driven site assembly is an elegant way to build websites if you can justify the scope of the project with the scope of your site. If you're sinking an exorbitant amount of time and money into simply keeping up with your content, moving to a modular publishing system is a smart step. If you simply want to move to a dynamic, data-driven site so you can add the latest buzzwords to your resume, it's probably not a good idea.

Optimizing graphics and animation for your website   Although there is a school of thought that advocates design through text and text alone, many website developers have discovered that using graphics sets a distinct look and feel for their site. There are also good information-depicting graphics that add to the content that the text is trying to convey. And once you've moved past using static images, other multimedia effects can enhance your site's content. Those multimedia effects can also heavily detract from the site by slowing down its performance. You'll learn techniques to ensure that your graphical, audio, and video effects work well across several different computer-browser combinations and on several different bandwidth frequencies. You'll also learn how to produce graphics and more sophisticated multimedia effects that accomplish their visual goal with very little trouble.

Using scripts to perform data transactions   Websites are most successful when they're giving users precisely what they want. Users are more sophisticated than many Web developers give them credit for, and they want an interface that allows them to perform sophisticated queries and get reliable results. These data transactions can be as basic as a keyword search or as complex as building a custom front door for a frequent user. They all operate on the same principle: reading a string of information a user gives and returning a page as a result. Using scripts to control page displays, organizing elements on a page, or organizing the path information takes as it moves between user and website and back again will all be covered.

Building tools to make your job easier   Most of the skills you learn on the job are geared toward making the client-side version of a website attractive and functional. However, producing a good product can be hard on the people who are working to create every new file. Part of the focus for maintaining or upgrading a website should be the question, "How can we improve this process for the people doing it?" Being able to wrap your brain around *why* you do things the way you do them, as well as *how* you do them, is an important tool. This tool will prove useful when it's time to re-evaluate the work you have done.

NOTE   Websites can be thought of as having two sides: the client side and the server side. The server side refers to the material and transactions that take place on the machines that serve website files to the public. The client side refers to the files that are displayed on the computer screens of the people who requested the files. In terms of file exchange, these people are referred to as "clients." The differences between client-side programming and server-side programming will be more thoroughly explored throughout the book.

Reevaluating Your Work

This step is crucial but rarely done. After finishing an intensive round of site work, you need to do two postmortems. This is not so people can say, "I told you so." This is so you can see how helpful the previous three steps of the cycle were and how you'd redo them. Since you're going to have to redo them anyway for the next round of repairs, it helps to solidify what works and what doesn't, so you can use what worked and learn from your mistakes.

The first postmortem is meant to capture the immediate thoughts of the people who worked on the latest Web development project. About a week after finishing repairs or pushing a relaunch live, sit down and discuss what went right and what went wrong. Ask the following questions:

- What was the most useful information that passed the evaluation step?

- What do you wish you had known, and what did you not find useful at all? The answers will all help you focus on a more effective round of information triage. They will also help you refine your evaluation process.

- Discuss what about the production process worked well for the people doing the work and what went well for the product being built. If your staff built a fabulous site, but the site drove the staff insane while they were building it, try to determine why the site was so hard to build, and ask if the reasons justify the mental health of the staff.

The second reevaluation should take place a month or so after the new site code has been running as the "normal" site and not the new kid on the server. This postmortem doesn't focus on the development process so much as the success of the final product over time. This time, the questions should focus on whether or not the stated goals—the *why* of what-why-how—have been met:

- Is the new site working better, or did it break more things than it fixed?

- Are the errors being repaired on your site the direct result of the recent site additions? Or are they errors from extant content?

- Determine whether the site repairs have decreased the maintenance work that the staff does.

- Decide whether the final product is one you're happy with, and begin to brainstorm what the next steps are toward beginning the cycle again.

Summary

Beginning the cycle again? Yup. Websites are never done, they're only built and maintained in stages. The four steps of the Web development cycle—information triage, evaluation, implementation, and reevaluation—allow you to get a handhold on the evershifting targets that comprise Web development.

The rest of the book sets forth implementation strategies and skills in the context of three distinct evaluation phases: building a technical foundation for your site; developing a data-structure–driven site; and moving to the cutting edge. You'll be able to see which factors ease the integration of new technology into a site and what technologies make each phase easy to work toward.

World (Wide Web) Domination through Better Planning: Establishing and Applying Standards

■ Defining your staff's duties

■ Getting the support you need

■ Establishing your standards

Building a website is easy. Maintaining or improving a website can present a real challenge. You have to keep up with the ever-accelerating pace of Web technology improvements. Learning HTML once will not be sufficient for building adequate websites. You need to keep up with the latest HTML standards; stay abreast of new protocols being proposed; find out what the trends are in website design, interface, and function; and learn how you can implement them on your site. The standard for an "adequate" site is raised every year.

Suppose that in 1995 you learned CGI scripting, in 1996 you learned more about client-side JavaScripting, and in 1997 you applied your previous scripting knowledge to acquiring DHTML skills. In 1998, you might tackle extended server-side includes, PHP, or XML.

In addition to filing these skills in your head, you also need to apply them wisely to your site. You have to figure out how to take the collection of files you threw together at the request of your boss back in 1995 and organize them into some sort of coherent product. You have to balance the attractiveness of multiple-mouseovers or style sheets with practical considerations: Are they going to solve pre-existing interface and design problems, or are they only perks? You have to create a product that continues to engage your audience without fully knowing who those users are or how they're viewing your site.

The beauty of overhauling a website (instead of simply maintaining it) is that you can radically alter the site to respond to increased information about your user without changing its physical location or the intangible "idea" of what the site is. The drawback to the write-over qualities of a website is that the fluidity that allows for quick data manipulation and improvisation often washes over any initial file structure or standards on the backend.

The Three-Legged Strategy

In this book, I'll base subsequent development strategies on the three-legged strategy pictured in Figure 4.1.

FIGURE 4.1:

The three-legged strategy
of site production

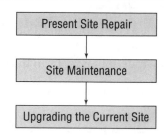

Present Repair

The first leg is *present repair*. Some sites are already built with self-archiving, persistent URLs and dynamic data generation in mind. However, not every site is so well-planned: Other sites are patching new contents and services onto a crumbling framework of 1994 code. Still other sites are adding more content without assessing the necessity or performance of past content. Any site that has ever experienced a jump in traffic, audience demand, or content probably has chunks of content based on hasty backend kludges.

These hasty patches and nonstandard solutions are akin to taping a car's radiator hose with duct tape rather than replacing it when it springs a leak. When something breaks on your car, you patch it temporarily so you can drive the machine to the repair shop for a permanent fix. When something breaks on your website, you may hastily repair it so the site still works, but you will eventually need to fix the source of the problem.

To perform site maintenance: Find these duct-tape code kludges and fix them. Even if the site works because of them, they're departures from the normal production procedure. They throw snags in site-wide repairs or maintenance scripts you want to run. They are an extra consideration in any site expansion or revision you have to do. Therefore, if you want to be able to perform optimal site maintenance—or upgrade your site without being driven nuts by the details—you need to identify those kludges, figure out why they were developed that way in the first place, and find a way to undo them and integrate the new code into the existing site structure.

Site Maintenance

Some sites are one-shot deals: Post the content, then forget about it. But for most sites, you'll need to perform a second leg: *site maintenance*. Site maintenance can involve a variety of tasks, from the simple to the complex:

- If you're linking to outside sites, you need to check the links to see if they're still live.

- If you're publishing new content under a persistent URL such as `http://this-is-my-site.com/news.html`, you need to figure out how to store old content without bogging down the system and how you want your readers to access it.

- If you have a copyright statement on your site, you need to amend it on a sitewide basis yearly.

- You need to find and fix links to content you may have moved or retired.

No matter the factor, realize that your website needs periodic checks to ensure that it is still performing up to the standards you've either setup or adopted over time.

NOTE   Site maintenance is different from present repair. Present repair involves backend work to tune your website for an acceptable performance level; maintenance is priming an already-tuned site.

Site Upgrading

The third leg is *site upgrading*. A good website usually meets two basic objectives:

- It provides an information exchange to its readers.

- It presents that information in an attractive, usable matter.

As Web-based data manipulation tools increase and HTML moves from a flat markup language to more finely controlled document design language, you'll want to capitalize on new technologies to increase the ability of your website to meet those two objectives.

For example, if your website that looked cutting-edge in Netscape 1.1 (granite-pattern background, 1-pixel-GIF leading, and heavily-tabled layout) looks old and outdated now, you need to update your design. If you're getting ready to migrate to a dynamic content-serving system, you need to increasingly compartmentalize the different site components.

Rather than rebuilding the site from scratch, capitalize on existing work. Use the hard-learned lessons from previous rounds of development to upgrade your existing product intelligently. If a site upgrade is done with foresight and planning, it's actually less work than rebuilding the site from scratch.

Writing about what ought to be done or drawing elaborate plans to keep your site in prime condition is much easier than actually sitting down with a few hundred `.html` files and `.cgi` files and trying to unravel the accumulated code that is your site.

The remainder of this chapter is devoted to accomplishing a step you must take before implementing any website repair or maintenance process: developing a set of baseline criteria for your site. These criteria constitute the minimum acceptable standard for the way your site looks and feels for the user and the amount of work and technical expertise the website workers must have. It's a pre-step for the three-legged development process. (How will you perform present repair—repairing the unacceptable kludges—if you don't know what is acceptable and what is unacceptable?)

These criteria will address different areas of website development and will aim to provide guidance for producing or refining a site that can act as a solid technical product. I'm going to outline the blueprint for producing a website that can stand alone as a good site or act as a platform from which to launch subsequent upgrades.

Personnel and Management Issues

Before you can build a site, you have to have the staff who will build it. And although I've covered personnel issues in the abstract in prior sections, now is the time to take a good, hard look at your own abilities and your staff's abilities.

You need to define who's going to own what in the project, what everyone's strengths and weaknesses are, and how you can structure workflow to play to those strengths and weaknesses. You also need to develop your approach to meeting deadlines—do you want to put in a lot of work up front, or do you want to put your site out quickly and fix the mistakes later?

Defining the Duties of Your Staff

The technical skills used to produce a transparent experience for the user are getting more complex and demanding. Therefore, don't just assume that a few long nights and some free pizza will be enough to induce your staff to bust their chops on a site. Start by brainstorming job descriptions for your Web team.

For example, the title *Webmaster* is ambiguous at best and deceptive at worst. The Webmaster can be anyone from an engineer devoted solely to making sure the server machines run smoothly, to the system administrator with the power to set up a direct T1, to the lone HTML jockey in a small office. There are no uniform technical criteria, nor is there any uniform background prerequisite.

As such, you need to have a grasp on who *your* Webmaster is and what his/her duties are. A Webmaster can be responsible for any one of the following:

- Setting up testing and live site areas
- Setting up and configure the hardware that will serve your site
- Arranging and maintaining the bandwidth connections in and out of your site
- Setting up sitewide permissions and directories
- Writing scripts for searching, forms, or page-generating templates
- Developing the site map, information organization, and backend
- Troubleshooting user problems
- Making technical evaluations for software and hardware purchases

Not all Webmasters will do all of these: Some are strict hardware folks, and some stick to being responsible for the user's perception of site performance. No matter what the Webmaster's role, make sure you and everyone on your team has a clear idea of what that role is. It will shape how each of you do your work.

NOTE To prevent the rest of this chapter from turning into a complicated mess, I'm going to define the Webmaster as the person responsible for smooth technical implementation of a finished website. A Webmaster is the person who can diagnose the problems in site performance and who has the wherewithal to fix them.

After you've established what your Webmaster will be doing, you'll need to assemble the people who will build the rest of your site. Here's a brief look at some of the roles team members may play in your site:

Content provider   Writes text for the site, edits text for the site, or copy-edits repurposed content from a print publication or company materials. Content providers typically write the material that goes on a site, find links to enhance the story, and make suggestion for where an article should be broken into two or more pages or how it can best be presented online.

Designer   Responsible for creating the visual look and feel of a site. This may include interface design, logo creation, or simply cranking out graphics for everyday page production. A designer is charged with accurately representing the site's information structure in an attractive visual package.

Information architect   Maps all the possible information flows from two different perspectives: how the content is organized from an editorial perspective and how the reader will be able to access that content.

HTML developer   Takes designs and translates them into code that a Web server can send out.

Technical developer   Works on "how-to" questions: moving data from server to client, generating pages dynamically, and implementing the design and code for the widest possible audience.

Remember that every site will have a different combination of people playing a variety of roles. In fact, the fluidity between different fields of Web design is what appeals to so many people.

Permissions and Security: Who Gets Access to What

After you've assembled your team, it's time to figure out how the work will flow between and among members. The most basic level of consideration is file permission: The ability to copy, move, or write over files is powerful, so be sure that you've set up a system that lets all parties know who has access to what files and where.

NOTE   For examples of building a backend that is conducive to workflow through better file management, visit Chapter 8.

The last thing you need is a designer tweaking font specifications on the live site, or an editor hastily re-editing an article on the live site. The basic considerations you need to have for staff access are task-appropriateness and version control.

Restrict file permissions on live site directories to a few people whose specific job it is to make live-site repairs. You can also restrict permissions to those who have passed a basic skills test, to make sure they fully understand the impact their code or commands might have on the site at large. Restricting permissions to people who only work directly on the file or who work in a group that deals exclusively with a project area, allows you to do two things:

- First, you can help control workflow through a project by setting file and directory permissions at every step of the project to reflect the personnel working on the files.

- Second, you can track version changes more easily, since the pool of candidates likely to make those changes is very small.

Version control is another issue to consider in setting up and maintaining the security of your site; you will want to be able to track not only what changes were made to any files, but who made them and when. This is not a step toward computer-assisted Big Brother management. This saves your coworkers time and sanity when they try to trace the evolution of an `index.html` page from a flat HTML document to a series of crosslinked server-side includes and database entries.

NOTE   You also need to consider what sort of security measures you're going to take against hackers. Chances are, someone who does not work at your company will probably want to alter your files for fun. (In an ideal world, the hacker would do the work you can't get your own staff to do. Unfortunately, that will never be the case.) You may want to dedicate some hardware to servers accessible on a read-only basis for the public. The tighter your permissions are on files, the less likely you will be to leave a back door open for hackers.

How Hard Should You (and Your Team) Work?

Hard work is one of the most visible badges of honor in an office today, but a question remains: How much of that work is really necessary, and how much is done just to satisfy some obtuse criteria handed down from someone in a corner office?

The answer, at least in Web development, is that there is ample hard work to be done, and there are ample opportunities to do it. The truly difficult aspect of this answer is best summed up in another question: How much work can your team do before they're burned out?

Burnout is a real problem and not just an excuse to spend a week surfing the Web. It can be incredibly frustrating to work on a project and then end up redoing the same site over and over for an ever-changing set of demands. Because the very nature of Web development tends to require redoing work frequently to maintain a public level of interest, your team may end up engaged in frequent, intense development cycles.

This makes Web development interesting—you learn something new all the time. But it also makes the field an interesting managerial challenge. If you are a developer or someone who manages other developers, your job is to draw lines. Don't be afraid to say when enough is enough and cut your team some slack. On the flip side, be able to push your team judiciously. Steer steady work instead of waiting to the last minute and pushing an all-night cram session.

Work More Now, Less Later

Be lazy. By that, I mean that you should figure out how much work you're willing to do in the short term to make long-term maintenance and development as painless as possible.

This sort of work philosophy sounds suspiciously like something your mom might have said, but it works. If you're looking at a team of contractors as your primary developing partners, or if you are a contractor yourself, you're going to want to build a site that will eliminate peeved customer calls after lanuch. If you're developing in-house, you're the best judge of how the workday flows and what your demands are. Chances are good that you don't have the time to do endless revisions and repairs on a site after you've put off three other projects to finish it.

Deadlines

When deadlines are part of your regular production routine, you may regard them either as necessary parameters, or minor ordeals. How you view them depends on how well your production routines and tools can accommodate the last-minute changes and chores that crop up. Examine how you and your development team deal with short-term and long-term deadlines. How flexible are the time constraints you're dealing with? What determines those deadlines: are you working on tight schedules to meet market demands, or are you working as a response to some upcoming event?

Being able to understand the ebb and flow of your work and being able to gauge what affects how well you deal with crunch times will help you evaluate both how you're building your site and what you're using to build it.

Getting the Right Level of Support Up Front

No matter how finely tuned your team, no matter how spare and elegant your production process, if you don't have a place to store your site and a way to get it to the outside world, your efforts are in vain. Below is a primer on the planning you should do to make sure the technical details for publishing your site are taken care of.

Selecting a Server

Although most of this book will focus on the really cool things you can do with the aid of your server, we need to talk about what you're actually looking for in a Web server. Part of the criteria may be dictated by simple market demand; the other portion will rise from the approach your organization takes toward Web development over time.

Don't look for a server that can meet your current website demands; look for a server that can meet your website demands two upgrades from now. Make sure your developers can work with it, that they can customize it and exploit its features to optimize the tasks your site performs. Make sure the server is well-supported and has a proven performance record. Ask yourself if the server as-is provides a solid basis for expansion or modification later.

Ultimately, you may not have much of a choice with Web servers, especially if your entire development system is already structured around an existing server. However, you should have an idea of what you're looking for in an ideal tool, so you can begin planning how to utilize your current server for optimal performance.

Selecting an ISP

Building a website is most of the battle, but pushing it live is the final coup. You need to find a bandwidth provider who can give you the physical address and pipeline you need. Once you've created a physical place for yourself on the Net, you need to make sure you keep your place. Your bandwidth provider should be scrutinized as closely as possible. They are, after all, responsible for making sure your site is seen by the public.

Decide what level of customer support you want from your ISP. Even if you've set up your host machines and IP addresses yourself, you're probably not going to be tapping directly into MAE-east or MAE-west. When you find someone who will, proceed with caution. Analyze their routemaps and see what sort of backup measures they have if their primary backbone connection goes out. Ask for client referrals and follow up on them. You will be paying someone to maintain your connection to the rest of the Net. Get your money's worth, and always keep in mind how their performance is going to affect the job you will be doing.

Establishing Standards for Your Website

There's been a groundswell support for the new Web Standards Project (`http://www.webstandards.org/`). This organization is building support for website developers who are arguing—correctly—that the lack of consistent W3C standards between competing browsers makes developing a site more difficult than it needs to be.

The push for simple adherence to established standards is a smart move for reducing work. Until we've got wider industry support for W3C standards, however, it's up to you as a developer to decide what rules you're going to follow, and what reasons you have for following them or breaking them.

In order to identify areas that need maintenance, you need to know why they're broken. Although some errors are immediately obvious, many are cumulative over time, and nobody notices because there are no *standards* to use as a measuring tool.

When I say, *standards*, I don't mean adherence to strict W3C specs (although some people believe that is incredibly important). By *standards*, I mean a set of criteria you can create and maintain to produce a high-performing site. Figure out what you will accept for:

- Sitewide data organization
- HTML layout
- HTML structure
- Modularity and reuse of code across the site
- Image size and dithering
- Page load time across various bandwidths
- Total page size including image files
- Other, highly individual factors

Once you have decided what is acceptable, reinforce it. Decide how far back in site history you want to reinforce the code.For example, if you are finally setting standards in 1998 for the site you started in 1995, you may want to limit standards implementation to the sections or content that is accessed most frequently. Reinforcing standards may also mean upgrading old code or files to run as smoothly as your content. Replacing interlaced GIFs with non-interlaced GIFs and set image height and width values is one example of upgrading a site to meet maintenance standards.

Make Sure the Backend Is Organized

Behind every website, there's a collection of files that are organized in some way. Scripts operate on these files, new files are created, old files are deleted. This whole tree of constantly shifting file interactions is your backend. Whipping those loose folders and lonely files into a cohesive, organized structure is one of the first things you'll want to do before undertaking any large-scale maintenance or upgrades.

Reorganizing your backend is probably the best ticket to finding all the kludges that have been gluing your site together. It is also the best way to get a mental grip on how your site's back parts will come together to create the client-end experience. You'll be able to better anticipate how further expansions and modifications affect your existing site too.

Storing Old Files and Data

Every time you add a new file or overwrite an old one, you're adding another item to be tracked and maintained to your website. If you have the kind of site that publishes several items daily, the number of items to keep track of is rising dramatically over the course of a year.

The question is: What do you do with all those old files once they've been replaced with more current content? How those files are built will continue to affect your new content. For example, if you're planning on moving to a database-driven website, you're going to have to determine what content is important enough to keep. You'll also have to figure out how to pull the content away from its formatting.

Another issue you're going to have to resolve is whether or not you actually want to store old content on your site. If you've published frequently since 1995, you're going to have hundreds, if not thousands, of files sitting on your Web server.

Determine whether or not there is an audience demand for those files. Decide how you're going to store the files so they don't get lost or inadvertently deleted.

Of course, if you decide to make only the most recent content available to your audience, you will need to set up a method to gently push your readers away from old files they've bookmarked. A redirect, or message page, should also be part of your backend storage system, so even if users don't get what they want, they just might find they get what they need.

Scripting and Your Site

Scripts are small, effective collections of commands that can do two different things: They can extend the functionality of the client-side Web page, or they can act as a functional glue between elements on the backend. As website production concerns move from what looks good to what can be done realistically, scripts can be your best friend. They can do the grunt work of searching and replacing, they can pull backend data into an HTML template, and they can glue several different backend parts together.

Examine the role that scripts play in your website. If applicable, determine the obstacles hindering fuller implementation of scripts. Begin developing with the assumption that markup language is only going to be the frontend of a set of tools allowing you to push information-rich sites to the public.

Handling Your HTML

HTML has been called the *lingua franca* of the Web or the *patois* of the Web. What this means is that it's a common vocabulary used to communicate ideas to a wide audience that speaks different tongues. Think of HTML as a pidgin language that mediates between computers and the browsers they use.

But pidgins only work if they have a base structure that everyone can understand. And just as a pidgin language has an agreed-upon vocabulary and word order, so should your HTML have a vocabulary and tag order that all browsers can understand.

The Importance of Flexible HTML

HTML files offer you the ability to constantly modify or add to the code in order to improve the final product. What appears in a user's window may be beautiful, but the backend product can quickly become a maze of additional chunks of code and kludges, rendering your code inflexible. Your site's functionality may hinge on a strange combination of code patched in over different revision rounds, and you may discover that it's difficult to divorce different functions from the entire body of code.

A well-maintained, easily-upgradable site is one where the code is flexible and can be easily modified without altering unrelated website functions.

Practice Defensive HTML

Making your site visually and structurally consistent is one step toward improved site usability. The next step is building code into your site that responds to extreme user situations.

Think like a driving instructor: Assume that everything that approaches your site is doing so under less than optimal conditions. Remember that the number of browser, hardware, and bandwidth combinations is almost infinite. The combination of circumstances means that your website is going to appear differently on different browser-computer combinations. How do you recognize that and work with or around it? How have you built your site to respond to these combinations? Are you exploiting all of the possible technologies to deliver a product that works well?

If you're limiting your technologies to a specific platform or standard, why? How are you dealing with users who do not adhere to your technological requirements? Having a good answer to these questions may be the best defensive HTML you can practice.

Set Up Data Structures with Conditional HTML

Most computer-based editorial material is online because the computer facilitates a degree of user interaction between the reader and the material that isn't possible with broadcast media. But most sites are still trying to migrate from a flat, paper-based paradigm to an input-and-feedback model. Have you begun considering whether or not this is appropriate for your site? Have you started building measures into your site to migrate toward data-driven sites?

Conditional HTML can help you begin to view your site as a series of structural organizations: Each organization is pulled together by a set of common criteria and composed of several unique parts. Conditional HTML allows you to identify these parts and to begin to use the browser to exert a greater degree of control over their appearance and performance within the finished page.

Image Optimization

Images can perform important interface functions, but they can also detract from the total interface goal by making the site less usable. In order to make sure images are working for your site and not against it, make sure you've adopted a workable pallette like the Netscape Color Lookup Table (CLUT—a collection of 216 colors that don't dither across browsers). The palette can reduce your image size by reworking the images to be mapped to fewer bits, and it can make sure your images reproduce equally well across browsers and computers.

You can also examine your animated GIFs to make sure you're using motion and frames as prudently as possible. You can optimize how you call your images if you're using the same types of images over and over.

In other words, images should be subject to the same rigorous standards you would apply to your code. You should make sure their palette, image size, and function are as efficiently utilized as the rest of the components building your pages.

Bandwidth Optimization

Bandwidth is a hot word among the Web crowd. Generally speaking, it's the capacity that users and servers have to send and receive requests over a specifically-sized pipe. In this case, bandwidth optimization is ensuring that your site gets to your users as quickly as possible.

Ask yourself the following questions:

- Do you cache frequently served files?

- Have you thought of ways to optimize the load that your server has to handle from clients?

- How do your employees access your server?

The first round of any site development should, of course, be plotting how you're going to plan your site. But part of executing site maintenance—the second leg of our process—should be how to execute your site with as little server strain as possible. You rely on that server to store files and push them out to a demanding public. Don't make its job any more difficult than it needs to be.

Subsequently, you may want to talk to your server admin and find out what (if any) limits there are to file sizes, script functions, or employee file access. If you are the server admin, you've probably already set these limits, but you may still want to take a look at Chapter 2 to see what development considerations you need to anticipate.

The Reader Experience

As we all know, the most important thing is how the site works for the reader. Your site may have a fabulous backend, but if the frontend is fraught with problems, no one will want to visit it. The two most important things to keep in mind are the transparency of media, and the interest your content holds for your readers. In order to catch their attention, you may want to find ways to model the user experience so it is memorable. The challenge is doing so in a way that lets the readers focus on the experience, and not the mechanism used to create the experience.

Or, to put it another way, think of your site as a roller coaster. You don't want the ride to be so dangerous that users are thinking of whether or not the rails are securely attached. You want to ensure that the ride is so technically perfect the users are only focusing on the thrills they get along the way.

Helping Your Readers Navigate All Those Links

In the abstract, one of the most basic appeals of hypertext is that it offers the reader a chance to control their own editorial narrative. Myriad experiences are available simply by varying where you click a page, and when.

Unfortunately, that same diversity of experience can make constructing a coherent content for your site quite a challenge. How do you advertise the depth of content on your site without sending the reader on an unguided, roundabout trip?

Some websites have responded by limiting hypertext options to a strict linear narrative, especially with longer articles that transfer easily to paper. Others try to balance a linear content approach with a sidebar of related links. Still others try to construct their content to be as "neutral" as possible, so a user approaching it from any angle will be able to jump in and find something.

Decide how much you want your user clicking through on your pages, and know why you want them to click. Being able to map the editorial flow early in the development process is important, because you can build to maximize that flow. Or, if called for, you can rebuild parts of your site to reflect a streamlined editorial flow. Whatever your strategy, remember that anticipating reader interaction helps you to build for it.

Multimedia and Plug-Ins

The ability to integrate different types of media into a Web page is tempting, but is it necessary? You may have had no choice with ad banner types, but incorporating animation, audio, or video onto your site may require more foresight than previously anticipated. Some audio or video formats require a dedicated server. Others work well only within certain browsers or on certain platforms. You also need to evaluate what kind of file formats and platforms you're going to support, and what you plan on doing to accommodate users who fall outside of your chosen parameters.

Many multimedia enhancements require your users to install plug-ins. Asking your users to independently download supplemental software just to view your site is a dangerous gamble. Although Shockwave, Flash, Quicktime, RealAudio, and other rich technologies allow users to process information beyond text and pictures, they have drawbacks:

- The plug-in installation process is relatively painless, but it *does* lead the user away from your site. You can't be certain that a user will return to your site once they've gone to the plug-in company's download page, downloaded the file, installed it, and restarted their browser.

- Another hazard is that your multimedia format could be different than their chosen plug-in. For example, there are two extremely effective audio formats, RealAudio and Liquid Audio. If a user already has RealAudio installed, they may not want to go out, find, download, and install yet another sound-based plug-in when they encounter a Liquid Audio file. Even if Liquid Audio is the optimal production tool for your site, if it's not the prevailing plug-in format among your user audience, you will not be able to promote your content effectively.

NOTE   One possible way around this dilemma is to write scripts that sniff for certain plug-ins; another is to provide your multimedia material in multiple formats. That adds additional production work to your development process and may require additional software or hardware resources.

- Finally, even if a user has installed the plug-in, the actual plug-in use may cause their browser to hang or crash. The last thing you want to do is have users associate your site with a core dump.

You may want to balance the experience plug-ins offer with the amount of work on both the client and production ends of the site.

Summary

These baseline criteria are meant to give you a broad overview of the skills and implementation issues you need to address when you want to build a technically savvy site. Each of these criteria is covered more in-depth in subsequent chapters. If you feel confident that your site is already turning in a solid technical performance, you may want to jump ahead to Part III, where you can see how resolving these baseline criteria allows you to begin restructuring your site as a dynamic data structure.

To read up on the maintenance, repair, and upgrade skills aimed toward building a technically savvy website, turn the page.

The Tools and Steps for Setting Up an Internet Presence

- ■ Understanding Internet protocols

- ■ Choosing an ISP

- ■ Amassing the necessary tools

- ■ Setting up your domain

This chapter is for anyone who is faced with building a website from the ground up and serving it to the general public, or for anyone who has been building sites for years without ever really thinking about how those sites get from their desktop to the public.

Use this chapter as a technical primer: It summarizes the underlying operations and protocols that drive day-to-day transactions on the World Wide Web.

What Is Web Access?

Access is one of the buzzwords in website development. Companies want access to the Web; individuals want access to the Web; people who work on Web-based products want to have increased access to machines, network space, and bandwidth. Obviously, access is in demand.

So what is access? As it relates to the Web, access is the means by which information moves from one machine to another. In this chapter, we will discuss how machines query and serve information and what tools we humans use to mediate our information requests with machines.

How Information Moves on the Internet

As you may already know, the Internet sprang from DARPANet, an experimental network that the Defense Advanced Research Projects Agency (DARPA) was using to exchange information. From the 1970s to the present, more research institutions were joining the Internet infrastructure, and in the early 1990s, the World Wide Web provided a graphical interface to the underlying Internet, thus leading to the proliferation of networked information and entertainment resources available today.

NOTE Interestingly enough, the `<IMG>` tag was not in original HTML, but was Marc Andreeson's brainchild. He came up with it when he was on the NCSA team, developing Mosaic. It began a long tradition of non-standard browser tags.

TCP/IP Transfers

Part of the reason the Web is so successful is that it uses underlying Internet protocols to move information from a server to a client quickly. The simple explanation is this: Packets of information are moved from a server to a client via specific, machine-connecting protocols. But this simple explanation doesn't really help anyone get a sense of how a Web page moves from the server to the client. So let's break it down, starting with TCP/IP.

- In order for files to move quickly, they have to be sent as binary information. The software you use to create or open files translates the 1s and 0s into the format you understand.

- This binary information is sent along the physical wires as a transmission of electronic data chunks called *packets*. *Packet-sending* was a revolutionary new way of sending data across a network; prior to the emergence of packet-sending technology in the late 1960s, computer networks used a technology adopted from the phone industry known as *circuit-switching*. Since a phone conversation can be transmitted as a continuous data stream, opening and closing a circuit is relatively efficient. However, since most computer data transmissions are completed in short intervals, circuit-switching isn't the most efficient way to use the network. The packet-switched technology is a more efficient way to transmit information because it stores all the packets, and then it forwards and assembles them when there's a network connection.

- Packets are only the data chunk plus a final address. There still has to be a way to move the packets from point A to point B. This is where *Transmission Control Protocol/Internet Protocol* (TCP/IP) comes in. This Internet protocol suite provides the information and specifications for moving packets. Each part of the suite has a distinct set of tasks it has to perform:

  - TCP works by breaking up the packets, sending them, reassembling them at their destination, and resending anything that got lost during the first transmission. To make sure that the correct packet sequence is being sent to the correct destination, TCP also keeps track of the order in which the packets are all supposed to be reconnected at the destination location. This task is called *demultiplexing*. To demultiplex a series of packets, TCP takes a file, breaks it down into packets, and attaches a header to each one that includes a destination port number and a message sequence number.

- IP works by taking the packets the TCP sent it, finding a route for the packets to follow, and using the port number as the destination that the packets will head to. In order to make sure that the packets are forwarded by any network system it goes through, IP adds another header. This header has the IP address for the source machine from which the packets came and the IP address to which the packets are supposed to go.

- The packets are sent when a TCP/IP application gives the go-ahead. These applications are commonly referred to as *layered applications*, because they contain four functional parts:

  - The application itself, such as e-mail or FTP

  - TCP, which provides the packet breakdown and assembly services

  - IP, which provides the route directions and relevant addresses

  - A network protocol such as Point-to-Point (PPP) or Ethernet

The layered application then attaches the appropriate headers to the packets so it can be sent off to the correct address.

NOTE   Another term for packets is *datagram*. The two terms are often regarded as interchangeable since both refer to units of data. However, the term packet also refers to a physical, singular item of data, whereas the datagram is a unit of data. The one time there is a clear differentiation between datagrams and packets is when TCP/IP is used on top of the X.25 interface. The X.25 breaks up the datagram into several discrete packets and then reassembles the packets into a datagram before passing it off to the TCP/IP protocols. You don't need to sweat the difference between datagram and packet though. The general network consensus is that it's more efficient to send one unit of data (the datagram) per physical packet.

HTTP Transfers

TCP/IP is only one set of protocols driving Internet information exchange. The other protocol—*Hypertext Transfer Protocol* (HTTP)—drives information exchange in the World Wide Web segment of the Internet. HTTP is the process that controls how Web clients and servers talk to each other, and it allows developers a window into what information the two are exchanging when files are requested or sent. HTTP tells computers what connections are open for sending and receiving files, then sets up a file exchange between a client and a server. It's one level removed from TCP/IP information transmission.

An HTTP transaction has the same steps every time:

1. The client contacts the server at a designated port number (the default port number is usually port 80). Take, for instance, the URL `http://my.foo.com:8080`. The 8080 part is the specific port to which users are being routed. Once the client is connected to the server, it sends a document request specifying a *method* (a type of HTTP command), a file path and name for the requested file, and an HTTP version number. The command `get /archive/index.html HTTP/1.1` tells the server to use the GET method to fetch `http://my.foo.com/archive/index.html`, according to the protocols set forth in HTTP 1.1.

2. After the client has sent the file request, it sends header information to the browser as well, including the browser and platform the client is using.

3. If the client is requesting data via a CGI script, that information gets sent either via GET or POST methods. This is because the HEAD sending method doesn't record any user input; it merely checks the header information any file has, like date requested.

   - If the server is running HTTP 1.0, the connection between host and client is closed once the request is answered.

   - If the server is running HTTP 1.1, the server maintains a connection with the client, which enables the client to make subsequent requests to the server.

Now that you know how information moves across the Internet in general and, more specifically, from Web server to client, you'll have a better idea of why network routes and fat bandwidth are so important to Web sites.

TABLE 5.1: Server Codes

Code	What It Means
1*xx*	Codes starting with 1 are informational; they indicate exactly what processes the server is undertaking.
100	Continue
101	Switching protocols

Continued on next page

TABLE 5.1 CONTINUED: Server Codes

Code	What It Means
2xx	The codes starting with a 2 indicate that the server has processed the request with success—even if the results aren't to your liking.
200	OK
201	Created
202	Accepted
203	Non-authoritative information
204	No content
205	Reset content
206	Partial content
3xx	Codes starting with 3 indicate when a client has requested a file that leads to redirection.
300	Multiple choices
301	Moved permanently
302	Moved temporarily
303	See other
304	Not modified
305	Use proxy
4xx	Codes starting with a 4 indicate a client error, like a query for a file that doesn't exist.
400	Bad request
401	Unauthorized
402	Payment required
403	Forbidden
404	Not found
405	Method not allowed
406	Not acceptable
407	Proxy authentication required
408	Request timeout
409	Conflict

Continued on next page

TABLE 5.1 CONTINUED: Server Codes

Code	What It Means
410	Gone
411	Length required
412	Precondition failed
413	Request Entity too large
414	Request-URL too large
415	Unsupported media type
5xx	Code starting with 5 indicate a server error. The request could not be processed for some reason.
500	Internal server error
501	Not implemented
502	Bad gateway
503	Service unavailable
504	Gateway timeout
505	HTTP version not supported

Figure 5.1 shows an HTTP transaction.

FIGURE 5.1:

The client and server in an HTTP exchange

The client makes a request to the address for a specific file.

This opens a connection between the client and server, per the HTTP protocol.

This is called a *request message.*

Server
www.gimme.com

Client
www.iwant.com

The server sends back the results of that request. It can be a server message like 404 (I looked for the file and it's not there), or it can be the requested file being transmitted back to the address that made the request.

Why Bandwidth Matters

Bandwidth is the blanket term describing a communication channel's capacity to move information. Radio was the first broadcasting medium, and because the frequency of sound limited the available resources, subsequent communication technologies and channels have also been subject to strict regulation.

The FCC is the chief arbiter of regulation for radio and television, with the most recent example of their work being the Children's Television Act of 1990, an affirmative action act mandating the inclusion of children's television programming. There is a rich history of Supreme Court regulation that goes back to the early 1940s. Basing an opinion on the 1919 contention that free speech was a marketplace of ideas, Associate Justice Felix Frankfurter wrote in 1943, "[radio broadcasting] facilities are limited; they are not available to all who wish to use them; the radio spectrum is simply not large enough to accommodate everyone," thus paving the way for a series of decisions justifying regulation for a resource perceived to be scarce.

NOTE   A small digression: Radio happens because sound is sent over radio waves, and we have equipment that can translate these waves into something we can hear. Radio waves and television waves are part of the electromagnetic spectrum. Two of the properties used to measure waves are frequencies and wavelengths.

Radios have the lowest frequencies, or rate of vibrations over time, in the electromagnetic spectrum, as well as the longest wave lengths. However, even though the range of frequencies is broad, from 30Hz to 3,000,000,000Hz, some of the lower frequencies are reserved for government use, and the total frequency range is still finite. Neither radio nor television frequencies are an expandable resource; they're a physical reality, like the size of the planet.

Data transfer on the Internet currently takes place over the same types of lines as telephones: Copper cables or other wires that can conduct and carry a series of electronic data transmissions over a limited spectrum. In fact, much of the physical infrastructure of the Internet—at least in America—is leased from Regional Bell Operating Companies. The co-opting of an existing physical infrastructure contributed to the explosive growth of the Net over the past few years. Of course, it has also stretched some phone operating companies to capacity as they discover that a Web-surfing session ties up a greater proportion of their network, and for longer, than a series of shorter phone calls.

Several cyberspace pundits are fond of pointing out that the Internet can comfortably exist on fiber-optic telecommunications networks, and that network infrastructure can expand to meet available demand. However, due to already-existing legislation in several countries, the range of telecommunications services that companies can offer is fairly limited.

As a result, the capacities of the physical infrastructure supporting the Internet are still somewhat restricted. This translates into occasional Net traffic jams and brownouts when a lot of client-server interactions are trying to take place at the same time.

NOTE   Check out this website: `http://www.internetweather.com` to see how the Internet is doing bandwidth-wise.

The number of transactions taking place aren't the only thing that will make your Internet connection choke: The size of the files counts too. The smaller the file size, the more quickly it can be transferred from one point to another. Table 5.2 provides a breakdown of how quickly certain file sizes transfer across the most common user connection speed.

TABLE 5.2: File Transfer Speeds

Page Size	14.4 Modem	28.8 Modem	56K Modem	ISDN
25	14 seconds	7 seconds	3.5 seconds	3 seconds
50	28 seconds	14 seconds	7 seconds	6 seconds

Why does file size count? Because every file you send, request, or receive goes through five different exchanges:

1. Your computer to your Internet Service Provider (ISP)

2. The ISP to its backbone provider

3. Your ISP's backbone provider to your destination's backbone provider

4. The destination's backbone provider to the destination's ISP

5. The destination ISP to the destination Web server

And then the process is repeated in reverse if the Web server is going to send a file back to you.

NOTE An ISP is a company that owns or rents the equipment necessary to set up a point-to-point connection to the Internet infrastructure, then makes money by selling access to that connection to individuals and businesses.

Subsequently, if you're serving websites, it's in your best interest to make small files. It is also in your best interest to find out who your ISP and backbone providers are and what sort of technology they're using to transmit packets. For example, MCI, which along with BBN and Sprint, provides backbone service to the United States, installed high-speed *Asynchronous Transfer Mode* (ATM) switches connected by fiber-optically delivered links, thereby increasing their speed and carrying capacity. If your ISP does something similar, you know your transfer speed will be enhanced even with slightly larger files. Ask your ISP who their backbone provider is and how their route maps are set, and you should get an idea of how long it will take your packets to travel from your site to the rest of the Internet.

Choosing an ISP

The most basic element in putting a website online is guaranteeing that you'll have the means to put it on a machine connected to the Internet. In order to do that, you need to embark on a business relationship with an Internet Service Provider (ISP). ISPs maintain the host Web servers that are connected to the Internet. Once you have an ISP, you have the means to make your website accessible to the public.

ISPs provide Web users with varying degrees of service at varying prices depending on a user's needs and the type of services the ISP is equipped to offer. A single user, such as a Web contractor, might use an ISP as a way to access the Web, send e-mail, or conduct other electronic file exchanges. A user with more diverse needs (such as a business) might use an ISP as the computer-based address for a domain name, or they may require a high-speed connection like an ISDN (Integrated Services Digital Network) or an ASDL (Asymmetric Digital Subscriber Line).

Many larger businesses have a different set of ISP concerns than other Internet users. Any company that relies on heavy traffic to their site to stay in business has moved beyond speed of connectivity and into actual access to the physical network driving the Internet. This kind of access is provided by a backbone provider, as opposed to an ISP.

Terms You Should Know

Memorize these terms. You'll be tested later.

Backbone provider   In network lingo, a backbone is the transmission path that smaller lines tap into in order to move data back and forth. The connection points between these data points are known as nodes; they're one level up from a ISP that allows you mediated access to a network path.

Speed of connectivity   The rate at which you can send and receive data on a network's infrastructure.

Physical network   A lot of web developers, me included, tend to think of the Net in content connections: who's linking to whom. What we're all forgetting is the physical network beneath it all—the geographic layout of wires and the connections that make data transfer possible. For an enlightening and humbling look at what it takes to put this physical network together, read Neal Stephenson's December 1996 article in *Wired*, "Mother Earth, Mother Board," available at http://www.wired.com/collections/connectivity/4.12_mother_earth1.html.

Regardless of the type of Internet hosting you elect to purchase, you will need to ask your ISP several questions to make sure you're getting the kind of service you need at a price you find reasonable. At the minimum, you should find answers to the following questions:

Will my site be sharing a server?   Some ISPs load several small sites onto one server, such as a Sun Microsystems Sparc 20 Unix box. If your site is small and without much in the way of graphics or server interaction, sharing a server may work. If your site contains pages heavy in server requests (like lots of graphics or multimedia files), you may want to insist on your own machine.

How many different connections does the ISP have to a backbone provider?   If the prospective ISP only has one T1 and 10 websites to serve, you may be better off moving to a better-connected ISP. A T1 is faster than ADSL and ISDN at 1.54Mbps.

What blocks of IP addresses does the ISP have?   Finding out whether or not the ISP has chunks of address numbers available is important, especially if you're planning on serving the site on your own machines and expanding the site over time.

What are the hardware specifics and protocols behind the ISP's connectivity?   Your ISP should be able to volunteer information about its network circuits, especially how many physical entrances there are for separating circuits. You should also know what type of routers the ISP is employing to connect to its backbone and whether those routers redistribute traffic in the event of individual machine load failures.

What are the physical facilities of the ISP like?   At the risk of being paranoid, you should make sure that the computers your ISP uses are in a secure environment. Check to see what precautions the ISP takes against fire, flood, and environmental temperature fluctuations. And find out if there is additional security in place to prevent theft and vandalism.

What kind of logging and reporting can you get?   Even if you're paying another company to do the heavy lifting, you'll need access to certain network records for precise website logging and ad reporting. You should specifically ask for access to server logs, and make sure that you turn on referrer information logging.

Will there be onsite technical support 24 hours a day, 7 days a week?   Again, if you're paying for someone else to host your site, you are also paying for them to host your site continuously and to ensure a bug-free hosting experience.

How long has the ISP been in business?   You want a company with some guarantee of permanence.

How frequently will your site files be backed up?   Even though you will be making backup copies on your side, you will want your ISP to back up your data frequently. Find out how frequently the company does backups and what methods they use.

TIP

Some ISPs may argue that you're better off purchasing a T1 connection from them. Remember that if you do opt to route your T1 through an ISP who will, in turn, route it through their backbone connection, you're adding another step in packet flow from your server to the rest of the world. Regardless of what your ISP tells you, you're better off with a backbone provider of your own.

Tools for Assembling a Website

In Chapter 2 you defined the scope and the technical parameters of your individual Web project. Now it's time to step back a level and determine the criteria and limits for the tools and protocols you'll use to serve your site to the public.

Back in 1994, you could walk into any software store and plunk down $20 for something called "Internet in a Box." It contained a collection of software tools, a beginner's manual, and a disk for connecting to an online service; the idea was that everything you needed to hook your computer up to the Internet was in one neat package.

The trend toward one-step connectivity has extended to Web servers as well. Several well known software companies, including Microsoft, include a Web server that you can run on your desktop. Unfortunately, running a professional-caliber website requires more than a PC and a dedicated ISDN. The remainder of this section outlines some considerations for integrating a collection of Web pages into an operational, reportable, computer-based product.

Assessing Your Performance Needs

You may find yourself in the not-entirely enviable position of being the only person in your office who knows anything about the Internet. As a result, you may field lots of questions about computers, browsers, and all things related to the World Wide Web.

Sooner or later, this knowledge of yours may cause your boss to ask for your recommendations on server software. Unless you're a hardcore hardware or software guru in addition to your Web prowess, you may not even know where to begin to find the answer to this question. So don't try to learn everything and explain it all to your boss. Instead, focus on the two most important considerations to start—speed and fault tolerance—and move on from there.

One of the most important factors in choosing a server is *speed*. Since your server is going to be the machine juggling all the incoming file requests and outgoing file responses, you want to make sure it can handle all that traffic quickly. (*Quickly* means about 10 times faster than the average desktop computer.) Several factors contribute to speed. The computer's processes, the storage devices it uses to store files, direct memory access, and the network interfaces are all vital to a smoothly performing server.

The consideration that runs a close second to speed is *fault tolerance*, or the server's ability to function as users and files burst into flames around it. You will want your server to be able to work continuously even as parts malfunction, users try to break your CGI-generated forms, and the applications you use to serve ads break. Most importantly, you want your server to maintain continuous power: This will reduce the likelihood of losing data if your server fails suddenly. Another way to stem data loss is to set up a hard-drive array. This way, multiple drives work together to compensate for the one that goes down—the server equivalent of driving with three good wheels and a spare.

Properly assessing your speed and fault tolerance needs will carry you through most of the server selection process, but you also need to focus on specific server parts. Also known as *subsystems*, these parts can rev up the performance of the server and make the difference between heavy traffic bringing your site to its knees and heavy traffic allowing you to start charging your advertisers more. The subsystem parts you want to focus on are:

Power supplies   You need multiple redundant power supplies for every server machine you have. These redundant systems can switch back and forth between live power sources (like uninterruptable power supplies) so you won't encounter a server shutdown in the event of an electrical failure.

Backup devices   It never hurts to be too paranoid about what could happen to the data on your server in the event of a power outage, fire, flood, or any other catastrophic event. The most common type of backup is done on magnetic tape such as Digital Audio Tape (DAT) or Digital Linear Tape (DLT). These large-capacity (35GB per tape, in the case of DLT), high-speed devices can give you the ability to swap tapes in and out to record all the data you need. You may also want to consider optical recording devices, since they're keeping up with the increasing storage capacities of servers themselves.

Storage capacity   Servers generate a lot of data you'll want to analyze later; they're also responsible for storing, assembling, and executing every conceivable file combination you make available to the public. The recommended minimum storage measure is to use Ultra Wide SCSI drive controllers; if you want to be really cutting-edge, you can research the feasibility of Storage Area Networking (SAN), a technology that relies on high-speed fiber optics to pass and store information between servers.

Memory   Like PCs, servers operate more effectively and efficiently when they have more memory. Cram your machine with at least 256MB.

Networking speed   It's folk wisdom in server circles that the server is the bottleneck for any network transaction. Make your bottleneck as wide as possible. Shoot for an Ethernet interface somewhere in the neighborhood of 100Mbps. Many people are now migrating from servers with Ethernet connectivity to direct fiber connections.

Assessing Your Physical Needs

Once you've established your performance criteria and subsystem criteria, it's time to focus on your *physical setup*. This encompasses everything from where in your office the server machines will be located, to how to keep that room secure, and how to power those machines.

First, consider where you're getting your power. Servers require more power than a typical desktop, so try to get a dedicated circuit for each server machine. This will help isolate the server from the rest of the building's power supply and reduce the chance of the server overloading the circuits or being overloaded thanks to another appliance.

Along those same lines, you should consider how you plan to ensure the server's continuous power. A rechargeable battery device, called an *uninterruptable power supply* (UPS), is one of the best investments you can make for your server's long-range performance.

Once you've tackled the power source and its maintenance, you then need to think about the side-effects of greater power consumption, namely, high levels of heat being given off from your server machines. You'll need to ensure that your servers have adequate ventilation and cooling; the optimal temperature for most servers is 70 degrees Fahrenheit (about 32 degrees Celsius).

Next, think about where you're going to keep your server machines. If they need to be in a cool place, they obviously also need to be in a climate-controlled room, preferably separated from the rest of your office facilities. And as long as you're sectioning off your servers, you should think about making their location physically secure so strangers can't just wander in and begin switching machines on and off at will. And you need a rack or shelf area to store your servers in your secure area.

And don't forget that there may be region-specific issues that you need to take into account. For example, I visited the Sierra Club's server room at their office in San Francisco and noticed that all of their servers are wired to shelves in the event of an earthquake. So whether your geographic location is given to flooding, hurricanes, lightning storms, or tsunamis, you should consider how to protect your server equipment.

Determining the Hardware You Need

Now that you've got a checklist of what to look for in a general Web server and an idea of what you'll need to do to make sure your server has a happy home, you need to go out and buy the necessary equipment. To reduce confusion and eliminate a lot of products you're not going to need, figure out what the server's primary tasks are and what you'll need to look for in a server to accomplish that task. This cheat sheet list will help you out:

Web servers store and dish out Web pages. You will want to pay particularly close attention to how much memory the machine has, how fast its networking speed and interfaces are, and how quickly the CPU works.

Mail servers receive, send, and log e-mail. The physical capacities are the same as for Web servers—any server that deals with large inter-network traffic has separate mail servers.

FTP servers provide an area for storing files for deposit or retrieval. The physical capacities are the same as for Web servers—any server that deals with large inter-network traffic has FTP servers.

Intranet servers act as firewall-protected local servers for storing and dishing out files within a company or organization. The physical capacities are the same as for Web servers—any server that deals with large inter-network traffic has intranet servers.

File servers work with Local Area Networks (LANs). Files and applications are stored on a hub machine that other machines could access; that hub is a file server. Because a file server is going to be accessed at any time by any one of a number of machines, you want to make sure it has large storage facilities and adequate backup equipment. Given that you'll probably have a steady stream of new users, you may also want to make sure that you have a high fault tolerance built into the system as well, so your fresh crop of interns doesn't bring the file server to its knees.

Print servers are crucial if you rely on multiple networked computers and printers. Since print servers store and process requests as a way of managing individual printer loads, the storage capacities for a print server are the top priority.

Database servers make up a dedicated area for storing database files and accessing them. If you are planning to buy a database server, be sure it can do computation, execute stored procedures, and handle binary data without balking. Be sure also to check how much storage capacity the disk has—your database server will need it if it is to do the many high-speed accessing and moving transactions you're asking of it.

Application servers are servers that let multiple users access and operate an application. Some e-mail and database applications live on an application server. Because application servers are basically file servers with live applications, you need to make sure yours has speedy network connections, lots of memory, and a fast CPU or three.

Now you should have an idea of what you're looking for, and you'll be able to ask intelligent questions of server vendors. Now the only thing you have left to do is ask your boss with a straight face for $3,000 to $300,000 for all of this equipment.

How Your Machine Can Have Its Own IP Address

In order to run a network or serve a domain to the rest of the Internet via your humble PC, you need to have a network card installed on your machine. Network cards all have unique hardware addresses.

When the machine starts, its network drivers send an electronic query called a *ping* to the domain; to be specific, the drivers are looking for a Dynamic Host Configuration Protocol (DHCP) to find a server that will allow the machine on the network. The drivers send a request; the DHCP server looks at the request and returns an IP address if the card is configured for DHCP. This positive confirmation is known as a DHACCEPT.

A DHACCEPT is marked with the DHCP server and the address on the network card. As a result, when a user makes an HTTP request, a packet is sent to the DHCP server, which in turn gets the information and returns it to the hardware address of your computer .

This process is known as *dynamic addressing*. The alternate type of addressing is *static addressing*, where a unique IP address is hard-coded into the individual machines hooked onto an IP address block.

Continued on next page

Like so many other methods and techniques in Web development, the two distinct addressing methods have strong allies and equally vociferous critics. Proponents of dynamic addressing argue that a pool of addresses, a pool of machines, and a method for matching the address with a machine logging into the network only increases the ease with which organizations can use IP addresses. Static addressing advocates argue that tracking which individual machines are using IP addresses is vital, and dynamic addressing allows people to sneak their machines onto a network or set up a competing DHCP server to hijack the network.

When it comes down to serving files on the Internet, just remember this: The Web server that answers to the publicly-known domain must have a permanent address, but the machines behind it can have dynamic IP addresses. The persistent IP address allows users to get a response from your site no matter what. The dynamic, behind-the-scenes addressing can be used to rotate a finite number of addresses among a pool of machines that may or may not be connected to the network at the moment.

Determining the Software You Need

Fortunately, the only software you absolutely need is a Web server software package. There is an infinite variety of these, from the open source server Apache (available on the companion CD-ROM) to expensive custom-developed software packages.

If you're going to be running the server yourself, consider an out-of-the-box solution. You're going to want something that offers plenty of flexibility in its various configurable options, so you can continue to refine how your server performs as you learn more about how to administer a server. You'll also want something well documented, so you can figure out how to install and run the software package yourself.

There really are two different paths you can take: You can host the pages on your own server, or you can let your ISP host your site on their server. If you're going to go for the first option, skip ahead to Chapter 8, where you'll find detailed documentation about different types of Web servers and their functions. If not, it's time to start grilling your ISP; see "Choosing an ISP," above, for concrete advice. If you do go with an ISP, be sure to set up a small desktop server—Microsoft bundles one into their NT platform—just so you can get a grasp of client-server transactions and improve your server savvy.

Setting Up Your Domain

Once you've got the bandwidth, the machines, and the site ideas in place, it's time to figure out what address to give your site. The URL is the human address, the name people will be typing into their browsers to find your site, and the address you will be printing on your business cards.

The centerpiece to the URL is the domain address. Currently, the InterNIC only recognizes addresses ending in .com, .net, .edu, .gov, and .mil, plus a host of foreign addresses like .fr (France), .jp (Japan), .cn (China), and .de (Germany).

You'll probably end up with a .com domain. In the next section, you'll find out how to name your domain, along with all the legal, technical, and usability aspects of selecting and registering a public domain.

Naming Your Domain

Choosing the name for your domain can take as much consideration as naming your first-born child. Your goal, ideally, is to have a domain name that's easy to spell, easy to remember, and that links your site name with your company's name and/or merchandise.

Here are some naming tips for URLs that are both memorable and accessible:

- Don't get creative with spelling unless it's absolutely necessary. Naming your site `phyrephlye.com` sounds a lot like "firefly.com" and keeps you from getting into nasty legal disputes, but every time you're reading the URL over the phone, you're going to have to spell it.

- Don't deliberately step on anyone's trademark. In other words, naming your site `malibubarbie.com`, `jaggedlittlepill.com`, or `kingsdominion.com` are likely to get you in trouble with Mattel, Maverick Records, or Paramount, respectively. Trademark law is a little tricky because it's not enough just to avoid directly infringing on trademark; you also have to make sure your name isn't so close to a preexisting trademark that leaves consumers confused. So naming your site `maliboobarbie.com` is also a trademark problem.

- On the other hand, if someone is using your pre-registered trademark, do not hesitate to ask for the name. Before you do, make sure you amend your existing trademark registration to include either Class 9 (computer goods) or Class 42 (computer services) categories. If you are having trouble getting someone to honor your preexisting trademark, ask Network Solutions, Inc. (NSI) to put the domain name on hold. NSI is the company that is responsible for the registration of `.com`, `.org`, `.edu`, and `.net` domains.

- Keep the URL as short as possible. Fifteen characters or less is ideal. If your product or brand name is well-established enough to keep a long name, or if you also provide multiple domains pointing to the same site, you can bend this rule a little. For example, Salon Magazine couldn't get the URL `www.salon.com`, so they initially went with `www.salon1999.com`. They also have `www.salonmagazine.com`. The shorter URL is easy to remember, and now that Salon has built a reputation for itself, the longer name doesn't prevent Web users from remembering the address.

- Avoid strange characters and underscores. There may be big differences between `rock-and-roll.com` and `rockandroll.com`, but a first-time user to the site that you *don't* own won't know that. Always have a Plan B. You may not get the address you want, so be sure you have a few extra addresses picked out that you can live with.

Understanding Host Address Assignment

Without easy-to-remember domain names, the Internet's daily operations would slow to a crawl. The Domain Name System (DNS) provides a system for assigning the hierarchy of simple domain names (for example, `eff.org`, `slip.net`, and `cnn.com`) to corresponding IP addresses.

The DNS assigns these addresses by running *name servers* that hold the information comprising the domain database. The domain database is split up into different zones, and the zones are distributed among individual name servers. Each zone is required to be available to the querying public on at least two different name servers, and each name server typically supports more than one zone. This recursiveness helps to ensure that all the zones are available all the time.

Individual zones within the DNS name servers have:

- data for the nodes—or individual machine connections—within each zone

- data that defines the top and bottom nodes in the zone

- data that lets name servers access the servers in the zone's delegated subzones

How IP Addresses Are Allocated

Before you can get a domain name, you have to get an IP address. This address is a globally unique set of numbers. You've probably seen IP addresses before—they are a string of numbers like 207.135.708.16. The addresses are set up in numeral sequence, so the address system can scale up as much as necessary.

IP addresses are regulated by the Internet Registry (IR) hierarchy. There are three levels to the hierarchy: the Internet Assigned Numbers Authority (IANA), regional IRs, and local IRs.

The IANA is the body that has authority over all the number spaces that comprise the Internet. It allocates different sections of number spaces to regional IRs depending on proven need.

Regional IRs operate in large geographic areas such as continents. There are currently three different regional IRs: Arin (American Register of Internet Networks) serves North America; the RIPE NCC serves Europe; and the AP-NIC serves the Asian Pacific region. The number of regional IRs is going to remain relatively small since the physical scope of the area they cover is quite large, and a regional IR can only be established under the authority of the IANA. For a breakdown of IP addresses, check out `http://ipindex.dragonstar.net/`.

Local IRs are usually national IRs. They're established by IANA and the regional IR that encompasses them. Local IRs are the governing bodies that assign IP address blocks to Internet Service Providers (ISPs).

There are two different ways to assign IP addresses. If the ISP is going to be directly exchanging information with other ISPs, and it has no other routes, the ISP can request blocks of address space from its local IR. However, all other IP address assignments fall under Classless Inter-Domain Routing (CIDR).

According to CIDR, ISPs have to request IP address space from their upstream provider and take what they're given. The only way around this is if:

- the ISP is directly connected to a major routing exchange. These exchanges are composed of four or more unrelated ISPs.

- the ISP has more than one physical connection to the Internet.

CIDR guideline stipulate that IP addresses be given to ISPs in blocks to ensure easier addressing.

The DNS database works by having root name servers point to master name servers. The master name servers host information for each top-level domain (top-level domains are names such as .com and .org). Specifically, master name servers contain the record- and name-server address for each domain. If a DNS server wanted to find the name-server address for sybex.com, it would ask the master name server for .com domains to find the name and IP address for the server that hosts sybex.com.

The machine that hosts sybex.com is the one that holds the IP address discussed a few sections back. This machine ultimately provides the DNS name server with the IP address for sybex.com.

NOTE You may be wondering why all IP addresses are configured like this: *XXX.XXX.XXX.XXX*. The periods separate the four constituent bytes of information that make up a discrete address. Since a byte can have a value ranging anywhere from 000 to 255, there are roughly 4,294,967,296 possible IP address combinations.

Registering Your Domain

Registering a domain is a lot like doing taxes; the earlier you do it, the better. Procrastination can lead to complications. Start a few months before you plan to launch the site.

Follow this step-by-step process to make registering your domain name simple:

1. Check to make sure your domain name isn't taken. This is really easy to do. Open a telnet window, connect to your local ISP, and type **whois *<proposed name>***. If nothing turns up, the name is probably open. *Probably* means either nobody has registered it, or someone is in the process of registering it. Sometimes ISPs have their own whois servers. Better yet, you can go to http://rs.internic.net/ and right on the front page you can perform a whois via the Web.

2. Get the domain application. The InterNIC site has it, as do most ISPs who offer domain-name hosting. You can fill this form out directly from the InterNIC website.

3. Establish your billing contacts and your network contacts. If you're going through the usual ISP routes, they are going to want to be your technical contacts. If you're building a site somewhere in academia, or you're running your own Web server, you may end up being your own technical contact.

4. Assign IP addresses and machines to the domain. Either your ISP or your friendly on-site MIS staff will know how to do this.

5. Take the information from steps 3 and 4, fill out your form, pay the necessary fee, and send the whole thing off to the InterNIC.

WARNING   Registering a domain takes anywhere from five days to six weeks, depending on many mysterious factors. Plan ahead.

Hosting a Domain

Paying someone else to host and administer your domain is a smart move if you're a solo developer or you work in a shop that cranks out websites for other companies. You don't have to babysit your machine and your Web server program, and you don't have to blow your Saturday night trying to figure out why your mail isn't being received. Nor do you have to pay the licensing fees for server software packages.

Fortunately, finding a commercial ISP to host and administer your domain is easy. Since you've already subjected your ISP to the rigorous qualification criteria described earlier in this chapter, you only have to do the following:

- Have your ISP contact the InterNIC and inform them that the ISP will be providing primary and secondary DNS services for your organization.

- Confirm that the ISP is going to enter a Mail Exchange (MX) record for your domain in its DNS database. The MX record has three parts: the name of the machine that accepts all the mail for your domain, the domain itself, and a preference for which machines should accept any mail for the domain.

- Confirm that you will get records for all the transactions that link your domain to the IP address it's served from.

- Get the IP addresses of the primary and secondary DNS servers so you can configure the machines you will be using to serve content and send e-mail.

Once you've taken these four steps, you'll be able to direct people to your publicly viewable domain name, send and receive e-mail to and from your domain, and collect records of all domain-related transactions.

Summary

This chapter gave you a thumbnail look at the technical basics underlying the URL you type and the results you see displayed in a browser. You should be able to sit in tech-heavy meetings now without feeling totally lost, and you should have an idea of the scope of technical work it takes to set up a site.

Once you've ironed out the technical specifics, it's time to begin fleshing out the structure on top of your server facilities. Read on to find out where to begin.

PART II

Building on the Foundation

CHAPTER

SIX

6

Maximizing HTML

- Understanding HTML's three roles

- Avoiding common complaints

- Optimizing code

- Using server-side includes

- Maintaining good code

HTML is the *lingua franca* that binds the Web together. Like most improvisational languages, it does a good job of communicating the basics, but falls short of communicating elegantly.

By elegant communication, I mean employing a full, rich vocabulary where synonyms have varying degrees of meaning, dependent on context. HTML still views the elements on a page as solid chunks of information; all the attributes that each chunk possesses are neatly recounted in the voluminous specs that are finalized about every 18 months.

But don't discount HTML as a powerful tool just because it has some solid and seemingly inflexible parameters. You can still use HTML to produce clear, comprehensible, and compelling content. The trick is in knowing how to look at HTML and the roles it can play, as well as how to manipulate it effectively and safely.

The goal of this chapter is to give you a thorough understanding of the three discrete roles HTML plays, and to tell you how to maximize each of those roles so your site benefits from compact, high-performing code.

The first role HTML plays is as a *structural language*. It lends a skeleton to a Web page, and can be the backbone of any good site. The second role of HTML (though unofficial) is as a *design language*; a savvy developer can use HTML to set up and maintain a rich visual lexicon throughout their site. The third role HTML takes is as a *content markup language*. The organizational structures and tags within HTML allow a writer or editor to pull seemingly disorganized content into coherent, organized information.

Note that HTML wasn't meant to play so many roles: It was developed first and foremost as a markup language and unwittingly assumed the other two roles as people began stretching the capabilities of the tags. In fact, later in the book we're going to look at the recommended approach for using HTML on your site: as a content markup language with Cascading Style Sheets filling in your design requirements.

The purpose of this section is to put your everyday use of HTML in context with the existing recommendations for using HTML standards.

These three roles are discrete, yet they complement each other. Without a decent interface (the province of design), the content is a lot less compelling. Without a solid structure defining the different parts of each Web page, and the site at large, the design is little more than a collection of jumbled visual items. And without some sort of editorial organization, there's no need for a solid structure.

But there is a difference between understanding the relationships these three discrete HTML roles have with each other and trying to mesh these roles into one multi-purpose kludge. A lot of HTML on well-known sites is a series of compromises between good design and good code. Any site that uses embedded tables strictly for visual placement is going to earn the wrath of an HTML structural purist; any site that doesn't set up a strong left-hand margin via spacer GIFs earns the disdain of designers who claim they're crippled in this medium.

This chapter won't solve all of the Web debates, but it will identify some of the common markup hacks out there and offer strategies on how to improve, rewrite, or ignore your code. In order to better understand the philosophy driving the development suggestions in this book, I'm going to start by taking a look at what HTML was created to do as a markup language and what it ended up doing instead.

And now, back to the very beginning...

A Brief History of HTML

HTML got its humble start as part of the WWW Project Proposal back in 1989. By 1992, the first version of HTML had been spec'd out, and the markup language has been evolving ever since.

HTML was written as a spinoff of Standard Generalized Markup Language (SGML). It's formally known as a Document Type Definition (DTD) of SGML. A DTD defines the syntax of an SGML-based language. It could be thought of as a dictionary for HTML, complete with a full description of element attributes and possible values.

> **NOTE** Pay attention to the acronyms here—Chapter 20 in Part IV tells you how SGML is still influencing Web data metalanguages today.

Anyway, HTML was written as a DTD, or explicitly specified document, of SGML. This means that HTML is specifying a document's physical layout and data organization, and assigning specific data attributes through specific tags. Heading are ranked in order of importance (<h1>–<h6>), ordered lists can be specified (<OL></OL>), and documents have discrete header and body sections.

HTML worked as a strict structural language for almost two years. The first browser to break free of line-mode Web surfing, Mosaic, debuted in 1994. Suddenly, how the information looked became as important as how it was structurally organized. People started looking at the physical rendering of tags. They noticed, for example, that you could alter the headline font sizes by forsaking <h1>–<h6> and writing something like:

```
<font size="4">I</font><font size="2">NTER</font><font _
size="4">C</font><font size="2">AP</font>
```

and having it render like this:

This was also a good example of how people began breaking out of standards if it meant their pages looked better. The <FONT> tag did not start out as part of an HTML standard. It was inserted by Netscape, violating the SGML rule of not being a formatting language but a structural language, and was included in HTML 3.2—which wasn't introduced until late 1994.

Web designers also broke away from hierarchical use of headlines and began using HTML for design effect. In 1995, the HotWired website posted an HTML document meant to mimic the eclectic typestyles of Colonial America at (`http://www.hotwired.com/special/lawsuit/`) and it relied solely on formatting markup tags like <font>, <B>, and <I> to assign attributes to the information within those tags.

1995 also saw a rise in graphics as a popular means of document structures and layout—although the results were only visible on the frontend. Sites began using tables and spacer GIFs to control margins and spacing between elements. As a result, many sites were launched without being in strict compliance with HTML specs.

Through the next few cycles of HTML spec updates and browser version upgrades, more features made their way onto the Web. Tables, originally intended to organize data relative to different categories, were quickly appropriated as layout grids. Frames, introduced by Netscape with their 2.0 browser, took the linking function that hypertext documents relied on for navigation and split the navigating experience into two or more windows within the same browser window.

1998 might well be remembered as the year of living conservatively: Although Netscape had released an alpha version of their 5.0 browser as of this writing, much of the Web development community worked on lobbying companies to comply with the existing HTML 4.0 standards. One noteworthy development in HTML use was a decreasing emphasis on traditionally structured documents as more people began exploring script-driven pages where content is composed or controlled via a series of programmed commands. However, even with a respite from a new HTML standard to adapt or a fresh browser to shake up the face of the Web, developers are still working on creating pages that perform consistently when accessed by even the pickiest users on the slowest modems.

Clearly, anyone who is developing for the Web at large needs some tools that explain how to do the most with the least code—and without sacrificing currency for accessibility.

The Three Guises of HTML

The current state of the Web is nearly as tumultuous as in 1994 and 1995. Fortunately, the browser battles have had one positive outcome: People are looking for reliable code that will reproduce well over the incredible array of browsers and browser versions people use to access the Web.

The back-to-basics rallying cry has coalesced in the recently-formed Web Standards Project (`http://www.webstandards.org/`), a group devoted to persuading browser makers to comply with and fully implement established W3C HTML standards. Even with the newly invigorated interest in writing standard, high-performing HTML, a host of challenges already exist for people building Web pages. This section outlines the roles HTML plays, how they came to play them, and how you can maximize those roles for the greater good of your own site.

As a Structural Language

Exactly how wide is the array of available browsers? As of late March 1998, Browsercaps (`www.browsercaps.com`) tracked 54 different browsers, from Acorn to Xchaos. The two biggest browser markets—Netscape and Microsoft Internet Explorer—had over 100 separate browser version/platform combinations. Browserwatch (`www.browserwatch.com`) reported over 182 different user agent/platform/version combinations of Microsoft Internet Explorer and 72 different user agent/platform/version combinations of Netscape.

With so many different types of browsers and access conditions, how do you design a page that looks consistent across any of them? The lo-res option is probably the neatest and easiest: Developers stick to the more basic structural markup tags to organizing the site. Two good examples of this are the Inquisitor Webzine site (`www.inquisitor.com`) and Jakob Nieslen's UseIt site, at `www.useit.com` (see Figure 6.1). Other sites opt to compartmentalize their elements, relying on the user's browser to be able to assemble them all on the fly. Examples of these sites include CNN (`www.cnn.com`) and CNet (`www.cnet.com`), both of which have a navigation bar coded as a vertical table on the left, and then embedded into a table used as the page layout grid. (Figure 6.2 shows the CNet site.) Still other sites use HTML merely as duct tape holding together interface experiences comprised of images, user choices via hypertext links, and frames or Dynamic HTML, also known as DHTML. Two models for this type of site are The Fray (`www.fray.com`; seen in Figure 6.3) and Word (`www.word.com`).

HTML can be used to do some eye-popping design. We'll discuss how in a few paragraphs. But the structural issue remains: HTML was meant to act as the framework that spelled out the physical arrangement of data and assigned informative attributes to the data via specific tags. When a site is built with HTML that only acts as a design and layout tool, you lose the ability to manipulate site elements quickly and efficiently. It's harder to maintain your pages. You can't adapt to new tags as quickly because your old code all hinges on some four-tables-deep layout. You've lost the simplicity that HTML initially offered.

I'm going to tackle specific areas of HTML 4.0 that offer solutions to the sticky development problems above. But first, a look at how and why HTML became a design tool.

FIGURE 6.1:

Basic structural design
from UseIt

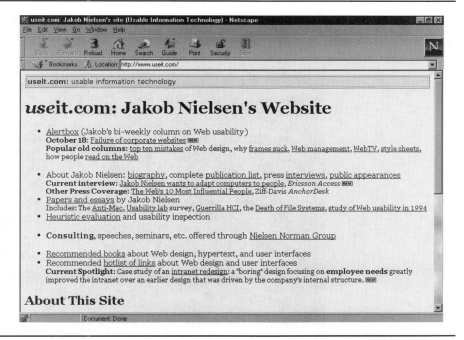

FIGURE 6.2:

The classic CNet layout
(www.cnet.com,
October 20, 1998)

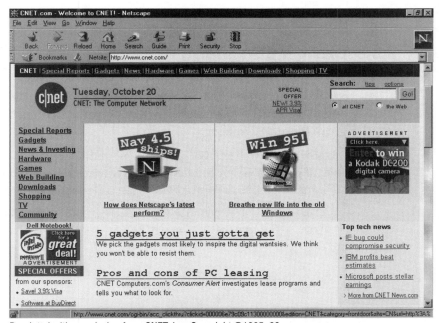

Reprinted with permission from CNET, Inc. Copyright ©1995–98. www.cnet.com

FIGURE 6.3:

Dynamic presentation from
The Fray

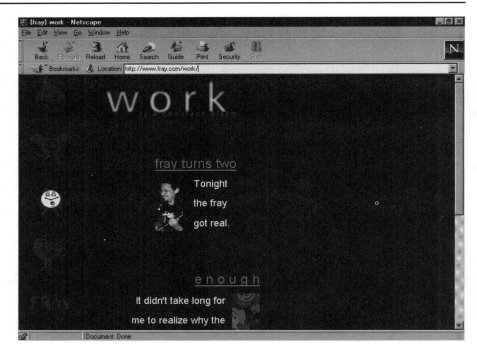

As a Design Language

Hardcore designers will tell you HTML isn't even a design language. In all honesty, it wasn't meant to be. But we do have tags that can be used to control key design elements—space and color—and to assign contextual meaning to data via use of those design tags.

Unfortunately, those design tags don't modify structural elements with as fine a level of granularity, or tight control, as most designers would like. Returning to the intercapping example of before, the code sequence:

```
<font size="4">I</font><font size="2">NTER</font><font
size="4">C</font><font size="2">AP</font>
```

reads like this:

and is the code of choice for visually-based Web developers because the code for attempted intercapping written as:

```
<H1>I</H1><H2>NTER</H2><H1>C</H1><H2>AP</H2>
```

ends up looking like this:

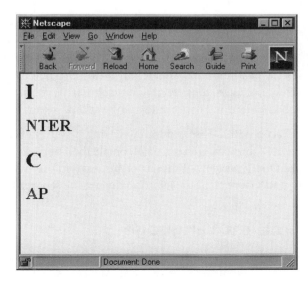

As you can see, some of the structural tags carry fixed physical properties. This does not lend incentive to people trying to convey a very specific visual look within their Web pages.

But is there a call for Web pages to have finely controlled visual looks? Yes, for several reasons:

- **Corporate sites may rely on a logo, font, or color scheme to retain their brand name image.** Think of the McDonald's website (`www.mcdonalds.com`). Would it remind you so strongly of the restaurant if the page were in black and white Times 14-pt. text instead of the red-and-yellow color scheme and restaurant-style font?

- **Reference sites may rely on different color schemes to indicate topical changes.** The page layout and data organization stay the same, but the different color cues you into realizing you've moved into a different area.

- **Different font faces and font sizes can provide a visual lexicon for users that is richer than the** <H1>–<H6> **hierarchy**. Consider how a font size can differ dramatically between the site subhead links and the explanatory blurbs for each subhead. This lets you know that the headline and blurb are related, but the blurb information is less relevant than the headline information.

Visual elements like color or space—anything that will attach the "different" quality to a significant element—provide contextual cues that can be quickly comprehended without having to read the document. They also hold a reader's attention longer and provide easier comprehensibility online.

Unfortunately, the HTML elements that provide the greatest degree of visual control are also those that have almost no structural value. <FONT> tags don't tell you where the item contained within fits relative to the rest of the page; <h1> tags indicate that it's the headline; <h2> that it may be a subordinate headline. The attribute tags—font sizes, font faces, font weight, font color, table color, table size, and others—format their content but don't contribute to the backend structure of the document at all.

Faced with a demand for increasingly automated, easily manipulated Web page content, how can designers reconcile their attribute tags with structural tags? There aren't any perfect solutions yet, but this chapter will later outline some steps to take to add visual attributes without losing the structural significance of a document.

As a Content Language

A third and final role of HTML is that of content editor. An often-forgotten secondary role of a structural language is that it can be used to organize and add context to text or images. As a result, HTML can impose order on information within a document.

The simplest examples of this are lists. Unordered lists <UL> and ordered lists <OL> allow a Web developer to collect items within the body of the document and organize them in a group that has one or more items in common. Further examples include dictionary definitions <DD>, <CAPTIONS>, and <BLOCKQUOTE>, all of which, being structural tags, are meant to add editorial context to the stuff within <BODY> tags.

There is a lot of effort devoted to trying to embrace the seemingly incompatible goals of utilizing a structural HTML-based data backbone, and adopting attribute tags that control the appearance of information within an HTML file. It's really easy to forget that the whole point of HTML was to provide both structure and context to the text and images being marked up. Take advantage of HTML's varied content-type tags to impose a little order on the flood of data you have to publish.

Avoiding Common Complaints

Now that I've thoroughly indoctrinated you into the school of HTML as structural markup, then confused you by saying, "but don't forget interface and actual content!" I'm going to pull this chapter out of the realm of theoretical discussion and back into the HTML-slinging world we all live in. The first step is to offer you a quick and heartless way to determine what development standards you're going to adopt. Pay attention, here it is:

You should support whatever HTML standard will cause the fewest user complaints possible and result in as little work as possible for you.

TIP

A general rule of thumb: the safest HTML standard to adopt is the one right below the current standard; most browser upgrades and standards upgrades take about a year to migrate all the way around the Web. Another factor to consider: As the Web audience grows to include large corporations and relatively inexperienced home users, corporate protocol or domestic contentment may impede the must-update urge that drives the Web development community. It's always good to incorporate new language or browser features after you've figured out an alternate implementation for slow or no-adopters.

A few words of caution: *user complaint* isn't limited to "This link is broken!" or "This frame shot me off onto some Mir Spacestation site!" Users can complain, legitimately, about any of the following:

- Page load time is too slow.
- The page is unreadable with the images off.
- Users can't find what they need.

These common complaints are dealt with in the following sections.

Slow Load Time

There are any number of reasons why your page is taking an excessive amount of time to load. It could be because you've written an extensive and well-documented resource that loads 346K worth of HTML into your document. You may have eight separate mini-forms on your page. You could have more graphics than you do actual typed characters in the HTML. Or you have eight tables nested one inside the other. A fabulous Java applet that allows pull-down menus and scrolling displays takes ten minutes to load on a T1. The Macromedia Flash or Shockwave site takes five minutes to load for a two-minute display.

Think hard: There's a reason you have all those slow-loading kludges in there. Did you post one gigantic document because you didn't have the time or resources to break it down into several smaller topical documents? Do all eight forms actually perform different functions, or are they all part of the same form? Why do you have all those graphics there? Is your site data primarily visual (like a fan page photo gallery)? Or do you rely on spacer GIFs, graphics-based headlines, and graphics pullquotes because it's the only way you can get your page to look consistent from browser to browser? Do the tables allow you to control precise placing of all the visual elements on your page? Do the Java or Flash applets allow you to add functionality that HTML just doesn't support?

Most of these complaint causes can be broken down into a few major categories: You want control over appearance; you want control over content flow and function; you want control over the user's entire site experience by directing the actions.

When you sit down with these three control issues and decide how to solve them, don't think complex or conditional. Think of a solution to your problem that lets your site stay as universal as possible, as quickly as possible. If your document is too big, ask yourself why; then figure out if it is prudent to drop in a splash page preceding the document to warn users that the following page will take their lunch hour to download (which requires that they access the document through one of your site gateways, versus coming in from a search engine). Or break the document down. Both solutions are low-tech and degradable.

If you want to finely control the appearance of your site across different browsers and platforms, you need to identify which is most important to you and your audience. The GIF-based site may be the most visually consistent, but that's true only as long as the images are turned on. Becoming fluent in different standards of HTML and browser bugs regarding those standards is probably a better long-term strategy. A 20K HTML file, well written, can keep visual consistency nearly as well as a 200K text-plus-images collection.

If you're more concerned with controlling your user's interaction with your site, map out what you want the user to do, then see if there's a way to do it in hyper-text. Are extra steps in the process going to disrupt the experience? Can you break down a Shockwave movie into a series of animations? Map out low-tech routes.

Regardless of what you decide, remember that your audience will feel the impact of your decisions as keenly as you do, if not more so. If, for some reason, you have difficulty persuading your boss to buy you eight or nine extra comput-ers and your own separate T1 line just for testing your website, you might want to look into a commercial software package that gauges how long your site will take to load at different connection speeds. SiteSweeper is one package worth looking into; go to `http://www.sitetech.com/`.

Excessive Use of Images

We've already touched on why desperate Web developers might resort to GIFs to guarantee the appearance of their page across the many browsers and platforms likely to access the site.

Ask yourself this question: Why are you designing pages that can't be repro-duced in HTML?

HTML is meant to act as a universal standard. The language itself doesn't change from browser to browser or platform to platform. What does change is how individual browsers or platforms read the HTML document. Earlier versions of a Web browser are not going to have the same support for certain tags as later browsers do. Some hardware reads Web pages differently: PCs have a default font size that is one point higher than Macintosh computers.

You need to design for a wide margin of flexibility. It's a function of designing for the Web. If the information you're trying to convey can only be presented in a very specific format, you need to reassess why you're putting it on the Web. You also need to brainstorm alternate routes for presenting that information, so users can make an informed, consenting choice before clicking the link to a page composed of a 500K image.

For example, if you are putting up a site containing visual data, like the Visible Human Project (www.madsci.org/~lynn/VH/), providing a text interface allowing users to choose what visual data to see is a good start. Another idea, also carried through on the Visible Human site, is a preview-type page where the visual options for large images or movie files are explained before users click on them.

If you're concerned about maintaining a specific look and feel on your site, and you feel that only a combination of colors, fonts, and images can do that, why not try and develop a lightweight version of your interface. Identify the key visual elements and play off those. For example, if McDonald's had really wanted to preserve a precise visual brand, they could have elected to replace all of their text content with imagemaps of menus. Instead, they bank on a color scheme similar to their restaurant, plus judiciously scattered images, to maintain a look and feel. The New York Times Digital section (www.nytimes.com/yr/mo/day/tech/) also appropriates only a few of the print elements on the website to let the reader see that the content is tied into the paper.

There are very few excuses for an all-GIF site. If you or your resident designer insists that only graphics can properly convey fonts and leading, why not build two sites: one low-bandwidth functional site, and one site that fully exploits style sheets and embedded fonts? We'll review how those two newest technologies work later in the chapter.

In the meantime, if you're still pondering ways to make a site accessible to the widest possible audience, check out Chapter 17.

Unruly Elements

Most framed documents are built by people who are courteous enough to provide a nonframed alternative. Not all do, and this is a mistake. Even if you do provide a nonframed alternative, be sure it has analogous information to everything that you offer in the frames. This means if you have a site with a navigation bar in the top frame and the content below, a nonframed option would still include a version of the navigation bar that led to nonframed pages.

Be sure to test your site even with key elements broken. If you've included a navigation bar on every page via a server-side include, that's great. You're recycling code and breaking down your site into a series of functional components. But if that nav bar doesn't work anywhere on the site, your user couldn't care less about how efficiently you're re-using code. If you have no alternate means for moving around the site or finding information in response to a specific query, you need to determine if this is a result of editorial/interface organization or a technology that doesn't degrade.

Ultimately, you will have to decide whether you want to spend more time creating low-tech solutions that speak to a large audience or refining higher-end solutions and finding a way to shepherd your audience toward adopting the technology to see your new and improved site.

Optimizing Code

Standards are beautiful things and a well-designed interface a work of art. But once you're over the initial thrill of creating something new, you're going to be faced with writing HTML that works in a wider variety of circumstances than Crazy Glue ever did.

You can do this one of two ways: You can code your page so thoroughly that the HTML leaves no room for breaking, or you can pick and choose your HTML so your pages use the best possible solution, as opposed to all the solutions at once. This section will pass on techniques for getting the most out of your site via smarter, situation-specific HTML.

These techniques are simple, flexible, and effective: ordering information, using tables, frames, style sheets, or block-level tags, and learning how to use server-side includes. Read on to begin.

Ordering Information

You've decided on your HTML standard, you've been given a big chunk of text to turn into HTML, and you're giddy with newfound insight. Time to slow down and ask yourself how you're going to accurately depict that information via hypertext.

You can take three different routes. First, you can opt for fine-grained visual control and develop a visual lexicon to convey the relationship each piece of information has with each other piece of information. Second, you can opt to use strict HTML tags and assign information meanings via the tags you use to bracket the information. Or, you can try for a happy medium between the two.

The advantage to developing your own visual lexicon and sticking to it is that you may be able to create an interface that echoes your company's print or broadcast identity. You may be able to appropriate a visual style that the marketing department has asked all public material to adopt. Or you may create a page that presents information on two different levels: the first level is a visual code, the second level is the actual content that the code is setting up. This last function is a lot like the intended purpose of structural HTML, except with a little more visual pizzazz.

The drawback to this option is that it is difficult to implement, difficult to maintain, and difficult to replace. You have to develop the specific code for every visual style, test that code for smooth integration with every other chunk of style-specific code, test it for consistent appearance across browsers and platforms, then find some place to drop the content in the middle of the formatting. Because each style is highly specific, there's a good chance it's comprised of a combination of different attribute-style tags. This nest of HTML will be difficult to troubleshoot line-by-line. It will also be tough to write scripts that can accurately search and replace strings of characters, especially if the pages were developed by different people over different times. And when you want to change the look of your site, you're going to have to go through every page on your site to strip out the formatting attached to each object, then find a new way to attach new formatting.

The second option is to stick to strict HTML-compliant tags. The advantage to this is that your code appears not to overtly favor one browser over the other, and it's easy to write maintenance scripts that check through the site based on given structural elements. It's also very easy to write scripts that drop database-stored content into an HTML frontend because you can write very simple one-to-one correspondences between data tables and structural tags. You'll win points for degradability, and proponents of text-based Web browsers will sing your praises.

On the down side, even if you write to spec, you're still not going to make every browser happy. There are two issues here: What version of the HTML spec did you write to, and what browser is accessing your site? If you're using strict

HTML 4.0, you're probably writing more stylistically elegant pages than people hacking together interfaces with GIFs, font tags, and custom formatting in HTML 3.2, but you're still excluding any audience using a 3.0 browser. Moreover, not every browser implements HTML equally well or to spec. Every browser is notorious for not supporting characters that are in the spec, so before you embrace `<CAPTION>` as the answer to the myriad chunks of `<font size="4" face="times roman, palatino" color="#666666"><I>`photo caption`</I></font>` littering your site, see what browsers support it. Appendix A includes a table listing which commonly-used tags are supported over browser type and version; check it before committing to any one structural scheme.

The third option is to try and combine the two previous strategies. Your combinations will depend on what components you deem most important for your site. If it's a one-time publication, like an annual report, you may want to invest heavily in an extremely formatted template and restrict your structural markup to the data dropped into each templated page. Another option would be to invest your visual customization only in the top and bottom site identifying elements and leave the body of your page subject to strict structural markup.

The following suggestions and examples provide platform and browser-safe information presentation options for browsers complying with HTML 3.0 on up.

Combine Two Different Specs

The example I'm going to show you combines the dictionary display (standard from HTML 2.0 on) with font colors. The dictionary tags are an often-forgotten way to use spacing and tabs to connote a visual hierarchy between information objects. In plain English: You can tell what's being defined and what the definition is by how they are indented relative to each other. The beautiful thing about this example is that the spacing is adequate for setting up a basic visual lexicon in case the page has to degrade down to a 2.0 browser, yet more advanced browsers will be able to extend the structural/visual association.

A few words about this code: I did not base any of my visual information attributes on anything that wasn't already structurally defined. This means that I went through and attached `<font color, face>` to `<H2>` and `<DT>`—two items that would have stood out anyway.

Figure 6.4 shows you what the code looks like on a low-end browser.

FIGURE 6.4:

Low-tech version

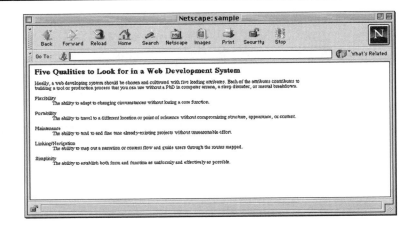

Compare this to Figure 6.5, which shows the same code on a higher-end browser.

FIGURE 6.5:

Hi-tech version

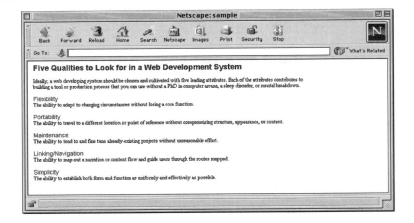

Here's the code I used:

```
<HTML>
<HEAD>
<TITLE>sample</TITLE>
</HEAD>
<BODY bgcolor="#FFFFFF" text="#000066" link="#006633" vlink="#003366"
alink="#330000">
```

```
<H2><FONT COLOR="#006633" FACE="arial, helvetica">
Five Qualities to Look for in a Web Development System</FONT></H2>
Ideally, a web developing system should be chosen and cultivated with
five leading attributes. Each of the attributes contributes to building
a tool or production process that you can use without a PhD in computer
arcana, a sleep disorder, or mental breakdown.
<P></P>
<DL>
<DT><FONT COLOR="#006633" FACE="arial, helvetica">Flexibility</FONT>
<DD>The ability to adapt to changing circumstances
without losing a core function.
<P></P>
<DT><FONT COLOR="#006633" FACE="arial, helvetica">Portability</FONT>
<DD>The ability to travel to a different location or point of reference
without compromising structure, appearance, or content.
<P></P>
<DT><FONT COLOR="#006633" FACE="arial, helvetica">Maintenance</FONT>
<DD>The ability to tend to and fine tune already-existing projects
without unreasonable effort.
<P></P>
<DT><FONT COLOR="#006633" FACE="arial,
helvetica">Linking/Navigation</FONT>
<DD>The ability to map out a narration or content flow and guide users
through the routes mapped.
<P></P>
<DT><FONT COLOR="#006633" FACE="arial, helvetica">Simplicity</FONT>
<DD>The ability to establish both form and function as uniformly and
effectively as possible.
</DL>
</BODY>
</HTML>
```

This is a pretty simple example; your site probably has a lot of these elements on every page, and you're trying to figure out how to deal with them all. Or, you may be unwilling to compromise what you see as irreconcilable structural attributes with your unmovable stylistic attributes.

Here's a mini-makeover showing how you can migrate from one font-driven system over to the handy dictionary markup.

Figure 6.6 is our before example.

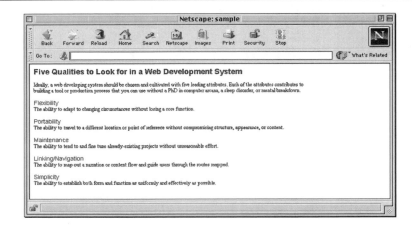

It's beautiful code—until you open the same file on a low-end browser, as shown in Figure 6.7.

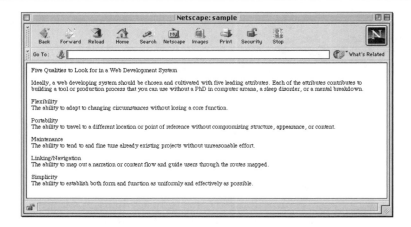

Why does this code not degrade? Take a look at it below:

```
<HTML>

<HEAD>
<TITLE>sample</TITLE>
```

```
</HEAD>

<BODY bgcolor="#FFFFFF" text="#000066" link="#006633" vlink="#003366"
alink="#330000">
<H2><FONT COLOR="#006633" FACE="arial, helvetica">Five Qualities to
Look for in a Web Development System</FONT></H2>
Ideally, a web developing system should be chosen and cultivated with
five leading attributes. Each of the attributes contributes to building
a tool or production process that you can use without a PhD in computer
arcana, a sleep disorder, or mental breakdown.
<P></P>
<FONT COLOR="#006633" FACE="arial, helvetica"
size="4">Flexibility</FONT><BR>
<FONT FACE="times, palatino" size="3">The ability to adapt to changing
circumstances without losing a core function.</FONT>
<P></P>
<FONT COLOR="#006633" FACE="arial, helvetica"
size="4">Portability</FONT><BR>
<FONT FACE="times, palatino" size="3">The ability to travel to a
different location or point of reference without compromising
structure, appearance, or content.</FONT>
<P></P>
<FONT COLOR="#006633" FACE="arial, helvetica"
size="4">Maintenance</FONT><BR>
<FONT FACE="times, palatino" size="3">The ability to tend to and fine
tune already-existing projects without unreasonable effort.</FONT>
<P></P>
<FONT COLOR="#006633" FACE="arial, helvetica"
size="4">Linking/Navigation</FONT><BR>
<FONT FACE="times, palatino" size="3">The ability to map out a
narration or content flow and guide users through the routes
mapped.</FONT>
<P></P>
<FONT COLOR="#006633" FACE="arial, helvetica"
size="4">Simplicity</FONT><BR>
<FONT FACE="times, palatino" size="3">The ability to establish both
form and function as uniformly and effectively as possible.</FONT>
<P></P>

</BODY>
</HTML>
```

See how it relies on nothing but font attributes to differentiate between terms and their definitions? Because the font is the only thing setting up a visual lexicon, the developer has to be extremely specific with the attributes for each element.

If we take our sample and add the font size attribute to all the <DT> tags, we get this page, as seen in Figure 6.8.

FIGURE 6.8:

New and improved with font size attributes

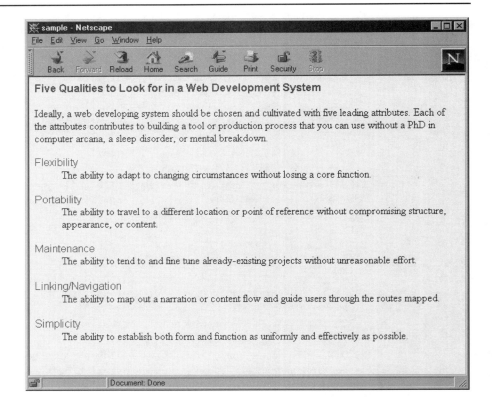

There is one difference: The definitions for each, signified as <DD>, are all indented. If you're trying to build a strong left margin, this is not what you're going to want to see. But if you want to measure this result against easy degradability, or the possibility of attaching a style that re-aligns the left edge of every <DD> element in your higher-end browsers, this is a solid solution.

Use Links

A lot of Web developers labor under the assumption that they have to cram all the relevant topical information for a site onto one page, or else they'll lose the reader. This is not true at all. The issue isn't forcing your readers to click to find the information they want, it's providing your readers with enough information to know what's going to happen when they click, and why.

In this example, I'm going to show you how you can combine hypertext linking and lists to break down one extremely long and unwieldy document into smaller chunks. I'm going to focus on degradability again and on providing a guided hypertext experience to the user.

Figure 6.9 shows the file we're going to make over.

FIGURE 6.9:

Poor ugly duckling

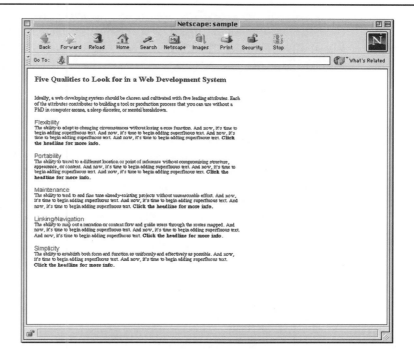

And here's the HTML.

```
<HTML>
<HEAD>
<TITLE>sample</TITLE>
</HEAD>

<BODY bgcolor="#FFFFFF" text="#000066" link="#006633" vlink="#003366"
alink="#330000">
```

```
<TABLE width=500 cellspacing=5 cellpadding=5 border=0>
<TR>
<TD valign=top align=left>
<H2><FONT COLOR="#006633" FACE="Arial, Helvetica">Five Qualities to Look
for in a Web Development System</FONT></H2>
</TD>
</TR>
<TR>
<TD valign=top align=left> <FONT COLOR="#006633" FACE="arial,
helvetica">
 Ideally, a web developing system should be chosen and cultivated with
five leading attributes. Each of the attributes contributes to building a
tool or production process that you can use without a PhD in computer
arcana, a sleep disorder, or mental breakdown.</FONT>
</TD>
</TR>
<TR>
<TD valign=top align=left>
<FONT COLOR="#006633" FACE="arial, helvetica" size="4"><A
HREF="#">Flexibility</A></FONT><BR>
<FONT FACE="times, palatino" size="3">The ability to adapt to changing
circumstances without losing a core function. And now, it's time to begin
adding superfluous text. And now, it's time to begin adding superfluous
text. And now, it's time to begin adding superfluous text. And now, it's
time to begin adding superfluous text. <B>Click the headline for more
info.</B></FONT>
</TD>
</TR>
<TR>
<TD valign=top align=left>
<FONT COLOR="#006633" FACE="arial, helvetica" size="4"><A
HREF="#">Portability</A></FONT><BR>
<FONT FACE="times, palatino" size="3">The ability to travel to a
different location or point of reference without compromising structure,
appearance, or content. And now, it's time to begin adding superfluous
text. And now, it's time to begin adding superfluous text. And now, it's
time to begin adding superfluous text. <B>Click the headline for more
info.</B></FONT>

</TD>
</TR>
<TR>
```

```
<TD valign=top align=left>
<FONT COLOR="#006633" FACE="arial, helvetica" size="4"><A
HREF="#">Maintenance</A></FONT><BR>
<FONT FACE="times, palatino" size="3">The ability to tend to and fine
tune already-existing projects without unreasonable effort. And now, it's
time to begin adding superfluous text. And now, it's time to begin adding
superfluous text. And now, it's time to begin adding superfluous text.
<B>Click the headline for more info.</B></FONT>
</TD>
</TR>
<TR>
<TD valign=top align=left>
<FONT COLOR="#006633" FACE="arial, helvetica" size="4"><A
HREF="#">Linking/Navigation</A></FONT><BR>
<FONT FACE="times, palatino" size="3">The ability to map out a narration
or content flow and guide users through the routes mapped. And now, it's
time to begin adding superfluous text. And now, it's time to begin adding
superfluous text. And now, it's time to begin adding superfluous text.
<B>Click the headline for more info.</B></FONT>
</TD>
</TR>
<TR>
<TD valign=top align=left>
<FONT COLOR="#006633" FACE="arial, helvetica" size="4"><A
HREF="#">Simplicity</A></FONT><BR>
<FONT FACE="times, palatino" size="3">The ability to establish both form
and function as uniformly and effectively as possible. And now, it's time
to begin adding superfluous text. And now, it's time to begin adding
superfluous text. <B>Click the headline for more info.</B></FONT>
</TD>
</TR>
</TABLE>

</BODY>
</HTML>
```

Although the tables will be readable if specialized form of software called a screen-reader accesses them and converts your printed material into an audio "reading" of the site, it's a cluttered and unwieldy way to present the information. It's also unnecessary; the reason the table is set at 500 px is to ensure that readers with 640x480 screens can see the whole table. If the information were un-tabled, it would wrap to fit the screenwidth. Moreover, as the items in each table row grow, the table gets longer, forcing the user to scroll down to digest everything. The only perk of using a table is that you can control the distance between different elements in the document. Still, from a structural perspective, none of these elements are significantly different from each other. The formatting is all that sets them apart.

The makeover, by contrast, reduces the information offered in the index page to one chunk of code outlining the framework, plus a clearly set up navigation scheme. The before and after shots are presented in Figures 6.10 and 6.11.

FIGURE 6.10:

Pre-makeover

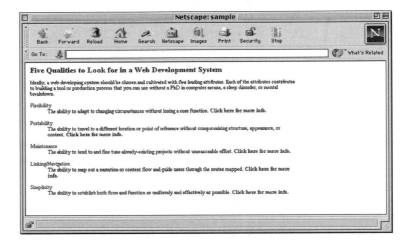

FIGURE 6.11:

Post-makeover

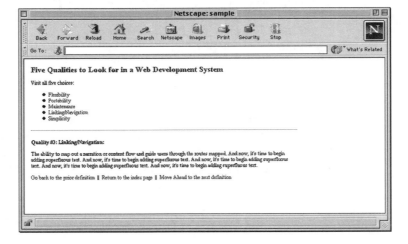

Notice that all of the navigation options for that data set are always open to the user. Note also that two different visual cues let them know where they are relative to the website as a whole: the placement of the content relative to the list, and the color of the links as they expire. The beauty of these two cues is that they degrade across browsers, and they allow room for adding and subtracting navigational sections without having to significantly alter all of the source code. Searching and replacing for repairs is quite simple.

The HTML for the made-over index page is below.

qualities.html

```
<HTML>
<HEAD>
<TITLE>sample</TITLE>
</HEAD>
<BODY bgcolor="#FFFFFF" text="#000066" link="#006633" vlink="#003366"
alink="#330000">

<H2><FONT COLOR="#006633">Five Qualities to Look for in a Web
Development System</FONT></H2>

Ideally, a web developing system should be chosen and cultivated with
five leading attributes. Each of the attributes contributes to building
a tool or production process that you can use without a PhD in computer
arcana, a sleep disorder, or mental breakdown.
<P></P>
<DL>
<DT><FONT COLOR="#006633"><A HREF="ul-
after2.html">Flexibility</A></FONT><BR>
<DD>The ability to adapt to changing circumstances without losing a
core function.
<B><A HREF="ul-after2.html">Click here for more info.</A></B>
<P></P>
<DT><FONT COLOR="#006633"><A HREF="ul-
after3.html">Portability</A></FONT><BR>
<DD>The ability to travel to a different location or point of reference
without compromising structure, appearance, or content. <B><A HREF=
"ul-after3.html">Click here for more info.</A></B>
<P></P>
<DT><FONT COLOR="#006633"><A HREF="ul-after4.html">Maintenance</A>
</FONT><BR>
```

```
<DD>The ability to tend to and fine tune already-existing projects
without unreasonable effort. <B><A HREF="ul-after4.html">Click here for
more info.</A></B>
<P></P>
<DT><FONT COLOR="#006633"><A HREF="ul-after5.html">Linking/Navigation
</A></FONT><BR>
<DD>The ability to map out a narration or content flow and guide users
through the routes mapped. <B><A HREF="ul-after5.html">Click here for
more info.</A></B>
<P></P>
<DT><FONT COLOR="#006633"><A HREF="ul-after6.html">Simplicity</A>
</FONT><BR>
<DD>The ability to establish both form and function as uniformly and
effectively as possible. <B><A HREF="ul-after6.html">Click here for
more info.</A></B>
<P></P>
</DL>

</BODY>
</HTML>
```

Note that it drops the table for a combination of dictionary definitions and
<P></P> tags. The formatting persists across different browsers and platforms
and has some structural meaning below the different visual attributes.

The HTML for one of the content pages is below.

content.html

```
<HTML>
<HEAD> <TITLE>sample</TITLE>
</HEAD>

<BODY bgcolor="#FFFFFF" text="#000066" link="#006633" vlink="#003366"
alink="#330000">

<H2><FONT COLOR="#006633">Five Qualities to Look for in a Web
Development System</font></H2>

<UL>
<LI><A HREF="ul-after2.html">Flexibility</A>
<P></P>
<LI><A HREF="ul-after3.html">Portability</A>
<P></P>
```

```
<LI><A HREF="ul-after4.html">Maintenance</A>
<P></P>

<LI><STRONG>Linking/Navigation:</STRONG>
The ability to map out a narration or content flow and guide users
through
the routes mapped.
And now, it's time to begin adding superfluous text.
And now, it's time to begin adding superfluous text.
And now, it's time to begin adding superfluous text.
And now, it's time to begin adding superfluous text.
And now, it's time to begin adding superfluous text.
<P></P>

<LI><A HREF="ul-after6.html">Simplicity</A><P></P>
</UL>

<P></P>
<A HREF="ul-after4.html">Go back to the prior definition</A>
 || 
<A HREF="ul-after1.html">Return to the index page</A>  || 
<A HREF="ul-after6.html">Move Ahead to the next definition</A>
</BODY>
</HTML>
```

Note that one of the cue methods—placing the text relative to the items preceding it and succeeding it in the sequence of events can be pitched if you're more interested in presenting the page differently.

You can separate out the navigational cue into a server-side include like this:

```
<HTML>
<HEAD>
<TITLE>sample</TITLE>
</HEAD>
<BODY bgcolor="#FFFFFF" text="#000066" link="#006633" vlink="#003366"
alink="#330000">
<!--#include virtual="nav-ul.htmlf" -->
<h4>Quality #3: Linking/Navigation:</h4>
The ability to map out a narration or content flow and guide users
through the routes mapped. And now, it's time to begin adding
superfluous text. And now, it's time to begin adding superfluous text.
And now, it's time to begin adding superfluous text. And now, it's time
```

```
to begin adding superfluous text. And now, it's time to begin adding
superfluous text.
<P></P>
<A HREF="ul-after4.html">Go back to the prior definition</A>
 || 
<A HREF="ul-after1.html">Return to the index page</A>  || 
<A HREF="ul-after6.html">Move Ahead to the next definition</A>
</BODY>
</HTML>
```

nav-ul.htmlf is just a fragment file.

---

nav-ul.html

```
<H2><FONT COLOR="#006633">Five Qualities to Look for in a Web
Development System</font></H2>
Visit all five choices:
<UL>
<LI><A HREF="ul-after2.html">Flexibility</A>
<LI><A HREF="ul-after3.html">Portability</A>
<LI><A HREF="ul-after4.html">Maintenance</A>
<LI><A HREF="ul-after5.html">Linking/Navigation</A>
<LI><A HREF="ul-after6.html">Simplicity</A>
</UL>
<HR>
```

I'll discuss server-side includes and the power they wield in a few more sections; I just wanted to point out that you can write and refine persistent, easily downgradable elements without too much trouble.

Tables

We are all guilty. Almost everyone has written a nav bar that was nothing more than a table with one row and six cells, or one column and six one-cell rows. Then, when faced with the question of how to make it fit into the rest of the page, you put it inside another table.

This is understandable, but dangerous. Not only are intricately tabled layouts hard to debug (leave off one <TD> and you could spend a few hours trying to figure out why no part of your layout is showing up), they can also slow down your page download time. Most browsers won't render the page until every item in every table is read—if you have more than four tables embedded, it's quite a bit of hang-time.

If that's not an argument against heavily embedding tables, here's a supporting argument. A lot of Web pages set up their layouts like this:

```
<HTML>
<HEAD></HEAD>
<BODY>
<!--insert ad call here -->
<IMG src="adbanner.html" width="486" height="60" alt="this is an ad
banner">
<!--layout starts here -->
<TABLE width=486 cellspacing=0 cellpadding=1 border=0>
<TR>
<TD>
<!--now there's a second table for nav bars -->
    <TABLE>
    <TR>
    <TD>
    </TD>
    </TR>
    </TABLE>
</TD>
</TR>
</TABLE>
</BODY>
</HTML>
```

The first thing that renders is the ad banner. Your sponsors may love you, but your readers may wonder. If you do insist on using multiple tables in your layouts, try to maximize the impact through some of the following tips.

Separate Your Tables

Well, at least as many as possible. In the example above, I embedded the second table within a table cell. If you can stack up a few tables on top of each other without embedding them, you'll improve rendering time.

Thus, our old example might now look like this:

```
<HTML>
<HEAD></HEAD>
<BODY>
<!--insert ad call here -->
```

```
<IMG src="adbanner.html" width="486" height="60" alt="this is an ad
banner">
<!--layout starts here -->
<!--nav bar first -->
<TABLE width=486 cellspacing=0 cellpadding=1 border=0>
<TR>
<TD></TD>
</TR>
</TABLE>
<!--now the headline + content -->
<TABLE width=486 cellspacing=0 cellpadding=1 border=0>
<TR>
<TD></TD>
</TR>
</TABLE>
</BODY>
</HTML>
```

Sift Out Your Table as Server-Side Includes

We'll cover includes more closely below, but here's a short working explanation:
Server-side includes are text files that contain HTML. These files are then called
by a master document, which assembles all the text file HTML into one coherent
file that the browser reads.

Our embedded table example would then look like this:

```
<HTML>
<HEAD></HEAD>
<BODY>
<!--insert ad call here -->
<IMG src="adbanner.html" width="486" height="60" alt="this is an ad
banner">
<!--layout starts here -->
<TABLE width=486 cellspacing=0 cellpadding=1 border=0>
<TR>
<TD>
<!--now there's a second table for nav bars -->
<!--#include virtual="navbar.htmlf" -->
</TD>
</TR>
</TABLE>
</BODY>
</HTML>
```

and the file `navbar.htmlf` would contain this:

```
<!--now there's a second table for nav bars -->
<TABLE>
<TR>
<TD>
</TD>
</TR>
</TABLE>
```

The advantage to using server-side includes is twofold. First, you can separate out each table and de-bug it separately. Second, when you move from a table-driven layout to one where <DIV> and style sheet specs allow you fine-tuned control over appearance, you'll be able to maintain the backbone of your document and only rewrite small server-side include files.

Avoid Intricate Table Code

Browsers render all the tables down to the level of detail specified. If you rely on one table to set the measurements for all of the elements inside, that's less code the browser has to churn through before rendering the page.

For example:

```
<TABLE width=500 cellspacing=0 cellpadding=0 border=0>
<TR>
<TD>
<TABLE width=498 cellspacing=0 cellpadding=0 border=0>
</TABLE>
</TD>
</TR>
</TABLE>
```

could probably be rewritten as follows:

```
<TABLE cellspacing=0 cellpadding=0 border=0>
<TR>
<TD>
<TABLE width=498 cellspacing=0 cellpadding=0 border=0>
</TABLE>
</TD>
</TR>
</TABLE>
```

The internal table will determine the size of the table cell for the external one.

Tables can be a good low-tech way to organize your page visually. Just try to minimize their impact on the structural organization of your page, and make sure they don't bog down your code on its way from server to client.

Frames

Let's commiserate on the following frustrating frame encounters:

- You find a framed site where the nav bar lies demurely on the left side of the browser window. Expecting to click on the nav bar and load new content into the gigantic right-hand content window, you discover instead that the new content loads into the left-hand nav window. Hitting the back button only takes you back to the document you visited before hitting the framed document.

- You find a framed site where some of the links in one frame seem to reference the content in a second frame, but the second frame's links launch a new window every time you click on one of the links.

- You encounter a framed document with a content window and a nav window. Clicking on a link in the content window pulls in another framed document—suddenly you have four tiny windows within your browser and no clue as to how to return your browser to one.

Frames proponents might look at the scenarios outlined above and snap "two words: link targeting." While it's true that providing a link target that matches the frame name is one of the easiest (yet overlooked) ways to control hypertext navigation through links, the issue of frames efficacy as a content-carrying device in hypertext remains.

The Argument for Frames

There are many good reasons to use frames. The most convincing ones follow.

Persistent Navigation Bars   If you look at *Salon* (`www.salonmagazine.com`), at press they had adopted a thin navigation bar that ran at the bottom of their site. This bar provides persistent links to *Salon*'s main sections, and doesn't impact the layout at all.

This thin, functional frame allows users to click at whim within the site and be able to return to key navigation points.

NOTE

Be sure to include backup navigation in the main document as well. A lot of people will want to print a page, or they simply prefer a no-frames site. You should make sure that your site is still easy to navigate when a user is viewing it without a frame.

A Great Place to Put Advertising   If you can't imagine altering your main content layout to accommodate advertising, why not alter the document layout and include a separate frame for ads? Not only does this allow you to "separate" ads—which makes setting up scheduling and tracking systems a little easier since they're almost self-contained—it also allows you to change the look and feel of your site while still maintaining an advertising presence.

A word about using frames for ads: A lot of Web sponsors will buy space on a site because they want to be featured in a specific section. If this is the case, a simple script can always pass the directory that the file is being called from so that the ad-serving mechanism serves an ad in response. We'll review more about advertising and your site in the next section.

A Truly Linear Hypertext Experience   Frames that control the loading of other frame contents through JavaScript and targeting can offer a developer myriad ways to create an associative hypertext site. This works well in sites that are promoting a specific content or editorial product, as opposed to a reference product. But you can also use a simple JavaScript to target links in two different frames and do something like change the ad in one frame when content changes in a main frame.

To demonstrate: You have a document—`index.html`. It looks like this:

```
<HTML>
<HEAD></HEAD>
<FRAMESET rows="550,*">
<FRAME name="text" src="content.html">
<FRAME name="ad" src="ad.html">
</FRAMESET>
</HTML>
```

Every time you click on a link in `content.html`, something new loads into the ad frame.

Here's a frame-by-frame/file-by-file breakdown of what you have to do:

```
frame name="ad"/src="ad.html"
```

Since this is a document being loaded into the frame, it doesn't need to have anything added to it.

```
frame name="text"/src="content.html"
```

You have to do two things: Target the link to load a new page into the "text" frame and tell the browser to load a new page into the "ad" frame. To do this, format all of your links in content.html to read like this:

```
<A HREF="newad.html" onclick="windown.self.location='newcontent.html'"
target="_ad">LINK</A>
```

What this does:

- It specifies that the file `newad.html` be loaded into the frame named "ad."
- It tells the browser that the window calling the link (`window.self`) wants a new file too.

You can also use this double frame-targeting trick to load a new nav bar into a window if you want to visually demonstrate to the user that she is moving up or down a level in your site tree. Another use is cueing sidebar frames to load when a new main frame loads, which is great for including related links or sidebars.

The Argument against Frames

But for every good use of frames, there's a use that turns horribly wrong. You may want to skip frames if any of the following problems comes to light:

Link Targeting Is a Nightmare   All it takes it one flawed link in a nav bar to load your content into the nav area and blow the user's faith in your site. If you're planning on cross-purposing the same content or navigation bar all over the site, you may have a hard time keeping file names and frame targets straight.

You Impose Frames on Users Unconditionally   As much as I love the Mining Company's HTML site (`http://html.miningco.com`), the one thing that drives me to distraction is their script that automatically resets a file to pull in the Mining Company's navigation frame. I understand that this script saves a lot of work on the production end and allows them to develop a complex editorial tree without having to check link targeting, but if I want to pull out a file and print it, I can't. Always offer your users both a nonframed alternative and a nonframed navigation device.

Frames can be a powerful way to extend the functionality of your site—just make sure that their addition enhances the way users navigate and use your site, rather than hinders it.

Block-Level Tags

Most early HTML focused on two things: putting HTML into predefined data categories like <body>, <blockquote>, or <DD>, and adding appearance modification to those data-labeled items via <EM> or <I>, and later <font> tags. As website design migrates toward a complex data structure, it makes more sense to start thinking of different chunks of content in terms of block-level tags.

A *block-level tag* is one that encloses a block of text or HTML. By itself, it doesn't have any outstanding data hierarchy or formatting characteristics. But it acts as a wrapper for content, so you can define a class or ID for the stuff within, and attach an appearance or action to the class or ID of the block-level tag.

Code within a block-level tag is affected by the properties that a block-level tag has. So if you define a block-level tag as having bold text, all of its contents will be bold. If you want to fine-tune the appearance or actions of items within block-level tags, you can do two things:

> **Take advantage of the nesting feature of block-level tag tags.** One block-level tag can hold several little block-level tags inside it.

> **Attach a <SPAN></SPAN> tag to items within the block-level tag.** The <SPAN> tag allows you to set those items apart and attach a different style or action to them. There will be more on that in the style sheets section.

I'm going to focus on three newer tags that act primarily as block-level tags..

<LAYER>

This tag is not specified in HTML 4.0: It's a Netscape extension and thus should be used with caution. A layer acts as a wrapping container for the stuff contained within. It is noted like this:

```
<LAYER>
<H1>This is a headline</H1>
<P></P>
this is text, and lots of it. Here is some <b>bolded text</b>.
</LAYER>
```

The text looks like this:

Note that the font is set to the browser's default face. If you were to add one small attribute to the layers tag:

```
<LAYER style="font-face:arial, helvetica">
<H1>This is a headline</H1>
<P></P>
this is text, and lots of it. Here is some <b>bolded text</b>.
</LAYER>
```

you would see this difference:

<DIV>

There are three differences between a <DIV> tag and a <LAYER> tag. <DIV> has been around since HTML 3.2, <DIV> is supported by Internet Explorer, and <DIV> is part of the 4.0 standard. These wrapping block-level tag tags behave *just like* layers:

```
<DIV style="font-face:arial, helvetica">
<H1>This is a headline</H1>
<P></P>
this is text, and lots of it. Here is some <b>bolded text</b>.
</DIV>
```

as you can see:

The only quirk in behavior is that Netscape 4.0 may render <DIV> tags with a line break after them, so closely lining up chunks of code via <DIV>s doesn't reproduce faithfully across browsers yet.

<OBJECT>

This tag is still a tag in spec only, and as of this writing, no browser has yet to implement it. The push for integrating <OBJECT> into working HTML is strong: You can write conditional objects within the <OBJECT></OBJECT> tag so that the browser serves whichever object content it can handle.

An object tag has two parts. The first is its attribute tag DATA. You can use OBJECT DATA to define what exactly it is that the object is reading. The second part is the material within <OBJECT></OBJECT> tags; this material is the alternative if the DATA cannot be read by the browser. Think of it as a data equivalent for the ALT in an image tag.

You can also embed objects for automatic browser degradation. For example, the .png graphic is a new format that is not fully supported on older browsers. If you find that the .png file gives you a great image, but you still want to accommodate lower-bandwidth users, you could write:

```
<OBJECT data="foo.png">
    <OBJECT data="foo_a.gif">
    <IMG src="foo_b.gif" alt="this is a gif">
    </OBJECT>
</OBJECT>
```

Here's what would happen—a browser that supported both the OBJECT tag and the .png format would render foo.png. A browser that supported the OBJECT tag but not the .png format would render foo_a.gif. A browser that didn't read the OBJECT tag at all would render foo_b.gif.

You should be able to use object tags to embed applets, HTML files, or other multimedia formats—they're all assembled on the client side instead of the server side.

NOTE   Hopefully, the 5.0 versions of browsers will support this tag, and you'll be able to use block-level tag tags to assemble intelligent HTML.

Style Sheets

I've already mentioned style sheets several times as the solution to a lot of design and structure dilemmas. But what are they, really?

Style sheet has become a generic term for *Cascading Style Sheets*, also known as CSS. CSS deal with assigning appearance-based attributes to structural objects in HTML. There is a small division in CSS, called CSS-P, that deals exclusively with positioning elements within a document. CSS-P is used primarily for DHTML.

Back to style sheets—it's one thing to talk about what they do: It's time to explain how.

A style sheet is really a collection of appearance specifications. Each specification has a unique name. If you want an object within a document to display a specification you wrote in the style sheet, all you have to do is match the name of the style sheet to the name of the object.

There are three different ways to match the object and the style. The first is to write the style to an object that is recognized as a block-level tag in the HTML 4.0 spec. These block-level tag tags are <BODY>, <P>, <OBJECT>, <DIV>, <TD>, <DD>, <DT>, <H1>–<H6>, <BLOCKQUOTE>—you get the idea. Anything that can contain text and be regarded as a block-level tag can be manipulated with a style sheet.

If you write a style sheet that says something like this:

```
<STYLE type="text/css">
<!--//
 .body          {font-size: 12 pt; line-height: 14 pt; font-face: verdana;
          font-weight: bold; color: #000000}

 .H1           {font-size: 36 pt; line-height: 40 pt;
```

```
                font-face: courier new, courier; font-weight: bold;
                color: #FF0000}
    //-->
    </STYLE>
```

You've just specified that all body text in your document is 12-pt Verdana with a leading of 14 pts, black and bold. Any text within the <H1> headline brackets will be much larger, courier, and red.

A few syntax notes: Style sheets are either linked from within the head of the document or placed there in their entirety. It helps if you tell the browser what type of style sheet you're using (you'll see why in a few paragraphs), and you should always include comment tags so older browsers don't read the code and display it. The technical term for the .H1 at the top of the page is the selector. The technical term for the attributes that live within the { } braces is properties.

Our style sheet example above would actually look like this:

```
<HTML>
<HEAD>
<STYLE type="text/css">
<!--//
.body         {font-size: 12 pt; line-height: 14 pt; font-face: verdana;
              font-weight: bold; color: #000000}

.H1           {font-size: 36 pt; line-height: 40 pt;
              font-face: "courier new", courier; font-weight: bold;
              color: #FF0000}
//-->
</STYLE>
</HEAD>
<BODY>
<H1>The Joy of CSS</H1>
Oh, I have slipped the surly bonds of ASCII. With style sheets I can make
a document look Photoshop-fresh. I no longer need to load huge gifs. Here
are the many ways I love style sheets ...
</BODY>
</HTML>
```

The second way to add a style to an object is to define a style for a class of objects. This is especially handy if you're planning on having a lot of things in your document that perform different, specific functions. For example, I want to continue my page singing the virtues of style sheets. I'm going to create one class of objects called "reason," and another called "example."

```
<STYLE type="text/css">
<!--//
.body        {font-size: 12 pt; line-height: 14 pt; font-face: verdana;
             font-weight: bold; color: #000000}

.H1          {font-size: 36 pt; line-height: 40 pt;
             font-face: courier new, courier; font-weight: bold;
             color: #FF0000}

.reason      {font-size: 12 pt; line-height: 14pt; font-face: verdana;
             color: #000000}

.example     {font-size: 12 pt; line-height: 14pt; font-face: verdana;
             color: #666666}
//-->
</STYLE>
```

Then I'm going to apply them within the body of our document:

```
<BODY>
<H1>The Joy of CSS</H1>
Oh, I have slipped the surly bonds of ASCII. With style sheets I can
make a document look Photoshop-fresh. I no longer need to load huge
gifs. Here are the many ways I love style sheets ...
<DIV class=reason>
Style sheets allow me to change font face
</DIV>
<DIV class=example>
```

Here's how to specify it:

```
.example            {font-size: 12 pt; line-height: 14pt; font-face:
verdana;
                    color: #666666}
</DIV>
</BODY>
```

All I did was attach a class to a block-level tag that was defined in the body of the document. The .reason and .example styles overrode the .body style because when a browser reads style sheet specifications, the properties of the last style specified are displayed.

Another way to demonstrate this: Let's say I have a really long style sheet—60 styles or so. It's 2 A.M., and I've forgotten whether or not I specified a `.body` style in my document. So I write another one, and my style sheet looks like this:

```
<STYLE type="text/css">
<!--//
.body           {font-size: 12 pt; line-height: 14 pt; font-face:
verdana;
        font-weight: bold; color: #000000}

.H1           {font-size: 36 pt; line-height: 40 pt;
        font-face: courier new, courier; font-weight: bold;
        color: #FF0000}

.reason       {font-size: 12 pt; line-height: 14pt; font-face: verdana;
        color: #000000}

.example      {font-size: 12 pt; line-height: 14pt; font-face: verdana;
        color: #666666}

<!--sixty lines deleted. Just pretend they're here -->

.body           {font-size: 12 pt; line-height: 14 pt; font-face:
courier;
        font-weight: bold; color: #000099}
//-->
</STYLE>
```

When I load my page, the style that's going to show up for the stuff within the <BODY> tag will be bright-blue courier font.

I'll return to the ways that a browser reads a style sheet; let's move on to the third way a style can be applied to something in an HTML document. The last and most specific way is to attach a style by an ID.

There is a distinct difference between an object's class and an object's ID. A class defines a group an object belongs to; an ID identifies a specific member of a class. For example, if I were writing my grocery list as a style sheeted document, I would write:

```
<!--//
.fruit      {taste: sweet; vitamins: yes; produce: yes}

.vegetable      {texture: crunchy; vitamins: yes; fresh: yes; produce: yes}
```

```
#carrots      {color: orange; taste: mild; raw: yes; juicy: no}

#oranges      {color: orange; taste; tangy; raw: yes; juicy: yes}

#grapes       {color: red; taste; tart; raw: yes; juicy: yes}
//-->
</STYLE>
```

And I would then write my list like this:

```
<BODY>
<div class="fruit" id="oranges">get 6 of these</div>
<div class="fruit" id="grapes">get a pound of these</div>
<div class="vegetable" id="carrots">get two pounds of these,
peeled</div>
</BODY>
```

There are several lessons here:

- You can apply both a class style and and ID style to an object.

- You can have one, or more than one, ID item in a class.

- You can use ID styles to distinguish between items in the same class.

- You can use classes to set up common characteristics for items, and save the specific details for IDs.

- Classes in style sheets are written .class.

- IDs in style sheets are written #id.

The first lesson—applying a class style and an ID style to the same object—demonstrates how you can apply multiple styles to the same object. This is where the "cascading" part of "Cascading Style Sheet" comes from.

Be sure to remember that the innermost style always wins. This is why the bright-blue courier font will display on your document with the sixty-line style sheet: It was the selector closest to the code. This is why, if you have two styles and one is expressed in a block-level tag that lives inside another, the innermost one affects the text within its block-level tag. For example,

```
<div id ="oranges"><div id="grapes">what are these?</div></div>
```

produces some grapes.

Applying Style Sheets

Now that you've got an idea of the three levels of specificity you can control when writing style sheets, it's time to find out the four different ways you can apply them.

Define All of Your Styles in the Head of Your Document   This is definitely a cleaner, neater way to define styles: The chunk of code allows for easy cutting and pasting, and it is very easily ignored by the browser if the browser doesn't have the ability to read style sheets. All of the examples we've been using show style sheets that are specified in the head of the document.

Use Inline Styles   With this option, instead of separating all of your styles into one chunk of code at the top, each tag in the document acts as a selector, and you can attach very specific styles to each tag as you approach it.

Using inline styles, our previous example of the Joys of CSS would now look like this:

```
<BODY style="font-size: 12 pt; line-height: 14 pt; font-face:
verdana;font-weight: bold; color: #000000">
<H1 style="font-size: 36 pt; line-height: 40 pt;font-face: courier new,
courier; font-weight: bold;color: #FF0000">The Joy of CSS</H1>

Oh, I have slipped the surly bonds of ASCII. With style sheets I can
make a document look Photoshop-fresh. I no longer need to load huge
gifs. Here are the many ways I love style sheets ...

<DIV class=reason  style="font-size: 12 pt; line-height: 14pt;
font-face: verdana; color: #000000">
Style sheets allow me to change font face
</DIV>
<DIV class=example  style="font-size: 12 pt; line-height: 14pt;
font-face: verdana; color: #000000">
Here's how to specify it:
.example          {font-size: 12 pt; line-height: 14pt; font-face:
verdana;
                color: #666666}
</DIV>
</BODY>
```

This negates the point of having one centralized style document to specify the appearance of your site, or separate appearance from structure.

There are a few good reasons for using inline style sheets. If you have three or four instances of the same structural tag on a page—four <h3></h3> subheadlines per section—and you want them to look extremely different from each other, you might want to apply inline style sheets. In addition, if you're looking at a huge chunk of text within the body of your document and you just want to set off one that you like, you can apply a style via the <SPAN></SPAN> tag, using SPAN as your selector and attaching all of the properties within that tag.

Link to an External Style Sheet   This is a truly powerful and efficient tool. If you set up one style sheet listing all of the styles for all of the objects likely to be on your website, then attach classes or IDs to all of your structural elements, you can swap styles in and out simply by retyping one line of code in one file. A little initial work setting up the site to respond to style specification saves you formatting and redesign work in the long haul.

Linking a style sheet that lives on your site is simple. The first step is to write the style sheet. If I wanted to set a universal site style, I'd make the file look like this:

```
<STYLE type="text/css">
<!-//
.body          {font-size: 12 pt; line-height: 14 pt; font-face:
verdana;
          font-weight: bold; color: #000000}

.H1          {font-size: 36 pt; line-height: 40 pt;
          font-face: courier new, courier; font-weight: bold;
          color: #FF0000}

.reason     {font-size: 12 pt; line-height: 14pt; font-face: verdana;
          color: #000000}

.example     {font-size: 12 pt; line-height: 14pt; font-face: verdana;
          color: #666666}


//->
</STYLE>
```

Then save it as `sitewide.css`.

The second and last step is to link to the style sheet in any document that you want to apply it. My HTML file would look like this:

```
<HTML>
<HEAD>
<LINK rel="stylesheet" type="text/css" href="sitewide.css"
title="sitewide">
</HEAD>
<BODY>
<H1>The Joy of CSS</H1>
Oh, I have slipped the surly bonds of ASCII. With style sheets I can
make a document look Photoshop-fresh. I no longer need to load huge
gifs. Here are the many ways I love style sheets ...
<DIV class=reason>
Style sheets allow me to change font face
</DIV>
<DIV class=example>
Here's how to specify it:
.example          {font-size: 12 pt; line-height: 14pt; font-face:
verdana;
             color: #666666}
</DIV>
</BODY>
</HTML>
```

The `<LINK rel>` tag in the head tells the browser what type of document is being linked relatively, where the document is located, and what title it has relative to the rest of the document. When the browser reads that tag, it will retrieve the style sheet file (`sitewide.css`) from the server, read it, then apply the styles to the data objects on the page.

Merge an External Style Sheet by Importing It   In this case, again, the style sheet is defined as a separate document from the HTML document in which it is appearing. But the syntax is slightly different:

```
<HEAD>
<STYLE type="text/css">
<!--//
@import url("css-import.html")
//-->
</STYLE>
</HEAD>
```

There are two significant differences between this command and the `<LINK>` commands. With the former, you're giving a style sheet address relative to the document calling the style sheet. With the latter, you're giving a style sheet address that is called from a URL location instead. The second difference is that the @import command is still buggy in both Netscape and Microsoft. The advantage that @import has over <LINK> is that you can merge several different style sheets into a document with the @import command, but you can only <LINK> one.

There are a few other rules governing how style sheets are applied throughout a website or a document:

- If there are conflicting styles defined for a class or ID of an object, the one closest to the actual object will be the one expressed.

- Inline style sheets will always be expressed over styles included in the head of a document.

- Inline style sheets will always be expressed over styles called via ID or class in a SPAN.

- A style defined (or excluded) in a SPAN has priority over one defined in the head of a document.

- The style sheet defined in the head of a document has precedence over a style sheet that is linked to the document.

- If you're going to import style sheets and define some styles locally in the head of your document, make sure you mention the imported documents first.

Dealing with Pre–Style Sheet Browsers

With that style sheet primer out of the way, your next question is likely to be "How do I write code that allows me to use style sheets and still allows control over the appearance of a document that is being viewed in an old browser?"

There are a few different strategies. The most elaborate would be to break out the code in your site so that the pages are generated either with or without the style sheet on the fly via conditional HTML. But unless you're already compartmentalizing your HTML so you can mix and match pieces, this solution is time-intensive and may require intensive restructuring of your document. The second suggestion is to nest your styles: If you're not sure who's going to be viewing your site and you want to make sure the contents look similar no matter what, you could write a chunk of code like this:

```
<p><font face="arial, helvetica" size="3" color="#006633">the text in
question</font></p>
```

The <p> style is called in the head of the document. Browsers that don't recognize style sheets will ignore the style sheet, but still format the text. This tactic allows you a degree of limited control over the appearance of your site for low-end browsers by pairing appearance-driven HTML tags with structural tags. A higher-end browser sees a document with a lot more control over the properties of each object.

The second solution is also a practical long-term solution for integrating style sheets into your site. As your audience shifts toward upgrades, you'll be able to strip out the relics among your formatting tags and add in more sophisticated object tags.

> **NOTE** For a list of complete style sheet attributes, the values you can specify for them, and the browsers that support them, visit Appendix E.

Server-Side Includes

Talking about including document code as a separate, universal file provides a wonderful segue into the world of *server-side includes*. These includes are two part tools you can use to create powerful, complex, and customized pages without hiring an army of interns.

The two parts of server-side includes (or SSIs) are the include call and the include itself. The *call* is the line of code you put in the file that you want to pull the include into. The *include* is an HTML fragment file. If you have an HTML document with a virtual include call in it, the server parses the included file into the HTML document, and pushes the blended file to the client.

This explains why you can't see server-side includes when you view source: They're processed on the server end before the file is loaded into your browser. So what may appear to be a complex HTML file like this:

```
<HTML>
<HEAD>
</HEAD>

<BODY bgcolor="#FFFFFF" text="#000000" link="#CC0000" vlink="#0000CC"
alink="#00CC00">
<!--this is where the nav bar goes-->
<TABLE>
...
</TABLE>
```

```
<!--this where the ads go-->
<A HREF="#"><IMG src=".."></A>
<!--this is where the headline goes-->
<h1><font face="arial, helvetica">Whither Server-side
Includes</font></h1>
<!--this is where the document content goes-->
<p>
insert text here ...
</p>
</BODY>
</HTML>
```

may actually appear like this to the production manager:

```
<HTML>
<HEAD>
</HEAD>

<BODY bgcolor="#FFFFFF" text="#000000" link="#CC0000" vlink="#0000CC"
alink="#00CC00">
<!--#include virtual="/navbar.html" -->
<!--#include virtual="/ads/sponsortop.html" -->
<!--#include virtual="code/headline.html" -->
<!--#include virtual="code/article.html" -->
</BODY>
</HTML>
```

There are a few things you should notice about the document above:

- All of the includes are stored on the same server. You can not link to a file that does not live on your server.

- Includes do not have to be in the same directory as the file that is calling them. So long as your server is configured to accept some sort of docroot at the top, you'll be able to set up your includes relative to the file in which they are being positioned.

- There are no hard returns in an include. If you put one in, or a stray ^M makes it in when the file moves from your designer's Mac to the Unix-based file server, the include will break. Instead of seeing the ad on a page, your user will see a set of brackets that read [error processing this directive].

- Includes are parsed into a document in the order that they appear in the document; the server reads top-to-bottom.

So how is it possible to have these includes? What do they really do? How powerful are they?

The most basic and universal include is the *virtual include*. A virtual include is a chunk of HTML markup, sans <HTML>, <HEAD>, or <BODY> tags, that contains code to be integrated into the page where the include is called. Virtual includes will work on almost any server; check with your server admin to see if you can use them.

To endear yourself to your server admin, here are a few things you should be aware of before bombarding her with your 50 new includes:

- In order for any type of server side include to work, the server's Options directive needs to be set so the Includes option is turned on.

- To make sure users can't piggyback the Includes option into a tour of your whole server structure, your server admin will also want to turn off that option, by using IncludesNoEXEC as the Options directive for off-limits directories. This might be a good thing to set up in subdirectories of a website section using server-side includes.

- The default no-includes server option is simply the Options directive without either option specified.

- Although includes use HTML, they are not the same as HTML files. Therefore, they need to be treated differently. You need to decide on a file extension to attach to your includes to tell them apart from your HTML files. Some commonly seen file extensions include .shtml, or .htmlf.

After you decide on the extension for your include files, you need to ask your server administrator to set the AddType to recognize and parse your files. She'll then write something like:

```
AddType text/x-server-parsed-html .htmlf
```

or

```
AddType text/x-server-parsed-html .shtml
```

The first command tells the server to parse .htmlf files into an HTML document that called them; the second tells the server to parse .shtml files into the requesting document.

Why bother being so nitpicky about which files are parsed? Because it reduces the chances of your server parsing any and all HTML files and thus driving server load through the roof.

After you've cleared using virtual includes with your server administrator, it's time to move on the harder stuff: Server-side includes that actually do more than simply call in HTML.

You can use SSIs to:

- define variables
- fill the values of variables
- execute scripts
- serve content in response to external variables
- pull information from one document into another

Before we launch into any of those tasks, I need to warn you: You need to clear up two things before you begin production. First, make sure you have an area on a test server to do any SSI development and testing. You cannot build an SSI-driven page on your desktop and expect it to work; when you view a file locally, there are no servers involved. Second, see what sort of environment variables the page is receiving. Make a page like this:

```
<HTML>
<HEAD></HEAD>
<BODY>
<pre>
<!--#printenv -->
</pre>
</BODY>
</HTML>
```

Then post it to your test server, and see what you get back.

Among the data you'll receive are the types of technologies your browser supports, what the browser user agent and platform are, and what base URI and URL the document is being called from. Granted, this is your information you're looking at, and not your user's, but it does provide you with diagnostic information about the types of environmental variables the page can query for and support.

Using those variables is half the battle in shrewd SSI implementation. The other half is making sure you've got your terminology straight. Let's define a few terms and get to work.

Using SSIs to Define Variables

If you want to use SSIs to serve efficient pages, or pages capable of responding to a user's browsing conditions, the first thing you must grasp is the way variables are written in SSI.

Variables do one of three things in SSI: They're either being defined, being set, or being printed. Printing a variable is usually the first thing browser-savvy developers learn. To print one of the environmental variables you found when you ran that print command in the last section, you'd write an HTML document like this:

```
<HTML>
<HEAD></HEAD>
<BODY>
<pre>
<!--#echo var="HTTP_USER_AGENT" -->
</pre>
</BODY>
</HTML>
```

These variables—including computer platform, domain, browser and browser version—can all be used to produced customized pages. We'll talk about how in a few sections. Just remember: These variables are only the most basic definition of SSI variable.

You can also define and produce your own variables. Any time you want to pull in a chunk of HTML, or a value for a line of markup, you have to define the variable, then print it.

To define a variable, just write :

```
<!--#set var="variablename" value="variablevalue" -->
```

For example: You want to make sure your headlines are all printed in Arial this week. You'd write:

```
<!--#set var="headline" value="arial" -->
```

But now that you've set the headline, how do you print it? The call for printing a variable on the client-side Web page is:

```
<!--#echo var="INSERT VALUE HERE" -->
```

So, printing your headline format would look like this:

```
<font face="<!--#echo var="headline" -->">
```

Note that includes can be called within other HTML tags.

But what about all those HTML fragments throughout the chapter? Do they need to have variables so a document can print them?

No. The syntax for pulling in entire chunks of HTML is different; instead of printing a specific variable, you can call the file as a virtual include. That syntax is:

```
<!--#include virtual="foo.shtml" -->
```

where `"foo.shtml"` is the fragment of HTML to be pulled into the document.

NOTE   You can also use specific variables within virtual includes and fragments. As long as the variables are defined, they will be printed.

For example, let's say I want to separate out all of a page's content from a structural template. I also want to make sure that the headline for the content is formatted to accept a SSI variable. Since the headline is in the include, here's how the code would be written:

The template document (`index.shtml`) would have this:

```
<HTML>
<HEAD>
<!--#set var="headline" value="arial" -->
</HEAD>
<BODY>
<!--#include virtual="content.shtml" -->
</BODY>
</HTML>
```

The content document (`content.shtml`) would have this:

```
<font face="<!--#echo var="headline" -->">This is the headline</font>
<P></P>
<!--content goes here -->
```

And when the browser reads the two documents, it will print the value for the variable in the include; the include will be merged into the rest of the `index.html` file.

Using SSIs to Fill the Values of Variables

Now that you know how to set and print variables, I'm going to show you how to set up multiple groups of variables and serve the correct one in response to a variable value set in a meta file. The practical applications for this are myriad: You can set up different color schemes for a document, pull in differing headlines or content chunks, even switch in new structural templates.

To start, figure out what needs to be set up as a group of variables. I'm going to do my example using color schemes. Let's say you have a company intranet, and the intranet features an event calendar. You want to change the calendar color scheme every month: it's black and white in January; red, white, and blue in July; orange and black in October; red and green in December.

You've identified what you want changed: the background color. It is written in HTML as: <body bgcolor>.

The key is to find where it is in the calendar document, and substitute the hard-coded values with variable names. So a chunk of code that looks like this:

```
<BODY bgcolor=#000000>
```

now looks like this:

```
<!--#set var="body" value='<BODY bgcolor=#000000> '-->
```

or this:

```
<!--#set var="body" value='<BODY bgcolor=#CC0000> '-->
```

or this:

```
<!--#set var="body" value='<BODY bgcolor=#00CC00> '-->
```

in the head of the document. The body tag has been replaced with:

```
<!--#echo var="body" -->
```

You can specify which background color to use by setting up the color schemes as if-then arguments. So your code ends up looking like this:

```
<HTML>
<HEAD>
<!--#set var="color" value="red" -->

<!--#if expr="$color = /black/" -->
<!--#set var="body" value='<BODY bgcolor=#000000> '-->
<!--#elif -->
<!--#if expr="$color = /red/" -->
<!--#set var="body" value='<BODY bgcolor=#CC0000> '-->
<!--#elif -->
<!--#if expr="$color = /green/" -->
<!--#set var="body" value='<BODY bgcolor=#00CC00> '-->
```

```
<!--#endif -->
</HEAD>
<!--#echo var="body" -->
</body>
</HTML>
```

The first line sets the variable value that the document recognizes as correct; the next chunk of code sets up all the possible variable value and corresponding conditions. The variable is finally called in the body of the document.

Using SSIs to Execute Scripts

As you know, server-side includes can call in files. So why not use them to call in JavaScript files and strip the code out of the template or structural HTML documents that they're sitting in? By separating out the script, you can easily rewrite or debug the script without having to worry about countless versions of earlier scripts popping up on the site, or without having to go through 50 files to cut and paste.

Server-side includes don't affect a script's execution abilities. You can just separate out the JavaScript or VBScript into a fragment file, then call it in the head of the document, which is where the code would live anyway.

Best of all, you can combine server-side includes with the if-elsif-else loop to create combinations of scripts and HTML that work from browser to browser. (See Chapter 14 for more on the script loops.) This allows you to capitalize on the latest advances in JavaScript or VBScript without worrying about the adverse effects for your lower-end users.

Using SSIs to Serve Content in Response to External Variables

If you jump back a few sections, you'll remember that you can use server-side includes to find out a wide variety of browser variables. You can also use includes to act as a broad filtering system and serve content only in response to certain variables.

For example, if I had a layout that only worked in 4.0 browsers, and yet I didn't wish to exclude anyone who was still happily surfing with their 3.0 browser, I'd use server-side includes to patch the correct page layout into the file for the users. Here's how.

The code goes in the head tags:

```
<!--#if USER_AGENT="Mozilla4.0" -->
<!--#include virtual="layout_hi.htmlf" -->
<!--#elif -->
<!--#include virtual="layout_lo.htmlf" -->
<!--#endif -->
```

And all it says is, "if the client's browser (USER_AGENT) is a 4.0 version, serve one include, or else serve the other. "Elif" is the server-side way of saying "or else"; if you were going to write "if you get to Parnassus Street, turn left, or else turn right," you'd write it "if Parnassus `<!--#include virtual="turn left" -->` elif `<!--#include virtual="turn right" -->`" The "endif" line is included to tell the server when to stop looking at if-else considerations when pulling in includes.

Using SSIs to Pull Information from One Document into Another

SSIs can control appearance and pull in scripts; they can also match text from one document to a template from another. This allows you to store all of your template files in one meta-type folder, and to set up a separate directory structure for your content. It also allows you to create a template once, and change the content week by week without having to do serious work.

The first way to do this is pretty basic: Format a hefty chunk of content in one server-side include, and call that chunk from within a style in another document. For example:

```
<HTML>
<HEAD></HEAD>
<BODY>
<!--ad goes here-->
<!--#include virtual="ad.htmlf" -->

<!--rest of content -->
</BODY>
</HTML>
```

but that means that ad.htmlf still has to be formatted something like this:

```
<A HREF="sponsor_click.html" target="_top"><IMG src="ad.gif"></A>
```

What if your ad—or, better yet, your entire content from headline to nav bar—was supposed to change frequently? How do you call in the content without having to change the template to call different chunks of content text/images every time?

The answer: Set up a template that prints the same set of variables no matter, then change the variable values in a second document.

For example, you could set up a template document like this:

```
<!--this is to line up questions and answers -->
<TABLE>
<TR>
<TD><!--#echo var="question1" -->
</TD>
<TD><!--#echo var="answer1" -->
</TD>
</TR>
<TR>
<TD><!--#echo var="question2" -->
</TD>
<TD><!--#echo var="answer2" -->
</TD>
</TR>
<TR>
<TD><!--#echo var="question3" -->
</TD>
<TD><!--#echo var="answer3" -->
</TD>
</TR>
```

And then set up the content document like this:

```
<!--#set var='question1' value='Have you used server-side includes to
set the appearance of the document?' -->
<!--#set var='answer1' value='Of course I did. I set up different color
schemes.' -->
<!--#set var='question2' value='Are you going to read ahead to the
section on condtional HTML?' -->
<!--#set var='answer2' value='Yup. I\'d like to figure out how to create
custom files using if-else statements and server-side includes.' -->
```

```
<!--#set var='question3' value='What do you think the biggest benefit is
to server-side includes?' -->
<!--#set var='answer3' value='You can target your work to include only
the most frequently changing files. Pardon the pun' -->
```

NOTE   Because the text is parsed, you have to escape (\) some characters out so they're not read as separate variables or commands. Those characters include single quotes ('), dollar signs ($), and ampersands (&).

Drawbacks to SSIs

There are some disadvantages to includes. They do constitute a security risk, because parsing an include may mean that the user is executing commands as the server's user. You can disable the exec option on the server side, but it is still something you should clear up before you push any SSI-driven documents live.

Another disadvantage is that includes can weigh down a server. If the server is loaded with a lot of traffic, having to parse several files together before sending a requested file out can slow the client-server connection. You may want to test how your pages perform during peak traffic hours before you push them out to the live site for users to actively request.

Finally, troubleshooting may be difficult in SSIs, especially if your pages are composed of multiple SSIs calling different variables from each other. For example, you have a page composed of a structural template include, a metafile include passing variables about the content to both the content include and the site's index page, a conditional HTML include setting up the color scheme for the file, and a content include. If the template SSI calls two other SSIs, like an ad SSI and a nav bar SSI, that's adding another troubleshooting step to your process if a link on the page is the wrong color, a meta variable is wrong, or the ad's link on the page is broken.

Despite these disadvantages, server-side includes may be a good way to separate out complex and persistent chunks of code so you don't have to keep copying and pasting or rewriting them. This separation has multiple advantages: You can refine a chunk of code and reuse it; you can alter one chunk of code and rest assured the changes took effect in every page that the include was called from; you can begin to map out the functional parts of your Web pages relative to the site as a whole. This mapping can help you if or when you decide to migrate to a databased content serving system.

Summarizing SSIs

You can use server-side includes to separate document structure from document style, to separate document content from document structure, and to separate document style from document content. The advantages to doing so are as follows:

- You can concentrate on writing individual chunks of complex code without "getting lost" in a huge file.

- You can swap styles in and out without changing the structure or content markup of a document (or site).

- You can swap content in and out of one basic template.

- You can customize content in response to browser variables.

The most important thing to remember about server-side includes is that they allow the development staff to add increasing complexity to a finished site by breaking down each page into very simple parts.

The two case studies at the end of Part III demonstrate how a flat HTML prototype page was broken down into a series of includes and how those includes were used to create different page combinations.

Conditional HTML

Now that you've mastered server-side includes and the if-else idea, you can take advantage of the code modularity and the if-else conditions to write documents that are custom-suited for certain browsers and platforms.

Conditional HTML is a strange hybrid beast in the world of Web development. If HTML is a structural language, and programming languages typically provide if-else conditions, then conditional HTML spans the gulf between the two.

How? In one of the most inefficient ways possible. You already got a sneak peak up in the server-side include section: The conditional part sets up the possible decision paths, and then big, discrete chunks of HTML are served in response.

You've already learned how to find out what sort of environmental variables you can pick up from the browser: browser type and version, the domain that the user is coming from, and the computer platform they're using are only a few.

For example, if you wanted to optimize the font size to look consistent from computer platform to platform (Macintoshes automatically default one font size larger than many PCs), you could write a chunk of code that looked like this:

```
<!--#if expr="($HTTP_USER_AGENT = /Mac/)" -->
<!--#set var='font_3' value='3' -->
<!--#elsif -->
<!--#set var='font_3' value='2' -->
<!--#endif -->
```

It will automatically adjust from platform to platform.

You could also use conditional HTML to automatically detect whether or not a user has a browser that supports frames:

```
<HTML>
<HEAD></HEAD>

<!--#if expr="$SUPPORTS_frames" -->
<frameset frameborder=no border=0 cols="200,*">
<frame marginwidth=0 marginheight=0 src="nav.html" noresize
scrolling="no" name="navigation">
<frame src="content.html"  marginwidth=5 framespacing=0 noresize
name="text">
</frameset>
<!--#else -->
<BODY bgcolor=#FFFFFF>
<!--insert nonframes layout here-->
</BODY>
</HTML>
```

Or, you could serve different types of content dependent on platform. This sample document calls in three different includes depending on what browser attributes are supported:

```
<HTML>
<HEAD>
<!--#if expr="$SUPPORTS_position" -->
<!--#include virtual="html4doc.htmlf" -->

<!--#elif expr="$SUPPORTS_table_color" -->
<!--#include virtual="html3doc.htmlf" -->

<!--#else -->
<!--#include virtual="html2doc.htmlf" -->
```

```
<!--#endif -->
</HEAD>
<BODY>
<!--default content goes here -->
</BODY>
</HTML>
```

The applications are numerous, and you can use them to offer your users rigorous code and content suited expressly for their browsers. Best of all, you can begin to lay the groundwork for migrating to a database-driven site by separating out your content into an include, then customizing content appearance by pushing it into a template controlled by conditional HTML.

Be aware that conditional HTML carries its own set of debugging glitches. You'll have to have access to a wide variety of browsers and platforms to test its efficacy with accuracy. And as your site gets more complex, the potential for a widespread bug—like a syntax mistake in a template file—going undetected increases.

Still, conditional HTML is a good way to create on-the-fly custom pages without relying on a database. For more examples of how to create conditional HTML pages without much extra work, check out the case study in Chapter 10.

Writing Cross-Platform and Cross-Browser Code

This section is negative: It tells you what to avoid, rather than what to embrace. But the intention is that you get the idea of the process of elimination for HTML development, and an understanding of some of my pet peeves running unleashed through the Web.

In order to accommodate both PCs and Macs, realize that they display colors and fonts differently. PCs tend to see the dark gray color #333333 as black, so if you're hoping to use a wide range of grays to convey subtle contextual clues, it's not going to work as well on a PC. In addition, dithered colors look a little less sharp. Stick with the colors that work across both platforms and browsers—defined in the 216 Netscape Color Lookup Table (CLUT), discussed in more detail in Chapter 7.

Many PCs display fonts one size larger than do Macintosh platform machines. Don't ask me why, they just do. If you're relying on font size to convey subtle distinctions between different levels of content, you might not want to do so in increments of one. Better yet, try and break free of <font> tags, period.

Always provide a low-standard alternative. Even if you've given up on converting your site with the whiz-bang conditional HTML that you hoped would deliver custom pages, you might want to drop a few lines of code redirecting users with hopelessly outdated browsers to an explanatory page. Expecting your users to automatically upgrade when they reach your page is counterproductive.

Shun browser-specific extensions. Why bank all your functionality and interface on only one browser?

For a complete cross-browser list of tags—what's supported in different versions of Netscape, Internet Explorer, Lynx, and Opera, please turn to Appendix B. The breakdown of tags is much more complete and more compactly presented than anything I could write here.

Incorporating These Steps into Large-Scale Web Production

By now you've got a full array of skills that will let you write code to meet almost any computer... assuming you have the time and inclination to revamp your site to accommodate server-side includes, style sheets, and conditional HTML. Few people are handed that sort of blank slate: Most of us are working with websites that vary wildly in look and feel over time and development.

The wild variations generally tend to be concentrated on the level of HTML used to mark up the site. As the designated maintainer or improver of the site, your job is to go in and make sure that the code is consistent and does the best job it can.

The job sounds daunting, but it isn't. It involves three basic parts:

- Identify the scope of the material to be maintained or improved. This is easy. It means surfing your site and taking note of what you see in different browsers, on different platforms, at different speeds. Once you've taken notes, go in and check the server-side source code and see if you can link the frontend appearance to the backend code.

- Identify the code that needs to be altered. This is a natural result of step 1. Very rarely will you take step 1 without segueing into step 2. On the off-chance that you have a running to-do list, this step may stem from you having crossed off everything else not related to rewriting large quantities of HTML.

- Rewrite the code. Because you are learning from experience, and most likely dealing with a much larger site than the one you originally launched, you're going to want to make the modifications as efficient as possible. For example: If you're reworking the nav bar across your site to reflect different content in each section, it makes a lot of sense to write one include per section, and drop one line of code in every file in that section, rather than cutting or pasting. If you wanted to be really efficient, you could write just one include, pack it with if-elsif-then variables, and drop the same line of code across your site (it will act as a default), then tack on the individual variables where needed. I'll show you how in the case study.

The point is, if you're going to be overhauling code, don't just rewrite the markup code—alter the document markup or process so it's not so much work next time. There will always be a next time, so make your repairs part of an ongoing effort to lessen the impact of next time's arrival.

General Rules for Good Code

Now that you have a good idea of the nuts and bolts—how to best utilize the basic as well as the advanced tools that HTML gives you—the larger issue at hand is when and how to implement your changes, as well as maintaining those changes with a solid team, clean organization, and a good set of the basic tools.

Assembling a Toolbox for Good Coding

Voluminous shareware archives aside, a development toolbox is not composed of software alone. You need to have an area for developing your code, and an area for testing the product before pushing it live. Ideally, these two areas are separate from each other, and neither of them is on the live server. The development area is important for trying out and testing new technologies before you whack them into 50-plus pages of HTML; the testing area can also serve as a backup copy of your site just in case you run across a bug you didn't catch during testing.

Once you've set up safe spaces for development and testing, you need to set up places to enforce good teamwork. This sounds a little silly, but let me explain: Any time you develop a website as a team, you're working in an environment where everyone has a different skill set and a different set of team responsibilities. And when more than one person is going to see your file, whether it's a graphic artist, copy editor, or resident JavaScript junkie, there's a chance they'll overwrite all the work you've done, or worse yet, lose the files. You need to prevent any worst-case scenarios by establishing a closed-access space for all team members to drop files. It's not just a big open directory. Impose order on it by creating a directory hierarchy that echoes the steps in your workflow process.

Here's an example. Your site development is supposed to follow the following steps: proposal, design mockup, code mockup, design review, code revision, editorial additions, copyedit, final QA. That's eight separate steps. Not everyone needs to have access to all of those steps. You can start by organizing those eight steps into four steps: initial development, revision, editorial review, final production. Drop the corresponding tasks into every category directory.

Make sure that this development tree is living on a machine somewhere on the company's network, preferably the development machine. This way, the file tree will get backed up whenever necessary. You can also exploit Unix's permission system to ensure that nobody inadvertently or deliberately writes over someone else's files. Give total tree ownership to the technical manager, since they'll be in a position to check and fix permissions. Then, assign each team member to a group. In this example, we have five groups—business, edit, copyedit, develop, and art. Each of those groups may or may not have write permission to the file tree. For example, the develop group may have permissions that look like this:

```
:/develop/projectX/1-initial_development> ls -l
rwx-rw--rw----       code_mockup/      jexe     develop     Sep 17 13:22
rw--rw--rw----       design_mockup/    jart     art         Sep 17 13:22
r---r---r------       proposal/         jdoe     business    Sep 17 13:22
```

This means that only the develop group can execute anything in the code_mockup directory, and they can only read the business proposal. The permissions displayed let all team members know which access privileges the author of the directory, the group that owns the directory, and a casual nonmember have. The permissions allow you to restrict access to a small group of people and allow you to exclude anyone who shouldn't be poking around those files.

WARNING   Do not assume that your development tree structure mirrors the site backend. It should not. The development tree is meant as a way to control versions of files through development as those files pass through several different groups. It's meant as an in/out box for the entire team. The site backend is meant to help the site serve finished products.

Once you've secured your testing and development space, set up a workflow between team members, and set up a general version control, it's time to take a look at your own personal arsenal of tools. Preferences for these vary widely from person to person and task to task.

The general categories you should touch on:

Connection Protocol   How are you accessing the Net, and what tools do you use to move files back and forth? A good telnet application is useful for plumbing the depths of your file system, and for performing sysadmin troubleshooting. If you happen to be a sysadmin, there are a whole set of Unix tools that make your life easier; I'll cover them in Chapter 8. An FTP application lets you move files between locations, which is handy for desktop-to-development tree moves. And check how you're connecting to the Net—ethernet hub, PPP protocol, or TCP/IP.

Text editors   There's a market for mind-to-screen coding software, but nobody's tapped it yet. So we're stuck with text editors for producing code. There are two different options for text editors—desktop apps like Notepad (on Windows) or SimpleText (on Macs), or text editors within your Unix shell account. Check your `.cshrc` file in your home directory to see how your shell is set up. If it's all gibberish to you, befriend a sysadmin and ask her to please check and make sure you can maneuver through your shell account. Another file to look for is `.emacs`. This lets you know that you have a set of preferences for running the Unix text editor emacs.

NOTE

There are three Unix text editors, and they are all different. Pico is a small, lightweight editor. The second, vi, is a powerful keyboard-driven text editor with two modes: edit text and insert text. Finally, emacs is a hybrid between standard UI-type point-and-click applications and the command-driven vi. vi is usually a sure bet on any Unix server, but it doesn't hurt to ask about emacs.

WYSIWYG editors   WYSIWYG stands for *what you see is what you get*. Some people rely on these specialized text editors like PageMill to produce Web pages quickly; some people use these tools as a way to ease into Web development. I will admit that I still hand-code all of my HTML, but that's because I'm a control freak.

The advantage to WYSIWYG editors is speed: Dropping and dragging elements or pointing and clicking is faster than typing the same code. The disadvantage is that many of them produce nonstandard HTML. There is a prominent editor that is notorious for embedded tables ten deep to produce the code for a dropped-and-dragged layout. Another disadvantage is that many of these editors insert proprietary tags into your code, which can produce problems for those developers aiming for cross-platform pages. And finally, the tools aren't quite up to the latest Web development standards: The only DHTML tool that was helpful at presstime was Macromedia's Dreamweaver, but even then most Web developers agreed it was only useful so long as you already had a strong background in coding by hand.

NOTE   A WYSIWYG editor can be a useful tool for quick jobs, or it can act as a friendly interface when you're doing development on your desktop. Just be wary of relying on it to produce rigorous HTML.

Browsers   Any good Web developer should have more than one browser installed on their local machine and know where to find or install more. Cross-browser testing begins with your desktop.

Graphics tools   If you need to deal with Web graphics, your best bet is to check out Chapter 7, which lists the issues for graphic design within website maintenance or development. But if you're dealing with them in a QA/repair way, or if you're trying to gauge file size for testing purposes, it doesn't hurt to have a few shareware apps that allow you to view graphics. GifBuilder 0.5 is a good Mac tool that allows you to view animated and static GIFs; its counterpart for PCs is GifConstructor.

Reference resources. Nobody develops in a vacuum. Every once in a while, you're going to run into a table alignment problem, a frames misload, or a server-side screw-up and not know what happened. Aside from reference books like this one, be sure you have a list of websites that provide standards, comparisons, and tutorials on any development issue that might affect you, from HTML to accessibility to Macintosh memory drains to JavaScript on Microsoft Internet Explorer. There are a number of good tables in the appendices for easy reference. You might want to dog-ear the following:

- The browser comparison chart (Appendix A) tells you what tags are supported on what browsers, by browser name and version.

- The HTML reference (Appendix F) is a gigantic HTML glossary.

- The style sheet reference (Appendix C) tells you what style sheet attributes are universally supported, and what attributes are browser-specific.

In sum, your toolbox should contain both software and workspace. Once you've settled on where you're going to do your work, and how, the rest should come easy—or relatively easy.

Finding the Right Time to Upgrade Your Code

There are two big indications, and both are external: Your boss or the resident code geek decrees that you're going to go to a consistent code format by x date, or you find a new spec or implementation at the W3C/Microsoft/Netscape that looks like it solves a long-term problem you've had with Web production. There are also a host of smaller, internal indications:

- You've gathered enough evidence that a particular markup hack is not working as well across browser and platform as you thought.

- You notice that a prior hack is requiring subsequent code modifications to be increasingly specialized and complex.

- You notice that your old hacks are largely browser-specific.

- You find a more elegant way of reworking the code.

- You are interested in migrating to a dynamically-generated site and want to begin breaking sections of your site down into different functional parts.

NOTE Please remember: A new browser version or standard does not mean you have some sort of obligation to immediately upgrade your site.

If your business or your site derives a lot of its identity from adopting new technologies early and with great innovation, then you will either have been testing these new modifications in beta, or you'll have built this new overhaul into your development schedule. If you want to gain in the early adopter/innovator market, you may want to start keeping tabs of the latest specs and versions and factoring in development time and resources around those releases. But if you're primarily concerned with maintaining a decent website for as large an audience as possible, view all upgrades with a critical eye. Read them with an eye toward how they solve interface or document structure problems you've had building the site. See how the people paid to be cutting-edge and early adopters are using new technology, and imagine how you might adapt that use toward your development priorities. But don't kill yourself being first to adopt a new technology. The cachet wears off in a few weeks, whereas a reputation for using solid technology well lingers for months, even years.

Maintaining Code Measures

There's a radical method for maintaining good code: Document what was done, what standards it complied to, and what files the change affected. This is radical in that it's time-intensive at first, but as you gradually document more of the maintenance you're doing, you'll notice that documenting is a small and pesky, yet extremely beneficial part of site maintenance.

Documentation can take several forms, including dated comments within HTML files, readmes dropped into directories, or full-blown formatted files in a central repository. The only two factors that are mandatory are that all of your developers know where to find the documentation and all of your developers note all relevant information when they make changes.

Insofar as maintaining the actual code, the skills in this chapter are meant to bring a site up to par with the broadest audience segment possible. The cutting-edge stuff is two sections ahead. This code is kind of like the color beige: useful, flexible, and a solid base for further developments, even if it isn't terribly exciting.

Summary

This chapter is meant to convey two main messages. First, website construction is more than using HTML: It's using HTML that retains its effectiveness over time and redesign. To do that well, you have to think about the process you use to build site, as well as the code you use to build each page.

Second, the skills in this chapter are meant to provide you with a basic toolbox. They're meant as the technical platform from which you can launch the next round of site maintenance. They're not exciting, but they will allow you to break your site down into easily upgradeable, fully functional parts. They'll also allow you to migrate to completely different methods of site development and serving, like DHTML or data-structure-based sites. Read ahead to find out how to enhance the structure of the site you just built.

Employing Intelligent Design

- Organizing your content

- Using space

- Using typography

- Using color

- Creating lightweight graphics

There are plenty of sites that are models of classic information organization. All of their content is neatly categorized in sitewide hierarchy, and all of their tags pass muster with the W3C's validators.

But no matter how pristine your code, if your information isn't presented attractively, few people will click twice. On the other hand, if you over-design your site, your users and your information may never meet. And if users can't decipher your graphics scheme, read the content through your palette and font size, or wait the 10 minutes it takes for each page to download, they don't have any incentive to come back.

Therefore, if you're doubling as both the developer and the designer for the site, you have a tricky job to do:

- You have to find a way to design the site attractively enough so users can find what they want without nodding off from boredom.

- You have to be able to ensure that your design doesn't hamper site performance.

- You want to develop a design that closely couples visual cues with a specific information organization function. As you may have surmised by now, information on the Web is useless unless it is coherently organized, both on an editorial level—like an outline—and on a visual level, like a page that broadcasts a specific factoid's context by placing emphasis within the body of the text (important) or on the margin (just trivial or tangential).

- Finally, you want to develop a distinctive design that surfers will come to associate with your site. That way, users will know when they're on your site and when a hyperlink has taken them off. A visual identity is a good way to brand your site onto people's eyeballs; as much as people howl about CNet's ubiquitous yellow nav bars, they also recognize whenever they're on one of CNet's sites thanks to that same layout and color scheme.

Pursuing these four goals only sounds daunting. The next section walks you through the basics for accomplishing them, and the remainder of the chapter goes over skills that will allow you to develop a distinctive graphical interface without sacrificing any of your site's speed.

Remember That There Is More Than One Browser on the Market

I cannot emphasize this point enough: there are many different browsers on the market, and many browsers have more than one version number. Someone using a browser type you've ever heard of will surely visit your site.

So be kind to your users. Do not design for a specific browser. Design good pages and then work on the code to guarantee that they'll look good in several different browsers.

Easier said than done, you say? Read on to discover what constitutes a good, browser-friendly design. The section on organizing your content and using space is a good starting point.

Standards versus Conventions

As we go through the rest of the chapter, you'll discover that a lot of the strategies listed are fairly vanilla. You may want to give in to elaborate nested tables and clear GIFs as margin buffers, because those are conventional ways of presenting a page.

There's a big difference between standards and conventions. A convention is "but everybody is doing it this way." A standard is "but the W3C says this is the legal way to do HTML." For example: Nesting tables is a big layout convention, but it's not a standard. Similarly, the `<object></object>` tag is a standard, but it's not part of Web building convention.

So how do you tell the difference between a standard and a convention? Think of it this way: A standard is a published, ratified specification from a recommendations body like the W3C. A convention is a widespread implementation of something that works in "the real world."

Your job as a Web developer and designer is to figure out how to use standards in a conventional context. One way to do this, for example, would be to clearly mark all your paragraphs as `<p>text goes here</p>`. Closing the container tags complies with the W3C ruling that the paragraph is a block-level tag, and doing so will not affect your page's rendering.

WebTV: New Considerations for Web Design

A lot of these design guidelines may need to be altered if you're planning on targeting WebTV users.

Unlike most computer monitors, WebTV monitors hew to a screen dimension optimized for the United State's National Television Standards Committee (NTSC): 420 pixels high by 560 pixels wide. Part of the screen is reserved for the WebTV interface menu and navigation controls, so you will typically have an area of 378 pixels high by 544 pixels wide.

What you put in that space is equally important. The saturated color palette that makes your site stand out on Netscape won't work for WebTV: it handles color differently and the page background will warp. Another area affected by the different display is contrast: Color combinations between different colors will be displayed less dramatically on WebTV. As a result, text may be harder to read if there isn't a great contrast.

But be wary of too much contrast. Red and orange colors tend to bleed out into surrounding areas, and the usability standby of black text on a white background is less easily read.

Color isn't the only area to consider. Because of the different screen size for WebTV, you'll also have to think about how items will be laid out on your screen. Avoid all of the following:

Complicated framesets   WebTV can display frames, but the more intricately you embed them, the more likely it is that the display will skew.

Long page <TITLE></TITLE> tags   Stick with short descriptions under 20 characters, so they can display in the WebTV controls

Long pages, period   WebTV doesn't have a scrollbar, so it's easy for users to get lost on your page.

Plug-ins   As of this writing, WebTV did not support plug-ins.

Organizing Your Content and Using Space

How you sort your content into something comprehensible to your readers, and how you present that sorted content can make or break a site. It doesn't matter how pretty your graphics or how striking your color scheme: If you've arranged information in a way that requires users to read your mind, they won't want to come back.

How Users Find Information on a Site

Even if you're trying for the spacious, minimalist website effect, you're going to want to provide your users with a congruous navigation system. It can be as simple as providing a set of hyperlinks moving a user forward or back through a series of pages or having a consistent set of hyperlinks at the top or bottom of the page.

More typically, you're going to face several navigation challenges within each individual page. The challenges usually include:

Challenge	Example
Moving readers up, down, and across through different levels of a site	For example, moving from an index page to a subtopic index, then to a second subtopic index, then to a specific content page within the subtopic is a simple 4-click process for your user but only if you provide the type of navigation that lets a user see where they are relative in the site hierarchy. An example of a good site hierarchy is Yahoo (`www.yahoo.com`): you are able to see how far down you've drilled in their index and what steps you can take to move over to another topic or subtopic.
Moving readers relative to other pages within a document	If you're trying to break up one long document into several pages or string together serial installments of one extended work, you may soon discover that you're considering two separate navigation systems. The first focuses on guiding your users through the specific series of pages, and the second focuses on guiding your users through different sections of the site. The challenge is in how to maintain both types of navigation without compromising the editorial flow of the site.
Diverting readers from old or retired sections of your site to the still-maintained areas without completely eliminating the links	This is a valid concern because you don't know how many readers rely on that section as a reference resource, or how many other Web pages have listed those retired areas in their pages. In addition, many Web indexes and search engines will continue to store the URLs and offer them as active pages for readers. Therefore, you need to design a navigation scheme that offers at least one route to retired sections and that can be transplanted to the retired sections as well so readers aren't taking a one-way trip on your site.

Challenge	Example
Providing a clear exit route at all times	If you're ever building a computer-based product, you need to give your users a clear-cut exit route so if they get lost they can return to home base and retrace their steps. Also remember that users will not always be entering your site from the index page or site map; therefore, you have to provide the page context relative to the site at large. A quick, compact, and informative way to do that is to provide all that context in your navigation: Hierarchical devices like different text sizes, arrows, or color blocks can quickly convey to your users exactly where they are and how to escape if necessary.

Once you've devised the navigation tools that your readers will use to whiz through your site, it's time to worry about how they're going to find specific items within individual pages. Although I've already covered the merits of placing specific items in a layout, I haven't yet broached the topic of information architecture.

Information architecture is the art and science of organizing your content and devising a plan for how that information will be presented, both on the page and throughout the site. A lot of websites don't adequately plan their information architecture, which explains why so many resource sites and directories meander off into dead ends or 404-Not Founds.

Because you brainstormed about the form and function of your website back in Chapter 2, you've already got the raw material for building a strong information structure.

The question is, What do you do with all that raw material?

First, figure out how you're going to organize it. A lot of sites rely on metaphors because they provide automatic parameters for classifying and organizing things. These parameters effectively limit how you identify the content within the site and the function each piece of content plays.

You can take this technique and transfer it to your own site. Some functional metaphors to consider:

A space mission   You can refer to new technologies (the space shuttle), the mission for these technologies, the research processes that creates these technologies (the folks at NASA), the people who will be building and using the technologies (the astronauts), and the people who run the company (Houston command).

A sleep-away camp   From the brochure (organizational information) to campfire stories (information about the company), there are plenty of analogs for a community-oriented or company-promotion site.

A library   From fiction to reference to periodicals to classification systems.

TIP   A metaphor must have some structure of its own before it can be used to apply structure to the goals and content for your own website.

There are many, many metaphors out there, but the ones you'll be interested in fall into three different categories: the *visual metaphor*, the *organizational metaphor*, and the *working metaphor*:

- An example of a visual metaphor is designing your site navigation to approximate a navigation scheme people use offline, such as turning the pages of a book or reading street signs.

- An organizational metaphor relies on a well-known grouping system and lifts the elements to the website. A good organizational metaphor (though maybe a touchy one) is SmithKline Beecham's Café Herpé site at `www.cafeherpe.com`; it uses a common culinary paradigm to pull its content into a public space. One of the dangers of using organizational metaphors is that a corporate site will often organize a site according to the company organization. Very rarely do your customers care where your meetings office is relative to the publications you put out—focus instead on organizing your content for someone who's not a company insider.

- The last type of metaphor, the working metaphor, is a way of transplanting a real-world process or routine to a website. One clever execution of a functional metaphor is Christopher Rywalt's site *It's Just Another Baby* (`http://www.westnet.com/~crywalt/pregnancy/`), in which the different events of pregnancy to a 9-month school year are mapped. It's a good way of capturing the sense of progression through the site's content without losing the readers in a jumble of medical information.

Once you've got the metaphor, hash out implementation. Going with a space shuttle metaphor may seem like a really good idea when you're starting to put boundaries on the 200 pages of printed content your boss wants to see online ASAP, but you also need to examine if it will hold up. Will you be able to flesh out your metaphor over the long run? Or will you end up with the space station Mir?

Using the Site Map to Reinforce Your Site Metaphor

Sometimes a site map is a schematic layout for website developers to figure out how many pages they have on a site, how those pages are grouped together, and what pages will reference to lead to other pages. You can also use a site map as a visual guide to show your readers what you have on your site, and how it's organized.

As websites become increasingly multileveled, providing your readers with a site map is one way to help them—and you—construct a mental model of all of the possible routes that users can take around your site.

But note that the site map is supposed to reinforce your site metaphor. It is not meant as a band-aid solution to a poorly organized site. It's a map of your site in the same sense that a map of the United States is an accurate representation of the country. A site map provides a visual metaphor, a conceptual tool for your users. It is not supposed to catalog every item in your site, just the landmark items, what those landmarks have, and how you can move from landmark to landmark.

Now that we've established how you can use site maps, how do you make one of these? It's simple; just follow the steps below:

- Remember that your site map is a visual metaphor. Design it so the relationships between various unique site elements are clear. This is especially easy when you're working with a site that has a clearly defined topical hierarchy, or a time-drive structure.

- Use a table of contents to flesh out the actual listing in your site map. Visual metaphors are useful, but only if they're driving an actual body of organized content.

- Approach automatically-generated site maps with caution. These handy little files often come with HTML editors or site content servers. While they're useful if your site is strictly hierarchical, they're not an effective tool for a differently organized site.

- The visual organization of your site map should reflect the logical organization of your site. Ignoring the organization of your site for the sake of a better-looking site map is counterproductive.

In practical terms, this is best accomplished by taking a look at the table of contents you've laid out for your site, asking yourself, "What hypertext routes cut across this linear table of contents?" and laying out your contents in a way that conveys both the contents and the possible routes between them.

Continued on next page

One excellent example of a good clean site map is on the Landor site (`http://www.landor.com/american/Home/Search/index.html`) pictured below. Notice that the left-hand side of the screen has a comprehensive table of contents listing and the right-hand side has a graphical representation of how all the information relates to each other.

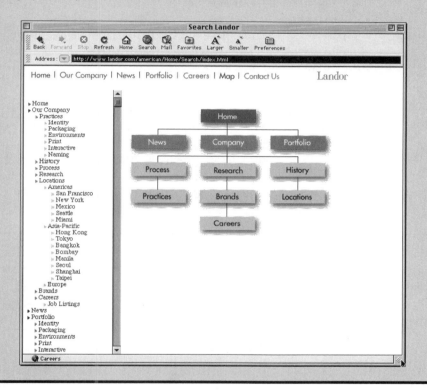

Once you've found a metaphor and wrapped your content goals, your content inventory, and your organization scheme into that same metaphorical container, it's time to apply all that theory to your actual site design.

First, figure out what's on every page. Typical page elements include:

- Site branding, to communicate to readers that they're still on your site
- Specific page headers, including graphics or headlines

- Specific page footers, including a text-only navigation system, contact information, or copyright notice

- Specific page content

- Sitewide navigation systems

Once you've figured out what your consistent elements are, it's time to map them to a grid. Yes, I know we've already discussed the differences between a grid layout versus an asymmetrical layout, but this is an important step *before* you start refining the visual look-and-feel.

Take all of your consistent elements, assign them each a box, and begin arranging boxes within a larger rectangle: The large rectangle represents the browser window. Your job is to see how to arrange the different elements spatially so none is ignored and you're getting the most out of a limited space. Remember that users can lengthen, widen, or narrow their windows dramatically, so it helps to think of your starting point as the upper-left corner, and design out from there. Look at Figure 7.1 for an example.

FIGURE 7.1:

A grid used to plot the placement of different elements of a website

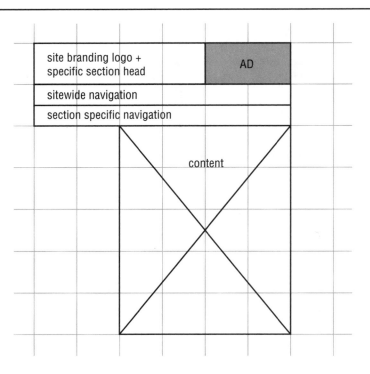

What's a Brand?

Over the past four years, the phrase *branding strategy* has become increasingly prominent. This doesn't mean that the World Wide Web discovered cow-punching; it means that many sites are now crafting plans to link a look, a feel, and a market niche with their URL.

Nike, for example, has built a name as a ubiquitous sporting-goods manufacturer by promoting its name and logo in venues where consumers are likely to be: athletic events and sporting magazines. A website faces a different set of considerations for a branding strategy.

Design frequently plays an important role in branding; think of where Nike might be if their patented swoosh logo weren't so distinctive and so easy to remember. You can bring the same traits—simplicity and visual distinctiveness—to your site so people come to associate a particular aesthetic with your site. Remember, online, your site is your brand name.

One of the best examples of creating a strong "brand" through design is the Fox television website (`http://www.foxworld.com/`), which manages to maintain a network-like identity through each of the individual show sections. The subsidiary shows like *The Simpsons* and *Ally McBeal* each carry the Fox branding strategy as well as their individual show identities.

After you've found a grid that works for you, it's time to flesh out the skeleton layout with a design. If you're bringing in designers to realize your information architecture, don't be surprised if they completely rebuild your grid. Unless the specific placement of specific elements is important, let them work. As long as all of the elements are included on all of the pages, go with it.

If you're doubling as your own designer, don't be afraid to re-arrange the items in your grid until you get a result you're pleased with. Then, mock up your design. You may have been mucking around with a graphics program even as you hammered out the information architecture for your site. If this is the case, it's time to merge your design vision with your grid, and to repeat the process until you have a result that's both easy-to-understand and attractive.

If you haven't even started *thinking* about your visual design, now is the time to start. Begin playing with the spatial arrangement of items on the page. Start experimenting with different font faces and colors. Just remember that you're going to need to maintain your color scheme and fonts across the site.

Great, you're saying. I can organize and grid to my heart's content, but what if my site is well-organized and visually boring? Worse yet, what if my site is gorgeous but clogs a user's 28.8Kpbs modem?

Read on for the practical how-tos in selecting colors and fonts for your designs, and for directions on making lightweight and functional images.

Space: The Initial Frontier

Good Web design involves using space intelligently. You can safely assume only one thing about your site and space: someone will always have a screen too small to see it.

> **NOTE** *Screen* can mean either of two things: the size of the monitor with which a user views any computer GUI, or the size of the browser window within the monitor. Bear in mind that both monitor size and the resolution with which a user accesses your pages will vary.

You're going to need to learn how to use a small space well because the only guarantee you have is that your users are going to have at least a small space in which to view your site. It is in your best interest to make that small space attractive to users.

Start by figuring out how your content is going to fit within that space. You're basically given a rectangular window (the browser), within another rectangle (the monitor). So you have two choices:

- Make your content a complimentary rectangle.
- Deliberately flout the rectangular layout.

Neither option is incorrect. Sometimes, the best way to convey information is to lay it out on a grid, with each specific chunk of data assigned to a specific area. This kind of layout is easy to generate and reproduce across large sites. For small screens, you'll have to test extensively to make sure your unconventional layout doesn't cause items to fall out of sight and cause confusion. A grid-based layout might scroll up or down more evenly. To see how well a grid-based layout works, see Figure 7.2.

FIGURE 7.2:

A grid-based layout

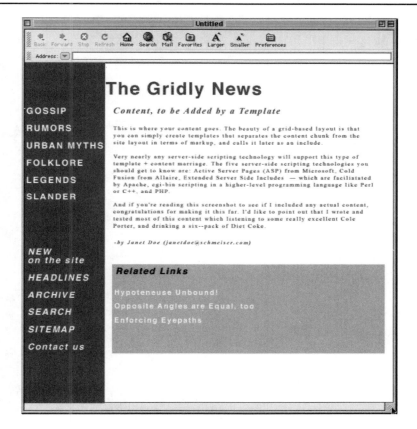

There are visually defined blocks for everything. The layout is reliable, and you can easily map every item in your site to these chunks. A user who has never seen the site before can decipher it within seconds because the placement of items is so consistent with other "standard" layouts on the Web like ZD-Net, CNet, and Wired.

Another option, illustrated in Figure 7.3, is to deliberately break out of a grid-type layout and arrange elements in a striking, non-rectangular layout. In Figure 7.3, notice that even though the elements are deliberately flouting any neat alignment, there is still a strong eyepath. The different elements all touch it, or are related to it, in some way.

This brings us to the only thing you need to know about spatial placement from a design perspective: All the items on a page should relate to each other in some way. A strong vertical or horizontal margin will provide a visual anchor for the entire page.

FIGURE 7.3:

An asymmetric layout

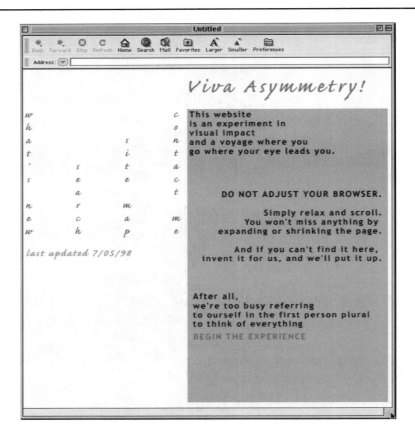

Your next challenge is to figure out how to maintain that eyepath, that visual anchor, through the page no matter what the screen size, window size, or monitor resolution. The key is simplicity. Less is more: Even if your site has a lot of "stuff" on it, if you place the stuff carefully, you'll create a layout that makes use of space and works on both small monitors and large. Figure 7.4 illustrates how to do that.

The eyepath for this site is a strong right vertical that holds up even if the browser window is very short; every element on the page has a visual connection to it somehow. All the text items are flush right, which sets up a margin, all the dingbats on the very right align left to the same margin that the text items recognize, and the whole layout forms a T with the bottom navigation bar.

FIGURE 7.4:

A page that manages to hold a lot of information and maintain a feeling of space

Contrast this with the site shown in Figure 7.5.

If you count the different items on the two pages, you'll notice that there are actually many more items on the former page, but that it still manages to look as though it has more space. How is that?

- In Figure 7.4, the strong vertical eyepath *reserves* space in the center as a resting point between actual content areas.

- The items in Figure 7.4 are broken up into main items and sub-items. Each clump of items constitutes a visual element. On the other hand, in Figure 7.5, the group of headlines is a big mono-formatted mess.

FIGURE 7.5:

The cluttered page. Somehow, although there is less information, the page feels more crowded.

- And more on the benefits of light: Lighter-looking items can fool the eye into thinking that there's a lot of space on a really crowded page. If the second screenshot had had a series of tiny, varied headlines, it would have looked cleaner.

- The elements were clearly organized, and that lets the reader build an information map in their head of what's on each page.

So space isn't solely about having few items on a page; it's about organizing the items you have so the eye creates relationships between them. You can do that by playing with leading—the space between lines of text, color, and layout.

Resolution and Screen Display

One of the greatest uncertainties of Web design is your user's monitor size and screen resolution. The settings on their machine can turn your carefully tiled and shaded graphics into something more closely approximating an Impressionist painting. Or, your website design could be so expansive that it doesn't fit on the screen.

The bad news is that you can't design a site to please all of the people all of the time. The good news is that you can still design a site with a clear idea of what limitations you have in the layout size. First, let's look at screen resolution. Assuming you have a color monitor, you may have a variety of settings for its output (the stuff you're seeing on the screen). The most significant is color depth: Depending on a monitor's capabilities, you will be able to view anywhere from 256 colors to millions. Naturally, the fewer colors your screen can see, the more limited your monitor's ability to process extremely subtle gradations in shade.

In addition to the assorted color displays, the size of the desktop area displaying these colors varies from machine to machine. Typically, most websites design for three different sizes:

- 640 pixels wide by 480 pixels tall

- 800 pixels wide by 600 pixels tall

- 1024 pixels wide by 768 pixels tall

The smallest dimension is usually the default for many smaller monitor sizes. Bear in mind that Web surfing is no longer restricted to desktop computers; people now surf the Web with laptops, hand-held PCs, or WebTV. Some laptops only display 640 pixels by 280 pixels; the picture on a hand-held PC is much smaller.

So how do you guarantee that your design will work well across a variety of screen sizes and color resolutions? The answer is to make sure that it degrades well over different dimensions. Most designers still aim for a 640×480 layout because that is the lowest common denominator for the largest Web surfing audience. The easiest degrading strategies are to make sure that you provide crucial context clues in the small, universally-viewed space at the top of the browser window and that your colors can gracefully display even on 256-color monitors.

Typography: The Web's Imperfect Art

Typography is an imperfect art on the Web. To begin with, a computer monitor displays everything broken down into pixels, so the beautifully rounded letters you have in your Photoshop program like this:

anti-aliased letters

are going to be rendered like this:

aliased letters

However, there are still ways to add a distinct set of visual characteristics to the text on your site. There are also good reasons to want to be able to do this:

- First, plain text is boring. Functional and easy to format, yes, but it is also as visually stimulating as watching a wallful of white paint dry.

- Second, the functionality of plain text is sharply limited—there are no visual cues to give readers an idea of what chunks of text perform specific duties within the site's information architecture. Contrast the two screens shown in Figure 7.6.

What Fonts Are Defaults

Most browsers include two types of fonts: a fixed-width font and a variable-width font. A fixed-width font such as `Courier` is composed of characters that have equal widths. This sort of font comes in handy when the user is viewing your site through a line-based browser like Lynx or Viola.

The variable-width font, which is usually something like Times Roman, is the default display font in your browser. You can change your individual display fonts by going into the preferences menu of your browser and changing the font face and size to something you find more aesthetically pleasing.

Remember, however, that you do not want to force your users to change their font preferences in order to view your site. You have two choices: Design your page so it looks good even if the user's default is set in 24-point Palatino font, or specify font sizes and faces to achieve a distinct typographic look. Read on for a primer on the tools you have at your disposal for website production.

FIGURE 7.6:

See how the second screen seems to have functionally different, visually separated areas? That's what exploring font attributes can add to your site without a lot of heavy graphic file overhead.

Font Face and Font Size

Structurally, the tags that specify font size and font space present problems. They're inline tags, meaning that they should be attached to block-level HTML elements like <P></P> and <DIV></DIV>. The <font> tag has also been recently deprecated in the HTML specification, meaning that there are other, better tags to accomplish the same thing.

However, a lot of websites are still designed and built using <font> tags. These tags typically look like this:

```
<font size="2">This is a smaller font</font>
```

or like this:

```
<font face="arial, helvetica">This is a sans-serif font</font>
```

or even like this:

```
<font face="arial, helvetica" size="4">This is a big, sans-serif
font</font>
```

Specifying font face is often a smart move for designers: you can use specific font types to connote different functions within a Web page. The default fonts most browsers and operating systems support fall into two categories: serif and sans-serif.

Serif fonts have little "feet" on them. Fonts like Times, Palatino, or New York are all serif fonts. Sans-serif fonts don't have the feet: Monotype, Arial, Helvetica, and Verdana are all sans-serif fonts. Examples of serif fonts and sans-serif fonts are shown in Figure 7.7. When you contrast sans-serif and serif fonts, there's a fairly clear difference between the two.

Therefore, using a serif font as the default for all of your text, and using a sans-serif font to set apart the persistent layout elements like the nav bar and headline, is a quick and easy way to set up a clear visual code for your site. After all, good design includes executing a clear design efficiently—and fonts let you do that.

Be careful how you use your serif and sans-serif fonts: Serif fonts like Times are easier to read in small text, and so are frequently used for body text, while sans-serif fonts like Verdana and Helvetica are used in headlines.

NOTE   Keep in mind that font tags are not to replace the structural tags like <H1> through <H6>. Instead, they're to be used to set attributes for block-level elements. If you're aiming your website design and development at people who are using older browsers, then scale your code to make sure that `<font>` tags are complementing your structural markup.

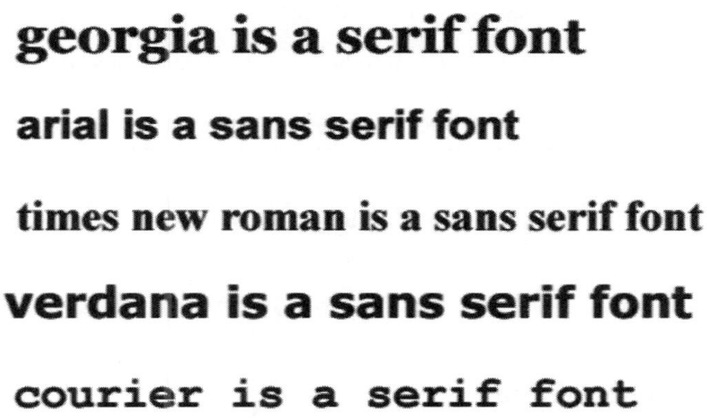

FIGURE 7.7:

Serif and sans-serif fonts

georgia is a serif font

arial is a sans serif font

times new roman is a sans serif font

verdana is a sans serif font

`courier is a serif font`

Both of the dominant browsers in the market, Navigator and Internet Explorer, support the font attributes for Cascading Style Sheets, as specified in HTML 4.0. Therefore, you can also easily insert typographic specifications via style sheet. And you can control more aspects of the font. Whereas the font tag only supported the attributes face, color, and size, any 4.0 browser supports the font style sheet attributes listed in Table 7.1.

TABLE 7.1: Font attributes for use with style sheets

Attribute	How It Works
`<font-family>`	This attribute is the equivalent of `<font face>`. You can specify the font appearance for a specific font like Verdana, or a generic font like sans-serif. There are five different font families: serif, sans-serif, monospace, cursive, and fantasy.
`<font-style>`	This attribute refers to the appearance of the font face whether the text appears as underlined, *italic*, or **boldface** text.
`<font-weight>`	You can set this attribute one of two ways: by specifying visual attributes like `normal` and `bold` or by attaching a weight value between 200 and 900.

Continued on next page

TABLE 7.1 CONTINUED: Font attributes for use with stylesheets

Attribute	How It Works
`<font-size>`	You can set this attribute in percentage, as in `font-size:20 percent` or you can use traditional measurement like points (**pt**) or pixels (**px**). Because of the way browsers and monitors render visual data, you'll end up with more consistent results if you set all of your font sizes to pixels. On the other hand, many readers with poor vision will have purposefully set their default font size as larger. If you use percentage font sizing, then your font will adjust itself relative to their default. You will need to balance aesthetics with usability.
`<color>`	This attribute sets the color of the font in question. Remember that you get more precise results if you use hexadecimal values, especially if those values fall within the 216-color browser-safe palette.

Remember that style sheets allow you to combine more than one attribute, so it's possible to write a tag like this:

```
{ font-family: verdana; font-style:bold; font-size:16px; color: #CCCCCC}
```

to specify the look for one specific chunk of text. And that's not even getting into the text alignment attributes.

NOTE   For a more complete overview of style sheet attributes, please see Appendix C.

Embedded Fonts

The phrase *embedded fonts* is deceptive because it's just not accurate. While it is true that 4.0 versions of Netscape Navigator and Microsoft Internet Explorer can hook non–system-installed fonts into a website displayed in their browser, the font itself isn't embedded in the browser.

Instead, a font file is embedded in the page, and the resulting data renders the items on your page with a specific font. There are two different ways you can offer this to your reader.

The first is Netscape's *Dynamic Fonts*, which relies on Bitstream's TrueDoc font rendering. This technology lets the designer record font information like character shape, store the recorded information in a portable font resource (pfr) file, then link the file into a website. The file is then downloaded in the background as the Web page is loaded, and the fonts are displayed within the Web browser.

The good thing—or bad, depending on your view—about implementing dynamic fonts is that the dynamic fonts appear on the screen via progressive rendering. This means that the page first loads without the font information, then reads the font data and redraws the text.

An alternate font-embedding technology is the OpenType format supported by Microsoft and Adobe. This format relies on an embedded open type object (.eot), which encodes all the relevant font information. To make .eot files, you need a program from Microsoft called WEFT. As of this writing, it was a Windows-only tool.

NOTE   Both font-embedding technologies tie the specific font information to a domain name, so someone else can't reference your font information files without providing a path to them. If someone on the Web is referencing your font files that way, it's easy to trace and stop.

Fortunately, you can incorporate both types of font-embedding technology into your Web page with no ill effects if the page is rendered in either platform. In order to do so, you'd write a file like this:

```
<HTML>
<HEAD>
<!--this is the OpenText font -- >
<STYLE TYPE="text/css">
<!--
@font-face {
font-family: Pineapple;
font-style: normal;
font-weight: 700;
src: url(pineapple.eot);
}
-->
</STYLE>

<!--this is the Dynamic Font fomat -- >
<link rel="fontdef" src="pineapple.pfr">
</HEAD>

<BODY>
<!-- the rest of your HTML goes here -- >
```

So is there one font-embedding technology that's better than the other? It depends on what you're looking for. For sites that are built to maximize unique browser technologies, OpenText is a good way to expand the font offerings on your site; it uses Unicode, the character set used to encode the visual ciphers for the world's languages, and so will handle browser conversions with ease. Moreover, it's got the support of both Microsoft and Adobe, so there's no escaping it.

NOTE   For more on Unicode, see Chapter 17.

However, TrueDoc has a lot going for it: More information gets packed into a smaller file format, and the TrueDoc anti-aliasing techniques mean that fonts look good across a wide variety of display conditions. In addition, TrueDoc is not a new technology; it's been adopted as the standard for several hardware and software tools, including network computers. Moreover, TrueDoc's small, fast technology works well with any font format or language and is optimal for small devices with limited memory capacity, like hand-held personal digital assistants.

So it's a draw between two equally capable technologies. Your best bet is to figure out what strengths each offers that play to the audience you're trying to reach with your site.

Using Color Intelligently

A picture may be worth a thousand words, but color can often act as a brief summary of what a picture is trying to say. You can use color to set a mood, to create a visual lexicon of your site's sections and functions, or to add visual panache to a boring website.

Fortunately, adding color to your website is fairly simple: You can use a set of HTML tags to specify a page background color, font colors, or large table cell blocks. Table 7.2 lists the tags that frequently have color attributes attached.

TABLE 7.2: The Most Color-Friendly HTML Tags

Tag	What It Affects
BODY bgcolor	The body background color
BODY text	The color of any text in the body of the document

Continued on next page

TABLE 7.2 CONTINUED: The Most Color-Friendly HTML Tags

Tag	What It Affects
BODY link	The color of any hyperlink in the page
BODY alink	The color of a link as it's being clicked on
BODY vlink	The color of any visited link in a Web page. This is a good way to visually separate links your user has seen from ones they haven't seen.
FONT color	An inline tag that sets the color of any text within its tags.

The color attribute can be attached to table cells too, from TABLE to TD.

For more precise color targeting, you might want to use style sheets instead. Bear in mind that doing so will limit the number of viewers who can see the full range of colors; attaching the color attribute tag will degrade down to 2.0 browsers.

Picking Colors for Any Browser

Thanks to the different ways that browsers read and reproduce the bits of information encoding color data for a file on different monitors at different color resolutions, there's little guarantee that your gorgeous, multi-hued picture of sunset on Maui won't end up on someone else's screen as a big orange blotch.

There are, however, different steps you can take to prevent that from happening. The most simple and easiest to follow is to set the color palette for all of your Web designs within the browser-safe color cube.

This 216-color cube is comprised of all of the colors that don't dither when displayed on a Microsoft Windows machine or within Netscape Navigator.

NOTE   *Dithering* is the process where a computer fills in color data with near-matching colors when it can't display the correct color value.

If you're using Adobe Photoshop to create your Web graphics, you're in luck. You can either import the 216-color palette via a color look-up table (CLUT), or fire up the 4.0 version of Photoshop, which already includes it. For more information on color-safe Web graphics, skip down to the graphics section later in this chapter. For more information on how to make the color attributes safe in HTML, read on.

A Bit of History, or Why Finger-Pointing Can Be Fun and Informative

216 is not one of the base-8 numbers that drives computing, but it is derived from 256 – 40. The 40 missing colors were reserved by Microsoft to be used as system colors. Needless to say, anyone using a PC is likely to notice when these 40 colors are missing.

But why should Macintosh users suffer? Because Netscape wrote code that built a 216-color display palette into their software, thereby limiting the number of colors anyone using Netscape can see.

Hexadecimal Conversions

Sooner or later, one of the following will happen to you:

- You'll be fooling around with different hex numbers, find a combination of numbers and letters you like, prepare to redo your entire site based on that value, then realize that you have no idea whether or not your perfect color fits into the browser-safe palette.

- You'll be making graphics in the graphics-building program of your choice, and you'll realize that you have no idea whether the RGB values you're entering for that stunning shade of blue are going to dither down to the browser-safe palette.

Fortunately, you can solve both dilemmas quickly and easily: Memorize the hexadecimal values that make up the browser-safe palette. Not all 216 color-hexadecimal value pairs, mind you, just the characters that make up the colors.

Each hexadecimal color value is made up of six characters: color="#CCCCCC", for example. These characters match up to red, green, and blue values. The first two digits represent red, the third and the fourth digits represent green, and the last two digits represent blue. So bright red is #FF0000, bright green is #00FF00, and bright blue is #0000FF.

In order for a color to fit in the browser-safe palette, each hexadecimal value for the red, green, or blue element of the color must be comprised of a pair of hexadecimal characters. There are only six different "safe" character pairs: FF, CC, 00, 33, 66, and 99. The key is how you combine those different characters: The combination #CCFFCC is safe; the combination #0C39F3 is not.

What Are Hexadecimal Numbers?

Computers use a slightly different counting method than we do. While we think of numbers as running from 1 to 10, a computer thinks in base-8, that is, numbers running from 0 to 8. To expand the numerals in a computer's number vocabulary, the hexadecimal number system was incorporated. This system has sixteen numerals: 0, 1, 2, 3, 4, 5, 6, 7, 8, 9, A, B, C, D, E, F. Needless to say, math takes on a whole new meaning: to learn more about hexadecimals, visit an excellent introductory article at `http://www.hotwired.com/webmonkey/html/97/17/index2a.html`.

"Marvelous," you're grumbling as you look at the color picker in your graphics program. "But my color selector only lets me fill in standard numbers like 0–255 for red, green, or blue."

Problem solved: You can quickly convert any RGB-valued color into its browser-safe hexadecimal equivalent by using Table 7.3.

Note that the hexadecimal values below do not comprise colors all by themselves. *They must be combined as three values in order to produce a color.* If the colors you're using have other hexadecimal numerals like A, 7, G, or 5, then your color is not browser safe.

TABLE 7.3: Failsafe Hexadecimal Numbers to Mix and Match for Browser-Safe Results

RGB Value	Hexadecimal Equivalent
00	00
51	33
102	66
153	99
204	CC
255	FF

Note: The values on the table are arranged from darkest (i.e., closest to black) to lightest (i.e., closest to white).

So if you wanted to code a bright, intense red, you'd specify your color to be #FF0000, which is the highest value possible for the red portion of RGB, and the lowest value possible for the green and blue. A deeper shade of red #990000 uses a mid-value R number. Similarly, a deep green like 003300 has a low hexadecimal value for the green (33) and even lower values—zero—for the red and blue.

Making Graphics That Won't Break Your Users' Browsers

The `<img>` tag blasted Web design out of a design model based on text-driven outlines of information. As a result, graphics are near-mandatory for any website design.

However, too many graphics can ruin your site. If your pages take too long to load, your users will flee to faster sites where they can get the information they need easily. If the colors you're using to make your graphics don't match any of the 216 colors that browsers can handle, then the images will look muddy or off-tone.

The following sections give you the basics for creating cleanly colored, lightweight graphics for your website.

Software Tools in Almost Every Graphics Toolbox

Making good graphics requires good tools. If you're determined to make an investment in your graphics work, I recommend any of the programs below:

BoxTop PhotoGif   An excellent tool for reducing already-created graphic palettes and making precise, transparent graphics. Go to `http://www.boxtopsoft.com` for more information on this application, which can be used either as a Photoshop plug-in or as a stand-alone application.

Photoshop (Adobe)   This is a near-standard graphics tool for anyone who's serious about making graphics for the Web. It is not exaggerating to say that Photoshop is the right-hand tool for any designer and the industry standard for graphics design. Now that it's available for the Mac OS, Windows, and two different flavors of Unix, your boss has no excuse not to buy it for you. Visit the Adobe website at `http://www.adobe.com/` to learn more about this tool.

DeBabelizer (Equilibrium)   Just as Adobe makes images, DeBabelizer polishes them, reducing file size with efficiency. Its scripting abilities allow you to create complex image-modifying routines with ease so you'll be able to perform complex cleanup jobs on large batches of images. Remember: efficiency is a goal for all Web development. The URL for DeBabelizer is: `http://www.equilibrium.com`. DeBabelizer is available on the companion CD-ROM.

Palettes for Web-Friendly Graphics

The information that comprises a graphics file seems deceptively simple: A graphics file consists of instructions for coloring specific pixels and for arranging all those uniquely specified pixels into a final product. However, if you've got a lot of color information, your file will end up being pretty big.

The key to well-colored, lightweight graphics is in palette reduction. We've already pared down your workable color spectrum to 216 colors; now it's time to reduce the colors an individual graphic is going to include in its palette information.

The key is in how many bits you map to a pixel. If you're converting an RGB graphic to a GIF format, you can actually specify how many bits of information you want to assign to each pixel. The drawback, of course, is that every reduced mapping reduces the number of colors that you can include in a graphic. How, then, do you balance multicolored graphics with lightweight file sizes?

Before I answer that question, let's back up and see how the color palette for a specific graphic gets built. I'll use Photoshop as an example.

In Photoshop, most graphic artists follow these steps:

1. Change the palette from RGB color to Indexed Color.

2. Select the 8-bit (256 color) option, plus no dithering.

3. Save the graphic.

This technique is effective, but it bundles in information for a number of colors the graphics artist is not, in all likelihood, using. Two other techniques are possible:

- The artist can save a graphic by reducing the number of bits per pixel (going from an 8-bit, 256-color palette to a 64-color 6-bit, for example).

- The artist can carefully dither the palette so that instead of containing fewer overall colors (like a 6-bit palette) it contains fewer *extraneous* colors.

This second option makes for more beautifully colored graphics in the long run. Best of all, the artist can exercise this option in Photoshop (thereby making the process more efficient) or in DeBabelizer (which guarantees that the color won't shift when you readjust the palette):

- Using Photoshop, all the artist needs is the series of Web Scrubber filters from Furbo Filters (`http://www.furbo-filters.com/`); the artist can install them as a Photoshop plug-in and then follow these steps:

    1. Pull out a test image in RGB mode. If it's a color-rich image, it will really illustrate the effects of image scrubbing.

2. Save the file as a GIF, twice. One of these images will be the experimental image, and the other will be the control image. When saving the image, be sure to save it to the smallest palette acceptable and don't dither it.

3. Open the experimental image again and switch to RGB mode. Select the graphic, then open the plug-in. The filter will appear in a Filter ➤ Xynthetic.

4. Fiddle with the slider until the color is balanced with image quality. Compare it to the control image. Index the image using the exact palette and save as a GIF.

- An artist using DeBabelizer should download the WebScrub algorithm script at http://www.verso.com/agitprop/dithering/. After unstuffing the script, they can go to DeBabelizer's Misc ➤ Scripts-Palettes ➤ Import menu to import the scripts and install then. Then the artist will follow these directions:

1. Open a GIF image in DeBabelizer, and save the file as a GIF, twice. One of these images will be your experimental image, and the other will be the control image. When you're saving the image, be sure to save it to the smallest palette acceptable and don't dither it.

2. Run the scripts—either 10 grit or 5 grit WebScrub—and compare the results with the test image. When you've reduced the palette without significantly affecting the appearance of the image, save your graphic.

So why is scrubbing images such a big deal? Because it lets an artist use colors that will dither down while still looking attractive. Scrubbing accomplishes this by using an algorithm that looks for colors whose R, G, or B values are within n (5 or 10) units of a multiple of 51. You'll recall from a few pages back that the R,G,B values within the 216-color palette all map to multiples of 51 (51, 102, 153); this algorithm finds colors near those values and dithers them as needed.

Transparency and Interlacing: Two Terms You Should Know

Whenever you're saving graphics in your handy graphics-making program, you'll inevitably be asked if you want to save your GIF as an interlaced graphic or if you want to save it as a transparent graphic. In this section, I'll explain what these two terms mean and how answering "yes" or "no" affects the graphic's performance on your site.

Transparency is the selective blanking out of a color within a graphic so that the graphic appears to be seamlessly integrated into the overall Web page. The transparent color is usually the dominant background color, so the graphic can appear to float on the Web page regardless of what color you or your user set the page's background color to be.

In Figure 7.8 below, the header image at the top does not have a transparent background, so it stands out in an awkward way when the user changes the Web page's background. In Figure 7.9, the background for the graphic is transparent so it appears to float no matter what.

FIGURE 7.8:

Here we see the graphic without a transparent background. This sort of production work can backfire if your user is surfing with a very different background color than you anticipated.

FIGURE 7.9:

Here's the same graphic with a transparent background. Now even someone who insists on viewing their pages through minty-green backgrounds will see elegantly floating images.

There are a variety of ways to make a graphic transparent—both Photoshop and DeBabelizer offer transparency as part of their graphics-saving options, and you can also find utilities like GifTransparency or PhotoGif on the Web to do the job. Whatever the application, the modus operandi is the same: You select a color to be "transparent," and the application blocks it out of the rendering process.

Your other saving option, *interlacing*, also refers to how a graphic will appear in a browser. In this case, interlacing refers to the way the graphic is loaded into the page. Interlaced graphics load into the page row-by-row; in the early days of graphic design on the Web, this was a desirable alternative to having the page hang until all of the image files downloaded.

Browser performance has since improved to the point where interlacing doesn't really affect a file download time, and it can interfere with dithering an image to an accurate palette.

The Different Types of File Extensions

There are only three types of graphics extensions you can use to put graphics on the Web, and they correspond to three distinct types of file formats. They are:

GIF (Graphics Interchange Format)   This is the most widely supported format for images on the Web and therefore still the most common. This is a highly compressed format that is designed to minimize file transfer time over phone lines, thus making it an ideal choice for low-bandwidth Web pages. GIF format only supports color-mapped images with 8-bit color or less.

JPG (Joint Photographics Experts Group)   Where gifs are encoded with 8 bits, JPGs are more densely encoded, with 24 bits per pixel. However, the way the data is compressed also makes information storage more efficient: The compression process identifies and discards data that is not visible to the human eye. This feature is great if you're converting a file to a JPG once, but if you try to decompress your JPG for further modifications, you'll end up with a file much different from the one you originally compressed. Don't let this limitation scare you off JPGs—they're great for putting photos on the Web without sacrificing a lot of the color because they store more color information per bit than the GIF format.

PNG (Portable Network Graphics)   A new kid on the block, this format doesn't enjoy the same widespread browser support as GIF or JPG, but that may change. Both Microsoft Internet Explorer and Netscape Navigator support PNG (provided you've installed the proper plug-in), and Adobe has given PNG the seal of approval. What makes PNG such a big deal? It compresses information 10 times more efficiently than GIFs do, and, unlike GIFs or JPGs, PNG can correct its own brightness by adjusting gamma levels depending on where it's displayed. Given the disparities between how a graphic is displayed from platform to platform and monitor to monitor, a PNG graphic will be able to ensure consistency at a level the best-scrubbed GIF cannot.

What Is Gamma Anyway?

If you pick up any graphics primer or noodle around any graphics-making program, you'll see the phrase *gamma correction* or *gamma level*. While gamma correction is not something you need to lie awake at night worrying about, it is handy to know what it is and how it affects graphics display.

Gamma level, gamma correction, and gamma control all refer to brightness control. The reason we don't just say "brightness control" is that the people who first started working with cathode ray tube displays (both televisions and monitors have CRT-based displays) discovered that a CRT produces a light intensity proportional to the CRT's input voltage raised to the power of gamma. That's a mouthful, so the handle *gamma* was used to refer to all matters of light display.

People who work with graphics on the Web are concerned with gamma levels not because they are avid CRT groupies but because the gamma levels that a monitor displays at change from platform to platform. The common gamma setting for a Mac is 1.8; for a PC it's 2.5.

Given the disparity, is it any wonder that PNG, with its self-adjusting gamma control, is gaining a foothold?

Animating Graphics

Sure, you could fill your website with a lot of well-composed, lightweight graphics. But sometimes, graphics aren't enough. Animation can draw a reader's eye to a section of the page, carry a short visual message, or provide extra information to the reader. A picture is worth a thousand words; perhaps an animation is worth a thousand pictures. Stylistic considerations aside, animation is also popular because it's easy to do. Read on to find out how to make your website move in no time.

The Basics

Just as the name suggests, animated graphics are basically a computerized version of those flip books you probably played with as a kid—little booklets with a single picture, or "frame" on each page, so if you flipped the pages, the pictures appeared to move. You can add as many frames as you'd like to achieve the effect you want, although there are a variety of low-bandwidth strategies that produce effective animation with a minimal amount of frames.

The first rule for animation is to tailor it to your audience's technical parameters. Remember that the people who are viewing your site hate to wait and that they will bitterly resent you for making them sit five minutes for an animated image. A corollary to the no-waiting rule is the no-bad-fit rule. Any animation you should put on the Web should be there because it is suited to the medium, not because you thought you had to have an animated graphic to stay on the cutting edge.

Make sure you know why you're creating animation:

- Are you doing it to add visual texture to a page?

- Is it an integral part of your page design?

Any sort of animation for the Web should take advantage of Web technology: Encourage interactivity or keep users guessing as to what they'll find on your page via a randomizing element.

Making Animation Lightweight

The best way to ensure that your animation is going to be small is to resolve to make it so. Set limits on file sizes and follow them assiduously. If you keep running over your limits, you need to re-evaluate the type of animation you want to create.

The easiest criterion you can use to re-evaluate whether or not you made a smart animation choice is tolerance for downloads. Asking your users to sit through 100K of animated GIFs is actually more annoying than expecting them to download a Quicktime movie—the users have no choice in waiting for the graphics, but the Quicktime movie is strictly a voluntary download.

If you're happy with your graphics format, it's time to think about speed. There are myriad tips and tricks for making graphics lightweight, but if your computer draws graphics slowly, then the slimmest animations are still going to crawl. If you decide to adopt a newer animation technology like DHTML, your file size may be smaller, but the rate at which the file is drawn in your browser may be affected.

After you've tucked this consideration into the back of your head, it's time to think of ways to get more bang for your animation buck. The key is to maximize the visual effect through as few frames as possible. More frames means a bigger graphic. Some of the most effective strategies for doing this are outlined below:

Close animation Use a background frame to set the size of the animated GIF, then make all subsequent frames small, focusing only on the area that

changes. For example, if you look at the front page of Red Meat (`http://www`
`.redmeat.com/`), the only part of the graphic that's animated is the eyeballs
blinking. An animator looking to decrease file size on that file would have
one base frame of a person's face, then two much smaller frames that focused
on different states of blinking. If you carefully position the frames, your audience doesn't have to know that there are only a few fragments animating the
entire thing.

Cutout motion   Remember those Monty Python animations where the
cut-out pictures moved jerkily and dramatically across the screen? These
animated frames do the same thing. Again, start with a base frame, then
make each subsequent frame jump dramatically from its predecessor. In
order to keep individual frame size small, you can make each frame invisible after it's been displayed. A program like GifBuilder (more on that
below) will help you to do that. The program will also help you set the
timing for loading each frame, thus making the animation look smoother.

Blur motion   Two frames, each indicating a separate motion. You can
give the appearance of dynamic, repeated motion simply by putting
together two frames that show different, blurred stages of a motion, then
looping the graphic.

Aligning Your Frames for Seamless Animation.

There are two different ways to optimize the arrangement of frames within an animated
GIF (also known as a gif89a). They are called *Frame Optimization* and *onion skinning*:

Frame Optimization   In GifBuilder, select Frame Optimization. Doing so will automatically eliminate areas of the frame that aren't being used or are redundant from
the previous frame.

Onion skinning   In onion skinning, you slide the frames over for more precise
alignment by positioning them with the arrow keys. To do this in GifBuilder, use the
Option + arrow keys to position the frames and Option + T to Step through animation. Note that I am referring to the Option key here—this means that these techniques are specific to GifBuilder, which is still only specific to Macs.

In addition to these design strategies, you can also use the following production tricks for keeping your animations lightweight:

- Restrict the number of frames you have in an animation. Three is usually enough to do the job.

- Avoid using an extensive palette. The fewer colors, the better—it makes assembling animations easier. Be sure that all the graphics in your animation are dithered to the same palette.

- Decide how you want to use the transparency and build accordingly. Keep your background frame full, and make all subsequent frames transparent to minimize file size.

Even with the animated graphics pros, there are also a few drawbacks. Gif89s don't run at the same speed on different browsers and browser versions. You can't pair sound with your animations. In addition, the speed that an animation runs at may be affected by how quickly it's loaded. Be sure to test the appearance of your page at several different connection speeds.

Software for Making Animated Graphics

For a low-cost, widely supported animation, you'll want to build a gif89a. These animations are simply a collection of GIF-formatted files played back in flip-style animation. There are three different tools for assembling these flip-books: GifBuilder, GifConstruction Set, and GifMation.

The URLs for the Biggest Gif-Building Software

If you're ready to foray into the world of digital animation, here are three low-cost, well-supported tools to get you started:

GifBuilder   MacUser loves it, thousands of people on the Web love it, and this handy, easy-to-use product is still free. You can download it at `http://iawww.epfl.ch/Staff/Yves.Piguet/clip2gif-home/GifBuilder.html`.

Gif Construction Set   For PC users everywhere, a gif89a builder app that includes its own wizard for assembling graphics. This shareware package can be downloaded at `http://www.mindworkshop.com/alchemy/gifcon.html`.

GifMation   Another product from the folks at Boxtop Software, this GIF builder software lets you assemble and tweak animated graphics with ease. Download it at `http://www.boxtopsoft.com/download.html`.

All three tools work by allowing you to add already-created GIFs to a slide-show-like window, and to control the speed with which the animation runs. You still need a basic graphics assembly package to make the constituent parts of an animated graphic. Insofar as animation software goes, the graphics assembly package is the least daunting to learn.

There are also alternatives to assembling gif89as for animation. One slow-motion effect for swapping out images is the lowsrc tag. This tag is bundled into your <IMG> tag as follows:

```
<img src="bigpic.gif" lowsrc="littlepic.gif" border="0" height="100"
width="100">
```

It works by loading a small placeholder type of image into the space that your large-file-sized, lengthy-downloading image will fill once it's downloaded. Lowsrc graphics are a great way to preview an image by providing a low-res or gray-scale version before the real deal loads. However, the two graphics you're using *have to* have the same height and width. Otherwise, you'll see horribly distorted graphics.

If you're looking for another way to make your graphics move, consider using JavaScript: this way people who have lower-version browsers will be able to screen out the JavaScript and it won't affect their page.

NOTE   For more on using JavaScript to control animation, see Chapters 14 and 15.

User Interface Considerations

As entertaining as a strategically-designed animated graphic can be, there are also times when it's annoying. Rapidly-set, continuously looping animation is the Web page equivalent of forcing your reader to surf your site under a strobe light, and so you should avoid this whenever possible.

Another reason to go easy on animation: if you carry ads, chances are good that they'll have animation as well. Because most ads are randomly served, you'll need to determine how many different animated graphics you can keep on the page before it's completely unreadable.

Imagemaps

So you've optimized your images, you've put links on them, and you've decided one link per image isn't enough. It's time to use imagemaps.

From a user's perspective, an imagemap is a way to click to multiple destinations from one specific image on a page. From a developer's perspective, an imagemap is a text file that links a series of anchor tags to an image tag.

Client-Side Imagemaps versus Server-Side Imagemaps

Imagemaps are like many Web techniques in that you can elect to do things on the server-side or client-side. Server-side technologies typically mean that any action requires a query to the server and back; with client-side technologies, all the relevant code gets bundled into the Web page and the user can execute it without having to rely a lot of client-server transactions.

Back in the early days of Web development, the only way to do imagemaps was to rely on server-side mapping. More recent browser versions support client-side mapping now, which is good for usability reasons we'll get into later.

> **NOTE**
> In these imagemap files, you can also include code comments, as long as they start with a hash mark (#).

Server-side maps are assembled like this:

1. You determine what your server software is.

2. You write an imagemap file that looks like the following:

```
rect one.html 10,10 70,70
rect two.html 70,10 100,70
rect three.html 10,70 70,100
rect four.html 70,70 100,100
default fallback.html
```

> **NOTE**
> URLs can be either relative or absolute. I put a default URL in this map to cover the possibility that users will click on an area that wasn't covered in the map coordinates above. Speaking of coordinates, they're written (x1, y1, x2, y2): the first set defines the top-left corner of your area and the second set defines the bottom-right corner.

3. Once you've written your map, you'll save it as a .map file—foo.map, for example—and call it from your image as follows:

```
<a href="/cgi-bin/foo.map"><IMG SRC="mapimage.gif" ismap width=100
height=100 border=0></A>
```

The items to note here are these:

- You're telling the browser to link an imagemap to the image file via the ISMAP tag.

- You are using an anchor tag to reference a document on the server that, in turn, provides corresponding coordinates and URLs for the image. This could cause a lot of back-and-forth browser-client interaction on your server.

- The imagemaps require a CGI script on the other end to parse the data request the user is sending.

Because a lot of site developers may not have the bandwidth or server access to support server-side maps, it's easy enough to use client-side imagemaps instead. To do so, follow these steps:

1. Write an imagemap file, as follows:

```
<map name="primary">
<area shape="rect" coords="25, 84, 144, 105"
href="../index.html"alt="[home]">
<area shape="rect" coords="25, 68, 144, 85"
href="../archive/index.html" alt="[archives]">
<area shape="rect" coords="25, 52, 145, 69"
href="../news/index.html" alt="[news]">
<area shape="rect" coords="25, 36, 145, 53"
href="../search/index.html" alt="[search]">
<area shape="rect" coords="25, 19, 145, 37"
href="../reference/index.html" alt="[references]">
</map>
```

2. Include it in the bottom of your document.

3. Reference it from your image as follows:

```
<img src="foomap.gif" usemap=#primary>
```

Regardless of the format you decide, there are a few relevant markup characteristics that are universal to imagemaps: The area shape tag determines the outline of the clickable area—you can have rectangles, ovals, or circles, among other shapes. The coordinates outline the parameters of a clickable area, and the href always refers the user to the file destination.

Usability and Imagemaps

From a strict usability perspective, client-side imagemaps are much better. This is because the <ALT> tag is required as part of the <AREA> tags; client-side image-maps let people using voice-based browsers determine where the imagemap is pointing. An ideal client-based HTML imagemap looks like this:

```
<map name="primary">
<area shape="rect" coords="25, 84, 144, 105"
href="../index.html" alt="[home]">
<area shape="rect" coords="25, 68, 144, 85"
href="../archive/index.html" alt="[archives]">
<area shape="rect" coords="25, 52, 145, 69"
href="../news/index.html" alt="[news]">
<area shape="rect" coords="25, 36, 145, 53"
href="../search/index.html" alt="[search]">
<area shape="rect" coords="25, 19, 145, 37"
href="../reference/index.html" alt="[references]">
</map>
```

See how the alt tags reflect where you're going? This is an easy way to make your sitemaps accessible to anyone.

Software for Making Imagemaps

Instead of squinting and trying to calculate the exact coordinates for imagemaps, use a shareware package instead. These applications are usually equipped with a viewing window for opening up the graphic, a tools palette that allows you to trace the area to be mapped, and a text window for entering the corresponding URL. Once you've finished drawing the coordinates for your imagemap, you hit a button and the application spits a finished map file at you.

Some of the best imagemap makers out there are WebMap, for Macintosh users, or MapEdit for PC users and Macintosh users . You can find WebMap at http://uiarchive.cso.uiuc.edu/pubindex/info-mac/comm/tcp/html/map-2-html-01b2.hqx.abs.html and MapEdit is available on the companion CD-ROM.

Summary

Graphic elements can enliven a well-organized site and elevate from a solidly-built site to a truly well-designed product. This chapter was a primer for all of us who didn't get a design education and need to figure out how design considerations affect everyday site performance.

I strongly recommend looking at the book *Web by Design* by Molly Holzschlag (Sybex, 1998) for a crash course in intelligent design for the Web. For the rest of this book, however, let's focus on refining your images and multimedia so your images both look and perform well.

CHAPTER

EIGHT

8

Building a Better Backend

- Retaining flexibilty

- Getting organized

- Managing files

- Rolling out the backend

- Exploring commercial and open source software

One of the most vital components of a website is also the most frequently overlooked and abused. Meet the backend of your site.

What is the *backend*? It's the term that describes the melange of files, scripts, and directories that compose your website. The backend is the server-end map of where you store the different parts of your website. There is a place for everything, and every item is defined, in some part, by the category or categories to which it belongs.

This chapter is going to talk about how to optimize your backend so you can add, delete, or move large chunks of your website without having to change a thousand hypertext links or provide "this page has moved" bandaids to users expecting to find a bookmarked item. I'm going to start by telling you why you should care about your backend, then move on to strategies for making the most of the file system you use to store the various parts of your website, and then go into the best way to introduce your new and improved backend. The last sections of this chapter will outline the software options that can help you maximize your backend's potential. Sounds dirty, but it's not!

Retaining Flexibility

A good backend is a lot like a good suspension bridge: It does a job—often under adverse conditions—without damaging any of the items currently depending on it to do their jobs. If a suspension bridge snaps under gale-force winds, cars plunge into the freezing river, and it's horribly obvious that the bridge didn't do its job. Granted, accidentally deleting your entire CGI directory doesn't fit on the same scale of human tragedy, but for the production folks stuck trying to rewrite CGI scripts and rebuild the parts of the site hosed by the deletion, it's a close second place.

What do bridges have to do with the random places you've stuck your website files? Think of it this way: A bridge links Point A to Point B. A backend links your concrete file structure to the organization of the site—the part your user sees and (hopefully) understands.

NOTE   Flexibility is the key element of any backend.

That's really important, so I'll say it again: Flexibility is the key element of any backend. The backend is the container for all of the elements that compose your website, and you will depend on an orderly system of object classification to find different site elements whenever you need to repair or upgrade part of your site. If that orderly system doesn't take into account new content, a new way of producing regular content, or a way of reorganizing files in response to a new production system or tool, it's useless the first time you do repairs. By the time you need to extract an old directory tree and send it to the archive, your antiquated backend and subsequent workarounds and hacks have made it impossible to gracefully extract any part of your site without suffering unfortunate consequences on pages all across the site.

So plan your backend with this principle in mind: Your site will change. You want a backend that can encompass new content without affecting the organization of the old content. You want a backend that will allow you to treat the different directory trees in your site as discrete units. You want a backend that allows you to anticipate any type of site modification and the work it will take to integrate that new modification.

So how do you set up this marvel of modern organization? Keep reading.

Setting Up a File Structure

All site organization starts with a coherent file structure. If you've inherited one of those corporate sites where each department is responsible for its own file structure, you may already be acutely aware of how difficult it is to efficiently administer a site that's built with several different organizational tactics. If you initially posted a ten-page site and named all of the pages after their contents (e.g., `myresume.html`, `abibliography.html`, `myfavlinks.html`), you may discover that organizing and linking your mysteriously expanded site is a lot more work than it needs to be.

Find a way to organize your site, do some brutal housecleaning, and then rigorously reinforce your new organizational structure. The best and most obvious way to execute these three tasks is to set up a file structure. Your file structure is like an outline: The top level directories are equivalent to the I, II, III headings; the directories contained within the top-level directories are like the topic headings A, B, C. The A, B, C directories contain files or directories that correspond to the 1, 2, 3 details. Some Unix books advise you to think of file systems as trees.

That'll work. Or think of them as branching outlines. A model of a file tree, with the subdirectories mapped to different levels of an outline, is shown in Figure 8.1.

FIGURE 8.1:

This is the model of a file tree.

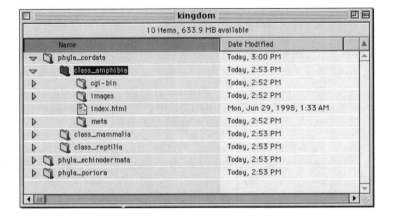

A file structure performs the following functions:

- It sets up a model for classifying and storing different items depending on their function.

- It provides you with a consistent system for storing and finding different files on your site.

- It contains a set of rules that allow you to add or delete content without affecting the overall operation of the website.

A file system can be organized in a number of ways. The basic idea is always the same: You have increasingly specialized categories the deeper you drill into the file structure. However, the criteria you use to create those categories are yours to devise and organize. The following sections outline some of the more common criteria.

Getting Organized

You've already learned the first tenet of organizing the backend (flexibility, remember?). There are two more: consistency and simplicity. Before you begin trying to plot your backend, consider how complex you want the file structure to be. Complexity has two attributes here: the *type of organization* you use to sort your backend, and the *degree* to which you want to carry your organization type.

TIP

It is important to remember that you should start out as simply as possible, while allowing yourself the flexibility of adding complexity later on.

The Linnean system, which classifies all living organisms, offers a great example of a coherent organization paradigm. The seven levels of Linnean classification would work well as a backend if you were trying to exhaustively categorize the contents of a site on frogs and toads. Why is it appropriate? Because the content requires a high degree of detailed distinction from item to item. If you were building a website on "My Friend, the Amphibian," you would probably want to make the content a little less specific.

Even if you've decided to restrict your site content to cataloging the myriad differences between frogs and toads, you may discover that the category-based backend you've devised isn't enough: You're adding a lot of new content regularly, and your What's New page is starting to list more information items than most of your frog pages. Or, you may discover that you are supplementing your frog and toad pages with an interactive identify-the-hopper learning tool, a frog search engine, and a virtual tour of a dissected frog.

NOTE

It's okay to make your backend a combination of different types of organization methods. The key is to decide which methods drive the site's primary structure, and which methods make navigating through the primary structure more feasible.

Continuing with our frog and toad website, we know that our content is restricted primarily to frogs in the genus *Rana* and toads in the genus *Bufo*, although we will have room in our backend to add frogs from different families or toads from different genuses if need be. But within the frog and toad divisions of the backend, there are a variety of supplemental organization tools.

For example, you add a new toad to the `bufo/` directory every Monday. Although you're introducing another item into a specific category, you're doing so on a regular, time-driven basis. So it might make sense to make your categories look like this:

```
/web/rana:> 98/ frog_tour/ hop_tool/
/web/bufo:> 98/ toad_quiz/
```

So you start out with a categorical backend, but provide a subcategory that is time-driven, and another that is functionally-driven. See how perfect science is? Don't worry, you haven't heard the last of Linnaeus. I'll get back to him later, in the section on organizing by subject.

When mapping the relationships that different parts of your site have to each other, consider how those parts function together and independently, and whether or not they do so over time. Also figure out what the bulk of your site work will comprise. Will you be adding new content frequently? Building new tools or applications for use within the site? Or expanding a timeless body of knowledge?

These questions can help you determine what your long-term tasks in maintaining the website are, and you can construct your backend accordingly to make completing those tasks more efficient for you and to lower impact on the already existing site.

Now that you have the general idea, let's get into a couple of the typical ways that you can organize your site.

Organizing By Date

Several sites, including the one I worked on as I wrote this book, use chronological file organization as the basis of their file structure. This works really well if you publish content on a regular schedule, or if you publish new content frequently. It does not work well if your site is not time-driven.

For example, if you publish a weekly digest of news stories about computer commerce, it makes sense to organize your backend according to publishing date. You could build your file structure like this:

/web/   This is the root.

/web/:> 96/ 97/ 98/   These are the contents of the /web directory. Note that they're time-driven but very broad. Let's look in one of them:

/web/96/:> 26/ 27/ 28/ 29/ 30/ 31/ 32/ 33/ 34/ 35/ ... 52/

This directory is listing weeks. If you want to write scripts to do things like publish or delete various directories during various weeks, listing your directories by week number is a great starting point.

The best thing about this file structure is that it can be mirrored for every subsequent year: You'll always have 1–52, and the persistence can allow you to do things like link back a year, or find something by date without having to open and read files.

Note how simple this system is: There are two levels of classification, yet you can find everything you need. Always strive for simplicity with your backend. If you publish more than once a week, you can always add one or two more levels of granularity to your backend. The first level would be day of the week, and the second, time of day. If you decide to push your newsletter from a weekly digest to a daily digest, you can always add another level to your backend, like this:

```
/web/96/26/:> sun/ mon/ tue/ wed/ thu/ fri/ sat/
```

NOTE

Note that the directory names are all lowercase. There's a good reason for that, which I'll get to in the section on filenames and linking. For now, it's enough to notice that all of your subdirectories should be consistently named and capitalized.

Now you can find your material by the day it appeared. So if you know that Monday is always the day you devote to running a reader Q&A, Wednesday is the day that you highlight new software tools targeted toward assisting Webmasters in setting a commerce-driven website, and Friday is the day that you interview some random executive in a commerce-driven website company, then you can find and repair items by category or date quickly.

TIP

In addition to your backend being simple, it should also be consistent.

I'll repeat myself: Your backend should be both consistent and simple. This will allow you to target content by subject or date, thus reducing the time it takes you to troubleshoot your site. The predictable targeting will also help you to perform site maintenance or overhauls on content areas without having to search every single directory for the targeted material. You'll save time and have less work.

The last thing you should remember about a time-based backend is that is should be as granular as you need it to be, but not overly divided. Extra levels of organization can increase the specificity of the category you're trying to create, but are merely superfluous if they're not needed.

For example, imagine that your Web commerce daily digest becomes so popular that you decide to publish an early edition and a late edition. You could do it one of two ways:

- Expand your backend file tree one more level, by adding two extra directories, like this:

```
/web/96/26/mon/:> morning/ evening/
```

All of your relevant files are either in the morning or evening directory.

- Build the time distinction into your filenames. This way you can keep the same directory structure and granularity, and drop in two distinct files without having to create yet another directory. The example is below:

  ```
  /web/96/26/mon/:> index_am.html     index_pm.html
  ```

The advantage to something like this is that you can always create a symlink from www.yourcommerce-digest.com/index.html to www.yourcommerce-digest.com/96/26/mon/index_am.html or www.yourcommerce-digest.com/96/26/mon/index_pm.html. Of course, you could also use symlinks even if you had the extra directory, but since I'm lazy, I prefer to keep the files in one sort of common container for as long as possible. For more info on symlinks, see "The Importance of Persistent URLs" section below.

A Word about Categorizing Your Website

Some websites are essentially periodicals that publish once or twice a month. You may want to embrace the chronological backend model, especially if your publishing schedule is marked by new editions of the website being delivered at reliable, regular intervals. But if you do a large number of topical issues, e.g., every one of your issues has a theme, you may want to consider a category-based approach.

Organizing By Subject

A chronological backend may not be for everyone. If you're posting a website with reviews of your various trips through each of the 50 states, you're not going to want to organize your travel accounts by date, you're going to want to organize them by subject. In this case, your subject is built in: you have 50 states. Your directory could look something like this:

```
/web:> /AL/ AK/  AR/ AZ/ CA/ CO/ CT/ DE/ ..
```

If you're not too crazy about 50 separate folders at the top level, then you could break them down into regions:

```
/web:> new_england/ midwest/ deep_south/ rockies/ alaska/
```

and then drop your state-by-state accounts into different regional folders like this:

```
/web/new_england:> ME/ NH/ VT/ MA/ CT/ RI/
```

The whole point to organizing your site by category is to devise a classification system that will allow you to include all content logically. Our content—the 50 states—is dealing with deliberately set parameters. You wouldn't include your trip to Germany in this file organization, because it doesn't fit into the file tree.

But you can alter the file tree to add new sections, or reassign the current categories to a new level in the file tree. Our old Web file tree assumed that we were only going to be publishing information about road trips through each of the 50 U.S. states. But if we're also including a trip through Canada, a backpacking expedition through continental Europe, and a week spent visiting Korea, we're going to need to expand the backend to reflect the new content.

How? Take a look at the categories you set up. The current file tree lists regions in the United States at the top level of the web. Just make them second-level directories, all living in the U.S. directory. So your new file tree looks like this:

```
/web:> united_states/ canada/ europe/ korea/
```

and the `united_states/` directory looks like this:

```
/web/united_states:> new_england midwest/ deep_south/ rockies/ alaska/
```

You can then apply the same country-region logic to your top-level `canada/` directory:

```
/web/canada:> maritime/ prairie/ northwest_territory/ pacific/
```

and then provide finer granularity:

```
/web/canada/maritime:> prince_edward/ newfoundland/ new_brunswick/ nova_scotia/
```

But what if you decide that the top level

```
/web:> united_states/ canada/ europe/ korea/
```

is categorically inconsistent, because Europe is a continent? No problem: Just bump the `united_states/` and `canada/` directory trees down a level and make your top level look like this:

```
/web:> north_america/ europe/ asia/
```

and continue your file structure from there. From this example, the need for flexibility, consistency, and simplicity should be evident.

NOTE An important note about category-based backends: Get only as specific as you need to.

So now you see how easy it is to add a new level of categorization to an already existing file tree. This comes in handy as your site expands. But you should always try to avoid micro-classifying your content. The more finely you divide it, the more work is required to do sweeping changes.

A helpful way to think of category-based backends is as a classification system for a really large group of objects. Let's get back to the Linnean system. Because I spent four years in college memorizing various scientific names for animals, I tend to think of my file trees like the Linnean system. This system has seven levels of increasingly specific categories, moving all the way from the kingdom the life form belongs to (animalia, protista, plant, etc.), down to the species name.

So if you're looking for the American toad specifically, you'll definitely want to get down to the two finest levels of classification, genus and species, and look for *Bufo americanus*. But if you're looking for animals with backbones, a childhood spent in water, and an adulthood spent on land, you can just stick with upper-level categorization: *kingdom animalia*, which eliminates plants, bacteria, slime molds, and other microscopic lifeforms; *phylum chordata*, which excludes any animals without backbones; *class amphibia*, which describes a category of animals who have an aquatic larval stage, soft moist skin, and egg-laying reproduction.

Not every category-based backend needs to reflect Linnean classification; I just included that example to indicate that different levels of specificity are adequate for meeting different types of information demands. As your site increases in size, or longevity, you'll need to modify your backend to serve these varying information demands.

Before we move into the methods that you can use to tailor backends to respond to different levels of organization, I'm going to repeat the two most important characteristics to remember about category-based websites:

- Get as specific as you need to.

- Different levels of specificity should be present only to meet different types of information demands.

A Word about Websites That Don't Fit Category, Issue, or Time

Even if your website doesn't slide neatly into any of the categories mentioned above, you can make one up. If your site is primarily application- or script-driven, you can always divide your backend by functionality, like so:

```
/web:> search/ calculate/ madlibs/ chat/
```

or by development language:

```
/web:> tcl_programs/ shell_scripts/ perl_cgi/ jscript_dhtml/
```

These organizational tactics may not be optimal if you're calling different types of applications or functions on the same page, but they will allow you to keep script libraries segregated by type, rather than by section category. They'll also allow you to add new applications carefully so you don't inadvertently break the apps you already have on the site.

And if your site is low-script and small-scale, you should still find and stick to a backend. A lot of personal sites grow into specific, well-trafficked resources, and maintaining or adding on the site is a lot easier when you have a clear map of what should go where.

Setting Apart Frequently Used Material

One of the most efficient things you can do is standardize the way things are done. This means applying a little critical thinking to how you deal with elements that are persistent from section to section on the site. Do you have a spacer GIF you use in every section? If so, does it live in only one images/ directory, or is there a copy in every branch of the file tree that calls it?

Setting apart the common elements in every directory is useful. You will be better able to canvas your site and eliminate redundant site elements; you'll also be able to perform more efficient site maintenance by setting apart functional elements like templates, graphics, or scripts.

For example, if you do build that U.S. roadtrip site mentioned a few sections back, you might have a backend organization like this:

```
/web/new_england:> ME/ NH/ VT/ MA/ CT/ RI/
```

But in addition to the topical organization, you'd also have directories like this:

```
/web/new_england:> ME/ NH/ VT/ MA/ CT/ RI/ templates/ images/
```

where the images/ directory holds all the images for the files living in ME/, NH/, VT/, MA/, CT/, RI/, and the templates/ directory holds all of the formatting templates for any content in the directory.

There are five big reasons for setting apart common elements:

- Finding elements will be easier if you know you can rely on the structure you've set up.

- Providing a discrete area for common elements allows you to easily centralize the elements that build the site.

- You'll be able to reduce the time you spend maintaining the site.

The last two reasons are so big, they gets their own sections: you'll reduce the load on the server and you'll find upgrading much easier.

Reducing Server Load

Centralizing your common site elements within the backend will let you reduce the load your server is pushing out every time a user makes a request.

For example, let's say you have a navigation bar that appears at the top of every page. Rather than copy the navigation bar code into every directory, and copy the same image into directory after directory, just write the code once, stick it in a central directory, and reference the code whenever you need it. Or, if all of your pages are formatted similarly, you can write one structural template, drop it in a central directory, and reference it on every page.

The advantage to both of these methods is that the file is only called from the server once, then cached. You'll be able to reduce the total number of files your server has to push to the average user. In the next chapter, I outline several different options for breaking down your Web pages into a series of modular, self-contained elements.

Facilitating Replacement and Upgrades

Another advantage to separating out frequently used site elements is that you reduce the number of places that you have to look when you want to replace chunks of code.

If you decide to add a section to your site, you're going to have to update your navigation bars to reflect the changes. Instead of having to check for a specific sequence of code that varies marginally from directory to directory, you would only have to change one file once and it would be reflected across the site.

Build your backend so it is modular, set apart the elements that are used sitewide, then make sure that the components that are section-specific have a clear path to the common site elements. Even better, try to standardize the file paths whenever possible. For example, if all of your pages have the same layout, you could write every page like this:

```
<!-#include virtual="/www/meta/templates/page_template.shtml" - ->
<!-#include virtual="content_file.shtml" - ->
```

The first line of code calls a template along a direct and highly specific file path; the second line of code calls a file within the directory that our two-line file lives in. The point is that the call to the template file is constant, no matter where the file lives. If you want to replace or update the template, you know where the file to be modified lives, and you're guaranteed that it will affect all of the files that call it.

By separating out common site elements or compartmentalizing the elements on your site that you anticipate changing frequently, you are saving yourself a lot of detective work and double-checking in the long run.

File Management

You can't stop once you have your metastructure down; consistently named and cleanly linked files can be just as important to the clarity and ease-of-management of your site.

Naming Files

Setting up a flexible and persistent file tree is one important and useful facet of building a backend. The second element that should be incorporated is the use of sensible filenames. This section lists guidelines for naming your files so any future maintenance scripts don't choke, and employees don't overwrite files unless they really try.

Use consistent case   InterCapping your company name may be really cool, but it rarely works in files. Developers end up trying to memorize non-intuitive combinations of uppercase and lowercase. Try to develop a consistent naming practice instead. All lowercase letters is probably your safest bet for naming both files and directories. If you worry that you or your developers will inadvertently overwrite the meta/ directory with a file named meta, then make your directories all caps. Just make sure your capitalization scheme is as simple as possible.

Avoid using nonstandard alphanumeric characters   Putting *, &, %, $, #, @, or ! in your filenames is only asking for trouble: Many operating systems use the * to indicate a special file status. In addition, CGI scripts are likely to try to read the filenames as a string of variables to be parsed. Using an underscore is permissible, and sometimes helpful if you're trying to distinguish between template.html, template_2.html, and template_2a.html.

Don't put spaces in your filenames   One of the reasons that system administrators shudder when someone tries to give them files fresh from a Macintosh is that they usually end up with filenames like:

```
This is the small gfx.gif
Index page b4 template.html
```

While, if they're lucky, look like this:

```
This\ /is\ /the\ /small\ /gfx.gif
Index\ /page\ /b4\ /template.html
```

The Unix operating system on my X-terminal helpfully inserted those slashes in there for me, since it can't handle spaces in a filename. These cumbersome filenames look wonderful on a Mac, where you can drop and drag files from one folder to the next, but they're murder on the wrists of your carpel-tunnel inflicted, command-line guru back in MIS.

The best solution is to keep your filenames short and simple. In the days before Windows 95, many computer users were constrained by the 8.3 rule: The name itself could only be eight letters long, and the file extension three. Try to maintain similar, brief names.

Develop and enforce a common naming scheme   For example, the opening page of every directory is index.html, the navigation bar template is nav.html, or if you're using HTML fragments as virtual includes (see Chapters 6 and 14 for more information) nav.shtml or nav.htmlf. Part of your success in maintaining an efficient, low-bulk backend will come from knowing what parts belong in what directories. Attaching consistent, functional names to each part will help you further tweak your backend.

Use your naming scheme to reflect your backend organization   If you've organized the backend chronologically, name your files to reflect dates: `home_mon.html`, `home_tue.html`, etc. If you're organizing the site by issue, name the files to reflect the issue number. The important thing is to extend the backend organization all the way down to the file level.

Linking Files

Another aspect of basic backend management is linking policy. There are several different issues to think about and resolve before laying down the first anchor tag. The two most important are:

- What sort of addresses do you want to present to your readers?

- What sort of link maintenance do you want to do on the backend?

The next two sections cover these issues in more detail.

A Word about External Link Policies

If you're building a site that relies heavily on links to external sites, you may want to research all of the legal implications of linking to, or incorporating content from, other sites. Providing a link to a specific file on another site is a commonly accepted practice, and is even desirable for some sites.

But setting up your site to display other pages as part of your own site may be treading on thin legal ice. Total News Inc. had to settle a law suit with *The Washington Post* and five other media companies and stop setting up its pages so the media companies' content was displayed within the Total News frame and URL.

Other legal issues—liability, consumer confusion, and copyright infringement—are beginning to raise their heads. Until these are all settled, you may want to play it safe and ask permission.

The Importance of Persistent URLs

The URL is frequently an inconvenient way to remember an address or location, especially if it's in cryptic Web-speak. Fortunately, most humans are flexible and can type several of their favorite addresses by heart. And bookmarks can't hurt. This is good news for your site, but it does raise a sticky issue: how do you keep those readers coming back for new content without changing the address constantly?

This isn't a problem, you say. Whenever I visit CNN or Salon, the content is different but the address is the same. So they're just writing over one file with another, right?

Wrong. Most sites maintain their individual files for archival purposes, or to exercise a form of version control, so if a new version of index.html doesn't work, you don't have to go back to the old one.

As more sites buy expensive dynamic content servers to assemble their pages, this becomes less of an issue since all you need to do to revive an old page is enter a combination of variables. Those of you who are running sites on your own Linux box, or who simply prefer building pages by hand, however, are going to be generating a lot of unique files. If you think that takes a lot of time, think of how much more time rebuilding those files takes.

So it's in your best interests to find a way to give your readers a means to quickly access a specific address like http://www.mysitehere.com/index.html, even if the actual contents marked up in index.html change daily.

The answer is to establish a permanent address, and change what goes there as often as you need to. You can do this one of two ways:

> **The time-intensive way**   Make your new file index.html, rename the old file to fit within your backend scheme, and keep cycling through new index.html files.

> **The efficient way**   Symlink a persistent address to ever-changing files. *Symlinks* are a handy Unix trick: They create a filename in the system that can be read and understood as a "file," even though it's only a virtual file.

The syntax is simple:

```
System/book/:> ln -s /98/17/chapter8.html index.html
```

To break it down:

- ln -s instructs the computer to make a symlink.

- /98/17/chapter8.html is the filepath and name of the real file.

- index.html is the symlinked address.

Users who go to /book/index.html will see the chapter9.html file. When they come back the next week, they may see a chapter9.html file. The important thing is, the address /book/index.html has been established, the address content itself is completely separate, and only the persistent URL pointer needs to change.

The Importance of Reliable Addresses within a Site

The prior section dealt with assigning persistent URLs for your user's ease. This section will talk about ways to make sure your long-term link maintenance is a minimal part of your backend maintenance.

What is link maintenance? It's largely composed of making sure that the internal hyperlinks on your site still work, even if sections are moved or deleted. Another function of link maintenance is making sure that any files or objects called from a file within your website (like graphics or multimedia files) can still be called if either file should move.

To prevent annoying maintenance tasks, like having to run a grep call for an old file string on your entire site tree, set up your file calls and links so they can be easily modified. The following tips will help:

Avoid relative file paths   When you're building a set of pages on your desktop, the relative file paths are convenient for checking page layout and hyperlinking. But if you push those pages live with relative links, you're assuming that everything you're linking to or calling (like an image) is going to stay in the same place no matter what. That's a dangerous assumption to make. If you decide to move all of your images to a central area, you'll have to comb every file for all the img src="../foo.gif" references.

NOTE   The only time you should break this rule is if you're building a site for a third-party client, and you have to make the site small and portable. Then, it's smart to make all your hyperlinks relative. But you should always reference images and includes with as much precision as you can.

Use absolute file paths   If you set up your server to have a base URL, like http://myserver.com, you can simply extend the file path and have absolute pointers like this: <img src="/98/17/chapter8.gif">. The beauty of this system is twofold: First, you have an absolute address, which is always easier to run search-and-replace scripts on. Second, you have an address system in place if you decide to move your images to a separate server. Your backend structure is already in place, so you can mimic the file paths on the image server and none of your pages on the content server are affected.

If the link is internal, set up a base URL on the server rather than including it on the page or in the anchor tag   This way, if you decide to change your site's domain name, or you're hosting several different sites that share similar resources, you will still be able to preserve the backend without doing any file editing.

TIP

There is an excellent program, called Site Sweeper, from a company called Site Technologies. It does a great job of going through an entire website checking for broken images, invalid or duplicate page titles, and broken links, both external and internal. Visit **www.sitetech.com** for more information, as well as a quick demo.

Expandability

A good backend is one that can handle the influx of new content without sacrificing old material. A great backend is one that simultaneously absorbs new content and neatly stores old content.

Fortunately, building a great backend is not hard. It requires a little forethought—which may be difficult to muster in the hectic project cycling that drives most Web development—but once you set everything up, the files just fall into place.

It's a mistake to assume you won't add new content to your site. Not only will you be adding new pages to existing sections, you'll probably be adding entire sections to the site. This leads to one driving question: How will the new content affect the older content?

Ideally, your new content shouldn't have any measurable impact on your old content at all (unless it was built specifically to do so). The reason for this is that you're going to be dropping it into your carefully set-up backend system. And thanks to the modularity of the system you set up (which we covered a few pages ago), you should be able to deduce where the new content will go in your existing backend structure.

Another benefit to using a modular backend with one persistent URL address is that archiving content is automatic. You won't have to move files to an /archive/ directory unless you want to: You can just build an archive index page and link to the rest of your site.

A final perk to maintaining a modular, self-archiving site is that entire sections of the site can be moved or deleted without affecting the site at large. For example: You run a site with six different urban restaurant directories. You sell one of the directories to a different company. They demand that you turn over all of your files and delete your copies at once.

If you had been using a system where all your old content went into an /archive/ directory, and you'd been overwriting your index.html files with new content, assembling and transferring all of the information might require a sitewide search, as well as some file-by-file HTML repair. But having one neatly organized directory allows you to copy over a near-perfect set of files, and run a few maintenance scripts on the remaining directories.

Using the Backend to Improve Workflow

A final benefit to having a well-organized, strictly enforced backend structure is that it can also double as an effective tool for getting your work done.

Having a separate development and testing area is crucial for a well-performing website. This area allows you to do things with your website that a desktop-only developer can't, and permits you to develop without airing your mistakes on the live site.

But just because it's not the "real" home of the site files doesn't mean it's not subject to the same considerations. If anything, your test site needs to be more organized, because it's executing more complex tasks.

A backend designed for hosting live sites and responding to client queries has one job: respond to requests with the correct results. A backend designed for testing and staging those sites has three different mandates:

- The backend has to be a copy of the live site, from content organization to server configuration.

- The backend has to provide a way to monitor file flow as the files move through various production processes.

- The system has to provide some sort of internal communication so employees know where files are and who's doing what to them.

But how do you accomplish the three mandates listed above? Read on.

Tools for Keeping Track of Your Backend

In order to use your backend as part of your daily production routine, you need to be able to keep track of files as they flow through the different areas of your work and testing space, and you need to be able to communicate file status to your fellow employees. There are two routes you can take: the DIY option, and the commercial software option. There are pros and cons to both systems.

The DIY Option

The most obvious benefit to setting up and running your own backend workflow system is that you can write the tools to meet your specific task requirements. You can even set up a backend system comprised of nothing more than an internal network and a series of e-mail aliases, then place the burden of moving files and e-mailing status updates on the shoulders of the people who are doing the actual tasks.

The DIY method works well on low-volume sites, or on sites that produce very specific content using a very specific process. However, DIY falls apart if site production becomes more complicated, more frequent, or higher volume. It also fails if the tools can't be built in time to perform tasks, or if those tools don't adapt to new site tasks.

Figure 8.2 shows a simple checks-and-balances system for producing files for your site. It works like this:

1. People drop their individual items into the words, code, or images folders in the 1_Rough folder. The production team will use the material they find in those folders to assemble the pages they will put in the 2_Draft\2_ToEdit folder.

2. People view the contents of 2_Draft\2_ToEdit and drop off revised or edited versions of content, images, or code in the 2_Draft\2_Edited directory. Production checks the revised content in the individual pages,

makes any changes, and drops the results in the 3_Production\3_ToEdit folder.

3. The copyeditors and QA folks take over. These people look at the content in 3_Production\3_ToEdit and move it all over to 3_Production\3_Working so the production people can keep dropping new material in 3_Production\ 3_ToEdit. Once everyone's done reviewing the material, they drop all edits and suggested revisions into 3_Production\3_Edited.

4. The production folks pull the pages out of 3_Production\3_Edited, make any necessary revisions, then drop them into 4_Revision\4_ToEdit. The QA and copyedit folks take another pass at the material and drop it in 4_Revision\4_Edited.

5. Production makes the final revisions if there are any, then drop all completed material into the 5_Final\Post folder. This tells anyone who's interested that the contents have been thoroughly reviewed and are ready for publication. At this point, the files can be moved from the workflow file tree into their places in your website file tree.

FIGURE 8.2:

Here is an example of a simple but thorough backend workflow system. You could set up a file tree like this on your test server and use it to control the process your team uses to build sites.

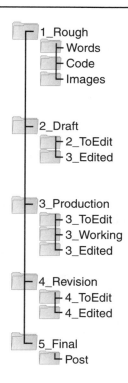

Integrating Third-Party Tools and Software into Your Backend

The other option is to use a software tool to produce, test, and publish the site. A lot of people are already doing this by using content tools like Vignette, ColdFusion, and OpenText.

If you're building the site from scratch, you'll be able to develop your backend to work symbiotically with the way each different tool stores and publishes files. But most of us are working with sites and backends designed before Web-publishing tools were even a serious idea. The real challenge is how to integrate a tool into a backend file structure that is already in existence, and into work routines that people are already used to.

Since each content publishing system is different, there's no one formula for meshing a new tool into your existing file structure. Instead, there is a set of criteria that you should think through before committing time and money to a content-publishing package.

Does the content publishing tool meet a specific task need, or are you adopting it as part of an overhaul of the way you do work on your site? If your new content tool is merely enhancing a process that's already in place, you're in luck. If you're planning on implementing a whole new way to move files from idea to publication, you need to ask:

- What will happen to old content?
- Will you have to separate old content because it is not assembled in the same way as the new content?
- Can you modify the tool to move the new files into the existing backend?

You don't want to make your backend a legacy structure that hampers new site production. Therefore, it's in your best interests to see how files flow through content tools before you integrate those tools into your site.

Rolling Out the Backend

Building a backend to increase your site's operational efficiency is great. Rebuilding your backend all over the live site is a fatal mistake. Your users don't care that a new and improved organizational system is coming soon. They care about their favorite bookmarks becoming 404s. When you reorganize your backend, you should do so in stages.

First, map out all of the functions your site is going to perform. Separate the items that are specific to certain directories. Then, plot a way to roll in the new and improved backend functions one at a time.

Before you roll any new backend file structures, templates, or page restructuring, test it thoroughly. On an ideal planet, you would be working on a website that had three distinct server areas. The first would be used for *testing*—developing the code and file systems that comprise your latest upgrade. The second would be used for *proofing* all content before it was ready for public viewing. And the third would be used for *pushing*: This is the server that pushes files to requesting clients, and it holds all of your public website files.

The three different areas work together in an assembly-line process. You develop and prototype any new website upgrades on the testing area. Once a prototype is functionally perfect, you set up its constituent parts on the proofing server. The proofing server is a mirror of the live site, you can use it as a testing ground to see how well the prototype content functions within the site as a whole, and to see how the prototype affects total site performance. You can also use it as the last-minute checkpoint for all content before it is pushed to the live site. The final step in the assembly line process is copying the files over to the pushing server.

WARNING No matter how strapped your resources, you should never do experimental development on your live server. Converting a spare PC or Macintosh to a desktop-run Web server is a safe alternative, and allows your developers to work within a test environment without affecting the live site.

The advantage to visibly separating the development processes into testing, proofing, and pushing is that you develop a distinct series of checks and balances for each different stage. Thus, you can continually ensure the integrity of the backend structure you've worked so hard to set up.

TIP Another alternative is to use the same server but duplicate the website in a sub-directory called Test. This would allow for the same effect if someone could not set up a second server. Often in small companies and higher education, people don't have a spare computer and/or network port lying around.

Fine-Tuning Your Backend

In order to maximize the machines and software you have serving your site, you need to be able to define what you need from your servers. You also need to know what tools will get those results, and how they work. You'll soon discover that another side benefit to having a more complex site is that troubleshooting involves a more complex body of knowledge.

You'll have to face facts: Your backend development is never going to be done. If you go ahead and apply some of the principles covered in the sections above to your own backend, file maintenance will be simple and straightforward. The next step is integrating content-serving and ad-serving software tools into your site's backend. These software tools reduce the total amount of people-hours that go into complex site construction and analysis. However, they will affect both your workflow and your machine performance.

The remainder of this section covers the two most likely paths for adopting backend software solutions. The first alternative, commercial software, wins points for out-of-box convenience and the fact that someone else already did the work to solve your problems. The second alternative, open source software, celebrates the time-honored tradition of building the types of tools you want to perform specific tasks.

Commercial Software Solutions

For a review of the basics for setting up a website and a distinct address on the Internet, refer back to Chapter 5. I assume that you have already set up an operational Web server, and are looking to jack up your site's performance and functionality to the next level.

What is this next level? Instead of serving a series of static Web pages, a next-level website builds pages on the fly, using a system of user input and server-side scripting to create sites that are easy to assemble and update. Many of the next-level sites are trying to exploit database-driven information on a Web browser frontend, and discovering that CGI scripting is slow, or too much of a drain on both the development team and the site server itself. Or, sites are trying to hold their readers by offering increasingly personalized content, like my.yahoo.com, as seen in Figure 8.3.

FIGURE 8.3:

my.yahoo.com, my style

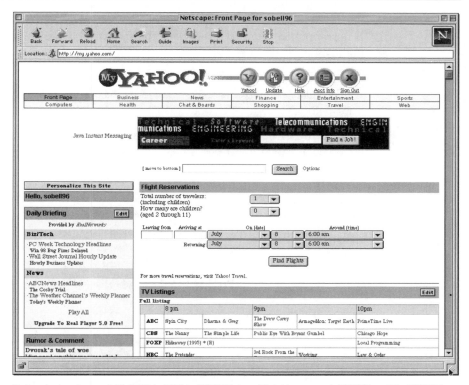

Text and artwork copyright ©1994–1998 by YAHOO!, Inc. All rights reserved. YAHOO! and the YAHOO! logo are trademarks of YAHOO!, Inc.

As a result, the tools you use to serve these sites are going to become increasingly more specialized. The rest of this section looks at the shrink-wrapped software options you have as a site developer, and at the freeware alternatives.

Exploring Your Options

You're going to be sinking a considerable amount of time, a not-small sum of money, and a significant amount of your development strategy into these software tools. Therefore, it is in your best interests to look at them carefully and make sure the software tool meets your specific needs before giving it the go-ahead.

Before you can begin to apply any type of stringent criteria to your prospective tools, it helps to know what is available. The software tools I'm going to present are all called *middleware*. As the name implies, middleware is software that mediates between two separate software products, connecting them to produce a final product. It is a unique class of software, and not to be confused with any sort of import or export function that you'll see in a software package like Microsoft Word or Adobe Photoshop.

There are four main categories of middleware: *application servers*, *content management tools*, *commerce servers*, and *personal tools*. These are all covered in the sections below.

Once you've determined what kind of software you need, you need to decide what specific brand-name application is right for you. If you're going to be buying your system off the shelf, consider the following:

Price   Are you paying for a tool that is well within your budget, or are you going to have to skimp somewhere else to afford the software? How much of a return on your investment do you anticipate? For example, if you're hoping to add a commerce server and increase sales for your catalog-based website, the investment is in line with your site's goals. But if you're planning on moving your corporate, media-kit-heavy website to a Vignette Story Server just because it would be cool, think again. More pricing considerations: What is the payment schedule? Do you pay on a per-use basis, quarterly, or yearly? Do you need to subscribe to support services?

Support and site licenses   How much money do you have to pay to allow your site to operate the software? And what sort of support agreement will you have with your software vendor? If your entire advertising software system goes down, your site is losing revenue while you labor to repair the damage. You'll need to work out support and maintenance agreements with the vendor ahead of time. Before you do even that, be sure you've decided among your team what level of support you expect: on-site consulting if a system crashes, free patches and upgrades, 24-hour response and paging.

Industry support   Is there any existing community-based support that you can turn to for tips on optimizing or debugging your tool? These kind of user-created websites, Usenet newsgroups or e-mail lists can be a valuable resource for anyone who wants to hear real-life tips from people who have walked in your shoes. If there aren't any online resources out there, find out why not.

Ease of integration   How easily will you be able to merge your new system into your extant Web tool suite? What protocols for data compression, file transfer, or file serving does each tool support? If you've chosen one specific vendor for all of your development needs, this is a moot point.

Ease of modification   Also known as *extensibility*. Can you add software patches or change the source code to customize the tool for your site? Remember, you're buying this software to serve your site production processes. You should not have to change your production processes to accommodate a new tool. The only exception to this rule: you've bought the software specifically to alter your production cycle.

Scalability   Will you be able to adapt the software to work if the size of your site changes scope? Can you run it across more servers if need be?

Features   Last but not least, make sure that the product offers support for site authoring and site publishing. How easy is it to separate your content from your formatting markup? Can you preserve templates without having to drop in actual content?

Another feature you'll end up paying for is workflow management. Check to see if there's any version control system that prevents two people from modifying the same file simultaneously. See if you can set up separate classes of users, and if you can attach specific file permissions to those groups, or even to individual users within a group. Finally, see if there's any way to track who's accessed what files, and what actions they took. These action logs will help you track down bugs and errors.

After you've settled personnel issues, figure out how the software package will affect the way you move files. Can you move files effortlessly from the 'creation' area to the staging server? Can you easily push specific files or batches of files live?

Of course, you'll want to be able to check your work too. Be sure you can preview and modify your content as well. Can you preview your work before pushing it live? More importantly, can you preview your work under a wide variety of conditions before pushing it live?

The following sections profile some of the more popular software products used in developing dynamic, data-driven sites. Some of these applications mediate between a deep database and a top-level server interface; others are a seamless package that handle everything from building databases to scripting pages. The software applications are broken down by the categories discussed above.

Application Servers

This is a catchall phrase for a software package that sits between the Web server and a backend database program. These packages can perform a wide variety of functions, from assembling pages via server-side scripting, to maintaining state information, to performing server load balancing. The market for application servers is highly fluid, with software packages moving from company to company as these companies merge, or get bought or sold. One of the more stable application servers is profiled below.

Netscape Application Server Netscape's Application Server is an intermediary piece of software that mediates between an external client request and a server-side database that provides information in a form the client is requesting. This extra layer makes the client-server transaction more of a three-tiered approach to serving information, but can be useful for pulling together lots of different data formats for Web-based distribution.

Don't think the Application Server is a glorified database interface. It's also a way to integrate varied technologies like load balancing (a way to ensure that traffic demands are distributed to prevent server overload) and dynamic page generation. How can an application server do all that? It provides a "space" where separate applications can exchange information or execute functions.

For more information, visit Netscape's Application Server page at `http://sitesearch.netscape.com/appserver/v2.1/index.html`.

Content Management Tools

These tools provide a visual aid and software medium for the production process driving your website construction. You may not write actual scripts here, but you may check files in and out of a prescribed workflow system, or use the content management interface to assemble individual templates.

ColdFusion by Allaire ColdFusion's own proprietary markup language, CFML, extends HTML functionality by adding tags for database queries. CFML also adds tags for formatting results pages if the user is going to be querying the site. For more information, visit Allaire's site at `http://www.allaire.com/`.

StoryServer by Vignette This content-managing system has its roots as an in-house application for the CNet website. It's now a software package designed to serve as a workflow tool: Editors can review or revise the content of Web pages while production types create or mix templates and systems folks hammer out sophisticated scripted programs to assemble different pages on demand.

To learn more about StoryServer, go to `http://www.vignette.com/`.

IIS by Microsoft   Microsoft's Internet Information Server is most frequently used as a "straight" Web server, but you can also use it to assemble and host Active Server Pages, which are more thoroughly explained in the sidebar. To learn more about IIS, I encourage you to read Peter Dyson's *Mastering Microsoft Internet Information Server* (Sybex, 1997).

What Is an Active Server Page?

Very nearly every definition of Active Server Pages (ASP) starts with a server-side scripting environment. This is about as illuminating as a dead flashlight. ASP is an assembly-line method for compiling browser-readable files from a lot of server-side bits and pieces. The glue that holds those pieces together is a scripting language that writes commands telling the server how to assemble the pieces before sending them as a file to the client.

ASP is a key feature of Microsoft's Internet Information Server (IIS). Just as the Apache server has the ability to parse includes from anywhere on the server into any file that calls them, IIS assembles the ASP files—which can be composed of HTML, scripts, and ActiveX objects—and pushes them live.

What Are Some of the Components of Active Server Pages?

The two items that make up the meat of an ASP-assembled site are sessions and objects.

Sessions identify a unique user's unique visit. Or, to put it less obliquely, if Joe visits your site Monday morning, then Wednesday afternoon, then Wednesday evening, he'll generate three discrete, unique session records—records that Jenn's three visits on Tuesday are completely dissimilar from. Sessions are not analogous to cookies, although cookies are used to maintain specific session objects. The data for a specific session is stored on the server, not on a cookie. Instead, the cookie is used to log a specific session ID, nothing more.

Objects are functional chunks that allow you to dictate the behavior of pages as they're processed by the IIS. Objects tend to be compact: One of the strongest arguments for using ASP is the ability of the ASP server to inject one line of code that spells out the HTML for part or all of a Web page. The browser capabilities (or *browsercaps*) are the ASP analogue to conditional server-side includes.

Continued on next page

What Are Some of the Advantages to Using Active Server Pages?

If you're used to working on a Windows machine and you're only beginning to move beyond HTML into database-driven site assembly, ASP combined with Microsoft Access to provide an interface for building database-driven applications with Microsoft SQL server—without having to become a database guru.

ASP also coddles the control freak on your developer team. Through the course of your Web development career, you will either work with or become the developer who insists on hand-coding their Web pages and applications. There's a lot to be said for the DIY school of Web development: You have a greater understanding of what every line of code does, and you'll be able to modify, add, or delete things with greater precision than a drop-and-drag tool affords you.

Still, slinging 1500 lines of code a day for weeks at a time can be difficult, and that's where ASP comes in handy. As a tool, ASP lets you tweak working Web applications well because it gives you the ability to extend the items you work with—scripting languages—beyond the defaults hard-coded in the application. So you can buy off-the-shelf extensions to ASP or build your own in any one of several programming languages.

When you can rewrite the application to better work how you want it to, there's less of a reason not to use it.

What Are Some of the Disadvantages to Using Active Server Pages?

Because ASP is part of IIS, they can only be served from the Windows NT platform. If your site currently lives on a Unix platform, you can't use ASP.

A more serious consideration is future development. If you are planning on moving your site to a Unix operating system, the work you've done in ASP is not easily salvageable unless you use an application like Chili!ASP. Therein lies the biggest drawback to ASP: It's not easily portable without the right off-the-shelf software tools.

If you're going to develop in ASP, you're making a commitment to a specific page building method and a specific operating system. This sounds about the same as committing to server-side includes on an Apache server, but there is one key difference: Apache offers versions of its server software for several different operating systems, and IIS only comes for Windows NT. Even if you're gung-ho about Windows NT, be warned: ASP is not a typical Windows-based technology. Final pages have to be accessed through a browser, and they have to reside in a virtual directory on the Web server.

Continued on next page

Is There Any Time When Using Active Server Pages Would Be Overkill?

The biggest advantages to using ASP are the easy SQL server transactions and the scripts to make your site more responsive to individual users. If you've got a series of static HTML pages, you'd do just as well building them out yourself. The same criteria you'd apply to any other facet of technical development also apply to your middleware solutions: use the best technology for the job. HTML still works for producing Web pages quickly. ASP works for producing database-driven sites that rely on querying and connecting facilities.

How Do I Get Started?

First, make sure your machine will support IIS and ASP. The only platforms that currently serve it are Windows NT 4.0 Server, Windows NT Workstation with Peer Web services, or Windows 95 with Personal Web Server.

Next, install IIS. This is usually an option in your desktop menu. After you've walked through installation, configure the server. You want to do this right off the bat because you need someplace to deposit all those `.asp` files you're going to create. Note that the file extension for files created and processed with ASP technology via IIS is `.asp`.

After you've set up your default file repository, build a `global.asa` file. This is the file you'll use to initialize your application objects, your session objects, and the connection string for SQL server. The `global.asa` file is optional later on, especially if you're trying to build items that don't pass or retain cookies. But use the `global.asa` at first until you're an ASP whiz.

Now that you've set up the basics, you're ready to romp through an SQL database and begin building tables and procedures to shape your dynamic Web pages. Assuming you know Microsoft SQL Server, that is.

Commerce Servers

A commerce server has a weighty task: It must provide the means to conduct most typical retail transactions, from cataloging inventory, to fulfilling purchase orders, to remembering a customer's purchase for service. The following list encompasses some of the basic tasks a commerce server has to fulfill:

Accurate tracking of customers through the site   Commerce servers must be able to track the pages visitors are hitting, and the products they're ordering. This helps the site developers focus on two things: store inventory and site construction. If you notice that a user is consistently checking out a specific brand-name vendor in every retail category, you can add a site navigation strategy that allows customers to find products by vendor and not just by category. As a result of tracking, you'll want to be able to reorganize your inventory to meet the surfing and ordering patterns of your customers. You also want to be able to merge, add, or delete categories whenever necessary.

Secure site   One of the bugbears of online commerce is the specter of Net hackers lifting credit card numbers off a commerce site and charging a trip to Tahiti on their stolen bounty. You'll want to invest in a secure server—both to alleviate your customers' fears about security breaches and to save yourself the work of taking constant, vigilant security measures.

Real-time credit card verification   One of the most prevalent complaints against e-commerce is that it offers no instant gratification since users aren't holding "stuff" after buying it. You can't alter the fabric of space and time by delivering physical objects over wires meant to transmit electronic packets, but you can let your users know that their credit card order went through successfully.

Expedient service   It is in your best interests to make sure that your user doesn't have to slog through several pages to make a purchase, therefore giving him more time to change his mind. If the grab-them-while-you-can argument doesn't work, consider this: If someone is ordering something they want right away, that alacrity is going to carry over to the ordering process too. You'll want to provide shopping cart functionality: Nothing is going to prevent big-ticket purchases more than having to perform several repeat transactions. A shopping cart allows potential customers to collect and review the items they want to buy, and to control their shopping experience.

Customizable environment   Online shopping sites present challenges that real-space stores don't have: The user doesn't have the same ability to easily navigate through their favorite store and find what they're looking for. In fact, plumbing the depths of your site's inventory may be a lot of work for even the most dedicated user. Offer your users as many ways as possible to mediate their environment. They should be able to set up lists of items to look for, to tag favorite brands or items, or to remember prior orders. In a related issue, you'll want to provide suggestions according to the customer's preferences, and display them on the customer's unique front page.

Meaningful organization and categorization of products   Before you make your commerce site public, you have to organize the products in a way that makes sense to your users and to the tracking system you're going to use to monitor inventory and purchases. Make sure your software can provide a suitably flexible organization framework, and that it allows for several levels of sub-categorization. Including a configurable search mechanism on your site can increase the speed with which users get to where they're going, as well as present results in a way that accurately reflects your site's organization.

Prominent display of products   One of the best ways to move merchandise is to put it someplace where users can't help but see it. Make sure your server offers a production interface for rotating different products on the front page of your site. And remember that there is some truth to the saying "A picture is worth a thousand words." If you're trying to sell something, having a visual aid can seal the sale.

Optional customer information   One of the advantages to online commerce is having the ability to record and store specific information about your customers next to their purchases. This is how you can find out what domains your users are coming from, where they live, and what purchases they've made recently. All of this information is valuable in helping you plan your inventory, or plot your subsequent site development work.

Real-time inventory checking   It is crucial that your customers have a clear idea of whether or not the products they are ordering are actually in stock. You will want to have a database system that allows multiple real-time queries and can accurately return results to your customers, without crashing the system. Sooner or later, someone is going to order something that isn't in stock. You'll want to be able to hold orders until they're filled, or for a reasonable time. You'll also want to indicate to your user the status of their order and generate a restocking request for your inventory tracking system.

Separate areas for production, staging, and development   This is already a priority for regular site development; it is equally important when your site is home to commercial transactions.

Content management work flow   As with any other website you'd build, you want to be able to parcel out your file flow to match the stages of production you're going through. This allows you to figure out who's done what where. Since a commerce site is going to be serving a lot of content in response to specific visitors, finding a way to track the files you're posting to the public is crucial.

Intranet ordering application What good is a commerce server if the people who build and maintain it don't have a way to order items off it as well? Provide the intranet ordering both as a gauge for system performance and a benefit of working for the organization.

Frequent shopper benefits A lot of real-life shops and restaurants offer frequent shopper perks—buy 10 cups of coffee and the eleventh is free, for example. Reward frequent shoppers on your site too. This means tracking the frequency of their orders, the amount of money they've spent, and the quantity of items they've bought. This way, you can pass on the promotions accordingly.

Now that you've got an exhaustive list of what to look for in a commerce server, let's take a look at one of the contenders, Miva Merchant.

Miva Merchant This application provides site administrators with the wherewithal for running a storefront or catalog. One of the most attractive features of Miva Merchant is that all the development is browser-based too, so developers can access the source code through their browser and can modify that code via the XML-based Miva Script. For more information on this application, go to `http://www.miva.com/`.

Personalization Tools

Personalization tools are going to become an increasingly important component in website development as more websites offer retail services, frequent-buyer promotions, custom catalogs, or even customized interfaces. As a result, developers are going to have to begin to ask how they can integrate customization in their website architecture.

Fortunately, the concepts behind personalization are straightforward: user-configurable characteristics, database-accessible customer information, and scalable service so the site can accommodate increasing numbers of visitors with personalized information.

The really thorny question is this: How do you implement these features on your website? You can either try to build a series of software programs that address each task, and try to integrate your programs, or you can buy a software package that addresses these issues for you already.

The one product I'm reviewing below, Group Lens by Net Perceptions, is a software package that relies on filtering customers' existing preferences to maintain customized pages or integrate suggested updates.

To do this, Net Perceptions uses a filtering engine to rank user preferences, find a correlation between a user's current preferences and possible new options, and suggest the findings to the user. For example, if your site sells graphic arts software, and one of your customers has bought several Photoshop plug-in and extensions accessories, the filtering engine might flag the customer's file with a notice the next time an upgrade of Photoshop is available. Another example of correlation-based filtering is slightly more user-directed: A site that sells music may ask its users to rank their favorite artists in order of preference, and use the results to suggest related artists that the user might be interested in. You've probably seen examples of filtering and ranking software on CD and bookstore sites already on the Web; Net Perceptions has been in use at one time or another at `Amazon.com`, E! Online (`Moviefinder.com`), Starwave and Music Boulevard. Figure 8.4 shows an example of ranking related artists on Music Boulevard.

What Are Intelligent Agents?

Intelligent agent is an umbrella phrase for a class of software devoted to collecting and filtering knowledge. A popular subclass of intelligent agents are spiders, which are agents that crawl a network and return information to a user. Most Internet search engines rely on spiders to crawl the World Wide Web and return new URLs and keywords for the search engine database. Another subclass, 'bots, are used for everything from chat conversations to shopping for the lowest price on software.

As the volume of raw information continues to rise on the Web, the ability to intelligently sort and present information will become increasingly valuable. Collaborative filtering, which you can read about in the body of this chapter, is one commercial solution for smart sorting. Intelligent agents are another.

NOTE   Net Perceptions does not provide you with a way to alter or extend the algorithms that drive the filtering engine; you have to use the algorithms provided to you in the application programming interface (API). But the API does come in Java, C/C++, and Perl. It works on the Windows NT, Solaris 2.51, and SGI IRIX operating systems, and merges with SQL or ODBC databases.

FIGURE 8.4:

Music Boulevard

Should You Buy Testing Products for Your Backend?

A growing niche market is website testing software. There's a reason this niche is justified: Sites usually grow beyond the abilities of one person to correctly antici-pate problems and gauge hang-ups. Site software can sift through the flow of incoming requests and outgoing responses and piece together the story of how your site works.

Most site testing software works by analyzing how your server responds to traffic and load increases. It looks for bottlenecks in file delivery and lags in server response time. To do all this, the software simulates an average user expe-rience, requesting files at the same frequency and volume as a human being might. Some software packages, like Astra Site Test from Mercury Interactive, can simulate a 50-user test.

While using a software package certainly seems to be less trouble than rounding up 50 different humans and asking them to stress-test your site, be aware that there are drawbacks to using these site testing packages. Not all software packages support the kinds of technologies you're serving to your public. Remember that the software development cycle tends to be slightly slower than the average website development cycle, so you'll have technical factors on your site that aren't incorporated into testing criteria yet.

Second, these packages can be expensive. Installation plus support can run $10,000. For that cost, you could hire 50 testers to bang on your site for a week—and support a contractor to diagnose the results. Again, there is a tradeoff between people-hours used to do work and collect data, and a software package that will hand you the results in much less time.

If you're going to invest in site-testing software, here are the criteria you should consider before you buy:

How will the software simulate client requests? Some software uses scripts that run actual client-server connections. Others use scripts of virtual clients connecting to the Web.

How much work do you have to do to set up the tester's "visitor" experience? Will you have to specify the pauses between file requests, or can you click on that option as part of the interface? Will you have to specify the number of files you want the "visitor" to hit, or can you estimate a range and let the software generate a random experience within those parameters? If you're trying to simulate 50 different users and you find yourself dictating the minutia of those visits to the software, you might be better off with a different application, or 50 live human beings.

How much control do you have over the technical parameters of the user experience? Can you specify whether or not the "visitor" is accessing your site with the images switched on or off? Can you specify the connection speed, platform, or browser client the user is approaching with? If the software package does not offer the options you need to mimic your audience's technical conditions, you will be better off with something else.

How easily can you set up the testing software? Some testing software is actually a suite of interconnected applications. Ask for a demo: Make sure that any modular software allows for smooth data flow between one application and the next. Also make sure that you don't need extraordinary amounts of RAM or a super-fast processor to make the software work.

How easily can you navigate the software's interface? You're going to be paying a lot of money for the software's special site-testing features. Make sure you can access and use them.

How are the results presented? How well-supported and well-documented are the types of results the software produces? Six screens' worth of line graphs may be impressive, but if you have no idea what's on the x- and y-axis, the graphs are useless. If you get a blank screen where a pie chart should be, you are going to want to know why you didn't get the results you wanted. A good software package contains documentation and support telling you how the results are presented, what is measured, and what units it is measured in.

How varied can the tests be? Can you set up the tests to run multiple times and increase the strain on the server? Can you deliberately target perceived weaknesses to see if the tests confirm your suspicions? Can you run multiple testing scenarios by mixing-and-matching different users, or do you have to assemble each test scenario from scratch? As in any other facet of Web development, the more prior work you can reuse, the better.

Open Source Software

There are alternatives to buying a middleware package. You can always use existing open source software to do the jobs for you. Known until recently as freeware, the name *open source software* was adopted for these code packages to convey the idea that the *source code* comprising the software's functions is free to the public and open to modification by anyone; that is, you can write your own modifications to customize the software.

Now that you're more tech-savvy than you were back in Chapter 5, you're probably thinking of your website in terms of executable functions and data sets. This is good—it means you're halfway to rewriting code. You're ready to assess software tools and decide if the time you're going to take in modifying them for your own use will suss out to a worthwhile return on investment.

The previous section was organized into the types of software you could purchase for your site; this section discusses some of the open source alternatives you can use to build your own tools.

The Apache Server

One of the first open source packages I'm going to discuss is the Apache HTTP server. Why Apache? Market share alone requires its mention in the book: More than 50 percent of the world's websites are hosted on Apache servers. As a Web developer, you've at least heard of Extended Server Side Includes (XSSI), an Apache-exclusive implementation of server-side includes.

NOTE   Apache comes on the companion CD-ROM.

Apache is based on an older version of the National Center for Supercomputing Applications's (NCSA) popular HTTP daemon. Work on the HTTP daemon was somewhat stalled after 1994, but many Webmasters continued to develop modifications and debugging methods for the server, all working independently. These code modifications—or any code modification meant to improve a software package—were referred to as *patches*.

By 1995, a group of these developers decided to pool their patches and any other enhancements they could find, tested the results, and released Apache 0.6.2 to the world. By December 1995, Apache 1.0 debuted on the Internet. The server software is now at version 1.3.2.

Besides being free, why is Apache such a big deal? Unlike several commercial server applications, Apache is available for a wide variety of computing platforms—Unix, Windows, even OS/2. Apache also lets its users delve into the guts of the code, in more ways than one. Unlike commercial software servers, Apache lets you access and modify the server code. This is nowhere near as fearsome as it sounds: Apache is organized into separate functional modules, each module (also known as a mod) specifying the behavior for a server feature like CGI scripting or secure socket layers. You can choose to compile only the features you need, or you can write your own server modes. Another way to peer into the inner workings of the server is through Apache's configuration files. These files are simply edited with a text editor like vi, so you know exactly what commands you wrote at what times. There's no GUI to get gummed up in.

Apache's homegrown roots and easily modifiable code aren't the only reasons to adopt it. The product has three powerful attributes that make it a good tool for any system.

- First, it's flexible. The code is sufficiently modular and can be pared down, modified, or expanded to meet the needs of sites ranging from simple e-zines to commerce-server sites. There are even commercial versions of the product out to support secure Web applications, C2Net Software being the leader in this field.

- Second, it's got the best features first. Thanks to the thriving freeware community, new patches for improved functionality are often available on the Web before any commercial server company has written and tested their commercial equivalent.

- Third, Apache is scalable. It can handle sites of very nearly every type of scope.

This is not to say Apache is perfect—like all other freeware, there is no automatic help desk available, so you're going to have to set aside the time and resources to develop a solid network of Web resources for question answering, plus time for playing with the code.

To learn more about Apache, go to `http://www.apache.org`.

Anatomy of a Multiprocess Web Server

Apache is unique among Web servers because it is a *multiprocess* Web server. What this means is that it has one parent process that coordinates the actions of all subsequent sub-processes (child processes).

What this translates to for client-server transactions is this: When a client request reaches the server, it is immediately handed off to a child process not currently engaged with another client request. If the same client makes another request, that second request may be handed to another child process. However, Apache can use a module like PHP to keep a persistent connection, meaning that if a client makes a database access request to the server (request1), then moves to another page and makes another database access request (request2), the child process from request 1 is still used instead of creating an all-new child process.

PHP

PHP (Personal Home Pages) is the scripting language equivalent of middleware: It allows you to generate on-the-fly Web pages after passing data back and forth from a database. A server-side scripting technology that emulates Perl's CGI-scripting abilities and Apache's XSSI functionality, PHP exists as an Apache server module.

PHP can access a wide array of commercial Web-data tools, including Microsoft Access, but works well when used as the frontend access tool for the open source database MySQL. PHP works in one of two ways:

- As a CGI-type *wrapper*, meaning that a file written using PHP opens a database query, finds what it needs, prints the results to the file, and serves it as a final product to the user. Since one of the most saleable points of PHP is its ability to maintain persistent database connections between queries and thus avoid having to burden your Web server by starting a new process every time a new query is sent to the server, this CGI-style implementation isn't the most efficient use.

- As a server module in the multi-process Web server Apache. Because multiprocessing relies on persistent database connections, this means that PHP is a good tool for building highly customizable or dynamic bases that rely heavily on databases.

The strongest argument for PHP is efficiency—both server efficiency and database efficiency. Servers are brought down if they're overwhelmed by too many client requests; databases grow sluggish if they have to open up and scan their files for new queries continuously. Persistent connections lessen the individual client requests and increase the operating efficiency of both your server and your database.

For more information on PHP, visit `http://www.php.net`.

Perl

That's right: one of the most commonly used CGI scripting languages is part of the freeware pantheon. Perl remains one of the Web's best examples of freeware for several reasons.

First, it solves a problem almost every website developer has: How do you sift through large amounts of text to get comprehensible results? Perl is excellent for handling those text-manipulating abilities. In addition, Perl's relatively simple syntax make it easy for developers to tag strings of text as objects to be manipulated via CGI scripts.

Second, Perl is well-supported, both by its original author, Larry Wall, and a wide and knowledgeable developer's community. Websites like perl.com are only the online extension of a suite of books documenting the ins and outs of the language.

Third, Perl is sufficiently modular, meaning that plenty of people can modify the language by adding to its core functionality without altering that same core functionality. Like Apache, Perl can be customized and enhanced through mods installed on a server.

Finally, Perl is easy to learn. Among the developers I've worked with over the last three years, people who wouldn't be able to tell Boolean algebra from a bowling ball are able to grasp the basics of arrays and statements, and rattle off CGI scripts with ease.

To learn more about using Perl in day-to-day production, visit Chapters 12 and 13. To learn more about Perl as a programming language, visit `http://www.perl.com`.

In Praise of Open Source Software

It is not an exaggeration to say that the World Wide Web runs on open source software. From the Apache server, which hosts more than 50 percent of the world's websites, to the operating system Linux, open source software provides low-cost, easy entries to anyone seeking to get online. Open source software is not synonymous with no-cost ware, but instead refers to source code access and distribution. Anyone can write, improve, manipulate, or modify the original source code for freeware. To quote the developers of the open source operating system GNU, "You should think of free speech, not free beer."

If the egalitarian aspects of open source software don't warm your heart, consider how freeware encourages software market growth:

- Open source software often creates markets of potential customers willing to upgrade to a specifically-featured retail version. There are a rash of companies that make their living selling customized versions of open source software.

- Open source software allows an ecology of ideas. People can write software to fill perceived voids in the market. In doing so, they may create new demands for software, or new models for how a specific task or operation should be performed.

- Open source software offers a low-cost way to test a potential market. Why spend a lot of money to develop, test, and market a software package if you can cast it to the net as a chunk of freeware?

- Conversely, open source software offers a way to be a shrewd software consumer. You can compare and contrast different software packages until you find the tool you want, and the budget overhead is minimal.

Continued on next page

- Open source software—either building it or using it—offers a do-it-yourself thrill. And because people often build the software for love of the product, many of the best free technologies out there have a passionate, well-supported developer's community.

Open source software isn't perfect: The features are often incomplete compared to commercial software packages, and it's rare to find 24-hour support when your free ad-serving script suite gets snarled. But it is a serious, viable option when building or upgrading your Web development suite.

Summary

Building a basic backend that can grow with your site is an investment in future work. It will let you impose simple QA controls on your files, and provide you with a framework for successfully expanding your site.

CHAPTER
NINE

Usability and QA

- Understanding usability

- Defining your audience

- Making your site user-proof

- Understanding quality assurance

- Developing a QA process

have spent the preceding chapters focusing on building websites intelligently. Now I'm going to turn the tables and focusing on building intelligent websites. The two areas I focus on—quality assurance (QA) and usability—are vital to any website maintenance or upgrade you do, especially if the site you're working on came into being during the "if we post it, they will come" period.

Usability is defined here as the intangible quality that makes surfing your site fun, useful, or vital for your target audience. This does not mean that usability equals content; usability equals the ability to construct your content for your user's maximum site-surfing experience. Again, the focus in this chapter is on how your site development, maintenance, or upgrades will affect your user.

This chapter will outline the most basic usability considerations you should have in mind when you build the site, from user interface to editorial bias to performance issues. It will provide a guide on how to define your audience and tailor the website accordingly, and how to present your content to the audience as effectively and attractively as possible.

Setting forth usability criteria early on in your Web development cycle will prove useful later: You'll have another parameter to use when sorting through your technology options for this round of site development, and you'll have a baseline from which to start on your next round of site revisions.

This chapter will also cover quality assurance. *Quality assurance*, or QA, is a simple idea with a lot of complex executions. QA means insuring that every element in a product meets quality standards. When applied to a website, QA can mean everything from checking every link in a hotlist to ensuring that every <TD> tag has included a `valign` and `align` value. Because most websites tend to be understaffed, the usual development emphasis is on building a site that breaks as little as possible; performing a structured battery of QA tests is the last thing on anyone's mind.

But if you're planning on maintaining your website more than six months past launch, or if you're faced with the task of renovating a website from the bottom up, setting up a baseline QA procedure can be one of the smartest things you can do to improve the site building process. Why? Because you'll find the wild inconsistencies from file to file first. You'll be able to determine the weak spots in the site, and prioritize future work. You'll have a few clues about what worked in your production processes, and what needs to be refined for next time.

This chapter will set forth some baseline QA procedures, a list of factors to mix-and-match for your QA process, and a website "stress test." Finally, the chapter will close with a few lists and QA charts that should aid in defining your audience and testing the site for them.

Usability: Why Bother?

There are plenty of websites out there that clearly haven't made usability a high priority. Some of them are still tolerable since their content is valuable and their users have enough free time to guess (and guess and guess...) what the site builders were thinking. Others are glaring candidates for *Web Pages That Suck* (by Vincent Flanders and Michael Willis, Sybex, 1998). Unless you're a sucker for any kind of publicity—even the bad kind—you're going to want to avoid website infamy and build a site that works as intelligently for your users as it does for you.

An ideal website is one that makes the user forget what browser she is using, what speed she is accessing the site with, and what computer she is using to do so. The site should be so easy for your user to maneuver through that she forgets there's several layers of computer and software between the server and her. The site should be so well organized that your user can perform her original tasks without having to suffer the distraction of acquainting herself with your way of thinking.

Short of hiring a squad of psychic HTML weenies, how are you going to accomplish this?

Simple. You're going to design the site with usability in mind. This is much easier than you think: All you have to do is design the site so people know what their options are when they reach your pages, and how they can find what they need.

Your first priority is to sit down and determine who your audience is. Once you've got an idea of who they are, you can figure out why they might want to visit you, and what you think they'll do once they get there. Then you can figure out what your screens look like on their end and how to build the site accordingly.

Does this sound a little overwhelming? I've broken the process down into three chunks: defining your current audience, defining your potential audience, and choosing which of the two you want to focus on. Read on to find out how you too can have a smartly built site that works smartly for the reader as well.

Defining Your Actual and Potential Audience

The first step is to figure out who's visiting your site. After you eliminate your staff, your mom, and any friends who are checking to make sure their bookmarks still work, you still have a lot of possibilities. Begin narrowing them down. You also need to decide who is missing out on your site, and how you can get them to visit. *Then* you need to figure out which side of the coin (exisiting visitors or potential visitors) you want to focus on most.

Who Visits Your Site Right Now?

This is directly related to the general question, who is your audience. You are building the site for people whom you know will need the information you offer. Just keep asking the question, and fleshing out the answer every time by determining the reasons for building the site. Jump into this little role-playing exercise, for a feel of what should be going on:

"Who are you building the site for right now?"

"I am building the site for middle school science teachers."

Good start. You've got a clearly defined audience. But what is it about this audience that tells you that there's a demand for a website targeted toward them?

"Who are you building this site for right now?"

"I am building the site for middle school science teachers. Fifty percent of our hits come from .edu domains in the United States. I am guessing those are science classes."

OK. It's a step in the right direction, but what made you guess that those hits came from science classes?

"Who are you building this site for right now?"

"I am building the site for middle school science teachers. Fifty percent of our hits come from .edu domains in the United States. I am guessing those are science classes. The reason I'm going with that guess is that most of the items in our referer log point to the Middle School Science Teacher Secret Resource website."

Stepping out of the example you can see that the site builder has constructed a picture of his existing audience by noting where they came from, and what tools they were using when they hit the site. But where is all this information coming from? That's where your referer log and server log come into the picture.

Using the Tools at Hand: The Referer Log and Server Log A good tool for slashing audience segments off your list is your referer log. Yup, it's spelled with only one *r*—you'll get used to it, even if your spellchecker never does. Another is your server log. The referer log will tell you who's been linking to your site, so you can do a little detective work and see what sort of folks are linking to you. The server log will tell you what files were called up by users, what browser and computer they were using to view your site, and where they were accessing you from ISP-wise, not webpage-wise.

We're going to focus on two main points: what information these logs contain, and how you're going to use it to determine who your audience already is. Figure 9.1 shows an excerpt from a raw referer log.

FIGURE 9.1:

A typical referer log

```
http://asamplesite.com  -> /archive/index?june.html
http://asamplesite1.com -> /archive/index?july.html
http://asamplesite2.com -> /archive/index?july.html
http://asamplesite3.com -> /archive/index?september.html
```

Read the data left to right: It will tell you who is pointing to you, and what page of yours they're pointing to. In our example, `http://asamplesite.com` is pointing to our `/archive/index?june.html` page. This tells you that someone browsing at `asamplesite.com` is linking to your archive page, and that's how users are getting to your site.

You can also do vanity search on some search engines, but as you can guess, grepping your referer log—or asking a sysadmin to do it for you—is a lot more accurate and effective, and takes less time.

So you've learned that your referer log tells you what locations are linking to you and what pages on your site they're linking to. The server log will tell you what pages were actually served, what browser and platform the person on the other end was using when they hit your site, and what page they visited prior to yours. This is a good, cheap way to get a demographic fix on your readership. A sample server log is presented in Figure 9.2: see how it differs from a referer log.

FIGURE 9.2:

A sample server log

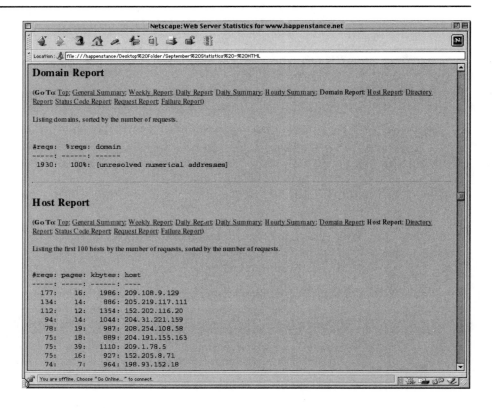

The steps above are a good way to determine who your current audience is, but you'll also want to figure out who your potential audience is.

You can glean a lot of data from a visitor, and it all takes up one line in a server log. But there are better ways to record and track that information than to make a team of interns go blind extracting and logging specific information.

WARNING   But first, an important caveat—this information can be spoofed or misrecorded, so it's best to assume a high degree of inaccuracy whenever you look at your recorded user info.

Now that you've established that you still want to sift through all of the information, the best way to go about this is to save all of the client data to a log file. The log file is going to see plenty of action. You're going to archive the files and dump all of the log information into a database.

That's right, a database. You can use anything from Apache's DBI logger to a SQL server. The important thing to remember is that you must have a Web server with the ability to dump data into database tables before you try writing your logs to your database. You can acquire this ability one of two ways: It can be built into the server (like Microsoft's IIS Server), or it can be added via server source code (this is how Apache does it).

> **NOTE** Remember that each discrete hit is counted as a discrete entry, but those entries all contain items of information that can be sorted down into separate tables. You can then run separate programs that pull data from specific tables, or look for specific values within different data tables.

Before you run out and sink several thousand dollars into a database system, consider what you will want out of the system:

Atomicity   Will you be able to record or undo a specific transaction when you need to?

Consistency   Database transactions should be permitted and completed only if the query conforms to the parameters set up by the system. In other words, if your database is only logging client agents and domains, you should not be able to enter or submit a query on server response codes.

Isolation   The different queries you run should never affect each other. For example, Janet runs a query to determine how many people logged in from .com domains at the same time Adam is running a query to check the traffic numbers on a certain section. Each should not know about the other's operations.

Durability   Once the query is composed and submitted, its results are permanently logged.

These four factors are called the *ACID* test; they're a staple in data processing circles. If you'd prefer your database considerations to be more oriented toward how to perform the data analysis you need, consider:

Indexing   In order to find any of the data that has to be queried, that data has to be classified in ways that make it easy to drop into "buckets" of specific information. When you're indexing files, remember that you want to be able to find information quickly, but you also need to be able to insert, modify, or delete information with alacrity.

Storing data   If you store only the data you'll need, or data that you antic- ipate being interested in, you'll be able to index and query your data much more quickly. You can triage your data by setting expiration dates on it— this way you don't have three-year-old logs cluttering your database.

Now, consider how to get it. You could always learn and use *Structured Query Language* (SQL). SQL is a small, compact programming language with an easy-to- grasp syntax; it is surprisingly powerful. A good hacker can write an SQL query for withdrawing data from a database in the same timeframe it takes program- mers to write a program looking for the same results. SQL is considered the most homegrown database management tool.

You could also build your own suite of database query and analysis tools. There are plenty of shareware and development sites on the Web that offer APIs, advice, and development how-tos. One of the most comprehensive database sites is `www.datawarehouse.com`. Alternatively, you could buy an off-the-shelf solu- tion. These database access tools are usually very easy to use, and often feature great interface perks like drop-and-drag data manipulation.

Unless you have an epic love for database programs, and you thrill to the possibil- ity that loading logs directly from your server to your database could cause either your database or your server to crash, it is best to invest in a database querying tool.

To recap: When you're just starting your site, going directly to the server and referer logs can tell you all about who's visiting your site, and how frequently. As traffic becomes more of a "selling point" for your site, or as you try to gauge audience capabilities for future editorial and technical decisions, you may want to start a more sophisticated traffic-logging system, such as putting your traffic logs in a database for more finely pinpointed inquiries.

In order to analyze your traffic data, you may want to look at a few commercial software applications that help you sift through the cold hard facts. WebTrends is one that's been repeatedly recommended by people I know who do this stuff all day. For more information, go to `http://www.webtrends.com/`.

Who Do You Want to Visit Your Site?

This is the kind of question you'll want to ask when you're getting ready to do site maintenance or to undertake a complete site overhaul. Is your current audi- ence still your highest priority? If it is, is maintaining your market share of your current audience a priority? Or is gaining a greater market share of your audience the reason for the site overhaul?

Let's get back to our science teacher example. We already asked, "Who am I building the site for?" and used data from the server and referer logs to construct a reasonable picture of the current audience. Now we're going to ask a few more questions that will help determine who the desired audience is:

> "Do I already have the market share among middle school science teachers that I want?"

Assessing your market share in any given audience is imprecise at best. Use of the Net grows exponentially every month, and a lot of users fall into several different categories simultaneously; some of those middle school science teachers you're trying to target might also be the weekend snowboarders that a different website is hoping to reach.

There's also the issue of how you define "market share." Are you shooting for a monetary goal, a traffic goal, a population goal, or some combination? And how do you evaluate your share—by comparing it to a similar website, or by finding another category that you feel is appropriate for contrast?

With our example, we have a very specific market: Our science teacher website builder is going to define share by doing a little market research. He checks some educational associations and discovers a survey. The survey says that 80 percent of all science teachers—45,000 people—have website access. If our science teacher's website has a hit count of only 20,000, he now has a benchmark audience and an idea of how much of an audience share he has, as opposed to how much he wants.

Which Audience Is Most Important to You?

In other words, who has the highest priority on your audience list? Is it your hard-core loyal audience, or is it the new and highly malleable niche market you just noticed thanks to your questioning and brainstorming? How do you decide whom to rank first?

To recap:

- Who uses the site right now?

- Who do you want to be using the site after this round of development?

- Which of those audiences are the higher priority?

Getting the Audience to Come to You

Creators of celebrity shrine websites have it easy: Their audience is self-selecting, and their editorial mission is simple—to provide a place of worship for like-minded fans. Unfortunately, the market for John Woo fan sites isn't as healthy as the market for profit-driven websites, so chances are high you'll be spending most of your time working on a website with a slightly less obvious audience-use goal.

The first step to determining how to mesh what your audience wants from you with what you want from them is to figure out *how* your audience is hitting your website.

Figuring out how your audience is reaching you is surprisingly easy. Take all the data you collected from your referer logs a few paragraphs back—that'll give you a preliminary snapshot of the other websites that provide a gateway to yours.

But while referer logs can provide you with an idea of where your users came from, you'll also want to know how your user is getting to you. This is where server logs come in handy. They can tell you what platform your users are coming from, and what browser and browser version they're using to get there.

Once you've figured out where your users are coming from and what tools they're using to visit you, you can begin to set the parameters for the experience you want your audience to have.

Of course, you want your audience to have the kind of experience that induces them to keep visiting over and over. This means you're going to have to focus your usability efforts on two goals: offering a product that honors the audience's technical parameters, and constructing an interface and information flow that gives the audience the ability to perform a given task on your site easily.

Let's look at the last point first. While there's a lot to be said for people hitting your site in a three-hour deadline avoidance session, the if-you-build-it-they-will-come technique may not be the best for encouraging repeat traffic. In fact, this strategy will probably work very poorly if you're trying to build up a new target market.

So a more productive strategy is to outline what tasks your users will want to accomplish on your site. You won't need a psychic for this, just some deductive skills and perhaps the list of questions below. The most important thing to remember is that people visit websites for some form of information exchange. The degree of information exchange can vary sharply:

- The user can visit your site with a very specific inquiry already in place, and then find a specific page to answer that inquiry. One example of this is a user visiting the San Francisco SPCA (`http://www.sfspca.org/`) to see if any housecats are available for adoption. In this case, the user already has a goal in mind (adopting a cat in the Bay Area) and knows exactly where to find the information, as seen below.

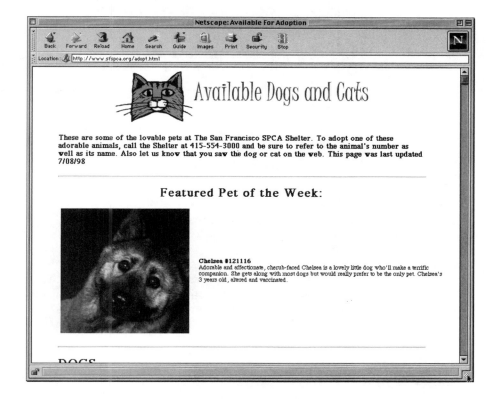

- The user can visit your site to find the means to answer a very specific inquiry, then gather the results to answer that inquiry. A good functional example of this is of a visitor accessing PCWebopaedia (`http://www.pcwebopadia.com/`) because they just read the phrase *RISC processor* and they want to find out what it is. Here, the user already has a specific question in mind, and a clear idea of where to answer that question. The information gathering is a two-step process: look for the answer on an index page, then read the actual answer on the corresponding entry.

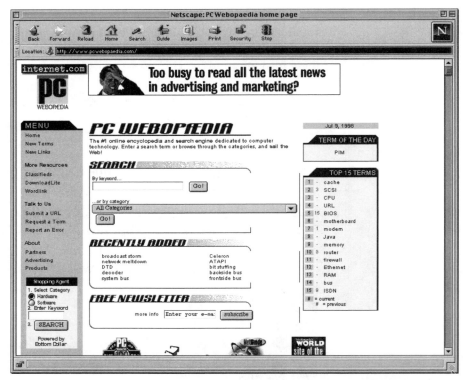

Originally appeared on Mecklermedia Corporation's "www.internet.com" website, Copyright ©1998 Mecklermedia Corporation, 20 Ketchum Street, Westport, CT 06880; http//:www.internet.com. All rights reserved. Reprinted with permission.

NOTE

In the first example, the user knew that they wanted a cat, and that the site might have the information on adopting a cat. In the second instance, the user had a general question and relied on a database to answer a question. The two surfing experiences are different in their specificity.

- The user can visit your website with a general inquiry, which they're hoping to focus into a more specific inquiry. For example, a user goes to Yahoo (http://www.yahoo.com/) hoping to find websites about Macintosh computers, and narrows her inquiry to shareware developed specifically for Macintoshes. In this case, the user comes to a general search site, picks a broad category (Macintosh computers), then users the results to narrow her search. She still hasn't found the end answer, but she has refined her query to a more manageable point.

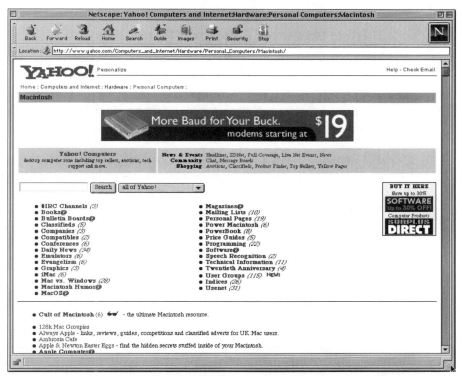

- The user can visit your website for specific information in response to a general query. Extending the example of our Macintosh-searching user, now that she's found a list of Macintosh shareware sites, she'll want to find the site that features FTP clients. Subsequently, she'll check the index page of each entry for a reference to her specific question. Note that this is different than the second example because (a) the user did not immediately think of the website as her first resource, and (b) she is not assuming that the answer she wants is at the website. Ironically enough, these users become repeat visitors if they're placated the first time around—even if they have no idea what they're looking for at first.

Once you've determined how your users are getting to the information on your site, you can begin to figure out how to make that information accrual easy for them. This means setting up an intelligent interface.

Interface and Design Issues

Interface design is a rich and well-researched field, which would explain why there are so many books about it. But within the context of this book, and of this chapter in particular, the only interface principals you need to consider are listed below, with explanations for why you need them and how they'll help your user have a better experience on your site.

Map Out the Entire Task   You must remember that your users won't have had the experience of building the site, and therefore won't automatically grasp what steps to take to obtain the information they want. Subsequently, it's up to you to map out the user tasks from beginning to end. Think about the following points in establishing how users will accomplish their intended task(s) on your site:

- What will you do to indicate the task's starting point?

- What is the first step?

- What is the expected result of the first step? What will happen if the first step does not lead to an expected second step?

- Is there a readily visible troubleshooting guide? Is this guide persistent from step to step of the user task process? Is the information in the guide appropriate to the step that the user is at?

- Is there a readily visible sequence of steps so the user has a clear understanding of what they've done so far, and what they need to do before the task is complete?

- How many steps will the user have to go through before reaching the end of the task?

- How will the user know it's the end of the task? What indication will there be?

- What will you do to indicate the task's exit point? What options will you offer the user at that point?

These may seem like a lot of options to consider, but they all make for a more humane interface. They're also a lot more intuitive than you think: Remember the last time you couldn't do exactly what you wanted on a website. What steps did you take to try and find your answer? And how did you finally find it? If you remember your most frustrating experience and why it was so frustrating, then apply that experience to the goal of making sure the same thing doesn't happen to your audience, you're halfway there.

Of course, you can never underestimate the power of a third-party opinion. We'll go over these in more detail later in the chapter when we talk about usability. But for now, remember that someone who hasn't been closely involved with developing and building the website can offer a fresh perspective on the process you've outlined for your users.

Limit Your User's Choices This seems almost counter-intuitive. After all, why would you want to deny your users the chance to find exactly what they're looking for, in exactly the way they want?

The answer is simple: The more choices you give a user, the less clear it is how they should perform a specific task. Think about a software package you use daily. When you first learned the package, you did so by figuring out the steps to a specific task and repeating those steps if they yielded the results you wanted. As you grew more familiar with the software, you began to combine tasks to produce specific results.

The point is, you weren't assaulted with all the options at once, and you learned in a self-contained environment. When developing a website, remember that you want to provide a sense of the task being performed in a discrete continuum— that is to say, you want your user to sense that they're making progress in the same area they started from.

By offering your users a lot of options at once, you're detracting from that consistent environment. You're also making it less clear to the user exactly what they can do on your site. If you want repeat visitors, it's in your best interests to convey what specific tasks they can do immediately, and then lead them to more complex information interaction later.

How do you do that? Once it's clear that the task is ended, you can indicate to the user that she has the option of performing another, more complex task. If she takes it, fine. If not, she didn't want to do it anyway. The user is still in charge of the entire site-surfing experience, and they have choices that allow them to effectively perform specific functions. This is much better than having several vague choices and no clear and unequivocal way to begin any of them.

Another way to limit your user's choices is to restrict the features per page. A nav bar with more than five or six choices is a bad idea—users tune out after the first few choices. One way to pack a lot of function into the limited context is to group your choices functionally, and present them as a discrete unit. For example, rather than list seven different subsections of a site plus a site map, a link to the search page, a link to the feedback page, a link to the front page, a link to the FAQ, a link to what's new, and a link to the archive (14 different choices) as clear and separate entries, why not group the choices: current content (the seven sections), old content (archive and search), new content (what's new), and info (site map, front door, FAQ, feedback). A helpful metaphor is the pull-down menu system in most Windows application: There are many different options, but you're not overwhelmed because they're grouped into sensible functional categories.

Take a look at Figure 9.3 below. It's an example of too many choices packed into one page.

Once your user's interface is restricted to an array of functional selections, consider further limiting the experience to provide only a few discrete chunks of content on the page, preferably one if you can help it. There is the temptation to maximize frames and pack in more content in the same screen real estate. Resist the temptation. The front page of a newspaper has six stories half-started because the user can easily flip back and forth through the paper. The hypertext experience isn't so similar; people associate clicking on a link with producing a functionally different result after clicking, and that breaks up any sort of page-flipping function.

Present Your Content Loud and Clear   One of the ways to clearly indicate what information tasks can be performed on the website is to present the information in a clear and unambiguous way.

Well, duh, you're saying. But it's harder than you think. Remember, the site has to be equally useful to both first-time visitors and daily returnees. When someone hits your site, they should be able to determine the following without a lot of work:

- What is the site's reason for being? Is the site a subject directory? A reference utility? An editorial work? Someone's personal digital art experiment?

FIGURE 9.3:

An over-crowded navigation bar

- What is the value of the site's content? Find a way to tie your site into a set of stated needs. For example, something like "This site offers a complete list of courier airline services in North America" instantly makes the site relevant to anyone living north of Panama who's interested in using a courier airline service. Of course, make sure you're telling the truth about the function and scope of your site's value relative to the user.

- What is the priority of content throughout the site? Sidebars are great devices, but when they're given more visual interest and a better spot on the layout than the main feature, their value relative to the value of the rest of site becomes really uncertain. Use strong visual cues to convey where each item of information stands in the site's hierarchy.

- How does the visual code assign priority throughout the site? You shouldn't add colors to your site unless you have a specific reason for them to be there. Users should be able to determine if a given color corresponds to a topical section, or a level of priority within the website. For example, if you look at *The Washington Post* website (`http://www.washingtonpost.com/`), each different editorial section has its own color scheme: If you're on a page with a yellow background, you're in Style Live; if you're on a orange page, you're in Sports; if you're on a purple-gray page, you're in the National section.

- What is the context of the content? For example, making users scroll up or down the page is acceptable if they remain in the same item of content that brought them to the page, like an article, or a list of items falling in a specific category. If you do break up your content into several pages, let the user know where they are relative to the rest of content chunk. In this case, if an article is broken up into several pages, label them: page 1 of 4, 2/5, etc.

- What functional role does each part of the screen play? For example, you can place the navigation bar in the same place every time, or place the headline and content in the same location relative to each other. The idea is to have your user land on any page in the site and understand where he is, what he's looking at, and how to move on to other tasks.

- What is the time frame for the content? If one of the selling points of your site is its frequently updated information, tell your readers. Find a way to prioritize your content by time, and to visually lead your users to the newest content.

Don't Bore Your Users   A lot of sites are models of good textbook usability, yet visiting them is as exciting as watching paint dry. One way to prevent that from happening to your intelligently designed website is to recognize that you need to involve the audience in your website. The content alone won't be that compelling; users have to be drawn into the entire site experience.

The way to engage your users is to construct your total site experience via a three-step process. This process will flow naturally after you've hammered out the task flows, the limits to the user experience, and the visual and contextual cues needed to direct your user to a maximum website experience. The three steps are:

1. Set up your users' goals for them. When you visit a site, it will usually tell you what it's there for and why you should want to use it. When you're developing a site, don't be shy about telling users what they should accomplish by visiting your site.

2. Provide your users with immediate feedback. This means providing hypertext links that lead to unambiguous, specific content, a search engine that provides accurate, ranked results, or a directory that offers a clear category system in response to a general search.

3. Once the site gets too easy, add another layer of complexity. Most news-related websites do this intuitively. Breaking news, which has the immediate appeal to both new and veteran visitors, is always featured prominently, and the site is built to allow users to move between a top layer of headlines and a second layer of corresponding breaking news articles. After a few trips, the user begins to notice that the news is divided into different beats, and that each beat acts as a separate self-contained section on the site to be explored.

Of course, your interface deals with the intelligent functional execution of design and content. There are still other considerations before you're off the usability hook; namely, now that you've got a great way of presenting your content, how do you create compelling material?

Editorial Issues

This section won't focus on the mechanics of good writing—there are enough books around to tell you how to write. But it will focus on ways to structure your content in order to have it convey what you want it to in a way that best exploits the peculiarities of the Web interface.

Note that I said *content* and not *writing*. While it's true that a lot of the best websites are heavy on the prose, the one-screen-at-a-time model of presentation has increased the role of effective information graphics in editorial presentation. These graphics add to written content and provide context for the content relative to the rest of the site.

Editorial graphics also provide another important role in websites: They keep our attention. Looking at a screen is visually demanding, and if the physical strain weren't enough, studies have shown we all have the attention span of four-year-olds when we're in a computer-mediated environment. We respond well to things that require us to make a decision, and one of the quickest ways to make us sit up is to provide some sort of visual stimulus.

This visual stimulus can help draw readers into a multipage article by propelling the reader into decision-making. The role of a good editor is to find a graphics/text relationship that lets the graphics and text complement each other. For example, a large, red, graphical pullquote in the middle of a page of text can push a provocative idea to the reader's attention and induce them to read through the rest of the story until they find the quote in question. The questions the readers have, "Where is this quote? How does it fit into the rest of the story?" automatically pull them into the content.

Take a look at the layout below, taken from CNet Builder.com (`http://www.builder.com/Authoring/Shafer/102698/?st.bl.fd.ts1.mbcol.1401`) on October 29, 1998. You can see how effective pullquotes can be in inviting the reader to delve into the smaller text.

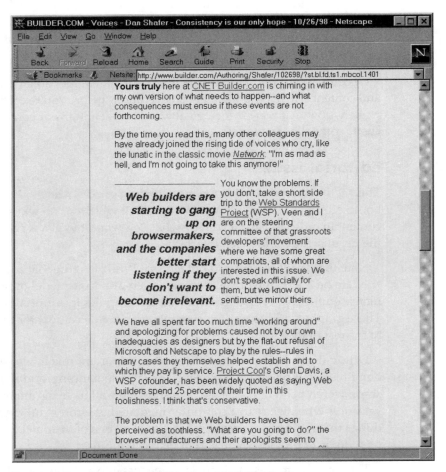

Reprinted with permission from CNET, Inc Copyright ©1995–8, `www.cnet.com`

Another way to improve the compel-factor of your content is to attach a time scale to it. If the content is new, feature it prominently. If it completes a series, show the series and the time it took so the user can get a sense of how the content has progressed over time. Another use of a time scale is to attach a sense of urgency to a piece of content. Breaking news is an example of this technique.

Finally, remember that there's a reason the inverted pyramid is still a journalistic standard. If you're packaging your content in one-screen chunks, you need to hook your reader in the first few sentences. In addition, the surfing style of most users is strictly functional, so you need to present a strong argument in prose quickly in order to register on your user.

No Two Users Are Alike

The final usability factor to consider is the performance experience your user is likely to have. While you can't control the browser your user views your site with, the speed with which she connects to your site, or the equipment which she is using to run her browser and connect to the Net, you can control how your site responds when faced with different user factors.

Why should you care what speed, software, or machine your visitor is using to hit your site? Because one of the goals in any computer-mediated environment is to make the product good enough to make the user forget she is using a complex tool to access the product. In other words, a user should not have to factor in her slow Net connection or tiny laptop screen when she looks at your site. As the developer, it's your responsibility to think about this stuff.

Pick a Resolution   Most computers have three or four standard screen size resolutions: 640 × 480, 800 × 600, and 1024 × 768 are the most common. The numbers refer to the number of pixels displayed on the screen; the larger or more expensive the monitor, the higher the resolution values can go. As a developer, you can use JavaScript to sniff out your visitor's monitor resolution and build your site to react accordingly by displaying one layout at one resolution, and another layout at a larger or smaller resolution. Another, less technical solution is to decide on a standard screen size for the site and design for that. For example, most of CNet's layouts (http://www.cnet.com/) work beautifully on the tiny 640 × 480 screen. Other sites may decide they only want to target higher-end users and deliberately design for 1024 × 768.

Whatever solution you decide upon, always remember to factor in both your target screen size, and a functionally acceptable result for viewers who are accessing your site with a different resolution.

FIGURE 9.4:

Comparing font sizes on a Macintosh versus a PC

Pick a Platform   The computer your viewer is using affects their perception of your site as well. For example, compare in Figure 9.4 how `<font size="3">` looks on a Mac versus a PC.

Some sites assume the differences in appearance are not sufficient enough to warrant building a site to respond to them. Others, like Hotwired (`http://www.hotwired.com/`), build their site to maintain a consistent appearance on both platforms.

Another area of user experience that platform affects is the plug-in category. Several subject-specific sites and gaming sites rely on specific plug-ins to present their content as effectively as possible. Moreover, not all functions extend to every possible platform: Little has been developed for the growing WebTV market. If you decide to include content that depends on a browser plug-in, plot out both the cross-platform compatibility of the plug-in, and what alternative you'll provide if there is no plug-in available for a specific platform.

NOTE   Chapter 6 offers specific scripts and development alternatives for platform issues in website development. Look there for step-by-step examples of how to implement the steps mentioned here.

Pick a Palette   Colors do one of two things on the Web: They dither or they don't. This is not to imply that a shade of blue spends its time on a monitor torn in an agony of indecision. When a color is *dithered*, it means that the computer monitor did not have the ability to display one of the components in the blend of red, green, and blue that makes up every color displayed on screen, and the computer substituted white or black instead.

As a result, a color can lose much of its distinctiveness—not a good thing if you're relying on subtle color gradations for indicating different types of content. There is some hope. Both of the Web's most popular browsers and the computers they work on recognize and display a universal palette of 216 nondithering colors. This palette is available in several places on the Web; if you'd like to have it in front of you, pick up the book *Web by Design*, by Molly Holschlag (Sybex, 1998). You can also deduce whether or not a hex value will display a nondithering color. The hex value of a color is a six-digit hexadecimal number: The first two digits tell the computer the numerical value for the amount of red in the color; the middle two digits dictate the amount of green in a color; the last two digits determine the amount of blue in the color. Any hex value where each of the red, green, and blue values is a double-repeat of any of the characters 0, 3, 6, 9, C, or F is a nondithering color. FFCC99, CCCCFF, and 003399 are nondithering colors; CF3609, FCCFFC, and 036993 are dithering colors.

It's All about Bandwidth   When you're working on a website in an office with its own T1, it's easy to forget that modems exist. But they do, and more than 50 percent of users still access the Web using a connection speed of 56K or less.

Subsequently, you'll want to make sure your page doesn't hang on a slow modem. The easiest way to insure this is to make sure the total file size for your page is relatively small. The total file size comprises both the markup file and any images the file is calling. According to the 7th Annual GVU Web Survey, located at `http://www.gvu.gatech.edu/user_surveys/survey-1997-04/`, 40K is the magic file size, although a lot of websites hover at 80K.

There are some tricks that work for improving download times, and some that don't. Using the same graphic for every navigation bar works, because the browser only has to call that specific file once, and then can keep pulling it out of the user's cache. Pre-loading all your site's graphics before even the first page loads doesn't work. Very few people are patient enough to sit through ten minutes of a blank browser screen for a site they haven't seen yet.

NOTE   Chapter 7 discusses some methods for producing effective multimedia and images without resorting to huge download times. Read those for step-by-step examples of how to implement the suggestions mentioned here.

Another way to reduce file load time is to take a look at the elements you have on a page. Severely nested tables (five or more levels deep) slow down a browser's rendering time, as many browsers don't display any tables until they've read the entire table. If you have five nested tables, that's five different, complete units to be read before display. Another slowing factor is the number of form elements—more than four or five different form elements on a page slows down the page download time. Finally, be wary of using Java on your site if you want the site to load quickly.

No, Wait, It's All about Browsers   Specifically, you need to determine which browsers you're going to develop for, and learn all you can about their capabilities. We'll go over the benchmark testing for browsers in the QA section of this chapter. For now, it's enough to keep in mind that each browser version, and each brand of browser, handles the same file differently.

Quality Assurance: Why Bother?

Quality assurance has an undeserved reputation as nitpicky grunt work. True, a good QA process is often detail oriented. But QA has the often thankless task of trying to break a product in order to make it better—and to point out room for improvement whenever necessary.

The role of QA in developing or maintaining a site cannot be overestimated. Website maintenance is a form of QA, making sure the product (your website) performs optimally for your users. But the QA process that takes place before you publish any live content is critical. This process must find any inconsistencies in interface, code implementation, navigation, content, and graphics. QA testers must be able to recreate bugs, and to recommend fixes for them. They must also keep their eyes peeled for inconsistencies that arise when the site is viewed at different download speeds, on different browsers, on different versions of the same browser, and on different platforms.

A good QA exam can throw a lot of work back at the people who built the site. Since most QA tends to be done during the penultimate stages of Web design, the results of a QA test often hit the development team right at a point where employees are already burnt out and hostile toward the idea of doing more work.

There are three possible solutions for this:

- Submit a perfect product the first time around.

- Ignore QA and resign yourselves to a flood of angry and insulting e-mail feedback from users.

- Incorporate a series of QA checkpoints into the development process from the beginning of site building so you're not stuck redoing all of your work the night before your new or improved site goes live.

Realistically speaking, what are the chances of submitting a perfect product the first time around? And do you really want to subject your customer support people to the e-mail abuse the second option holds?

The remainder of this chapter will focus on the third possibility—incorporating QA into your entire development cycle. I'll start by taking a look at the factors you should consider while developing or revamping the site.

QA Factors to Consider

I won't resort to the old cliché about the ratio of prevention to cure, but I will tell you this: The sooner you consider and accommodate the factors listed below, the less arduous your last-minute revisions before pushing the site live will be. Interacting with a website is a surprisingly complex action. In order for it to appear simple to the user, it's up to the developer to make sure every aspect of the site-visiting experience has been checked for maximum performance.

Let's move on to the QA factors. The items listed below are the categories you should keep in mind as you develop your site. Note that QA is designed to make the process of site maintenance almost as painless as the process of visiting the site.

Site Building

Initial development   What can you do to make the site production as efficient as possible?

Expansion   How can the site expand while staying within the parameters of the site's backend structure?

Backend work   What will need to be done to maintain the functional infrastructure through maintenance/upgrading?

Graphics performance   How can you optimize the quality and usability features of your graphics?

Reproducible bugs   How are bugs discovered, and can you retrace the steps to recreating them?

Usability Considerations

Consistency across browsers   Does the site look and perform the same when viewed with different browsers?

Consistency across platforms   Does the site look and perform the same when viewed with different computers?

Degradability   How well does the site perform when viewed in sub-target conditions? How does it look?

Navigation   Is the navigation both functional and consistent? Is it persistent through the site?

Action and Results

Interface   How does the arrangement of all the interface items lend itself to intuitive task execution? Can users dive right into the site without explanation?

User impressions   What are the users' opinions of this site, and what led them to those opinions?

Model QA Processes

Typically, testing is done as part of a larger development cycle. An ideal QA test involves the following interrelated parts to assist in sharpening everything from the site's focus to the site's performance:

Performance analysis   These are the conclusions drawn after a team of QA testers reads through the results of user tests, and their observations of those tests. The goal of a performance analysis is to determine if the user's performance met your expectations, if it met the user's expectations, what the difference between your expectations and your user's expectations are, and if extra instruction needs to be added to the task.

Task analysis   This is a step-by-step breakdown of the task the QA team asked the user to do. It is a descriptive list that itemizes the actions and desired outcomes. This acts as a baseline for what you want from user behavior.

Critical incident analysis   This is a post-test analysis of what glitches and crashes happened during the test. This test determines how many of these negative incidents are a result of a user acting within expectations, and how many of these are the result of a user acting outside of the task's stated steps and scope. This test also provides you with the means for finding out exactly what the trouble indicators are for task misfiring.

Target population analysis   This is audience analysis based on adjustment for things like self-selecting population, performing population, and nonperforming population. You use this to figure out who is using your site, as opposed to whom you had intended it to be built for.

Goal analysis   Everyone should have a little goal analysis in their corporate life: It's the point where you take abstract goals and define them clearly in action steps. This is where you define your user's main performance as an area of testing focus, and you begin to set priorities for your user within that performance.

Note that this is all analysis. You can't get to the point where you're providing six well-reasoned theses without doing hands-on testing. The scope and type of your testing will vary greatly. Some of the factors determining your test will be simple but big, like time and budget. Others depend on what you want from a test. QA tests are not the same from step to step in a development cycle, and the results you get will be a direct result of when you choose to do the test. I've broken the process down into seven steps:

1. Decide what type of testing is appropriate to each style of development. Computer-based testing, where you watch a user zoom through an interface, is pretty useless when you haven't developed a product-specific interface yet. A black-box test, where you sit the user down with no instruction or indication of product function and watch the results, is best left to the stage of development when you've completed both the task set and interface for the website. But you can, at different points in development, test people to see if they think parts of the interface mean the same thing that the designers think they do. You can test people on a task-by-task basis to see how they execute desired tasks. Think about what you want to know at every step of the process, and design your user test accordingly.

2. Determine how to best distribute testing throughout the process of site development. This may be decided by drawing a simple relationship: The more work you're doing on a particular development step, the more likely it is you'll need to test. In other words, factor in testing when you're getting ready to pull a major backend overhaul or interfacelift.

3. Once you've figured out when you're going to be testing, make sure the timing and contents of each test create some sort of relationship between the

different tests at different stages, i.e, they flow in a natural progression. Ideally, you should be using the results from each test to hone your product and therefore refine the test after it.

4. Next, assess the merit of testing the site during different stages of development. If you're still storyboarding the site and writing content, there's not a lot of QA. If you're beginning to build or revise the backend, there's probably some procedural QA you could be doing to ensure that future site maintenance and upgrades don't mean hosing the work you're doing now.

NOTE   Note that the type of process QA I just talked about is completely different from user-based testing. Both are equally important—one helps you refine your product, and the other helps you refine your process.

---

5. After you've determined what to test, when to test, and how the tests complement each other, determine the amount of testing you need to do. If your latest round of Web development is primarily backend maintenance, you may only need to do a series of specific, performance-related tests. If you're launching an upgraded, redesigned site, you'll need to factor in new user testing, as well as user tests that assess how well the new product integrates with the old one.

6. Once you've hammered out the testing conditions, it's time to take a look at your goals. Decide what skills your users need in order to complete testing successfully. This isn't confined to the users' skills—you also need to assess what skills your Web-building staff needs to have to maintain the work they're doing. Once you've decided what skills everyone needs, ask yourself how they're going to get those skills. Are the users (or builders) adding to knowledge they already possess, or is your website going to be imparting those skills from the ground up?

7. You've got everything clearly stated, and you're convinced that QA will make your product invincible. Now it's time to convince your managers and bosses. The last step in QA should be to calculate the costs and benefits of the QA process relative to the resources you're going to use while testing. You need to be able to evaluate the resources you're going to use, and to justify why those resources are important enough to sink into testing. One of the most potent arguments for cost-benefit returns on QA testing is this: The sooner an error is corrected, the cheaper it is to fix it.

Summary

Now that you've got seven steps that will carry you through QA testing, you're equipped to take your usability goals and begin cross-training your site for optimum performance.

CHAPTER

TEN

Case Study #1: Moving to a Technically Proficient Site

This chapter takes all of the skills and considerations discussed in this part's previous chapters and applies them to a *bona fide* website. Since the chapters in Part II all focus on fine-tuning your website for technical proficiency, we're going to focus on smarter ways to build run-of-the-mill websites.

There are three main sections in this chapter. The first section focuses on building a technically proficient site, the second section focuses on modifying the layout for a fresher look and feel, and the third section adds scripting functionality to the site.

> **NOTE**   Some of the skills discussed in this case study are explained in more detail in subsequent chapters. If I mention a skill or technique here that has not yet been covered, I will provide the chapter where you can find more information.

The idea behind this chapter structure is to show how a site can move through several different revisions. Each section focuses on easing from one mode of production to another. Best of all, we build or revise a complete site in each section, so you can see how any upgrade or maintenance checks carry over from page to page. The source code for each site is available on the CD-ROM included with the book.

Let's get started!

ACME ISP, Round 1: Building the Site

Every one of our case studies is going to start with the inception of a site, then follow the site-building process through the steps from brainstorm to completion. Our first site is for a small ISP that simply wants to put up a "we're here!" sign on the Web.

Why Build the Site

Every scenario has their everyman or everywoman, and ours is called Sarah Smith. Sarah is a freelance Web developer who makes her living building and maintaining smaller-scale websites for local business. She's been hired to pull together a site for Acme ISP as a barter deal: She does the site, and in return, she gets free server space for her own business site.

Although Sarah's the site developer for an ISP, she doesn't get special access privileges for the Web servers: She has to develop a portable site within the technical specs she's wangled from her contact at Acme ISP and deliver the complete product to them.

Since Sarah's flying blind here, we're going to start by having her organize a lot of print material and late-night napkin notes into a workable site.

What Development Decisions Were Made

Since the site has to move from Sarah's computer to the ISP's designated site directory without much extra effort, the site has to be portable and self-contained. In other words, it has to be able to move from machine to machine without links or image file references breaking.

The best way to do this is to set up a site structure that allows Sarah to check her file structure at a glance. Before she can do that, however, it's best to figure out the scope of her site—what content it is supposed to encompass, and how she plans on providing all that content.

The Scope and Technical Requirements for the Site

In order to get a grasp on the day-to-day basics of building the site, Sarah sat down with the Acme ISP founder's notes on what he wanted from the site. Here's what she had to work with:

Selling ISP to New Customers

- Explain how dial-up access works.
- Show areas that can dial in locally.
- Walk customer through ordering service.
- Provide instructions for setting up PC for Dialin.

Selling ISP to Savvy Customers and Businesses

- Detail the different levels of service, from shell accounts all the way to T1 access.
- Show area that can dial in locally.

- Show network maps for business customers.

- Walk customer through ordering service.

- Point customers to page for software downloads, etc.

Customer Support

- Divide into different areas: dialing in, installing software, using software, tech capabilities.

- Provide different pages for each area.

- Link all four pages to the human contacts page for further questions.

Translated into English, this outlines the three editorial focuses of the site: selling the ISP to Internet novices, selling the ISP to seasoned Internet users, and providing support to current customers. Keeping this in mind, Sarah designed a site structure that she felt could grow to support any further site changes. She's going to use this both as a backend and as a site tree for readers.

The beauty of creating a reference structure like this early on is that the site tree diagram allows Sarah to answer questions like:

- Is that information already on the site?

- If it's already on the site, is it clearly marked for the user to find?

- Is it easy to find the answers to specific questions a customer has about service details?

- Does a page corresponding to each step in the path exist?

- Are there links or text cues already supporting the paths she mapped out, or do they need to be built?

- What paths already exist between the different pages on the site?

How Site Templates Were Built

The first step Sarah took was to build a page that she liked to look at. This page served as the first draft for her site. Because she knew it was going to have both vertical and horizontal margins set by table cells, she concentrated on setting up all the elements in a grid before refining alignment and spacing. Figure 10.1 shows her first layout attempt.

FIGURE 10.1:

First draft

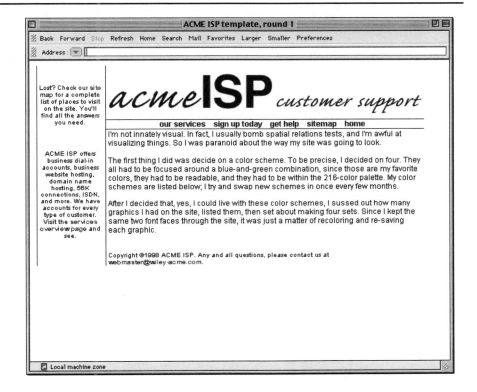

And here's the source code, with "greeked" text to give her an idea of what the site would look like.

---

siteplan.html

```
<html>

<head>
<title>ACME ISP template, round 1</title>

</head>

<body bgcolor="#FFFFFF" text="#000000" link="#990000" vlink="#003366">

<!--the layout is tabled so we can have a vertical sidebar as well as
horizontal site elements. All hail colspan and rowspan elements!
In addition, the table size is set so the entire site fits in a 640x480
screen.-->
```

```
<table width="600" cellspacing="0" cellpadding="0" border="0">
<!--remember to number your rows so you can keep track of what's going
where. When I build templates, I like to turn the borders on and de-
compact code so I can see exactly what's doing on the layout -->

<!--row 1-->
<tr>
<!--this sets a narrow white margin-->
<td rowspan="8" valign="top"> </td>
<!--this sets the dark-blue vertical margin I want-->
<td rowspan="8" valign="top"bgcolor="#003366">
<img src="../images/spacer.gif" alt="..." align=right width="1"
height="10" border="0">
</td>
<!--this is where all the vertical sidebar features are going to go. -->
<td rowspan="8" width="20%" align="center" valign="middle">
<!--insert sidebar copy here. This is going to change from site to site --
>
<small>
<p>
Lost? Check our <strong><a href="#">site map</a></strong> for a complete
list of places to visit on the site. You'll find all the answers you need.
</p>
<!--this is the spacing elements that separates the sidebar slugs.-->
<p>
 
</p>
<p>
ACME ISP offers business dial-in accounts, business website hosting,
domain name hosting, 56K connections, ISDN, and more. We have accounts for
every type of customer. Visit the <strong><a href="#">services overview
page</a></strong> and see.
</p>
</small>
<!--end of inserted sidebar copy -->
</td>
<!--here's the other dark-blue margin. I'm going for a clean, outlined
look. -->
<td rowspan="2" valign="top"bgcolor="#003366">
<img src="../images/spacer.gif" alt="..." align=right width="1"
height="10" border="0">
</td>
```

```
<!--this sets a narrow white margin. I only set the rowspan for two rows
so I could make the horizontal blue margin bump up next to it.-->
<td valign="top"> </td>

<!--this sets the width for the content -->
<!-- the header is made up of two different images: the logo, and a
subhead-type image on the right that indicates what section we're in. When
I compact the HTML, the two will tile nicely. I've measured the heights of
all the images to make sure that the leading is even. -->
<td width="75%" valign="bottom">
<img src="../images/logo.gif" alt="ACME isp" align=left width="260"
height="85" border="0">
</td>
<td align="left" valign="bottom">
<img src="../images/cussupp_subhead.gif" alt="customer support"
align=right width="227" height="40" border="0">
</td>
</tr>

<!--row 2-->
<tr>
<td colspan="3" bgcolor="#003366" align="left" valign="top">
<img src="../images/spacer.gif" align=right width="1" height="1"
border="0">
</td>
</tr>

<!--row 3-->
<!--this is where the nav goes -->
<tr>
<td bgcolor="#003366" align="left" valign="top">
<img src="../images/spacer.gif" align=right width="1" height="1"
border="0">
</td>
<td colspan="3" valign="middle" align="middle"><font face="arial,
helvetica"><strong><a href="#">our services</a></strong>   
<strong><a href="#">sign up today</a></strong>    <strong><a
href="#">get help</a></strong>    <strong><a
href="#">sitemap</a></strong>    <strong><a
href="#">home</a></strong>
</font>
</td>
</tr>
```

```
<!--row 4-->
<tr>
<td colspan="4" bgcolor="#003366" align="left" valign="top">
<img src="../images/spacer.gif" align=right width="1" height="1"
border="0">
</td>
</tr>


<!--row 5 -->
<tr>
<td rowspan="4" bgcolor="#003366" align="left" valign="top">
<img src="../images/spacer.gif" align=right width="1" height="1"
border="0">
</td>
<td colspan="3" align="left" valign="top">
<img src="../images/spacer.gif" align=right width="1" height="1"
border="0">
</td>
</tr>


<!--row 6 -->
<!--white spacer before content -->
<tr>
<td rowspan="3" bgcolor="#FFFFFF"align="left" valign="top">
<img src="../images/spacer.gif" align=right width="1" height="1"
border="0">
</td>
</tr>



<!--row 7 -->
<!--content! woo-hoo! -->
<!--but first, the little white margin-->
<tr>
<td colspan="3" valign="top" align="left">
<!--any text-->
<font face="arial, helvetica">
<!--start with a small bump-->
<p>
I'm not innately visual. In fact, I usually bomb spatial relations tests,
and I'm awful at visualizing things. So I was paranoid about the way my
site was going to look.
</p>
```

```
<p>
The first thing I did was decide on a color scheme. To be precise, I
decided on four. They all had to be focused around a blue-and-green
combination, since those are my favorite colors, they had to be readable,
and they had to be within the 216-color palette. My color schemes are
listed below; I try and swap new schemes in once every few months.
</p>
<p>
After I decided that, yes, I could live with these color schemes, I sussed
out how many graphics I had on the site, listed them, then set about
making four sets. Since I kept the same two font faces through the site,
it was just a matter of recoloring and re-saving each graphic.
</p>
<p>
 
</p>
</font>
</td>
</tr>
<!--row 8-->
<!--copyright-->
<tr>
<td colspan="4" valign="bottom">
<font face="arial, helvetica"><small>Copyright &copy;1998 ACME ISP. Any
and all questions, please contact us at <strong><a
href="mailto:webmaster@wiley-acme.com">webmaster@wiley-
acme.com</a></strong>.</SMALL>
</font>
</td>
</tr>
</table>
</body>
</html>
```

After she looked at both the finished page, and the HTML, she decided that she had to modify the design. There were two specific areas that she wanted to refine: the sidebar on the left of the screen, and the navigation bar running underneath the site graphics. Sarah also wanted to pad the margins for the sidebar; however, she couldn't add cellpadding to the current table because it would throw off the narrow blue lines.

The answer was to build a separate table, add cellpadding there, then drop the table back into the table cell. In addition to controlling the appearance of the content, she could then make a "library" of sidebars and drop the appropriate ones in the appropriate files. This also solved a troublesome UI problem: How would Sarah incorporate secondary navigation into the site? The sidebar would offer links to each page in the section.

Sarah was also going to table the horizontal navigation bar so she could control its spacing and appearance as well. In addition, by setting the size of that table, she could maintain a minimum width for the content area and maintain layout consistency.

Why did Sarah elect to embed two separate tables into her main table? It was done reluctantly, and only because style-sheet support was still quite inconsistent when the site was built.

Figure 10.2 shows the new, improved layout.

FIGURE 10.2:

Second draft

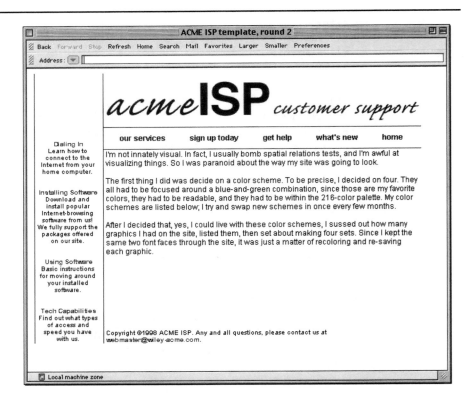

And here's the source code for the file.

template2.html

```html
<html>

<head>
<title>ACME ISP template, round 2</title>

</head>

<body bgcolor="#FFFFFF" text="#000000" link="#990000" vlink="#003366">

<!--the layout is tabled so we can have a vertical sidebar as well as
horizontal site elements. All hail colspan and rowspan elements!
In addition, the table size is set so the entire site fits in a 640x480
screen.-->
<table width="600" cellspacing="0" cellpadding="0" border="0">
<!--remember to number your rows so you can keep track of what's going
where. When I build templates, I like to turn the borders on and de-
compact code so I can see exactly what's doing on the layout -->

<!--row 1-->
<tr>
<!--this sets a narrow white margin-->
<td rowspan="8" valign="top"> </td>
<!--this sets the dark-blue vertical margin I want-->
<td rowspan="8" valign="top"bgcolor="#003366">
<img src="../images/spacer.gif" alt="..." align=right width="1"
height="10" border="0">
</td>
<!--this is where all the vertical sidebar features are going to go.
-->
<td rowspan="8" width="20%" align="center" valign="middle">
<!--insert sidebar copy here. This is going to change from site to
site. I indented the code so I could tell this table from the one that
shapes the entire site. -->
        <table width="100" cellspacing="0" cellpadding="2"
border="0">
        <!--row1-->
        <tr>
        <!--spacer goes here to match up with logo height -->
```

```
<td valign=top align=middle>
<img src="../images/spacer.gif" alt="..." align=right
width="1"         height="100" border="0">
</td>
</tr>

<!--row2-->
<tr>
<!--first nav option goes here -->
<td valign=top align=middle>
<font face="arial, helvetica"><small>
<p>
<strong><a href="http://wiley-acme.com/dialin.html">Dialing
In</a></strong><br>
Learn how to connect to the Internet from your home computer.
</p>
</small></font>
</td>
</tr>

<!--row3-->
<tr>
<!--spacer goes in between every nav option -->
<td valign=top align=middle>
 
</td>
</tr>

<!--row4-->
<tr>
<!--second nav option goes here -->
<td valign=top align=middle>
<font face="arial, helvetica"><small>
<p>
<strong><a href="install.html">Installing
Software</a></strong><br>
Download and install popular Internet-browsing software from
us!     We      fully support the packages offered on our site.
</p>
</small></font>
</td>
</tr>
```

```
<!--row5-->
<tr>
<!--spacer goes in between every nav option -->
<td valign=top align=middle>
 
</td>
</tr>

<!--row6-->
<tr>
<!--third nav option goes here -->
<td valign=top align=middle>
<font face="arial, helvetica"><small>
<p>
<strong><a href="http://wiley-acme.com/using.html">Using
Software</a></strong><br>
Basic instructions for moving around your installed software.
</p>
</small></font>
</td>
</tr>

<!--row7-->
<tr>
<!--spacer goes in between every nav option -->
<td valign=top align=middle>
 
</td>
</tr>

<!--row8-->
<tr>
<!--fourth nav option goes here -->
<td valign=top align=middle>
<font face="arial, helvetica"><small>
<p>
<strong><a href="http://wiley-acme.com/tech.html">Tech
Capabilities</a></strong><br>
Find out what types of access and speed you have with us.
</p>
</small></font>
```

```
            </td>
            </tr>
        </table>
<!--end of inserted sidebar copy -->
</td>
<!--here's the other dark-blue margin. I'm going for a clean, outlined
look. -->
<td rowspan="2" valign="top"bgcolor="#003366">
<img src="../images/spacer.gif" alt="..." align=right width="1"
height="10" border="0">
</td>
<!--this sets a narrow white margin. I only set the rowspan for two
rows so I could make the horizontal blue margin bump up next to it.-->
<td valign="top"> </td>

<!--this sets the width for the content -->
<!-- the header is made up of two different images: the logo, and a
subhead-type image on the right that indicates what section we're in.
When I compact the HTML, the two will tile nicely. I've measured the
heights of all the images to make sure that the leading is even. -->
<td width="75%" valign="bottom">
<img src="../images/logo.gif" alt="ACME isp" align=left width="260"
height="85" border="0">
</td>
<td align="left" valign="bottom">
<img src="../images/cussupp_subhead.gif" alt="customer support"
align=right width="227" height="40" border="0">
</td>
</tr>

<!--row 2-->
<tr>
<td colspan="3" bgcolor="#003366" align="left" valign="top">
<img src="../images/spacer.gif" align=right width="1" height="1"
border="0">
</td>
</tr>

<!--row 3-->
<!--this is where the nav goes -->
<tr>
<td bgcolor="#003366" align="left" valign="top">
```

```
<img src="../images/spacer.gif" align=right width="1" height="1"
border="0">
</td>
<td colspan="3" valign="middle" align="middle">
<table width="480" cellspacing="5" cellpadding="5" border="0">
<tr>
<td valign="middle" align="center">
<font face="arial, helvetica"><strong><a href="#">our
services</a></strong></font>
</td>
<td valign="middle" align="center">
<font face="arial, helvetica"><strong><a href="#">sign up
today</a></strong></font>
</td>
<td valign="middle" align="center">
<font face="arial, helvetica"><strong><a href="#">get
help</a></strong></font>
</td>
<td valign="middle" align="center">
<font face="arial, helvetica"><strong><a href="#">what's
new</a></strong></font>
</td>
<td valign="middle" align="center">
<font face="arial, helvetica"><strong><a
href="#">home</a></strong></font>
</td>
</tr>
</table>
</td>
</tr>

<!--row 4-->
<tr>
<td colspan="4" bgcolor="#003366" align="left" valign="top">
<img src="../images/spacer.gif" align=right width="1" height="1"
border="0">
</td>
</tr>

<!--row 5 -->
<tr>
<td rowspan="4" bgcolor="#003366" align="left" valign="top">
```

```
<img src="../images/spacer.gif" align=right width="1" height="1"
border="0">
</td>
<td colspan="3" align="left" valign="top">
<img src="../images/spacer.gif" align=right width="1" height="1"
border="0">
</td>
</tr>

<!--row 6 -->
<!--white spacer before content -->
<tr>
<td rowspan="3" bgcolor="#FFFFFF"align="left" valign="top">
<img src="../images/spacer.gif" align=right width="1" height="1"
border="0">
</td>
</tr>


<!--row 7 -->
<!--content! woo-hoo! -->
<!--but first, the little white margin-->
<tr>
<td colspan="3" valign="top" align="left">
<!--any text-->
<font face="arial, helvetica">
<p>
I'm not innately visual. In fact, I usually bomb spatial relations
tests, and I'm awful at visualizing things. So I was paranoid about the
way my site was going to look.
</p>
<p>
The first thing I did was decide on a color scheme. To be precise, I
decided on four. They all had to be focused around a blue-and-green
combination, since those are my favorite colors, they had to be
readable, and they had to be within the 216-color palette. My color
schemes are listed below; I try and swap new schemes in once every few
months.
</p>
<p>
After I decided that, yes, I could live with these color schemes, I
sussed out how many graphics I had on the site, listed them, then set
```

```
about making four sets. Since I kept the same two font faces through
the site, it was just a matter of recoloring and re-saving each
graphic.
</p>
<p>
 
</p>
</font>
<!--end any text-->
</td>
</tr>
<!--row 8-->
<!--copyright-->
<tr>
<td colspan="4" valign="bottom">
<font face="arial, helvetica"><small>Copyright &copy;1998 ACME ISP. Any
and all questions, please contact us at <strong><a
href="mailto:webmaster@wiley-acme.com">webmaster@wiley-
acme.com</a></strong>.</SMALL>
</font>
</td>
</tr>
</table>
</body>
</html>
```

Once Sarah decided that this was the file she wanted to go with, her next step was to figure out how to build it better. In other words: How could she streamline and template the page for daily production or for easily reproducing the page design for several subsequent new pages?

How the Templates Were Modified for Daily Production

The easiest way to template your site is to pick apart the items that comprise each individual page, figure out how frequently each item is going to have to be modified, then find a way to build "shells" that hold your not-frequently-modified items in place and allow you to swap your frequently modified items in and out. For a real-life example of how you'd go about doing this, check out the diagram below.

Constant on every page

Constant on every page

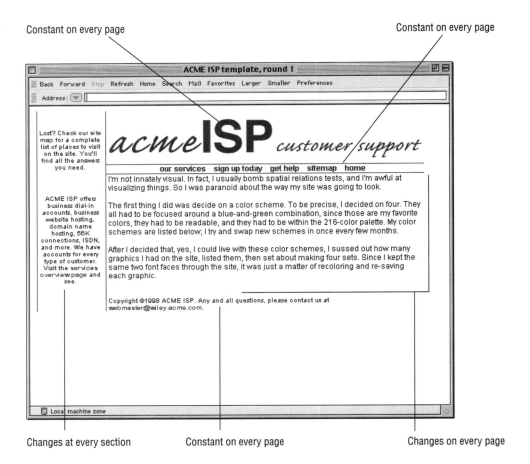

Changes at every section

Constant on every page

Changes on every page

Note that Sarah printed out a page, then sorted the page elements into three categories:

1. Items that are persistent and unchanging from page to page.

2. Items that are persistent and open to change from page to page.

3. Items that do change from page to page.

The persistent and unchanging item for each page was the layout. Since this is built out with the table structure, she could use this as the base for a day-to-day template for any page on her site. The Acme ISP logo is also unchanging, so it should be built into the template as well.

The next step was finding the persistent and changing items for each page. There are four: the primary and secondary navigation bars, the copyright notice, and the headline for each page. Each item changes under different conditions: The copyright notice only changes once a year, the primary navigation changes only if a section is added or taken away, the secondary navigation changes from section to section, and the headline changes from page to page. However, all four items have two things in common: They appear on every page, and they must be accessible because they are subject to change.

Finally, Sarah identified the items that change from page to page. The one thing that stood out for her was the content: Some pages are form-driven, some are composed of a giant list, others are blocks of text. The layout and type of content varies wildly from page to page, so it's best to set up sitewide.

Once Sarah identified all these different pieces, she looked at the source code for her template and began figuring out how to break it down into parts that would permit her to do two separate things:

- Maintain the pages she had to build for the first iteration of the site
- Build new pages that fit into the existing site seamlessly

The first thing she did was strip all the changing items out of the site template, leaving only a structural skeleton.

The next thing she did was save each of the persistent items as a separate HTML fragment. These fragments comprise a site-building library, which is efficient because individual elements are in one central place for easy updating and reference.

Finally, the last thing Sarah does is write a style guide for the different types of content—forms, lists, text, and graphics—so she has a set of visually consistent rules to apply to all the content areas across her site. She can then format each page's content as a virtual include, and change the filename for the content include call in each "shell" template.

In a nutshell, here's how her new template system works:

1. Each file a user sees in their browser (`http://www.acmeisp.com/services/index.html`) is composed of a shell file (`index.html`) that calls a bunch of virtual includes.

index.html

```
<html>

<head>
<title>ACME ISP template, final</title>

</head>

<body bgcolor="#FFFFFF" text="#000000" link="#990000"
vlink="#003366">

<table width="600" cellspacing="0" cellpadding="0" border="0">
<!--remember to number your rows so you can keep track of what's
going where. When I build templates, I like to turn the borders on
and de-compact code so I can see exactly what's doing on the layout
-->

<!--row 1-->
<tr>
<!--this sets a narrow white margin-->
<td rowspan="8" valign="top"> </td>
<!--this sets the dark-blue vertical margin I want-->
<td rowspan="8" valign="top"bgcolor="#003366">
<img src="../images/spacer.gif" alt="..." align=right width="1"
height="10" border="0">
</td>
<!--this is where all the vertical sidebar features are going to go.
-->
<td rowspan="8" width="20%" align="center" valign="middle">
<!--insert sidebar copy here. -->

<!--note that this is not the only sidebar we have - I just elected
to use this one. There are several others, with source code listed
in the chapter. I elected to store all the sidebars in the /meta/
directory, reasoning that they were more like site-wide elements
than page-specific ones. However, you may want to keep directory-
specific elements in the same directory as the pages they're being
included on. -->

<!--#include virtual="meta/sidebar.htmlf" -->
```

```
<!--end of inserted sidebar copy -->
</td>

<td rowspan="2" valign="top"bgcolor="#003366">
<img src="../images/spacer.gif" alt="..." align=right width="1"
height="10" border="0">
</td>

<td valign="top"> </td>

<td width="75%" valign="bottom">
<img src="../images/logo.gif" alt="ACME isp" align=left width="260"
height="85" border="0">
</td>
<td align="left" valign="bottom">
<!--#include virtual= "headline.htmlf" --></td>
</tr>

<!--row 2-->
<tr>
<td colspan="3" bgcolor="#003366" align="left" valign="top">
<img src="../images/spacer.gif" align=right width="1" height="1"
border="0">
</td>
</tr>

<!--row 3-->
<!--this is where the nav goes -->
<tr>
<td bgcolor="#003366" align="left" valign="top">
<img src="../images/spacer.gif" align=right width="1" height="1"
border="0">
</td>
<td colspan="3" valign="middle" align="middle">
<!--include the main nav bar now. -->
<!--#include virtual="meta/nav.htmlf" -->
</td>
</tr>

<!--row 4-->
<tr>
<td colspan="4" bgcolor="#003366" align="left" valign="top">
```

```
<img src="../images/spacer.gif" align=right width="1" height="1"
border="0">
</td>
</tr>

<!--row 5 -->
<tr>
<td rowspan="4" bgcolor="#003366" align="left" valign="top">
<img src="../images/spacer.gif" align=right width="1" height="1"
border="0">
</td>
<td colspan="3" align="left" valign="top">
<img src="../images/spacer.gif" align=right width="1" height="1"
border="0">
</td>
</tr>

<!--row 6 -->
<!--white spacer before content -->
<tr>
<td rowspan="3" bgcolor="#FFFFFF"align="left" valign="top">
<img src="../images/spacer.gif" align=right width="1" height="1"
border="0">
</td>
</tr>


<!--row 7 -->
<!--content! woo-hoo! -->
<!--but first, the little white margin-->
<tr>
<td colspan="3" valign="top" align="left">
<!--now bring in your content include. You can go one of two ways
with this: you can keep all your content includes in the directory
where the actual file names are, or you can stuff them all in the
meta directory and save yourself the trouble of figuring out file
paths. I encourage putting the content includes in their topic-
specific directories, and making sure all of your stuff is pulled
together with absolute URLs. This way, you can use the same template
over and over, and you don't need to worry about paths. -->

<!--#include virtual="buy/content.htmlf" -->
```

```
</td>
</tr>
<!--row 8-->
<!--copyright-->
<tr>
<td colspan="4" valign="bottom">
<!--this is where the copyright include goes. -->
<!--#include virtual="meta/copyright.htmlf" -->
</td>
</tr>
</table>
</body>
</html>
```

2. The shell file calls individual includes. These are assembled by the server before they go out. Here is the source code for each of the includes being called.

sidebar.htmlf

```
<table width="100" cellspacing="0" cellpadding="2" border="0">
<!--row1-->
<tr>
<!--spacer goes here to match up with logo height -->
<td valign=top align=middle>
<img src="../images/spacer.gif" alt="..." align=right width="0"
height="100" border="0">
</td>
</tr>
<!--row2-->
<tr>
<!--first nav option goes here -->
<td valign=top align=middle>
<font face="arial, helvetica"><small>
<p>
<strong><a href="http://wiley-
acme.com/services/contact.html">Contact us</a></strong><br>
We now have a 1-888 number for your urgent queries.
</p>
</small></font>
</td>
```

```
</tr>
<!--row3-->
<tr>
<!--spacer goes in between every nav option -->
<td valign=top align=middle>
 
</td>
</tr>
<!--row4-->
<tr>
<!--second nav option goes here -->
<td valign=top align=middle>
<font face="arial, helvetica"><small>
<p>
<strong><a href="http://wiley-
acme.com/services/routemap.html">Routemap</a></strong><br>
See where ACME lives on the Internet's physical cable network.
</p>
</small></font>
</td>
</tr>
<!--row5-->
<tr>
<!--spacer goes in between every nav option -->
<td valign=top align=middle>
 
</td>
</tr>
<!--row6-->
<tr>
<!--third nav option goes here -->
<td valign=top align=middle>
<font face="arial, helvetica"><small>
<p>
<strong><a href="http://wiley-
acme.com/service/corp.html">Corporate Accounts</a></strong><br>
Do you want to connect your business to the 'Net? We offer T1
pipes, 56K lines, and other flexible business options.
</p>
</small></font>
</td>
</tr>
```

```
<!--row7-->
<tr>
<!--spacer goes in between every nav option -->
<td valign=top align=middle>
 
</td>
</tr>
<!--row8-->
<tr>
<!--fourth nav option goes here -->
<td valign=top align=middle>
<font face="arial, helvetica"><small>
<p>
<strong><a href="http://wiley-
acme.com/services/isdn.html">Personal ISDN</a></strong><br>
Personal web acounts now come with an ISDN connection option. We
also host websites, and offer domain name hosting.
</p>
</small></font>
</td>
</tr>
</table>
```

nav.htmlf

```
<table width="480" cellspacing="5" cellpadding="5" border="0">
<tr>
<td valign="middle" align="center">
<font face="arial, helvetica"><strong><a href="#">our
services</a></strong></font>
</td>
<td valign="middle" align="center">
<font face="arial, helvetica"><strong><a href="#">sign up
today</a></strong></font>
</td>
<td valign="middle" align="center">
<font face="arial, helvetica"><strong><a href="#">get
help</a></strong></font>
</td>
<td valign="middle" align="center">
```

```
<font face="arial, helvetica"><strong><a href="#">what's
new</a></strong></font>
</td>
<td valign="middle" align="center">
<font face="arial, helvetica"><strong><a
href="#">home</a></strong></font>
</td>
</tr>
</table>
```

headline.htmlf

```
<img src="../images/cussupp_subhead.gif" alt="customer support"
align=right width="227" height="40" border="0">
```

copyright.htmlf

```
<font face="arial, helvetica"><small>Copyright &copy;1998 ACME
ISP. Any and all questions, please contact us at <strong><a
href="mailto:webmaster@acmeisp.com">
webmaster@acmeisp.com</a></strong>.
</font>
```

content.htmlf

```
<p>
A paragraph full of text goes here. Note that it does have closing
tags, so if Acme ISP ever decides to roll out stylesheets, they
can attach styles to the block-level paragraphs.
</p><p>
A paragraph full of text goes here. Note that it does have closing
tags, so if Acme ISP ever decides to roll out stylesheets, they
can attach styles to the block-level paragraphs.
</p><p>
A paragraph full of text goes here. Note that it does have closing
tags, so if Acme ISP ever decides to roll out stylesheets, they
can attach styles to the block-level paragraphs.
</p>
```

Why Use Apache Server-Side Includes?

I made this decision for a number of reasons, all of which I believe are firmly rooted in real-world experiences I've had and discussed with Web developers both in AND outside of multimedia gulch.

The predominant model for building sites—and it's a good one—is server-side assembly of separate site parts. I did not want to pick any specific closed-source software product for server-side site assembly.

Apache is open source, and it's the most widely used Web server. Therefore it makes sense both in a hacker way and in a practical way to build sites to a prevailing industry standard, instead of a software package readers may or may not have.

I have learned, through teaching at Seybold, handing off sites to clients, and building sites for both content-driven and marketing purposes, that server side includes are an excellent way to introduce people to two important site-building skills:

- assembling pages from separate parts

- practicing if-else logic for "dynamic" page assembly

Every time I approach component site-building by using SSI as an example, the learning curve for my unwitting pupils went through the roof after a thorough bout with SSI. So learn SSI and you'll have a leg up on whatever server solution you elect to use in the long run.

NOTE   This is just one chunk of text being formatted for an example. What we need to remember from Sarah's example is that the content is a discrete, well-formed, and valid chunk of HTML.

The Source Code for the Whole Site

The following files are available on the companion CD-ROM:

- `index.html`

- `fax.html`

- `phone.html`

- `web.html`

- `contact.html`
- `dialin.html`
- `install.html`
- `tech.html`
- `using.html`
- `bandwidth.html`
- `corporate.html`
- `domain.html`
- `personal.html`
- `web_business.html`
- `web_personal.html`
- `aboutus.html`

Remember that each of these files are composed of:

- One shell file
- One page-specific content include
- One page-specific headline include
- A section-specific sidebar include

As a result, I am showing how each shell file looks when it calls every individual item.

The following files compose the include library:

- `nav.htmlf`
- `headline.htmlf`
- `copyright.htmlf`
- `Linked_list.htmlf` (content include)
- `form_sample.htmlf` (content include)
- `text_excerpt_short.htmlf` (content include)
- `text_excerpt_long.htmlf` (content include)
- `ordered_list.htmlf`

I elected to show content includes that addressed specific formatting issues, like forms, long chunks of text, or items in a series, so each content "type" is represented as a different include that can be edited as appropriate for a page. These library components make filling in client-approved content easier.

ACME ISP, Round 2: Giving the Site a Facelift

The Acme ISP site launched successfully, and thanks to Sarah's template library and style guide, she was able to quickly build and refine all the pages. However, now that her bosses have a website, they want to make it look better.

Why Build the Site

Now that Sarah's built a serviceable site, it's time to make it a little more visually attractive. Sarah also discovered that there were too many indistinguishable navigation features in her last site design, so she's simplifying the interface and offering a number of straightforward, linear links for readers. How is she going to overhaul her site? Read on ...

What Development Decisions Were Made

The navigation made no note of primary and secondary levels of navigation because the two different levels were in two separate places on the page. While the reader was able to move comfortably within a specific subdirectory, they couldn't move from section to section as easily, unless they had decoded the visual distinction between the primary and secondary navigation. A site for online goods and services needs to sell both the product and support for the product, but with the difficulty navigating from one section to another, Acme ISP wasn't selling either product or support effectively.

Another flaw in the interface: It was long on space, but short on making information stand out memorably. While the basic grid layout did a good job of making sure that specific information occupied specific spaces on the page, it didn't provide enough visual distinctiveness between the different sections to give readers an instant eyeball assessment.

Therefore, the biggest priority in the project was to find a clean, fast-loading design, then impose it on the rest of the site. Once the design was set, the next step was to figure out how to easily implement it. After all the careful planning, it's time to put your mouse where your mouth is and begin merging old content with a new site.

The Scope for the Site

One of the biggest complaints Sarah's bosses had about the old site was that it was too confusing to pick out the navigation for the different sections. Instead of offering users the option of going to all the different pages within a section, they reasoned that having one central index page and subsequent "child" pages springing from the main page was a smarter strategy since users were less likely to get confused.

Sarah's bosses were on the right track. Primary navigation, where you move among index pages in different sections of a site, is a must. Secondary navigation, where you reveal the contents of the individual sections in a separate or expanded navigation device, is helpful, but not always necessary. When would secondary navigation be necessary? If the contents of an individual section are all long, bulky, or so disparate as to be non-intuitive. If you're updating items chronologically, secondary navigation can be useful in letting users move back and forth within a calendar period. Figure 10.3 illustrates this idea.

However, Acme ISP has a fairly limited array of items in each different directory, so a secondary navigation, while nice, is going to be discarded in favor of a more visually distinct primary navigation. Sarah went back to the drawing board, and came up with the design changes listed below.

How This Site Differs from the Earlier Site

The most dramatic differences between the old site and the new site are all in the layout. They can be summed up below:

Introducing a vertical color bar to give the navigation bar greater prominence. This sends a clearer visual signal to the reader that the area to the left is not content, but part of the interface *framing* content. This vertical bar is actually a background graphic Sarah made; a user surfing with the images off doesn't see it.

FIGURE 10.3:

FIGURE 10.3:

Here's an example of primary and secondary navigation on the Relevance website (http://www.relevance.net/). The vertical menu to the left is the primary navigation, and the horizontal navigation is the secondary navigation.

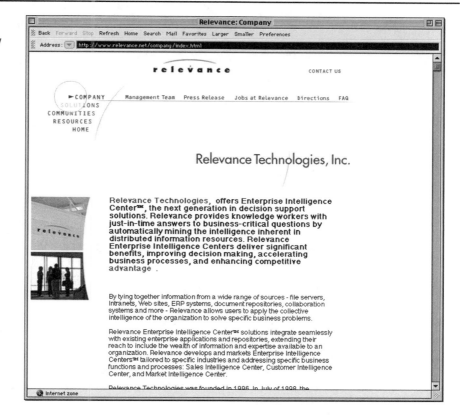

The old code:

```
<body bgcolor="#FFFFFF" text="#000000" link="#990000" vlink="#003366">
```

The new code:

```
<body background="../images/nav_bg.gif" bgcolor="#FFFFFF"
alink="#990000" link="#990000" text="#333333" vlink="#003366">
```

Removing a level of granularity in the vertical nav bar. Instead of changing the vertical nav bar so it reflects whatever is in a specific directory, a single, top-level nav bar lets users move from section to section. If users want to move within a section, they make that decision on the index page of the section. By sharply restricting the different paths one can take through a site, the Web developer is able to tightly control the site tree and work on providing clear paths between existing options.

In the old code there were two distinct navigation sections. The site-wide navigation was tucked underneath the headline graphic like this:

```
<td width="75%" valign="bottom">
<img src="../images/logo.gif" alt="ACME isp" align=left
width="260" height="85" border="0">
</td>
<td align="left" valign="bottom">
<img src="../images/cussupp_subhead.gif" alt="customer support"
align=right width="227" height="40" border="0">
</td>
</tr>

<!--row 2-->
<tr>
<td colspan="3" bgcolor="#003366" align="left" valign="top">
<img src="../images/spacer.gif" align=right width="1" height="1"
border="0">
</td>
</tr>

<!--row 3-->
<!--this is where the nav goes -->
<tr>
<td bgcolor="#003366" align="left" valign="top">
<img src="../images/spacer.gif" align=right width="1" height="1"
border="0">
</td>
<td colspan="3" valign="middle" align="middle">
<!--include the main nav bar now. -->
<!--#include virtual="meta/nav.htmlf" -->
</font>
</td>
</tr>
```

with the code for nav.htmlf inserted underneath. The second navigation device, a vertical list that varied from section to section, was called in the code even before the primary navigation, at the beginning of the table layout:

```
<!--row 1-->
<tr>
<!--this sets a narrow white margin-->
```

```
<td rowspan="8" valign="top"> </td>
<!--this sets the dark-blue vertical margin I want-->
<td rowspan="8" valign="top"bgcolor="#003366">
<img src="../images/spacer.gif" alt="..." align=right width="1"
height="10" border="0">
</td>
<!--this is where all the vertical sidebar features are going to
go. -->
<td rowspan="8" width="20%" align="center" valign="middle">
<!--insert sidebar copy here. -->
<!--#include virtual="meta/buy.htmlf" -->

<!--end of inserted sidebar copy -->
</td>
```

The new and improved navigation is a simple include called in the first row of the table, like this:

```
<table width="600">
<tr>
<td rowspan="6">
<!--#include virtual="nav.htmlf" -->
</td>
</tr>
<!--insert the row where the brand goes-->
<td>
<img src="../images/brand.gif" alt="[acme isp]" width="400" height="73"
border="0">
<p> </p>
</td>
</tr>
```

And then a separate navigation include is called in to provide the vertical navigation bar. That include, nav.htmlf, is provided in full below.

These navigation changes illustrate one of the great truths of upgrading a site: You don't necessarily add to the old code. Instead, you may streamline your layout to the point where it's all of five lines, and four of them are references to modular includes you built earlier.

Sarah's not that efficient, but she did manage to save herself from a mess of content updates when she finally built out her design. To find out how, keep going.

How Site Templates Were Built and Modified for Daily Production

Since Sarah built the first version of the site with the content separated from the page structure, it should be easy for her to repurpose the content. In fact, she's still using the same model for site production as she did last time. If something works, don't fix it unless you really, really have both the time and the burning desire.

To recap that model briefly: The pages are made up of a "shell" document that provides a document structure for all the elements contained within it. This shell document calls a number of HTML fragments, each of which contain some specific element on the page like a navigation bar or a copyright notice. The fragments are there so Sarah can change one file and have the change take effect sitewide, rather than going through countless files to change the same thing over and over.

In order to come up with the new look and feel for Acme's site, Sarah decided to re-lay out the page as if it weren't broken down into parts at all, then deconstruct the page to fit her daily production model. Here's the source code for her mockup of the new and improved layout:

```
<html>

<head>

<title>Welcome to ACME ISP</title>

<!--insert stylesheet-->
<style type="text/css">
<!--//
A:link      {font-family: helvetica, arial, sans serif; font-
weight:bold; font-size:10px;}
A:visited   {position: absolute; font-family: helvetica, arial, sans
serif; font-size:10px;}
body {font-family:helvetica, arial, sans serif; font-size:10px; line-
height:12px;}
//-->
</style>


<body background="../images/nav_bg.gif" bgcolor="#FFFFFF"
alink="#990000" link="#990000" text="#333333" vlink="#003366">

<table width="600">
<tr>
```

```
<td rowspan="6">
<p> </p>
<p><a href="../services/corporate.html"><span style="font-size:14px;
font-weight:heavy;">CORPORATE ACCOUNTS</span></a></p>
<p> <br></p>
<p><a href="../services/personal.html"><span style="font-size:14px;
font-weight:heavy;">PERSONAL ACCOUNTS</span></a></p>
<p> <br></p>
<p><a href="../services/domain.html"><span style="font-size:14px; font-
weight:heavy;">WEB HOSTING</span></a></p>
<p> <br></p>
<p><a href="../services/bandwidth.html"><span style="font-size:14px;
font-weight:heavy;">BANDWIDTH LEASING</span></a></p>
<p> <br></p>
<p><a href="../buy/web.html"><span style="font-size:14px; font-
weight:heavy;">ORDER NOW!</span></a></p>
<p> <br></p>
<p><a href="../help/contact.html"><span style="font-size:14px; font-
weight:heavy;">NEED HELP?</span></a></p>
<p> <br></p>
<p><a href="../us/contact.html"><span style="font-size:14px; font-
weight:heavy;">CONTACT US</span></a></p>
<p> <br></p>
<p><a href="../us/aboutus.html"><span style="font-size:14px; font-
weight:heavy;">ABOUT US</span></a></p>
<p> <br></p>
</td>
<!--insert the row where the brand goes-->
<td>
<img src="../images/brand.gif" alt="[acme isp]" width="400" height="73"
border="0">
<p> </p>
</td>
</tr>

<tr>
<!--insert the div for the individual page title-->
<td>
<img src="../images/about_subhead.gif" width="400" height="50"
border="0">
<p> </p>
</td>
</tr>
```

```
<tr>
<!--insert a blue rule 'cause it looks cool-->
<td bgcolor="#003366">
<img height="2" width="400" src="../images/spacer.gif" alt="...">
</td>
</tr>

<tr>
<!--now insert the content-->
<td>
<p>
Living away from the folks has many benefits, but the one immediately
<a href="#">apparent drawback</a> is that I now have to compete with
roughly 5000 people for the washers and dryers in my building. This has
meant two things: I have had to get over my long-standing belief that
laundry can be done as you sleep sweetly, and I have had to adjust my
schedule so I can do laundry before the overzealous apartment manager
locks the laundry room for the night.
</p><p>
On an <a href="#">abstract level</a> - the same level that discusses
"society's" problems and all that - I understand why the laundry room
must be locked. Evil, sick people are in the habit of dragging innocent
victims back into unlocked laundry rooms late at night and doing things
best left unmentioned. To prevent these hideously deranged people from
perpetrating their crimes here, the laundry room must be locked.
</p><p>
But for those of us who are insomniacs, or who believe that it never
kills garments to let them tumble-dry overnight, this whole "safety"
thing is inconvenient. And since I'm the one likely to be most affected
by any sick perverts in the laundry room late at night, what with
proximity being a strong argument since it means the perv won't have
far to drag my lifeless body, I think that anyone who's willing to take
that chance should be able to do <a href="#">perilous late-night
laundry</a>.
</p>
</td>
</tr>

<tr>
<!--the ad div goes here-->
<td>
<img src="../../../general/ad-banner.gif" alt="[468x60 banner]"
width="468" height="60" border="0">
</td>
```

```
</tr>

<tr>
<!--the copyright div-->
<td>
Copyright &copy; 1998, Acme ISP. For more information, <a
href="../us/aboutus.html">go here</a>.
</td>
</tr>
</table>

</body>
</html>
```

This is what it looks like in a browser:

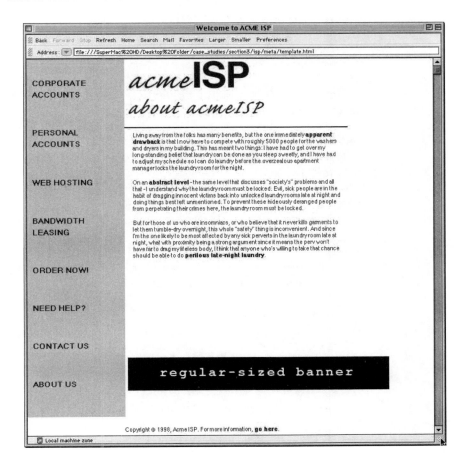

Sarah then decided to break up the code to see if she could realistically expect to maintain or expand the site within the new design. She started by pulling out the elements she had previously identified as persistent to each page but suspect to change: the primary navigation bar, the copyright notice, and the headline for each page. She also pulled out the content.

Here are the source code samples for the resulting "frame" index page, and each of the subsequent fragment files.

template_index.html

```
<html>

<head>

<title>Welcome to ACME ISP</title>

<!--insert stylesheet-->
<style type="text/css">
<!--//
A:link      {font-family: helvetica, arial, sans serif; font-
weight:bold; font-size:10px;}
A:visited   {position: absolute; font-family: helvetica, arial, sans
serif; font-size:10px;}
body {font-family:helvetica, arial, sans serif; font-size:10px; line-
height:12px;}
//-->
</style>

<!--insert any scripts-->

<body background="../images/nav_bg.gif" bgcolor="#FFFFFF"
alink="#990000" link="#990000" text="#333333" vlink="#003366">

<table width="600">
<tr>
<td rowspan="6">
<!--#include virtual="nav.htmlf" -->
</td>
</tr>
<!--insert the row where the brand goes-->
<td>
<img src="../images/brand.gif" alt="[acme isp]" width="400" height="73"
border="0">
```

```
<p> </p>
</td>
</tr>

<tr>
<!--insert the div for the individual page title-->
<td>
<!--#include virtual="subhead.htmlf" -->
<p> </p>
</td>
</tr>

<tr>
<!--insert a blue rule 'cause it looks cool-->
<td bgcolor="#003366">
<img height="2" width="400" src="../images/spacer.gif" alt="...">
</td>
</tr>

<tr>
<!--now insert the content-->
<td>
<!--#include virtual="content.htmlf" -->
</td>
</tr>

<tr>
<!--the ad div goes here-->
<td>
<!--#include virtual="ad.htmlf" -->
</td>
</tr>

<tr>
<!--the copyright div-->
<td>
<!--#include virtual="copyright.htmlf" -->
</td>
</tr>
</table>

</body>
</html>
```

subhead.htmlf

```
<img src="../images/about_subhead.gif" width="400" height="50"
border="0">
```

nav.htmlf

```
<p> </p>
<p><a href="../services/corporate.html"><span style="font-size:14px;
font-weight:heavy;">CORPORATE ACCOUNTS</span></a></p>
<p> <br></p>
<p><a href="../services/personal.html"><span style="font-size:14px;
font-weight:heavy;">PERSONAL ACCOUNTS</span></a></p>
<p> <br></p>
<p><a href="../services/domain.html"><span style="font-size:14px; font-
weight:heavy;">WEB HOSTING</span></a></p>
<p> <br></p>
<p><a href="../services/bandwidth.html"><span style="font-size:14px;
font-weight:heavy;">BANDWIDTH LEASING</span></a></p>
<p> <br></p>
<p><a href="../buy/web.html"><span style="font-size:14px; font-
weight:heavy;">ORDER NOW!</span></a></p>
<p> <br></p>
<p><a href="../help/contact.html"><span style="font-size:14px; font-
weight:heavy;">NEED HELP?</span></a></p>
<p> <br></p>
<p><a href="../us/contact.html"><span style="font-size:14px; font-
weight:heavy;">CONTACT US</span></a></p>
<p> <br></p>
<p><a href="../us/aboutus.html"><span style="font-size:14px; font-
weight:heavy;">ABOUT US</span></a></p>
<p> <br></p>
```

ad.htmlf

```
<img src="../../../general/ad-banner.gif" alt="[468x60 banner]"
width="468" height="60" border="0">
```

---

copyright.htmlf

```
Copyright &copy; 1998, Acme ISP. For more information, <a
href="../us/aboutus.html">go here</a>
```

Sarah decided to keep the content files from the old site iteration, since they can be plugged into the new layout without any problems. Because of this modular site approach, she eliminated a lot of extra work.

The Source Code

Remember that each of files these is composed of a series of includes. The individual "shell" files are:

- index.html
- fax.html
- phone.html
- web.html
- contact.html
- dialin.html
- install.html
- tech.html
- using.html
- bandwidth.html
- corporate.html
- domain.html
- personal.html
- web_business.html
- web_personal.html
- aboutus.html

And the include files:

- `subhead.htmlf`
- `nav.htmlf`
- `ad.htmlf`
- `copyright.htmlf`
- `Linked_list.htmlf` (content include)
- `form_sample.htmlf` (content include)
- `text_excerpt_short.htmlf` (content include)
- `text_excerpt_long.htmlf` (content include)
- `ordered_list.htmlf`

ACME ISP, Round 3: Adding Leading-Edge Features

Now that Acme ISP has a serviceable, workable site, why not try to add a few bells and whistles to the basic performance? This section outlines an experiment Sarah Smith did to add DHTML functionality to the navigation bar of the site.

Why Build the Site

Sarah's happy with her site, but she wants to pull it kicking and screaming into the world of DHTML. Her contact at Acme ISP has given her a short leash, so she's got to figure out how to incorporate her newly-acquired JavaScript abilities into a site that her client is already happy with.

What Development Decisions Were Made

Sarah elected to do only two new things: She modified the code for the site so that each element had its own style-sheeted block-level container, and she attached a slide-in, slide-out function to the navigation bar.

She figured that so long as something as integral as site navigation was tied to a specific technology, she might as well pull the entire site layout into 4.0 standards and abandon tables as layout devices in favor of style-sheeted <div>s. Sarah didn't do this just because she's a devout believer in HTML standards: She also reasoned that converting all her includes to self-contained <div>s would allow her to add further scripts across the site if the need arose.

Since she will be running the entire DHTML-converted site as a proposal for her boss as a trial suggestion, Sarah is going to forgo worrying about compatibility issues with lower-end browsers. This is an experiment for her to see how well she can translate her design into DHTML.

The Scope and Technical Requirements for the Site

The technical parameters required of users were raised when the DHTML navigation was introduced. Because the navigation bar's functionality relies on a browser that can read and render scripted events, and because every item on the page is placed according to a position specified in a style sheet, the Acme ISP pages wouldn't work on anything less than Netscape 4.0 or Internet Explorer 4.0.

Sarah built the sites using Netscape Navigator and Microsoft Internet Explorer as her benchmark software, because those two browsers still make up at least 85 percent of the market according to September 1998 survey conducted by IGD. In order for the navigation to be incorporated into the existing site, the DHTML had to meet the following criteria:

- The code had to be portable, meaning it could easily be extracted from a page without affecting the rest of the page.

- The code had to work reliably across both dominant browser packages.

- The code had to be easy to understand, in case Sarah had to hand the site off to another contractor.

Keeping this in mind, Sarah experimented with JavaScript until she found code that would move a <div> back and forth on a user's mouse gesture, then retrofitted the existing Acme site with the new code. Assuming her boss likes the extended functionality and wants her to take it live, she may go back and find a way to serve pages based on browser capabilities. For now, she's assuming that the DHTML experiment is a small-scale effort.

How This Site Differs from the Earlier Site

There are two differences between this site and its prior incarnation, but they're only apparent on the backend.

First, there are no more tabled layouts for low-end browsers; the entire site is done in <DIV>s.

The old layout was pulled together by tabling discrete elements:

```
<table width="600">
<tr>
<td rowspan="6">
<!--#include virtual="nav.htmlf" -->
</td>
</tr>
<!--insert the row where the brand goes-->
<td>
<img src="../images/brand.gif" alt="[acme isp]" width="400" height="73"
border="0">
<p> </p>
</td>
</tr>

<tr>
<!--insert the div for the individual page title-->
<td>
<!--#include virtual="subhead.htmlf" -->
<p> </p>
</td>
</tr>

<tr>
<!--insert a blue rule 'cause it looks cool-->
<td bgcolor="#003366">
<img height="2" width="400" src="../images/spacer.gif" alt="...">
</td>
</tr>

<tr>
```

```
<!--now insert the content-->
<td>
<!--#include virtual="content.htmlf" -->
</td>
</tr>

<tr>
<!--the ad div goes here-->
<td>
<!--#include virtual="ad.htmlf" -->
</td>
</tr>

<tr>
<!--the copyright div-->
<td>
Copyright &copy; 1998, Acme ISP. For more information, <a
href="../us/aboutus.html">go here</a>.
</td>
</tr>
</table>
```

This new layout assigns each of the elements their own block-level container, and treats them as discrete items occupying the same browser window. So instead of relying on the grid set up by the table, the <div>s all have their own coordinates, listed below:

```
<html>

<head>

<title>Welcome to ACME ISP</title>

<!--insert stylesheet-->
<style type="text/css">
<!--//
A:link   {font-family: helvetica, arial, sans serif; font-weight:bold;
color:#990000; font-size:10px;}
A:visited   {position: absolute; font-family: helvetica, arial, sans
serif; color:#003366; font-size:10px;}
```

```
body    {background-color:#FFFFFF; color:#333333; font-family:helvetica,
arial; font-size:10px; line-height:12px;}
//-->
</style>

<!--insert any scripts-->

<body>
<!--insert the div where the nav bar goes. -->
<div id="nav" style="position:absolute; z-index:40; left:0; top:0;
width:175px; height:600px; background-image:url(../images/nav_bg.gif);
background-color:#6699FF; font-family:helvetica, arial; color:#990000;
font-weight:bold; font-size:14px; line-height:21px;margin:10px; ">
<p> </p>
<p><a href="../services/corporate.html"><span style="font-size:14px;
font-weight:heavy;">CORPORATE ACCOUNTS</span></a></p>
<p> </p>
<p><a href="../services/personal.html"><span style="font-size:14px;
font-weight:heavy;">PERSONAL ACCOUNTS</span></a></p>
<p> </p>
<p><a href="../services/domain.html"><span style="font-size:14px; font-
weight:heavy;">WEB HOSTING</span></a></p>
<p> </p>
<p><a href="../services/bandwidth.html"><span style="font-size:14px;
font-weight:heavy;">BANDWIDTH LEASING</span></a></p>
<p> </p>
<p><a href="../buy/web.html"><span style="font-size:14px; font-
weight:heavy;">ORDER NOW!</span></a></p>
<p> </p>
<p><a href="../help/contact.html"><span style="font-size:14px; font-
weight:heavy;">NEED HELP?</span></a></p>
<p> </p>
<p><a href="../us/contact.html"><span style="font-size:14px; font-
weight:heavy;">CONTACT US</span></a></p>
<p> </p>
<p><a href="../us/aboutus.html"><span style="font-size:14px; font-
weight:heavy;">ABOUT US</span></a></p>
<p> </p>
</div>
```

```html
<!--insert the div where the brand goes-->
<div id="brand" style="position:absolute; z-index:70; top:55px;
left:175px; width:400px; height:75px; border-style:solid; border-
color:#FFFFFF; border:1px;">
<img src="../images/brand.gif" alt="[acme isp]" width="400" height="73"
border="0">
</div>

<!--insert the div for the individual page title-->
<div id="subhead" style="position:absolute; z-index:50; left:175;
top:105px; width:400px; height:75px; border-style:solid; border-
color:#FFFFFF; border:1px;">
<img src="../images/about_subhead.gif" width="400" height="50"
border="0">
</div>

<!--insert a blue rule 'cause it looks cool-->
<div id="blue" style="position:absolute; z-index:50; left:175;
top:126px; width:400px; height:2px; border-style:solid; border-
color:#003366; border:1px; background-color:#003366;">
</div>

<!--now insert the content-->
<div id="content" style="position:absolute; z-index:40; left:180;
top:135px; width:395px; height:100%; background-color:#FFFFFF; border-
style:solid; border-color:#FFFFFF; border:1px; margin: 10px;">
<p>
Content goes here
</p>
</div>
<!--the ad div goes here-->
<div id="ad" style="position:absolute; z-index:50; left:180; top:600px;
width:468px; height:60px; border-style:solid; border-color:#FFFFFF;
border:1px;">
<img src="../../../general/ad-banner.gif" alt="[468x60 banner]"
width="468" height="60" border="0">
</div>

<!--the copyright div-->
```

```
<div id="copyright" style="position:absolute; z-index:50; left:175;
top:675px; width:400px; height:30px; border-style:solid; border-
color:#FFFFFF; border:1px; background-color:#FFFFFF;">
Copyright &copy; 1998, Acme ISP. For more information, <a
href="../us/aboutus.html">go here</a>.
</div>
</body>
</html>
```

Sarah also added style sheets in the head of the document to control the behavior of all the text in the document. Since style sheets are meant to cascade, meaning one works on top of the other, this means that any separate text formatting must be called out specifically within the document, which she did do for the links in the navigation section:

```
<p><a href="../services/personal.html"><span style="font-size:14px;
font-weight:heavy;">PERSONAL ACCOUNTS</span></a></p>
```

Sarah also got rid of the background graphic and assigned it to the <div> that holds the sliding navigation bar:

```
<div id="nav" style="position:absolute; z-index:40; left:0; top:0;
width:175px; height:600px; background-image:url(../images/nav_bg.gif);
background-color:#6699FF; font-family:helvetica, arial; color:#990000;
font-weight:bold; font-size:14px; line-height:21px;margin:10px; ">
```

Second, the nav bar she revamped in the last round of site improvement is now a sliding navigation bar, thus freeing up more real estate for the site content.

Here's what the JavaScript for the slide-out menu looks like.

slide_menu.html

```
<script language=javascript>

function animate(onOrOff) {
    if (onOrOff == 1) {
        button.mouseIn = 1;
        timer = window.setTimeout("moveButton(1);", 0, "JavaScript");
    } else {
        button.mouseIn = 0;
        timer = window.setTimeout("moveButton(0);", 0, "JavaScript");
    }
}
```

```
function moveButton(onOrOff) {
    if (onOrOff == 1 && button.mouseIn == 1) {
        if (button.style.posLeft < 0) {
            button.style.posLeft = button.style.posLeft + 10;
            timer = window.setTimeout("moveButton(1);", 0,
"JavaScript");
        }
    } else {
        if (button.mouseIn == 0 && button.style.posLeft > -200) {
            button.style.posLeft = button.style.posLeft - 10;
            timer = window.setTimeout("moveButton(0);", 0,
"JavaScript");
        }
    }
}
</script>
```

And here's a line-by-line commented breakdown of how it works:

```
<SCRIPT language=javascript>

//this function determines the state of the //layer called in the
function. The layer
//is named "button," the value 0 is the //hidden state, and the value 1
is the showing //state.
//this function says, "if the state is 0 //pass the value 0 to the
moveButton function.
//if the state id 1, pass that value to the //moveButton function."
function animate(onOrOff) {
    if (onOrOff == 1) {
        button.mouseIn = 1;
        timer = window.setTimeout("moveButton(1);", 0, "JavaScript");
    } else {
        button.mouseIn = 0;
        timer = window.setTimeout("moveButton(0);", 0, "JavaScript");
    }
}

//this function is what moves the meu div in and out depending on mouse
cue.
//If you jump down to the HTML, you'll notice that the numbers one and
zero
```

```
//play a big role: mouseIn=0 onMouseOver=animate(1)
//onMouseOut=animate(0)
//this is to cue this function: if mouseIn = 1, then move the function
out; if
//mouseIn=0, then move the function in.
function moveButton(onOrOff) {
    if (onOrOff == 1 && button.mouseIn == 1) {
        if (button.style.posLeft < 0) {
            button.style.posLeft = button.style.posLeft + 10;
            timer = window.setTimeout("moveButton(1);", 0,
"JavaScript");
        }
    } else {
        if (button.mouseIn == 0 && button.style.posLeft > -200) {
            button.style.posLeft = button.style.posLeft - 10;
            timer = window.setTimeout("moveButton(0);", 0,
"JavaScript");
        }
    }
}
```

```
</SCRIPT>
```

How Site Templates Were Built and Modified for Daily Production

Instead of the navigation bar being part of the site's tabled layout, Sarah included it as a <div> titled "button." Then she set up a style sheet to specify the beginning point for "button" and a position for "button" relative to the rest of the site, and she enclosed the navigation bar in that <div>.

This affected the shell document that specifies all the components on the page. If Sarah's experiment takes off, she'll end up adding the JavaScript and style sheet to all of the shell files for each individual address on the site (an address being http://www.acmeisp.com/service/corp.html), and reformatting the shell files to accommodate the new method of laying out site elements.

However, Sarah's goal is to easily transition her existing collection of modular site components into this new page layout structure. Fortunately, this is easy: All the includes are well-formed and valid, meaning that any open tags get closed in the same file, and the HTML can be integrated into any block-level container. Her original template looked like this:

```
<html>

<head>

<title>Welcome to ACME ISP</title>

<!--insert stylesheet-->
<style type="text/css">
<!--//
A:link       {font-family: helvetica, arial, sans serif; font-
weight:bold; color:#990000; font-size:10px;}
A:visited    {position: absolute; font-family: helvetica, arial, sans
serif; color:#003366; font-size:10px;}
body {background-color:#FFFFFF; color:#333333; font-family:helvetica,
arial; font-size:10px; line-height:12px;}
//-->
</style>

<!--insert any scripts-->

<body>
<!--insert the div where the nav bar goes. -->
<div id="nav" style="position:absolute; z-index:40; left:0; top:0;
width:175px; height:600px; background-image:url(../images/nav_bg.gif);
background-color:#6699FF; font-family:helvetica, arial; color:#990000;
font-weight:bold; font-size:14px; line-height:21px;margin:10px; ">
<p> </p>
<p><a href="../services/corporate.html"><span style="font-size:14px;
font-weight:heavy;">CORPORATE ACCOUNTS</span></a></p>
<p> </p>
<p><a href="../services/personal.html"><span style="font-size:14px;
font-weight:heavy;">PERSONAL ACCOUNTS</span></a></p>
<p> </p>
<p><a href="../services/domain.html"><span style="font-size:14px; font-
weight:heavy;">WEB HOSTING</span></a></p>
<p> </p>
<p><a href="../services/bandwidth.html"><span style="font-size:14px;
font-weight:heavy;">BANDWIDTH LEASING</span></a></p>
<p> </p>
```

```
<p><a href="../buy/web.html"><span style="font-size:14px; font-
weight:heavy;">ORDER NOW!</span></a></p>
<p> </p>
<p><a href="../help/contact.html"><span style="font-size:14px; font-
weight:heavy;">NEED HELP?</span></a></p>
<p> </p>
<p><a href="../us/contact.html"><span style="font-size:14px; font-
weight:heavy;">CONTACT US</span></a></p>
<p> </p>
<p><a href="../us/aboutus.html"><span style="font-size:14px; font-
weight:heavy;">ABOUT US</span></a></p>
<p> </p>
</div>

<!--insert the div where the brand goes-->
<div id="brand" style="position:absolute; z-index:70; top:55px;
left:175px; width:400px; height:75px; border-style:solid; border-
color:#FFFFFF; border:1px;">
<img src="../images/brand.gif" alt="[acme isp]" width="400" height="73"
border="0">
</div>

<!--insert the div for the individual page title-->
<div id="subhead" style="position:absolute; z-index:50; left:175;
top:105px; width:400px; height:75px; border-style:solid; border-
color:#FFFFFF; border:1px;">
<img src="../images/about_subhead.gif" width="400" height="50"
border="0">
</div>

<!--insert a blue rule 'cause it looks cool-->
<div id="blue" style="position:absolute; z-index:50; left:175;
top:126px; width:400px; height:2px; border-style:solid; border-
color:#003366; border:1px; background-color:#003366;">
</div>

<!--now insert the content-->
<div id="content" style="position:absolute; z-index:40; left:180;
top:135px; width:395px; height:100%; background-color:#FFFFFF; border-
style:solid; border-color:#FFFFFF; border:1px; margin: 10px;">
<p>
```

Living away from the folks has many benefits, but the one immediately
<a href="#">apparent drawback</a> is that I now have to compete with
roughly 5000 people for the washers and dryers in my building. This has
meant two things: I have had to get over my long-standing belief that
laundry can be done as you sleep sweetly, and I have had to adjust my
schedule so I can do laundry before the overzealous apartment manager
locks the laundry room for the night.
</p><p>
On an <a href="#">abstract level</a> - the same level that discusses
"society's" problems and all that - I understand why the laundry room
must be locked. Evil, sick people are in the habit of dragging innocent
victims back into unlocked laundry rooms late at night and doing things
best left unmentioned. To prevent these hideously deranged people from
perpetrating their crimes here, the laundry room must be locked.
</p><p>
But for those of us who are insomniacs, or who believe that it never
kills garments to let them tumble-dry overnight, this whole "safety"
thing is inconvenient. And since I'm the one likely to be most affected
by any sick perverts in the laundry room late at night, what with
proximity being a strong argument since it means the perv won't have
far to drag my lifeless body, I think that anyone who's willing to take
that chance should be able to do <a href="#">perilous late-night
laundry</a>.
</p>
</div>
<!--the ad div goes here-->
<div id="ad" style="position:absolute; z-index:50; left:180; top:600px;
width:468px; height:60px; border-style:solid; border-color:#FFFFFF;
border:1px;">
<img src="../../../general/ad-banner.gif" alt="[468x60 banner]"
width="468" height="60" border="0">
</div>

<!--the copyright div-->
<div id="copyright" style="position:absolute; z-index:50; left:175;
top:675px; width:400px; height:30px; border-style:solid; border-
color:#FFFFFF; border:1px; background-color:#FFFFFF;">
Copyright © 1998, Acme ISP. For more information, <a
href="../us/aboutus.html">go here</a>.
</div>
</body>
</html>

After she stripped out the different modular parts, Sarah had the following files for easy site assembly:

```
<html>

<head>

<title>Welcome to ACME ISP</title>

<!--insert stylesheet-->
<style type="text/css">
<!--//
A:link        {font-family: helvetica, arial, sans serif; font-
weight:bold; color:#990000; font-size:10px;}
A:visited     {position: absolute; font-family: helvetica, arial, sans
serif; color:#003366; font-size:10px;}
body {background-color:#FFFFFF; color:#333333; font-family:helvetica,
arial; font-size:10px; line-height:12px;}
//-->
</style>

<!--insert any scripts-->

<body>
<!--insert the div where the nav bar goes. -->
<div id="nav" style="position:absolute; z-index:40; left:0; top:0;
width:175px; height:600px; background-image:url(../images/nav_bg.gif);
background-color:#6699FF; font-family:helvetica, arial; color:#990000;
font-weight:bold; font-size:14px; line-height:21px;margin:10px; ">
<!--#include virtual="nav.htmlf" -->
</div>

<!--insert the div where the brand goes-->
<div id="brand" style="position:absolute; z-index:70; top:55px;
left:175px; width:400px; height:75px; border-style:solid; border-
color:#FFFFFF; border:1px;">
<img src="../images/brand.gif" alt="[acme isp]" width="400" height="73"
border="0">
</div>

<!--insert the div for the individual page title-->
```

```
<div id="subhead" style="position:absolute; z-index:50; left:175;
top:105px; width:400px; height:75px; border-style:solid; border-
color:#FFFFFF; border:1px;">
<!--#include virtual="subhead.htmlf" -->
</div>

<!--insert a blue rule 'cause it looks cool-->
<div id="blue" style="position:absolute; z-index:50; left:175;
top:126px; width:400px; height:2px; border-style:solid; border-
color:#003366; border:1px; background-color:#003366;">
</div>

<!--now insert the content-->
<div id="content" style="position:absolute; z-index:40; left:180;
top:135px; width:395px; height:100%; background-color:#FFFFFF; border-
style:solid; border-color:#FFFFFF; border:1px; margin: 10px;">
<!--#include virtual="content.htmlf" -->
</div>
<!--the ad div goes here-->
<div id="ad" style="position:absolute; z-index:50; left:180; top:600px;
width:468px; height:60px; border-style:solid; border-color:#FFFFFF;
border:1px;">
<!--#include virtual="ad.htmlf" -->
</div>

<!--the copyright div-->
<div id="copyright" style="position:absolute; z-index:50; left:175;
top:675px; width:400px; height:30px; border-style:solid; border-
color:#FFFFFF; border:1px; background-color:#FFFFFF;">
<!--#include virtual="copyright.htmlf" -->

</div>
</body>
</html>
```

All she had to do to re-assemble the page is drop in the style-free, valid chunks of HTML she created in the last round of site revision: subhead.htmlf, nav.htmlf, content.htmlf, ad.htmlf, and copyright.htmlf.

The final look of the site won't be any different than in round 2, other than the sliding nav bar. Figure 10.4 shows both versions (with the nav bar and without).

FIGURE 10.4:

The final version of the site, including a sliding nav bar

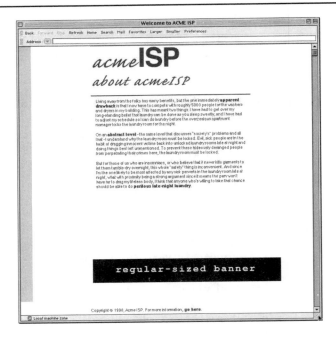

The Source Code

Again, the source files (available on the companion CD-ROM) are:

- `index.html`
- `fax.html`
- `phone.html`
- `web.html`
- `dialin.html`
- `install.html`
- `tech.html`
- `using.html`
- `bandwidth.html`
- `corporate.html`
- `domain.html`
- `personal.html`
- `web_business.html`
- `web_personal.html`
- `aboutus.html`
- `contact.html`

And the include files are:

- `subhead.htmlf`
- `nav.htmlf`
- `ad.htmlf`
- `copyright.htmlf`
- `Linked_list.htmlf` (content include)
- `form_sample.htmlf` (content include)
- `text_excerpt_short.htmlf` (content include)
- `text_excerpt_long.htmlf` (content include)
- `ordered_list.htmlf`

Constants for the Entire Site-Development Process

Although this site went through three incarnations, there were a lot of site development factors that stayed constant from site to site. The two factors Sarah dealt with every time were the Acme ISP style guide, and the QA process for checking the site. Each of these is discussed in more detail below.

Style Guide

Although Acme ISP went through distinct redesigns, the color scheme and markup formatting for the content stayed basically the same from site to site, which greatly eased the upgrading effort for Sarah. Whenever you build a site for a client, a site that you may not be directly maintaining, or a site that you maintain or upgrade only sporadically, it's a good idea to write down any style guidelines that you use to preserve the site's structure or look. The specific items in Acme ISP's style guide are all listed below.

Color Guide

The ACME ISP site relies on a blue and red scheme to preserve its all-American look and feel. The red is #990000 (153-0-0 in RGB values), and the blue is #003366 (0-51-102). In order to highlight the navigation area without overwhelming the page, she washed out the blue to 20-percent opacity in Photoshop. The resulting values were not browser-safe, so Sarah made a 1 pixel GIF, dithered it to 4 bits per pixel for optimum size and reproduction across different platforms, then used it as a background image for the table cell/div that envelopes the navigation area. The background color is white (#FFFFFF in hex value and 255-255-255 in rgb), and the text is dark gray (#333333 in hex value and 51-51-51 in rgb).

Top-Level Headlines

All of these are graphics and they're all dithered down to 4 bits per pixel. All graphics are made in colors from the browser-safe palette, and those colors are the same as the red and blue we use for the body links. All graphics also have descriptive ALT tags, and the height and width values are listed as well.

Subheads

All subheads are denoted with H2, and the following style sheet designation:

```
{color:#003366; font-weight:bold; font-family:helvetica, arial, sans-
serif; font-size:24px; line-height:30px;}
```

Body Text

The style sheet for the body text is:

```
font-family:helvetica, arial; font-size:10px; line-height:12px;
```

Items in a Series/Items in a List

There are two formats for these: unordered lists and definition lists. The archive entries are all definition lists. The unordered lists are saved for brief summaries on index pages. Neither list method has a specific style; they inherit the body text style. All of the tags are standard HTML tags, with no special formatting.

Images

All of the images stick to the browser-safe color palette. The images are dithered down to a 4 bit/pixel palette. All subsequent images should be as lightweight.

QA Process

You should never post a site without checking to see how it works. Here are the steps Sarah took in cleaning up this site. Take note—this applies to you too!

Validate the HTML. This is easy to do, and can teach you a lot about "good" HTML coding practices. You can elect to validate a document one of two ways:

- Include a doc-type declaration at the top of your document. These declarations look like this:

```
<!DOCTYPE HTML PUBLIC "-//W3C//DTD HTML 4.0//EN"
"http://www.w3.org/TR/REC-html40/strict.dtd">
<!DOCTYPE HTML PUBLIC "-//W3C//DTD HTML 4.0 Transitional//EN"
"http://www.w3.org/TR/REC-html40/loose.dtd">
<!DOCTYPE HTML PUBLIC "-//W3C//DTD HTML 4.0 Frameset//EN"
"http://www.w3.org/TR/REC-html40/frameset.dtd">
```

You only need to pick one. Then, enter the URL of the page you wish to validate at `http://validator.w3.org/`. Your page must be publicly accessible from a Web server—no checking pages that live only on your desktop or on a password-protected server.

- If you don't think this is a feasible step for your site, you can put an include like this into the bottom of all your files:

```
<div id="check"><a href="http://validator.w3.org/check/referer"
class="offsite">Check this page</a>
```

This sends a query to the validator at `http://validator.w3.org/`, querying a specific site.

Check the sites across different browsers. It never hurts to look at a site on at least four different browser/platform combinations:

1. Netscape 4.*x*/Mac

2. IE 4.*x*/Mac

3. Netscape 4.*x*/Windows

4. IE 4.*x*/Windows

Since the sites is being targeted for lower-end browsers, it was also checked against these browsers:

1. Netscape 3.*x*/Mac

2. IE 3.*x*/Mac

3. Netscape 3.*x*/Windows

4. IE 3.*x*/Windows

After you've checked to make sure the HTML is consistent from browser to browser, check to see how the site loads with the images off. Then, dump your browser cache and time how fast the page loads with and without images.

Once your site looks consistently lovely across all the different platforms, and loads relatively quickly, you're set to publish it.

Summary

This section showed you one site that moved through three distinct stages: initial building, revision, and modification of the revised design. In each distinct site mode, you saw the pragmatic production decisions our case-study heroine made, and you saw how those decisions altered previous code.

One of the over-arching themes that ran through all three site iterations was this: You can never be too lazy (also known as "efficient") when it comes to re-using code. For example, in order to prevent having to re-code her entire template parts library when she moved from a tables-driven layout to a <div>-driven site, Sarah had already built out all her site components as strictly formatted chunks that could easily be repurposed. She anticipated site development by asking herself what parts of the site she would need to use over and over.

Anticipation and laziness are two of the greatest attributes any site developer can possess. Once you've busted your tail picking up all the skills on how to build a site properly, use those skills intelligently to prevent having to re-do your work in the future. Recycling code is healthy for your mental environment.

PART III

Moving from Static to Dynamic Website Production

Applying the Document Object Model (DOM) to Your Site

■ Understanding object models

■ Breaking your site apart

■ Putting your new and improved site back together

Now that you know about XML and the rest of the metadata gang, you're ready to rewrite your site and stride boldly forth into the brave new world of data models.

That is, you'll be ready as soon as you find the time to rewrite your site. W3C-approved standards are excellent resources for understanding what software developers were thinking when they put together the latest browser, and they're perfect for explaining the underlying reasons behind such mysteries as why tables never look perfect on the first try. But they are often tricky to implement in real life.

This chapter is a bridge between the last 30 pages of standards and data models and the next ten chapters of how-tos. This chapter is going to tell you everything you need to know to start thinking of your site as a dynamic data collection instead of a series of facts stored in discrete files.

We'll start with how you and your browser should think of individual documents, then we'll move up to how to think of the site itself. Next, we'll break down all the work you just did in Part II and put it back together in a new and improved data-driven model.

Thinking Like a Web Browser: Viewing a Document as an Object Model

Your browser thinks of every document it sees as a collection of *objects*. This is because browsers operate on an object model, meaning that there's a set of specific rules that describe what can live in a browser and what sort of attributes the residents of the browser can have. Those specific rules, plus the items that live in the browser, comprise an *object model*.

The benefits of an object model are simple and powerful: By making everything in the browser part of an object model, you have a label for each discrete item. Those items also have properties, or traits. So you can write markup code that outlines different object relationships. You can also write scripts that manipulate objects.

Thinking of your website in terms of objects is exactly what you have to do when you move from a static site to a database-driven site. Therefore, start by thinking of an individual page or document in your browser the same way a browser does: Look at each page as a collection of objects rather than as one big object.

WARNING   Netscape Navigator and Microsoft Internet Explorer don't think of a document in the same way. But they do share a little common ground.

The Common Ground between Microsoft Internet Explorer and Netscape Navigator

Both Navigator and IE look at object models as being composed of a browser window (e.g., the big thing with changing content) and an array of basic objects contained within the window, as shown in Figure 11.1. When a browser implements the DOM, it does so on a page-by-page basis. Therefore, when I'm talking about the object models, I'm going to refer to the browser-eye view. Because the window contains the object, it's referred to as the *parent*; the objects are called *children*.

FIGURE 11.1:

The Document Object Model

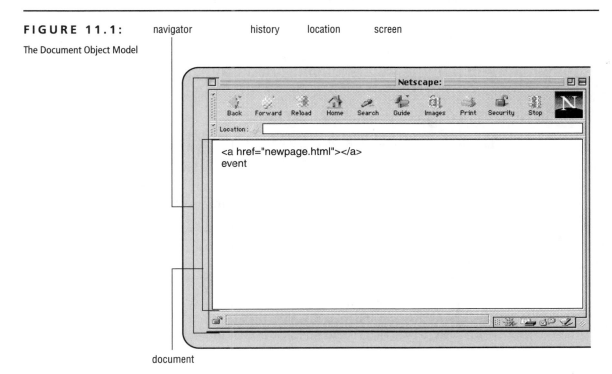

The child objects of the window are the following:

The document object   The file in the browser window. Because this chapter is about applying the Document Object Model to your site at large, we'll discuss the document object in more detail later.

The event object   The object that adds action. It provides a beginning point (state) of an object and offers a scripting "hook" to change that beginning status.

The history object   The previously visited URLs are all stored in this object.

The location object   The network address of the document currently in the window. Also known as the "you are here" attribute.

The navigator object   Tells the window what browser application is open and is viewing the document in the window. Even IE calls it the navigator object, as part of an effort to maintain consistency between the two Document Object Models.

The screen object   Tells the window what the screen resolution and capabilities for display are. The screen object is a big player in DHTML, especially if your focus is on visually tweaking a site's presentation.

Where Navigator and IE Differ

There is an old saying, "The devil is in the details," and it holds true with this section too. IE and Navigator's DOMs differ in several ways.

The first is the way that groups of objects are organized. The IE DOM calls groups of objects *collections*; Navigator calls groups of objects *arrays*.

TIP   This semantic difference is useful to remember when writing scripts or looking through documentation.

The second noticeable difference is the number of items in the each of the browsers' DOMs and the roles that they play. Figure 11.2 displays the two DOMs next to each other; read on to view their differences item by item.

FIGURE 11.2:

Contrasting and comparing
the two DOMs

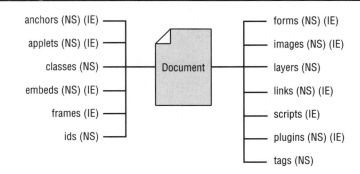

The other significant difference is Netscape's inclusion—and Microsoft's exclusion—of the layers tag in the DOM. Netscape has a more inclusive interpretation of what belongs in the DOM. IE, on the other hand, prefers to attach styles to documents in code syntax.

The result for you? A lot of allowances for syntax whenever you try to write cross-platform DHTML. To that end, I've included a few workarounds in Chapter 14.

NOTE   DHTML, or Dynamic Hypertext Markup Language, is a Web development technique that combines client-side scripting, the Document Object Model, and Cascading Style Sheets (CSS) to build sites that can change after the files have loaded into the browser. This is a departure from websites that depended on server-side pushes to update a page's appearance or data after a user performs an action on the page.

Moving from Theory to Practice: Applying the DOM to Your Site

The reason the DOM has received so much attention is that it provides site developers with a perfect framework for moving their website from a collection of static, templated pages to a browser-based application.

This paradigm shift is relevant even if you host a site that focuses on text, like an e-zine or another Web counterpart to a print publication. In thinking of your website as a browser-based application, what you're doing is shifting your time and attention from building sites that were merely marked up to approximate a user interface, to sites that can offer features that *extend* the user interface.

Consider this: A book offers users the ability to flip forward or backward while maintaining the current page via a bookmark or strategically-placed finger. Desktop software programs let you drag, drop, cut, and paste data. Both the book and the user desktop operate within certain medium-specific parameters: Books have pages and they turn in a given direction. Desktop software programs usually arrange menu bars and pull-down menus in places that users reflexively mouse to, like the upper-left corner of the user interface.

On the Web, the browser application provides a type of shell interface: Users can manipulate the browser to control the appearance of the pages within or specify what sites they want to access. However, there is very little in the way of user interface on many websites. Until the emergence of the DOM, neither developers nor users had the tools to manipulate the data within.

Clearly, a tool for imposing parameters on a website is necessary. Why? If you're going to present information, or tools for manipulating information to a wide audience, you have to make your site easy to understand for anyone who stumbles onto it without any prior knowledge. Setting limits on the behaviors that your users will be able to execute, and defining clear parameters on the routines or editorial paths a user can take ultimately make the site more comprehensible to the user.

Because the DOM provides a structured scheme for labeling data items and specifying rules of behavior for those data items, it's a first step toward giving developers a tool for true user interface work.

The DOM spells out what specific data objects are, and what sort of behaviors can happen around and to these objects. In terms of site development, the DOM sets up the rules for how scripts reference different elements within a document; how scripts can alter or install specific attributes on different elements in a document; and what specific attributes may or may not be applied to elements in a document.

More plainly put, the DOM provides the vocabulary for identifying objects, slapping style-sheeted attributes on each object, and using JavaScript to change those styles on a user cue. Because DHTML, or database-driven site assembly, can be daunting if viewed one page file at a time, the DOM also makes your life easier by giving you the means to write sitewide behaviors. Remember: Your goal is to do as little work as possible in the long run.

Breaking Your Site Apart

In Part II, you did your best to assemble a site that works well and is easy to maintain. Now it's time to take that site apart. Don't worry—we'll put it back together in the next section. But the purpose of this section is to show you how you can map your site onto the DOM and begin taking the steps toward developing a website *cum* application instead of a collection of pages under one domain.

With luck, you've already done half of the work without realizing it. If you've moved your site production process to template-plus-content assembly, the foundation is in place for mapping out your site according to the DOM.

Start at the document level—in this case, the specific, unique file at the end of a URL. Each file is made up of this basic structure:

```
<HTML>
<HEAD></HEAD>
<BODY></BODY>
</HTML>
```

with the really interesting stuff happening between the <BODY> tags.

The <BODY> tags serve a very important purpose: They bookend the document object. In other words, a file with only the code mentioned up top is a valid document, since it has both the requisite <HTML> and <HEAD> tags, and the <BODY> tags that the browser interprets as the "container" for the document. According to the DOM, everything within the <BODY> tags can be broken down into child objects branching off from the document object.

An HTML page with real code in it can be broken down into a document object and a series of child objects branching off the document. Here's one example.

Chocolate1.html

```
<HTML>
<HEAD></HEAD>
<BODY>
<H1>Chocolate: the Sixth Basic Food Group</H1>
<P>
This paragraph extols the virtue of chocolate as a valuable part of a
balanced diet. It will lead in to explanations of how to integrate
chocolate into your daily routine.
</P>
```

```
<H2>Chocolate: the Breakfast Food</H2>
<P>
This paragraph lists all the different breakfast options for chocolate,
including mochas, pop-tarts, and the half-melted candy bar you found in
your car as you were driving to work.
</P>
<P>
This paragraph gives a recipe for chocolate-chip buckwheat pancakes for
all the folks at home concerned about their fiber.
</P>
<H2>The Chocolate Generation</H2>
<P>
<IMG align=left alt="[brownies]" src="brownie.gif">This paragraph
talks about all the portable chocolate options for people who claim
they're too busy to eat properly. If anyone is going to take chocolate
seriously as a food group, they need to make allowances for it in
their diet.
</P>
</BODY>
</HTML>
```

In the source code above, there are seven different objects that are children of the document object: four paragraphs, two subheads, and one headline. In order to make each object accessible to style sheets and scripting, we're going to assign it an ID. The source code for that is below.

Chocolate2.html

```
<HTML>
<HEAD></HEAD>
<BODY>
<H1 name="headline">Chocolate: the Sixth Basic Food Group</H1>
<P name=P0">
This paragraph extols the virtue of chocolate as a valuable part of a
balanced diet. It will lead in to explanations of how to integrate
chocolate into your daily routine.
</P>
<H2 name="subhead0">Chocolate: the Breakfast Food</H2>
<P name="P1">
This paragraph lists all the different breakfast options for chocolate,
including mochas, pop-tarts, and the half-melted candy bar you found in
your car as you were driving to work.
```

```
</P>
<P name="P2">
This paragraph gives a recipe for chocolate-chip buckwheat pancakes for
all the folks at home concerned about their fiber.
</P>
<H2 name="subhead1">The Chocolate Generation</H2>
<P name="P3">
<IMG align=left alt="[brownies]" src="brownie.gif" name="brownie">This
paragraph talks about all the portable chocolate options for people who
claim they're too busy to eat properly. If anyone is going to take
chocolate seriously as a food group, they need to make allowances for
it in their diet.
</P>
</BODY>
</HTML>
```

As you can see, dropping IDs into different child objects isn't terribly difficult, nor will it alter the way the document is rendered in your browser.

By now, you may have noticed that one of the paragraphs has an IMG tag in the middle of it. The IMG is not a child of the document object, but a child of the P3 object. So if you wanted to access the P3 to change the font or set a specific style, you'd call it: document.P3.

If you wanted to access the image via a script or any other syntax that sets behaviors for objects, you'd write: document.P3.brownie.

See how the DOM allows for nesting objects within a document hierarchy? This means it's also applicable to the types of page assembly that you're already doing. If you've got a page like this:

```
<HTML>
<HEAD></HEAD>
<BODY>
<!-#include virtual="doctitle" -->
<!-#include virtual="docnav" -->
<!--# include virtual="doccontent" -->
<!--include virtual="docfooter" -->
</BODY>
</HTML>
```

the HTML objects in every include become child objects of the document in which the include is contained. If the docnav include listed above looked like this:

```
<TABLE width=250 cellspacing=0 cellpadding=0 name="navtable">
```

```
<TR>
<TD valign=top align="left">
<IMG width="250" height="25" alt="[home]" border="0" name="homegif"
src="home.gif">
</TD>
</TR>
<TR>
<TD valign=top align="left">
<IMG width="250" height="25" alt="[sitemap]" border="0" name="mapgif"
src="map.gif">
</TD>
</TR>
<TR>
<TD valign=top align="left">
<IMG width="250" height="25" alt="[search]" border="0" name="searchgif"
src="search.gif">
</TD>
</TR>
</TABLE>
```

you would write the syntax for the navigation table as `document.navtable`; the individual images are called as `document.navtable.napgif`.

Ultimately, document object syntax is determined by the document that the object ultimately ends up being called in, not the physical file where it may reside.

The first two examples listed in this section all list fairly basic HTML, which you probably surpassed long ago. So how do you apply the data-driven, hierarchical labels to sites that may feature embedded tables two or three levels deep, plus font tags instead of heading tags, or any of the other markup kludges that make Web pages look pretty even if they're nonstandard?

To put it more bluntly, where does the single-pixel GIF trick fit into the DOM?

If you follow these guidelines when mapping out your pages to the DOM, you'll be able to solve that sort of dilemma on your own:

- Break down the code on your page into functional chunks. If your headlines look like this:

  ```
  <font face="verdana, arial, helvetica" size="4" color="#FF0099">
  <b>H</b></font><font face="times roman, palatino" size="3"
  color="#000099"><I>eadline</I></font>
  ```

you can drop comments into the source code above and below that mess, reading `<!--start headline--><!--/end headline-->`. These labels will help you to pull out the code later, or find a way to wrap a container for easy handling of the object in scripts.

- Speaking of containers, <DIV> tags are recognized by both Netscape and IE 3.*x* and up. You could elect to wrap a <DIV> tag around the headline mess above as follows:

```
<div id="headline0">
<font face="verdana, arial, helvetica" size="4" color="#FF0099">
<b>H</b></font><font face="times roman, palatino" size="3"
color="#000099"><I>eadline</I></font>
</div>
```

The <DIV> tags provide the same neat separation as the comment tags, but they also provide a handle to which you will attach the headline's unique name. Now you can begin to set up a rough DOM that can serve as a model for every file on your site: document, headline.

- Balance your need to design for late adopters and lower-end users with your need to build a hierarchical site. The primary factor in your decision should be the software with which users are already accessing your site. Because the browsers that support both style sheets and DIV elements are over 1 year old, the HTML available for DOM markup is hardly new.

- You could always move your DOM focus up a level from individual documents to multiple versions of the same document served to the user depending on the user agent that the client sends. If this is the case, the best strategy is to find and identify the common elements in every version (e.g., headlines, content, images, a sitewide navigation bar), and label those elements to maintain consistency between your different document versions. You'll also have to resign yourself to doing one of two things with your lower-bandwidth pages: not fully applying the DOM in order to preserve the appearance of your site, or streamlining the code in your site so the content can be integrated into the DOM.

Once you've tagged discrete and functional chunks of code, take a look at what you have left. If you've got a plethora of single-pixel GIF tricks, ask yourself why they're there. Are they working to provide leading between different paragraphs, or between lines of text? Are you using the GIFs to force table cell size and thus set up margins? All of these style tricks can be grafted onto style sheet specs for the objects they modify.

For example, instead of using tables to set the margins of your page, you could write:

```
<BODY>
<DIV id=wrapper>
<!--put content here-->
</DIV>
</BODY>
```

and set the style of the wrapper object to have a prescribed width. The effect is the same as using a table to specify content width without having to resort to tables.

Or, you could specify padding around individual objects within a document to space the objects evenly. The point is, you've been using tables and single-pixel GIFs to create specific and consistent layouts and now you can stop. Stripping out those extraneous tables and GIFs will clean up your DOM in a hurry.

When you're done, you should have something the DOM shown in Figure 11.3, which corresponds to the Web page shown in Figure 11.4. Your HTML will look like the code shown in MySite1.html.

FIGURE 11.3:

The DOM for a typical Web page

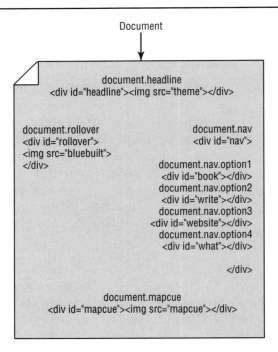

<!-- insert theme here -->

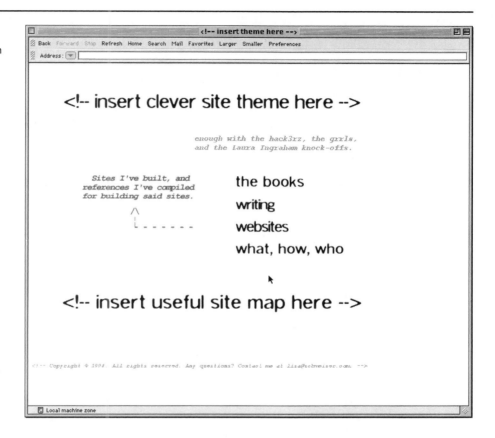

FIGURE 11.4:

The Web page specified in Figure 11.3

MySite1.html

```
<HTML>
<HEAD>
<TITLE>
 s c h m e i s e r.com: sitemap
</TITLE>
<META http-equiv="Content-Type" content="text/html; charset=iso-8859-1">
</HEAD>
<BODY bgcolor="#FFFFFF" text="#000000" alink="#FFFF33" link="#003366"
vlink="#6699CC">
<TABLE width="448" border=0 cellspacing=0 cellpadding=0>
<!--row1-->
```

```
<!-- insert headline -->
<TR>
<TD colspan=4 valign=middle align=right>
<IMG SRC="../IMAGES/sitemap_headline.gif" ALT="[site map]" ALIGN=RIGHT
WIDTH="224" HEIGHT="56" BORDER="0">
</TD>
<TD>
<IMG SRC="../IMAGES/spacer.gif" ALT="[spacer]" ALIGN=LEFT WIDTH="56"
HEIGHT="56" BORDER="0">
</TD>
<TD>
<IMG SRC="../IMAGES/spacer.gif" ALT="[spacer]" ALIGN=LEFT WIDTH="56"
HEIGHT="56" BORDER="0">
</TD>
<TD>
<IMG SRC="../IMAGES/spacer.gif" ALT="[spacer]" ALIGN=LEFT WIDTH="56"
HEIGHT="56" BORDER="0">
</TD>
</TR>
<!--row2-->
<!-- insert content -->
<TR>
<TD>
<IMG SRC="../IMAGES/spacer.gif" ALT="[spacer]" ALIGN=LEFT WIDTH="56"
HEIGHT="56" BORDER="0">
</TD>
<TD>
<IMG SRC="../IMAGES/spacer.gif" ALT="[spacer]" ALIGN=LEFT WIDTH="56"
HEIGHT="56" BORDER="0">
</TD>
<TD>
<IMG SRC="../IMAGES/spacer.gif" ALT="[spacer]" ALIGN=LEFT WIDTH="56"
HEIGHT="56" BORDER="0">
</TD>
<TD valign=top align=middle>
<A HREF="new.html" onMouseOver="(window.status='the latest and greatest
additions to the site'); return true">
<IMG SRC="../IMAGES/new.gif" ALT="[NEW]" ALIGN=MIDDLE WIDTH="56"
HEIGHT="56" BORDER="0">
</A>
</TD>
<TD>
```

```
<IMG SRC="../IMAGES/spacer.gif" ALT="[spacer]" ALIGN=LEFT WIDTH="56"
HEIGHT="56" BORDER="0">
</TD>
<TD valign=top align=left>
<IMG SRC="../IMAGES/left_star.gif" ALIGN=LEFT WIDTH="56" HEIGHT="56"
BORDER="0">
</TD>
<TD>
<IMG SRC="../IMAGES/spacer.gif" ALT="[spacer]" ALIGN=LEFT WIDTH="56"
HEIGHT="56" BORDER="0">
</TD>
</TR>
<!--row3-->
<TR>
<TD>
<IMG SRC="../IMAGES/spacer.gif" ALT="[spacer]" ALIGN=LEFT WIDTH="56"
HEIGHT="56" BORDER="0">
</TD>
<TD>
<IMG SRC="../IMAGES/spacer.gif" ALT="[spacer]" ALIGN=LEFT WIDTH="56"
HEIGHT="56" BORDER="0">
</TD>
<TD colspan=2 valign=middle align=right>
<A HREF="../write/index.html" onMouseOver="(window.status='Click here to
read stuff I wrote'); return true">
<IMG SRC="../IMAGES/write.gif" ALT="[writing]" ALIGN=RIGHT WIDTH="112"
HEIGHT="28" BORDER="0">
</A>
</TD>
<TD>
<IMG SRC="../IMAGES/spacer.gif" ALT="[spacer]" ALIGN=LEFT WIDTH="56"
HEIGHT="56" BORDER="0">
</TD>
<TD valign=top align=right>
<IMG SRC="../IMAGES/right_star.gif" ALIGN=RIGHT WIDTH="56" HEIGHT="56"
BORDER="0">
</TD>
<TD>
<IMG SRC="../IMAGES/spacer.gif" ALT="[spacer]" ALIGN=LEFT WIDTH="56"
HEIGHT="56" BORDER="0">
</TD>
</TR>
```

```
<!--row4-->
<TR>
<TD>
<IMG SRC="../IMAGES/spacer.gif" ALT="[spacer]" ALIGN=LEFT WIDTH="56"
HEIGHT="56" BORDER="0">
</TD>
<TD align=right valign=top colspan=3>
<font size=2>
<A HREF="../write/index.html" onMouseOver="(window.status='Sarcastic,
analytic, never dull'); return true">
Articles and Editorials
</A>
<P>
</P>
<!--A HREF="../WDTS/index.html" onMouseOver="(window.status='Jump-start
your creativity'); return true" -->
<I>
Web Design Templates Sourcebook
</I>
<!--/A-->
<P>
</P>
</font>
</TD>
<!--missing third cell cause of content-->
<!--missing fourth cell cause of content-->
<TD valign=top align=left>
<IMG SRC="../IMAGES/tinystar_flip.gif" ALIGN=LEFT WIDTH="56" HEIGHT="56"
BORDER="0">
</TD>
<TD>
<IMG SRC="../IMAGES/spacer.gif" ALT="[spacer]" ALIGN=LEFT WIDTH="56"
HEIGHT="56" BORDER="0">
</TD>
<TD>
<IMG SRC="../IMAGES/spacer.gif" ALT="[spacer]" ALIGN=LEFT WIDTH="56"
HEIGHT="56" BORDER="0">
</TD>
</TR>
<!--row5-->
<TR>
<TD>
```

```
<IMG SRC="../IMAGES/spacer.gif" ALT="[spacer]" ALIGN=LEFT WIDTH="56"
HEIGHT="56" BORDER="0">
</TD>
<TD colspan=3 valign=middle align=right>
<A HREF="../build/index.html" onMouseOver="(window.status='I do this
stuff so you don\'t have to'); return true">
<IMG SRC="../IMAGES/site.gif" ALT="[site building]" ALIGN=MIDDLE
WIDTH="168" HEIGHT="28" BORDER="0">
</A>
</TD>
<TD>
<IMG SRC="../IMAGES/spacer.gif" ALT="[spacer]" ALIGN=LEFT WIDTH="56"
HEIGHT="56" BORDER="0">
</TD>
<TD valign=bottom align=left>
<IMG SRC="../IMAGES/left_big_star.gif" ALIGN=LEFT WIDTH="56" HEIGHT="56"
BORDER="0">
</TD>
<TD>
<IMG SRC="../IMAGES/spacer.gif" ALT="[spacer]" ALIGN=LEFT WIDTH="56"
HEIGHT="56" BORDER="0">
</TD>
</TR>
<!--row6-->
<TR>
<TD>
<IMG SRC="../IMAGES/spacer.gif" ALT="[spacer]" ALIGN=LEFT WIDTH="56"
HEIGHT="56" BORDER="0">
</TD>
<TD align=right valign=top colspan=3>
<font size=2>
<A HREF="../build/12-step.html" onMouseOver="(window.status='You\'ll be
granted the serenity to accept the browser wars'); return true">
12-step websites:
</A>
addictive site hacks
<P>
</P>
The ultimate
<A HREF="../build/toolbox.html" onMouseOver="(window.status='Shareware,
specs, and more'); return true">
website toolbox
```

```
</A>
<P>
</P>
<A HREF="../build/colophon.html" onMouseOver="(window.status='It\'s
aliiiiiiiiiiiiiiiiiive!'); return true">
Colophon:
</A>
how I built this site
</font>
</TD>
<!--missing third cell cause of content-->
<!--missing fourth cell cause of content-->
<TD>
<IMG SRC="../IMAGES/spacer.gif" ALT="[spacer]" ALIGN=LEFT WIDTH="56"
HEIGHT="56" BORDER="0">
</TD>
<TD>
<IMG SRC="../IMAGES/spacer.gif" ALT="[spacer]" ALIGN=LEFT WIDTH="56"
HEIGHT="56" BORDER="0">
</TD>
<TD valign=top align=left>
<IMG SRC="../IMAGES/tinystar.gif" ALIGN=LEFT WIDTH="56" HEIGHT="56"
BORDER="0">
</TD>
</TR>
<!--row7-->
<TR>
<TD>
<IMG SRC="../IMAGES/spacer.gif" ALT="[spacer]" ALIGN=LEFT WIDTH="56"
HEIGHT="56" BORDER="0">
</TD>
<TD colspan=3 valign=middle align=right>
<A HREF="../misc/index.html" onMouseOver="(window.status='Stuff that
defies categorization'); return true">
<IMG SRC="../IMAGES/odds.gif" ALT="[odds&ends]" ALIGN=MIDDLE WIDTH="168"
HEIGHT="28" BORDER="0">
</A>
</TD>
<TD>
<IMG SRC="../IMAGES/spacer.gif" ALT="[spacer]" ALIGN=LEFT WIDTH="56"
HEIGHT="56" BORDER="0">
</TD>
```

```
<TD>
<IMG SRC="../IMAGES/solid_star.gif" ALIGN=RIGHT WIDTH="56" HEIGHT="56"
BORDER="0">
</TD>
<TD>
<IMG SRC="../IMAGES/spacer.gif" ALT="[spacer]" ALIGN=LEFT WIDTH="56"
HEIGHT="56" BORDER="0">
</TD>
</TR>
<!--row8-->
<TR>
<TD>
<IMG SRC="../IMAGES/spacer.gif" ALT="[spacer]" ALIGN=LEFT WIDTH="56"
HEIGHT="56" BORDER="0">
</TD>
<TD align=right valign=top colspan=3>
<font size=2>
STP: Rights for the families
<BR clear=all>
of murder victims
<P>
</P>
<A HREF="../misc/self.html" onMouseOver="(window.status='Yep, check here
to see whether I\'m a 14-year-old cheerleader from Kansas, or a
400lb.hitman'); return true">
Obligatory personal information
</A>
</font>
</TD>
<!--missing third cell cause of content-->
<!--missing fourth cell cause of content-->
<TD valign=top align=left>
<IMG SRC="../IMAGES/tinystar_flip.gif" ALIGN=LEFT WIDTH="56" HEIGHT="56"
BORDER="0">
</TD>
<TD>
<IMG SRC="../IMAGES/spacer.gif" ALT="[spacer]" ALIGN=LEFT WIDTH="56"
HEIGHT="56" BORDER="0">
</TD>
<TD>
<IMG SRC="../IMAGES/spacer.gif" ALT="[spacer]" ALIGN=LEFT WIDTH="56"
HEIGHT="56" BORDER="0">
```

```
</TD>
</TR>
<!--row9-->
<TR>
<TD>
<IMG SRC="../IMAGES/spacer.gif" ALT="[spacer]" ALIGN=LEFT WIDTH="56"
HEIGHT="56" BORDER="0">
</TD>
<TD>
<IMG SRC="../IMAGES/spacer.gif" ALT="[spacer]" ALIGN=LEFT WIDTH="56"
HEIGHT="56" BORDER="0">
</TD>
<TD colspan=2 align=right valign=center>
<A HREF="../work/resume.html" onMouseOver="(window.status='I build
sites, write copy, do UI/QA'); return true">
<IMG SRC="../IMAGES/hireme.gif" ALT="[hire me]" ALIGN=MIDDLE WIDTH="112"
HEIGHT="28" BORDER="0">
</A>
</TD>
<TD>
<IMG SRC="../IMAGES/spacer.gif" ALT="[spacer]" ALIGN=LEFT WIDTH="56"
HEIGHT="56" BORDER="0">
</TD>
<TD valign=bottom align=right>
<IMG SRC="../IMAGES/left_big_star.gif" ALIGN=LEFT WIDTH="56" HEIGHT="56"
BORDER="0">
</TD>
<TD>
<IMG SRC="../IMAGES/spacer.gif" ALT="[spacer]" ALIGN=LEFT WIDTH="56"
HEIGHT="56" BORDER="0">
</TD>
</TR>
<!--row10-->
<!--insert nav bar -->
<TR>
<TD valign=top align=left colspan=7>
<TABLE width=392 border=0 cellspacing=0 cellpadding=0>
<TR>
<TD valign=bottom align=left colspan=7>
<IMG SRC="../IMAGES/schmeiser.gif" ALT="[schmeiser.com]" ALIGN=BOTTOM
WIDTH="392" HEIGHT="41" BORDER="0">
</TD>
```

```
</TR>
<TR>
<TD valign=top align=left>
<A HREF="http://www.schmeiser.com/content/sitemap.html"
onMouseOver="(window.status='sitemap'); return true">
<IMG SRC="../IMAGES/sitemap_nav.gif" ALT="[sitemap]" ALIGN=BOTTOM
WIDTH="56" HEIGHT="15" BORDER="0">
</A>
</TD>
<TD valign=top align=left>
<A HREF="http://www.schmeiser.com/write/index.html"
onMouseOver="(window.status='writing'); return true">
<IMG SRC="../IMAGES/writing_nav.gif" ALT="[writing]" ALIGN=BOTTOM
WIDTH="56" HEIGHT="15" BORDER="0">
</A>
</TD>
<TD valign=top align=left>
<A HREF="http://www.schmeiser.com/build/index.html"
onMouseOver="(window.status='site building'); return true">
<IMG SRC="../IMAGES/building_nav.gif" ALT="[building]" ALIGN=BOTTOM
WIDTH="56" HEIGHT="15" BORDER="0">
</A>
</TD>
<TD valign=top align=left>
<A HREF="http://www.schmeiser.com/misc/index.html"
onMouseOver="(window.status='odds and ends'); return true">
<IMG SRC="../IMAGES/odds_nav.gif" ALT="[odds&ends]" ALIGN=BOTTOM
WIDTH="56" HEIGHT="15" BORDER="0">
</A>
</TD>
<TD valign=top align=left>
<A HREF="http://www.schmeiser.com/work/resume.html"
onMouseOver="(window.status='r&eacute;sum&eacute;'); return true">
<IMG SRC="../IMAGES/hire_nav.gif" ALT="[hire me]" ALIGN=BOTTOM
WIDTH="56" HEIGHT="15" BORDER="0">
</A>
</TD>
<TD valign=top align=left>
<A HREF="mailto:site@schmeiser.com">
<IMG SRC="../IMAGES/mail_nav.gif" ALT="[mail me]" ALIGN=BOTTOM
WIDTH="56" HEIGHT="15" BORDER="0">
</A>
```

```
</TD>
<TD valign=top align=left>
<IMG SRC="../IMAGES/cright_nav.gif" ALT="[&copy;1998]" ALIGN=BOTTOM
WIDTH="56" HEIGHT="15" BORDER="0">
</TD>
</TR>
</TABLE>
</TD>
</TR>
</TABLE>
</BODY>
</HTML>
```

Astute readers will notice that yes, my old site map page had a lot of tabling. You will also notice that I had three different includes: one for the head, one for the content, and one for the navigation. That means there were two different things going on here:

- I assemble the site via templated parts.

- I have a much different DOM than my HTML indicates.

Can this Web page be saved? Stay tuned, true believers. In the next section, I'll overhaul all this code.

Putting Your Site Back Together

Once you've figured out the hierarchy within your pages and collected all that data in one place, it's time to think of how to reassemble your site so the hierarchy still applies and you can access and reuse as many of the objects as possible.

Before you do, let's stop and recap what you should have done to prep your site for integrating the DOM:

- You should have inventoried the chunks of code, including scripts, server-side includes, and templates, that comprise your site.

- You should have mapped out the logical hierarchies of every object on your page.

NOTE   Remember that the inventory and the logical hierarchy don't have to look alike.

So, using my site map page as a model, Figure 11.5 shows how the new and improved DOM organizes my page.

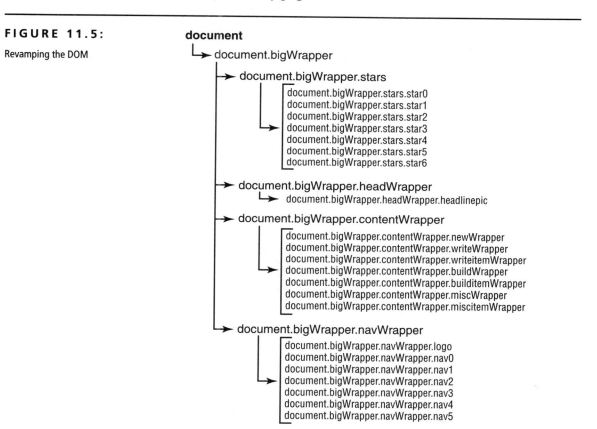

And the source code follows. Of course, there are a lot of changes between the original page and the new, DOM-madeover site. They're listed below:

- I got rid of tables and moved to <di v> tags. Strictly speaking, tables are supposed to be used only to organize data. I used them for the initial layout because HTML 3.2 doesn't offer any other way to hack positioning coordinates onto items. Since I rewrote the page to take advantage of the Document Object Model, I decided to also take advantage of other HTML 4.0 features like style sheet positioning.

- Moving to <div> tags as a way to "wrap" individual items also allows me to set up relationships between items on the page. In the old layout, the document consisted of the <body>, the <table> as a child object of the <body>, and everything else as a child object of the <table>. There was no way to sort items by function, like I did with the document.bigwrapper.navwrapper items. There is also no way to set up a hierarchy. If I wanted to manipulate items on my page according to function, like every star turning yellow on mouse-over, I wouldn't be able to do it as easily.

- I got rid of the spacer graphics. I could do this because they're no longer needed.

- Every item on the page has a name and a style. The style attributes dictate what the item looks like; the name allows you to attach specific styles to it later, or to manipulate the item via script.

- As a result, the page is much lighter. I printed out the before and after code, and the source code dropped from six pages to three. Moreover, it was easier to functionally identify everything after I had moved all the items on the page to a DOM-driven markup.

As for doing the actual work and converting the page from a table-driven layout to a DOM-driven page, once I had done the detective work and figured out what each table cell held, setting up the style sheet attributes for the individual objects was easy. Then I looked at the page, figured out all the functional relationships between the items, and began grouping the individual items by function: all the graphic stars were grouped in one <div>, all the navigation items were grouped in another. I then checked my styles to see what cascaded down from "container" <div> tags like bigwrapper and headwrapper to affect the constituent items. Once I had squared all the styles away, I was done with the page.

MySite2.html

```
<HTML>
<HEAD>
<TITLE>
 s c h m e i s e r.com: sitemap
</TITLE>
<META http-equiv="Content-Type" content="text/html; charset=iso-8859-1">
<STYLE type="text/css">
```

```
.body    {font-family: times new roman; palatino;
         font-size: 12 px;
         font-color:#000000;
         line-height: 13 px
         }


</HEAD>
<BODY bgcolor="#FFFFFF" text="#000000" alink="#FFFF33" link="#003366"
vlink="#6699CC">

<DIV name=bigWrapper style="width:448; position:absolute; top:25; left:25">

<!--insert stars -->
<DIV name=stars style="postion: absolute; top:25; left:350; width:56">

<IMG name="star0" style="position:absolute; left:0; top:0"
SRC="../IMAGES/right_star.gif" ALIGN=RIGHT WIDTH="56" HEIGHT="56"
BORDER="0">

<IMG name="star1" style="position:absolute; left:39; top:60"
SRC="../IMAGES/tinystar_flip.gif" ALIGN=LEFT WIDTH="56" HEIGHT="56"
BORDER="0">

<IMG name="star2" style="position:absolute; left:0; top:120"
SRC="../IMAGES/left_big_star.gif" ALIGN=LEFT WIDTH="56" HEIGHT="56"
BORDER="0">

<IMG name="star3" style="position:absolute; left:39; top:180"
SRC="../IMAGES/tinystar.gif" ALIGN=LEFT WIDTH="56" HEIGHT="56" BORDER="0">

<IMG name="star4" style="position:absolute; left:0; top:240"
SRC="../IMAGES/solid_star.gif" ALIGN=RIGHT WIDTH="56" HEIGHT="56"
BORDER="0">

<IMG name="star5" style="position:absolute; left:39; top:300"
SRC="../IMAGES/tinystar_flip.gif" ALIGN=LEFT WIDTH="56" HEIGHT="56"
BORDER="0">

<IMG name="star6" style="position:absolute; left:0; top:360"
SRC="../IMAGES/left_big_star.gif" ALIGN=LEFT WIDTH="56" HEIGHT="56"
BORDER="0">
```

```
</DIV>
<DIV name=headWrapper style="position:absolute; left:0; top:0; width:224">

<!-- insert headline -->
<IMG NAME="headlinePic" SRC="../IMAGES/sitemap_headline.gif" ALT="[site
map]" ALIGN=RIGHT WIDTH="224" HEIGHT="56" BORDER="0">

</DIV>
<DIV name=contentWrapper style="position:abolsute; left:0; top:60;
width:350">

<!-- insert content -->
<DIV name=newWrapper style="position:absolute; left:0; top:0">

<A HREF="new.html" onMouseOver="(window.status='the latest and greatest
additions to the site'); return true">
<IMG name="new" SRC="../IMAGES/new.gif" ALT="[NEW]" ALIGN=MIDDLE WIDTH="56"
HEIGHT="56" BORDER="0">
</A>
</DIV>
<DIV name=writeWrapper style="position:absolute; left:0; top:60">

<A HREF="../write/index.html" onMouseOver="(window.status='Click here to
read stuff I wrote'); return true">
<IMG SRC="../IMAGES/write.gif" ALT="[writing]" ALIGN=RIGHT WIDTH="112"
HEIGHT="28" BORDER="0">
</A>
</DIV>
<DIV name=writeitemWrapper style="position:absolute; left:0; top:90">
<A HREF="../write/index.html" onMouseOver="(window.status='Sarcastic,
analytic, never dull'); return true">
Articles and Editorials
</A>
<P>
</P>
<A HREF="../WDTS/index.html" onMouseOver="(window.status='Jump-start your
creativity'); return true" >
<I>Web Design Templates Sourcebook</I>
</A>
</DIV>
<DIV name=buildWrapper style="position:absolute; left:0; top:120">
```

```
<A HREF="../build/index.html" onMouseOver="(window.status='I do this stuff
so you don\'t have to'); return true">
IMG SRC="../IMAGES/site.gif" ALT="[site building]" ALIGN=MIDDLE WIDTH="168"
HEIGHT="28" BORDER="0">
</A>
</DIV>
<DIV name=builditemWrapper style="poaition:absolute; left:0; top:150">
<A HREF="../build/12-step.html" onMouseOver="(window.status='You\'ll be
granted the serenity to accept the browser wars'); return true">    12-step
websites:
</A>
 addictive site hacks
<P>
</P>
 The ultimate
<A HREF="../build/toolbox.html" onMouseOver="(window.status='Shareware,
specs, and more'); return true">
website toolbox
</A>
<P>
</P>
<A HREF="../build/colophon.html" onMouseOver="(window.status='It\'s
aliiiiiiiiiiiiiiiiiive!'); return true">
Colophon:
</A>
 how I built this site
</DIV>
<DIV name=miscWrapper style="position:absolute; left:0; top:180>
<A HREF="../misc/index.html" onMouseOver="(window.status='Stuff that defies
categorization'); return true">
<IMG SRC="../IMAGES/odds.gif" ALT="[odds&ends]" ALIGN=MIDDLE WIDTH="168"
HEIGHT="28" BORDER="0">
</A>
</DIV>
<DIV name="miscitemWrapper" style="positon:absolute; left:0; top:210">
<A HREF="../misc/self.html" onMouseOver="(window.status='Yep, check here to
see if I'm a 400lb.hitman'); return true">Obligatory personal information
</A>
<P>
</P>
<A HREF="../work/resume.html" onMouseOver="(window.status='I build sites,
write copy, do UI/QA'); return true">
```

```
<IMG SRC="../IMAGES/hireme.gif" ALT="[hire me]" ALIGN=MIDDLE WIDTH="112"
HEIGHT="28" BORDER="0">
</A>
</DIV>
</DIV>
<!--insert nav bar -->
<DIV name="navWrapper" style="position:absolute; left:0; top:300;
width:392">
<IMG name=logo style="position:absolute; left:0; top:0"
SRC="../IMAGES/schmeiser.gif" ALT="[schmeiser.com]" ALIGN=BOTTOM
WIDTH="392" HEIGHT="41" BORDER="0">
<A HREF="http://www.schmeiser.com/content/sitemap.html"
onMouseOver="(window.status='sitemap'); return true"><IMG IMG name=nav0
style="position:absolute; left:0; top:41" SRC="../IMAGES/sitemap_nav.gif"
ALT="[sitemap]" ALIGN=BOTTOM WIDTH="56" HEIGHT="15" BORDER="0"></A>
<A HREF="http://www.schmeiser.com/write/index.html"
onMouseOver="(window.status='writing'); return true">
<IMG IMG name=nav1 style="position:absolute; left:56; top:41"
SRC="../IMAGES/writing_nav.gif" ALT="[writing]" ALIGN=BOTTOM WIDTH="56"
HEIGHT="15" BORDER="0"></A>
<A HREF="http://www.schmeiser.com/build/index.html"
onMouseOver="(window.status='site building'); return true"><IMG IMG
name=nav2 style="position:absolute; left:112; top:41"
SRC="../IMAGES/building_nav.gif" ALT="[building]" ALIGN=BOTTOM WIDTH="56"
HEIGHT="15" BORDER="0"></A>
<A HREF="http://www.schmeiser.com/misc/index.html"
onMouseOver="(window.status='odds and ends'); return true"><IMG IMG
name=nav3 style="position:absolute; left:168; top:41"
SRC="../IMAGES/odds_nav.gif" ALT="[odds&ends]" ALIGN=BOTTOM WIDTH="56"
HEIGHT="15" BORDER="0"></A>
<A HREF="http://www.schmeiser.com/work/resume.html"
onMouseOver="(window.status='r&eacute;sum&eacute;'); return true"><IMG IMG
name=nav4 style="position:absolute; left:224; top:41"
SRC="../IMAGES/hire_nav.gif" ALT="[hire me]" ALIGN=BOTTOM WIDTH="56"
HEIGHT="15" BORDER="0"></A>
<A HREF="mailto:site@schmeiser.com"><IMG IMG name=nav5
style="position:absolute; left:280; top:41" SRC="../IMAGES/mail_nav.gif"
ALT="[mail me]" ALIGN=BOTTOM WIDTH="56" HEIGHT="15" BORDER="0"></A>
</DIV>
<!--end wrapper div -->
</DIV>
</BODY>
</HTML>
```

The code is much simpler than the tabled stuff you may be used to, although writing and debugging it can be nerve-wracking until you're used to attaching styles to everything. Remember the following points:

- Pages built with table-driven layouts put all their items in a grid. The table provided the horizontal and vertical rules for the grid, and you could move the page parts around like the little plastic ships in the game Battleship. The grid was really two-dimensional: You didn't have an easy way to overlay items. And finally—because I haven't beaten up on tables-as-layout enough—the table layout method does not allow you to establish items relative to each other, unless you want to embed another table. The DOM allows you to create connective relationships: The sidebar `<div>` lives inside the article `<div>`, for example. This allows you to mirror the information relationships you're conveying to your readers on the client-side.

- When you build connective relationships within a page, you can begin looking at pages to see how many of those connective relationships can be carried across a site. If you always have a sidebar in your articles, you can start writing your pages to include that and writing your code so the sidebar formatting is automatically called into every page. This is where server-side assembly options come in handy, because they can let you format all the pieces individually then re-assemble them on a page.

- A final word of warning about bringing in included child parts: they are automatically integrated into the current page's DOM. If you've written a JavaScript that tells the included navigation graphics `body.navWrapper.nav1.gif` and `body.navwrapper.nav2.gif` to turn colors on mouseover, don't forget to check whether or not those included graphics are part of a wrapper `<div>` that lets you swap includes in and out. In the case of the code above, the navigation graphics actually live in `body.bigWrapper.navWrapper`, so the targets would have been all wrong.

Now that I've walked you through a total code overhaul and DOM mapping, you may be wondering how the made-over site looks. The final site is shown in Figure 11.6.

FIGURE 11.6:

The new and improved, super-organized site

Summary

The Document Object Model provides a handy way of putting all of your Web content into neatly categorized buckets. It's analogous to the index cards and drawers that used to make up a library's card catalog system: All of the tools are there, and it's up to you to fill in the content and impose organization.

What you should remember above all else is that the DOM gives you a way to grab hold of anything on your Web page and make it do what you want. And if you can do that, you can give your users a way to make anything on the page do anything that *they* want.

Moving Data between You and a User: Forms

- ▇ Understanding what forms do on your site

- ▇ Designing forms

- ▇ Using scripts

- ▇ Writing cookies

- ▇ Debugging scripts and forms

- ▇ Using POST and GET

One of the most elementary aspects of a website is the exchange of data between the client and the server. A form is one way to specify and extend the types of information that the website and visitor want from each other.

If you've been building websites for some time, you've run across forms. Maybe you've even built a few. But as websites become increasingly compartmental, the data a form collects and the page it spits back as a result may be out of step with the way you're building the rest of your site. Writing form interface and results pages tends to be difficult for Web developers who are shaky about altering scripts; as a result, forms often don't get updated or modified with the rest of the site.

Websites are becoming increasingly unique-user oriented. That is, instead of providing a single view that is displayed to any user that accesses the site, each individual user may experience a slightly modified version of the site, based on several different criteria. If you want to provide a specific user with a customizable interface, you're going to need to set up and maintain that interface. You're also going to need to start building site compartmentalization into your forms so they can adapt to an ever-shifting site structure.

This chapter focuses on how to treat forms and scripts as mix-and-match components for a website interface, and how to use scripts on the backend to handle data intelligently over a wide variety of conditions. I'll start by looking at the impact a form has on user interface and server performance, and I'll finish by showing you some task-specific script examples.

The Impact a Form Has on User Interface and Site Performance

Forms can make or break your site, especially if you rely on user feedback or user input to showcase your site's best features. Before you go scattering form elements hither and yon through your site, consider how they're going to affect your site performance.

The last big media site I worked on was also the home of my last big forms revelation. We were launching a new section, and one page featured many, many pull-down forms that permitted the reader to choose specific site sections. In addition to the many pull-down forms, we also had one or two search fields thrown in for good measure.

The head of design came down to ask if we'd be willing to add three or four more forms to the page. The head of production vetoed it, saying that too many forms on a page slow down the page rendering time. We tested this, and discovered that after four separate forms are included on a page, the time a page will take to load in your browser increases significantly.

The moral here? Be judicious with how many form elements you put on your page. It will affect your site's download time, and user-perceived performance.

NOTE　　Speaking of the user, remember that forms need instructions and context to work well. Plopping a text box and a "Submit" button on a page will not let your readers know that you want them to give you feedback; add context within the page. You can do this by actually telling your readers what the form is, what the different elements in the form are, and what data users can enter for anticipated results.

For more on smart form design, read on.

Designing Your Forms: Creating an Interface Your Users Won't Hate

There are several things you can do to make your forms more pleasant for your readers:

- Hide the inner workings of a form from your readers.

- Provide all the information the users need to fill out the form on the same page as the form.

- Make sure that neither the form nor the page containing the form takes too long to load.

The only part of a form your reader should see is the interface they have to deal with. They should not have to notice that the CGI script takes 10 minutes to process their input, they should not have to wonder if their information went through, nor should they have to guess what data strings will or won't be accepted by the script.

Imagine the experiences—good and bad—that you've had filling out forms on the Web. A useless, badly planned form just presents loosely labeled form elements, and it's up to the reader to psychically infer whether or not to put dashes in their phone number, or what information fields are mandatory. A well-designed form, however, through a few simple editing additions, manages to make filling out your name and address much simpler.

When you are creating a form, you should make sure that all of the information the user needs to have to fill out the form is on the same page as the form. Doing so will save your reader the hassle of flipping back and forth between pages, trying to track down the information they need.

- Travelocity (`http://www.travelocity.com/`), for example, fails in this respect: To make a reservation, you need to enter the three-letter code of the airport you want to travel to. If you don't know the code, you need to go through three separate pages to find the specific data and then hit the Back button to return to the form and type in your required three-letter code.

- Southwest Airlines (`http://www.iflyswa.com/`), on the other hand, lists all of its airports on the reservation page, so you can fill out your request without having to refer to another site first. Take a look at Southwest Airlines' scheduling page and note that the airport codes are all listed.

In addition, make sure that neither the form nor the page containing the form takes too long to load. The more forms or form elements you have on a page, the slower the page will load. If you're using several tiny forms as navigational aids for your site, balance the number of forms and form elements with the total page load time. If you're using a form to complete a complex data-exchange between you and a customer, consider breaking the form up into several discrete chunks and giving each chunk its own page. By doing so, you'll save the reader time; later on, you can easily customize the data flow or the components in a multi-form process.

WARNING   Always provide feedback for your user. If they don't think a form has been submitted, they're going to hit the button again and again. If a form breaks, tell them why it broke, or what they need to fill in. Creating these simple HTML pages is the biggest interface favor you could do for your audience.

Will Your Form Slow Down Your Server?

Before you create your first form, you'll want to consider the impact it will have on your server. Most forms are driven by CGI scripts. CGI stands for *common gateway interface*; it's an acronym that indicates how the data moves between client and server.

A *gateway* is a two-way phenomenon:

- It's a tool that helps translate data for a Web server. It accepts user input and presents it to the server in a form the server can understand.

- It takes server information and presents it to the user.

Gateways are a fantastic way to mediate between servers and clients, but they do take a toll—every time a CGI script is called, it starts a new server process. In addition, depending on what that script does, or what databases it accesses, back-end databases must be accessed, queried, and processed, before the results are returned to the browser.

So before you add forms all over your site, consider how much they will slow down your server. Make sure your backend can handle thousands of server processes forking simultaneously and that your databases can handle a lot of hasty open-and-shut queries.

Forms and Function: Creating Forms That Do What You Want Them to Do

Writing a form in HTML is easy; getting it to do what you want it to do may be tougher.

Forms are made up of three basic elements: the <FORM> tag, the <INPUT> area where the user is to enter information, and the <SUBMIT> button, which sends any input back to the server. Figure 12.1 shows a basic form you can create using the code below.

Form.html

```
<FORM method="get">
Please type your favorite color: <INPUT type="text" name="color"
size="40">
<INPUT type="submit" value="submit">
</FORM>
```

FIGURE 12.1:

A basic form viewed in a browser

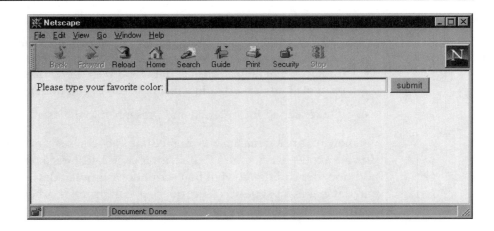

NOTE
If you need to brush up on the formula and HTML elements that tell a browser to render a form, refer to Appendix F, which provides a review of various HTML tags.

This section will focus on the relationship an HTML form has to a script and the types of scripting languages and tools that are available to you.

How Scripts Work

CGI scripts all operate on the same basic formula:

1. The script writes a content header to tell the server what to expect. This is so the server knows to anticipate text, HTML, JavaScript, whatever.

2. It also defines the QUERY_STRING for the data that's coming in. This sets up a context for the rest of the script. As a QUERY_STRING comes in from a user, it may be parsed, mailed, sorted, or recorded. But before it can, it must be defined.

3. It parses the data according to the commands the script author wrote.

4. It writes the results.

As a developer, you're going to be concerned with how that data is parsed and what is done with it. I'm going to concentrate on writing scripts that demonstrate backend data storage, and frontend writing.

Choosing a Backend Script Language

There are a number of different programming languages you can use to write CGI scripts. The only factors you need to consider are:

- What skills do you or your teammates have?

- What platform will you be using to serve the scripts?

- How much traffic do you expect the form to generate?

The most popular scripting language for CGI scripting is Perl; most books and samples are written with this language. The examples I am going to use through the rest of the chapter all rely on Perl. I chose Perl because it's fairly basic to pick up and it's one of the best-supported languages on the Web. The many FAQs, samples, and tutorials are a great support system for new scripters, or old scripters on new deadlines. For an easy and comprehensive introduction to all things Perl-related on the Web, go to `http://www.perl.com/`.

You can use almost any interpreted computer language though, so something like Tcl or C will work too.

Tcl—it's pronounced *tickle*, and stands for *Tool Command Language*— is another interpreted computer language that can be used for scripting. It's generally used to provide command enhancements to other tools or programs, such as editors and debuggers—or in our case, shell environments on a Web server. Tcl is a favorite among some programmers because its abilities as a language are augmented by its custom Tcl code libraries. To learn more about Tcl, start at `http://www.sco.com/Technology/tcl/tcl.html`.

C is yet another option for writing scripts, although probably not a good option for those of us who learned programming by hacking apart shareware CGIs on the Web. The same strengths that make C such an attractive development language— it is very close to a machine-level assembly language and therefore allows developers to write efficient code—also make it difficult to learn for those without any programming background or time to acquire one. If you do want to take the time to learn this language, you could start with a Web-based tutorial at `http://www.iftech.com/oltc/c/c0.stm`.

NOTE   Any interpreted computer language such as Perl or Tcl must have the interpreter installed on your servers, so check with your system administration about installation. Make sure you clear any and all CGI scripting activity through them before you design your latest and greatest site. CGI scripts are usually kept in their own `cgi-bin` directory on the server; this separation ensures that the permissions that a sysadmin needs to set up for a CGI script don't affect the security of the rest of the site. If you're hosting sites on a third-party ISP, you will need to ask them whether or not you can author your own scripts, or if you have to use their pre-written, or "canned" samples.

The Relationship between Your Form's HTML and Your Form's Script

Behind every working form on a website there is a CGI script. Since scripts do not make a form alone, you have to toss an interface—in the guise of an HTML-generated form page—in front of it. The form and the script each affect the other. If you're going to use HTML to add new information-gathering fields to your form, you'll need to write a command for handling those fields into your script. If you're going to eliminate a CGI script function, you will want to edit your form accordingly.

Forms and scripts communicate primarily through a mutual vocabulary of named data fields. If you look at the HTML behind any form, you'll see something like this:

```
<FORM method="post" action="sample.cgi">
<INPUT type="text" size="20" name="keyword">
<P></P>
<INPUT type="text" size="20" name="month">
<P></P>
<INPUT type="submit" value="submit">
</FORM>
```

In this example, the <INPUT> tag is telling the browser what type of user input field to display, how it should look, and what its value will be. It's telling the CGI script what the name and value of the user input getting sent back to it will be.

TIP

> If you're going to use forms and scripts across your site, it's a good idea to get a filename policy set up and in place. Brevity is the soul of sanity. You'll be typing those names into scripts, so make them short, descriptive, and relevant to their place in the site hierarchy.

Not all input fields are visible to the user. Some are deliberately left hidden, as a way of passing tracking data about a user while they're filling out a form. You would use this if you wanted to track a specific location or function that a CGI script was performing for you.

For example, if you're using a pull-down menu for navigation between sections, but wanted to gauge what section had the most navigational referrals in it, you'd attach an <INPUT> tag to the menu form in every section, and make that <INPUT> tag hidden, like this:

```
<INPUT type="hidden" name="leaving" value="archive">
```

The user doesn't see the tag, but you know that the pop-down menu in the archive was accessed because the data was passed to you.

Hidden data fields are useful for tracking where users are going and how they're getting there. They can also be useful in attaching user interface function names to scripts. The idea is to collect the information, see what the most useful menus and scripts are, and revise the site as necessary.

Maintaining State: What It Means, Why You Care

The whole point of pairing forms with CGI scripts is that you want to provide the reader with an interface so they can provide you with specific information. You may want the information for a variety of reasons, but for this exercise, I'm going to assume you want it so you can collect data for site analysis purposes.

In order to use the information you've collected, you have to keep that information accessible no matter where it's called from. If the data is collected in page1.html and passed to the server, your site still needs to be able to reach back to the area on your server where you store user input and regurgitate that user-entered information on page 4 (or wherever).

Here's a real-life example of maintaining state from page to page in a site. If you go to a search engine like AltaVista (http://www.altavista.com/) and type in **airline strike**, every subsequent page of results is going to pass the information "airline strike" back to the server to remind it what data the user input. When I queried AltaVista, the first five pages of results all had URLs with Airline+ Strike:

```
http://www.altavista.com/cgi-
bin/query?pg=q&kl=XX&q=Airline+Strike&search=Search
http://altavista.digital.com/cgi-
bin/query?pg=q&q=Airline+Strike&stq=10&c9k
http://altavista.digital.com/cgi-
bin/query?pg=q&q=Airline+Strike&stq=20&c9k
http://altavista.digital.com/cgi-
bin/query?pg=q&q=Airline+Strike&stq=30&c9k
http://altavista.digital.com/cgi-
bin/query?pg=q&q=Airline+Strike&stq=40&c9k
```

This is known as *maintaining state*. A classic dilemma for maintaining state on the Web is how to write a form that can keep referencing and passing data from any one of multiple entry points.

There are three notable ways to maintain state when using a CGI script, a form, and multiple ways to access or leave the form. The first is to add a session ID as a hidden field in the forms, the second is to use path information passed via the URL, and the third is to use cookies.

- The first method is the easiest to implement. Just type a hidden field into the form; the browser will parse the input and pass it along with any user generated input, and you'll have a "tag" telling you where the input came from. The syntax for this is:

```
<INPUT TYPE=hidden NAME=state VALUE="response generated from the
widgets.html page">
```

> **NOTE**   I use this method in `Script3.cgi` in the site navigation section that follows.

- A second way to maintain state between different pages on a form is to pass the information as text in the URL. If the text appears after a CGI call, it will be passed and printed in the script, providing another handy tag. This method has limits, however, primarily concerning how much data can be passed through the GET form action.

- The final way to maintain state between different parts of the site relies on cookies.

Cookies are an often-debated technology used to pass on information to users and retrieve that information later.

According to the Netscape spec, "cookies add a simple, persistent client-side state." What this means in English is that:

1. A user accesses a Web page with a cookie-making CGI script.

2. The script is activated when the page loads.

3. The cookie is then generated by the script, and it contains a unique cookie ID number for tracking, the name of the cookie, the domain that can recognize and retrieve the cookie, and a specific path for the cookie.

4. That cookie lives in a cookie file within your browser folder on the user's hard drive.

The cookie resides on the user's machine, and it only starts working the second time the user visits a site. The idea is that the cookie file maintains the state between the user and the website—giving the Web server a place to look up that user time and again, either during a prolonged session or on subsequent visits. Here's how it works:

1. The user visits a specific URL, like `http://www.surfatwork.com/sneaky/index.html`.

2. Loading that file sets the CGI script in motion, which creates and writes the cookie entry to the user's cookie file. That cookie would include unique ID # 1001, the domain `surfatwork.com`, and the path `sneaky/index.html`.

3. The next time the user visits the `/sneaky/index.html` path on the website, the script will look in the user's folder for any cookies from `surfatwork.com` and see if there are any from the `/sneaky/index.html` path.

4. When the server reads the cookie and finds the previous entry, a notation in a log file can then be generated, indicating that a return visit occurred.

WARNING   Cookies are still a controversial technology because they can be used to track user traffic on a site, and unless a user has their cookie alert option on their browser open, the user may not realize she's being tracked. Another, even more controversial application is cookies via ad-serving systems. Ad networks that spread similar ads across several sites can use cookies to track users across more than one site, since the cookie is being passed back to the ad network. For more information that debate, visit Chapter 16.

Writing a Cookie

Despite the privacy debate, cookies are still a useful technology. They can allow you to pass information from one page of a multiple-page form to another, or serve a page in response to a frequent user. They're the backbone to shopping-cart applications.

For those of you who haven't taken the plunge into the wild world of online shopping, shopping carts are a Web page/cookie/form combination that permit you to view the items you have selected to buy on the shopping site you visited.

Typically, after you select items, you go to a separate page to survey your shopping cart.

Even if you decide not to use them, advertisers on your site might, so it would be smart to learn how to write cookies.

First, Set the Cookie

The cookies have to be recognized by the browser's HTTP header. There are two ways to make this happen. The first is to edit the server's HTTP header files. To do that, you would write:

```
Set-Cookie: variable=value; expires=date; path="/path/";
domain="domain pattern"
```

replacing the italicized terms as follows:

`value`	The ID number or information you want to pass on from the Web-browsing session to the server
`date`	The date that the cookie expires, for example: Mon, 19-Oct-1998 15:45:320 GMT
`/path/`	A unique path, like /sneaky/
`domain pattern`	The domain that can read and record the cookie, like surfatwork.com

So the complete cookie could be:

```
Set-Cookie: variable=foo; expires=Mon, 19-Oct-1998 15:45:320 GMT;
path="/sneaky/"; domain="surfatwork.com"
```

NOTE   You can only assign one variable per cookie. If you want to track more than one information item, you will need more than one cookie.

The code you just wrote tells the server to pass the cookie on to anyone requesting a specific file in the URL and path.

If you can't edit the header file, you can also set the cookie in the <HEAD></HEAD> of an HTML document as follows:

```
<HEAD><META HTTP-EQUIV="Set-Cookie" CONTENT=" variable=value;
expires=date; path="/path=";domain="domain pattern"></HEAD>
```

An Alternative Cookie-Programming Method

You can also use JavaScript to program cookies. You may want to do so if your ISP or MIS department discourages using cgi-bin scripting. A sample JavaScript cookie setter is below:

Cookie3.html

```
<SCRIPT LANGUAGE = "JavaScript">
<!--

function getCookie(name){
var cname = name + "=";
var cc = document.cookie;
    if (cc.length > 0) {
    begin = cc.indexOf(cname);
        if (begin != -1) {
        begin += cname.length;
        end = cc.indexOf(";", begin);
            if (end == -1) end = cc.length;
            return unescape(cc.substring(begin, end));
        }
    }
return null;
}

function setCookie(name, value) {
var now = new Date();
var then = new Date(now.getTime() + 31536000000);
document.cookie = name + "=" + escape(value) +
"; expires=" + then.toGMTString() + "; path=/";
}
</SCRIPT>
```

The two functions in this JavaScript cookie perform different duties: One sets cookies if necessary, and the other retrieves any previously set cookies. You can use these cookies to validate data entry in forms or to track users.

Three Task-Specific Script Examples

All of the scripts in this section will rely on the Perl module CGI.pm. A *module* is a collection of functions that make programming tasks easier. A module might include commonly used but programmatically complex calculations. This would allow the programmer to then simply pass a request to the module for processing, rather than including or rewriting that chunk of code each time it's needed.

> **NOTE**   To get `CGI.pm`, go to `ftp://ftp.rge.com/pub/languages/perl//modules/by-module/CGI/`. It must be installed on your server before any of your scripts work.

Most of the intricacies of dealing with HTML and the CGI interface for the GET method of passing data are hidden when you use CGI.pm, so you won't have to worry about writing specific subroutines to tell the server what to do.

The First Example: Feedback on the Fly

In this section, I'll show you a script that takes data from an entry form, attaches a label to each item so that it can be stored in a database, and reprints it on a results screen for the user to see. This is like the one I showed you earlier in the chapter, with the addition of buttons.

> **NOTE**   The script in this section relies on the Database Interface (DBI) module. DBI calls specific database drivers on a server and allows you to link executable CGI calls to specific types of databases. To download DBI for installation, go to: `http://www.hermetica.com/technologia/DBI/`.

The Script

The source code for the script is below. I've broken it up so you can see how it works. This script has three different parts: it sets up a form, it parses the results for the developer on the backend, and it prints the input the user entered into a Web page.

The first line of the code tells the program where to find Perl on the Web server; on a Unix server, this line is required, so it's a good idea to include it no matter what. The second and third lines call specific Perl modules. The DBI module is one that you download and install to give Perl the ability to sort and write data to a database.

```
#!/usr/bin/perl5

use CGI;
use DBI;
```

Because writing to a file always requires permission, you will want to set up your database files so a specific user can write to them. In the following lines, we do so with a user ID and password. The last line, my $dbd, identifies the type of database you're going to push the user-entered information into. In addition to Oracle, you can use regular SQL-driven databases. Check out the DBI module for more information, and be sure to talk to your sysadmin about it. To learn more about the DBI module, go to ftp://ftp.rge.com/pub/languages/perl//modules/by-module/.

```
my $database_name = 'register';
my $user_id = 'web';
my $password = 'insecure';
my $dbd = 'Oracle';
```

The next section of code produces a page on-the-fly if there is no information to pass to the database. The lines print a new HTML document and generate it.

```
$query = new CGI;

print $query->header;
print $query->start_html (-title=>'Sample Form',
                          -meta=>{'keywords'=>'database cgi'},
                          -style=>{'src'=>'/style/style.css'},
                          -bgcolor=>'#FFFFFF');
```

The next few lines verify the user's input after they've entered data. It does this by reprinting the user's input—represented as variables—as a line of text on the page.

```
if(param()) {

my $name=$query->param('namefield');
my $address=$query->param('addressfield');
print 'You entered $name and $address. Thank you for filling this out.\n';
```

Now we're going to connect to the database:

```
$db_handle = DBI->connect($database_name, $user_id, $password, $dbd);
```

The next section checks for errors:

```
if (!$db_handle) {
print 'Error - couldn't connect to database: $DBI::errstr\n';
print $query->end_html;
exit;
}
```

In the next section, we create a statement handle. A statement is a direction for the computer to take, so the statement handle attaches a "hook" or circumstance for the direction to be executed.

```
$st_handle = $db_handle->prepare('insert into register (name, address)
values(?, ?)');
$st_handle->execute($name, $address);
if ($DBI::err) {
print 'Error: $DBI::errstr\n';
print $query->end_html;
exit;
}

}
```

The last section of code produces a page on-the-fly if there is no *new* information to pass to the database:

```
else {
print $query->start_form;
print 'Name:';
print $query->textfield(-name=>'namefield',
-maxlength=>50);
print '<p>';
print 'Address:';
print $query->textfield(-name=>'addressfield';
-maxlength=>100,
-size=>50);
print '<p>';
print $query->submit(-name=>'submit');
print $query->end_form;

print $query->end_html;
```

Script2.cgi

```
#!/usr/bin/perl5

use CGI;
use DBI;
my $database_name = 'register';
my $user_id = 'web';
my $password = 'insecure';
#this tells the DBI that we're using Oracle's database engine
my $dbd = 'Oracle';
$query = new CGI;

print $query->header;
print $query->start_html (-title=>'Sample Form',
                          -meta=>{'keywords'=>'database cgi'},
                          -style=>{'src'=>'/style/style.css'},
                          -bgcolor=>'#FFFFFF');
if(param()) {

my $name=$query->param('namefield');
my $address=$query->param('addressfield');
print 'You entered $name and $address. Thank you for filling this
out.\n';
$db_handle = DBI->connect($database_name, $user_id, $password, $dbd);
if (!$db_handle) {
print 'Error - couldn't connect to database: $DBI::errstr\n';
print $query->end_html;
exit;
}
$st_handle = $db_handle->prepare('insert into register (name, address)
            values(?, ?)');
$st_handle->execute($name, $address);
if ($DBI::err) {
print 'Error: $DBI::errstr\n';
print $query->end_html;
  exit;
}

}
else {
```

```
print $query->start_form;
print 'Please fill out your name and e-mail address so we can notify
you of any updates. Thank you.';
print <p>;
print 'Name:';
print $query->textfield(-name=>'namefield', -maxlength=>50);
print '<p>';
print 'Address:';
print $query->textfield(-name=>'addressfield';
                        -maxlength=>100,
                        -size=>50);
print '<p>';
print $query->submit(-name=>'submit');
print $query->end_form;
}
print $query->end_html;
```

Figure 12.2 shows the results of Script2.cgi; note that the initial screen and the results screen pick up some of the same HTML elements. You should be able to modify the code to maintain your site's distinctive look and feel.

All of the HTML for the page is contained within the print statements in the script. If we were going to print out the page *without the script,* it would look like this:

```
<html>

<head>
<title>sample form</title>
<meta name="keyword" content="cgi">
<style src="/style/style.css">
</head>

<body bgcolor="#FFFFFF">
<form>
Please print out your name and email address so we can notify you of
any updates.
<p>
Name: <input type="text" name="namefield" maxlength="50">
<p>
Address: <input type="text" name="addressfield" maxlength="50">
<p>
<input type="submit" value="submit">
```

```
</form>
</body>

</html>
```

But all of these HTML commands are included in the form script.

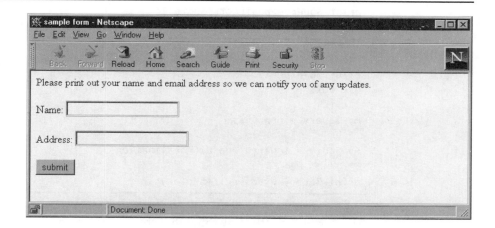

The Second Example: Site Navigation

Instead of relying on image maps or long HTML tables, you can use a CGI script and a pull-down menu to provide a compact and effective navigation device. The action the script performs is simple: it reads the value that the user has selected, and it serves a Web page in response.

The Script

The first line of the code tells the program where to find Perl on the Web server. The second line calls the specific Perl modules.

```
#!/usr/bin/perl5
use CGI;
```

The next line initializes a CGI object; the query contains the information passed to the script.

```
my $query = new CGI;
```

Next, you need a line that tells you that the selection, goto, is getting passed as a query to spit back a corresponding destination page.

```
my $goto = $query ->param('destination');
```

And finally, the last line sets the http header and sends an HTTP1.1 message to the server:

```
print $query->redirect("$goto");
```

Script3.cgi

```
#!/usr/bin/perl5
use CGI;

my $query = new CGI;

my $goto = $query ->param('destination');

print $query->redirect("$goto");
```

This script is a little, tiny thing that should live in your CGI directory and get called from your main page. A sample HTML page that would call it would be written like this:

```
<html>
<head>
<title>sample pull-down menu with CGI</title>
</head>
<body bgcolor="#FFFFFF" text="#333333" link="#330000" vlink="#000033">
<font face="verdana">
<h1>sample pull-down menu used for navigation</h1>
<p>
This is the first page of content. If a user wants to navigate to any
other page on the site, they can use the pull-down menu below to have
their way.
</p>
<p>
<form action="script3.cgi">
<select>
<option value="archive.html">Archive
<option value="news.html">News
<option value="feature.html">Features
```

```
</select>
</form>
</font>
</body>
</html>
```

The Third Example: Searching

In this section, there are actually two discrete scripts: the first script indexes all of the files in a website's directory structure by reading the keyword metatags, and the second script passes a user-entered keyword to the script and prints out the filenames and URLs of any Web pages in the directory that match the keywords.

The Script

This script will search all of the files in the directory in which it is run for keyword metatags, and update a central index for use by a Web-based search tool. This script will work in either Perl 4 or Perl 5.

Script4.cgi

```perl
my $index_filename="/cgi-bin/data/index";

#create a list of .htm and .html files in this directory
@html_files=glob("*.htm*");

#open the indexfile
dbmopen(%INDEX,"$index_filename",0666);
foreach $html_file (@html_files) {
open THIS_FILE "$html_file";
while (<THIS_FILE>) {
if (/\<META NAME="KEYWORD" CONTENT="(.+)"\>/i) {
$keywords=$1;
$keywords=~s/\s//g;
@keywords=split(/,/,$keywords);
foreach $keyword (@keywords) {
#Add each keyword to the index
$INDEX{$keyword}=$INDEX{$keyword}.":".$html_file;
}
}

}
```

```
close THIS_FILE;
}
dbmclose(%INDEX);
#!/usr/bin/perl5
use CGI;
$query = new CGI;
my $base_ref=Error! Bookmark not defined.;
my $index_filename="/cgi-bin/data/index";
print $query->header;
print $query->start_html
(-title=>'Sample Form',
-meta=>{'keywords'=>'search cgi'},
-style=>{'src'=>'/style/style.css'},
-bgcolor=>'#FFFFFF');
if(param()) {
#The form passes the script a search term for which to search
my $searchterm=$query->param('searchterm');
dbmopen(%INDEX,"$index_filename",0666);
$matching_files=$INDEX{$searchterm};
dbmclose(%INDEX);
# $matching_files looks like:   #:file1.html:file2.html:file3.html
$matching_files=~s/^\://;   # get rid of first colon
@matching_files=split(/:/,$matching_files);
# Create urls for each file
foreach $matching_file (@matching_files) {
$this_url=$base_ref.$matching_file;
print "<a href=\"$this_url\">$this_url<\a><br>\n";
}
print $query->end_html;
}

#! /usr/bin/perl
```

This line tells you where to find the index file that you're going to write all the results to.

```
my $index_filename="/cgi-bin/data/index";
```

This line tells you how to create a list of .htm and .html files in whatever directory just called the script.

```
@html_files=glob("*.htm*");
```

This line tells you to open the index file so you can begin writing information to it.

```
#open the indexfile
dbmopen(%INDEX,"$index_filename",0666);
foreach $html_file (@html_files) {
    open THIS_FILE "$html_file";
    while (<THIS_FILE>) {
        if (/\<META NAME="KEYWORD" CONTENT="(.+)"\>/i) {
            $keywords=$1;
            $keywords=~s/\s//g;

@keywords=split(/,/,$keywords);
                foreach $keyword (@keywords) {
#!/usr/bin/perl5
use CGI;

$query = new CGI;
```

These lines reference the database index file we opened and wrote, then looks in that index file for the keywords queried.

```
my $base_ref=Error! Bookmark not defined.;
my $index_filename="/cgi-bin/data/index";
```

These lines print out HTML. You should remember them from `script2.cgi`.

```
print $query->header;
print $query->start_html (-title=>'Sample Form',
                    -meta=>{'keywords'=>'search cgi'},
                      -style=>{'src'=>'/style/style.css'},
                    -bgcolor=>'#FFFFFF');

if(param()) {
```

This line sets up the search term that the user sets in the form, and that the script will use to search the index file.

```
my $searchterm=$query->param('searchterm');
dbmopen(%INDEX,"$index_filename",0666);
$matching_files=$INDEX{$searchterm};
dbmclose(%INDEX);
```

```
$matching_files=~s/^\://;  # get rid of first colon
@matching_files=split(/:/,$matching_files);

# Create urls for each file
```

Once you've found matching files, make and create URLs for all of them.

```
foreach $matching_file (@matching_files) {
    $this_url=$base_ref.$matching_file;
    print "<a href=\"$this_url\">$this_url<\a><br>\n";
}
print $query->end_html;
        }
```

Debugging CGI Scripts and Forms

Unless you're possessed of amazing natural talent for scripting (or a computer science degree), you're occasionally going to write something that doesn't work. Fortunately, most CGI scripts can be easily debugged. Just ask yourself the following questions:

- Are the pointers to all locations correct? In other words, does your script point to /usr/bin/perl when your perl modules live in /usr/tools/cgi/?

- Are all the permissions set correctly? It's not enough to tell a script where to write data—you have to make sure the permissions on the directory are set to allow writing. In addition, you have to set the permissions so the script is executable. You may need to take special care to do this, especially if your .cshrc (your user profile file on a Unix system) is set to only read and write files. Finally, you need to remember to set the permission so that the server can write to your CGI data files as well—this is how data is recorded.

- Did you check the server error logs? You can open up the error log in a telnet window and run the command tail -f as you try to execute the script. You'll get a printout of what kind of error you're getting, and the location of the error in the script.

- Did you remember to use correct syntax, end every line with a semicolon (;) and return lines (/n) when printing?

Most CGI scripts can be debugged with a few minutes of careful detective work. Just run through every possible reason, take notes on how the script is breaking, and start tracing the reason for the break back through the code and script set-up.

Sending Your Form to the Server Using GET or POST

Forms can be sent to the server in one of two ways, GET or POST. This is known as the method for sending data, and it is usually set in the form tag.

POST passes data to the server as one big block. It's a good way to send data if you're working on a low-tech site and you just want to e-mail data from the site to a designated address.

GET is used with forms that rely on CGI scripts for handling. It requires an "action," which is usually called as an address for the script that handles the form. GET allows you to parse data from a data block into specific fields. This is handy if you're passing data to a database, or trying to call specific data from a database. It's also easier to organize data by categories and query it if you're working with flat text files.

Forms and Security

Any time you send or receive data over the Internet, you're conducting an information transaction in a less-than-secure environment. Your information, which gets sent as packets, can be intercepted and read by anyone who has the knowledge and inclination.

CGI-run forms present an extra security risk because CGI scripts open a two-way gate between a client and a server. An improperly written or executed script can be exploited by hackers. They'll use it as a Trojan horse to enter the rest of your site.

So before you post any CGI scripts on your site, take security precautions. Some of the more common methods for securing your CGI script are listed below.

- Put all of your CGI scripts in one directory. You should always separate your CGI scripts from the rest of your site; this way, you can set the permissions the CGI scripts require without compromising the rest of your site. If you have CGI scripts scattered through the site, a hacker could create a random `.cgi` program and call it via URL to gain entry into your site.

- Remove or turn off server-side includes if you're running them in the same directory that you're running CGI scripts.

- If you're writing CGI scripts, limit your use of `eval`—the command that allows you to construct a string of data and have the server execute the string. If you do not clearly specify and limit what that string can contain, a user could have the server process a string of data that allows them access to the backend.

- If you're writing CGI scripts, don't give away information about your site. If the data can't be obtained by running a HTTP-env call, it shouldn't be on your site.

- If you're writing CGI scripts, don't ever write a line that allows unchecked remote user input. The syntax to watch out for is any line using `system ()`, `exec ()`, and `open ()`. Never make asuumptions about the input your user is going to try.

- Provide absolute paths in any system references. Relative paths are security holes waiting to be exploited.

If you want to borrow someone else's CGI scripts, exercise extreme caution. Find out if the specific areas where files are read and written will compromise your site security or directory permissions. See if the script requires interactions with other server programs—these interactions could also open a security hole.

Summary

Forms are an excellent way to pass data back and forth between a server and a client, and to make sure that users have a tool that allows them to actively participate in their Web surfing process. As a Web developer, you'd do well to start thinking of forms as more than collections of checkboxes; instead, start thinking of forms as a way to pass and manipulate data. In the overarching theme of this section, the scripting technology driving forms may be the equivalent of a good toolbox for building a dynamic data-driven site.

CHAPTER

THIRTEEN

13

How to Provide Information on the Fly: Scripting and Website Production

- Pages on the fly via conditional HTML and includes

- Pages on the fly via JavaScript

- Pages on the fly via CGI scripts

In the first chapter on markup languages, I explored how to partially automate your site assembly process by breaking down your site components into virtual includes, then writing files that assemble those includes into a complete page. You should be comfortable with the idea of your site as a collection of functioning components to be assembled according to spec. Now that you can break down your site into pieces, it's time to learn how to write the rules for reassembling those pieces.

On-the-fly Web page building means that the page is assembled as it is sent from the server to the client, based on variables that the client has already passed to the server. When you make a query on a search page, the results page is generated on the fly based on the search term (a.k.a. the variable) you passed to the server.

This chapter will cover three ways to build pages on the fly. The first is by advanced use of templates, conditional HTML, and virtual includes. The second method relies on JavaScript to create and display your site. The third focuses on using CGI scripts to format data from a database and push it through a template before publishing.

All three methods—includes, JavaScript, and CGI scripting—are based on some common principles. They are:

- The content of the document is completely separate from the structural or design markups that build the site.

- The structure of the site has been mapped and clear relationships between different data objects are established and followed.

- The style and attributes that comprise site design are all template-driven. They are not embedded in the content.

- Each data object can have attributes attached to it. Part of dynamically controlling a site is being able to grab an object based on its attributes and perform some action.

Keep these principles in mind as you read the rest of the chapter. They will recur; the only thing that changes is the way those principles are executed.

Using Conditional HTML and Includes to Build Pages on the Fly

There are varying levels of on-the-fly page building. The most basic is a page that is assembled based on a single variable, like color or browser type. A combination of virtual includes and conditional HTML can provide these on the fly pages. I'm going to give you three basic examples of how to assemble a page on the fly in response to a variable.

Example 1: Changing Color Schemes

Sites that rely on colors to tell different sections apart use three or four attributes to create a different color scheme. Those attributes are all attached to objects within the document: the <body> tag controls the bgcolor, text, link, alink, and vlink attributes; <font> tags can specify a specific color; and <table> and <td> tags can support background colors.

You can substitute hard values for these attributes with server-side include variables, then write conditional HTML to change the values of these variables.

In this example, we are going to change the color scheme of a page.

Color.html

```
<HTML>
    <HEAD>
    <TITLE>This is the Color-Change Example</TITLE>
    <STYLE type="text/css">
    <!--//
    #10        {position: absolute; left:10px; top:50px}
    #9         {position: absolute; left:12px; top:60px}
    #8         {position: absolute; left:14px; top:70px}
    #7         {position: absolute; left:16px; top:80px}
    #6         {position: absolute; left:18px; top:90px}
    #5         {position: absolute; left:18px; top:100px}
    #4         {position: absolute; left:16px; top:110px}
    #3         {position: absolute; left:14px; top:120px}
    #2         {position: absolute; left:12px; top:130px}
    #1         {position: absolute; left:10px; top:140px}
    #headline        {position: absolute; left:10px; top:30px}
```

```
//-->
</STYLE>

<!--this is where the include variables go -->
<!--#if expr="$color = /white/" -->
<!--#set var="body" value='<BODY  bgcolor=#FFFFFF alink=#FFFF00 _
link=#660000 vlink=#CC3300 text=#000000>'-->
<!--#set var="headstyle" value="#0066FF" -->
<!--#endif -->

<!--#if expr="$color = /blue/" -->
<!--#set var="body" value='<BODY bgcolor=#99CCFF alink=#330066 _
link=#003399 vlink=#330066 text=#000033>' -->
<!--#set var="headstyle" value="#003366" -->
<!--#endif -->


<!--#if expr="$color = /green/" -->
<!--#set var="body" value='<BODY bgcolor=#99FFCC  alink=#996666 _
link=#009966 vlink=#996666 text=#003333>' -->
<!--#set var="headstyle" value="#006633" -->
<!--#endif -->

<!--this sets the variable -->
<!--#set var="color" value="white" -->
</HEAD>
<!--#echo var="body"-->

<div class="headline"><font color="<!--echo var='headstyle' _
-->">Top Ten Reasons to Get a PDA</div>
    <div id="10">10. instant geek chic, even in Silicon Valley</div>
    <P></P>
    <div id="9">9. glow in the dark screen means you can work even in _
movie theatres</div>
    <P></P>
    <div id="8">8. the buttons are fun to click</div>
    <P></P>
    <div id="7">7. it has its own development platform</div>
    <P></P>
    <div id="6">6. grafitti counts as a second language</div>
    <P></P>
```

```
    <div id="5">5. they're a lot more portable than a desktop _
computer</div>
    <P></P>
    <div id="4">4. even the carrying cases are cool</div>
    <P></P>
    <div id="3">3. infrared ports mean you can play hearts during _
meetings</div>
    <P></P>
    <div id="2">2. more apps than most desktop platforms</div>
    <P></P>
    <div id="1">1. you may actually use it to organize things</div>
    <P></P>
</BODY>
</HTML>
```

What Are the Variables?

The two variables are *body* and *headstyle*. All of their possible values are defined in the code in the head of the document:

```
<!--this is where the include variables go -->
    <!--#if expr="$color = /white/" -->
    <!--#set var="body" value='<BODY  bgcolor=#FFFFFF alink=#FFFF00 _
link=#660000 vlink=#CC3300 text=#000000>'-->
    <!--#set var="headstyle" value="#0066FF" -->

    <!--#elif expr="$color = /blue/" -->
    <!--#set var="body" value='<BODY bgcolor=#99CCFF alink=#330066 _
link=#003399 vlink=#330066 text=#000033>' -->
    <!--#set var="headstyle" value="#003366" -->

    <!--#else expr="$color = /green/" -->
    <!--#set var="body" value='<BODY bgcolor=#99FFCC  alink=#996666 _
link=#009966 vlink=#996666 text=#003333>' -->
    <!--#set var="headstyle" value="#006633" -->
    <!--#endif -->
```

The conditional area is the if-elif-else construction in the set of variable definitions. This defines the conditions that can be affected by a changing variable value.

Note that the variable value that is going to be passed to the browser for on-the-fly assembly is already built-in:

```
<!--#set var="color" value="white" -->
```

How Are the Templates Built?

In this case, the only part of the file that is templated is the formatting. The content is hard-wired into the code. A further step in templating the whole page would be to separate out the contents of each <div> as a separate content file, and call them as another series of server-side variables. An excerpt of the code would look like this:

```
<!--#echo var="body"-->
<div class="headline"><font color="<!--echo var='headstyle' _
-->">Top Ten Reasons to Get a PDA</div>
<div id="10"><!--echo var="ten" --></div>
<P></P>
<div id="9"><!--echo var="nine" --></div>
<P></P>
```

A separate document would have

```
<!--#set var="ten" value='instant geek chic, even in Silicon Valley' _
-->
<!--#set var="nine" value='glow in the dark screen means you can work
even in movie theatres' -->
```

What Does the End Result Look Like?

In Figure 13.1, you can see the final product.

Example 2: Changing Page Layout Based On Browser Version

Another way to use if-else conditional HTML is as a response to environmental variables passed in the browser header, like browser type and version number. You may have already used this kind of if-else code to support non-frames-reading browsers. You can also extend that to other types of parameters. In this example, we're going to set up a document that uses style sheets if the browser is a version 4 browser, and formatted <font> tags if the browser is not.

FIGURE 13.1:

Compare these two versions of the final page. In the top, the body variable was set to *white*. In the bottom, the body variable was set to *blue*.

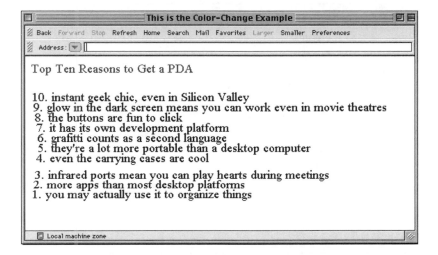

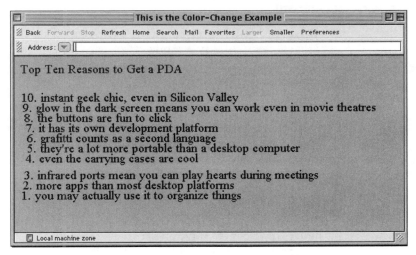

There are several separate files that assemble the one page. `index.html` decides what formatted content will be pulled in. This is the file that will be built on the fly for the user. `stylesheets.shtml` formats the text using inline style sheets, and `fonts.shtml` provides the default text.

index.html

```
<HTML>
<HEAD>
<TITLE>Content Change Example</TITLE>
<!--#if expr="$SUPPORTS_position" -->
<!--#include virtual="stylesheets.shtml" -->
<!--#else" -->
<!--#include virtual="fonts.shtml" -->
<!--#endif -->
</HEAD>
<!--echo var="body -->
</BODY>
</HTML>
```

stylesheets.shtml

```
<P style="font-family:arial; font-size:12px; color:#003333">
I have been so busy writing this book
that I have not yet had time to download
helper applications for my Pilot.
</P>
<P style="font-family:arial; font-size:12px; color:#003333">
When I get time, I want to download
something that will help me balance my
checkbook, and an index of maps in the U.S.
</P>
<P style="font-family:arial; font-size:14px; color:#CC0000">
Road trip here I come!
</P>
<P style="font-family:arial; font-size:10px; color:#000033">
(after I meet this deadline, that is)
</P>
```

fonts.shtml

```
<font face="arial" size="2" color="#003333">
<P>
I have been so busy writing this book
```

```
that I have not yet had time to download
helper applications for my Pilot.
</P>
<P>
When I get time, I want to download
something that will help me balance my
checkbook, and an index of maps in the U.S.
</P>
</font>
<font face="arial" size="4" color="#CC0000">
<P>
Road trip here I come!
</P>
</font>
<font face="arial" size="1" color="#000033">
<P>
(after I meet this deadline, that is)
</P>
</font>
```

What Are the Variables?

In this case, the only variable is the browser capability, which is implicitly set in the statement:

```
<!--#if expr="$SUPPORTS_position" -->
<!--#include virtual="stylesheets.shtml" -->
<!--#else" -->
<!--#include virtual="fonts.shtml" -->
<!--#endif -->
```

supports_position is an attribute for 4.0-generation browsers, since it is attached to style sheets. Therefore, anything that does not support positioning is going to get the default include, fonts.shtml.

How Are the Templates Built?

The index page acts as the template for every file, since it sets up the conditional statement; you may want to make stylesheets.shtml and fonts.shtml separate templates. However, the focus in this section is on setting up the conditional HTML in the index page. Therefore, use that as your template.

What Does the End Result Look Like?

Figure 13.2 shows the final product.

FIGURE 13.2:

Two versions of the final page, depending on the browser client. On the top is the style-sheeted layout; notice that there really isn't much difference between the 12 px. type and the 14 px. type. On the bottom is the layout for browsers that don't support style sheets. Notice that there's a lot more difference between font sizes.

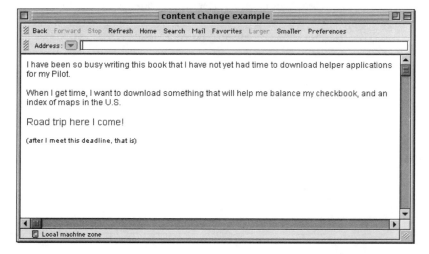

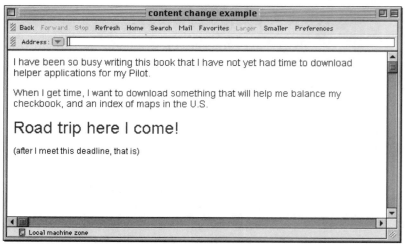

Example 3: Changing Content Based On a User-Selected Variable

This example is useful if you provide a reference library of resources or links to your site. In this case, the library is broken down into one persistent "frame," and the user-selected entries are clicked via a navigation bar at the top. The navigation bar passes a variable to the server as a query, and the server sends out a newly constructed page in response.

Swap.html

```
<html>
<head>
    <title>swapping content</title>
</head>
<body>
<!--#if expr="$QUERY_STRING" -->
<!--#include virtual="./${QUERY_STRING}.htmlf" -->
<!--#else -->
<!--#include virtual="./a.htmlf" -->
<!--#endif --><br><br>
<a href="./index.html?a">A</a> <a href="./index.html?b">B</a> _
<a href="./index.html?c">C</a>
</body>
</html>
```

a.htmlf

```
<p>
This is the content that loads when I select <b><big>a.htmlf</big></b>,
or if I've loaded the page for the first time.
</p>
```

b.htmlf

```
<p>
This is the content that loads when I select <b><big>b.htmlf</big></b>
</p>
```

c.htmlf

```
<p>
This is the content that loads when I select <b><big>c.htmlf</big></b>
</p>
```

What Are the Variables?

The variables are all included in the navigation bar.

Index.html?a, index.html?b, and index.html?c all carry variable values *a*, *b*, or *c* back to the server. These then get read by the index.html shell file, which pulls in the corresponding include.

These variables are all accessed in the $QUERY_STRING, which exists for the sole purpose of having values passed to it. Since the variables are a, b, c, and they correspond to files a.htmlf, b.htmlf, and c.htmlf, the if-else code is a very neat way of writing "when you are given a specific variable, cram in the include that happens to share the same name as the variable."

How Are the Templates Built?

The index page acts as the template, since it contains the conditional statement that will load content in response to user clicks, and it is also the framework in which each fragment—a.htmlf, b.htmlf, and c.htmlf—will be loaded. The stuff that you'll want to cut and paste every single time you make the template is the HTML structure you see up at the top. As a shell, it's your best bet for template building.

What Does the End Result Look Like?

Figure 13.3 shows the final product.

FIGURE 13.3:

The three choices users can select within the shell page to get new content

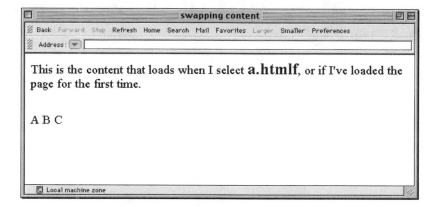

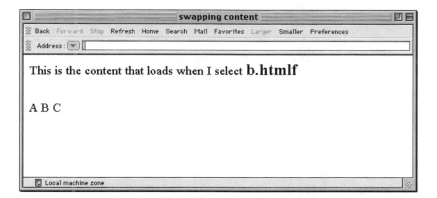

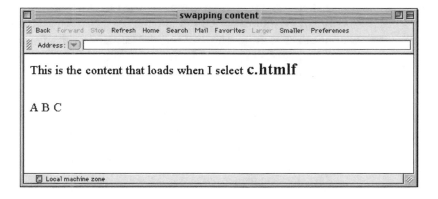

Using JavaScript to Build Pages on the Fly

Virtual includes and conditional HTML rely on variables being passed back and forth between the server and the browser, and the process is restricted by a lack of active viewer input, as is the case for the color and layout examples. JavaScript-generated pages differ because they can create new pages based on user-driven events.

Unlike HTML, JavaScript is an object-oriented language, so it recognizes elements on the page as document objects, and attaches events to them. You can control those events and use them to create new HTML pages.

Why would you want to do that? If you want to control where your user clicks on a page and the display they see, you can. You can control the window size, cause footnote windows to pop up in hypertext essays, or create pages to give feedback for data you entered into a form.

The three examples I'm going to go through demonstrate how to use objects and events to generate pages in response to user actions. Unlike the previous examples, I will not be following the four-section format presented in the server-side assembly section. Instead, I will be focusing on the bare-bones commands that allow you to enrich your pages via user input and client-side scripting.

Example 1: Clicking a Hyperlink to Generate a New Page

A certain free home page provider has become notorious for popping up small windows with new documents whenever you load a page on their site. This pop-up method is annoying, but the technology behind it—using JavaScript to cue a new browser window—can be very useful. If you have a photo gallery, a sidebar, a tutorial, or a floating navigation bar as a pop-up cue, you have more freedom in how you structure your existing pages within the browser frame.

Building user-cued new pages into your existing site is an easy, four step process. I'll walk you through the steps one by one.

First, write the JavaScript function that will make the new window pop up.

```
<script language="javascript">
<!--//
function popup ()
{
```

```
window.open ("urlhere.html", "new_window", width="200", height="200", _
menubar="0", location="0", status="0", titlebar="0", toolbar="0", _
scrollbar="1" resizable="1");
}
//-->
</script>
```

This tiny script does four things:

1. It defines the function that will be called when a user clicks a specific area.

2. It opens a new window with the command `window.open`.

3. It calls a URL (`"urlhere.html"`).

4. It specifies the physical appearance of the new window. All the properties mentioned—width, height, menubar, location, status, titlebar, and toolbar—dictate how big the window will be, whether or not it will have a location bar (the area where you type in or see the URL), and other items typically found in a browser page. All of these traits are accessible via the Document Object Model (DOM). For a more thorough look at the DOM, visit Chapter 11. The way you set the values and specify whether or not you want a specific browser attribute manifested is by the value assigned: 0 equals "no," and 1 equals "yes." So in this example, scrolling through the window is permitted, but there is no titlebar.

After you've written the function, write the "hook" that will call the JavaScript function into your HTML. I'm going to use a hyperlink:

```
<a href="javascript: popup();">Click here to launch a new window</a>
```

You'll note that there is no URL in the hyperlink. That's because the new file to be loaded into the new window is specified in the pop-up function (`"urlhere.html"`).

So you're halfway home: You have the script, and you have the hook that calls the pop-up script. The next step is to write the HTML for the content you'll be pulling into your new window. You already have a good grasp of HTML, so let's move on to the last step: giving your users a way to get rid of that pop-up window they cued.

To give users a way to wipe out that window, all you need to is attach another JavaScript cue to a hyperlink within the file that got loaded into your pop-up window. The command for this is:

```
<a href="javascript: self.close();">Click here to close the window</a>
```

All this does is tell the browser to close its own window. You could even include this command in your main window— but you'd end up ticking off your readers as they shut down their open browser windows. It's best to save this function for auxiliary windows that you include in the site as bonuses to the main content.

Here's the HTML I used for Figure 13.4:

```
<html>
<head>
<title>generating a new page via j-script link</title>
<script language="JavaScript" type="text/javascript">
function popup()
{
window.open
("1303.html","new_window","width=200,height=200,location=0,menubar=0,_
resizable=1,scrollbars=1,status=0,titlebar=0,toolbar=0,hotkey=0");
}
</SCRIPT>
</head>
<body>
<h1><a href="javascript:popup();">Click here to launch a new
window</a></h1>
</body>
</html>
```

FIGURE 13.4:

An example of a pop-up window being called by a parent page. The small window is the pop-up window; the large window with the big hyperlink is the parent window.

Example 2: Writing a New HTML Page Using JavaScript-Passed Data

This script example shows what you can do when you use the DOM to write data to a brand new Web page. In order to do this, our script has to do the following:

1. Open a new document.

2. Specify that actual HTML plus information is to be written to the document.

3. Take advantage of the DOM to write information to the document.

Here's the script that does all three steps:

```
<script language="javascript">
<!--//
function diagnose()
{
diagnoseWindow = window.open("","DiaWindow");
diagnoseWindow.document.write(<HEAD><TITLE>New data being
written/TITLE></HEAD>);
diagnoseWindow.document.write("<BODY>");
diagnoseWindow.document.write("window.parent.document.title");
diagnoseWindow.document.write("is the title of the file that called _
this script");
diagnoseWindow.document.write("window.document.title");
diagnoseWindow.document.write("is the title of this window.");
diagnoseWindow.document.write("</body>");
diagnoseWindow.document.write("</html>");
}
//-->
</script>
```

In order to cue this marvelous script, you must call it from an HTML page. I did this like so:

```
<html>
<head></head>
<body>
<form onsubmit="diagnose();">
<input type="submit" value="diagnose page">
</form>
</body>
</html>
```

Figure 13.5 shows the script after it was cut-and-pasted into a simple HTML document.

FIGURE 13.5:

The window of the script after it was cut-and-pasted into a simple HTML document

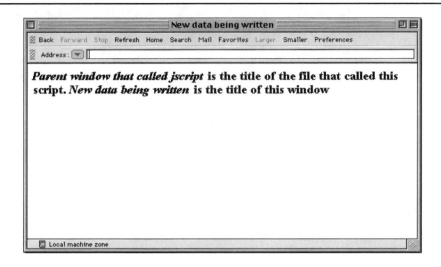

The most important thing to take away from this is that the JavaScript function was called by a user action: submitting the form. You could also write a hyperlink to do the same thing: `<a href="javascript:diagnose();">Click here to diagnose</a>`. So long as the JavaScript has a handle for the user to trigger it, this script works.

And here's how the script works: The first line opens a new document. The subsequent lines have two parts: the `diagnoseWindow.document.write` command tells the script where to write the HTML—to the specific window mentioned in the first line—and the second part specifies that the browser should render either HTML (`"<body>"`) or information the script can grab off the browser's DOM, like the title of the document being loaded into the browser.

You could probably tweak this script and use it as a QA tool to check for specific items on a page, or you could use it to test what the DOM objects really look like in your browser.

Example 3: Writing New Information to an HTML Page Using JavaScript

Before we begin invoking scripting magic, let me define "new" information: I mean new to your user; you'll have seen or anticipated everything beforehand.

This example is perfect for those sites that rely on simple mathematical displays of information for their users, like commerce sites.

In order to provide users with this information, you have to take the following steps:

1. Define the type of information you'll be able to present to your users (this is the "new" part).

2. Find a way to store that information—or the means to calculate that information—until it's needed, on the client side of the server-client interaction.

3. Find a way for users to input data leading to the generation of new information.

4. Define a cue to load the new data being presented in the page.

We can do this for one easy example, and then for one hard one. Let's warm up with the easy example: clicking on an image to load some pre-defined data into a page.

In order to make this work, you need to define your "hook" for cueing the new data. We're going to do this by wrapping an image in an anchor tag, and calling the information-displaying JavaScript from the anchor like this:

```
<a href="javascript:newinfo();"><img src="clickme.gif"></a>
```

Now, we need to write the function `newinfo()`:

```
<script language="javascript">
<!--//
function newinfo()
{
document.info.value=
"As you click, new information is displayed here.\n
This is an excellent way to pair images and facts about those images.\n";
}
//-->
</script>
```

This script is really basic: It defines the information to be displayed on the page, and specifies where on the page the information is to be displayed. The information is the two-sentence blurb with the new line breaks (\n) within quotation marks; the location is the area on the page named "info."

The HTML for the page to display the script would look like this:

```
<html>
<head><!--insert script--></head>
<body>
<a href="javascript:newinfo();"><img src="clickme.gif"></a>
<div="info">
</div>
</body>
</html>
```

Remember, that was our warm-up example; let's look at a more complex way to store information for users and display it on a cue.

We're going to create an *array*, or set of related information items, store our data in the array, and return array values when called. Here's the script:

```
<script language="javascript">
<!--//
function arraySet()
{
array[0]=new pair("Virginia Tech", "Hokies");
array[1] =new pair("West Virginia", "Mountaineers");
array[2] =new pair("Rensselaer", "Engineers");
array[3] =new pair("Kent State", "Flashes");
return this;
}
function teamName(school, mascot)
{
this.school=school;
this.mascot=mascot;
return this;
}

function calculateMascot(pairValue)
{
var index=0
var result=0
var temp=0
if (schoolValue.toUpperCase() ==schoolGuide[index].name)
{result = schoolGuide[index].mascot;
}
index++
}
//-->
```

```
</script>
And in order for the script to work, it needs HTML:<html>
<head><!--insert script here--></head>
<body onload ="schoolGuide=new arraySet();">
<form name="mascotform">
School: <input type="text" name="school" size="30" OnChange="if _
(mascotEntered) { calculateMascot(mascot.value);}">
<br>
Mascot: <input type="text" name="mascot" size="30" OnChange="if _
(mascotEntered) { calculateMascot(this.value);}">
</form>
</body>
</html>
```

Here's how it works: There are three functions, and they are all interdependent. The function arraySet provides the structure for the array of data and actual values to populate that structure. These values will be referenced later. Function teamName squares away some syntactical naming, so if a value like school or mascot is referenced later, the script knows exactly what's being referred to. The last function, calculateMascot, specifically looks for items that match any of the pair values in the array set up by the arraySet function, and if there's a match, prints out the corresponding school-mascot pair.

The HTML for the page calls up the calculateMascot function if there's a change in the page—like a user inputting data into the form—and produces results. By linking the onChange action to the form field, we've found a neat way to pass data from form to script. Figure 13.6 shows the end result of this script.

Using CGI Scripting to Build Pages on the Fly

The last method for building pages on the fly is via CGI scripts. Like JavaScript, these pages can be created in response to user input, but like server-side include pages, they can also be done on the server-side before a user even loads a page.

What are the arguments for using CGI scripts? For all of the flexibility and functionality that JavaScript offers, it is still voluntary for users, and if a user elects to turn off their JavaScript, your page loses its functionality. CGI, on the other hand, is server-side and can be controlled by the developer (that is, you).

FIGURE 13.6:

This is an example of how the JavaScript works. In the first window, I entered the value "Virginia Tech." Fortunately, there is a value for "Virginia Tech" in the array, so the page returns the mascot name "Hokies."

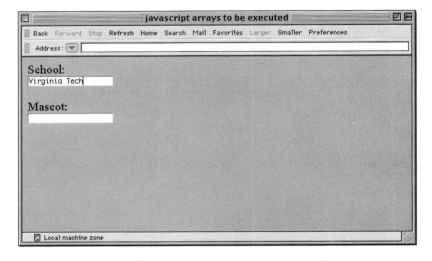

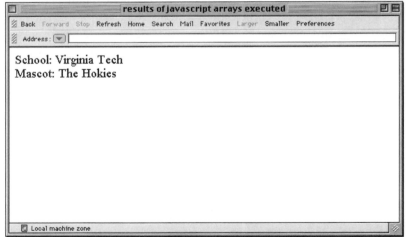

So what advantage can CGI have over server-side includes? Some servers may not support includes, or be able to fully take advantage of them. CGI scripting is a lot more universal by platform, and offers greater data-manipulation capabilities.

The three examples we are going to go through demonstrate how to write a script that can assemble your pages on the backend, recognize a previous visitor, or respond to user feedback. Again, I'm not going to follow the four-section format presented in the server-side assembly section. Instead, I will be focusing on the bare-bones commands that drive user input and subsequent page generation via CGI.

Example 1: Assembling a Page via CGI

The advantage to writing a page via CGI is that you can later build upon your first scripts to do sophisticated text processing or page generation built on variables. But you have to learn to walk before you can run, so here's a basic example of how to write a CGI script that prints out HTML for a browser to read.

Here's the code:

```
#!/usr/bin/perl/cgi-bin/
print "Content-type: text/html\n";
print "<BODY bgcolor=#FFFFFF text=#000000 link=#CC0000
vlink=#0000CC>\n\n";
print "<h3>This is a subheadline</h3>\n";
print "<p></p>\n";
print "This is the text that fills in the blanks.\n";
print "</BODY>\n";
```

Figure 13.7 shows how the browser will render it.

FIGURE 13.7:

The source code for the script-generated page

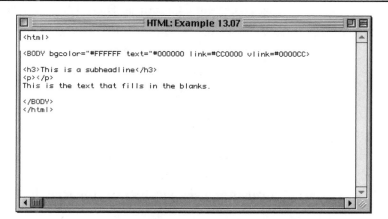

Figure 13.8 shows how the page looks.

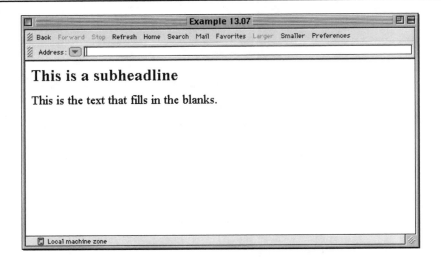

This script only has three basic functions, but they're the key to writing good CGI-based Web pages:

- `#!/usr/bin/perl/cgi-bin/`

  Don't forget that scripts need to start with the directory where you're storing all of your CGI scripts. This address is where the server is going to look for the script.

- `print "Content-type: text/html\n";`

  This line tells the server to read the output as a text-HTML file, and adds a line break. The line break is to make reading the output easier for you.

- `print "<p></p>\n";`

  Note the syntax: Everything in quotes is going to be read as source code. Each statement ends with a semicolon. And, notice that the \n tells the server to insert a line break and start a new line. Again, these line breaks are here to make sure that you can read the source code.

See how easy building pages via a CGI script is? You've just mastered the basics in three easy lines.

Example 2: Assembling a Page with Variable Content via CGI

The script above showed you the basic principles for writing a script that specifies an HTML output. While that's a handy chunk of code to append to the end of a feedback form or a guestbook script, it's not very illustrative of how to use scripts to automate site production.

In order to use CGI scripts as automated templating tools, think of the process this way:

- There is a chunk of HTML that has variables embedded in the form.

- There is a script that matches values to the variables.

Here's the code for the HTML:

```
<html>
<head></head>
<body bgcolor="#FFFFFF" text="#000000" alink="#330000" link="#330000" _
vlink="#000033">
<h1>$title</h1>
<p>$sentence1</p>
</body>
</html>
```

The two variables $title and $sentence are going to be filled in with a value that the user puts in a separate tool. The script for putting the values into the HTML is a simple one:

```
#!/usr/bin/perl/cgi-bin/
open (TEMPLATE "html file name");
local($/) = undef;
$template = <TEMPLATE>'
close (TEMPLATE)
$template =~ s/\$TITLE/$title/g;
$template =~ s/\$SENTENCE1/$sentence1/g;
print $template;
```

The $template variable is defined as the HTML file that calls the other variables—the HTML code in the very beginning of this example. You should remember the $title and $sentence1 variables from their inclusion in the HTML template as well; each line is saying, "For every defined variable, pull in and print the value."

It's effectively a search-and-replace script: Pair it with an input tool that allows you to enter specific values for each variable, and assemble a page from the entered values (See Figure 13.9).

FIGURE 13.9:

These three screens illustrate how one might embed the sample script into a Web-based interface, use it to enter new data, and generate a Web page—in that order.

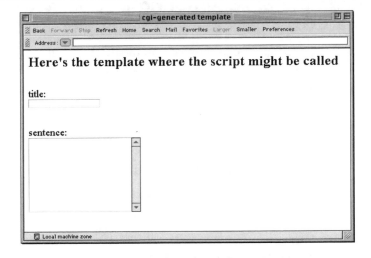

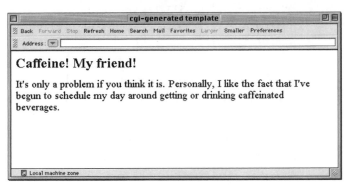

Example 3: An Input Form and a Response

Now that you know how Perl-driven scripts print out HTML, and how they drop variable values into HTML to be printed out, it's time to focus on how to get those values recorded for future fun and games.

The first step is to define your variables, since you'll be calling them in the script later:

```
<html>
<head></head>
<body bgcolor="#FFFFFF" text="#000000" alink="#330000" link="#330000" _
vlink="#000033">
<form action ="input.cgi" method="post">
<p>
<input type="text" size="20" maxlength="40" name="fname"><br>
First Name
</p>
<p>
<input type="text" size="20" maxlength="40" name="lname"><br>
Last Name
</p>
<p>
<input type="submit" value="submit">
</p>
</body>
</html>
```

In this case, the variables we're defining are fname and lname. The next step is to write input.cgi.

input.cgi

```
#!/usr/bin/perl/cgi-bin/
$fname=$in('fname');
$lname=$in('lname');
print "Content-type: text/html\n";
print "<html><head></head><body bgcolor="#FFFFFF" text="#000000"
alink="#330000" link="#330000" vlink="#000033">
";
print "Your firstname is $fname and your lastname is $lastname.";
print "</body></html>";
```

Figure 13.10 shows a sample output for the CGI script.

FIGURE 13.10:

An example of the output for the CGI script. In other words, this page was assembled in response to user input.

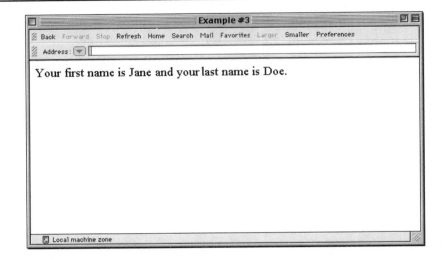

Summary

These are all very basic page assembly techniques meant to demonstrate how you can break down your Web page code and maximize it so you can change designs, change content, or assemble pages based on external input. Experiment with these basic techniques to find a way to make these low-cost, open-standard site-assembly methods work for you.

CHAPTER
FOURTEEN

DHTML: Every Action Is Scripted

- Understanding DHTML

- Using JavaScript and VBScript to code in DHTML

- Applying DHTML to your site

Dynamic HTML, or DHTML, is one of the most recent Web-development buzzwords, and a genuine behind-the-browser phenomenon. Every iteration of HTML and every new browser version introduces a new code or design concept that separates it from the "accepted" majority practice. In 1995, tables and background images changed the face of the Web; in 1996, table colors and finer font controls changed it even more. Those were all changes focusing on marking up existing items; those changes did not affect the behavior of any objects loading into your browser window. DHTML, on the other hand, not only changes how stuff looks in your browser, it changes how it behaves as well.

Why? Because DHTML is a combination of scripting, HTML tags, Cascading Style Sheets, and distinct file formats that allows developers to provide a more application-oriented website. The *dynamic* in DHTML refers to the shifting appearances, time-based presentations, and information-input features that static HTML pages cannot provide. These front-end features set DHTML-equipped websites apart from the others.

The backend of a DHTML-enhanced website is also different from that of a standard, static website. Since DHTML is made up of a collection of parts, how those parts work independently and together must be considered, as must how those parts are assembled on the front end. The development and production process for DHTML is different too.

This chapter outlines the basics of DHTML, starting with the parts that comprise it, and moves on to the different ways you can incorporate DHTML into your website.

DHTML: A Working Definition

DHTML is really a catchall name for the combination of scripting, HTML-specified style sheets, and the Document Object Model that builds dynamic Web pages. DHTML really moves beyond HTML because it breaks out of marking up site attributes and objects, and moves toward attaching behavior to those objects.

In a nutshell, the difference between HTML and DHTML is the ability to code a table on a Web page, and the ability to control data display on a Web page, from its appearance to how much data appears, and under what conditions. HTML allows you to mark up the structure of each page's content; DHTML allows you to mark up the behavior and appearance of the HTML-marked content.

Tools for Building and Testing DHTML

DHTML was designed to take advantage of newer W3C specs, among them style sheets and the DOM. As a result, it's not viewable with just any browser. The two browsers that are currently battling for DHTML dominance are Netscape and Microsoft Internet Explorer. Both of those browsers incorporated different aspects of DHTML when they released their version 4.0 browsers in the summer of 1997.

As a result, if you want to view any DHTML, you need to use either Netscape 4 or IE 4 or higher. If you want to develop DHTML, however, there may not be as many tools to help pull together the different components.

HTML editors may not recognize the style sheet and object tags; as for scripts, those are usually written by hand. The early forerunner for a WYSIWYG DHTML editor is Macromedia's Dreamweaver editor, available on the companion CD-ROM.

Dreamweaver is novel among WYSIWYG editors because it lets hard-core developers (you know, the ones who think any HTML tags not typed by hand are weak and suspect) monkey around in the code *and* view the results at the same time. You can then attack your page by tweaking the source code and eyeballing the results as you work, or by shaping the site in the preview window and watching how the code is coming along.

Best of all, Dreamweaver lets you customize your HTML preferences, so you can make it write code the way you would if your brain was a K-6 processor. You can also use the same preferences to load your coworkers' files into Dreamweaver and "correct" their coding style for a uniform site standard.

In addition to the time-saving customization, Dreamweaver has a library that lets you import or build chunks of HTML or JavaScript that you can use over and over. The Web also provides a lot of online support for the product; Webmonkey (`http://www.hotwired.com/webmonkey/`) maintains a series of scripts in their JavaScript library that you can easily munge into Dreamweaver, and Macromedia's home site (`www.macromedia.com`) points to several resources.

Dreamweaver exemplifies a lot of Web development tools and processes: after an initial investment in time and planning ahead, you'll be able to execute your tasks with efficiency.

Let's look at the three distinct parts of DHTML—scripts, style sheets, and the DOM—more closely.

Scripts

Scripts are small programs that can be embedded in a Web page, or linked to a Web page, and executed on the client side of the website-surfing experience, namely, the browser. When writing a script in DHTML, you're likely to write your scripts in JavaScript or VBScript.

DHTML provides a way to link in, or embed, scripts in a file via the <SCRIPT> </SCRIPT> tags. The attributes that you will want to take note of are:

<SCRIPT language> The scripting language that the code is written in. for example, <SCRIPT language="JavaScript">.

<SCRIPT src> The pointer to an externally linked script. For example, <SCRIPT src="nav.js">.

The reason scripts are an integral part of DHTML is because they take HTML and change it from a markup language to a way to control the way objects on a page behave. This allows developers to start extending the way the data on a site can be manipulated, and to control the appearance of a site more closely.

I'll go to go over scripting basics throughout this chapter.

Style Sheets

Style sheets can add appearance-driven attributes to objects that are defined. They work on two different levels:

- First, they provide metacategories of class and ID to different styles and objects. This allows the developer to apply a specific style to a group of objects, or to one specific object.

- Second, they provide specific and explicit instructions on how an object should look. These instructions include an object's position, its length and width, whether it is layered over or under other objects, what color or font it is.

DHTML can pair scripts with style sheets to manipulate or change the appearance of objects, as long as the object is specified in both the style sheet and the script.

This chapter is going to assume fluency in the Cascading Style Sheet Recommendation; for a working primer on how you can apply CSS to your site, flip back to Appendix C. If you're not certain about how to write style sheets, or what you can use style sheets to specify, turn to Chapter 6 for a review, or Appendix F for a complete tag listing.

Document Object Model

In order for scripts and style sheets to act on the objects in DHTML, those objects have to be defined. Enter the Document Object Model (DOM).

The Document Object Model is a W3C recommendation that identifies the objects that a developer can use to define objects which are later manipulated via script. For DHTML purposes, the DOM defines things like the window a Web page fits in, the total document, and the objects within the files.

A DOM also defines the attributes that an object can have. Remember that attributes are often things like "width," "visibility," and "id." So attributes can be specified via the DOM, yet the values for those attributes are defined via style sheet.

For more on the DOM and how it affects site structure, turn to Chapter 11.

Scripting Basics for DHTML

Scripts work by defining a group of objects and dictating actions that the objects perform, or actions that are performed on objects. When you incorporate scripting into your website, you have to shift the way you think about the markup that defines your Web pages.

In order to start thinking about your websites as a collection of objects and actions, it helps to become familiar with the jargon that goes with a script-driven, object-based site. The following sections review all of the different terms you need to become familiar with.

Variables

Every time you read a definition of a variable, it always reads something like "a variable is a placeholder." While the definition is accurate, it's not really illustrative. Instead, try this definition:

> *A variable is a symbolic representation of a value that you expect to modify or manipulate.*

For example, you could write the sentence, "I ate X cups of chocolate frozen yogurt." X can be a value ranging from 0 to infinity. But the important thing is that you can set conditions that make X change. You could write two sentences:

"I ate X cups of chocolate frozen yogurt last Friday."

"I ate X cups of chocolate frozen yogurt yesterday."

There is no guarantee that the two sentences share the same value for X; the *value* for X can be changed by the day of the week, or whether or not I even like chocolate frozen yogurt.

Arrays

An array is a collection of items. An alphabet can be said to be an array of letters. A starting team is an array of seven-foot-tall basketball players.

> **NOTE** An important thing to remember is that an array can be treated as an item to be manipulated, or that the individual members of an array can be manipulated.

Another important thing to remember is that arrays don't have to have a clear and definite limit on the number of items contained within it. You can create *dynamic arrays* which shrink or expand according to certain scripted actions. Note that these arrays change size within pre-known array lengths; the point is that you can add and subtract array items within the parameters of the dynamic array.

Arrays can also have varying levels of organization. There are simple arrays and complex arrays. *Simple arrays* are usually built on a 1:1 counting system, like this:

The StartTeam Array

Index	Player
0	Johnson
1	Jordan
2	Williams
3	Pippen
4	Barkley

There are two things to notice about this array. First, the value that we use to start counting is 0, not 1. This is because most computer languages start their arrays with 0, and it makes sense to extend that trait here. Second, there is only one value for each item in the array. The first item has the value "Johnson," the second item has the value "Jordan," and so on.

TIP One word that I should also define is the *index* of an array. The index is how an array organizes the items, much like an index of a book organizes the individual topics in a book. This is sometimes called an array of objects.

Complex arrays can have different values assigned to every item in the array. If we were to expand the StartTeam array to become a complex array, we could also add starting position and free throw percentage to the values per each item in the array, like this:

The StartTeam Array

Index	Player	Starting Guard	Free Throw Percentage
0	Johnson	No	80
1	Jordan	No	100
2	Williams	No	100
3	Pippen	Yes	70
4	Barkley	Yes	60

Arrays can be as complex as you want to make them—just remember that you'll be tracking what the values for the items in them are, and how those values can be affected by variables.

Built-In Functions, Built-In Objects

Most scripting consists of performing actions on variables. Some of these actions are operations you will define and write yourself; others are already specified in the language as built-in functions or built-in objects. If you're writing your DHTML in VBScript, you can call on a library of built-in *functions*; in JavaScript, you have a library of built-in *objects*.

All about Functions

VBScript has more than 80 built-in functions to do everything from change the case of your text to computing the sine of a number. Rather than run down each function, I'm just going to highlight a few that will come in handy when scripting DHTML, in Table 14.1.

TABLE 14.1: VBScript Functions for DHTML

Function	What It Does
CDate(expression)	This function converts an expression or variable to a date.
Date	This function allows you to return the date value.
Now	This function allows you to return the user's date and time.
Rnd(number)	If you invoke this function, it returns a random number between 0 and 1.
	If the value or variable calling the Rnd function is less than 0, then the function uses the same seed, or starting number, every time it is called. If the seed number is greater than 0, then Rnd uses the random number supplied as the seed for successive random numbers.
	You can use the different seed values to produce wildly disparate results based on a script.
MsgBox (prompt, buttons, title)	Prompt allows you to control the string that gets displayed in a message box. You could type anything like, "Click here!" or "Press retry if you like Hal Hartley films." Buttons allows you to specify the number and type of buttons you want to display in a message box. You can do this by assigning number values:
	0 - displays OK button only
	1 - displays OK and Cancel buttons
	2 - displays Abort, Retry, Ignore buttons
	3 - displays Yes, No, Cancel buttons
	4 - displays Yes and No buttons
	5 - displays Retry and Cancel buttons
	Title allows you to control the string of text that appears in a pop-up box's title bar.
Trim(*String*)	This removes any blank spaces before or after the string of characters being passed to the function.
Left ("String", x)	X number of left-most characters in the string x will be passed by the function.
Right ("String", x)	X number of right-most characters in the string x will be passed by the function.

All about Objects

JavaScript also has a number of built-in tools for performing actions on variables. You can use objects to manipulate strings of characters, to perform mathematical calculations, or to manipulate the message boxes in a way similar to VBScript's MsgBox function. Some of the most useful objects for writing DHTML are listed in Table 14.2.

TABLE 14.2: Javascript Objects for DHTML

Object	What It Does
anchor(name)	This turns (name) into an HTML anchor tag.
fontcolor(color)	This changes the object's font color to the color specified within the parentheses.
random()	This returns a semi-random number between 0 and 51.
Round()	This rounds a number up or down to the nearest integer.
getDate() getDay() getTime() setDate()	These are all objects that allow you to manipulate the date and time; getDate and getDay return the day of the month and the day of the week respectively. GetTime returns the time value, and setDate allows you to set the day of the month, if necessary.

Operators

An *operator* is another type of scripting symbol. Just as variables are symbols for values that can be manipulated, operators are symbols for the types of actions that can affect variables.

For example, the sentence x+y includes two variables and an operator. *x* and *y* are variables; + is an operator that tells the computer to add *x* and *y* together.

Operators come in three varieties: arithmetic, comparison, and logical. *Arithmetic* operators allow you to perform different types of classical math transactions like addition or subtraction. *Comparison* operators offer you a way to contrast two or more variables and use the difference to cue an event. *Logical* operators allow you to set up conditions like if a NOT b or if a OR b, and cue an event to happen if those conditions are met. These are sometimes referred to as branching IF THEN statements.

The two primary DHTML scripting languages are VBScript and JavaScript. Since JavaScript is more widely supported across browsers, we're going to do all of our examples in it, but Tables 14.3, 14.4, and 14.5 below do list the different types of operators by script language.

TABLE 14.3: Arithmetic Operators

Operator	Name	VBScript or JavaScript?
-	Negation	Both
*	Multiplication	Both
/	Division	Both
+	Addition	Both
-	Subtraction	Both
&	String concatenation	VBScript
^	Expontentiation	VBScript
\	Integer division	VBScript
Mod	Modulus	VBScript
%	Modulus	JavaScript
++	Increment	JavaScript
—	Decrement	JavaScript

TABLE 14.4: Comparison Operators

Operator	Name	VBScript or JavaScript?
<	Less than	Both
>	Greater than	Both
<=	Less than or equal to	Both
>=	Greater than or equal to	Both
=	Equality	VBScript

Continued on next page

TABLE 14.4 CONTINUED: Comparison Operators

Operator	Name	VBScript or JavaScript?
= =	Equality	JavaScript
<>	Inequality	VBScript
!=	Inequality	JavaScript
Is	Equivalence (more than one variable refers to the same item)	VBScript

TABLE 14.5: Logical Operators

Operator	Name	VBScript or JavaScript?
Not	Negation	VBScript
And	Conjunction	VBScript
Or	Disjunction	VBScript
XOr	Exclusion	VBScript
Eqv	Equivalence	VBScript
Imp	Implication	VBScript
!	Not	JavaScript
&&	And	JavaScript
||	Or	JavaScript

Controlling Event Sequence

The last scripting element you need to know about is controlling the flow and sequence of events in a script. Translated into English, this means that you need to be able to specify what happens, and when it happens.

The most basic mechanism for controlling when events happen is being able to specify what a script will do when it is presented with a decision. These critical junctures are known as *decision points*. The way a program handles a decision point is called a *control structure*.

If-Then/If-Else Statements

You have probably already worked with one classic control structure: the *If-Then* statement. This is a good statement to use if the decision point does not need to offer a lot of alternatives. Naturally, VBScriptand JavaScript handle the If-Then structure differently.

Here's an example of VBScript's If-Then structure:

```
If condition = true Then
    Action
    Action
    Action
End If
```

or

```
If condition = false Then
    Action
    Action
    Action
End If
```

The first line sets up a parameter for the script: if or when `condition` is true or false, then perform the following actions. This is the longhand syntax for VBScript. You can also write it like this:

```
If condition Then
    Action
End If
```

or

```
If Not condition Then
    Action
End If
```

VBScript assumes the `condition` is true or false depending on whether you have Not in the statement.

JavaScript handles If-Then statements differently. For one thing, the formal syntax is `if-else`. Second, you can write actions to take place *if* a condition is being met without *else* being required. Instead, *else* is used to extend the power of the control structure; *if* only trigger events when a certain condition is met, but *else* allows you to be very specific about what is to happen when that certain condition is not met.

To better illustrate the distinction, here are two examples.

JavaScript's `if` structure

```
if (condition) {
    action;
}
```

Here, if the *condition* is met, then *action* takes place. If not, nothing happens. If you want to control exactly what happens when the condition is not met, then use the `else` statement.

JavaScript's `if-else` structure

```
if (condition) {
    action1;
}
else{
    action2;
}
```

There is an extra degree of specificity in the statement. Should you want to add yet another layer of specificity by outlining what you want the script to do when the decision point returns multiple options, you could use an *if-elseif-else* statement.

JavaScript's `if-elseif-else` structure

```
if (condition) {
    action1;
}
elseif{
    action2;
}
else{
    action3;
}
```

See how there are now multiple specific options? VBScript has a similar control structure.

VBScript's `If-Then-Else` **structure**

```
If condition Then
    Action1
Else
    Action2
End If
```

Loop Structures

Once you've determined how events are going to progress if and when certain conditions are met, you can begin to set the frequency of certain scripted events. This is done by *looping* events. Loops allow you to repeat events as often as necessary.

VBScript has three ways of letting you loop things. They're outlined and explained in the examples below.

VBScript `Do-Loop` **structure**

```
Do
    Action1
    Action2
    Action3
Loop
```

You can use the `Do` statement to set a limit on the number of times you loop the actions, but this brings in a `While` statement. `While` sets up the loop to act so long as a condition is true (or false).

VBScript `Do-While-Loop` **structure**

```
x = 2
Do While x<50
        x*x+2
Loop
```

The last way to set up a repeating action within VBScript is to assign a `For-Next` structure to it. This statement sets up the premise that *For* every condition stated, an action will be taken; once the conditions are no longer true, the *Next* action will take place.

VBScript For-Next structure

```
For x=1 to 1000
    Action1
    Action2
Next
```

If you're using arrays, the structure looks like this:

```
For Each Index in Array
    Action1
    Action2
Next
```

Aren't you glad you know what index items and arrays are now?

If you're writing DHTML in JavaScript, then you'll be using a different set of structures. The first one is the most fundamental structure: the for loop.

JavaScript's for loop structure

```
for (starting condition; conditional item; updated condition;) {
    Action1;
    Action2;
    Action3;
}
```

for is a big deal because you can set the condition to be a starting condition, a conditional item (like x<100), and an updated condition, so all three conditions can have specific actions assigned to them. If you're thinking on a slightly smaller scale, you can use a while loop. while works a lot like VBScript's for-next structure: while a condition is true, perform an action.

JavaScript's while loop structure

```
while (conditional expression) {
    Action1;
}
```

As we get further in the chapter, we'll be using a lot of these structures to control the timing of events.

This section should give you a good overview of the pieces you need to understand before you begin scripting in DHTML. For an extremely thorough look at DHTML, try *Dynamic HTML: Master the Essentials* by Joseph Schmuller (Sybex, 1998).

The Differences between VBScript Syntax and JavaScript Syntax

As you look at the examples in this section, you may have noted that the VBScript examples and JavaScript examples look very different from each other. This is because each language was developed with its own set of syntactical rules.

To help you keep the differences between the two straight, and to assist you if you should decide to write DHTML in both VBScript and JavaScript, here is a list of helpful pointers for writing in either language.

- JavaScript statements end with a semicolon (;). Spaces and breaks are ignored by the JavaScript interpreter, but a semicolon signals the end of a statement no matter what.

- JavaScript variable names are case sensitive: `PictureCaption` and `picturecaption` are regarded by the JavaScript interpreter as two different objects. You will want to establish a capitalization policy early, and stick to it. VBScript is *not* case sensitive; `PictureCaption` and `picturecaption` are regarded by a VBScript interpreter as the same thing.

- Neither JavaScript variables nor VBScript variables can start with a number; they must start with a letter or underscore (_) character.

- VBScript does not allow periods as any part of the variable.

- VBScript has two types of procedures: *functions* return values (print x+2 for x <100 is a function that returns a value for x), and *subroutines* do not return values.

- JavaScript regards every procedure as a function. It also requires that its functions be surrounded by curly braces ({}).

- VBScript comments are written with an apostrophe (') commenting them out, like this:

  ```
  ' this is a comment.
  ```

- JavaScript comments are written with a double slash (//) preceding them, like this:

  ```
  //this is a comment.
  ```

Using DHTML to Control Site Appearance

One of the most useful things DHTML can do is add cause-and-effect appearance changes to your site. This allows you to set up your website content so it is presented as a series of prescribed events. What we're going to focus on, however, is using DHTML to link site appearance to user-driven events.

In plain English, this means that certain items will change colors, flash, or otherwise change appearance when your user performs some sort of action on them. This is just an extension of the color-changing properties many developers set up for their hyperlinks.

The sections below will outline how to perform some specific tasks in DHTML. Before we can get to the nitty-gritty and start writing code that turns your website into a slick, usable interface, we're going to review the role style sheets play in DHTML. In general, style sheets work to define the appearance of specific items on a page. In DHTML, style sheets provide the appearance descriptions, and they provide "hooks" which a script can access to change an object's look in certain situations.

Style Sheets and DHTML

The tyranny of tables as a layout tool is over. You can use a wide variety of style sheet filters to control precisely how your page is laid out—from measuring the spaces between objects to placing items on top of each other like so many cards. The trick is in Cascading Style Sheets Positioning (CSS-P). Although CSS-P is only a W3C Working Draft—as opposed to a Recommendation—the alternatives proposed in the CSS-2 recommendation aren't widely implemented in the current browser market, so you'll want to read up on the workable practices for positioning items.

CSS-P: Cascading Style Sheet Positioning

Let's begin with the most basic idea: how items are positioned within a window. The upper-left corner of your browser window has the coordinates (0,0). The first zero refers to the vertical axis, and the second zero refers to the horizontal axis.

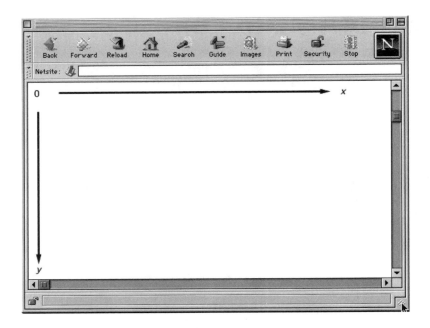

Any specifications for positioning items include a *top* attribute, which corresponds to the vertical axis, and a *left* attribute, which corresponds to the horizontal axis. Positive values move things down and to the right, negative values move them up and to the left. There are two different ways you can set your positions: absolute or relative.

Absolute positioning means that an object's left and top coordinates stay the same regardless of window size or screen resolution; if your user shrinks his screen to 300 pixels by 300 pixels, the nav bar you've written at top:400 px is off the immediate screen. The advantage to using absolute positioning is that you will always be guaranteed that your objects on a page stay precisely where you want them to be. Moreover, you will always be guaranteed that objects stay certain distances from each other. Absolute positioning is fixed positioning, which, while a boon for designing control freaks everywhere, can impede accessibility issues. Like many other things in Web development, you have to balance the benefits and drawbacks for your site.

Relative positioning is the other alternative. It means that any left and top coordinates are set up relative to the size of the display screen, using percentages. Figure 14.1 illustrates how this translates in real-life code.

FIGURE 14.1:

The size of the browser window opened up by 50 percent. Note that the placement of the big black box moved accordingly.

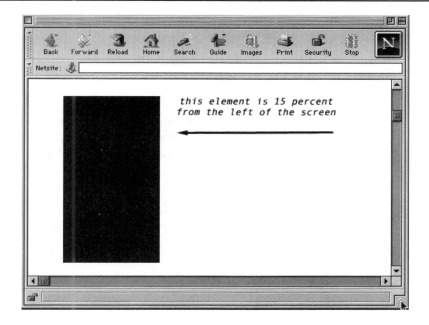

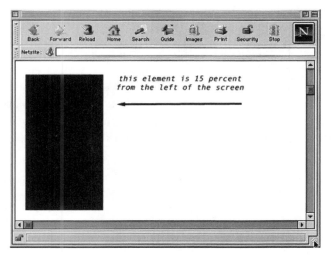

The code for the big black box reads:

```
<DIV id="sample" style="position: relative; left: 10%; top: 25%;
bgcolor:#000000">
```

The box stays in the same position relative to the browser window's dimensions, but it may change in relation to the other objects in the window.

Relative positioning is best used if you're trying to preserve the spatial relationships between items and include them on a page regardless of screen size. It does not allow you the same degree of appearance control as absolute positioning, but it does allow you to "resize" the page layout automatically.

But how do you attach positioning to the items in your site? One way is to attach styles to every tag on your site, but that makes attaching a style sheet inefficient, and opens the potential for losing track of all of the different styles you have throughout the site. A better way to ensure a uniform, consistent style across your site is to use block-level tags to set a uniform layout, and attach positioning attributes to those tags.

Another advantage of block-level tags is that they can be a handy way for you to start thinking of your site as being built like a deck of cards, rather than an eternally spreading flat piece of paper. This shift in perspective allows you new freedom in layout.

Sometimes, you want to use a block of color to set apart a specific page element, or to add a visual cue that ties the content into the rest of the layout. You just want to slip a little extra color behind the rest of your layout.

Using the z-order properties in CSS-P, you can. *Z-order* specifies the stacking order of page elements. If no value is specified, the browser just assumes that the element is sitting on the same field as every other element in the page, at a default value of zero. If a z-order value for an element is negative, the item is sitting behind other items; if it's positive, it may be in front of other elements. The third iteration of the Society for Cognitive Dissonance website in Chapter 18 demonstrates positioning. Here's how it works:

```
<div id="cframe" style="position:absolute; z-index:40; left:20 px; _
top:20px; width:500px; height:500px; border:1; bordercolor:#003366; _
background-color:#003366;">
<div id="content" style=" position:absolute; z-index:80; left:4px; _
top:4 px; width: 492px; height:492px; border:1; bordercolor:#FFFFFF; _
background-color:#FFFFFF;">
</div>
</div>
```

The rule of thumb for z-order values is the higher the value, the closer to the top of the page element "stack" the object is. Since the "content" div has a z-index value of 80, it will always sit on top of its green counterpart.

Style Sheet Filters and Transitions

Style sheets are being touted primarily as a way to control an object's conventional attributes like font face or background color. This is only one step toward increased control over site appearance via code. Another, more sophisticated approach is to use DHTML to create visual effects that offer low-bandwidth alternatives to GIFs. You can do this via filters. A *filter* refers to a program that processes a specific type of data and outputs the results. In the case of style sheet filters, these programs take control of an item's visual properties and allow you to manipulate the output. For example, an opacity filter lets you determine if something is see-through, hazy, or opaque.

For really high-tech effects, couple the filters with timed transitions to create a dynamic visual presentation.

Let's start with the syntax for including a filter:

```
<DIV STYLE = "filter: filterName (properties=values);">Filtered _
text</DIV>
```

It's just like any other inline style sheet property. The code syntax above illustrates how to add a filter to an object within a document, but you could easily set up your filters in a master style sheet. And like other style sheet IDs, you can apply several specific filter styles to the same object. There are only two things you need to remember when you use filters. First, in order for them to work, you need to specify both the height and the width of the object to be modified. Filters are easy to use if you've got a Windows/IE 4 development environment; they're not as easily implemented in Netscape.

I'm going to review the different filter styles, and show you the syntax and values for each of them. Because the heading of this section is about transitions, I'm also going to demonstrate how different filters can be coupled with transitions.

Alpha   The alpha filter allows you to control the intensity of an object's color or appearance. You use this if you want to make things fade in and out, or if you want to fade the appearance of an object for a static visual effect.

The syntax is pretty basic:

```
<DIV ID = "alphaEx1"
STYLE = "width: 100; height: 10; font-size: 24pt; color: #0000CCC; _
filter: Filter: alpha(opacity=80)">
```

```
Old websites don't die…they just 404.
</DIV>

<DIV ID = "alphaEx2"
STYLE = "width: 100; height: 10; font-size: 24pt; color: #0000CCC; _
filter: Filter: alpha(opacity=80, finishOpacity=30, style=1, _
startX=0%, startY=0%, finishX=30%, finishY=30%)">
Old websites don't die…they just 404.
</DIV>
```

The alpha filter has a number of different properties you can control:

opacity   This specifies how opaque or clear the object is. Opacity is the quality that controls the faded appearance. This attribute is required: Why else apply the alpha filter if you're not going to alter the intensity of the object?

If you want to control the fade or intensity of an object over time, you'd use the following attributes:

finishOpacity   This is the final value for an object's opacity. The beginning opacity is specified by the initial opacity tag. In order for an object to fade or grow more intense, the browser reads the two values and alters the gradient accordingly.

startX, startY   These are the starting points of the opacity gradient. They can be set in percentages or pixels.

finishX, finishY   These are the ending points of the opacity gradient. They shape the end result of fading over a gradient.

style   You can actually determine how you want the fade to appear on your object. Style=0 sets a uniform gradient across the area to be affected by the filter; style=1 applies a linear gradient (a line), and style=2 applies a radial (circling outward) gradient.

You can use JavaScript to control the fade gradient over time. Remember that this only works for Internet Explorer.

```
<SCRIPT LANGUAGE = "JavaScript">

// Detect IE 4
isIE4 = (navigator.appName == "Microsoft Internet Explorer");
```

```
// Run the function for the first time
if (isIE4) doFade(100, 0, 1, 0, 0, 0, 0);


// This is how to set up the fade.
function doFade(opacity, finishOpacity, style, startX, startY, _
finishX, finishY) {
if (finishX < 100) {
finishX += 4;
document.all.fadeText.style.filter = "alpha(opacity=" + opacity + ", _
finishOpacity=" +
finishOpacity + ", style=" + style + ", startX=" + startX + ", _
startY=" + startY + ",
finishX=" + finishX + ", finishY=" + finishY + ")";
}
}

</SCRIPT>
```

Chroma   This filter works a lot like a GIF transparency application: You use it to select a specific color and tell the browser to render it transparent.

The syntax for the tag is pretty basic: The image that the filter is going to be affecting is specified, plus the color of the filter, and—as always—the height and width of the object to be filtered. Unlike the alpha filter, the chroma filter only has one property that you can manipulate. That property—color—can be manipulated to select parts of an odd-shaped image, then paired with another filter.

```
<IMG ID = "example1"
STYLE = "filter: chroma(color=#FFFFFF)" SRC = "cliff.gif" HEIGHT = _
"100" WIDTH = "100" BORDER = "0">
```

Drop Shadow   This is a typical effect—setting a shadow behind text or another image. Unfortunately, setting up a shadow effect on a website used to require bandwidth-crunching GIFs.

As with the other filters, the syntax is fairly basic:

```
<DIV ID = "dropShadow"
STYLE = "width: 100; height: 100; font-size: 18pt;
font-family: courier new, courier; color: #CC0000;
```

```
filter: dropShadow(color=#000000, offX=10, offY=10, positive=1)">
Shadow
</DIV>
```

The filter syntax has a few properties that are fun to manipulate. The first is color—this allows you to set the color of the shadow behind the filtered object. The next two properties—offX and offY—determine how far from the main object the shadow will be. positive determines whether the shadow is inside the text, or set outside and behind it.

If you wanted to do something really cool, you could change a drop shadow filter on a JavaScript cue. For example, you could set the initial drop shadow filter to be the same color as your text, then have it slowly filter into a separate, contrasting color. Here's how:

```
<DIV ID = "dropShadow"
STYLE = "width: 100; height: 100; font-size: 18pt;
font-family: courier new, courier; color: #CC0000;
filter: dropShadow(color=#CC0000, offX=10, offY=10, positive=0)">
Shadow
</DIV>
```

and here's the JavaScript:

```
<SCRIPT LANGUAGE = "JavaScript">
document.all.dropShadow.style.filter = "dropShadow(color=#000000, offX=10,
offY=10, positive=1)";
</SCRIPT>
```

Here, we use the Document Object Model to tell the script that any object within the document named dropShadow should have a black filter. This could be used instead of attaching filters to individual objects on a page. In other words, you could create a set of templates, include the filters, and change the filters as necessary.

Before you start applying drop shadows to all of your filters, you should see whether you want to animate those filters as well. Here's how:

```
<SCRIPT LANGUAGE = "JavaScript">

// Detect IE 4
isIE4 = (navigator.appName == "Microsoft Internet Explorer");

// Run the function for the first time
if (isIE4) doShadow(20, 20, 1);
```

```
// Function to bring the shadow closer
function doShadow(offX, offY, positive) {
if (offX > 1) {
offX -= 1;
offY -= 1;
document.all.dropText.style.filter = "dropShadow(color=#009000, _
offX=" + offX + ", offY=" +
offY + ", positive=" + positive + ")";
}
}

</SCRIPT>
```

Glow   The glow filter does precisely what it says: It makes things glow. Note that the syntax only includes two attributes: the color that the object is to glow, and the strength of the glow.

```
<DIV ID = "glowShadow"
STYLE = "width: 100; height: 100; font-size: 12pt; color: #000000;
filter: glow(color=#FFFF00, strength=10">
Illuminating
</DIV>
```

If you wanted to make the glow pulsate eerily, you would manipulate the strength property through JavaScript:

```
<SCRIPT LANGUAGE = "JavaScript">

// Detect IE 4
isIE4 = (navigator.appName == "Microsoft Internet Explorer");

// Run the function for the first time
if (isIE4) doGlow(10);

function doGlow(strength) {
if (strength < 10) {
strength += 2;
}
else {
strength -= 2;
}
```

```
document.all.glowShadow.style.filter = "glow(color=#FFFF00, _
strength=" + strength + ")";
}
</SCRIPT>
```

This lets you change the strength of the glow from 8 to 12 and back again.

Mask   If you pair the mask filter with the chroma filter, you can create outlines of the invisible portions that you selected.

```
<IMG STYLE = "filter: chroma(color=#000000) mask(color=#FFFFFF)"
SRC = "cliff.gif" HEIGHT = "100" WIDTH = "100">
```

The mask filter has only one property: color. In order for you to use the mask filter correctly, you do need to pair it with the chroma filter.

Motion Blur   Before the advent of the motion blur filter, you could only create an illusion of motion on a Web page via gif89s. However, the filter has an advantage over gif89s, because it can be applied to plain HTML text. Once again, the filter offers a low-bandwidth alternative to a graphics-heavy design.

The syntax is:

```
<IMG ID = "blurGif"
STYLE = "position: absolute; left: 0; top: 20 px;
filter: blur(add=0, direction=45, strength=40)"
SRC = "cliff.gif" HEIGHT = "100" WIDTH = "100">
```

There are three attributes: add determines whether or not the image is put in the middle of the "blur." Direction determines the path that the blur goes in—in this case, 45 degrees. The strength factor identifies the intensity of the blur.

Adding Animation over Time

One of the most gratifying ways to spend your learning-about-DHTML time is to mock up a page where items move over time. Jargon junkies prefer to think of this as "animation," since animation does concentrate on changing an image's appearance over time. To introduce you to the world of telling things how to look—and how to change that look over time—we're going to work on a simple animation example where we use JavaScript to move an item from one side of the screen to another.

We're going to start by moving a simple <DIV> tag from the right of the page to the left. The idea is to get you comfortable with using programming to dictate the actions an item within a page file takes.

Here's the code. There are two different parts to focus on: the HTML markup, and the JavaScript that's going to affect the marked-up object.

The HTML markup is fairly simple:

```
<div id="sample" style="position:relative; left:500px; width:50px; _
height:50px;">
zooming text goes here!
</div>
```

Note that I attached the <DIV> tag's attributes as an inline style sheet rather than separating them and sticking them in a style sheet at the top of a document. This is just to illustrate how you can use JavaScript to manipulate the attributes of a given <DIV>.

Speaking of which, here's the JavaScript:

```
<script language="JavaScript">

function moveSample() {

    if ((document.layers) || (document.all)) {
      setTimeout('moveSample()', 100);
    }

    if(document.layers) {
       document.sample.left = - 5;
       if (document.sample.left <0) {
         document.sample.left = 500;
       }
    } else if (document.all) {
       sample.style.left = parseInt(sample.style.left) - 5;
       if (parseInt(sample.style.left) < 0) {
         sample.style.left = 500;
       }
    }


    }

</script>
```

Since there are two competing document object models, the script structure is written to say, "If the browser supports `document.layers`, then move the layer object called `sample`; if the browser supports `document.all`, then move the HTML object named `sample`." Note that the browser-specific actions are wrapped up in a non-browser-specific JavaScript. Because of this, you also need to stick a subroutine in the script that tells browsers not to execute either of the routines if the browser doesn't support either the `document.layer` or `document.all` object.

So the script does this:

> *If* the browser is Netscape and supports the `document.layers` object, move the `sample` object.

> *Or else*, if the browser is MSIE and supports the `document.all` object, move the `sample` object.

> But before you do, check to make sure the browser supports either `document.layers` or `document.all`, and if it does, then launch the subroutine `moveSample` on a timeout.

The basic mechanics of the script are all hammered out. So only two questions remain:

- How do you set up the timing so that the animation moves?
- How do you change the object's left position attribute over time?

Let's look at the way each subroutine answers these questions.

```
if(document.layers) {
    document.sample.left -= 5;
    if (document.sample.left <0) {
      document.sample.left = 500;
    }
  }
```

The subroutine starts by grabbing the left value of the object sample, and subtracting 5. So long as the value stays above zero, the script will keep subtracting 5. Once the value dips to 0 or below, the loop is reset.

```
else if (document.all) {
    sample.style.left = parseInt(sample.style.left) - 5;
    if (parseInt(sample.style.left) < 0) {
      sample.style.left = 500;
    }
  }
```

This subroutine identifies the `style.left` selector set for the object `sample`. Once it's identified, the routine starts subtracting 5. So long as the value stays above zero, the script will keep subtracting 5. Once the value dips to 0 or below, the loop is reset.

So what cues either of these scripts? The first subroutine does:

```
if ((document.layers) || (document.all)) {
    setTimeout('moveSample()', 100);
}
```

After the subroutine checks to make sure that the browser in question supports either of the document object models that drive DHTML, it takes a positive feedback value to count down to launching the animation in `moveSample`.

NOTE You'll remember that Netscape and Microsoft differ significantly in their DHTML syntax. Netscape identifies their objects as `document.sample`, meaning that the object sample is a child of the document currently in the browser window. Microsoft defines its object's style attributes by telling the browser, "Hey! This is an attribute!" They do it like this: `sample.style.left`.

But how is this useful for my site, you ask. First, remember that the code I showed you is just a simplified, isolated example meant to show how you can use JavaScript to create cross-browser DHTML. In order to apply the basic principles of this example, you could make this animation a function of your introductory pages.

Simply clean up the code so your DIVs are calling a style defined in a sitewide style sheet. Then create a JavaScript library document. This library document would hold the code for all of the routines on the site. Since your routines will all have different names (the routine `moveSample` is only one example), they would not misfire on unintended document objects. An added advantage to setting up your site for both a style library and a script library is that you can standardize actions and appearances across your site. In addition, performing maintenance is easier because you only have to tweak one master file to affect the site as a whole.

Extra Points for Programming

One of the reasons that this works so well is because the page is really simple. But your website construction is going to be much more complex. You may have embedded <DIV>s within <DIV>s, and trying to keep track of all your embedded objects may get tricky.

For example, if you have the following structure:

```
<DIV id = sample>
    <DIV id=example>
        <DIV id=instance>
        move this text!
        </DIV>
    </DIV>
</DIV>
```

You're trying to target the `<div>` instance, so you're going to end up writing a subroutine for `document.sample.example.instance`. If I may speak frankly, I only want to type that once in my life; I can't imagine anyone else would want to do so repeatedly in the name of DHTML.

However, rather than tell the browser you don't really feel like typing, you're going to have to tell it how to regard the object `document.sample.example.instance`. The smartest way to do it is to help the browser make the association between `document.sample.example.instance` and your nickname for it, bunky.

How? By writing a separate script to help the browser make the association:

```
<script>
function setup(){
    if(document.layers){
    bunky = document.sample.example.instance;
    } else if(document.all) {
    bunky = instance.style;
    }
}
</script>
```

The beauty behind this script is that bunky translates into whatever object the browser needs to read it as. Therefore, you can probably slim down our earlier script by rewriting it as:

```
<script language="JavaScript">

function moveSample() {

  setTimeout('moveSample()', 100);
```

```
bunky.left = parseInt(bunky.left) - 5;
      if(parseInt(bunky.left) < 0){
bunky.left = 500;
}

}
```

Those conditional subroutines we used in the first round are separated out in the function `setup() script`, and then called in the function `moveSample()`. Since the object bunky has already been defined for any browser that supports either IE or Netscape's DOM, it doesn't need to be recalled.

Again, the impatient Webmaster wants to know, what does this do for me? Templates, template, templates. You could write a series of elegant set-function scripts to define the different object hierarchies you're using across your site, then drop the new, improved, and abridged code into the pages that need it most. In order to take maximum advantage of this, you must have plotted out your site well in advance, including:

- The page structure and the object hierarchies contained within each page.

- How many common objects you will have across the site, and how many objects are unique to each page.

- How you're going to assemble pages comprised of both page-unique objects and site-wide objects.

- How you're going to name all your different objects. It is imperative that you keep track of names, since your scripts will rely on them.

- What style and appearance parameters you have, what parameters you can alter, and what parameters remain fixed across the site.

Appearance Changes Based On User Events

Remember the event handler? It's about to become your best friend. The following three examples all illustrate how to use JavaScript's event handlers to manipulate the appearance of your site. Event handlers, for those of you keeping track of the jargon at home, are "hooks" within JavaScript that allow you to attach significant actions to specific user actions.

Mousing Over Items

One of the first tricks anyone learns when they begin coding in JavaScript is the onMouseOver event handler. A typical example:

```
<A HREF="http://www.schmeiser.com/content/sitemap.html" _
onMouseOver="(window.status='sitemap'); return true">
```

This changes the status bar in the browser so the user sees that the link leads to a sitemap.

However, the status bar cue that readers are getting may be a little too subtle. You can use DHTML to make images or text swap appearance whenever a user mouses over them or off them.

Let's start with how to change the appearance of a text-based link on mouseover. The first thing we'll do is decide how the text is going to look when you mouse over it, and when you mouse off it.

In this case, I decided I wanted two different styles:

```
<STYLE type="text/css">

.mouseon     {font-family:arial, helvetica; font-weight: bold; _
font-size:24px; font-color:#CC0000}

.mouseout    {font-family:arial, helvetica; font-weight: bold; _
font-size:18px; font-color:#CCCCCC}

</STYLE>
```

The class mouseon shows the appearance of the text when someone moves their mouse over it; the class mouseout defines what happens when a user moves their mouse away.

The next step is to attach those styles to the object that you want them to modify:

```
<A HREF = "link.html"  CLASS = "off" onMouseOver = "this.className _
='mouseon';" onMouseOut = "this.className = 'mouseoff';">
Roll over me to see the text change!
</A>
```

Here's what they look like.

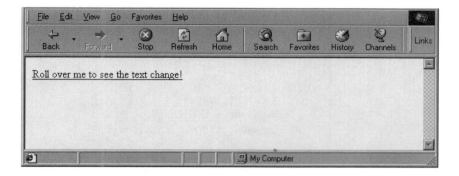

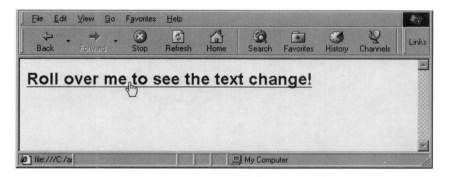

One of the drawbacks to user-driven text changes is that the browser still has to recognize the changeable object as a hot spot, i.e., an area on the page that is supposed to parlay a reaction after the user inputs it. So you could still use the trick above, even with no destination URL, like this:

```
<A HREF = "#"  CLASS = "off" onMouseOver = "this.className ='mouseon';" _
onMouseOut = "this.className = 'mouseoff';">
Roll over me to see the text change!
</A>
```

Another, more popular application for DHTML-rollover scripts is one where images are swapped in and out as a user rolls her mouse over the site.

To do the magic switcheroo, you need to remember the following: for every rollover, there's a rollout. Each image-rollover is actually dual images. The image that's called during the user rollover is called `imgAover.gif`; the default image is called `imgAout.gif`.

There are two parts to the rollover—the JavaScript and the HTML. Let's go over the JavaScript first:

```
<SCRIPT LANGUAGE = "JavaScript">
<!--//

        if (document.images) {
            imgAover = new Image();
            imgAover.src = "imgAover.gif";

            imgAout = new Image();
            imgAout.src = "imgAout.gif";

        }


function imgOver(imgName) {
        if (document.images) {
            document[imgName].src = eval(imgName + "over.src");
        }
}


function imgOut(imgName) {
        if (document.images) {
            document[imgName].src = eval(imgName + "out.src");
        }
}
// -->
</SCRIPT>
```

There are three different subroutines in the script. The first defines the images that are being moved in and out. The second and third subroutines are proof that we're planning ahead; they describe a function that says, "If this image is being called, produce the source with [image name]+over, or [image name]+out."

The advantage to this is that you've already defined these sources in the first subroutine. If you wanted to continue to perform image-swapping for another three images, all you would have to do is tack on more image source definitions, thus making the subroutine look like this:

```
if (document.images) {
                imgAover = new Image();
```

```
        imgAover.src = "imgAover.gif";
        imgBover = new Image();
        imgBover.src = "imgBover.gif";

        imgAout = new Image();
        imgAout.src = "imgAout.gif";
        imgBout = new Image();
        imgBout.src = "imgBout.gif";

    }
```

Now, let's take a look at the HTML for the image swap:

```
<!--insert HTML formatting -->

<A HREF = "foo.html"
 onMouseOver = "imgOver('imgA')"
 onMouseOut = "imgOut('imgA')">
<IMG NAME= "imgA" BORDER = 0 HEIGHT = 71 WIDTH = 500 SRC = "imgAout.gif">
</A>
```

Remember that we defined the functions imgOver and imgOut as the second and third subroutines. So the anchor tag is doing three things:

1. It sends an event handler (onMouseOver, onMouseOut) to the browser.

2. It cues a corresponding function (imgOver, imgOut) depending on the event handler.

3. It passes a value to the function, telling it what image corresponds with the action that the function is going to take.

So the <A HREF> tag provides all the information that the image-swapping JavaScript needs. Why bother with the IMG tag at all?

Because you need a browser default. The JavaScript is event-based, which means that the user has to do something to trigger it. More importantly, the JavaScript needs to know what image it's affecting. Hence the IMG NAME (imgA): This tells both the browser and the script what the default image value for the site is.

Dragging and Dropping Objects

The last DHTML skill I'm going to cover pairs event handlers with the physical coordinates of an object—dragging and dropping. Once you've mastered this, you can pair the drag and drop with cookies or CGI scripts to give your users customizable interfaces.

But before you run away with the cool interface award, learn how to walk. In this case, learn how to write DHTML that lets you plot how to drag and drop items. This is one area where it is especially important that you plan every step ahead of time.

Our example is the Mondrian collage toy: The page is a collection of bright rectangles that users can rearrange to make their best approximation of a post-Impressionist painting. The steps we're going to take are:

1. Define the objects to be dragged and dropped.

2. Define the action of dragging.

3. Define a way to tell the browser that you've stopped dragging the object.

4. Give the user a way to repeat steps 2-3 as often as they like.

The first step actually breaks down into a few substeps. The first is the creation of the HTML objects to be dragged and dropped. We're going to do this by defining the styles of the Mondrian blocks in the style sheet, then by making objects in the body of the document.

```
<STYLE type="text/css">
<!--//

#block1    {position: absolute; z-index:2000; visibility: visible;
left:25; top:25; height:60; width:150; background-color:#FF0000}
#block2    {position: absolute; z-index:1750; visibility: visible;
left:50; top:50; height: 120; width:120; background-color:#00FF00}
#block3    {position: absolute; z-index: 1500; visibility: visible;
left:100; top:100; height: 100; width: 250; background-color:#0000FF}
#block4    {position: absolute; z-index:1250; visibility: visible;
left: 250; top:250; height:30; width:50; background-color:#FF00FF}
#block5    {position: absolute; z-index: 1000; visibility: visible;
left:400; top:400; height: 75; width: 150; background- color:#FFFF00}

//-->
</STYLE>
```

```
<!--insert HTML formatting here -->

<div id="block1"> block1</div>
<div id="block2">block2</div>
<div id="block3">block3</div>
<div id="block4">block4</div>
<div id="block5">block5</div>
<div id="block6">block6</div>
```

Once you've created those substeps, the next step is to start your script by setting the number of drag-and-drop objects you want to be able to manipulate:

```
<SCRIPT language ="JavaScript">
var totalblocks=5;
</SCRIPT>
```

There's more to the script—the remaining three steps are nothing but scripting.

We're going to be manipulating five different block objects, represented by uniquely named <DIV>s. As with the rest of the DHTML we've written, we want to write the code with as few lines as possible, and we want to write stuff that can continue to work if we change the number of objects it's acting on, like expanding our block collection to 25 objects.

WARNING   Naturally, because we're trying to be efficient, we are going to run into complications. The biggest one is this: MSIE and Netscape deal with event handlers and moused events much differently. Therefore, the functions for dragging and dropping objects are much different for the two browsers; we're going to include them as an `if-else` in our script.

Before we write our code, let's think the dragging-and-dropping thing through a little more carefully. First, we don't want one dragging action to erase the previous actions. Therefore, we will need to specify that old objects selected are null whenever the user triggers a new event.

So the script below defines the DIVs (or, as Netscape prefers to think of them, layers), and it creates global variables to keep track of the mouse's position, the actively selected layer, and the number of layers that can be manipulated. Then, it tells the browser how to capture the mouse clicking down and releasing again.

Here's the script, broken up into easily digestible pieces:

```
<SCRIPT language=JavaScript>
```

First, define those global variables. These keep track of mouse position and which layer is currently selected.

```
var oldX, oldY, objSelected="null";
var totalblocks=5;
```

Next comes code for registering the mousedown and mouseup events. When a user clicks the mouse on an object, that signals the beginning of the drag. When they release the click, it's the end. Note that this code only works in Netscape, as specified by the first line.

```
if (navigator.appName == "Netscape") {
        document.captureEvents(Event.MOUSEUP|Event.MOUSEDOWN);
        document.onmousedown=begindrag;
        document.onmouseup=enddrag;
}
```

Here's a function that allows the browser to determine which object layer just got clicked. This is crucial to figuring out what object to move. clickX and clickY are mouse coordinates. The first line sets up a loop, and the eval statement sets the variable object equal to whatever is being clicked on by attaching the current index to block. All the next two lines say is, "If the user clicks anywhere within the left or top parameters of the block, tell me." The last line kills the drag-and-drop functions if it turns out that the user was clicking on a dead area (return value null).

```
function getSelectedElement(clickX,clickY) {
        for (var i=1; i<totalblocks+1; i++){
eval('obj=document.layers["block' +i+ '"]');
                if ( (clickX > obj.left) && (clickX < _
obj.left+obj.clip.width)
                                && (clickY > obj.top) && (clickY < _
obj.top+obj.clip.height)){
                        return obj;
                }
        }
        return ("null");
```

Now that you've set up the global variables and a way to detect the clicked object, write a function that begins the dragging sequence.

NOTE   **e** is an event being passed, and **e.pageX** and **e.pageY** are the mouse's coordinates at the moment it is clicked. In other words, they're the beginning coordinates. The rest of the function specifies that a non-**null** value (remember, the **null** value means the user is clicking on dead space) triggers the function drag on **mousemovement**.

```
function begindrag(e) {
        objSelected=getSelectedElement(e.pageX,e.pageY);
        if (objSelected != "null"){
                document.captureEvents(Event.MOUSEMOVE);
                document.onmousemove=drag;
                oldX=e.pageX;
                oldY=e.pageY;
                return false;
        }
}
```

Next, write the drag function that you just called. Note that event **e** is being called again and that the **offset()** method is what's moving the layer by calculating the difference between the old XY coordinates and the current XY coordinates.

```
function drag(e) {
        obj.offset(e.pageX - oldX, e.pageY - oldY);
        oldX = e.pageX;
        oldY = e.pageY;
}
```

Okay, we've got the groundwork laid down. Now it's time to write the function that begins the drag sequence. **e** is once again invoked as the event to be handled, and the second line registers both the initial mouse position and whether or not it lands on a draggable object. If the mouse is on an object, it sets the initial XY coordinates oldX and oldY (you say those in the drag function).

```
function begindrag(e) {
        objSelected=getSelectedElement(e.pageX,e.pageY);
        if (objSelected != "null"){
                document.captureEvents(Event.MOUSEMOVE);
                document.onmousemove=drag;
                oldX=e.pageX;
                oldY=e.pageY;
                return false;
        }
```

Now it's time to wrap this up with the end function. The `releaseEvents` line tells the browser and script that event **e** is over, so the layer being dragged stops moving after the user lets go of the button.

```
function enddrag(e) {
        document.onmousemove=0;
        document.releaseEvents(Event.MOUSEMOVE);
        objSelected="null";
        return false;
}
```

Finally, because IE handles mouse events differently, here's the code for hashing out the same drag-and-drop functions in IE. This is adapted straight from the Microsoft website. This `if` statement maps out the sequence of functions the browser is going to call.

```
if (navigator.appName != "Netscape") {
  document.ondragstart = doDragStart;
  document.onmousedown = doMouseDown;
  document.onmousemove = doMouseMove;
  document.onmouseup = new Function("curElement=null")
 }
```

This sets a loop based on the drag object's name.

```
function doDragStart() {
   if ("IMG"==event.srcElement.tagName)
      event.returnValue=false;
   }
```

This ends the sequence by passing a finished value to the browser. That value is calculated in the **doMouseMove** function.

```
function doMouseDown() {
    if ((event.button==1) && (event.srcElement.tagName=="IMG"))
       curElement = event.srcElement
   }
```

This function performs the same role as the function **getSelectedElement** way up at the top of the script. The only difference is that this performs that function for IE.

```
var curElement;
function doMouseMove() {
  var newleft=0, newTop = 0
  if ((event.button==1) && (curElement!=null)) {
        // position object
```

```
                    newleft=event.clientX-document.all.OuterDiv.offsetLeft-
(curElement.offsetWidth/2)
            if (newleft<0) newleft=0
            curElement.style.pixelLeft= newleft
            newtop=event.clientY -document.all.OuterDiv.offsetTop-
(curElement.offsetHeight/2)
            if (newtop<0) newtop=0
            curElement.style.pixelTop= newtop
            event.returnValue = false
            event.cancelBubble = true
       }
    }
```

```
</SCRIPT>
```

So the script is a bit of a mind-boggler, but it's just as portable as you need it to be. Think of it as the capstone to your DHTML skills. Just in case you got a little cross-eyed trying to string together the code between explanations, here's the whole thing again, complete and uncommented.

dropdrag.js

```
<script language="javascript">
var oldX, oldY, objSelected="null";
var totalblocks=5;
if (navigator.appName == "Netscape") {
  document.captureEvents(Event.MOUSEUP|Event.MOUSEDOWN);
  document.onmousedown=begindrag;
  document.onmouseup=enddrag;
}
function getSelectedElement(clickX,clickY) {
        for (var i=1; i<totalblocks+1; i++){
eval('obj=document.layers["block' +i+ '"]');
                if ( (clickX > obj.left) && (clickX <
obj.left+obj.clip.width)
                                    && (clickY > obj.top) && (clickY <
obj.top+obj.clip.height)){
                        return obj;
                }
        }
        return ("null");
function begindrag(e) {
        objSelected=getSelectedElement(e.pageX,e.pageY);
        if (objSelected != "null"){
```

```
                        document.captureEvents(Event.MOUSEMOVE);
                        document.onmousemove=drag;
                        oldX=e.pageX;
                        oldY=e.pageY;
                        return false;
                }
        }
        function drag(e) {
                obj.offset(e.pageX - oldX, e.pageY - oldY);
                oldX = e.pageX;
                oldY = e.pageY;
        }
        function begindrag(e) {
                objSelected=getSelectedElement(e.pageX,e.pageY);
                if (objSelected != "null"){
                        document.captureEvents(Event.MOUSEMOVE);
                        document.onmousemove=drag;
                        oldX=e.pageX;
                        oldY=e.pageY;
                        return false;
                }
        }
        function enddrag(e) {
                document.onmousemove=0;
                document.releaseEvents(Event.MOUSEMOVE);
                objSelected="null";
                return false;
        }
        if (navigator.appName != "Netscape") {
          document.ondragstart = doDragStart;
          document.onmousedown = doMouseDown;
          document.onmousemove = doMouseMove;
          document.onmouseup = new Function("curElement=null")
         }

        function doDragStart() {
           if ("IMG"==event.srcElement.tagName)
             event.returnValue=false;
         }
        function doMouseDown() {
           if ((event.button==1) && (event.srcElement.tagName=="IMG"))
             curElement = event.srcElement
         }
```

```
var curElement;
function doMouseMove() {
  var newleft=0, newTop = 0
  if ((event.button==1) && (curElement!=null)) {
        // position object
        newleft=event.clientX-document.all.OuterDiv.offsetLeft-
(curElement.offsetWidth/2)
        if (newleft<0) newleft=0
        curElement.style.pixelLeft= newleft
        newtop=event.clientY -document.all.OuterDiv.offsetTop-
(curElement.offsetHeight/2)
        if (newtop<0) newtop=0
        curElement.style.pixelTop= newtop
        event.returnValue = false
        event.cancelBubble = true
    }
  }

</SCRIPT>
```

Using DHTML to Control Information Display

The most valuable function DHTML can perform is as a means to control information display. By information display, I mean how information looks, and how much of it is visible to the user at any given time.

With DHTML, there are two ways to control information display. The quickest and easiest way is to control the visibility, and have the specific data appear or disappear on a user cue like clicking. The MediaDiet case study in Chapter 24 sets up an example of this.

The second method, which I'm going to go into here in greater detail, is via tabular data control. Rather than focusing on the appearance attributes, Tabular Data Control, or TDC, focuses on ways to sort information so it's available only when certain criteria are met. This sounds like any website option—check a few boxes, hit a submit button, see what happens—but there is one key difference: TDC is a strictly client-side feature, so there are no secondary queries to the server.

Read on for more detailed information about TDC and how to implement it.

Tabular Data Control

Tabular Data Control (TDC) is an ActiveX control that allows you to provide both data and controls for displaying that data on the client side of a website. This is both good and bad: good in that it allows a user to manipulate data, and bad in that it is currently an ActiveX control, and thus is only accessible to people who are running IE 4 with ActiveX controls turned on.

Although the mechanism for TDC automatically limits the audience, the idea behind it—eliminating long client-server exchanges in favor of giving the client viewing a site the tools to control their own data display—is a good one, and therefore deserves to be explained here.

The idea behind TDC is to provide both a data structure and a preprogrammed filter for manipulating the items in a data structure, to bundle those two items into a Web page, and to push the file and the objects out to the client. All of the data the client needs, plus a filter for customizing their data, is on their machine.

> **NOTE**
> This is analogous to going to a travel site, downloading all of the possible flight schedules for a specific route, then playing with date and time results without having to requery the server.

In order to set up a document that can use TDC, a Web developer has to follow several steps. They're outlined below.

Step 1: Store Your Data

Most data on a page is displayed in the midst of HTML tags. It can be hard-coded in, like this:

```
<TD valign=top align=left>Virginia's capital is Richmond</TD>,
```

or called in via script like this:

```
"print <TD valign=top align=left>$statecap</TD>"
```

The point is that you're used to thinking of data as something to be displayed within markup. Readjust your perspective about 45 degrees, and start thinking of data as a separate, organized file, For our example, we're going to create a text file like this:

```
States, Capitals
Virginia, Richmond
```

```
South Carolina, Columbia
Maryland, Annapolis
New York, Albany
California, Sacramento
```

We're going to call it `caps.txt`. Note that every row of text should have a hard return after it.

Step 2: Write Your Markup

We're going to display the data in the `caps.txt` file as a two-column table. A normal table without TDC would look like this:

```
<TABLE>
<TR>
<TD>Virginia</TD><TD>Richmond</TD>
</TR>
<TR>
<TD>South Carolina</TD><TD>Columbia</TD>
</TR>
<TR>
<TD>Maryland</TD><TD>Annapolis</TD>
</TR>
<TR>
<TD>New York</TD><TD>Albany</TD>
</TR>
<TR>
<TD>California</TD><TD>Sacramento</TD>
</TR>
</TABLE>
```

But since we're calling in the data file, we've got to add a few extra elements. The first is a table head to mark off the beginning of the table, and a table body to mark off the table data:

```
<THEAD>
<TR><TD colspan=2>States and Capitals in the U.S.A</TD></TR>
</THEAD>
<TBODY>
<TR>
<TD>Virginia</TD><TD>Richmond</TD>
</TR>
</TABLE>
</TBODY>
```

The second element is an ID to be connected to the TDC. This file gets called in the TABLE tag:

```
<TABLE width=400 Datasrc=#tdcCapdata>
```

Step 3: Add the TDC

This is the object that the browser is going to read and recognize. The syntax is as follows:

```
<OBJECT ID=tdcCapdata
CLASSID="clsid:333C7BC4-460F-11D0-BC04-0080C7055A83">
        <PARAM NAME="DataURL" name="caps.txt">
        <PARAM NAME="UseHeader" value="True">
</OBJECT>
```

The `object ID` corresponds to the ID that you set up in the table. The `CLASSID` tells the browser which ActiveX control is being used, and the `PARAM` values set up conditions for reading the data. The first `PARAM` tells you the name of the file to draw data from, and the second `PARAM` tells the browser to read `caps.txt` as a header file, then data.

The Different Parameters for the TDC Object

Throughout the rest of the chapter, I will be pulling in different <PARAM> types and telling you what they do for the object. I'm not making this up as I go along—there are predefined <PARAM> properties that can make your TDC object extremely specific.

<PARAM NAME="Filter">

This filter allows you to sift out entire data fields.

<PARAM NAME="Sort">

If you want to be able to compare one column of data against the other, use this parameter. This parameter is often used in tandem with the **UseHeader** parameter listed below; that header specifies the names of different columns, and the **Sort** parameter can specify whether a column is going to be organized in ascending (+) or descending (-) order. The syntax is <PARAM name="Sort" value="capitals; +population">.

Continued on next page

\<PARAM NAME="UseHeader">

This gives you the option of including header information at the beginning of your data file. The option comes in handy if you're trying to sort data by categories. The normal syntax is \<PARAM NAME="UseHeader" value="true"> if you're going to use a header. If not, make the value false.

\<PARAM NAME="DataURL">

All this does is provide a pointer to the separate data file that the TDC is going to access. It's a simple function, but an important one.

\<PARAM NAME="RowDelim">

This tells the TDC when one row of data has ended and a new one should be displayed. This parameter was developed in response to the problem of spitting out neat data rows in not-so-neat HTML tables. The syntax is usually \<PARAM NAME="RowDelim" value="newline">, thus cueing the TDC to treat each new line as a new row of data.

\<PARAM NAME="FieldDelim">

This is how the TDC distinguishes between data fields. The syntax is usually \<PARAM NAME="FieldDelim" value=","> which means that the TDC will use commas as separators.

\<PARAM NAME="AppendData">

If you have more than one DataURL file, the AppendData parameter tells the TDC whether the new file should be appended to the old one, or simply replace the old one. The syntax for adding the new file to the old one is \<PARAM NAME="AppendData" value="true">; to replace one data file with the new one, make the value false.

\<PARAM NAME="CaseSensitive">

This parameter allows you to decide if the TDC views lower- and uppercase versions of characters as different entities. If you want to be able to draw a distinction between TLC and tlc, set the value to true like this: \<PARAM NAME="CaseSensitive" value="true">; if you don't want to make your data case sensitive, set the value to false.

\<PARAM NAME="CharSet">

Just in case you don't plan on using the standard ISO character set, you can set a new character set, like Cyrillic, using this parameter.

Continued on next page

<PARAM NAME="Language">

This is another parameter that shines if you're trying to handle multilingual data requests. You'll be able to specify different languages as a value if need be; the default for any TDC where this parameter isn't set is English.

<PARAM NAME="EscapeChar">

If you're setting your data fields to separate on characters like commas and quotation marks, you might have difficulty convincing the TDC object that you want to enter "Bobo the small, insane, dancing monkey" as a discrete string. So you want to specify an escape character which will cue the TDC to read the following character as part of a string, not a row or field delimiter. We would write <PARAM NAME="EscapeChar" value="/">, and then make sure Bobo made it into the TDC by writing "Bobo the small/, insane/, dancing monkey."

<PARAM NAME="TextQualifier">

This is an optional way to set the limits on what a single chunk of data is in a field. For example, the TDC might assume that the data fields are delimited by commas, but if I wanted to have "Sacramento, CA" and "Carson City, NV" read as two objects and not four, I'd set the TextQualifier to recognize the stuff within quotes as a discrete data chunk. To do so, the syntax is <PARAM NAME="TextQualifier" value=""">.

Step 4: Delete Some Data

The next step is to delete the hard-coded data in the table and cue the browser to pull in the data from caps.txt.

```
<TABLE width=400 Datasrc=#tdcCapdata>
<THEAD>
<TR><TD colspan=2>States and Capitals in the U.S.A</TD></TR>
</THEAD>
<TBODY>
<TR>
<TD><DIV datafld="state"></DIV></TD>
<TD><DIV datafld="capital"></DIV></TD>
</TR>
[÷]
</TBODY>
</TABLE>
<OBJECT ID=tdcCapdata
```

```
CLASSID="clsid:333C7BC4-460F-11D0-BC04-0080C7055A83">
      <PARAM NAME="DataURL" name="caps.txt">
      <PARAM NAME="UseHeader" value="True">
</OBJECT>
```

All of the table cells lose their state capitals or states, but they gain a data field spec. The data in the text file gets pulled in through two columns. The results of your new and improved file are below:

Step 5: Filter the Data

Our first file only had five lines of text; in order to better demonstrate how the filtering works, we're going to rewrite the file with more data:

```
Region, State, Capital
New England, Maine, Augusta
New England, New Hampshire, Concord
New England, Vermont, Montpelier
New England, Rhode Island, Providence
Mason-Dixon, Maryland, Annapolis
Mason-Dixon, Virginia, Richmond
Mason-Dixon, North Carolina, Raleigh
Mason-Dixon, South Carolina, Columbia
Mason-Dixon, Georgia, Atlanta
```

```
Mason-Dixon, Florida, Tallahassee
West, Wyoming, Cheyenne
West, Colorado, Denver
West, Sacramento, California
West, Nevada, Carson City
```

Now, save the file as `caps.txt`. The object that corresponds with this file is:

```
<OBJECT ID=tdcCapdata
CLASSID="clsid:333C7BC4-460F-11D0-BC04-0080C7055A83">
        <PARAM NAME="DataURL" name="caps.txt">
        <PARAM NAME="UseHeader" value="True">
</OBJECT>
```

This is just the basis of the object. You can add different filters to display different pages:

```
<OBJECT ID=tdcCapdata
CLASSID="clsid:333C7BC4-460F-11D0-BC04-0080C7055A83">
        <PARAM NAME="DataURL" name="caps.txt">
        <PARAM NAME="UseHeader" value="True">
        <PARAM NAME="Filter" Value="Region = Mason-dixon">
</OBJECT>
```

which gives you this:

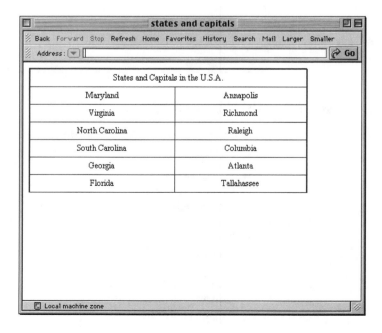

If you wanted to extend the features of your filter, you can add extra criteria using an ampersand (&) to join the criteria, like this:

```
<OBJECT ID=tdcCapdata
CLASSID="clsid:333C7BC4-460F-11D0-BC04-0080C7055A83">
        <PARAM NAME="DataURL" name="caps.txt">
        <PARAM NAME="UseHeader" value="True">
        <PARAM NAME="Filter""Value=Region = Mason-Dixon & West">
</OBJECT>
```

The second filter combines two different criteria under the "region" category.

As a result, you get this:

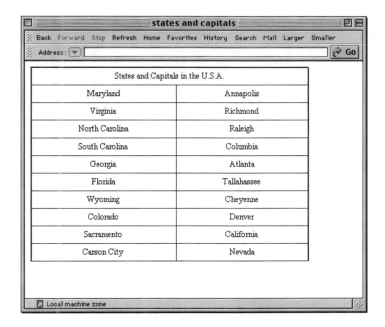

Step 6: Sort the Data

The filter parameter allows you to set limits on the data displayed by letting you specify what value for the filter can be displayed. The sort parameter allows you to organize the data in the file.

In this example, we're going to sort the Mason-Dixon region states alphabetically. To do so, we'll add an extra line to the <OBJECT> below.

```
<OBJECT ID=tdcCapdata
CLASSID="clsid:333C7BC4-460F-11D0-BC04-0080C7055A83">
        <PARAM NAME="DataURL" name="caps.txt">
        <PARAM NAME="UseHeader" value="True">
        <PARAM NAME="Filter" "Value=Region = Mason-Dixon">
        <PARAM NAME="SortColumn" Value="State">
</OBJECT>
```

The SortColumn parameter specifies that the information in the "state" column is to be alphabetized. See the graphic below for results.

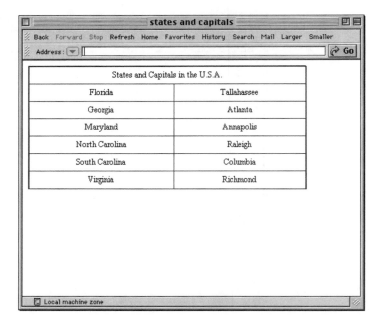

Step 7: Add Dynamic Filtering and Sorting

Now that you know how to set up filters and sorting criteria, how do you turn over the controls to your users?

The answer lies in how you set up your data area, and how you allow your user to access the data filters. The process involves three steps: setting up the markup to be receptive to different data tags; specifying the data tags that users can access; writing a script that pairs user selections with TDC filters.

Let's start with the relevant markup:

```
<LABEL class="headers" FOR=selectCat>Region</LABEL>
<SELECT id=selectCat>
<OPTION selected value=all>ALL
<OPTION value=1>New England
<OPTION value=2>Mason-dixon
<OPTION value=3>West
</SELECT>
```

The LABEL assigns a name to the pull-down menu; the menu itself has an ID for future reference and the parameters users can use to limit their data display.

The next step is making sure the data tags are clearly specified. This means making sure that the table explicitly spells out what is supposed to go into each cell:

```
<TABLE id=tblRegions width=400 Datasrc=#tdcCapdata>
<THEAD>
<TR><TD colspan=2>States and Capitals in the U.S.A</TD></TR>
</THEAD>
<TBODY>
<TR>
<TD span datafld="region"></TD>
<TD span datafld="state"></TD>
<TD span datafld="capital"></TD>
</TR>
</TBODY>
</TABLE>
```

The final step is writing a script that allows the machine to take user-selected criteria from the pull-down menu and match it up with data in the file caps.txt. Here's the total script:

WARNING   This is the only script in the chapter written in VBScript.

```
<SCRIPT language=VBSCRIPT>
' This section tells the browser which criteria to filter by
sub selectCat_onclick()
tdcCapdata.FilterColumn = "Region"
if selectCat.selectedIndex = 0 then
```

```
                tdcCapdata.FilterCriterion = "<>"
                tdcCapdata.FilterValue = "no value"
        else

                tdcCapdata.FilterCriterion = "="
                select case selectCat.selectedIndex
                case 1
                tdcCapdata.Filtervalue ="New England"
                case 2
                tdcCapdata.Filtervalue ="Mason-Dixon"
                case 3
                tdcCapdata.Filtervalue ="West"
                case else
                MsgBox "Pick one"
                end select
        end if
        tdcCapdata.Reset()
        end sub
        </SCRIPT>
```

This script lives in the head of the file. The total code for the exercise follows.

---

region.vbs

```
        <HTML>
        <HEAD><TITLE>TDC and regions and states</TITLE>

        <SCRIPT language=VBSCRIPT>
        ' This section tells the browser which criteria to filter by
        sub selectCat_onclick()
        tdcCapdata.FilterColumn = "Region"
        if selectCat.selectedIndex = 0 then
                tdcCapdata.FilterCriterion = "<>"
                tdcCapdata.FilterValue = "no value"
        else

                tdcCapdata.FilterCriterion = "="
                select case selectCat.selectedIndex
                case 1
                tdcCapdata.Filtervalue ="New England"
                case 2
                tdcCapdata.Filtervalue ="Mason-Dixon"
                case 3
                tdcCapdata.Filtervalue ="West"
```

```
          case else
          MsgBox "Pick one"
          end select
end if
tdcCapdata.Reset()
end sub
</SCRIPT>

</HEAD>
<BODY>

<OBJECT ID=tdcCapdata
CLASSID="clsid:333C7BC4-460F-11D0-BC04-0080C7055A83">
          <PARAM NAME="DataURL" name="caps.txt">
          <PARAM NAME="UseHeader" value="True">
          <PARAM NAME="Filter" "Value=Region = Mason-Dixon">
          <PARAM NAME="SortColumn" Value="State">
</OBJECT>

<LABEL class="headers" FOR=selectCat>Region</LABEL>
<SELECT id=selectCat>
<OPTION selected value=all>ALL
<OPTION value=1>New England
<OPTION value=2>Mason-Dixon
<OPTION value=3>West
</SELECT>

<TABLE id=tblRegions width=400 Datasrc=#tdcCapdata>
<THEAD>
<TR><TD colspan=2>States and Capitals in the U.S.A</TD></TR>
</THEAD>
<TBODY>
<TR>
<TD span datafld="region"></TD>
<TD span datafld="state"></TD>
<TD span datafld="capital"></TD>
</TR>
</TBODY>
</TABLE>
</BODY>
</HTML>
```

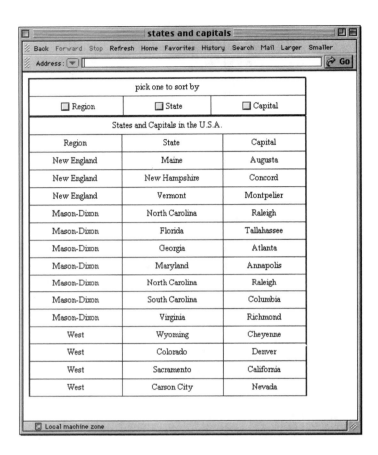

Summary

As you've seen by the varied skills demonstrated throughout the chapter, DHTML offers developers a whole new way to separate your site data from your site presentation. Remember that there are three discrete parts to DHTML: style sheets, scripting, and the Document Object Model. You can use these different parts to manipulate the data on your page, and allow your readers greater functionality as they look over your site.

CHAPTER

FIFTEEN

Bells and Whistles: Incorporating Multimedia into Your Website

- Exploring your multimedia options

- Gathering the necessary hardware and software

- Adding sound and animation to your site

- Reviewing Macromedia's multimedia offerings

You're a whiz in Photoshop, and your site is so visually tuned, it practically sings. You may decide it's time to move on to greater multimedia challenges. Fine, you say. But what exactly is multimedia, and why would I want it on my site?

Multimedia is the combination of different types of information-presenting media into one package. Truthfully, any Web page with images could be considered multimedia since it combines both text (media type #1) and images (media type #2). However, in Web parlance, multimedia indicates the inclusion of audio and video clips, in addition to images.

Historically, multimedia on the Internet is synonymous with "bandwidth hog." The file formats for encoding the data are immense compared to simple text or image files, and the act of sending or receiving a bundle of these files could bring a server to its knees.

So why do people persist in trying to bring multimedia to the Web? First, because sometimes it is the best medium for the message, and second, because there are ways to format your multimedia so it doesn't eat an entire T1 line.

Multimedia is a good way to provide the edge that certain content needs. A tour of the human body, slice by slice, makes for a riveting website, but the site where you fly through a frog courtesy of video is downright memorable. And what's the point in posting a page on diplomatic speeches or spoken-word contests if you don't have audio samples of what went on? Multimedia is one step closer to the broadcast media model that currently drives Net development.

And the formatting? It's called compression. This is a process that relies on algorithms to weed out the data that corresponds to frequencies the human ears can't detect or spectrum colors the human eye can't perceive. Once the unnecessary data are filtered out, the file is squished and formatted for sending across the Net.

There are two drawbacks to compression. First, because you're filtering out data—no matter how imperceptible to the human senses—you're taking away file refinement and degrading the data slightly. Second, many compression algorithms and techniques are proprietary to the software tool you use to compress them, so the finished files are only accessible to users who have a playback applet made by the same folks who made your compression tool. Universal multimedia isn't quite here yet.

However, multimedia as a key content delivery component keeps rising. The rest of this chapter focuses on different types of multimedia for the Web, the software tools you can use to create these files, and the tools you can use to play them back.

Multimedia Vocabulary Terms You Should Know

Here are some of the more commonly tossed-around terms. In order to understand specific software instructions or editing routines, learn these words and the concepts they embody.

8-bit/16-bit   The "word length" of a data bit in a file. The longer the word length, the closer to the original audio/video source the file is.

bps/Kbps   Bits per second/kilobits per second. These are the units of measurement for data transfer rates. Since rate of transfer is often dependent on file size over a given transfer mode (like a modem or an Ethernet connection), it's important to keep these transfer rates in mind when you're building big files. ˜

Channels   The number of data streams in a specific multimedia file. For example, stereo data has two different data streams.

Codec   *Compression/decompression* algorithm. Also known as the technology that makes multimedia go round: this is the technology for compressing multimedia files and then decompressing them on feedback.

Frame rate/fps   The number of frames per second that a video file shows. The standard for American television broadcasting is 30 fps.

Sampling frequency   A crucial measurement in calculating the quality of a sound file. The highest pitch an audio file produces is exactly half the sampling rate, so higher sampling frequencies produce a wider range of pitches, and in all likelihood, better sound files.

Making Movies

Video remains the Grail of Web-based multimedia. It's a great idea, but an incredible time-sink in practice. Fortunately, putting video on the Web doesn't require a passel of men in armor to get to the goal: It just requires time, patience, and the correct suite of tools.

Gathering the Tools

The first step is to gather your movie-making toolbox together. The first basic piece is a video capture card. Some Macintosh models may come with these preinstalled; others allow you to purchase a board from a third-party vendor such as Radius (`http://www.radius.com/`). PCs need to have at least a 486 processor and sound and video cards.

The next step is to check your machine's RAM: 40MG will be tolerable for small-scale production of multimedia files, but you should shoot for at least 80–120MG.

Bear in mind these are the basic requirements: two people I talked to who really know what they're doing recommended at least 64MG of RAM for smooth animation, plus at least a Pentium 90 processor and a video card for smooth visual rendering. A video card refers to the card used to send the output to the monitor or display.

Next, consider storage. Remember that you're going to be the one compressing those video files, and the uncompressed, huge files have to go somewhere. Your hard drive is the most likely candidate. Therefore, it's in your best interest to have the kind of disk space that can handle uncompressed files playing at the rate of 1MG per second. A gigabyte or two of external hard drive storage space is probably a good idea.

Finally, you need to find a way to transfer the actual images from camera to computer via a digital transfer. This means that you need a patch cord for the machine connection and video capture software. You can pick up the patch cord at a hardware or computer supply store; video capture software is available from a wide variety of Web-based suppliers, including Radius.

Software

Once you've set up your basic video production lab, you'll need the tools to digitize your video clip. First, of course, you'll have to find the video clip you want to digitize. Because your images will be going through several different processing steps, it's a good idea to start with a high-quality video format like Hi8, instead of VHS.

NOTE   If you're shooting video specifically for the Web, remember that the target screen is much different than a television or movie projection screen. You want to shoot for a small, closely composed picture so it compresses well. A 160x120 pixel screen is the safest size.

After you have your video, it's time to import and edit it. It's best to invest in an off-the-shelf software package like Adobe Premiere; Premiere costs about $525 dollars. If you plan on creating streaming video using the RealNetwork format, you'll need to buy the RealPublisher (as of this writing, RealPublisher 5.1 was going for $79.98) and the RealPlayer, which costs $29.99. You can also get a RealPublisher plug-in for your Adobe Premiere package for $99.99.

Premiere is considered the tool of choice for video editing files to Web-readiness. You can import multiple files and splice them together, sync audio files with video playback, and incorporate static Photoshop or Illustrator files. Once you've accomplished your professional obligations via Premiere, you can import the file into Adobe's After Effects for more visual fun. After Effects is to video what Photoshop is to images: a way to apply filter and visual effects for eye-popping results. Of course, Macromedia has an entry in the video-editing field, with Director (Macromedia products will be covered later in the chapter).

Once you've edited your film, focus on the sound quality—it helps if you treat the soundtrack as a separate element to be edited. If you're using Quicktime, the MoviePlayer application will separate the audio and you can export the file in .aiff format. Listen to the audio and edit as necessary for clarity; a more detailed description of audio editing is below.

After you've edited both the audio and video portions of the movie you want to post, it's time to compress the file for the Web. Radius makes a cross-platform package called Cinepak that performs both compression and decompression.

Functionality Via Plug-ins

While we're talking about software, it's a good time to consider the plug-in conundrum. Web developers are going to have to begin cracking down on the functionality within their websites. By *functionality*, I'm referring to the Web page experience above and beyond HTML. Functionality encompasses any actions over time that take place within a site; these actions include audio playing for the user, video playing for the user, or animation that contributes to a page interface or information.

Although plug-ins were hailed as the best hope for extending the functionality of a Web page, they're not necessarily the best solution for controlling the functionality of your pages. Like the CD-ROM-styled "system requirements" that many Web designers tried to get their readers to adopt, relying on plug-ins to supply the functionality for your website assumes a user's responsibility for controlling their own browser enhancements.

Continued on next page

Remember: Plug-ins aren't mandatory. Users have to make the effort to go to the plug-in home page, follow the download and installation instructions, and then reboot their browser and return to your page. The installation effort can easily diminish your traffic; if a plug-in is improperly installed, or isn't supported on the user's machine or operating system, the user is left with the frustrating feeling of having just completed an extra-effort task with no payoff.

Further adding to the plug-in conundrum: There are no standards for any of the extensible abilities that plug-ins offer. Site developers who want to install audio on their sites can choose from RealAudio and LiquidAudio, among many; if a site developer wants to add a video-like element to a news story, they can play a Quicktime movie, a Shockwave sequence, or any file format ending in `.avi` or `.mpeg`. So even if a user already has a number of plug-ins, there's no guarantee that they have the plug-in you are requiring them to have to fully experience your page in all its functionality.

This section isn't meant to bash plug-ins: they do a great job of allowing users to customize their browsers, and allow users to have Web-surfing tools tailored toward their own functionality interests. Plug-ins also provided the first somewhat reliable way to allow users to experience audio and video without having to leave their browsers. And, plug-ins are a first step toward total browser functionality.

However, they are not a perfect solution. Developers are forced to decide whether to permit users to leave if they don't choose to install a plug-in, or to provide a filter or a scripting kludge that will provide an alternate website experience. When you're planning on incorporating an extra-HTML functionality into your website content, you may want to consider these factors:

Can a limited version of that functionality be incorporated via new HTML specs?   For example, DHTML can provide motion of certain elements over time. If you want to have different page elements fade in and out when a user clicks on them, you could write a DHTML script that allows them to do so. If you want to move text across the screen, you could write a script that changes the coordinates of the text container over time (see Chapter 14 for details on these features). Granted, frame-by-frame video is best served within an application like Quicktime, but for controlling simple interface motion, DHTML may be a viable option.

Can you provide the experience as a separate part of the content, or does it have to be integrated?   An animated graphic may provide a cognitive model for an instructional website; does a theme song do the same thing? If you want to use video or audio as an illustration of an idea, it may make more sense to have the files as a link that the user actively clicks. For example, if you're writing a website comparing different Seattle grunge bands, you may want to include various sound clips from Nirvana, Mudhoney, and Screaming Trees at the bottom of the page, instead of playing "Smells Like Teen Spirit" as a MIDI file throughout the entire page load.

Continued on next page

What sort of technology requirements do you have? Do they fit into your current user profile? If you're looking at an audience that already adopts any new technologies early and often, then it may be a safe gamble to persuade your users to use plug-ins. If you're targeting a large general audience, you may want to reassess how you plan to use plug-ins. You may want to provide a separate, deliberate path toward pages containing plug-ins so your users can make deliberate choices to access that content.

What sort of plan B do you have for your users? If you do decide to use plug-ins, you ought to provide an alternate site experience for users who elect not to use plug-ins, or who don't want to go to the trouble of downloading the plug-in you require. You can do this the easy way: Provide two separate and clearly marked content paths that permit users to choose whether or not to access the plugged content. Or, you can do this the hard way by incorporating a plug-in-sniffing script on the pages that do use plug-ins. Whichever way you decide, make sure it works for the users on the low end of your target technology range.

Plug-ins don't have a complete lock on extra-browser functionality. Java has been used to incorporate many of the same functions plug-ins serve. Java-based applications can control image display, produce animation, or provide on-click functionality to items embedded in your Web page. Java differs sharply from plug-ins in its browser-based presence; both Internet Explorer and Netscape have a built-in Java engine in their browser versions from 3.x on up, so users don't have to go out and download a Java-reading application. However, Java does have one thing in common with plug-ins: its use is optional. Any user can access their preferences and elect to turn Java off.

Current Java implementation is far from perfect; pages relying on Java to drive user events or appearances are often slow to load, and can cause memory leakage. However, Java applications are a step toward the future. Extending browser functionality is best done with scripts that can be written once, tested everywhere, then embedded into a Web page. The alternative—expecting users to run out and fix their browser abilities to suit a Web page—is a recipe for low traffic or an incomplete site experience.

Putting the Video on Your Webpage

Now that you've made a file suitable for public viewing, it's time to put it where the public can see it. It's going to be an embedded file, and the syntax goes like this:

```
<embed src="sample.mov" height=30% width=50% controller=false
autoplay=false pluginspage="download.html" loop=palindrome>
```

So what do all those tags after `src` mean? Here's a quick rundown:

height=pixel/percent   This is the viewing height for your movie.

width=pixel/percent   This is the viewing width for your movie.

autoplay=true/false   The autoplay tag determines if the video begins streaming as soon as the user loads the page (read: the server query and response are cued when the host file is called), or if the user decides when the movie is played.

controller=true/false   This adds controls so your user can play, stop, fast-forward, or rewind the film. Since the area is considered part of the movie viewing area, you'll want to add about 20 extra pixels to the height to include the space for the controller.

loop=true/false/palindrome   These are your options for replaying the movie. It will loop continuously if set to true, it will play forward-to-back and back-to-forward if set to palindrome, and loop not at all if set to false.

pluginspage="download.html"   If users don't have the correct player for viewing your movie file, this page will whisk them to a site where they can download it. Note that you still have to make the page yourself.

Competing File Formats for Movie-Making Online

There are currently three different file formats for making movie files on the Web. They are:

Quicktime movies (`.mov`)   This is the most ubiquitous video file format on the Web, and has the best developer community support. Quicktime is also easily converted to `.avi` format, so it's a great base for cross-platform compatibility production plans.

Moving Picture Expert Group (`.mpeg`)   This format has the highest output image quality, possibly because of its much higher compression ratio. You get 30 frames per second, which is the standard for American television. Of course, you also get slightly larger file sizes.

Audio Video Interleave (`.avi`)   This is a Windows-oriented format that hasn't quite taken off, possibly because the audio-video synchronization reminds people of a badly dubbed kung fu movie.

Tips for Better Cinematography

I love the show *Homicide: Life on the Streets*, but I suspect its jerky, jump-cutting editing style wouldn't please a majority of Web-surfing multimedia types. To produce some of the smoothest cuts on the Web, follow these filming tips:

Avoid hand-held cameras.   Tripods make for smooth, steady focuses into a scene or pans across a scene.

Use a tightly focused scene.   Space is not good, since your viewers don't have the screen real estate to appreciate it anyway. Instead, hone in on your subjects.

Avoid busy backgrounds.   Avoid anything that will visually distract the viewer from the subject. Also avoid really dark or really light backgrounds since your camera's light meter will probably try to overcompensate.

Turn off the timestamp in your video camera.   Unless that tape is all that stands between you and a trip to the gallows, few people are going to care when it was made.

Avoid sudden movements.   Your audience will get vertigo, which is hardly a usability asset.

Use jumpcuts sparingly, if at all.   Few homegrown cinematographers can pull off the *Homicide* effect without a lot of practice, and most of them unintentionally achieve it because they haven't thought the whole video sequence through. Prevent jumps by plotting the entire sequence of your video beforehand, and plot your transitions between shots to reinforce a fluid viewing experience.

Allow for long transitions between scenes.   It's better to edit down than to not be able to edit thanks to a lack of footage.

Keep it simple.   This is going on the Web; the less data that the compression algorithm has to process, the better.

Therefore, most people who work in video concentrate in `.mpeg` or `.mov` formats. Since `.mpeg` formats require special editing equipment to create the files, and the quality of `.mpeg` playback varies wildly from machine to machine, it may not be your best bet for universal video.

Deciding what file format to use depends on how the file is going to be viewed on your user's machine. Obviously, the file is going to have to be stored in a standard format so any user's machine and software package can recognize and play it. An *architecture* sets up that standard format; multimedia architectures support file formats, data storage, and playback formats, and let you specify how you're going to compress the video for compact files.

Two of the most common architectures on the Web are Quicktime and RealVideo. Quicktime is the elder of the two, and age has bred ubiquity. Files are encoded using the Quicktime architecture; then after the user has downloaded the entire file, he can play it. RealVideo, on the other hand, is a streaming technology, meaning that the user can see the video file as it's downloading. This format allows users to view or listen to events as they are broadcast.

In addition, setting up shop to create Quicktime movies is relatively inexpensive: some Macintoshes come with video capture cards that allow you to produce your own videos.

A Few Words about Compression

In order to transfer video data to a computer file format, it is necessary to compress it , or compact it, so the data fits in a small amount of file data storage. Since even a second of uncompressed video in the NTSC video standard format would take up 30MB of storage space, you have to compress the video data as you convert it to a computer-readable format.

You do this using a codec, or compression/decompression scheme. A codec can be a software package or a piece of hardware; both work by using a series of complex algorithms to *compress* video files for reasonable computer storage sizes.

Compression comes in one of two flavors:

Spatial compression deletes information that is common to a sequence within a video file, or common to the entire file. For example, if you have the same puffy white cloud in the upper-left corner of your screen, the information encoding this cloud is coded at the beginning of the sequence, then deleted from subsequent portions of the tape. Since the cloud status doesn't change, neither should the encoding data.

Temporal compression pares down any scenes or sounds that are not necessary for continuity. If your background scene never changes, that scene is tagged as a key frame, and all subsequent scenes are compared against that frame to see if anything changes. The next time the background changes, a new key frame is set.

This is just a cursory look at how to compress files. For more information, I recommend visiting a Web development site such as `webdeveloper.com`; there are great basic tutorials and links to further information.

Multimedia Extensions

File formats can be some of the most frustrating and ambiguous three-letter acronyms you run into. Here's a quick rundown on what some of the most commonly encountered file formats are.

Graphics Files

`.gif`	Graphics Interchange Format—the most common graphics format on the Internet. This is a highly compressed format (using LZW compression) that is designed to minimize file transfer time over phone lines. GIF format only supports colormapped images with less than 8 bit color.
`.jpeg` or `.jpg`	A more densely encoded format—24 bit encoding. Joint Photographics Experts Group (JPEG) compression economizes on the way data is stored and also identifies and discards "extra" data, that is, information beyond what the human eye can see. Because it discards data, the JPEG algorithm is referred to as "lossy." This means that once an image has been compressed and then decompressed, it will not be identical to the original image. In most cases, the difference between the original and compressed versions of the image is indistinguishable. One advantage of JPEG compression is that you can select the quality when compressing the image. The lower the quality, the smaller the image but the more different it will appear from the original.

Audio Files

`.au`	A binary file format for sound files.
`.aiff`	A binary file format for sound files.
`.rm`	The RealAudio format for sound files. For more information, go to http://www.realnetworks.com/.
`.wav`	A binary file format for sound files.

Video Files

`.mov` or `.qt`	The Quicktime movie format. The QT format is native to the Mac, but it's also a binary format and so plays well on PCs.
`.mpg`	The standard movie format on the Web.

Continued on next page

Other Formats

`.bin`	A Macintosh binary encoded file, often used for formatting shareware.
`.gz`	A file compression format most often found on Unix systems.
`.hqx`	The extension for the BinHex file compression format.
`.pdf`	The Adobe Acrobat *portable document format*. For more information, go to `http://www.adobe.com/`.
`.sit`	A StuffIt archive format: this is usually a Macintosh format that is used for compacting one or more files for storage.
`.sea`	*Self Extracting Archive* format. This is usually a Macintosh format that is used to store applications that "launch " themselves after a click.
`.tar`	A Unix file format that bundles several files into one compact archive file.
`.zip`	A Windows compression format that bundles one or more files into a more compact archive or storage format.

Streaming Video

Having your user click on a video icon, sit and wait for it to download for ten minutes, then play a video by clicking the correct control is one way to expose your users to the video experience. The next level of video technology is the streaming video experience. The difference for the end user is that the file is delivered and played in a much smoother sequence of events than the old download-and-play model. Really good streaming video over a wide bandwidth pipe can handle a live video feed. To make an analogy about standard video formats on the Web versus streaming video, it's the difference between taping a television show and watching it later, and tuning in to watch the show as it's being broadcast.

For the developer, streaming video translates into server modifications. Streaming video works by installing compression software on a Web server so the video files can be compressed for bandwidth limits and transmitted on-the-fly. Of course, this compression scheme works only if the viewers have complementary software, but the players are usually free to encourage a large user base. The server software, on the other hand, can be pretty pricey.

Exploring Your Options

There are a handful of competing streaming video technologies worth checking out:

Xing Technology (www.xingtech.com) was the first out of the gate with Stream-Works (it debuted shortly after RealAudio's streaming audio technology caught on).

NetVideo has a streaming video technology called VDOLive.

Digigami (www.digigami.com) entered the field with CineWeb and won points for its nonproprietary format.

VivoActive (www.vivo.com) joined the streaming video field with its .avi compression format.

GEO Interactive's Emblaze (www.emblaze.com) is a promising newcomer. (See below for more on Emblaze.)

Streaming video is a great way to deliver on the promise of you-are-there immediacy, but it can present problems for you as a site developer and maintainer. For one thing, in order for streaming media to keep working, the client must make and maintain a persistent connection with the server. As the number of extended client-server connections adds up, the performance of the server will slow down. Since streaming servers are regarded as separate "entities" within the Web server system, this may not affect your overall site performance, but it could wreak havoc on your streaming server. And, if you've put your streaming server and your Web server on the same physical machine, one server could bring down the machine that houses both of them.

But crashing servers is just the least of your site administration concerns. Streaming video takes up approximately 10 times the bandwidth of streaming audio; 10 to 12 extended connections to a streaming server can tax a dedicated T1 line. So your server may actually get clogged with traffic before you can even get it to the point where it crashes, unless you've considered scalable server solutions as a baseline criteria for implementing multimedia.

Scalable is a synonym for "more." Consider adding more RAM, more physical machines, a T3 instead of a T1. Because multimedia files require a lot of space to read and write files, be sure to leave a lot of room for overflow and error—at least 25 percent of your overhead is ideal.

Another way to prevent server freeze is to restrict the number of simultaneous connections permitted at any one time, and set that number well below the max-out number for the streaming server. You can't freeze the server then, since the traffic will never be permitted to grow large enough to do so. Remember that your goal in life is to prevent your server from crashing: If it does, any prospective surfers are going to get a connection failure error message on their browser, and blithely sail off, never to be heard from again.

Streaming Video Example: Emblaze

GEO Interactive recently introduced a streaming technology that doesn't rely on user-installed plug-ins to view videos. This technology, called Emblaze, may revolutionize the way website builders can compress and serve video to a large audience.

Emblaze doesn't require that the user download any extra plug-ins, and it doesn't require the installation of server-side compression tools either. What it does require is a Java-capable browser, since the video is run via a downloaded Java applet.

Emblaze also saves audio as a separate .avi file, which allows developers a finer degree of control over the quality of the sound and video synchronization, and also allows users the option of viewing videos with or without sound.

Unfortunately, Emblaze isn't available in demo form, and developers have to pay for it. However, it may be worth investigating as a next step technology for streaming video.

Streaming Video Example: RealVideo

As part of RealNetworks suite of tools for delivering streaming video over the Web, RealVideo enjoys both a broad user base and a capable suite of developer tools for making videos. Creating streaming videos in the RealVideo format is surprisingly easy. Follow the steps below.

1. Make your digital video file. Set the target frame rate at 30 frames per second, and make the display 320 × 240 pixels. These are both standard numbers for optimal video playback.

2. Shrink the film. This is analogous to creating an image in Photoshop and then shrinking it to 80 percent. Set the standard video frame size to the RealVideo encoding specification: 177 × 144.

3. Encode the video file for playback on a RealNetworks product. You can encode both low-bandwidth (28.8kbps) and high-bandwidth (56kpbs)

versions, and customize the video and audio rates for both. The encoding tool is bundled into the RealVideo developer kit.

4. Play your product back; if you don't like what you see, you can change different encoding parameters until you're happy with the final product.

5. Once you've encoded the video to the point where you're happy with it, set a target bit rate. It should be roughly 4/5 your actual bandwidth target rate. For example, a target bit rate for a video clip on a 28.8kbps modem connection should be 19.

6. If there are still instructions to follow, you aren't finished. Put the video on your server, and include a link on your pages. For RealAudio, the file extension is .ra; for RealVideo, the file extension is .rm.

The Two Tools You'll Decide You Can't Live Without

Encoding streaming files and playing them back require two separate tools from RealNetworks (www.real.com). You will come to rely on them like you rely on your e-mail and Telnet clients now. They are:

RealPlayer This is the tool you use to view streaming video and listen to streaming audio. The trial version, which is plenty good for viewing files, is free.

RealEncoder This is the utility that compresses your files by removing extraneous layers of data. There are a variety of user options that let you tweak the quality of the compression and therefore accommodate low-bandwidth and high-bandwidth users.

Clickable Video

One of the cool functions in RealVideo is the image-mapping function. This pushes video beyond a passive playback experience and into the realm of interactivity.

If you're going to use this technology, you have to decide if is there any earthly reason to include imagemapping on your film. Most people enjoy film specifically because it allows them to sit back in a guided experience; if you add a degree of active participation, you also have to consider how to move your viewers through the new interactive level as well as the traditional film level.

One possible use for clickable video from a creative standpoint might be as a way to have individual characters in a narrative "branch off" and offer their specific perspectives on a shared story. When a user clicks, they're taken from a group scene to an interview with a specific character. A more pragmatic user might be willing to drill down to different levels of information, to topics that are tangential, or more details than the overall pace of the narrative allows for.

Once you've decided why you're including clickable video, the only obstacle left is how to include it.

The first step is basic: Begin assembling your film for editing. Once the film is edited to a point where you're pleased with it, find the individual frames you want to map, and create a map file.

Your map file is going to go above and beyond the conventional imagemap files, because it maps the clickable areas against the duration of the film. A clickable area is mapped out against the beginning and end of a specific instance in a video timeline in addition to the spatial hotspot for clicking.

Here's what a sample imagemap for a 5-minute film clip looks like:

```
<MAP START=0:0:0:0:0 END=0:0:5:00:00 COORDS=0, 0,100,100>

<AREA START=0:0:0:0:0 END=0:0:0:45:00 SHAPE=RECTANGLE COORDS=0, 0,100,100
URL="destinationsource1.html" ALT="The first clickable area" >

<AREA START=0:0:0:45:00 END=0:0:2:00:00 SHAPE=RECTANGLE COORDS=0 ,0,100,100
URL="destinationsource2.html" ALT="The second clickable area" >


<AREA START=0:0:2:30:00 END=0:0:4:59:59 SHAPE=RECTANGLE COORDS=0 ,0,100,100
URL="destinationsource3.html" ALT="The third clickable area" >
</MAP>
```

In order for the map to work, you have to have values for all five time fields— days: hours: minutes: seconds: milliseconds. If you don't put at least a zero in each field, the map won't work.

After you've created the map file, you have to merge it with your video file. This currently requires a Windows machine, since you'll be using DOS. The steps are as follows:

1. From a DOS command prompt, go to the directory where your RealVideo Encoder is installed. If you're like me, it will be in C:\applications\REAL\ RVENCODER.

2. Enter the following command:

   rmmerge -f rmimap.dll imagemap_text_file output_rm_file

3. When Done appears, it means the files have merged and you've created an imagemap .rm file.

4. Merge the imagemap .rm file with a RealAudio (.ra) or RealVideo (.rm) file by typing the following command:

   rmmerge output_rm_file audio_or_video_ra_or_rm_file final_output_file

5. Verify the final_output_file by playing it with RealPlayer.

A few words on mapping and videos: It's still as inexact as other video production methods, so be sure to build in an ample cushion for users to process their options and click to act upon them. In addition, different movie files for different bandwidths stream at different speeds, so you may want to create different maps for different times.

Still, clickable video may well be the first visual application for the hypertext model. If you can find a novel way to make it work, good!

NOTE   There is a new Web video technology called SMIL (Syncronized Multimedia Integration Language), pronounced smile. It allows the user to control syncronization of video, text streaming, still graphics, and sound. Check out `http://www.justsmil.com`, or jump to Chapter 20 for a debriefing.

How Do All Those Webcams Work?

So you've decided that the right warm-and-fuzzy touch for the office website would be an action-camera update of what everyone in your office is doing every five minutes. Or you've read about the plethora of people who broadcast everything from coffeemakers to their social lives via a webcam and you decided that you had to know how to do that too.

Never fear, instruction is here. Web cameras transmit live images from the camera home port to your website during regularly specified intervals—provided the camera is on.

First, get a Web camera. The most frequently used model is the Connectix QuickCam; it installs effortlessly on PCs and Macintoshes.

Once you've got the QuickCam, you need to install the QuickCam VC driver. Be sure to install the software before plugging in your camera.

After installing the driver and plugging in your camera (for more specific pointers, check your owner's manual), it's time to download and install the software that pushes your QuickCam images live to the rest of the Web. My favorite package is the WebCamToo, hosted at `http://webcam.paperjet.com/`.

WebCamToo is currently a Macintosh-only product. However, if you're bound and determined to have a Windows copy, the source code for the software was just made available, so you can always bribe a friend to write one for you. The software itself—the Mac version—is a Web server that serves individual images as documents. Fortunately, you can control the parameters of the document by setting image height, width, method for publishing, and even camera number if you have more than one camera you want to publish.

WARNING   You need to have an IP address available before you can fully configure WebCam for publishing images live. Remember, the software acts as a server, therefore it needs an address.

So the steps are, briefly: Set an IP address for your machine; install the Quick-Cam; install the WebCamToo; check to make sure everything is working by entering your IP address in the browser and seeing what happens.

Once you have everything up and running, you can customize your presentation using any one of WebCamToo's wide variety of parameters.

Making Noises

Sound plays a vital part in many computer-mediated experiences. Whether or not you realize it, you've probably become attuned to certain audio cues to indicate if you've performed a transaction successfully: When you save a file, the machine chimes. When you empty the trash or recycling area of your desktop, a different beep goes off. We develop functional associations between sound and tasks.

You can also use sound to enhance the user's website visiting experience, albeit in a slightly different way. Sound files can add an extra dimension to a user's perception of content. They can augment the main point of the text on a page or be the main content.

Read on for ways to produce palatable sound files for your audience.

Gathering the Tools

Thankfully, the hardware required for making audio files on the desktop is the same as for making video files, so you don't have to worry about building a replica of Brian Eno's studio in your basement.

You do, however, have to consider the software tools you'll need. Foremost among these is a software tool called an audio editor to open and refine sound source files.

Macromedia—a company that makes a variety of multimedia tools more thoroughly covered later in this chapter—makes a tool called SoundEdit that works on the Macintosh. If you're using a Windows OS, go with ProTools (`www.digidesign.com`). These two tools allow you to edit your files without altering the original sound source, and they permit direct digital transfer to other types of digital media like DAT.

NOTE   Like visual multimedia, audio files tend to be large, so make sure you've got plenty of disk space for those files.

Once you've got your equipment set up, it's time to start manipulating actual sounds. The first thing to do is transfer your sound source to your desktop.

If the sound you want is coming from a tape, be it digital or cassette, you will need to connect your sound machine to the computer. To do this, find the audio out port of your DAT machine or stereo receiver, and plug in a patch cord. As I said in the video section, these cords are available at hardware stores and computer stores. Next, find the audio in port on the back of a computer equipped with an AV card.

Once the computer and sound machine are connected, you can transfer the sound to the computer, open it up in your sound editor, and begin cleaning up the sound. Jump on down to "Cleaning Up Audio Files" for instructions on eliminating snaps, crackles, and hisses from your files.

Competing File Formats for Audio Online

Sound software and encoding formats are as numerous as the different types of graphics formats. There are four different formats you need to concern yourself with:

.wav   The Windows audio standard for Waveform Audio Files.

.aiff   The Sun audio standard. It can only encode 8 bit data (see the terms above for a definition) instead of longer, more detailed 16 bit data.

.au   The Apple audio standard, also known as Audio Interchange File Format.

.ra   This is the proprietary RealAudio format, which you can use for streaming sound. The biggest contrast between .ra and the preceding three file types is that .ra files are compressed for fast transfer (for more on this, see the "Streaming Audio" section) and .wav, .aiff, and .au files are not.

Format actually matters when you decide to put sound on the Web. The delivery process will always be the same—sound is converted from an audio source to a digital file, then compressed via encoding. But the encoding affects the sound in two different ways: It compresses the file in a proprietary format that requires a specific playback technology, and it tosses out data through the compression process (also known as "lossy" compression).

Therefore, it's in your best interest to clean up your files as much as possible before encoding them. Read on for smooth editing techniques.

Cleaning Up Audio Files

Even the best sound-editing application is possessed by a devil. How else to explain the audio artifacts—those bubbles of hissing noise—that appeared on your perfectly clean audio source.

Fortunately, exorcising those artifacts is easy. They're visually distinctive, so you should be able to see them in your sound editing software control window, as shown in Figure 15.1.

FIGURE 15.1:

The sharp, high vertical lines show an artifact in the middle of a sound wave.

Provided the artifact is on the end of a file, you can simply chop out the offending sound by selecting and deleting. Your file plays a little shorter, but no one but you is the wiser. Other artifact exorcism tactics include opening the audio file in a different format and trying to re-save it, or opening a backup copy in a different sound-editing application.

It's not the world's most solid bug-zapping strategy, but it's all we've got. The occasional artifact shouldn't stop you from performing quality control on the rest of your sound files. You won't go wrong if you follow these basic quality controls:

- Use headphones as your primary output. This way, you can hear what your users are most likely to hear.

- Amplify and normalize your audio source. It will up the values for both amplitude and volume so that the peak values in your audio file—parts that are louder or more intense—average out to a 95-percent range. This prevents you from blowing out someone's RealPlayer unintentionally.

- Equalize your files. This prevents a file from choking on extreme treble (high) or bass (low) notes.

- Be sure to make a lot of backup copies. These come in handy for many reasons. Two of the most immediate reasons are for when the audio editor introduces more artifacts than the Smithsonian houses and as extra copies for experimentation and recovery.

- Keep your recordings simple. The simpler the files, the less likely something will muddy the track.

Streaming Audio

RealAudio pioneered this field and continues to have the largest user base. This is important to you as a developer because you'll want to encode your audio files in a format that reaches the largest possible audience.

Fortunately, setting up a streaming audio file is really easy: once you're done cleaning up your file, you just open the RealAudio encoder (visit their website at `http://www.realnetworks.com/` for downloads and information), select your target bandwidth (14.4 kbps or 28.8 kbps), and choose your audio source file.

Because this is streaming audio, you have two choices—a live stream or a digital file. Once you've selected a source, the Encoder does two things: it attaches the `.ra` suffix to your newly formatted filename, and it saves it to the RealAudio server of your choosing.

NOTE   There are two different ways you can add a RealAudio server to your site. The first is best for getting your feet wet: download the free RealNetworks Basic Server (`http://www.real.com/server/basic/index.html`) and set it up to host your streaming media files. For faster performance and more robust backend features, you may want to consider buying a RealNetworks server like the Basic Server Plus (`http://www.real.com/server/basic/plus.html`). Both products are available on the Web at the URLs listed here.

Another cool feature in the Encoder is its ability to bundle file information via a text tag that you format. This way, you can include things such as sound name, author, and copyright notice as necessary.

How Does Live Audio Work?

A server-side application known as a Live Transfer Agent (LTA) is responsible for making it all happen. The LTA lives on the same machine as the RealAudio server, so it can take any incoming audio streams and encode them on-the-fly for quick server delivery.

You do need to beware: For every bandwidth playback option you offer, such as 14.4kbps or 28.8kbps, you will need a separate LTA to handle the conversion requests. You don't, however, have to have the LTA if you're doing *live* audio streaming, and if you have a `.ra` or `.rm` file format, you can stream your media via HTTP instead.

Embedding Sound on a Web Page

There are two definitions for embedding. The first relies on the `<embed>` tag—a way to link discrete RealAudio or Shockwave files into a Web page. The second links a browser-readable audio file format into your Web page.

The three file formats discussed above—`.wav`, `.aiff`, and `.au`—are all safe for instant file reading, since they are unconditionally supported by both Netscape and Microsoft. However, remember that they'll download into the page the same way a graphic file does, so if your sound file is very large, it will make the whole page hang until the client application has received all of it.

You should now be able to import, edit, stream, and embed audio files with some ease. Becoming a digital mixmaster will take more time, practice, and skill than we can go into here: for more information, look into one of the books available on the subject, such as *Audio on the Web: The Official IUMA Guide*, by Jeff Patterson and Ryan Melcher.

Macromedia Overview

You should definitely be aware of Macromedia: They keep turning out one great multimedia product after another. If you're a strict coding geek, you may know the name primarily by their Dreamweaver software, but people who work in pulling together multimedia presentations have been using Director for everything from film editing to graphics-based multimedia trips.

Director has a long, rich history as a multimedia tool: people were using it to pull together CD-ROM presentations while early Web users were still using command-line browsers. Its many editing facilities and script-based object coordination make it a natural for migrating complex multimedia to the Web.

But Director may be too much of a good thing, especially if you're trying to create simple multimedia files. If this is the case, the newly emergent Flash application may be your cup of tea; the vector-based graphics offer ease of scaling that bitmapped images do not. The overall result is more information in fewer bytes.

But whether you elect to go with Dreamweaver (see Chapter 14 for a review), Director, or Flash, there's probably a Macromedia product you'd be better off knowing. Read on to find out more about their multimedia offerings.

Director

Director's multimedia plug-in Shockwave colonized the Web in 1995 and still continues to hold sway over multimedia formatting on the Web. If you want to make Shockwave presentations, it's important to know Director.

Director is also a great way to model user experiences for your website; by writing a script that anticipates all possibilities and plots them accordingly, you've set up a dynamic page model for your developers. Finally, Director is a great multipurpose tool for any sort of multimedia presentation.

Are you convinced that you need a working knowledge of it? Let's get started.

Director has a window where everything plays, also known as the stage. You control the elements on the stage via a Control Panel, which has the same types of controls your CD player has: forward, back, stop, play, volume, and playback rate.

Sounds simple enough? Time to move on to the Score. This is where you will coordinate all of the items that appear in your presentation. These items are referred to as cast members (extending the theatre metaphor—Director, stage, etc.). You control the cast members by using various options in the Score to dictate their behavior. Some of the Score options include:

Tempo channel   This sets the pace, in frames per second, that your Director movie runs at.

Color palette   This sets the colors for all the cast members.

Transitions palette   How will your cast members appear and disappear? Through transitions such as fades, wipes, and dissolves.

Sound file channels   These two channels are where you'll store your audio cast members.

Script channel   If you write scripts in Lingo, the Director programming language, you'll drop them in this channel.

You place the cast members in various channels and sequence them so they'll run through the presentation on stage.

How do you load cast members into a stage for working? There are two routes: you can create your cast members within Director, using their Tool palette, the Text window, and the Paint window, or you can import files from another application.

Since a lot of Director presentations rely on outside media sources, let's review the steps you'd take to do this. First, open the Cast window, and select the empty cast members that will house your files. Then, go to the File menu and select Import. Using the menu interface, find and select your file. You've just imported the file, and can manipulate it on the stage however you wish.

What you do on stage is up to you; this is a rudimentary explanation of what Director can do. Because comprehensive Director instruction is beyond the scope of this book, I recommend that you read *Mastering Macromedia Director 6*, by Chuck Henderson (Sybex, 1997) for more comprehensive instruction.

Cast Members and Their Properties

Once you're whizzing through Director's interface and you've begun to plot your ultimate demo, you're going to want to be able to manipulate cast members with impunity. This table tells what you can do to cast members to maximize your presentation. All of the properties listed below are fully manipulable by you, for any media-type cast member.

- fileName of member
- media of member
- name of member
- palette of member
- purgePriority of member
- scriptText of member

Some of your cast member media types may be bitmaps. If that's the case, you can set `paletteRef of member`, `picture of member`, and `regPoint of member`.

Your digital video cast members have the following manipulable properties:

- controller of member
- crop of member
- directToStage of member
- frameRate of member
- pausedAtStart of member
- preLoad of member

Flash

Unlike Director, which gains some of its more powerful and novel effects from scripting, Macromedia Flash doesn't require a lot of scripting savvy to create neat effects. In fact, the easy-to-understand interface and gratifying instant results make this an ideal tool to adopt if you've never used Director before. Another bonus about Flash's results: they're relatively tiny (5–100K) compared to Shockwave-embedded Director movies, and they're browser independent.

Flash is a tool for building animated graphics via a vector format. This doesn't seem like a big deal unless you know the difference between the two ways one can create digitally-based graphics.

The first method is bitmapping: the graphic is basically mapped onto a grid, and the different squares on the grid have different colors to render the graphic. The intensity of the shade of color is often what allows subtle changes in color from one grid square to another; the size of individual grid squares also allows you to cram more finely detailed shading into one place.

However, when you enlarge some bitmapped graphics, they look terrible: Figure 15.2 presents the comparison for you.

FIGURE 15.2:

A GIF, stretched to five times its normal size; see all the individual squares?

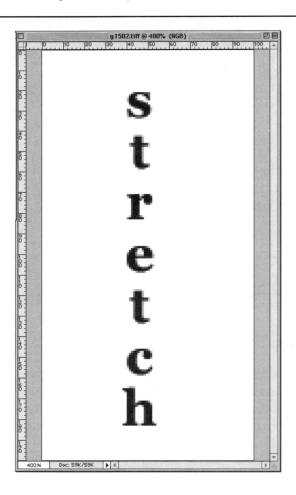

Needless to say, GIFs don't scale well, which can present layout problems when you're trying to make a page that expands or contracts with the browser window.

Enter the vector graphic format. Instead of relying on a specific number of colored squares to make up a mosaic-like image, vector graphics encode a set of instructions telling the graphics-rendering engine to display a given image through a series of lines. Vector graphics require less overall file information, and they scale more elegantly.

Although Microsoft Internet Explorer supports its own brand of vector-based graphics (generated through ActiveX objects and lots of lines of code), Flash is only visible if you've got the Shockwave plug-in from Macromedia installed already. Still, Macromedia has announced its support for the Flash image vector format as a Web-wide standard, so it's possible that there will be browsers with fully integrated vector graphics viewing by the summer of 1999.

To prepare against that day, here's a quick-and-dirty cheatsheet on everything you need to know about Flash.

1. Download the application. A full, bells-and-whistles version of the application is going to set you back about $300, but you can download a thirty-day trial demo from the Macromedia website at `http://www.macromedia.com/shockwave/download/`.

2. Decide to make a movie. This will acquaint you with the most critical menus in Flash.

3. Take a moment to look at the floating toolbar palette. It looks very similiar to other graphics applications like Photoshop. You'll be able to draw, fill, crop, and move graphics with ease. Now look at the big blank area—this is where you'll draw your graphics for movie making. We're starting small.

4. Look at the menu bar at the top of the page. There's a library palette. Select Create Symbol and select the Make Movies option. When you select the Movie Clip, you open the edit window for manipulating whatever is going to be on your movie. When the movie window is open, you can draw whatever is going to be on your movie.

5. Set the animation in motion. You do this by going to the layer pop-up menu at the top of your window (it's next to the timeline) and selecting the Add Motion Guide option. Then, draw the path you want the object to move in.

6. Meet the Key Frame: these are specific reference points that the application uses to connect the dots between animation motions. The key frames are the dots between *tweening*, or drawing motion between the start and end of the animation sequence. To plot the trajectory of your animation as smoothly as possible, you'll want to insert a lot of key frames. Note that this step is a balance between smooth animation and large file size.

7. Tween! The word itself deserves to be said out loud a few times while you do this step, because it's so amusing. The step itself is a little more tricky—you need to identify the motion you want your tweening to make over the course of the timeline.

8. Make your viewers do some work. By this, I mean give them control of the animation—the power to stop, start, or pause it. Like any other user-driven action, the button will have an "up" state when it hasn't been touched yet, a "down" or action state, a mouseover state, and a "hot" area or event that triggers the button. You define all of these in the area to the right of the main stage. To actually make them work when a user clicks, drag your entire button construction back into the movie frame and save it.

9. Test your work. This is a handy feature in Flash: you can go to the Control menu and select the Test Movie option to see how well your movie performs. It beats embedding the file on a page and loading it into a browser.

That's Flash in a nutshell. Like any other complex and multifunctional tool, it works best when you invest some time to just play around in it.

Including Flash or Shockwave Files on a Website

Including a Shockwave or Flash file on a Web page is surprisingly easy: Simply embed it like you would any other external file to be displayed. The only difference between including an image and including a Shockwave or Flash file is the tag designation.

Here's the basic syntax:

```
<OBJECT CLASSID="clsid:D27CDB6E-AE6D-11cf-96B8-444553540000"
CODEBASE="http://active.macromedia.com/flash3/cabs/swflash.cab#version=
3,0,0,0">
<PARAM NAME="MOVIE" VALUE="flash.swf">
<PARAM NAME="PLAY" VALUE="true">
<PARAM NAME="LOOP" VALUE="true">
<PARAM NAME="QUALITY" VALUE="autohigh">
```

```
<EMBED SRC="flash.swf" WIDTH="400" HEIGHT="300"  PLAY="true" LOOP="true"
QUALITY="autohigh" PLUGINSPAGE="http://www.macromedia.com/shockwave/
download/index.cgi?P1_Prod_Version=ShockwaveFlash">
</EMBED>
</OBJECT
>
```

And here's the breakdown tag by tag:

- The OBJECT tags embed the ActiveX control that lets Microsoft Internet Explorer read Shockwave and Flash files, if the correct plug-in isn't already installed. The PARAM tags define behavior parameters for the OBJECT; you'll notice that the attributes are repeated later in the EMBED tag. Note that I said Microsoft Internet Explorer: this means that these tags, while not supported widely across other browsers, are included for this specific browser.

- The EMBED tag is the anchor for the Macromedia file (denoted with a .swf extension).

- The attribute tags are fairly straightforward: PLAY tells the browser whether to stop the movie after the first frame or keep on rolling (true means to keep playing); LOOP indicates whether or not the movie is supposed to loop; QUAL-ITY refers not to content but to image-antialiasing.

NOTE   You don't have to do all this by hand. Macromedia has also made an application called AfterShock that automatically formats the HTML objects for you. It's still important to know what all the tags do.

Summary

You've seen the varied types of multimedia that will make your pages sing and dance—literally. This chapter should have also given you an overview of the media-specific considerations and vocabulary you need before committing to a multimedia strategy, plus some equipment pointers for creating multimedia.

Go forth and create. Just make sure it doesn't kill your server. For more pointers on optimizing your backend performance for your more complex site, read on.

CHAPTER

SIXTEEN

16

Accommodating Advertising

- Appreciating the need for advertising

- Understanding basic banner production

- Tracking and reporting ads

- Adding co-sponsorship

- Choosing ad-serving software

Advertising may be the bane of the Web, or it may be a sign of a fledgling media's legitimacy. Regardless of how you feel about advertising, it's not going away. In fact, it's only going to get bigger: The Internet Advertising Bureau estimates that $907 million dollars' worth of advertising business took place on the Web in 1997.

Planning to run, rotate, and report ads is important; integrating the systems you use to do advertising production into the rest of your Web production process is crucial.

Planning and maintaining successful ad space on your website is not as simple as throwing an image tag on a Web page. Production concerns where outside revenue is involved go beyond optimizing HTML or reducing the number of frames in a GIF. You have to start thinking of things such as tracking the number of times a banner is going to be viewed, tracking the number of times a user clicks on a banner, and reporting that data to a third party.

Integrating advertising and website production is an ongoing process. Both sides of the transaction have a number of standards they expect to see followed, and those standards are always evolving. This chapter focuses on how to execute advertising smoothly on your website, while considering the expectations of the people who are paying for the advertising space.

Why Advertise at All?

Some websites are unabashedly commercial, and the people who produce them are working to parlay the site into a business. Some websites are less fiscally oriented. And some exist for pure self-entertainment. In the Web advertising game, the motivation for building a site is almost irrelevant. No matter why you built the site, you're going to want to advertise.

For one, advertising brings you more traffic. This is how Geocities and Tripod promote the varied user content on their site—they have their Web page publishers cross-promote it. You can use advertising to cross-promote your site, or to tie your site into a loose confederation of similar sites.

If you're on the Web to make money, improving your site traffic will ultimately improve your bargaining power when you incorporate commercial advertising on your site.

Most online ad agencies won't even touch a site that gets less than 10,000 hits per month.

If you're lacking hits, making sure your website is listed in search engines is not going to be enough to make traffic start pouring in. The Web is so vast and disorganized that you have to make an active pitch to potential viewers. A system of banner-swapping with similar sites will help to attract and build a larger readership. Even if you're not aiming for commercial attention, the larger audience will help to guarantee you steady employment.

Banners and Beyond

Advertising on the Web seemed like a bad idea for a long time: The amount of money it took for a Web ad to reach a consumer was much higher than the amounts advertisers spent on television, radio, or print. Yet despite the low cost-to-return ration, advertisers kept pouring money into the Web.

Unlike the more traditional media forms, the World Wide Web allows site developers and advertisers to carefully track their target audience. Cookies can provide data on someone's Web-surfing habits, the pages they hit on a particular site, and the frequency with which they visit. Server logs can tell what domains are accessing a site. All of these different data-gathering methods allow advertisers to more carefully target their audience. This one-to-one marketing can be handy if an advertiser wants to promote brand-name awareness among a very specific consumer demographic.

For more information on cookies, check out Chapter 12, and for more on server logs, see Chapter 9.

All the backend analysis is still fronted with the ubiquitous banner. These square or rectangular graphics are the dominant form of advertising on the Web. Although advertising agencies have been pushing for a new ad model "beyond the banner," many of their innovations—forms, games, and multiple-choice input—have made it into banner-sized spaces on a Web page.

This first section of the chapter is a survey of banner-based advertising. It will be a crash course in ad production, starting with a brief rundown of the vocabulary you need to know to talk ads, moving through a survey of production concerns to be addressed when putting ads on a site, and ending with recommendations for ad-serving tools and strategies.

Production Concerns

I'm going to start off this section with a small personal story. I agreed to take a job as an advertising production manager back in the dark ages of Internet advertising (this was 1996). I thought the job would focus on the technical aspects of advertising production, like the ways we could optimize banners or analyze data for client reports. I knew nothing about the business end of online advertising. This didn't worry me, and it should have.

I spent the first few months of my job learning about the concerns that drive advertising: scheduling multipart ads, precisely controlling the placement and time an ad was slated to run, and finding ways to mine server data for the numbers needed to make clean, comprehensive reports. I spent the next few months trying to balance everything that my advertising clients wanted with the realistic site standards the website developers maintained.

Learn from my mistakes. Keep reading to see what you'll need to know to make both advertisers and site developers happy—or at least to prevent them from being actively discontent.

A Short Vocabulary Test

If you're used to talking W3C, document object model, and embedded includes with your production buddies, check that vocabulary at the door. Web-based advertisers speak in a different set of keywords. Here's what you need to know to understand what they're saying:

Campaign   An advertisement, or collection of advertising, all centered on a specific theme over a finite time period. A non-Internet example of an ad campaign is the series of television commercials Microsoft ran with the slogan "Where do you want to go today?" An Internet example of an ad campaign is the series of banners Microsoft ran on websites, with each banner featuring a different helper icon from Microsoft Office.

Continued on next page

Click-through   The Holy Grail of banner advertising. When a user is compelled to click the banner to the Web page that the banner is requesting, it's called a click-through. Recent studies by the research firm Millward Brown Interactive have shown that click-throughs may not be as effective as previously thought, but they're still measured in an advertiser traffic report.

CPM   Cost per thousand. The M is a throwback to Roman numerals. Ad impressions are typically sold in lots of one thousand, and the pricing for these ad runs is done by the thousand. So a typical ad sale might be for 50,000 impressions, at $20 per 1,000. The price goes on record as being $20 per CPM.

Creative   The catchall phrase for an ad. Banner ads, buttons, microsites are all referred to as "creatives."

Impressions   This is a slightly more specific definition than page view. While a page view measures how many times a particular file-plus-ad combination was requested from the server, an impression counts how many times an ad banner was loaded. If a banner is scheduled to run on the archive page and two content pages, it is entirely possible for it to have 9,000 total impressions on the site. Those impressions are broken down by page view: 5,000 on the archive page, 2,000 apiece on the content pages.

Page views   A term for how many people viewed a file when it was displaying a particular ad. This differs from page traffic because more than one ad can be rotated into a specific ad space. For example: Your archive page has one area at the top of the page designated for an ad banner. That area is occupied by either a software company banner (A), a free home pages banner (B), or an in-house promotional banner (C). The page can have a traffic number of 10,000 unique visitors, but banner A will only report 5,000 page views, banner B gets 3,500 page views, and banner C gets 1,500 page views.

Scheduled run   The length of time an advertisement is going to appear on a website. A scheduled run may also include the number of impressions to be delivered, as well as a list of pages where the ad is to be seen.

Traffic   This is the umbrella term for the number of visitors who hit a given page, a website section, or the section itself. Traffic numbers are what you sell and what you promise to advertisers.

Scheduling Advertising

Putting a banner ad on a page may seem as simple as putting an <IMG> tag on a page, but banner placement rides on a variety of factors.

One of the most important factors is the scheduled run of an ad. Bear in mind that making sure a banner goes up and comes down on the appointed beginning and ending dates is not the end of your responsibility. There are a wide variety of other factors to consider, including:

Making sure an ad delivers the promised numbers in the promised time period. Ads are usually sold in lots of 1,000, and sales numbers can be highly specific. Part of the balancing act in scheduling ads is making sure they hit the impressions goals set in the sales agreement. Therefore, if you're placing ads, one factor you need to always keep in mind is the number of impressions the sale is good for.

Scheduling an ad to appear a specific number of times (impressions). In addition to fulfilling the general ad delivery numbers, most ad properties come with a specific number of impressions attached. An advertiser may submit several banners and ask that each one be scheduled to receive a certain number of page views. So a second factor to keep in mind is how many impressions each creative gets.

Scheduling multiple banners for an advertiser (campaigns). Very few ad campaigns come with only one banner. There may be as many as fifty banners per campaign. Those banners may be staggered over the course of the advertising run, so in addition to counting impressions per banner, you also need to make sure banners go up when they're supposed to. Each specific banner is another piece of data to keep track of.

Scheduling multiple campaigns in a given piece of real estate. Once you've figured out how many banners there are, and you've figured out how many impressions a banner must get over the course of its run, it's time to match the dates and numbers with location. In addition to garnering so many impressions over time, many ad buys are also made with the specific condition that the banner be displayed on certain pages or sections of the site. Balancing location and impressions per creative per campaign is easy; your job will be balancing those criteria for multiple sponsors who have all requested the same location over the same time period.

Reporting the results of the scheduling and user interaction. Now that you've served those ads, it's time to prove to the advertiser that you did. All of the data factors listed above—the campaign's scheduled beginning and ending date, the number of impressions per banner, and the location where those impressions were to be served—need to be reported.

This means that in addition to juggling all of those factors mentioned above, you must also record how you juggled them. Scheduling and record-keeping software is an integral part of advertising production. You will need to balance the demands of multiple client schedules, record how their ads were served, and take care of the technical details of Web production.

Basic Banner Production

Those small graphic squares take a lot of thought. Although the majority of your efforts might be detail-oriented, focusing on what URLs go with what properties where, you may also find yourself having to create banner ads or assess the tools you use to serve ads. The sections below cover the most general concerns for anyone involved in the implementation process for advertising on a website.

Banner Specs Back in the Dark Ages of Web advertising (1996), each website that took ads also took them only in certain sizes. This led to one of two common problems:

- The ad agencies in question racked their brains and exhausted their staff trying to create an ad banner campaign that would work equally well across 50 different banner sizes.

- Production staff at specific sites would start bickering with ad agencies when agencies said, "I don't care if your banner size is four pixels shorter than what we made. Fix it yourself if it doesn't meet your specs."

Either way, everyone was working more than they needed to, and nobody was happy.

Enter the Internet Advertising Bureau (`http://www.iab.net/`). In early 1997, the first thing they did was set up a list of recommended standard sizes for banners. There are eight different sizes, listed below.

- **468 x 60 pixels:** Full banner size

468 x 60

- **392 x 72 pixels:** Full banner with vertical navigation bar

392 x 72

- **234 x 60 pixels:** Half banner

  234 x 60

- **120 x 240 pixels:** Vertical banner

  120 x 240

- **120 x 90 pixels:** Button 1

  120 x 90

- **120 x 60 pixels:** Button 2

  120 x 60

- **125 x 125 pixels:** Square button

  125 x 125

- **88 x 31 pixels:** Micro button

  88 x 31

Banner Effectiveness   Less is more. Banners are basically tiny billboards. Just as the most successful billboards are ones that create clear messages, so should your banner do the same. If you've just inherited the job of designing advertisements, here are some tips to make sure your banner doesn't crash and burn.

Decide on the message you want to send.   Do you simply want to raise brand-name awareness? Have people associate the name of your site with a logo? Or do you want to send a specific message about your site?

Decide how to send that message.   Are you going to go for a minimalist approach with just a name or logo? Or is your message more specifically tailored to a special promotion or message you want associated with your site? However you decide to send your message, remember that less is more.

Decide what you want the result of that message to be.   "Increased brand awareness" is a fine answer: Just be sure that you know how to measure that increased awareness. You may want the result of your message to be an increase in clicks on the site.

Knowing *what* you're going to say, *how* you're going to say it, and *what results* you expect it to yield should be clear before you begin making your banner.

Once you've nailed down your objectives, begin producing banners. Obviously, you should be creative. But even if you tend to balk at trying to "be creative," rest assured. You can do it. In order to be creative, all you need to do is to find a clear way to present your message. Brevity counts. Remember the beer slogan "Tastes great, less filling." It's concise, it's clear, and it's memorable. Try to attach the same type of qualities to your ad.

For example, if you run a website for a moving company, you could do a banner ad like, "Packing up is hard to do." The slogan is a riff on an old pop song (without infringing on royalties, which is always good), and it has a clear premise (packing), so it is more memorable than "Click Here for a Thousand Boxes."

Another way to be creative is to utilize animation. This may increase your banner size, but it won't make too much of an impact if you do it carefully. Restrict the motion on your banner to a few smaller frames within the larger frame. Reduce the number of frames that the total animation takes—a jerky, campy effect might send a more effective animated message than a smoothly flowing scene. Finally, make sure your animation is relevant to your message.

For an example of relevant animation, let's return to the moving banner. The first frame reads "Packing up is hard to do." Then, a plate breaks into two separate pieces over the slogan (see Figure 16.1). You've just done two things: invoke one of the difficulties of packing for a move, and reminded the reader of the song the slogan is borrowed from. As for irrelevant animation, imagine this: The same moving banner features the slogan "Packing up is hard to do" plus a slow fade of a smiling face morphing into a frown. We get the message that packing is distasteful to someone, but we have no really compelling reason to find out who.

FIGURE 16.1:

Effective banner usage

Packing up is hard to do.

Packing up is hard to do.
Let us do it. Packrats.
http://www.packrat.com

Even after you've found the perfect mix of creative slogans and animation, test the banner's usability. Is the font easy to read on a busy page? Remember, this banner is only a small part of a page, and it's not a part of the page that the reader came specifically to see. Therefore, you need to make it as easy to read as possible. You also need to simplify your color palette as much as possible. Your audience will not care that you are extending your college thesis on the Fauvists to the banners you create today; they want a few simple, high-contrast colors. After you've streamlined your banner's fonts and palette, test it to make sure it loads quickly. And a final note: test where you want the banner to click through to. Linking to your front page works only if you're promoting a general brand for your site; you may want to link to a specific feature or campaign on your website.

What's a Nice Guy like You Doing Designing Banners?

As I mentioned previously in the chapter, becoming part of a site network can help drive up your traffic. Banners help increase the likelihood that your site will be seen by someone other than your friends or people following the URL at the bottom of a newsletter or ad.

So even if the thought of using a graphics program leaves you shivering, it doesn't hurt to learn how to make basic, functional banners you can use as self-promotion until you gain enough traffic or exposure to barter your site services for an afternoon of a graphic artist's time.

NOTE

Now that you've mastered banner production basics, I'm going to complicate your life by pointing out that there's more to Internet advertising than the banner. Most ad banners are within IAB specs, and you're likely to see the 468 × 60, 234 × 60, and 125 × 125 sizes. However, there are other ways to squeeze paid advertisers on to your site. For example, if you've got a deal with a software company, you could make a download button for the product and include it on your page. Or you could include a link on your front door to a series of co-produced advertiser pages. The possibilities are only going to expand.

HTML Banners   Banners were originally little more than billboard-style advertisements for their sponsors. As online commerce vendors got into the advertising game, they wanted to extend the functionality of a banner. Since you can't make a GIF double as an order form, setting up a banner via HTML seemed to be a logical choice.

The setup for an HTML banner is very basic: It's a table set to an IAB width, with a spacer GIF to set the height, plus whatever elements couldn't fit inside a GIF. One of the most popular functions for these banners is as a search form, like the banner below.

Implementing these banners isn't too difficult. Most ad-serving software systems usually work by pulling in a fragment of code, much like a server-side include, that includes the ad, the URL, and any CGI variables the software needs to track and report ad placement. The only complication is the number of formatting tags you'll need to compose these banners. Some ad-serving software systems may not be programmed to handle more than a specific, single-tag label for an ad property.

JavaScript Banners   Some banners rely on a combination of HTML, images, and JavaScript to pull together their message. These banners have the same serving constraints as HTML banners: They must be able to be served as a discrete code fragment.

WARNING People serving JavaScript banners should beware: Some versions of JavaScript have difficulty working when the script is embedded two tables deep. If your page layout relies on tabling an ad at the top or the bottom, you may need to re-arrange your code or reassess how to accomplish your JavaScript effect.

Shockwave Banners   These banners can provide smooth animation and sound, but they're also bandwidth-heavy and they need a plug-in in order to work. If you can find a way to serve the ad with a sniffer script, you're good to go. (See below for more on sniffer scripts.)

Java Banners   Unless you've got an on-site Java expert, you might be better off passing up on these. Although a memorable game-playing banner can give your site and your sponsor technical credibility, the headache of trying to cram a 20K banner—complete with Java classes and images—onto a page is painful.

In addition, remember that your site is going to hear any complaints if the banner breaks on a particular platform, or mistakenly tries to load on a low-end user's machine. The issues to using a Java banner are similar to those in using plug-in banners. Even if you rely on an outside ad network to set up sniffer scripts and smooth out any serving difficulties, the banner is still going on your site, and you'll have to deal with errors immediately.

How to Sniff for Low-Tech Users

If you want to move beyond GIF banners into more technically sophisticated banner advertisements, you need to have a Plan B in place. Plan A is targeted toward serving your new and improved multimedia ads to the audience that has the hardware and software to view them; Plan B is targeted toward delivering ads to users who don't or won't use the tools you require for them to view your ads.

The first and most obvious tactic is to serve your ads conditionally, using browser variables such as browser make or version to determine the technical level that your users are accessing your site with, and to serve appropriate ads in response. But advocates of multimedia ads must fight a little harder: Some of the more cutting-edge techniques require plug-ins like Shockwave or Flash. If a site is hesitant to use plug-in-required content because it doesn't want to lose traffic, how can you prevent an advertisement from directly contradicting that policy?

The answer is to use a *sniffer script*. These scripts, commonly written in JavaScript, look for a particular plug-in or browser feature such as Java being enabled, and serve an ad in response to what they find.

For specific information on how to write a sniffer script, check out this site: `http://developer.netscape.com/docs/manuals/tools/devguide/devtech .htm`. You'll need to scroll down to the section on "Compatibility Techniques," but you may find interesting stuff on the way. The scripts usually operate in this order: They test to see if a plug-in is present. If it is, they serve one specific ad. If it is not, then they serve another. The real challenge for sniffer scripts is deciding how they're going to be included in the ad serving process.

The biggest production stipulation is control, since some advertising networks insist on using their own sniffer scripts with plug-in ads. This saves you the work of having to write a sniffer script, but takes the ability to repair or modify it out of your hands. If the script doesn't work, it's not the ad network that angry users will be e-mailing, it will be you. Balance the factor of site control versus that of having a specialized ad agency set up a sniffer and banner.

Placing and Inserting Ads

Regardless of the format you have for your ads, you're going to have to find a way to integrate them into your site. There are two factors you need to resolve to ensure that your ads rotate smoothly.

First, find out where the ad is going to live on the page layout. You need to know this because it's the first step in integrating your ad-serving code into the document structure or template. You also need to know this because some sites or sponsors may go with an external window pop-up, where loading a page causes a new, precisely sized browser window to pop up and display an ad. If your site is going to go with this route, you also need to consider where to put the ad pop-up code (most frequently JavaScript) to track which ad popped up as a result of a specific page loading, and you'll have to find an alternative ad-delivery method for sites that don't support the Java or JavaScripting you use to launch your extra-layout ad.

The second factor you have to resolve is how you're going to insert the ad on a page. Is it going to be a hard-coded tag listing a specific graphic and URL? Is it a call to a database that passes on a filename, user domain, and browser type before returning an ad? Is it a JavaScript calling for a pop-up window and a call for a specific ad? You need to know what code is going to call your ad, and how it works.

Knowing how the ad code works helps you to pinpoint trouble when it strikes. It also helps you to optimize how to serve ads without hindering the rest of your site production.

Rotating Ads

Embedding an ad in a page is only part of the ad-serving challenge. The other part is rotating those ads on schedule. You have three basic options. First, rotate the ads by hand. This works well only on an extremely small, low-maintenance site. You could also rely on CGI scripts to rotate the ads based on a stated variable such as page location, sponsor banner number, or date. These offer a larger degree of automation and specificity.

Cookies: How and When to Use Them

One of the key tools for gathering data about the viewers who visit the site—and the ads served— is the Magic Cookie. Ad-serving systems often rely on cookies to establish:

- whether this is the first time a user has seen an ad, or if it's a repeat viewing

- how many other pages in the same ad network a user has visited, and what those pages are

- how many different ads a user has seen from a specific ad network

- which pages on a specific website a user visits

Then, the data collected by cookies can be used to moderate how many times a user sees a specific banner, or what specific banners are displayed on specific sites for a unique visitor.

NOTE   It is important to note that the current use of ad-delivered cookies to profile a user may actually be in violation of United States law, unless full disclosure to website viewers is made and full consent from those viewers is obtained. So be wary how you're using cookies until a clear standard for user profiling and privacy is established.

For samples of cookie scripts (plus an overview of the debate about cookies and web-surfer privacy), check out Chapter 12.

How Ads Affect Site Backend

One of the final technical considerations you need to take into account before serving ads is how well the tools you use to serve ads mesh with the rest of your site production tools.

NOTE   For more information on ad-serving software, see the "Choosing Ad-Serving Software" section, below.

First, find out if the ad-serving software you want to use is compatible with your Web-serving software, or if it will require a separate server. You may want to isolate your ad server anyway, especially if it's a complex ad-serving system. This way, if there's a system crash, the site still serves content, and you only have to worry about getting the ads back up again. If you're dealing with a lot of advertising revenue, you may want to invest in a backup system for ads. This will help if you're rolling in new ad-serving or ad-reporting software; you can test or serve the ads while reducing the likelihood that the ad-serving system will crash.

Next, find out how the ad calls can be rolled into the site assembly process. If you build your site by cutting-and-pasting new text into established templates, how are you going to call or incorporate the code that calls an ad? If you rely on a content-serving tool like Vignette's Storyserver or Allaire's ColdFusion, do you need a separate ad-call template? If so, is the syntax for composing the ad fragment going to affect the way your ad-serving tool reads and responds to the code calling an ad?

Finally, find out how ads are affecting the performance of your page. Does the ad call slow down the total page load time? Is the image slow to load? Since ads are a part of your site, they need to be subject to the same usability considerations you apply to the rest of the site.

Financial Concerns

Serving ads accurately is a technically impressive accomplishment, and a commendable one. But it may not be a billable accomplishment unless you can prove to the client's satisfaction that you actually did it successfully.

How do you prove you served ads? By reporting them. Ad sponsors want to hear about everything—from what ads were served on what pages, to what time the ads were served every day. Below is a guide on what to look at when setting up ad production so reporting is relatively painless.

Tracking and Reporting Ads: The Factors Advertisers Look For

When reporting to ad sponsors, you need to know that they don't really care about how you managed to connect the ad banner with the page. They care about the actual ad serving event, and the details of that event. More specifically, when you're setting up your ads for reporting, you need to consider each of these separate factors:

- Frequency of a specific ad banner being served. Some advertising sponsors want to limit the number of times a specific user sees their ad.

- Number of discrete ad units in a specific advertising campaign. Some agencies like to compile data on the traffic for a campaign as a whole. You'll need to remember to find a way to identify ad properties as belonging to a specific campaign, especially if a sponsor on your site is running several different campaigns.

- What domains users were coming from when they saw the ad. This is especially handy if you have a contract that specifies only one or two specific domains.

- Where the ad was being served from. Another stipulation of sale may be a specific location within the site; you need to be able to schedule the ad, then reliably report that it was served there.

- How many times the ad was served, in total. Whether the ad was split into two domains, across five different areas of the site, or if it only appeared on one specific page, you're going to need to add up how many times it was served.

- Whether or not the ad was clicked on. Click-through is usually held as a benchmark for the success of an ad campaign. Therefore, it must be tracked.

Reporting these separate factors is only part of the reporting task; the other part is being able to combine statistics and turn up complete ad-serving profiles. Telling an advertiser that 60 percent of their ad viewers came from a .com domain is somewhat useful; telling the advertiser that all of the .com viewers visited the same two pages helps the advertiser narrow their focus and plot more successful ad campaigns.

Auditing a Site's Ad Serving

No matter how thorough your ad-serving software, you're not infallible. Part of the advertising agreement between a site and an advertiser includes third-party auditing.

The advantage to auditing websites is that a third-party audit provides an independent assessment of how ads are being served on a site. An audit can verify a site's traffic numbers, the ad-serving traffic numbers, and the veracity of a site's reporting system. Before you begin thinking of a third-party audit as bookkeeping's answer to the secret police, consider this: audits also lend credibility to the sites that agree to them, and help establish their legitimacy as serious business models.

The process of completing a third-party audit is relatively straightforward. Depending on who you hire to do your audit, you will probably have to do the following:

- archive your server logs for a few consecutive months
- provide site counting and accounting figures on request
- install an auditing software package on the live Web servers
- provide a schematic breakdown of what machines serve ads, content, or multimedia, and what IP addresses and domains those machines use

There are two different auditing programs that currently lead the market in third-party auditing: I/PRO and Audit Bureau of Circulations (ABC).

Recording and compiling data comprises the bulk of reporting, but the data still has to be rendered into something presentable for the client. Do not rely on an Microsoft Excel spreadsheet and two team workers. Instead, look for an ad-serving system that will also provide scheduling and reporting tools. These tools will allow you to process and present data by taking advantage of the software, not your coworkers.

Should You Pay Someone Else to Serve Your Ads?

For a lot of websites, the tasks of scheduling, producing, and reporting the results of an ad campaign fall to different members of the same ad production team. Ad serving is only going to become more complex and targeted, so the tools and time required to fulfill complex requests are going to grow in proportion.

If you don't have the means or motivation to hire and maintain an advertising production staff, you can still offer first-rate advertising service on your site by entering into an agreement with an advertising network like Doubleclick or an ad rep firm like 27/7 Media.

These firms usually provide the following production and business tasks:

- national advertising sales
- ad serving
- ad targeting to specific audiences
- ad scheduling
- ad reporting
- ad/traffic auditing

But there is a tradeoff; these firms usually work on commission, and commission can be steep. If you're a small-market or extremely specialized site, you may not want to make the investment for this kind of service. But if you're a general interest site or part of a larger site network, using an ad network may be a good way to offer sophisticated ad services without having to build your own advertising department.

How to Choose a Third-Party Ad Firm   You've decided to sink your company equipment and personnel into building the site, and you've figured that outsourcing your advertising sales and serving is probably your best bet. How do you choose an ad firm that you can work with, without losing money?

First, do your homework. Research the firms you'd be interested in working with. See how long each firm has been in business. Find out who their advertisers are. Find out who their other clients are and ask those clients for references. When you're asking for references, ask if the ad firm is immediately responsive when there are technical difficulties, and ask how careful and reliable the ad rep's reporting procedures are.

Second, sell yourself. An ad firm is going to sell space on your site only when they know enough about the site to be able to make a pitch. Subsequently, you have to pitch yourself. Try the following:

- Give them a few months of consistent traffic reports, so your ad firm knows how many visitors you get, and at what rate they return.

- Produce a demographic sketch of your reader: geographic region, domain, profession. Remember those annoying forms you had to fill out whenever you downloaded a plug-in from a software site? They're for reporting demographics. You'll need to begin gathering demographic data as well.

Third, find a firm with a mutually agreeable selling policy. Most ad firms are going to want exclusive rights to the real estate on your site for anywhere from three months to a year. They're also going want a percentage of the ad sales—again, the number can be anywhere from 15 to 50 percent. Finally, you'll need to make sure you're both conversant with the firm's payment procedures.

The idea is to enter a mutually beneficial relationship. Your role is to produce saleable content, using the editorial and technical expertise you and your coworkers have. Their role is to sell ads, using the marketing and technical expertise they have.

Adding Co-Sponsorships to Your Site

If you've ever sat in on an advertising meeting, you've heard the phrase *co-branding*. This is a stealthy approach to combining commercial revenue and content: sites that are co-branded are usually built to have a specific identity, and a single underwriting sponsor. Intel's MediaDome (`http://www.mediadome.com/`), originally created at CNet, is an example of a co-branded site—Mediadome is the specific content identity, yet Intel owns the site.

Co-branding is one type of a site revenue strategy known as *sponsorship*. Just like the television sponsorships of the 1950s, website sponsorships attach one specific commercial sponsor to a content area.

Sponsorship can take many forms. HotWired's first two sponsorships were its humanities-geared commentary site Packet (`http://www.hotwired.com/packet/`) and the job-hunting site Dream Jobs (`http://www.hotwired.com/dreamjobs/`). Both sites had a persistent sponsor-only logo banner on the front door of the site, plus a supplemental microsite linking the sponsors to the content. A typical example of sponsorship is in effect at the Minty Fresh record label's site (`www.mintyfresh.com`). Here you can link to CDNow and buy Minty Fresh's latest releases. See Figure 16.2.

FIGURE 16.2:

CDs from the Minty Fresh record label can be bought through CDNow.

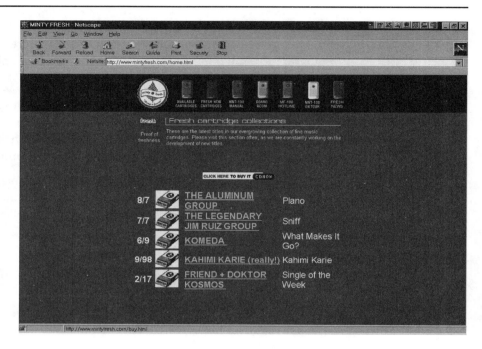

So sponsorship can go all the way from a company orchestrating and approving content for the sponsored site, to a small and exclusive service presence on the pages. The remainder of this section covers how to handle integrating sponsorships on your site.

Integrating a Sponsorship

To a commercial sponsor, one of the benefits of a content site sponsorship is that it allows the content and sponsor to team up and highlight their best features. For example, a travel e-zine might have a sponsorship with an online travel agency, and demonstrate that service exclusively throughout its articles. Or, a Web tools site may be part of an ad-sharing network, and the four sites share a common navigation bar at the top of each page.

No matter the degree of involvement, or how cleverly the sponsor and content are merged on the frontend of the site, the people who run the backend of the site are going to have to be prepared to start doing production for two—two sites, that is. Sponsorships often involve tracking software, co-branding logo calls, or even shared code between sites. Subsequently, some of the factors you need to consider for peaceful sponsorship production are:

Integration of sponsorship elements into the site's daily production tools and code.   If your sponsorship agreement calls for a persistent logo or link on the site, it makes sense to integrate that permanent element into your site templates or code. But how do you accomplish this? Adding the element as a virtual include makes modifying it quickly on client request easy. It also makes it easy to remove a sponsorship element should the sponsorship end. However, you may need to take a look at other site elements that are not so easily pulled in and out. If you've had to incorporate a new logo into your site banners, you're going to need to keep track of what elements in your site have been altered so you can upgrade or remove them as necessary.

Co-branding between specific sites or services.   This usually entails your site displaying their site logo—and vice versa—when visitors from your site are referred to theirs or from their site to yours. You need to find a way to combine a server variable like referring domain, plus a layout feature that does or doesn't display the co-brand when needed. If you've got three different co-branding deals for one section, you want those deals to be visible at different, specific times. Determine how to use elements like conditional HTML, ad-serving software, or virtual includes to customize your pages for sponsors.

Reporting of sponsorship elements.   The reason your site is entered into a sponsorship agreement is that you can deliver the demographic your sponsor wants to reach. This means you're going to have to prove your demographics constantly. Invest in a reporting system, and use it. You're going to have to consider a third-party auditing system like the ones discussed above. It will help ensure that you and sponsor are both getting benefits from the sponsorship.

Choosing Ad-Serving Software

If you want to be able to offer extremely specific and dynamic ad targeting, you may want to invest in ad-serving software. Ad-serving software adds a saleable element to your site: if you can offer an extra degree of ad targeting, an extra aspect of specificity to your reporting, or an extra ability to support something above and beyond the basic GIF banner, you've got an edge over your competition.

TIP

Software packages range in price and technical complexity from $35 to $35,000. The price usually corresponds to the number of features and amount of technical support offered per package. Only you can decide what criteria you need. One of the best comparative ad server software sites is Mark Welch's Banner Server Software Site (`http://www.markwelch.com/bannerad/baf_ad_sw.htm`), with links to varied packages plus pricing information.

Before you select a system you'll need to ascertain a few factors. Some pertinent ones are as follows:

Technological Issues

Is the ad-serving technology compatible with the rest of the site's production technology? For example, if your ad system doesn't support or recognize server-side includes, yet the rest of your site lives and dies by Apache, you may have a problem. If you are faced with two incompatible technologies, are you willing to invest the time and money to make them work together in producing your complete site?

What sort of scripting language will you need to know to use the site? Some ad-serving systems require you to know regular expressions, others require a basic grasp of Perl, still others require JavaScript. You'll want to pick an ad-serving system that you and your existing staff can competently operate.

NOTE

Ad-serving scripts usually let you rotate banners based on one or two simple, parsable variables. They're CGI scripts, so they rely on the server to open a connection, pass on relevant information, then pass back an appropriate response to users. CGI-rotating scripts are a good tool to use if you're offering limited ad targeting, or if you're not especially concerned with the number of connections or processes your server has to run. One of the best places to look for ad-serving scripts is Matt's Script Archive (`http://www.worldwidemart.com/scripts/`).

What kind of tags or information will you have to start including on your pages in order to accommodate the ads? More importantly, can this data be easily found and replaced if you need to update or change ad systems?

And most importantly, can this data sit separately from the rest of the page structure? Can you build modular, indexable pages that aren't absolutely dependent on the ad call for completion?

How will you enter data into the ad tool?   Is there an easy-to-load interface? Can you log in and use the tool via a Web-based interface remotely, or is it platform-specific software restricted to one machine? How you access the ad tool to enter data can affect how effectively you and your staff can use it to modify or repair ads.

How do the systems report a successful ad serve?   Is it based only on the page being served through the point of the ad call? Or is it when the entire banner was served? You need to establish what counts as a served ad—the definition could affect how you report ads and thus fulfill your contractual obligations. Over-reporting ad service ruins an advertiser-client relationship; under-reporting ad service causes you to lose possible ad possibilities.

How easily can you access Web statistics?   Can you check the statistics every day or several times a day if necessary? If you're working on a short, time-specific ad campaign, being able to check how well it's serving is important.

How does the software count the number of ads being served?   There's a reason that the top of a Web page is considered prime real estate: it often loads more quickly than the rest of the page, so the chance of a user seeing the ad rises. Some ad-serving tools count any call for an ad as an ad served. If that ad call is at the bottom of a page and a user moves on to a new page before the old page is completely loaded, you've just counted an ad that the user didn't even see. Find out if the ad serving software simply requires the ad call to be summoned, or if it logs only those ads that have loaded completely.

How does ad counting affect the rest of your site operations?   Depending on how ads are counted, you may want to physically separate your ad files from the content files. If you're logging the call to a specific ad and its successful load, it's easier to read and record signals from a separate machine. The drawback: Your ad server is going to cost money because it's an extra machine. Moreover, you're going to have to provide the same kinds of backup and duplication plans that you have for your regular content.

How many different factors does the ad-serving software log? You'll want to find out what sort of data the software promises to log, and how it does it. If you've got software promising to stick unique ads on unique pages in the site, how is the ad-serving software going to keep track of pages and ads?

Logistical Issues

How much will it cost the company to install and use the ad-serving system? The initial software license and support costs are only the tip of the iceberg. Do you have to purchase separate servers to support the ad-serving system? What about backing up the separate system? Will you have to hire someone with specific expertise about the ad-serving system? How easy will it be for employees to install and interact with the ad-serving system? How much time and money will go into training?

Is the ad system scalable? Can it handle an increase in the number of ads, an increase in the number of pages where ads must be served, or the addition of another tracking data point? You will need to determine what the traffic and load breaking points are for your ad system. These parameters will help you determine if you can expect to use an ad system over a fair-sized time interval.

Is the ad system portable? Portability takes two guises: how easily specific ad calls on a unique site file can be removed, added, and modified; and how easily you can move the entire ad-serving system to new machines or new operating systems. You don't want to be married to specific technology simply because it's the only one your ad-serving software will work on.

What factors does the ad system allow you to target? Ideally, your new ad-serving software should let you serve ads based on a combination of criteria, such as user domain, time of day visiting, and specific file being visited. If you can't mix and match the criteria, or if they're not that specific, you might be better off with a series of server scripts.

What extras will the ad system require you to install on the rest of your backend? One well-known ad-serving system works via a series of Perl scripts; in order for the ad server to work, you have to have at least one machine where Perl is installed and running. Make sure that the technical parameters for your site are compatible with the technical parameters the ad-serving software requires. If they're not, evaluate the cost of acquiring those parameters relative to the revenue the new ad system will help you generate.

> **NOTE**
>
> This cannot be emphasized enough—how will the ad serving software affect the rest of your backend? Will you be able to merely include specialized ad calls to the ad-server as part of your regular page assembly? Do you have to install a site indexing system that your ad server recognizes? Determine how ad serving and tracking affects the rest of your site by determining how it records data.

Can you serve ads across multiple sites or servers? A sophisticated, specific ad-targeting system is useless if it can't expand with your site. You need to buy an ad server for the site that you anticipate maintaining a year from now, as well as for the site that you're currently maintaining.

Advertising on the Web is a booming business, and it gets more technically complex every year. Your ad serving and reporting systems keep your current advertising clients happy, but they also serve as selling points to future clients. If an advertiser isn't happy with reports they're getting, or isn't happy with how incomplete the data are, they'll pull their dollars and find a site that gives them what they want.

Balance the demands of the advertiser against what you can reasonably provide. Even though advertising drives many sites, it wouldn't even be around if the sites weren't visited. Before you bend over backwards to meet a client, consider what it's going to cost your backend to do so.

Summary

Web-based advertising is a far more complex industry than was outlined in this chapter, but you should come away with a basic understanding of the factors that drive the Web advertising industry, and the production concerns you have to address when you decide to put ads on your website.

If you're a contractor who works on varied sites, it can only help to prepare your clients for ad sales, or to build your site to work well with their ad-serving system. If you're a production manager who thinks of advertising as a third-party concern, this chapter should have provided some insight into how to integrate advertising into your site without a lot of pain.

Money and content are going to have a long, intertwined relationship on the Web; learn how to build your site to withstand the twists and turns that relationship takes.

CHAPTER
SEVENTEEN

Accessibility for All Users

- ■ Maintaining a culturally accessible site

- ■ Maintaining a physically accessible site

- ■ Streamlining your QA process

Now that you've set up a website backend that can rise to most user challenges, it's time to use your skills and site setup to address two common problems among data-structure-driven websites. The first problem is a usability one; the second addresses the increased level of quality assurance (QA) a website needs when it migrates to a data-driven model.

We took an introductory look at usability in Chapter 9 of the previous part. The primary focus was on how to figure out who your audience is, and how to bridge the gap between user expectations and developer expectations. The usability portion of this chapter will focus on bridging another gap: making the site accessible for audiences with differing physical abilities. You'll be able to recognize some usability issues, and learn some strategies for incorporating accessibility into your existing site. You'll also focus on making the site accessible and comprehensible to audiences coming from a much different cultural perspective.

The quality assurance portion of this chapter will extend what we discussed in Chapter 9. Before, we talked about the basic considerations for developing a QA process that could be integrated into website development. Now, we're going to talk about the considerations for QA when the site is migrating to a data-structure model. There will be an increased emphasis on the development process, because the site is getting more technically complex.

Now—let's start focusing on accessibility.

The Accidental Visitor

There are two different definitions of accessibility. The first is cultural accessibility, the second is physical accessibility. *Cultural accessibility* is little more than simple courtesy—providing clear units of measurement for time, money, and temperature, and writing your HTML so it can be read by browsers that render in different foreign languages. *Physical accessibility* requires a little more planning, and it affects every aspect of site functionality.

So why bother making the site accessible for people who don't fall into a "typical" user group? If you're dealing with different cultures, it's common courtesy to make the World Wide Web as universal as possible. It's also common courtesy to consider the working environment of all of your users—and that environment extends from the computer to the user as well.

If courtesy doesn't sway you, consider this: There are over 11 million Americans alone who have some sort of vision impairment. Would you deliberately exclude any other audience segment of 11 million just because you didn't want to alter your HTML?

Integrating accessibility measures into your website doesn't have to be difficult. The remaining sections will discuss different accessibility issues, how they contribute to website accessibility, and how their incorporation affects the rest of your site.

Maintaining a Culturally Accessible Site

The World Wide Web is often derided as being anything but. This is not due so much to a preponderance of English-speaking sites as the underlying assumption that everyone online speaks the same language we do, and gets the same cultural references. This goes far in explaining why website directories tend to be mono-lingual—it's hard to index content you can't comprehend.

However, there's a strong chance that your audience will extend past the geographic and linguistic boundaries you know. How do you make sure your site is readable and comprehensible to someone in Germany, South Africa, or Thailand? You consider the contextual references to your culture, and the HTML you use to build your site. The categories below outline some of the items that you should consider when trying to integrate cross-cultural accessibility into your site.

Units of Measurement

America is one of the few nations that hasn't converted to the metric system. While an intimate knowledge of conversion values isn't required for the nuts and bolts of site-building, it is a content usability issue. Any website whose content relies on quantifiable values should remember that units of measurement should never be assumed. In other words: A dollar is not equal to a yen is not equal to a franc, nor is a meter equal to a yard.

Mark your measurements clearly, and provide conversions when relevant. Some areas where measurement marking should be absolutely mandatory are:

- Anything mentioning a money figure. If the figure is in dollars, be sure to mention whether it's U.S. dollars or Canadian dollars; if the figure deals with an amount of money spent, earned, or lost in another country, include the money amount in both the currency of the country where said money was lost or gained, and the currency of the country where your readers are. Reading about someone losing ¥128,000,000 doesn't register with U.S. readers—reading about someone losing $1,000,000 U.S. dollars does. Conversely, a Japanese reader might not care about someone losing $1,000,000 U.S. dollars, but she will pay attention when the amount is shown to be equal to ¥128,000,000.

- Anything mentioning a temperature. The Celsius temperature scale is the metric standard that most of the world—and many technical professions—use as the de facto measuring scale. The United States uses Fahrenheit. Extremely dedicated physicists may use Kelvin. If you're going to mention temperatures, at least provide the Celsius and Fahrenheit values.

- Anything mentioning volume or weight. Reading about the 350 kilogram alligator who escaped from the zoo is a little less compelling to American readers than reading about that same alligator weighing in at 771 pounds. Similarly, a punchbowl that was filled with 600 gallons of sangria won't register with European readers the same way a punch bowl filled with 2,727 liters would.

- Anything mentioning distance. Most countries measure the distance between two cities in kilometers; Americans tend to do their distance calculation in miles. Thus, a three-hour 300 kilometer roadtrip (186 miles) is nothing like the five-hour 300 mile (483km) roadtrip. Any website looking to act as a travel resource might want to consider their international audience.

There are a few great metric conversion sites on the Web, so converting your values to reach a larger audience should be no problem. A little time and effort to add cultural context cues can make your site much more relevant to users who think in different units of measurement.

Language Issues

You may be reading this book in English; but you may be reading it in Chinese, in Arabic, in French. Translation is an issue that must be dealt with, whether you're publishing a book or a website. There are a number of steps that can be taken to ensure that your site gets the maximum cultural range.

Automatic Language Detection

Browsers are capable of amazing feats, but guessing the native language of website developers is not one of them. As a result, what looks like beautifully rendered Cyrillic to someone in Moscow, Russia may come off looking like the cat walked across the keyboard to someone in Moscow, Idaho. So how do developers tell browsers in which language to render their markup? Currently, people who are writing HTML for non-English-speaking audiences have to rely on a lot of ISO characters to get the job done.

There is one future solution to this, and one real-world one. The future one is the `<lang>` tag; it's currently part of the HTML 4 specification. Its purpose would be simple: the `<lang>` tag is an attribute tag attached to a container tag like `<p>`, `<BODY>`, or `<DIV>`. `<Lang>` specifies that the content contained within the container tag it's modifying be rendered as a specific language. For example, `<div lang ="fr">QUOTE</div>` produces a French quote.

The real-world solution is slightly more limited. It involves sticking this meta tag in the header of your document:

```
<meta http-equiv="Content-Type" content="text/html; charset= [value]">
```

where `[value]` equals an encoding scheme supported by at least one browser. For example, the tag

```
<meta http-equiv="Content-Type" content="text/html; charset=SHIFT_JIS">
```

specifies that the character encoding scheme is a Japanese alphabet.

HTTP headers are set up to pass language rendering information to the browser. The old HTTP 1.0 protocol included a charset parameter "Content-Type" to specify the language the document was written in. This parameter was optional, so it was largely ignored and therefore ineffective. In HTTP 1.1, however, the charset parameter specifying language is mandatory. Therefore, documents now provide that information. Users who have set their browser language preferences to receive documents with a specific language might stand a better chance of getting a document in the language of their—not the site developer's—choice.

Future Technology

The implementation of these technologies is still in the "we (heart) the idea!" stage from most browser makers. International URLs, Unicode, and non-Western URLs are all in development.

International URLs   Most URLs are restricted to the standard ASCII printable alphabet. At 95 characters, it's not enough, nor does it allow for characters with accents, or characters in any language that doesn't use the written Roman alphabet. Needless to say, a lot of international companies must translate their company name into a different language in order to devise a domain name and URL. The W3C is currently deciding whether or not a working group is going to revise the URL protocol to include non-Roman characters. To monitor the progress on this issue, go to `http://www.w3.org/International/O-URL-drafts.html`.

Unicode   All languages are encoded so that their characters are either stored as 7 bits of information, or 8 bits of information. Because each language has a number of characters that are unique to that language (like the German ß), there are a number of character encodings that are unique to the language set. Extending our example, ß is unique to the language set called the German alphabet.

The International Standards Organization (ISO) stepped in and created a series of character sets. These character sets are meant to do two things: accommodate the wide number of unique language characters, and establish a standard set of character encodings that all software could recognize and accurately render. There are five predominant character sets:

Latin 1 (which we know as ASCII)	(ISO 8859-1)
Cyrillic	(ISO 8859-5)
Arabic	(ISO 8859-6)
Greek	(ISO 8859-7)
Hebrew	(ISO 8859-1)

All of these character sets are comprised of 8-bit chunks of data, so they have a limit of 256 different, individual data units total. That's only 256 characters. This works fine with the relatively limited Roman alphabet, but what about languages like Japanese or Chinese, with tens of thousands of discrete characters? What about languages whose written expression consists of pictographs instead of alphabet units?

The answer is to rethink the way the data is encoded. Instead of relying on 8-bit character encoding, move to a 16-bit encoding schema. Then the number of characters an ISO alphabet could have would jump from 256 to 65,536. This could open up the encoding possibilities for many alphabets; it could also serve to unify a number of alphabet series into one ISO standard that can be used by Web developers everywhere.

That's where Unicode comes in. It's a standard based on the 16-bit scheme, and its goal is to assign every alphabet character a unique octet (8 bits equals one octet). Unicode is already part of the HTML 4.0 standard, and it looks to be a rising player in accommodating specialized alphabets, especially since one of its roles is to provide a translation-type role between the ISO encodings, and other alphabet encodings like the Japanese SHIFT_JIS.

The issue of pictographic languages still hasn't been resolved by Unicode or the W3C. Since the Web is becoming increasingly global, however, more attention is being paid to the issue of non-alphabet-based written language systems.

Non-Western Layout   Reading left to right isn't the only way people digest information: Hebrew and Arabic are read right to left, and many Asian languages are read top to bottom. Since most older browsers were developed by people who worked in primarily left-to-right-reading cultures, the browsers automatically display information left to right, top to bottom.

In order to accommodate different layouts, the W3C has suggested using style sheets to specify information flow. Although the current implementation of Cascading Style Sheets doesn't have any explicit directions for making text flow one direction or the other, a complex ISO scheme called *Document Style Semantics and Specification Language* (*DSSSL*) does. DSSSL handles bidirectional text flow, which makes it useful to languages that read right to left. So if you write your style sheets in DSSSL, you might be able to set up an approximation of non-Western formatting. However, DSSSL is inherently complex—its creators have admitted as much at `http://www.w3.org/International/O-CSS.html`—and so is not currently supported in the browser market.

Another soon-to-be-implemented-within-browsers solution is the Unicode-based `<dir>` attribute. When combined with the `<lang>` tag, this attribute can tell the browser which direction to render your text. For example:

```
<div lang="Fr" dir="ltr">Quote</div>
```

specifies a French-language quote rendered from left to right (hence the "ltr" value for the `dir` tag). This example:

```
<div lang="He" dir="rtl">Quote</div>
```

provides a quote in Hebrew, rendered right to left.

With any luck, attributes that allow a Web builder more control over her layout will be incorporated into future browsers.

Content flow isn't the only directional consideration you will have. Your navigational elements may be equally culture-specific, and therefore a little difficult for non-natives to negotiate. For example, navigation bars at the left of the page not only make the site physically less accessible (more on that in the accessibility sections), but also assume your users read left to right and top to bottom. Granted, this is now such a common interface standard—from pull-down menus to websites—that most readers can interpret the information easily.

But if you're trying to build a website with a distinctly international audience, you may want to consider alternatives. One such alternative is to place your navigation scheme horizontally, and immediately below your page headline. Other schemes can be based on contextual cues: A document broken up into several pages can give readers a sense of where they are both absolutely and relatively by displaying a page tally at the top (1 of 6, 2 of 6, etc.). You can also convey the intended direction of editorial material by labeling your links "back to prior page" and "forward to next page," thus coupling context with direction. The goal you are trying to meet is to pass along two items of information: where the user will be going, and how it relates to where she is currently.

Maintaining a Physically Accessible Site

According to the 1990 U.S. census, almost 50 million people in America have disabilities; since you're reading this nearly 10 years later, the number is sure to have gone up. At the time of the census, people with visual impairment counted for 7 million of those disabled; the number has since climbed to 11 million.

Maintaining a physically accessible site isn't just a matter of political correctness. There are other large population groups for whom physically accessible sites are becoming important: Senior citizens, and "ordinary" people suffering from arthritis or carpal tunnel syndrome are making up an increasingly large percentage of the Web population. Well-funded movements to make the Web more accessible to senior citizens, and organizations like SeniorNet (`http://www.seniornet.org/`) and Third Age (`http://www.thirdage.com/`), plus an inevitable jump in the number of online users as America's baby boomers approach retirement, mean that you'll be designing for an audience that won't stand for gray 8pt type on a black background just because it's cool.

The World Wide Web provides a medium where people who have a wide range of physical capabilities can find information and support, expand their opportunities, and participate in the same sort of entertaining, data mining world we develop sites in. As site developers, it's important to provide a product that can be used by the widest possible audience; if the product can't be used as is, it's important to provide an adaptation.

The sections below discuss different accessibility issues, how they affect physical interaction with the site, how these issues can be addressed, and how their accessibility solutions affect the rest of your site.

NOTE   Please note that the accessibility issues the visually impaired face are not the same accessibility issues the cognitively impaired face, nor are the issues the mobility-challenged face in Web surfing the same as the ones hearing-impaired face. None of the sections below is a panacea for all accessibility problems, but each one highlights a different, common aspect of Web development that impacts different groups in unexpected ways.

Color

A lot of website designers rely on color to distinguish between different sections, cue site users regarding different site functions, and create a cohesive look and feel for the entire site. Most of the time, this is a good idea. There are, however, some color considerations to make if you want to make your site physically accessible.

First, make sure that your color scheme takes color blindness into account. Color blindness, or the inability to distinguish between different colors, affects roughly 9 percent of the general U.S. population. The most frequent type of color blindness is an inability to distinguish between red and green. Therefore, it's probably sound usability practice to ensure that any functional color scheme have a backup method for visual identification, like spatial placement. For example, if you have a navigation bar with several primary colors indicating the different sections, you would make sure that the color areas stayed in the same position on the nav bar throughout the site, so the color of the nav bar option wasn't the only way users could visually identify the functions offered to them.

A less extreme, but still important, color consideration is the variance and shades of the colors you're using. Some people with visual impairment may not be able to perceive color contrasts, or differences among several different shades in the same color family. Again, if you're relying on color as a visual cue for different site functions, make sure you have an equally effective backup measure as well—like text labels on nav bar elements, or consistent spatial arrangement. If you do want to use color, one option is to use extreme contrasts to indicate a change of state, such as a sky blue nav bar button that turns dark blue when clicked. Another option is to assign dramatically different colors to different functions—yellow to search pages, green to index pages, blue to archive pages—and provide a text-based labeling system as backup.

Font Size and Font Face

Fixed font size is a great way to control the precise layout and spatial arrangement on a page, but it wreaks havoc on users who rely on large type in order to read. If you set a font size, like `<font size="3">`, you take the font control out of the hands of your users. Besides, as Cascading Style Sheet implementation becomes more widely supported by the browser makers—so far, Opera does a better job than either Netscape Navigator or Microsoft Internet Explorer—you should be specifying more of your content's appearance attributes via CSS. In addition to relieving font size issues, CSS will also allow you to set up specific color schemes for different viewing situations.

The most commonly suggested alternative for font sizing is relative sizing, such as putting `<smaller>` and `<larger>` around different chunks of text. The size differences can still be used as visual indications of functional differences, and users can adjust the font size to meet their visual requirements.

The other font trouble that visually impaired users run into is the mixing and matching of different font faces. While you may be able to tell the difference between the rounded, short Verdana font and its skinnier sans-serif cousin Helvetica, someone with poor vision sees only a sea of sans-serif characters. If you're relying on font face to convey specific functions, like picture captions, sidebar text, or navigation scheme, pick two fonts that are dissimilar enough to be easily told apart, or revise your visual scheme so the site still works with only one font.

If you still want to offer as rich a typographic experience as possible without sacrificing accessibility, use the traditional heading tags (`<H1>`–`<H6>`), which come in a variety of sizes, and document container tags like `<BODY>`, `<P>`, and `<DIV>`. You can assign each different heading and container a style in a Cascading Style Sheet; your targeted readers will still get the visual experience you anticipated, and the visual design degrades smoothly across differently configured browsers.

Finally, be wary of using font size as a way of controlling text flow. Not only are all sorts of users accessing your sites with different window sizes, thus wrecking the spacing scheme you set up, the different text sizes you set in browser sizes allow users to shrink or expand even tabled text, so the caption that fits a 9pt.

Helvetica in one line on your screen may end up as a two-line 15pt. Times tidbit on someone else's. Anticipate design degradation, and restrict typography to conveying a level of information from <H1> to <H6>.

Tables

Tables can be a great way to control the relative spatial positioning of layouts. You can drop a nav bar along the left vertical margin, provide sub-navigation at the top or bottom of a document, and align text and images.

Too bad that it renders the page unreadable by a lot of screen readers and text synthesizers. Although HTML purists have repeatedly warned that tables should be used only for data organization, most pages today rely on some sort of tabling to maintain a reliably consistent look and feel across browsers and platforms.

For example, this code:

```
<TABLE>
<TR>
<TD>
Site map<P></P>
Archive<P></P>
What's New<P></P>
Search<P></P>
Return to Index<P></P>
</TD>
<TD>
Welcome to MY site. It's filled with cool trivia about tabby cats,
especially those that still have claws and enjoy kneading their owner's
scalp with those claws at 4 a.m.
</TD>
</TR>
</TABLE>
```

reads like this on a tables-supported visual browser:

Site Map	Welcome to MY site. It's filled with cool trivia about tabby cats, especially those that still have claws and enjoy kneading their owner's scalp with those claws at 4 a.m.
Archive	
What's New	
Search	
Return to Index	

but like this when read aloud by a screen reader:

> Site map Welcome to MY site. It's filled with
>
> Archive cool trivia about tabby cats, especially those
>
> What's New that still have claws and enjoy
>
> Search kneading their owner's scalp with those
>
> Return to Index claws at 4 a.m.

Notice how both the function and context of the various parts has been completely ruined, simply because the screen reader moved one line at a time, left to right. This is only a simple two-cell table: Imagine how embedded tables would read.

You can still use tables on your site, provided that you are using them for strict data-presenting purposes or provide a non-tables layout for browsers.

If you're set on trying to maximize your current site without resorting to the options above, consider adding the <THEAD>, <TBODY>, or <TFOOT> attributes. These will assign a meaningful data tag to those positions, so people hearing your site understand what the head, body, and bottom of your document are. Note that the data contained within <THEAD></THEAD>, <TBODY></TBODY>, and <TFOOT></TFOOT> are still presented in horizontal rows, but at least you've attached some functional context to it.

Here's how each of the tags works:

- <THEAD> defines the "head" of the table. This is analogous to the title of a table.

- <TBODY> defines the data that comprises the table. Figure 17.1 shows four cells in the <TBODY>.

- <TFOOT> defines footer material. This can be used for a table caption.

No matter what option you choose, as long as table data doesn't form multiple text columns, and it can be understood regardless of the direction it's read in, you'll be safe.

FIGURE 17.1:

An example of a table with THEAD, TBODY, and TFOOT markup

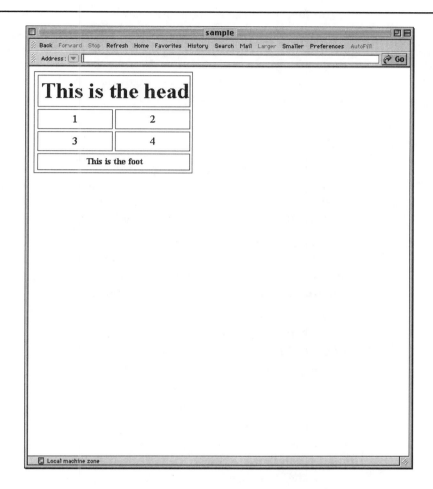

White Space

By now, you may be getting a little frustrated with the various no-nos for site accessibility: no subtle palettes, no table-driven layouts, no specific font sizes. Fortunately, there is at least one layout technique you can use to create visual connections between content and function, and still maintain an aurally, visually accessible site. The key is white space, and lots of it. By making "islands" of content on a page, you can separate out the different page elements by function, and allow people who are visually impaired to better focus on individual items.

Another benefit to using white space is that you can design pages that remain consistent across the site. This consistency not only raises the total usability quotient across your site for seasoned info-gatherers, it also provides a framework for those with physical or cognitive disabilities to comfortably negotiate their way about the site. Knowing where sitewide features like navigation will be is important if pointing and clicking from one page to another is not just a reflexive task.

Frames

When frames first hit the browser scene, some designers hailed them as the best means to create a multi-branching hypertext story; a lot of us just figured frames would provide that perfect, persistent means of providing a navigation element. It turns out that when it came to usability and accessibility, both sides were wrong.

Remember that experiment with the screen reader and the tables, a few paragraphs back? Screen readers yield the same results if a frames document is read aloud. So even if your navigation scheme is persistent, all you're doing is adding persistent gibberish to the rest of the page as it's read aloud.

The most obvious, and easiest, solution is one you're probably already offering: a <NOFRAMES> alternative. You can go really low-tech with this one by having users deliberately select that option as they alight on your page, or you can use conditional HTML to detect a non-frames browser and serve up the correctly formatted page without being asked.

The only possible exception to the no-frames rule might be a thin, narrow frame placed at the top or bottom of a page, so it's read as a horizontal chunk of data either first or last. The primary drawback is that it's not a persistent navigation element for users who are hearing the page; a secondary drawback may be the aesthetic value and linking scheme for the rest of the site.

If you're going to use frames, be sure that you include the <title> tag in all documents so your user can independently load pages and still have an idea of what you're doing.

Links

Hyperlinking is one of the most basic appeals of the World Wide Web: The ability to collect or cruise through information with the click of a mouse is what initially made the Web so enticing to many people.

However, hyperlinking presumes a basic level of sight to see the links, and the mobility to aim for and hit the links. And while your arthritic or carpal-tunnel-riddled audiences may be able to see the links, moving a mouse to click on them is another issue. Whenever you present hyperlinks in your site, you need to make sure both your sight-impaired and your motion-impaired audiences can use them.

The first, and lowest tech, solution is to make your link area as large as possible, both in area and in meaning. There is a well-know dictionary (which shall remain nameless) that only hyperlinks the tiny dots next to the text labels on its navigation bar, rather than hyperlinking the bullet and the label. Don't copy this site—make your links large enough for someone with limited motor control to aim for. Accessibility evangelist Terry Sullivan suggests testing your link area this way: Switch to your nondominant hand, and try to hit all the links on your site. If it takes you multiple tries, it's time to rethink your linking areas.

Picking on the dictionary site again, only the bullets next to the word categories are highlighted, not the categories. How is a blind user supposed to know where they're clicking? Your second link consideration is context. There are a lot of sites that want to add editorial depth or randomness to their site, and provide hyperlinks specific to one word. This works fine for sighted viewers, but many blind users frequently set their screen-reading software to read only the links. If you can't see the page and the only clues you have to go on for links are "[image], [image], [image]," what's going to compel you to follow any of those links? Links should be able to be understood independently of the context they're placed in, and should give a reader an idea of where they're going to go if they click on the link.

After you've solved your linking context problems, it's time to renew your focus on link accessibility. There are two higher-tech ways to make your links more accessible to the mobility-impaired. Both require using HTML tags, and both are supported by HTML 4.0. How well they are supported by browsers is another issue: for the browser compatibility with each tag, check Appendix B.

The first HTML tag is the `<input type="tabindex">` tag. This simple tag is an attribute tag that modifies a lot of tags—A, AREA, OBJECT, INPUT, SELECT, TEXTAREA, and BUTTON. What it does is simple: It tells the browser to let the user hit the tab key to move from data field to data field in the order that the fields are coded in the HTML with a tabindex value.

Note the order. If your forms are coded as follows:

```
<FORM action ="..." method="post">
<P>
First name <input type=text tabindex=1>
```

```
</P>
<P>
Last name <input type=text tabindex=2>
</P>
<P>
Phone number <input type=text tabindex=3>
</P>
</FORM>
```

the user moves from first name to last name, in a simple one-two-three. But if the code reads like this:

```
<FORM action ="..." method="post">
<TABLE>
<TR>
<TD>
<P>
First name <input type=text tabindex=1>
</P>
</TD>
<TD>
<P>
Phone number <input type=text tabindex=2>
</P>
</TD>
</TR>
<TR>
<TD>
<P>
Last name <input type=text tabindex=3>
</P>
</TD>
</TR>
</TABLE>
</FORM>
```

the first and last names are aligned together, but the user will move from first name to phone number, because of the order of tags. In order to make sure a user moves from first name to last name, then to phone number, you'd reassign the tabindex to the values listed below:

```
<FORM action ="..." method="post">
<TABLE>
```

```
<TR>
<TD>
<P>
First name <input type=text tabindex=1>
</P>
</TD>
<TD>
<P>
Phone number <input type=text tabindex=3>
</P>
</TD>
</TR>
<TR>
<TD>
<P>
Last name <input type=text tabindex=2>
</P>
</TD>
</TR>
</TABLE>
</FORM>
```

If a tabindex value isn't specified, most browsers will usually default to the order we saw in the first tabled example: first name, phone number, then last name. Tabindex can also be used to allow a user to skip from section to section of a document using the <A NAME> tag set. This would come in handy if you have a long document broken up into separate topical sections.

The next type of tag is the `<accesskey>` tag. This tag is another attribute tag, and it can modify the <A>, <LABEL>, <CAPTION>, and <LEGEND> tags. What this means in practical terms is that you can slap an `<accesskey>` tag onto a link, or any of the data containers mentioned above, and map the keyboard keys to that area. In strict accessibility terms, you've just allowed a user an alternative to mouse-driven navigation. In more fully realized accessibility terms, you could assign different keys to different hyperlinks and therefore create functional associations between accesskeys and the actions they perform.

For example:

```
<BODY>
<P>
<A accesskey="T" HREF="toc.html">Press the T key to visit the table of
contents</A>
```

```
</P>
<P>
<A accesskey="S" HREF="search.html">Press the S key to visit the search
page</A>
</P>
</BODY>
```

Note that each different link had its own accesskey assigned to it, and that each link told the user what key to press, and what results the action would produce. If you're going to implement accesskeys, be sure to let your user know, and repeat the feature on every page you've included it in. In the example above, I paired the accesskey and the function. You could also include an accesskey table, like this:

```
<BODY>
<P>
This website allows you to navigate through the pages using access
keys. The pages each accesskey leads to are listed below. If you're on
a PC, press the [ALT] key plus the stated accesskey; if you're on a
Mac, press the [cmd] key plus the access key.
</P>
<P>
S - search <BR clear=all>
T - table of contents <BR clear=all>
B - archive <BR clear=all>
E - new <BR clear=all>
</P>
<!--content-->
<!--navigation area-->
 
<A accesskey="S" href="search.html>Search</A>  
<A accesskey="T" href="toc.html>Table of Contents </A> 
<A accesskey="B" href="archive.html>Archive </A> 
<A accesskey="E" href="new.html>New</A> 
```

Note that the accesskey tag still modifies the link, even though there is a user key in a much different part of the page.

You can also use accesskeys to let users move through different sections of a form. In this case, the assigning of the accesskey seems a little removed: you create a table of keys and labels for the keys. Then, in the form code, you assign the input areas names that correspond to the key labels. The chain of control goes like this:

ACCESSKEY is brought into focus by a key-specific LABEL which also tells the key which INPUT to act on because it has the same NAME.

The following example will show you how it works in hands-on code:

```
<FORM action ="..." method="post">
<P>
<LABEL for "fname" accesskey="3">
First name
</LABEL>
<INPUT type="text" name="fname">
</P>
<P>
<LABEL for "lname" accesskey="6">
Last name
</LABEL>
<INPUT type="text" name="lname">
</P>
<P>
<LABEL for "pnumber" accesskey="g">
Phone number
</LABEL>
<INPUT type="text" name="pnumber">
</P>
</FORM>
```

A final note about accesskeys: They are usually activated when the user types both the stated accesskey, plus the Alt button on a PC or the Cmd button on a Macintosh. Since a lot of system shortcuts for browsers and operating systems are also used by mapping letters to the Alt or the Cmd keys, you'll want to make sure none of your accesskeys affect the browser or desktop at large.

If the ideas of inadvertently closing a browser window or relying on an HTML tag with spotty support make you nervous, there is an even more technical solution: Write a simple JavaScript that maps the keys in tab order. The only drawback? JavaScript is still a purely optional browser feature.

Navigation

We've already established some of the cultural connotations in left-to-right and top-to-bottom navigation. We've already talked about some of the pitfalls users may encounter with a page layout with tabled nav bar elements. And we've already talked about the pitfalls of frames.

Is it possible to have an effective, accessible navigation system? The answer is yes, but there are no perfect solutions.

First, consider document size. If you have an especially long, or multitopic document, you may want to provide a little intradocument navigation after each section. This sort of navigation typically offers the readers the option to click back to the top of the document, to skip to the previous topic, or to continue to the next topic. If the reader chooses the top of the document, they have the choice of exiting the document completely, or reviewing the contents of the document and re-entering the document body. For a good example of intradocument navigation that still remains accessible, go to the Yosemite Information Page at `http://ourworld.compuserve`
`.com/homepages/jrabold/yos_qr.htm`. (See Figure 17.2.)

FIGURE 17.2:

Easy navigation

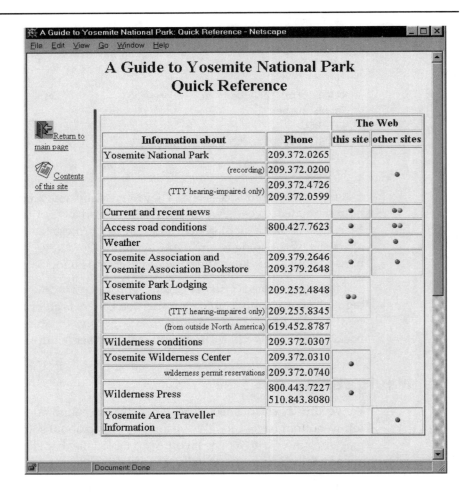

The biggest drawback to the example I cited: The navigation buttons are especially small, which makes it difficult for people with impaired mobility to accurately point and click. Still, even if the execution isn't perfect, the tool principle works really well.

If you don't think intradocument navigation is an issue, you still have to consider how you're going to set up an accessible site navigation scheme. First, you need to have a good sitewide understanding of how your site is structured. This may seem obvious, but most sites tend to branch off over time into different directories that may or may not maintain the same linking scheme, or develop otherwise labyrinthine structure. Once you've figured out what the main branches in your site tree are, and what the important documents are within those branches, set those links aside.

Use those links to create a centralized, text-only site map. It will provide a comprehensive guide for all of your readers, and be the default link-back area for your accessible navigation scheme.

Then, determine how much of that site tree you want to include on your navigation bar. You may do best to stick with one simple, top-level scheme, like a chunk of HTML offering to take users either to the site map, or to the top-level index of your site. This type of simple scheme works well if you have a site with a wide, shallow content model: one or two pages of information per category, and lots of categories. You could also elect for a simple, one-row table at the top or bottom of your page. The table, which would read accurately left to right, or right to left, could offer links to a few key top-level categories, plus the site map and the top of the site. This navigation scheme works well if you have a few deep categories, and each category index page leads to another index listing.

The key to navigation is to place it where people who are hearing your site can remember where it is, and to keep the options simple and therefore memorable. Now is not the time to demonstrate your command of Tabular Data Control and ActiveX; now is the time to offer access to the top-level pages of your well-structured directories.

A final note on navigation: If you're going to offer image-based or imagemap navigation, offer a text alternative. A series of images as a navigation tool can easily be reproduced by a text nav bar sitting immediately above or below the images. If you're going to use an imagemap, be sure to make it a client-side imagemap, and link the navigation areas so that they default to taborder. If this isn't possible, specify a taborder in each anchor. As long as you ensure that your navigation works when the images are turned off, you should be fine.

Imagemaps and Accessibility

Imagemaps are a compact and elegant solution to a lot of hyperlinking and navigation dilemmas, but they don't win many points for usability. Some of the things you can do to improve the overall accessibility for your imagemaps:

- Make them client-side imagemaps. Not only will they load faster, you can pack in `alt` tags for every link, thus making them readable to people with adaptive software or no images. A sample client-side imagemap looks like this:

```
<map name="primary">
<area shape="rect" coords="25, 84, 144, 105" href="../
index.html" alt="[home]">
<area shape="rect" coords="25, 68, 144, 85" href="../
archive.html" alt="[archives]">
</map>
```

- Provide smaller text links beneath the imagemap.

Applets and Scripts

JavaScript is becoming increasingly ubiquitous on websites as developers discover its ability to control window appearance, visibility of images and content, and timing of events. As DHTML gets incorporated less buggily into standard browsers, the script+markup combination will become even more commonplace.

This will present a small accessibility dilemma to some users. The solution for you as a developer is to provide some sort of conditional DHTML that recognizes different browsers and provides a scriptlet-free alternative to browsers that don't support DHTML.

If you're dealing with embedded page applets, the best alternative is a two-step alternative: Post a text description, then lead users to pages that mirror the applet function. For example, you can mirror the function of a feedback form by providing a section telling the user how to accomplish the same feedback via phone, snail mail, or e-mail. Just let your users know what the applet was, and what similar functions they can perform on your site; this is where the ubiquitous and ever-useful `alt` tag comes in handy.

Images

In order to be considered a functional part of any Web page, images should be self-explanatory. Site builders should also provide an alternate means of explanation for people who can't see images and are relying on aural browsers or text-only browsers. A short and descriptive `<alt ="">` within the image tag is good form, common courtesy, and highly functional. It's also worth noting that the `alt` attribute is required in HTML 4.0, and the only thing standing between hundreds of sites and invalid HTML is the charity of browser makers.

Providing an `alt` tag can also warn aural browsers what's coming next on the screen. For example, if you have a horizontal navigation bar at the bottom of the page, and it's an imagemap (which you shouldn't be doing unless you're also offering a text-based alternative in the immediate proximity as well), an `alt` tag saying, "Image nav bar—text links below," lets a visually impaired person know what was there, what function it served, and what alternative is being offered.

Implementing informative `alt` tags—even on spacer GIFs—adds no significant development or maintenance time to your website. If you pair the `alt` tag label with adding or changing GIFs to pages, it's a small and expected part of site QA. Providing informative alternatives to imagemaps may be much more difficult, but should still be mandatory; even if a user isn't blind, they may be surfing on a text-only browser or with the images turned off, and your site should be equally functional then too.

Sound

There is a small but annoying genre of websites that use background music or open their sites with a barrage of related sounds. User-control issues aside, adding extraneous sound effects to a website can muddle a user's ability to comprehend the rest of the site if they're visiting via an aural browser.

This is not to suggest that you strip sound from your site. There are a number of sites where sound is not only appropriate, it's part of the user experience. For example, there are currently 1,100 U.S radio stations providing 24-hour broadcast on the Web, and the sound experience is integral to those station's website functions. However, broadcasting sound via your Web pages should be a user-driven experience, so it doesn't interfere with aural instruction. If you still contend that your background sound won't affect the Web page, try reading the page aloud while the sound is playing, to someone who isn't familiar with the site. Their reaction should provide a gauge of how welcome the background noise is.

Finally, be sure to indicate whether or not there even is sound on your site. If you're trying for a closed-media experience and relying on sound cues to tell your readers when to click back or forth within the narrative, deaf readers won't be able to follow your cues. Visually indicating sound options alerts them to your cueing system, and allows deaf readers to find an alternate navigation option.

If you're using streaming sound on your site, offer a text-based transcript in addition to any sound files. One proposed standard that merges textual transcripts—which are descriptive—with a soundtrack is Synchronized Multimedia Integration Language (SMIL). An SMIL-encoded file is able to access images, audio or video clips, and formatted text and play it back in a bandwidth-friendly format.

Best of all, major movers and shakers in the Web development business are supporting SMIL markup by offering tools to create sites using SMIL. Allaire's Home-Site 4 (available on the CD-ROM) will provide SMIL support, and RealNetworks offers a SMIL-interpreting browser. For more on SMIL basics, see Chapter 21.

To view the W3C proposal for SMIL , go to `http://www.w3.org/TR/1998/PR-smil-19980409/`. To go to a developer's site that provides the latest in SMIL tools and news, visit `http://www.justsmil.com/`.

Multimedia Effects

Many websites offer video clips as a feature to enhance the overall presentation of the site. Like all other motion and sound presentations across other forms of media, Web-based multimedia needs to accommodate the hearing- and sight-impaired as well.

If you are featuring an audio interview or a movie with dialog, provide a text-based transcript. Not only does this accommodate your deaf users, it allows users with low-end computers and browsers to benefit from the content as well. Real-Player allows you to close-caption your video images for the hearing-disabled, so they can still watch the video and perceive the entire content with a minimum of disruption. Providing a descriptive scene-by-scene transcript of a video allows sight-impaired users to determine what those contents are.

Meet Bobby

If you're especially concerned about making sure your HTML leads to accessible pages, test them using Bobby. Bobby is an HTML tag checker developed by the Center for Applied Special Technology (CAST). CAST's primary mission is to develop ways to use computers as a way to expand the capabilities of learners, especially individuals with disabilities; Bobby is one of the tools they use to help optimize the Web for a widely varied audience.

Bobby offers two different testing modes. In the first, users go to the Bobby website (`http://www.cast.org/bobby/`), enter the URL of the site they want to test, then select the browser they want to check their site against for display quality. Bobby offers several different versions of the AOL, Mosaic, Netscape, Internet Explorer, Lynx, and WebTV browsers, as well as pure HTML standards. Output can be an annotated version of the page or a text-only list of the problems.

The second Bobby test involves downloading and installing a local Bobby application that checks a large website in a single pass and allows testing prior to putting a site on the Web. This Bobby software is available for the three largest developer platforms—Unix, Macintosh, and Windows 95/98/NT. The advantage to this is that it doesn't require a constant Net connection.

But why bother testing with Bobby, in addition to the other HTML tag checkers out there? There are several reasons: Bobby is the only tag checker designed explicitly to test for accessibility. It presents its results via ranking, with the most serious accessibility site violations listed first, and it attaches an explanatory error message to each chunk of offending code.

Bobby checks everything from `alt` tags to client map links. It ranks the site's usability based on factors including how clearly the hyperlinks are worded, how frequently tables appear on the site, and whether or not the forms are accessible without a mouse. As if that weren't enough, Bobby also checks for general browser/HTML compatibility.

In short, Bobby is currently the closest thing the Web development community has to a tool for building accessible sites. Even if Bobby doesn't build the sites for you, it provides enough pointers for you to be able to identify hot spots and begin to develop alternative site presentation methods.

Other Accessibility Benefits

If you've read through the preceding sections and you still think none of the issues raised are relevant to your site's design concerns, think again: Universally accessible design carries over to mainstream users.

Think about all the ways people access the Web: through big monitors, tiny laptop screens, and even smaller PDA screens. People also surf in less than monastic conditions, checking out sites in crowded airports, busy offices, university computer labs, or in the midst of real-life activities.

By focusing on clear, accessible design, you'll be doing all your users a favor, not just the ones who don't fit in your "typical" demographic.

Quality Assurance: Process Counts

Now that your site probably contains a number of templated parts and a mechanism to mash them all together, troubleshooting live site errors is part exercise in deductive reasoning, part damage control for entire sections. This section of the chapter is going to go over some ways to integrate QA into the development process as a whole, in order to prevent massive post-publishing site emergencies. We'll discuss the importance of documentation and why it's necessary on a website, and outline a model QA test for a data-structure-based site.

Designing a Good QA process

The last QA chapter (Chapter 9) made the argument for quality assurance as an element of site developing, and provided a checklist of issues that a good QA process should encompass. That section should have provided a foundation for assuring the quality of the product your user sees. This section will concentrate on using QA to improve the production processes within your site.

Why focus on the behind-the-scenes stuff? There are two reasons. First, as the site gets more complex, there are more areas introducing the potential for something to break, and therefore a longer post-production troubleshooting process if something does get broken. Second, if someone's not doing their job right in the middle of site production, not only does their step of the process deteriorate, so do all the subsequent steps. Going back to repeat work is nobody's idea of fun, so the more quickly you eliminate that possibility, the more efficiently you're going to work in the long run.

The first step for establishing production process QA is to figure out what steps need it the most. This may be blindingly obvious—all of your user complaints center on the incredibly inaccurate "related links" sections at the bottom of each page. Or it may be incredibly subtle, since you never have the same user complaint twice. If the answer is very obvious, you can install temporary QA measures focusing on the troublesome step until you've got a beginning-to-end QA process in place. If it's not so obvious, collect the complaints you've been getting, sit down, and begin plotting where to incorporate QA during production.

If you want to be especially thorough, incorporate a QA process at the end of every task a site builder executes. Most workers do this unconsciously—almost everyone who works with computers and code knows to "check their work" before passing it off to someone else. But double-checking processes vary from person to person, so you may want to formalize it according to task. Therefore, as a QA developer, your job is two-fold: Identify each discrete task from beginning to end, and determine what QA steps must be taken. The idea is to keep the QA process as simple and non-intrusive as possible, so the site builder can incorporate it effortlessly.

Therefore, you want to try and coordinate the QA steps for each process with the goal of the task the site builder is trying to achieve. If it's someone's job to hunt down related hyperlinks and cut-and-paste the results into a template, ask yourself if the job successfully ends when the person finds links, or when they paste those links in the template, or when the chunk of HTML filled with working links makes it to the live site. Since most websites tend to be strapped for personnel, it would be easy for a manager to make the argument that the link-finder also has to test his formatted findings.

This leads us to the primary consideration of intraprocess QA: How do you accurately test your work? Back in the dark ages of the Web, all you had to do to test your work was hit reload on your browser a few times. But then the dinosaurs went extinct, we had the Renaissance, and suddenly, people were using frames, server-side includes, and databases to create sites. Subsequently, someone may be working on a fragment of HTML or a data table that works fine in an isolated context, but breaks when integrated into the whole.

Returning to the link-pasting example, let's say our link-checker (we'll call him Len) has been using a search engine to find his related links. Len then cuts and pastes them into his template, hits submit on the form-based tool, and begins searching for the next set of links. What Len doesn't realize is that the URLs with characters like &, ?, and %, are getting parsed by the site's template assembler, and emerging without the &, ?, and % that identify them as unique locations within the site database. So although Len does check the links, he doesn't do so in a live site setting, and so is completely missing the realization that his work breaks when it hits the template assembler.

Clearly, having Len test his work would accomplish two positive QA steps here: It would correct the flawed content, and it would identify an execution flaw in the template assembler. If Len were to test his links in a staging area where all the live site tools and processes were mirrored before live site assembly, he'd notice that the URLs he's seeing are not the same ones he's entered, and the site team could take steps either to reformat Len's URL entry, or fix the template parsing mechanism.

So having a testing environment that reflects the live site as accurately as possible is an important element in process-wide QA. Not only does it let you know how well constituent website parts mesh with each other, it allows people to refine their individual tasks as well. Once you've found a way to break down your website into a series of production processes and created an environment in which to test how those processes work separately and together, you've implemented an important part of a production QA process.

A Helping Hand with QA

You don't have to spend your QA time devising complicated tests, co-opting banks of computers, and honing every little thing by the sweat of your brow. There are actually companies that will test your site for you, if you have the time, means, and inclination to pay someone else. Otivo, Inc. is one company that specializes in QA processes for websites; they're at `http://www.otivo.com`.

If you'd prefer to buy a software tool or two, consider using something like Site Technologies Site Sweeper (you can read more about it at `http://www.sitetech.com/`). This tool goes through your site and checks for bad images, bad links, and site download speed over a wide variety of conditions.

Enforcing a Good QA Process

After you've identified the steps of site assembly, the goals of each individual task that is performed during assembly, and the clashes between the different parts of the process, you've reached a plateau in site troubleshooting.

Naturally, this is where the trouble starts. Once the bugs get worked out of a system, people are confident that the production process is perfect. Nothing could be further from the truth: The current process is nearly perfect, and people are trained to look for errors on all subsequent products of that process, but you have an entire website to check—including old material, material on lower-end browsers, and conditional material you may have set up in an effort to evangelize or accommodate different audience segments.

Keeping New Material up to Spec

Your first step is to make sure current QA processes at the end of each discrete task are still being performed. Once site builders catch on to what processes produce the best results as quickly as possible, they're going to refine those processes until they're rote for them. Rote process produces the occasional error, and therefore site builders should still do a little aggressive testing just to ensure their product hasn't deteriorated over the course of refining daily production processes.

Your next step is to ask whether current QA processes are being performed over all the user conditions you're hoping to reach. A test server usually produces a site as it would appear to a user with the same set of computer conditions: Browser, domain, and bandwidth are all picked up by the server and reflected back to the tester. As a result, most people who are viewing their test site through the same computer they used to develop the site are seeing a working product. Then, when someone tries to access the site using a different computer, browser, bandwidth speed, or top-level domain, the site breaks for them. Since most user complaints aren't filed like controlled-run bug reports, diagnosing the problem may be difficult.

The answer is to develop a test bank that allows you to mix and match conditions. One way of doing this is to set aside a number of machines with specific test configurations—a few PCs, a few Macintoshes, each with different browser versions and different connection speeds. If you're stuck with one machine, set aside a block of time for installing and uninstalling different browsers for testing, draw up a list of concrete criteria (visit the QA process a little later in this chapter for ideas), and devote a day to testing.

You may not have to test every document under every different combination. Ideally, you should test any new material you're launching or relaunching first, so you have an idea of how it performs before it makes its public debut. If you publish similarly formatted material on a frequent basis (if you run a news site or directory, for example), you may want to test a batch of material as a means of setting a benchmark, then use the results as a way of eyeballing and evaluating your subsequent content.

And if you didn't check your old material with the same combination of conditions, now is the time to do so. You can see what features in your old material have held up over time and what features were bad ideas in retrospect. You can also see if implementing any new sitewide features, like a sitewide copyright footer, have broken or otherwise adversely affected your content. You newest material isn't the only material users are going to judge you on: It's in your best interests to do occasional testing and maintenance checks on the performance of your old material too.

Standardizing the Process

Once you've stabilized the new material and found a performance benchmark that extends back to your older material, it's time to integrate your older material into the newer site, and to make sure the QA standard is uniform for all your content. You'll already know the difference between user-driven QA results, like appearance and links, and developer-driven QA, like site assembly, thanks to the QA steps you've just integrated into your current production processes. It is obviously too late to perform active process QA on retired or "old" material. But you can deduce what steps were made routine, and what was done on the fly in every document by taking a look at the source code.

Check out the code for several different files in the same directory; if the material you're looking at published on a regular schedule, like a travel column, check out several sequential files. Look for areas that are obviously the same: Was the code for the nav bar obviously copied in from a template file every week? Are all of the layouts based on the same table setup? Are there comments indicating what elements to anticipate in the source code next?

If you're lucky, you'll be working on a site where someone (maybe even you) had the foresight to template and comment persistent site elements early in the life of the site. When this is the case, your job is much easier; you can use a few choice Unix commands to grep and replace any parts that you want to update.

If you're unlucky, you inherited a site where every page is resolutely individual. In this case, you must decide if it's worth the effort to go through each individual page, extract the content, and cram it into a sitewide template, or if you're better off rearranging your backend and providing both a visual divider and a URL structure that act as an alert to the reader.

Regardless of how you treat sitewide standardization issues, there are page-to-page issues. Links decay over time; the directory of related links you set up a year ago may be only 70 percent live now. You can have an intern check pages that you deem a priority for maintaining currency, or you can run a robot link checker over the site and fix anything the robot reports as broken. A robot is faster, but a human may be able to find and reconnect a broken hyperlink to a new, equally appropriate source, so you may want to combine your resources.

Another page-to-page issue is stray error. No matter how carefully you set up your backbone, and how structured your image calls, nav bar referrals, and intra-directory navigation is, there are going to be a slew of errors excepting the rules. This may be due to a section of your site relaunching, and reintroducing a whole new backend; this may be due to a newly integrated ad-serving system; this may be due to someone having a busy or hectic day and kludging a link or image call rather than follow a directory structure. The point is, for every sitewide search-and-repair you do, you need to be prepared to spend time looking for exceptions and repairing them to fit the norm you've established for your site.

The difficulty in anticipating how smoothly old and new production methods can be integrated is usually due to one factor: lack of documentation.

Establishing Sitewide Documentation

Apparently the digital revolution was neither televised nor documented. There are a number of factors that contribute to this. Here are a few typical scenarios:

- This now-ubiquitous resource site used to be a one-person affair. That one person knew what she was doing at all times so she didn't write anything down for posterity. When the site expanded, more people came on gradually, and what the primary developer knew diffused across the staff. It wasn't until after she left, and the site did its first relaunch without her, that anyone noticed there was a lot of unexplained fossil code.

- This news site was launched to compete with an already-established, similar product. It wasn't so much developed as launched and developed after the fact. Since the production staff was dealing with both user-driven QA issues like the interface, and backend issues like producing and publishing new material on time, they concentrated on trying to cross off their multiple tasks. Once the staff finally established a working equilibrium, they began looking at a way to improve and streamline the site. That's when they realized the entire site was produced via a series of inconsistent kludges. No-one could say why anything was developed as it was, because nobody could remember the circumstances under which anything was developed.

- The site was created by an outside contractor, and it was assumed that it would be a one-time job. However, over the course of the next year, the company changed names, expanded its product line, and wanted to use its website as a direct marketing tool. The contractor and his image files weren't available for the site upgrade during the window of time the company wanted the site done.

The common denominators in these stories are staff and time. Staff turnover on many websites tends to be high; if a series of contractors worked on producing a large-scale website, the turnover is even higher. The second issue is time: Websites have the dubious distinction of being required to perform like software under news media deadlines. As a result, they're frequently developed the same way you'd write a news story on short notice: The important stuff happens first, and any long-term details get tossed in later.

In a classic software development process, the product is spec'd out, designed, developed, tested, and documented before release. A software development cycle can also take years; few websites are in development longer than three months. Software also benefits from having fixed versions; the features in WordPerfect 5.0 set it apart as a discrete product from WordPerfect 4.0. Very few websites benefit from the same version freeze. New content is constantly being added, old content is being revised, and all of it is being redesigned.

Is it any wonder few Web developers have time for documentation?

Unfortunately, as websites and their staff expand, the site developers need to make more of an effort to document what they did and why they did it. Not only does documentation assist the developers in future projects, it also allows the staff to examine their current development process and eliminate any redundant work.

At the very least, site developers should document:

- What they're creating from scratch. When a future developer has to come in and reconstruct the now-old site, they'll be glad to know what came into existence when, where it lived, and what files each file was created to complement.

- What they're modifying. Not only is this information useful for future developers trying to trace the production processes of their predecessors, it can also be a red flag to existing site staffers who may have crucial information on the files you modified. For example, a current employee may take a look at the list of files you just modified and identify other files that need to be modified in response.

- How they modified existing files. This goes along with determining whether other, seemingly unrelated files need to be modified as well, and with seeing whether any work is being duplicated unnecessarily.

- Why the modifications and additions were made. Old, cryptic code is often called *kludgy* when no one can figure out why it's written the way it's written, and brilliant when there's documentation backing it up. By providing the motivation behind modification, you reduce guesswork, and the likelihood of future kludges.

Development documentation doesn't need to be complex. It just needs to provide enough information to refresh your memory, or to clearly inform a coworker about the methods to your madness. It's the capstone of good production process QA.

Improving an Existing QA Process

The following bulleted QA process is meant to give you a baseline from which to base your own QA process. I've broken down the entire list into function-specific areas, from editorial quality to technical performance. You may want to rearrange things to reflect your own production processes or roles. So feel free to mix, match, and modify to make this fit your own site.

Editorial Issues

- Has the content been through a final edit?

- Has the content been through copyedit at least once?

- Is there a sitewide style guide?

Interface Issues

- Is there a clearly defined navigation scheme on each page?

- Does this navigation scheme work when the user drills down several levels in the site?

- How is the navigation structure included on every page?

- Does the navigation structure degrade over different browsers?

- Does the navigation accurately reflect the different options the developer wants the user to have?

- Does the navigation accurately reflect the different tasks the user wants to perform?

- Are the user goals for each section of the site clearly defined?

- Do users meet the goals? Are they reasonable goals? Are there varying levels of user interaction to maintain user interest?

- Have developers and designers had a chance to assess user reaction to the site, and modify site design and performance in response?

Image Issues

- Is each image dithered to the same palette?
- Is each image dithered to the smallest possible palette?
- How much file compression is there per image?
- If the images serve a functional purpose, is there a non-image alternative?
- If the images are animated, is each frame as small as possible?
- How are the images served—is there a central image directory, specific image directories for each distinct site section, or a number of image directories that may or may not contain duplicate files?
- Do the images have descriptive alt text?
- Does each image have the height, width, border, and alignment specified?

Backend Structures

- Does the backend structure support the conceptual organization of the site?
- Does the backend structure support a functional organization of the different parts of the site?
- Does the backend structure support completely new subsections?
- Does the backend structure support the expansion of a section over time?
- Does the backend structure provide a means of separating current content from archived content?
- Does the backend structure provide a means of separating live content from content being tested and developed?

Linking Scheme

- Does every page have a base HREF?
- How are internal links structured? What's the most common base unit between two links?
- How are external links structured? How are they targeted?
- Does each document rely on internal linking for the user to navigate within the document?
- If so, how are the intradocument links kept separate from the extradocument links?

Standard Page Features

- Is there a clearly marked title on each page?
- Is there a copyright notice on each page?
- Is there a site contact method on each page?
- Is there a clearly marked navigation scheme on each page?
- Can you tell where each page is relative to its topical section?
- Can you tell where each page is relative to the rest of the site?
- Are there visual cues to let the user know they're still on your site?

Browser Performance

- Is there a significant difference in page loading time on the different browsers?
- Is there a significant difference in page color palette on the different browsers?
- Is there a significant difference in font appearance on the different browsers?
- Is there a significant difference in content layout on the different browsers?
- Is there a significant difference in form element appearance on the different browsers?

Platform Performance

- Is there a significant difference in page loading time on a PC versus a Mac?
- Is there a significant difference in page color palette on a PC versus a Mac?
- Is there a significant difference in font appearance on a PC versus a Mac?
- Is there a significant difference in content layout on a PC versus a Mac?
- Is there a significant difference in form element appearance on a PC versus a Mac?
- Is your layout and functionality still preserved on Unix and Linux platforms?

Bandwidth Performance

- Does the site load quickly on a T3? A T1?

- Does the site load at a reasonable speed on a 14.4 modem? A 28.8 modem? A 56K line?

- Have you tested the loading times of your top index page at several speeds?

- Have you tested the loading times of your site map at several speeds?

- Have you tested the loading times of a typical content page at several speeds?

- Have you tested the response times of any feedback forms-based page at several speeds?

- Have you tested the response times of any search engine forms-based page at several speeds?

- Does turning off the images dramatically lower page load time?

- Do increased numbers of server-side includes make the page load more quickly, or more slowly?

- Have you tested the performance of all the key pages mentioned above against the key pages of your competitors under the same conditions?

Final Copy Performance

- Does the total site performance adhere to the developers' expectations?

- Does the total site performance adhere to the users' expectations?

Summary

The World Wide Web isn't going to be an accurate name for anything we develop until more site developers begin putting accessibility issues on the same priority level as they do cross-platform compatibility and other end-user performance issues. There are a number of small steps you can take to improve the accessibility of the site; don't hesitate to begin incorporating them.

Remember, even when you've packed the site with easy-to-access features, that they all have to work. Testing and QA are critical for a site; use these processes to fine-tune your work and save yourself a few panic-fueled changes later.

CHAPTER

EIGHTEEN

18

Case Studies #2 and #3: Two Sites That Evolve in Response to Changing Standards

In the first case study, we followed one contractor's work through three separate site iterations. But not all websites are self-contained, portable file collections, nor do all websites represent the debut of a business or organization.

This chapter features two more case studies, and each separate case study highlights a different type of Web-development environment. In the first, the Web developer is given the responsibility of representing a non-wired organization online; he works in an office where networked information technologies—like online file transfer or e-mail—aren't practiced much. In the second case study, two Web workers are building their website as a saleable property. They rely on a lot of external links, so in addition to budgeting time for developing the code for their site, that team must also budget time for frequent content maintenance and updates.

Read on and see how each Web developer responded to a very different set of circumstances.

Case Study #2: The Society of Cognitive Dissonance

This case study looks at how one person working in a decidedly non-wired organization negotiates content and posts a product that his old-media bosses like, while still producing a product he won't mind putting on his new-media resume. This site will go through three different iterations, but let's start off with the task of trying to organize and transfer regularly scheduled paper publications to an online media.

Cognitive Dissonance, Round 1: Building the Site

The Society for Cognitive Dissonance is a small non-profit organization hoping to use their website as a way to augment their current communications efforts. The site is being put together by an intern with carte blanche. The intern, Jason Johnson, is supposed to assemble a site that closely reflects the paper communications organs for the Society for Cognitive Dissonance.

He has been given roughly a week's start-up time, plus a time allowance of ten hours per week to add to and maintain the site. Therefore, Jason needs to build a site that's easy to build out and to expand. What decisions did he make to do so? Read on.

What Development Decisions Were Made

Before he could begin to build the site, Jason had to assess the scope of the project. He figured out that the content could be loosely sorted into four separate categories. Then, he assessed whether each category needed to be archived or not.

Here's how he broke down all the potential content in his notes:

Company Information

This information is permanent: Once it's posted, it's not going to be added to. The actual contents may be modified, but it won't be deleted or expanded. Therefore, there is no need for archiving.

Meeting Information

This section exists to provide website viewers with information on forthcoming real-time, real-world events. It's the equivalent of a bulletin board. Therefore, Jason decided the content doesn't need to be archived, since the whole point is to act as advance notice for each of the upcoming events.

Organization News

Like the meeting section, this section also provides timely content. But in this case, the content is written up as individual news articles, and so will be archived for future reference.

Excerpts from Society Publications

Like many nonprofit or academic organizations, the Society for Cognitive Dissonance has a flagship publication that its members rely on for an authoritative voice in its field. Because subscription to this publication is an incentive for paying membership dues, the Society for Cognitive Dissonance doesn't want to give away its number-one draw on the Web. However, the Society director wants to post one or two articles as an effort to entice Web surfers to join the organization. Therefore, one or two selected articles from every issue should be available, and new articles will be added every time a new issue of the journal is published.

So Jason has two types of content that don't need to be archived, and two types of content that do need to be archived. Therefore, he's going to set up a file tree that allows him to automatically archive old material whenever he adds new material.

Jason set up the file tree as outlined in Table 18.1.

TABLE 18.1: Cognitive Dissonance File Tree

index.html (top of site)			
co_info/	meeting/	news/	pub/
index.html	index.html	index.html	index.html
award.html	schedule.html	news1.html	article1.html
contact.html	links.html	news2.html	article2.html
		archive.html	
		archive/	

The index.html page for each section also serves as a secondary table of contents, listing the items in the section.

After Jason had laid out the site's structure, he had to ask himself—and answer—the question: How can I balance the site's development against the time I'm allotted for maintaining the site?

The answer is to template anything that's going to be updated on a regular basis. The specifics for developing all the templates are detailed below.

The Scope and Technical Requirements for the Site

Jason is dealing with two separate conditions that shape his site's code: the technical limitations of his perceived audience, and the time constraints for building and updating the site.

To give a better idea of what Jason has to do in a week, let's outline his task list and how many hours he can allot per task.

> **Preliminary design for the site** Jason has to find a page design and layout that prominently features the Society's logo and duplicates the feel of the printed material. This design has to contain elements that can be transferred from printed materials like meeting announcements and magazine articles to Web only items like archive link pages. Once Jason's designed the site, he has to get it approved by his department head, then make any modifications. He's allotted himself 12 hours, or a day-and-a-half to do this.

Preliminary code mock-ups   Once Jason gets final design approval, he's got to set the design in code and make sure it works in Netscape Navigator, Microsoft Internet Explorer, and Lynx. This takes him another day. Jason's used up two-and-a-half days of his allotted week, and has two-and-a-half days left.

Building site templates   After Jason's ironed out a bugproof version of his HTML design, he's going to look at ways to break down the HTML template so the parts can be mixed and matched. This takes about half a day; Jason's got two days left.

Populate the templates with content   Let's assume a best-case scenario: The Society for Cognitive Dissonance produces all of their flyers and publications via electronic files that can be easily dropped into HTML templates. If this is the case, Jason can spend one day formatting all 16 files. In a worst-case scenario, Jason will end up retyping content. If this is the case, he's going to need to add time to his one-week deadline. But for the sake of the case study, we're going to assume that he's good to go with electronic versions of all the content.

Perform final QA on the site before posting it to the Web   Jason should spend his final day checking every page on the site to make sure all links work, and that the site looks good in a wide variety of browsers. The entire day is necessary: Jason can fix any errors that he finds without the stress of someone breathing down his neck.

This is a really tight schedule. In order to accommodate it, Jason's going to make the following time-saving efforts:

- Keep the design as simple as possible: The layout is the same from page to page, with only content markup distinguishing different pages from one another.

- Template the pages as much as possible for quick updates.

- Design the site for the lowest-common-denominator: Jason will be designing the site for browsers that support HTML 3.2, meaning that anyone with a 2.0 or higher browser version will be able to read the site.

- Design the site with as few images as possible. This saves on production time, both at the initial start-up, and during site maintenance.

So what does Jason's minimally designed site look like? The how-tos follow.

How Site Templates Were Built

Jason set up the template so it featured the following: the site logo, a central navigation tool, a specific page heading, content, and a copyright notice. Figure 18.1 shows his final design.

FIGURE 18.1:

The templated Cog Diss site

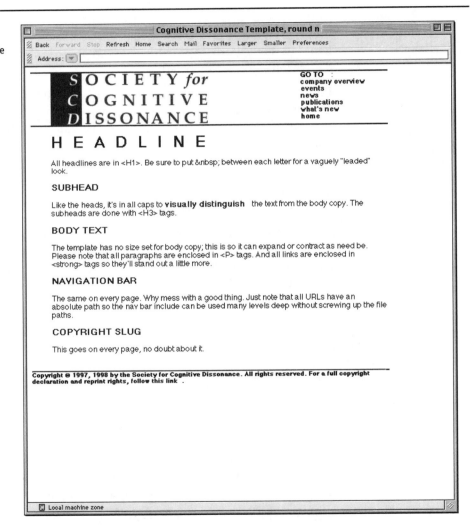

FIGURE 18.1:

The templated Cog Diss site

And here's the source code.

cog_diss_template.html

```
<HTML>
<HEAD>
<TITLE>
 Cognitive Dissonance Template, round n
</TITLE>
<META name="keywords" content="science, technology, test tubes, lab
monkeys, people in white coats">
<META http-equiv="Content-Type" content="text/html; charset=iso-8859-
1">
</HEAD>
<BODY bgcolor="#FFFFFF" text="#000000" alink="#FFCC00" link="#003333"
vlink="#003366">
<TABLE width=550 cellspacing=0 cellpadding=0 bgcolor="#FFFFFF"
border=0>
<TR>
<TD valign=top align=left bgcolor="#003333" colspan=3>
<IMG SRC="../images/spacer.gif" ALT="[spacer]" WIDTH="545" HEIGHT="2"
BORDER="0" align=left>
</TD>
</TR>
<TR>
<TD valign=top align=left bgcolor="#FFFFFF">
<IMG SRC="../images/spacer.gif" ALT="[spacer]" WIDTH="25" HEIGHT="1"
BORDER="0" align=left>
</TD>
<TD valign=top align=left>
<IMG SRC="../images/logo.gif" ALT="[Society for Cognitive Dissonance]"
WIDTH="247" HEIGHT="83" BORDER="0" align=top>
</TD>
<TD valign=top align=left>
<font face="helvetica, arial">
<small>
<P>
<STRONG>
 GO TO
</STRONG>
  : 
<BR clear=all>
```

```
<A HREF="http://center-for-cogdiss.org/co_info/index.html">
<STRONG>
company overview
</STRONG>
</A>
<BR clear=all>
<A HREF="http://center-for-cogdiss.org/events/index.html">
<STRONG>
events
</STRONG>
</A>
<BR clear=all>
<A HREF="http://center-for-cogdiss.org/news/index.html">
<STRONG>
news
</STRONG>
</A>
<BR clear=all>
<A HREF="http://center-for-cogdiss.org/pub/index.html">
<STRONG>
publications
</STRONG>
</A>
<BR clear=all>
<A HREF="http://center-for-cogdiss.org/new.html">
<STRONG>
what's new
</STRONG>
</A>
<BR clear=all>
<A HREF="http://center-for-cogdiss.org/index.html">
<STRONG>
home
</STRONG>
</A>
<BR clear=all>
</P>
</small>
</font>
</TD>
</TR>
<TR>
```

```
<TD colspan=3 valign=top align=left bgcolor="#003333">
<IMG SRC="../images/spacer.gif" ALT="[spacer]" WIDTH="545" HEIGHT="2"
BORDER="0" align=left>
</TD>
</TR>
<TR>
<TD colspan=3 valign=top align=left bgcolor="#FFFFFF">
<font color="#FFFFFF" size="2">
 
</font>
</TD>
</TR>
<TR>
<TD valign=top align=left bgcolor="#FFFFFF">
<IMG SRC="../images/spacer.gif" ALT="[spacer]" WIDTH="25" HEIGHT="1"
BORDER="0">
</TD>
<TD colspan=2>
<font face="helvetica, arial">
<H1>
 H E A D L I N E 
</H1>
<P>
 All headlines are in &lt;H1&gt;. Be sure to put   between
each letter for a vaguely "leaded" look.
</P>
<H3>
 SUBHEAD
</H3>
<P>
 Like the heads, it's in all caps to
<strong>
<a href="##">
visually distinguish
</a>
</strong>
 the text from the body copy. The subheads are done with &lt;H3&gt;
tags.
</P>
<H3>
 BODY TEXT
</H3>
```

```
<P>
 The template has no size set for body copy; this is so it can expand
or contract as need be. Please note that all paragraphs are enclosed in
&lt;P&gt; tags. And all links are enclosed in &lt;strong&gt; tags so
they'll stand out a little more.
</P>
<H3>
 NAVIGATION BAR
</H3>
<P>
 The same on every page. Why mess with a good thing. Just note that all
URLs have an absolute path so the nav bar include can be used many
levels deep without screwing up the file paths.
</P>
<H3>
 COPYRIGHT SLUG
</H3>
<P>
 This goes on every page, no doubt about it.
</P>
<P>
  
</P>
</font>
</TD>
</TR>
<TR>
<TD colspan=3 valign=top align=left bgcolor="#003333">
<IMG SRC="images/spacer.gif" ALT="[spacer]" WIDTH="545" HEIGHT="2"
BORDER="0" align=left>
</TD>
</TR>
<TR>
<TD colspan=3 valign=top align=left>
<h6>
<font face="helvetica, arial">
 Copyright &copy; 1997, 1998 by the Society for Cognitive Dissonance.
All rights reserved. For a full copyright declaration and reprint
rights,
<A HREF="http://center-for-cogdiss.org/meta/legal.html">
follow this link
</A>
```

```
</font>
</h6>
</TD>
</TR>
</TABLE>
</BODY>
</HTML>
```

How the Templates Were Modified for Daily Production

Jason is not working in an environment where he can use includes to slice out the dynamically-updated content. His best bet for this round of development is to comment his code like crazy, so he can scan it for sections that need to be updated or swapped out. If he needs to make global changes across the site, he can rely on a WYSIWYG editor that permits regular expressions or greps for text strings, and change his code that way; BBEdit is an excellent tool for this. If you look at the source code for the index page, you'll see the well-commented template elements that are repeated from page to page on the site.

index.html

```
<HTML>

<HEAD>

        <TITLE>Cognitive Dissonance Template, includes version</TITLE>

        <!--insert keywords -->
        <META name="keywords" content="science, technology, test tubes,
lab monkeys, people in white coats">

        <!--insert doctype -->
        <META http-equiv="Content-Type" content="text/html; charset=iso-
8859-1">

</HEAD>

<!--all the colors are within the 216 palette. -->
```

```
<BODY bgcolor="#FFFFFF" text="#000000" alink="#FFCC00" link="#003333"
vlink="#003366">

<!--a few words about the include syntax: I used absolute pathways to
guarantee that you could copy the template code and use it on
absolutely any level of the site. Note also that each include starts
with the comment beginning and a pound (#) sign, and that thre is a
space after the include file name and the end of the comment tag. -->

<TABLE width=550 cellspacing=0 cellpadding=0 bgcolor="#FFFFFF"
border=0>

<!--label your rows so you can troubleshoot later-->
<!--row 1-->
<TR>
<TD valign=top align=left bgcolor="#003333" colspan=3>
<IMG SRC="../images/spacer.gif" ALT="[spacer]" WIDTH="545" HEIGHT="2"
BORDER="0" align=left>
</TD>
</TR>

<!--row 2-->
<TR>
<TD valign=top align=left bgcolor="#FFFFFF">
<IMG SRC="../images/spacer.gif" ALT="[spacer]" WIDTH="25" HEIGHT="1"
BORDER="0" align=left>
</TD>
<TD valign=top align=left>
<!--start logo -->
<IMG SRC="../images/logo.gif" ALT="[Society for Cognitive Dissonance]"
WIDTH="247" HEIGHT="83" BORDER="0" align=top>
<!--end logo -->
</TD>
<TD valign=top align=left>
<!--begin nav -->
<font face="helvetica, arial">
<small>
<P>
<STRONG>
 GO TO
</STRONG>
```

```
 : 
<BR clear=all>
<A HREF="http://center-for-cogdiss.org/co_info/index.html">
<STRONG>
company overview
</STRONG>
</A>
<BR clear=all>
<A HREF="http://center-for-cogdiss.org/events/index.html">
<STRONG>
events
</STRONG>
</A>
<BR clear=all>
<A HREF="http://center-for-cogdiss.org/news/index.html">
<STRONG>
news
</STRONG>
</A>
<BR clear=all>
<A HREF="http://center-for-cogdiss.org/pub/index.html">
<STRONG>
publications
</STRONG>
</A>
<BR clear=all>
<A HREF="http://center-for-cogdiss.org/new.html">
<STRONG>
what's new
</STRONG>
</A>
<BR clear=all>
<A HREF="http://center-for-cogdiss.org/index.html">
<STRONG>
home
</STRONG>
</A>
<BR clear=all>
</P>
</small>
</font>
```

```
<!--end nav-->
</TD>
</TR>

<!--row 3 -->
<TR>
<!--the horizontal green spacer, repeated. The top and bottom green
horizontal lines are part of the design, as a way of anchoring the
header to the page while maintaining a visual separation from the
content below. -->
<TD colspan=3 valign=top align=left bgcolor="#003333">
<IMG SRC="../images/spacer.gif" ALT="[spacer]" WIDTH="545" HEIGHT="2"
BORDER="0" align=left>
</TD>
</TR>

<!--row 4 -->
<TR>
<TD colspan=3 valign=top align=left bgcolor="#FFFFFF">
<font color="#FFFFFF" size="2"> </font></TD>
</TR>

<!-- row 5 -->
<!--content -->
<TR>
<TD valign=top align=left bgcolor="#FFFFFF">
<IMG SRC="../images/spacer.gif" ALT="[spacer]" WIDTH="25" HEIGHT="1"
BORDER="0">
</TD>

<TD colspan=2>
<!--start content -->
</TD>
</TR>
<!--end content. -->

<TR>
<TD colspan=3 valign=top align=left bgcolor="#003333">
<IMG SRC="images/spacer.gif" ALT="[spacer]" WIDTH="545" HEIGHT="2"
BORDER="0" align=left>
</TD>
```

```
</TR>

<!--row 7 -->
<!--copyright -->
<!--It's always a good idea to have a legal disclaimer on your site,
because then you have a leg to stand on if someone tries to steal your
source code and pass it off as their own. Ours is an include -->
<TR>
<TD colspan=3 valign=top align=left>
<h6>
<font face="helvetica, arial">
 Copyright &copy; 1997, 1998 by the Society for Cognitive Dissonance.
All rights reserved. For a full copyright declaration and reprint
rights,
<A HREF="http://center-for-cogdiss.org/meta/legal.html">
follow this link.
</A>
</font>
</h6>
</TD>
</TR>
<!--end copyright -->
</TABLE>

</BODY>

</HTML>
```

The Source Code

The source code for each of the files on the Society for Cognitive Dissonance site is available on the CD-ROM. I've included general content includes as examples in the fragment library after the individually formatted files; remember that Jason will assemble the site by pasting the correctly formatted include into the file at the

```
<TD colspan=2>
<!--start content -->
</TD>
</TR>
<!--end content. -->
```

section.

These are the individual files that are available:

- `index.html`
- `archive.html`
- `news_index.html`
- `news1.html`
- `news2.html`
- `arch1.html`
- `arch2.html`
- `article1.html`
- `article2.html`
- `pub_index.html`
- `meeting_index.html`
- `links.html`
- `schedule.html`
- `co_info_index.html`
- `award.html`
- `contact.html`

And here are the fragment files:

- `list_plus_text.htmlf`
- `text_items.htmlf`
- `general_text.htmlf`
- `linked_items_in_list.htmlf`

Cognitive Dissonance, Round 2: Giving the Site a Facelift

Six months after Jason built a site reflecting the paper communications formats for the Society for Cognitive Dissonance, his bosses have taken a look at it and decided that it doesn't take advantage of the medium. They've asked Jason to give the site a distinctive visual identity. Jason has a week to come up with a new design and implement it.

NOTE   Our fearless site builder's latest bright idea will require him to work on practical strategy after he's figured out what technical limitations he has, so our standard model of development decisions before scope and technical requirements is turned around. Site builders are allowed to be flexible.

The Scope and Technical Requirements for the Site

Jason's recently discovered the doctrine of the W3C, and has decided to try and move away from using tables as layout devices. He did an initial mockup of his new design using block-level `<div>` containers and attaching style-sheeted visual attributes to each container.

Unfortunately, a sizeable percentage of the site's viewers still rely on 2.0- or 3.0-generation browsers. Jason then had to see if his design would hold up when converted back to a table-driven layout. After discovering that it did, he had to answer a few questions: Should he create a high-bandwidth site and a low-bandwidth site? How could he ensure that audiences saw a site optimized for their specific browser version?

To answer these questions, Jason had to push for more technical support from the Society's information systems department (IS). Like many companies who are exploring how to best represent themselves on the Web, each department in the Society has its own "microsite" that it is responsible for creating. After each site is created, the files are turned over to the sysadmin, who drops them into the overall site.

Therefore, Jason has to go plead his case with the sysadmin. The decree: Turn in two separate sites, and the sysadmin would set up a way for the correct set of pages to be served.

Serving Pages in Response to Different Browser Clients

In all likelihood, the sysadmin is going to do one of two things:

- Give each cluster of pages its own set of distinct filenames, then write a CGI script that checks a user's browser version, then automatically serves the right pages in response. For an example of a CGI script that snoops to find the user's browser version, go to `http://www.hotwired.com/webmonkey/geektalk/96/41/index3a.html`.

- Rip out the guts of each page (everything between the **<body>** tags), create a set of includes, then write a chunk of conditional HTML in the top of each file that serves an include in response to the user's browser client.

Each method has its advantages and disadvantages: the CGI script method allows Jason to continue developing his sites in tandem without having to keep track of lots of little pieces. The downside to serving sites via CGI is that unless the script is set to fire anytime someone makes a request for a file, a user may try to access a deep-site URL they found via a search engine and end up staring at a page of gibberish. The server-side include method maintains one set of end-user file addresses, which is a good thing. However, developing the site becomes a little more complicated because any work has to be done on a server (to test how the includes work) and if the two separate includes also call site-wide include elements like ads or copyright statements, troubleshooting becomes complex.

What Jason then did is develop both low-bandwidth and high-bandwidth templates for the site.

What Development Decisions Were Made

Since Jason is going to be developing two parallel page sets, he wants to pool as much code as possible. Therefore, he's going to take the following steps as he designs the site:

1. *Develop a design that looks more dynamic*. Jason did this by "boxing in" the content: The content is framed within a green border, instead of simply sitting in white space. This sets finite borders on the material, and presents it nicely to the viewer. The headlines are now contrasting serif italics, instead of sans-serif. This is still easy to produce, and is entirely dependent on standard HTML tags. There is a strong green margin on the left side that echoes

the green width in the logo. This does a good job of tying the logo into the rest of the design, as opposed to having it float out in the middle of a sea of white space.

2. *Draft both low-tech and high-tech versions of the site design.*

3. *Look over both site templates and find common elements to pull out.* Recycling the code between the two templates saves on work in the long run.

4. *Build practical templates for widespread site conversion.* Once a library of shared code is established, it is easy to go through and build templates that can call from this library, thus stripping each individual version of the template down to the elements that make it distinct. Creating bare-bones templates, especially if they're differing versions, has two benefits. First, it allows you to identify all those elements that differ within versions. Second, it allows you to pull out the items that will persist across the site as a whole, regardless of whether or not they're couched in a high-end or low-end template.

5. *Convert the site.* This is the most work-intensive portion of the project, since it will involve stripping out old content and dropping it into new templates.

Jason decided that the best way to proceed with steps 3–5 of his plan would be to see if he could use virtual includes. He went back to his sysadmin and got permission to do so, then decided to build his templates with this development criteria in mind.

How the Site Changed

If you look at Figure 18.2, you'll see the low-end template for the site redesign on the left, and the high-end redesign for the template on the right. You can note that they look different from the first site iteration, but not from each other. This is a good thing.

This section is going to go over how Jason overhauled the templates, and what the low-end and high-end templates look like.

Accommodating Advertising   The site has been redesigned to accommodate advertising. The Society now has a banner exchange going on with similar sites, and as such, needs to find a way to incorporate banner ads into their site as well. Here's what the high-tech template version did to pull in the banners:

```
<div id="ads" style="postion:absolute; left:10; top:5; background-
color:#FFFFFF; border-color:#FFFFFF; border-style:solid; border:1px;
width:475px; height:60px; ">
```

```
<img src="ad-littleban.gif" alt="[234x60 banner]" width="234"
height="60" border="1">
<img src="general/ad-littleban.gif" alt="[234x60 banner]" width="234"
height="60" border="1">
</div>
```

And here's what the low-tech version looks like:

```
<table width="475" border="0" cellspacing="0" cellpadding="0">
<tr valign="top" align="left">
<td><img src="../../../general/ad-littleban.gif" alt="[234x60 banner]"
width="234" height="60" border="1"></td>
<td><img src="../../../general/ad-littleban.gif" alt="[234x60 banner]"
width="234" height="60" border="1"></td>
</tr>
</table>
<br>
```

The high-tech version relies on Cascading Style Sheet Positioning (CSS-P) to place the ads container; the low-tech version relies on a browser dropping one table on top of the other when it renders the page.

Framing the Content   There is now a strong left margin on the pages, to more clearly frame the content. In the high-tech version of the template, Jason sets up the margin by doing a two div overlay: the first div is the green background, and it acts as a container for everything within it. The second div is white, and it acts as a canvas for all of the printed material on the page:

```
<!--insert the big green background for the page. Tres chic!-->
<div id="back" style="position:absolute; z-index:30; left:10px; top:
180px; width:475px; height:600px; border-style:solid; border-
color:#003333; border:1px; background-color:#003333;">
<!--and here goes the white canvas for all the content.-->
<div id="canvas" style="position:absolute; z-index:50; left:50px;
top:3px; width:423px; height:592px; border-style:solid; border-
color:#FFFFFF; border:1px; background-color:#FFFFFF;">
<!--insert content -->
<!--end canvas-->
</div>
<!--end green background -->
</div>
```

The markup is nested; note that the z-index value for the green div is smaller than the value for the white div, which means that the white div will always sit on top of the green one.

In the low-tech version, on the other hand, the strong green margin on the left is set by creating a green column in a tabled layout like this:

```
<!--insert the big green background for the page. Tres chic!-->
<table width="475" cellpadding="2" cellspacing="0" border="0"
bgcolor="#003333">
<!--here's how we make the green margin on the left-->
<td valign="top" align="left">
<img src="../images/spacer.gif" width="46" height="1" border="0">
</td>
<!--and here goes the white canvas for all the content.-->
<td valign="top" align="left">
    <table width="100%" cellpadding="0" cellspacing="0" border="0"
bgcolor="#FFFFFF">
<!--content goes in table here -->
</table>
</td>
</tr>
<!--this is for the green margin at the bottom-->
<tr>
<td colspan="2" valign="top" align="center">
 
</td>
</tr>
</table>
```

NOTE   Notice that the canvas is actually a nested table within the green background; the code is still "layered" in a way, but it can be read and rendered attractively by lower-end browsers.

Note that the headings have changed too: Jason got tired of stuffing nonbreaking spaces between each letter, and decided it would be easier to simply present all headings as <h1></h1> tags. In the style-sheeted version, he specifies the character traits for <h1>:

```
h1          {position:absolute; left:10px; margin:10px; font-
family:times, palatino, serif; font-weight:bold; font-style:italic;
font-size:27px; line-height:33px; color:#003366;}
```

And in the low-end version, he wraps font tags with the relevant information around each tag:

```
<font color="#003366" face="times, palatino, serif"><i><h1>Archive
</h1></i></font>
```

This way, the structural markup of the document is preserved, and if the browser can read font attribute tags, the headline looks formatted. Figure 18.2 shows the two versions, though to actually see the difference you will have to study the code.

FIGURE 18.2:

Low-end vs. high-end: Can you tell the difference?

FIGURE 18.2:
CONTINUED

Low-end vs. high-end: Can
you tell the difference?

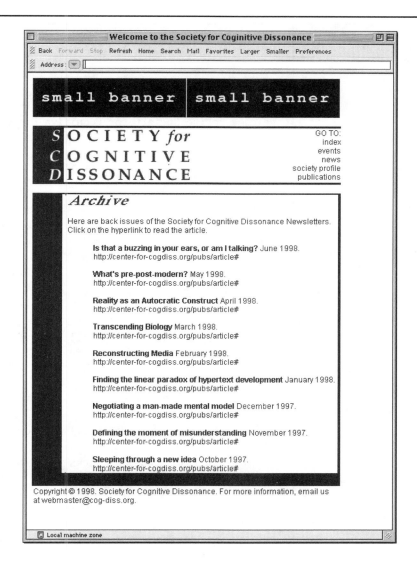

How Site Templates Were Built

As you are well aware, there are two different site templates: One for browsers
that support HTML 4, and one for browsers that do not. Here they are in their
entirety, before common elements were pulled out for ease of production.

lo-tech.html

```
<html>

<head>

<title>Welcome to the Society for Cognitive Dissonance</title>

<!--insert any caveats for includes -->

</head>

<body color="#FFFFFF" text="#333333" alink="#003366" link="#003366"
vlink="#003333">

<table width="475" border="0" cellspacing="0" cellpadding="0">
<tr valign="top" align="left">
<td><img src="../../../general/ad-littleban.gif" alt="[234x60 banner]"
width="234" height="60" border="1"></td>
<td><img src="../../../general/ad-littleban.gif" alt="[234x60 banner]"
width="234" height="60" border="1"></td>
</tr>
</table>
<br>

<table width="475" cellpadding="0" cellspacing="0" border="0">

<!--insert a green rule 'cause it looks cool-->
<tr>
<td colspan="2" valign="top" align="left" bgcolor="#003333">
<img src="../images/spacer.gif" width="475" height="3" border="0">
</td>
</tr>
<tr>
<!--insert the logo for the site-->
<td valign="top" align="left">
<img src="../images/brand.gif" alt="[Society for Cognitive Dissonance]"
width="248" height="87" border="0">
</td>
<!--insert the navigation for the site-->
```

```
<td valign="top" align="right">
<img src="../images/spacer.gif" alt="..." width="100" height="1"
border="0"><br>
<font face="arial, helvetica, sans serif">
GO TO:<br>
</span>
<a href="../index.html">index</a><br>
<a href="#">events</a><br>
<a href="#">news</a><br>
<a href="#">society profile</a><br>
<a href="#">publications</a></br>
</font>
</td>
</tr>

<!--insert a second green rule to hem in the brand and nav divs-->
<tr>
<td colspan="2" valign="top" align="left" bgcolor="#003333">
<img src="../images/spacer.gif" width="475" height="3" border="0">
</td>
</tr>
<tr>
<td colspan="2" valign="top">
 
</td>
</tr>
</table>

<!--insert the big green background for the page. Tres chic!-->

<table width="475" cellpadding="2" cellspacing="0" border="0"
bgcolor="#003333">
<!--here's how we make the green margin on the left-->
<td valign="top" align="left">
<img src="../images/spacer.gif" width="46" height="1" border="0">
</td>

<!--and here goes the white canvas for all the content.-->
<td valign="top" align="left">
    <table width="100%" cellpadding="0" cellspacing="0" border="0"
bgcolor="#FFFFFF">
        <tr>
```

```
                    <td>
                    <font color="#003366" face="times, palatino,
serif"><i><h1>Archive</h1></i></font>
                    <font face="arial, helvetica, sans serif">
                    <p>Here are back issues of the Society for Cognitive
Dissonance Newsletters. Click on the hyperlink to read the article.
                    </p>

                    <p><DL><DD><strong>Is that a buzzing in your ears, or am
I talking?</strong> June 1998. <a href=" http://center-for-
cogdiss.org/pubs/article#"> http://center-for-
cogdiss.org/pubs/article#</a></DD></DL></p>


                    <p><DL><DD><strong>What's pre-post-modern?</strong> May
1998. <a href=" http://center-for-cogdiss.org/pubs/article#">
http://center-for-cogdiss.org/pubs/article#</a></DD></DL></p>

                    <p><DL><DD><strong>Reality as an Autocratic
Construct</strong> April 1998. <a href=" http://center-for-
cogdiss.org/pubs/article#"> http://center-for-
cogdiss.org/pubs/article#</a></DD></DL></p>

                    <p><DL><DD><strong>Transcending Biology</strong> March
1998. <a href=" http://center-for-cogdiss.org/pubs/article#">
http://center-for-cogdiss.org/pubs/article#</a></DD></DL></p>

                    <p><DL><DD><strong>Reconstructing Media</strong>
February 1998. <a href=" http://center-for-cogdiss.org/pubs/article#">
http://center-for-cogdiss.org/pubs/article#</a></DD></DL></p>

                    <p><DL><DD><strong>Finding the linear paradox of
hypertext development</strong> January 1998. <a href=" http://center-
for-cogdiss.org/pubs/article#"> http://center-for-
cogdiss.org/pubs/article#</a></DD></DL></p>

                    <p><DL><DD><strong>Negotiating a man-made mental
model</strong> December 1997. <a href=" http://center-for-
cogdiss.org/pubs/article#"> http://center-for-
cogdiss.org/pubs/article#</a></DD></DL></p>
```

```
            <p><DL><DD><strong>Defining the moment of
misunderstanding</strong> November 1997. <a href=" http://center-for-
cogdiss.org/pubs/article#"> http://center-for-
cogdiss.org/pubs/article#</a></DD></DL></p>

            <p><DL><DD><strong>Sleeping through a new idea</strong>
October 1997. <a href=" http://center-for-cogdiss.org/pubs/article#">
http://center-for-cogdiss.org/pubs/article#</a></DD></DL></p>
            </font>
            </td>
        </tr>
    </table>
</td>
</tr>

<!--this is for the green margin at the bottom-->
<tr>
<td colspan="2" valign="top" align="center">
 
</td>
</tr>
<!--whoops! can't forget the copyright div.-->
<tr bgcolor="#FFFFFF">
<td colspan="2" valign="top" align="left">
<font face="arial, helvetica, sans serif">
<p>Copyright &copy; 1998. Society for Cognitive Dissonance. For more
information, email us at <a href="mailto:webmaster@cog-
diss.org">webmaster@cog-diss.org</a>.
</font>
</p>
</td>
</tr>
</table>

</body>

</html>
```

hi-tech.html

```
<html>

<head>

<title>Welcome to the Society for Cognitive Dissonance</title>

<!--insert any scripts-->

<!--insert any stylesheets -->
<style type="text/css">
<!--//
body       {background-color:#FFFFFF; color:#333333; font-
family:helvetica, arial, sans serif; font-size:12px;}

A:link      {font-family: helvetica, arial, sans serif; font-
weight:bold; color:#003366; font-size:10px;}

A:visited     {position: absolute; font-family: helvetica, arial, sans
serif; color:#003333; font-size:10px;}

p            {position:absolute; left:10px; margin:10px;}

h1           {position:absolute; left:10px; margin:10px; font-
family:times, palatino, serif; font-weight:bold; font-style:italic;
font-size:27px; line-height:33px; color:#003366;}
//-->
</style>
<!--insert any caveats for includes -->

</head>

<body>

<!--insert div for ads. This can stay the same for both the lo-tech and
hi-tech versions of this site. Since the ads are separate from the page
layout and the <div> tag is recognized in 3.0 browsers as a container
tag, the end result will stll be similar.-->
```

```
<div id="ads" style="postion:absolute; left:10; top:5; background-
color:#FFFFFF; border-color:#FFFFFF; border-style:solid; border:1px;
width:475px; height:60px;">
<img src="../../../general/ad-littleban.gif" alt="[234x60 banner]"
width="234" height="60" border="1">
<img src="../../../general/ad-littleban.gif" alt="[234x60 banner]"
width="234" height="60" border="1">
</div>

<!--insert a green rule 'cause it looks cool-->
<div id="green1" style="position:absolute; z-index:50; left:10px;
top:80px; width:475px; height:3px; border-style:solid; border-
color:#003333; border:1px; background-color:#003333;">
</div>

<!--insert the logo for the site-->
<div id="brand" style="position:absolute; z-index:40; left:10px;
top:79px; width:248px; height:87px;">
<img src="../images/brand.gif" alt="[Society for Cognitive Dissonance]"
width="248" height="87" border="0">
</div>
<!--insert the navigation for the site-->
<div id="nav" style="position:absolute; z-index:40; left:400px;
top:85px; width:100px; height:87px;">
<span class="navhead" style="font-family:helvetica, arial, sans-serif;
color:#003366; font-size:18px; line-height:22pt; font-weight:bold;">
GO TO:<br>
<a href="../index.html">index</a><br>
<a href="#">events</a><br>
<a href="#">news</a><br>
<a href="#">society profile</a><br>
<a href="#">publications</a></br>
</div>

<!--insert a second green rule to hem in the brand and nav divs-->
<div id="green2" style="position:absolute; z-index:50; left:10px;
top:165px; width:475px; height:3px; border-style:solid; border-
color:#003333; border:1px; background-color:#003333;">
</div>

<!--insert the big green background for the page. Tres chic!-->
```

```
<div id="back" style="position:absolute; z-index:30; left:10px; top:
180px; width:475px; height:600px; border-style:solid; border-
color:#003333; border:1px; background-color:#003333;">

<!--and here goes the white canvas for all the content.-->

<div id="canvas" style="position:absolute; z-index:50; left:50px;
top:3px; width:423px; height:592px; border-style:solid; border-
color:#FFFFFF; border:1px; background-color:#FFFFFF;">

<h1>Archive</h1>

<p>Here are back issues of the Society for Cognitive Dissonance
Newsletters. Click on the hyperlink to read the article.
</p>

<p><DL><DD><strong>Is that a buzzing in your ears, or am I
talking?</strong> June 1998. <a href=" http://center-for-
cogdiss.org/pubs/article#"> http://center-for-
cogdiss.org/pubs/article#</a></DD></DL></p>


<p><DL><DD><strong>What's pre-post-modern?</strong> May 1998. <a href="
http://center-for-cogdiss.org/pubs/article#"> http://center-for-
cogdiss.org/pubs/article#</a></DD></DL></p>

<p><DL><DD><strong>Reality as an Autocratic Construct</strong> April
1998. <a href=" http://center-for-cogdiss.org/pubs/article#">
http://center-for-cogdiss.org/pubs/article#</a></DD></DL></p>

<p><DL><DD><strong>Transcending Biology</strong> March 1998. <a href="
http://center-for-cogdiss.org/pubs/article#"> http://center-for-
cogdiss.org/pubs/article#</a></DD></DL></p>

<p><DL><DD><strong>Reconstructing Media</strong> February 1998. <a
href=" http://center-for-cogdiss.org/pubs/article#"> http://center-for-
cogdiss.org/pubs/article#</a></DD></DL></p>

<p><DL><DD><strong>Finding the linear paradox of hypertext
development</strong> January 1998. <a href=" http://center-for-
cogdiss.org/pubs/article#"> http://center-for-
cogdiss.org/pubs/article#</a></DD></DL></p>
```

```
<p><DL><DD><strong>Negotiating a man-made mental model</strong>
December 1997. <a href=" http://center-for-cogdiss.org/pubs/article#">
http://center-for-cogdiss.org/pubs/article#</a></DD></DL></p>

<p><DL><DD><strong>Defining the moment of misunderstanding</strong>
November 1997. <a href=" http://center-for-cogdiss.org/pubs/article#">
http://center-for-cogdiss.org/pubs/article#</a></DD></DL></p>

<p><DL><DD><strong>Sleeping through a new idea</strong> October 1997.
<a href=" http://center-for-cogdiss.org/pubs/article#"> http://center-
for-cogdiss.org/pubs/article#</a></DD></DL></p>

</div>

<!--end back div-->
</div>

<!--whoops! can't forget the copyright div.-->
<div id="copyright" style="position:absolute; z-index:90;left:10px;
top:800px;">
<p>Copyright &copy; 1998. Society for Cognitive Dissonance. For more
information, email us at <a href="mailto:webmaster@cog-
diss.org">webmaster@cog-diss.org</a>.
</p>
</div>

</body>

</html>
```

How the Templates Were Modified for Daily Production

There are a few elements in each template that share two very important traits:

- They must be on every page.
- They're subject to change.

These elements are important because they affect the way Jason does his work. Since he has to update and expand the site frequently, it's in his best interests to build the site so he has to do very little nit-picky updating work. Therefore, Jason's going to pull out any template element he sees as having these two traits. He identifies the following elements:

- the advertising block at the top of the page
- the navigation—it might change if the site is reorganized
- the main content
- the copyright

As a result he has this library of includes; there are two ad formats, since one relies on the HTML 4 standard, and the other is tempered for lower browsers:

ad_hi.htmlf

```
<div id="ads" style="postion:absolute; left:10; top:5; background-
color:#FFFFFF; border-color:#FFFFFF; border-style:solid; border:1px;
width:475px; height:60px;">
<img src="ad-littleban.gif" alt="[234x60 banner]" width="234"
height="60" border="1">
<img src="general/ad-littleban.gif" alt="[234x60 banner]" width="234"
height="60" border="1">
</div>
```

ad_lo.htmlf

```
<table width="475" border="0" cellspacing="0" cellpadding="0">
<tr valign="top" align="left">
<td><img src="../../../general/ad-littleban.gif" alt="[234x60 banner]"
width="234" height="60" border="1"></td>
<td><img src="../../../general/ad-littleban.gif" alt="[234x60 banner]"
width="234" height="60" border="1"></td>
</tr>
</table>
<br>
```

nav.htmlf

```
<a href="../index.html">index</a><br>
<a href="#">events</a><br>
<a href="#">news</a><br>
<a href="#">society profile</a><br>
<a href="#">publications</a><br>
```

There are two different content includes, because one must include information for the heading and body font formatting.

content_lo.htmlf

```
            <font color="#003366" face="times, palatino,
serif"><i><h1>Archive</h1></i></font>
            <font face="arial, helvetica, sans serif">
            <p>Here are back issues of the Society for Cognitive
Dissonance Newsletters. Click on the hyperlink to read the article.
            </p>

            <p><DL><DD><strong>Is that a buzzing in your ears, or am
I talking?</strong> June 1998. <a href=" http://center-for-cogdiss.org/
pubs/article#"> http://center-for-cogdiss.org/pubs/article#</a></DD>
</DL></p>


            <p><DL><DD><strong>What's pre-post-modern?</strong> May
1998. <a href=" http://center-for-cogdiss.org/pubs/article#">
http://center-for-cogdiss.org/pubs/article#</a></DD></DL></p>

            <p><DL><DD><strong>Reality as an Autocratic
Construct</strong> April 1998. <a href=" http://center-for-cogdiss.org/
pubs/article#"> http://center-for-cogdiss.org/pubs/article#</a></DD>
</DL></p>

            <p><DL><DD><strong>Transcending Biology</strong> March
1998. <a href=" http://center-for-cogdiss.org/pubs/article#">
http://center-for-cogdiss.org/pubs/article#</a></DD></DL></p>
```

```
<p><DL><DD><strong>Reconstructing Media</strong>
February 1998. <a href=" http://center-for-cogdiss.org/pubs/article#">
http://center-for-cogdiss.org/pubs/article#</a></DD></DL></p>

<p><DL><DD><strong>Finding the linear paradox of
hypertext development</strong> January 1998. <a href=" http://center-
for-cogdiss.org/pubs/article#"> http://center-for-cogdiss.org/
pubs/article#</a></DD></DL></p>

<p><DL><DD><strong>Negotiating a man-made mental
model</strong> December 1997. <a href=" http://center-for-cogdiss.org
/pubs/article#"> http://center-for-cogdiss.org/pubs/article#</a></DD>
</DL></p>

<p><DL><DD><strong>Defining the moment of
misunderstanding</strong> November 1997. <a href=" http://center-for-
cogdiss.org/pubs/article#"> http://center-for-cogdiss.org
/pubs/article#</a></DD></DL></p>

<p><DL><DD><strong>Sleeping through a new idea</strong>
October 1997. <a href=" http://center-for-cogdiss.org/pubs/article#">
http://center-for-cogdiss.org/pubs/article#</a></DD></DL></p>
        </font>
```

content_hi.htmlf

```
<h1>Archive</h1>

<p>Here are back issues of the Society for Cognitive Dissonance
Newsletters. Click on the hyperlink to read the article.
</p>

<p><DL><DD><strong>Is that a buzzing in your ears, or am I
talking?</strong> June 1998. <a href=" http://center-for-
cogdiss.org/pubs/article#"> http://center-for-
cogdiss.org/pubs/article#</a></DD></DL></p>
```

```
<p><DL><DD><strong>What's pre-post-modern?</strong> May 1998. <a href="
http://center-for-cogdiss.org/pubs/article#"> http://center-for-
cogdiss.org/pubs/article#</a></DD></DL></p>

<p><DL><DD><strong>Reality as an Autocratic Construct</strong> April
1998. <a href=" http://center-for-cogdiss.org/pubs/article#">
http://center-for-cogdiss.org/pubs/article#</a></DD></DL></p>

<p><DL><DD><strong>Transcending Biology</strong> March 1998. <a href="
http://center-for-cogdiss.org/pubs/article#"> http://center-for-
cogdiss.org/pubs/article#</a></DD></DL></p>

<p><DL><DD><strong>Reconstructing Media</strong> February 1998. <a
href=" http://center-for-cogdiss.org/pubs/article#"> http://center-for-
cogdiss.org/pubs/article#</a></DD></DL></p>

<p><DL><DD><strong>Finding the linear paradox of hypertext
development</strong> January 1998. <a href=" http://center-for-
cogdiss.org/pubs/article#"> http://center-for-cogdiss.org/pubs/
article#</a></DD></DL></p>

<p><DL><DD><strong>Negotiating a man-made mental model</strong>
December 1997. <a href=" http://center-for-cogdiss.org/pubs/article#">
http://center-for-cogdiss.org/pubs/article#</a></DD></DL></p>

<p><DL><DD><strong>Defining the moment of misunderstanding</strong>
November 1997. <a href=" http://center-for-cogdiss.org/pubs/article#">
http://center-for-cogdiss.org/pubs/article#</a></DD></DL></p>

<p><DL><DD><strong>Sleeping through a new idea</strong> October 1997.
<a href=" http://center-for-cogdiss.org/pubs/article#"> http://center-
for-cogdiss.org/pubs/article#</a></DD></DL></p>

copyright.htmlf
<p>Copyright &copy; 1998. Society for Cognitive Dissonance. For more
information, email us at <a href="mailto:webmaster@cog-diss.org">
webmaster@cog-diss.org</a>.
</p>
```

Once the library items were separated out, the templates were reformatted.

lo_tech.html

```
<html>

<head>

<title>Welcome to the Society for Cognitive Dissonance</title>

<!--insert any caveats for includes -->

</head>

<body color="#FFFFFF" text="#333333" alink="#003366" link="#003366"
vlink="#003333">

<!--#include virtual="ad_lo.htmlf" -->

<table width="475" cellpadding="0" cellspacing="0" border="0">

<!--insert a green rule 'cause it looks cool-->
<tr>
<td colspan="2" valign="top" align="left" bgcolor="#003333">
<img src="../images/spacer.gif" width="475" height="3" border="0">
</td>
</tr>
<tr>
<!--insert the logo for the site-->
<td valign="top" align="left">
<img src="../images/brand.gif" alt="[Society for Cognitive Dissonance]"
width="248" height="87" border="0">
</td>
<!--insert the navigation for the site-->
<td valign="top" align="right">
<img src="../images/spacer.gif" alt="..." width="100" height="1"
border="0"><br>
<font face="arial, helvetica, sans serif">
<h5>GO TO:</h5>
<!--#include virtual=" nav.htrnlf" -->
</font>
```

```
</td>
</tr>

<!--insert a second green rule to hem in the brand and nav divs-->
<tr>
<td colspan="2" valign="top" align="left" bgcolor="#003333">
<img src="../images/spacer.gif" width="475" height="3" border="0">
</td>
</tr>
<tr>
<td colspan="2" valign="top">
 
</td>
</tr>
</table>

<!--insert the big green background for the page. Tres chic!-->

<table width="475" cellpadding="2" cellspacing="0" border="0"
bgcolor="#003333">
<!--here's how we make the green margin on the left-->
<td valign="top" align="left">
<img src="../images/spacer.gif" width="46" height="1" border="0">
</td>

<!--and here goes the white canvas for all the content.-->
<td valign="top" align="left">
    <table width="100%" cellpadding="0" cellspacing="0" border="0"
bgcolor="#FFFFFF">
        <tr>
            <td>
            <!--#include virtual="content_lo.htmlf " -->
            </td>
        </tr>
    </table>
</td>
</tr>

<!--this is for the green margin at the bottom-->
<tr>
<td colspan="2" valign="top" align="center">
 
```

```
</td>
</tr>


<!--whoops! can't forget the copyright div.-->
<tr bgcolor="#FFFFFF">
<td colspan="2" valign="top" align="left">
<font face="arial, helvetica, sans serif">
<!--#include virtual="copyright.htmlf" -->
</td>
</tr>
</table>

</body>

</html>
```

hi_tech.html

```
<html>

<head>

<title>Welcome to the Society for Cognitive Dissonance</title>

<!--insert any scripts-->

<!--insert any stylesheets -->
<style type="text/css">
<!--//
body      {background-color:#FFFFFF; color:#333333; font-
family:helvetica, arial, sans serif; font-size:12px;}

A:link     {font-family: helvetica, arial, sans serif; font-
weight:bold; color:#003366; font-size:10px;}

A:visited     {position: absolute; font-family: helvetica, arial, sans
serif; color:#003333; font-size:10px;}

p          {position:absolute; left:10px; margin:10px;}
```

```
h1            {position:absolute; left:10px; margin:10px; font-
family:times, palatino, serif; font-weight:bold; font-style:italic;
font-size:27px; line-height:33px; color:#003366;}
//-->
</style>
<!--insert any caveats for includes -->

</head>

<body>

<!--insert div for ads. This can stay the same for both the lo-tech and
hi-tech versions of this site. Since the ads are separate from the page
layout and the <div> tag is recognized in 3.0 browsers as a container
tag, the end result will stll be similar.-->

<!--#include virtual="ad_hi.htmlf" -->

<!--insert a green rule 'cause it looks cool-->
<div id="green1" style="position:absolute; z-index:50; left:10px;
top:80px; width:475px; height:3px; border-style:solid; border-
color:#003333; border:1px; background-color:#003333;">
</div>

<!--insert the logo for the site-->
<div id="brand" style="position:absolute; z-index:40; left:10px;
top:79px; width:248px; height:87px;">
<img src="../images/brand.gif" alt="[Society for Cognitive Dissonance]"
width="248" height="87" border="0">
</div>
<!--insert the navigation for the site-->
<div id="nav" style="position:absolute; z-index:40; left:400px;
top:85px; width:100px; height:87px;">
<span class="navhead" style="font-family:helvetica, arial, sans-serif;
color:#003366; font-size:18px; line-height:22pt; font-weight:bold;">
GO TO:<br>
<!--include virtual="nav.htmlf" -->
</div>

<!--insert a second green rule to hem in the brand and nav divs-->
```

```
<div id="green2" style="position:absolute; z-index:50; left:10px;
top:165px; width:475px; height:3px; border-style:solid; border-color:
#003333; border:1px; background-color:#003333;">
</div>

<!--insert the big green background for the page. Tres chic!-->

<div id="back" style="position:absolute; z-index:30; left:10px; top:
180px; width:475px; height:600px; border-style:solid; border-
color:#003333; border:1px; background-color:#003333;">

<!--and here goes the white canvas for all the content.-->

<div id="canvas" style="position:absolute; z-index:50; left:50px;
top:3px; width:423px; height:592px; border-style:solid; border-color:
#FFFFFF; border:1px; background-color:#FFFFFF;">

<!--#include virtual="content_hi.htmlf" -->

</div>

<!--end back div-->
</div>

<!--whoops! can't forget the copyright div.-->
<div id="copyright" style="position:absolute; z-index:90;left:10px;
top:800px;">
<!--#include virtual="copyright.htmlf" -->
</div>

</body>

</html>
```

The Source Code

The following round two code files are available on the CD-ROM:

- index.html
- archive.html

- news_index.html
- news1.html
- news2.html
- arch1.html
- arch2.html
- article1.html
- article2.html
- pub_index.html
- meeting_index.html
- links.html
- schedule.html
- co_info_index.html
- award.html
- contact.html

And these fragments:

- ad_hi.htmlf
- ad_lo.htmlf
- nav.htmlf
- content_lo.htmlf
- content_hi.htmlf
- copyright.htmlf
- list_plus_text.htmlf
- text_items.htmlf
- general_text.htmlf
- linked_items_in_list.htmlf

NOTE   There are two different content includes, because one must include information for the heading and body font formatting.

Cognitive Dissonance, Round 3: Adding Leading-Edge Features

Now that we have a functional site, it's time to see what Jason can do when he gets a blank check for DHTML.

Jason's managed to convert his entire office to the cult of the Web. His boss now wants to know if he can develop a cooler version of the website, something that takes advantage of scripting and style sheets. Jason has been given carte blanche to create a site that exploits the most recent browser versions' capabilities, and he's going to use it to create a visually interesting site.

What Development Decisions Were Made

Jason's tired of copying over old site files, dropping in new content, and renaming the files. He feels—correctly—that there's a lot of room for error: He might end up inadvertently writing over work he's already done, or repeating a lot of specialized formatting from file to file.

One possible solution to Jason's growing dissatisfaction is to break down the site into a series of includes, or at least separate the content out into includes called from individual files. This way, Jason doesn't have to worry about copying over the live files he's using as a model for new pages. Instead, he can have one template file, and create a new content file to be called into that template as often as necessary.

But first, Jason has to come up with a new site design.

The first two iterations of the Society for Cognitive Dissonance's website focused on presenting information within a functional layout. The first site was built for an audience that could best be described as "late adopters." The second site used some HTML 4 technology, but stayed relatively restrained in its use of newer Web development techniques. This site, however, finally moves into the latest ratified version of HTML to build a cleaner, less blocky look.

The new look is geared to breaking out of the blocky, symmetrical style that the previous two site incarnations supported. The final look and feel should be more "designed" and reflect some sense of a unique visual style, as opposed to the grid-like layout most information-based websites aim for.

Jason decided that simple HTML-specified spatial layout would be more visually effective than a tiled graphic effect. He also decided that the best way to serve this focus on space would be to tightly control the positioning and layout. This meant resisting the idea of a flowing layout—one that resizes and repositions itself according to the window size—and deciding instead that the layout elements are fixed in definite relation to each other, and maintain the same sizes and proportions no matter how big or small the window is.

The next step was to find a way to make these precisely spaced elements stand out. Jason decided the best way to do this would be to greatly simplify the layout: Instead of trying to include a few different kinds of information in an eye-pleasing arrangement, he would revert to a "simpler" medium. He also decided that a letter would be a good example of this simple format: You have a letterhead identifying the sender (branding), plus content, in a simple package.

To make the letter stand out, he set it on a green mat. In order to maintain consistency between old layouts and color schemes, and the new design, he kept the same green that dominated the old layout in horizontal rules. Jason also decided to subtly detail the letter's outline by adding a blue outline around the central content area as well. This echoes the second color in the "letterhead" logo, and gives the appearance of the letter being lifted off the page.

Since the spacing and borders are the primary visual draw in the layout, the content area stayed deliberately simple. In fact, were it not for the style-sheeted `<div>`s outlining the content, the text could easily transfer from an HTML 2 design to a 4.*x* design. Which, come to think of it, is the whole point to a well-done design: crucial parts can easily migrate up or down the browser spectrum.

But wait, you're saying. Before you go telling me how well-done this design is, where are the ads? And where is the site navigation? The ads are placed below the layout, so the user gets the full impact of the spacing first, that's where. Although this runs contrary to some sponsors' wishes regarding page placement, you ultimately need to decide what's best for your page layout; if the site isn't compelling, you're not going to have traffic anyway and nobody will visit at all.

As for the navigation, Jason decided to use DHTML to make a pop-down menu. This is a space-saving solution that helps to carry the letter analogy a bit further. Since the design is so streamlined, it would only detract from the overall look to include "traditional" vertical or horizontal navigation bars. As we begin to nudge websites toward an application model, emulating typical Windows or Macintosh UI menu behavior is an evocative step toward that new way of thinking.

There is a very small, very discreet text navigation area immediately above the copyright statement. This is to provide a backup system if the user has her JavaScript turned off.

The Scope and Technical Requirements for the Site

The major technical consideration for this site was the introduction of DHTML. Of course, by whole-heartedly adopting DHTML, Jason runs the risk of losing his audience; this move isn't recommended unless you're (a) experimenting with DHTML; (b) confident your audience will take the plunge; or (c) planning on serving up different versions of the site depending on the user's browser client.

If Jason has the same comfortable working relationship with his sysadmin that he established during the last round of site revisions, he could probably debut this site iteration without worrying about losing his low-tech audience.

How the Site Changed

A number of changes have been made.

Placement of the Ads The ads were moved from the top of the page to the bottom of the page, to more clearly separate the difference between the content and the ads.

In the old template, the ads were the first container loaded after the body tag; here, they're stashed at the bottom, as you can see from the style sheet attached to the <div>:

```
#ads            {position:absolute; top:675px; left:70px; background-
color:#FFFFCC; background-color:#FFFFFF; border-color:#FFFFFF; border-
style:solid; border:1px; width:475px; height:60px;}
<!--insert ads div here. we moved them down to give more visual
prominence to the organization logo.-->
<div id="ads">
```

```
<img src="../../../general/ad-littleban.gif" alt="[234x60 banner]"
width="234" height="60" border="1">
<img src="../../../general/ad-littleban.gif" alt="[234x60 banner]"
width="234" height="60" border="1">
</div>
```

Layout Shape   The shape of the layout was changed completely: Instead of hemming in the page via a left-hand green margin and separating the heading with green rules, the heading and the content were grouped together and placed in a green and blue square "frame."

```
<!--everything lives inside backblock -->
<div id="backblock">
    <div id="cframe">
        <div id="content">
        <!--don't forget the society logo. it has its own style-->
            <img id="brand" src="../images/brand.gif" alt="[Society
for Cognitive Dissonance]" width="248" height="87" border="0">

            <div id="include">
            <!--#include virtual="PUT TEXT FOR SECTION HERE" -->

            </div>

        </div>
    </div>
</div>
```

Floating Navigation Bar   The navigation is no longer glued to the header section of the page. Thanks to DHTML, it can pop up or down as necessary. It's now an image that pops in and out of visibility on a JavaScripted cue. The old menu was a stack of text links; the new one looks like this:

```
<div id="clickButton">
<a href="javascript:showHideLayerSwitch('clickMenu');">
<img src="../images/clicknav.gif" alt="[click here]" width="100"
height="12" border="0">
</a>
</div>
<div id="clickMenu">
```

```
<img src="../images/menu.gif" USEMAP="#click" alt="[click to go
somewhere cool.]" width="100" height="100" border="0">
</div>
```

with an imagemap at the bottom of the page:

```
<!--imagemap for popdown menu-->
<map name="click
click">
            <area shape="rect" coords="-7, 79, 99, 100"
                href="http://center-for-cogdiss.org/pub/
index.html">
            <area shape="rect" coords="-3, 58, 99, 79"
                href="http://center-for-cogdiss.org/co_info/
index.html">
            <area shape="rect" coords="-2, 38, 100, 58"
                href="http://center-for-cogdiss.org/news/
index.html">
            <area shape="rect" coords="-2, 16, 99, 39"
                href="http://center-for-cogdiss.org/meeting/
index.html">
            <area shape="rect" coords="-2, -4, 100, 17"
                href="http://center-for-cogdiss.org/index.html">
        </map>
```

Getting Hi-Tech   There is no longer a low-end version of the page. To view the page properly, you need a browser that supports version 4 technologies.

All of the style-sheeted attributes were moved to one document at the top of the page. Jason did this to reflect this site version's commitment to HTML 4 execution. In the old template, he had restricted his `<head>`-contained stylesheet to text attributes and included it in the lo-tech template because many of the elements can still be read and parsed on version 3 browsers, but not positioning. The new-and-improved style sheet for the document looks like this:

```
<style type="text/css">
<!--//
body    {font-family:helvetica; arial; sans-serif; color:#333333;
font-size:10px; line-height:12px; background-color:#FFFFFF;}
A:link    {font-family: helvetica, arial, sans serif; font-weight:
bold; color:#003366; font-size:10px;}
```

```
A:visited     {font-family: helvetica, arial, sans serif;
color:#003333; font-size:10px;}
p             {position:absolute; left:10px; margin:10px;}

h1            {position:absolute; left:10px; margin:10px; font-
family:times, palatino, serif; font-weight:bold; font-style:italic;
font-size:27px; line-height:33px; color:#003366;}


#backblock    {position:absolute; z-index:10; left:50px; top:50px;
width:500; height:500px; border:1; bordercolor:#003333; background-
color:#003333;}

#clickButton  {position:absolute; z-index:1000; left:375px;
top:10px; width:100px; border-color:#003366; border-style:solid;
border:1px; width:100px; height:18px;}
#clickMenu    {position:absolute; z-index:1000; left:390px;
top:22px; width:100px; border-color:#003333; border-style:solid;
border:1px; width:100px; height:100px; visibility:hidden;}

#cframe       {position:absolute; z-index:40; left:20 px; top:20px;
width:500px; height:500px; border:1; bordercolor:#003366; background-
color:#003366;}
#content      { position:absolute; z-index:80; left:4px; top:4 px;
width: 492px; height:492px; border:1; bordercolor:#FFFFFF; background-
color:#FFFFFF;}
#brand        {position:absolute; z-index:40; left:10px; top:10px;
width:248px; height:87px;}
#include      {padding:5px; position:absolute; z-index:40; left:10px;
top:100px;}
#ads          {position:absolute; top:675px; left:70px; background-
color:#FFFFCC; background-color:#FFFFFF; border-color:#FFFFFF; border-
style:solid; border:1px; width:475px; height:60px;}
#copyright    {position:absolute; z-index:90;left:10px; top:750px;}
#textnav      {position:absolute; z-index:90;left:10px; top:730px;}

//-->
</style>
```

Figure 18.3 shows the revised site, with the floating nav bar shown in the second shot.

FIGURE 18.3:

The Society for Cognitive Dissonance, now with a floating nav bar

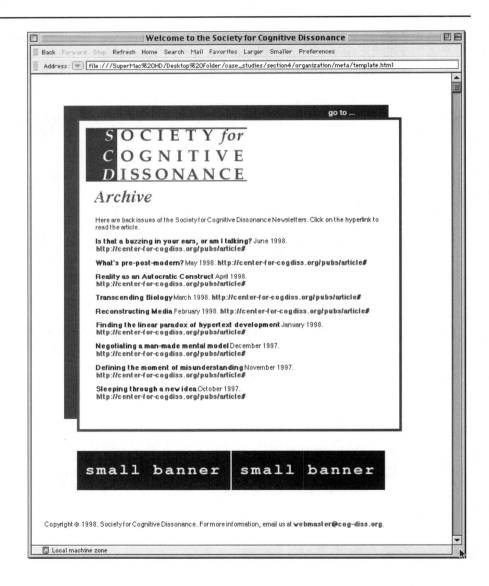

FIGURE 18.3:
CONTINUED

The Society for Cognitive
Dissonance, now with a
floating nav bar

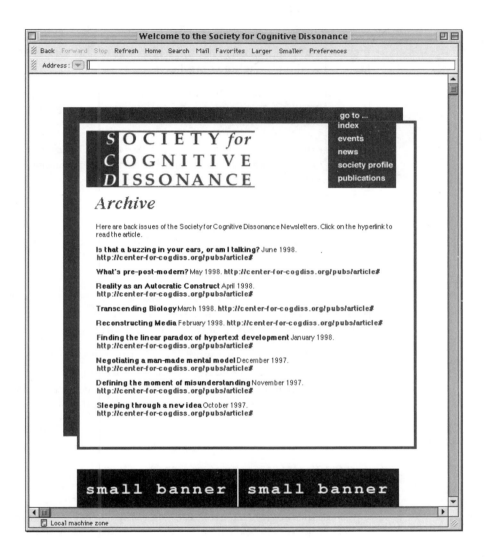

How Site Templates Were Built

Jason worked on perfecting the pop-down menu first. He liked the menu because it's an elegant solution to the ever-present problem of limited screen real estate for a Web page, and because it echoes the user experience of using pull-down menus in a Windows-type desktop environment.

After Jason's menu code was debugged, he worked on gracefully integrating the menu into a general layout. We're going to take a look at the HTML, then the JavaScript, then the whole template file.

In our template, the scripts are already added. But a review of what goes into making them work won't hurt. Let's look at the HTML first.

```
<div id="clickButton">
<a href="javascript:showHideLayerSwitch('clickMenu');">
<img src="../images/clicknav.gif" alt="[click here]" width="100"
height="12" border="0">
</a>
</div>
<div id="clickMenu">
<img src="../images/menu.gif" USEMAP="#click" alt="[click to go
somewhere cool.]" width="100" height="100" border="0">
</div>
```

The hook for the JavaScript function that makes the menu appear and disappear is attached, via a link, to a button. The button lives in the object container "clickButton". The function is called showHideLayerSwitch.

In order to tell the script what layer to make visible or invisible, the handler passes the value "clickMenu". Notice that the object with the id immediately below the button is called "clickMenu". This is the <div> that holds the menu, and turns visible or invisible when you click on the button object.

Now that you know what all the handlers in the HTML are doing, let's look at the script. The easiest way to do this is to reprint the script with comments:

```
<SCRIPT LANGUAGE="JavaScript">

        var visibleVar="null";
//Remember this function from the layers documentation?
//It's what allows the script to mediate through two different
//implementation of the document object model and apply
//stylesheet modifications to them.
        function init(){
            if (navigator.appName == "Netscape") {
                    layerStyleRef="layer.";
                    layerRef="document.layers";
                    styleSwitch="";
                    visibleVar="show";
            }else{
                    layerStyleRef="layer.style.";
```

```
                        layerRef="document.all";
                        styleSwitch=".style";
                        visibleVar="visible";
            }
    }
//This line defines the function and its parameter (the layer name).
//The rest of the function checks the layer's visibility property
//and responds accordingly: if the layer is visible, then it calls
// the hideLayer function; if the layer is invisible, then the function
//calls the showLayer function.
    function showHideLayerSwitch(layerName){
            if
(eval(layerRef+'["'+layerName+'"]'+styleSwitch+'.visibility ==
visibleVar')){
                hideLayer(layerName);
            }else{
                showLayer(layerName);
            }
    }
//This shows whatever layerName value gets passed to it. In this
//case, it's the layername (article+number) concatenated
//with a visibility style call.

    function showLayer(layerName){

eval(layerRef+'["'+layerName+'"]'+styleSwitch+'.visibility="visible"');
    }
//This hides whatever layerName value gets passed to it. In this
//case, it's the layername (article+number) concatenated
//with a visibility style call.
    function hideLayer(layerName){

eval(layerRef+'["'+layerName+'"]'+styleSwitch+'.visibility="hidden"');
    }

</SCRIPT>
```

The HTML for the template is completely <div>-driven and style-sheeted. Here's what the whole file looks like:

```
<html>
<head>
<title>
Welcome to the Society for Cognitive Dissonance
```

```
</title>
<!--insert stylesheet-->
<style type="text/css">


<!--//
body      {font-family:helvetica; arial; sans-serif; color:#333333;
font-size:10px; line-height:12px; background-color:#FFFFFF;}
A:link     {font-family: helvetica, arial, sans serif; font-
weight:bold; color:#003366; font-size:10px;}
A:visited      {font-family: helvetica, arial, sans serif;
color:#003333; font-size:10px;}
p          {position:absolute; left:10px; margin:10px;}

h1          {position:absolute; left:10px; margin:10px; font-
family:times, palatino, serif; font-weight:bold; font-style:italic;
font-size:27px; line-height:33px; color:#003366;}


#backblock     {position:absolute; z-index:10; left:50px; top:50px;
width:500; height:500px; border:1; bordercolor:#003333; background-
color:#003333;}

#clickButton     {position:absolute; z-index:1000; left:375px;
top:10px; width:100px; border-color:#003366; border-style:solid;
border:1px; width:100px; height:18px;}
#clickMenu          {position:absolute; z-index:1000; left:390px;
top:22px; width:100px; border-color:#003333; border-style:solid;
border:1px; width:100px; height:100px; visibility:hidden;}

#cframe          {position:absolute; z-index:40; left:20 px; top:20px;
width:500px; height:500px; border:1; bordercolor:#003366; background-
color:#003366;}
#content     { position:absolute; z-index:80; left:4px; top:4 px;
width: 492px; height:492px; border:1; bordercolor:#FFFFFF; background-
color:#FFFFFF;}
#brand          {position:absolute; z-index:40; left:10px; top:10px;
width:248px; height:87px;}
#include     {padding:5px; position:absolute; z-index:40; left:10px;
top:100px;}
#ads          {position:absolute; top:675px; left:70px; background-
color:#FFFFCC; background-color:#FFFFFF; border-color:#FFFFFF; border-
style:solid; border:1px; width:475px; height:60px;}
```

```
//-->
</style>
<!--insert any javascript -->
<SCRIPT LANGUAGE="JavaScript">

    var visibleVar="null";
    function init(){
       if (navigator.appName == "Netscape") {
                 layerStyleRef="layer.";
                 layerRef="document.layers";
                 styleSwitch="";
                 visibleVar="show";
       }else{
                 layerStyleRef="layer.style.";
                 layerRef="document.all";
                 styleSwitch=".style";
                 visibleVar="visible";
          }
     }

    function showHideLayerSwitch(layerName){
          if
(eval(layerRef+'["'+layerName+'"]'+styleSwitch+'.visibility ==
visibleVar')){
              hideLayer(layerName);
          }else{
              showLayer(layerName);
          }
     }
    function showLayer(layerName){

eval(layerRef+'["'+layerName+'"]'+styleSwitch+'.visibility="visible"');
    }

    function hideLayer(layerName){

eval(layerRef+'["'+layerName+'"]'+styleSwitch+'.visibility="hidden"');
    }


</SCRIPT>
</head>
<body onLoad="init()">
```

```
<div id="backblock">
<div id="clickButton">
<a href="javascript:showHideLayerSwitch('clickMenu');">
<img src="../images/clicknav.gif" alt="[click here]" width="100"
height="12" border="0">
</a>
</div>
<div id="clickMenu">
<img src="../images/menu.gif" USEMAP="#click" alt="[click to go
somewhere cool.]" width="100" height="100" border="0">
</div>
<div id="cframe">
<div id="content">
<!--don't forget the society logo. it has its own style-->
<img id="brand" src="../images/brand.gif" alt="[Society for Cognitive
Dissonance]" width="248" height="87" border="0">
<div id="include">
<h1>
Archive
</h1>
<p>
Here are back issues of the Society for Cognitive Dissonance
Newsletters. Click on the hyperlink to read the article.
</p>
<p>
<strong>
Is that a buzzing in your ears, or am I talking?
</strong>
 June 1998.
<a href=" http://center-for-cogdiss.org/pubs/article#">
 http://center-for-cogdiss.org/pubs/article#
</a>
</p>
<p>
<strong>
What's pre-post-modern?
</strong>
 May 1998.
<a href=" http://center-for-cogdiss.org/pubs/article#">
 http://center-for-cogdiss.org/pubs/article#
</a>
</p>
<p>
```

```
<strong>
Reality as an Autocratic Construct
</strong>
 April 1998.
<a href=" http://center-for-cogdiss.org/pubs/article#">
 http://center-for-cogdiss.org/pubs/article#
</a>
</p>
<p>
<strong>
Transcending Biology
</strong>
 March 1998.
<a href=" http://center-for-cogdiss.org/pubs/article#">
 http://center-for-cogdiss.org/pubs/article#
</a>
</p>
<p>
<strong>
Reconstructing Media
</strong>
 February 1998.
<a href=" http://center-for-cogdiss.org/pubs/article#">
 http://center-for-cogdiss.org/pubs/article#
</a>
</p>
<p>
<strong>
Finding the linear paradox of hypertext development
</strong>
 January 1998.
<a href=" http://center-for-cogdiss.org/pubs/article#">
 http://center-for-cogdiss.org/pubs/article#
</a>
</p>
<p>
<strong>
Negotiating a man-made mental model
</strong>
 December 1997.
<a href=" http://center-for-cogdiss.org/pubs/article#">
 http://center-for-cogdiss.org/pubs/article#
</a>
```

```
</p>
<p>
<strong>
Defining the moment of misunderstanding
</strong>
 November 1997.
<a href=" http://center-for-cogdiss.org/pubs/article#">
 http://center-for-cogdiss.org/pubs/article#
</a>
</p>
<p>
<strong>
Sleeping through a new idea
</strong>
 October 1997.
<a href=" http://center-for-cogdiss.org/pubs/article#">
 http://center-for-cogdiss.org/pubs/article#
</a>
</p>
</div>
</div>
</div>
</div>
<!--insert ads div here. we moved them down to give more visual
prominence to the organization logo.-->
<div id="ads">
<img src="../../../general/ad-littleban.gif" alt="[234x60 banner]"
width="234" height="60" border="1">
<img src="../../../general/ad-littleban.gif" alt="[234x60 banner]"
width="234" height="60" border="1">
</div>
<!--small text nav.-->
<div id="textnav" style="position:absolute; z-index:90;left:10px;
top:730px;">
<p>
<a href="http://center-for-cogdiss.org/pub/index.html">
publications
</a>
 + 
<a href="http://center-for-cogdiss.org/co_info/index.html">
society
</a>
```

```
 + 
<a href="http://center-for-cogdiss.org/news/index.html">
news
</a>
 + 
<a href="http://center-for-cogdiss.org/meeting/index.html">
meetings
</a>
 + 
<a href="http://center-for-cogdiss.org/index.html">
home
</a>
 + 
</p>
</div>
<!--whoops! can't forget the copyright div.-->
<div id="copyright" style="position:absolute; z-index:90;left:10px;
top:750px;">
<p>
Copyright &copy; 1998. Society for Cognitive Dissonance. For more
information, email us at
<a href="mailto:webmaster@cog-diss.org">
webmaster@cog-diss.org
</a>
.
</p>
</div>
<!--imagemap for popdown menu-->
<map name="click click">
<area shape="rect" coords="-7, 79, 99, 100" href="http://center-for-
cogdiss.org/pub/index.html">
<area shape="rect" coords="-3, 58, 99, 79" href="http://center-for-
cogdiss.org/co_info/index.html">
<area shape="rect" coords="-2, 38, 100, 58" href="http://center-for-
cogdiss.org/news/index.html">
<area shape="rect" coords="-2, 16, 99, 39" href="http://center-for-
cogdiss.org/meeting/index.html">
<area shape="rect" coords="-2, -4, 100, 17" href="http://center-for-
cogdiss.org/index.html">
</map>
</body>
</html>
```

How the Templates Were Modified for Daily Production

The template mockup you saw had text dropped into it so Jason could gauge how much content he could fit on a page. When he gets ready to remodel the real site, he's actually going to rely on the content include system he set up in the previous revision round to drop the content into the HTML; the resulting "everyday" template he's using is actually coded like this:

```
<html>
<head>
<title>Welcome to the Society for Cognitive Dissonance</title>

<!--insert stylesheet-->
<style type="text/css">
<!--//
body      {font-family:helvetica; arial; sans-serif; color:#333333;
font-size:10px; line-height:12px; background-color:#FFFFFF;}
A:link    {font-family: helvetica, arial, sans serif; font-
weight:bold; color:#003366; font-size:10px;}
A:visited     {font-family: helvetica, arial, sans serif;
color:#003333; font-size:10px;}
p          {position:absolute; left:10px; margin:10px;}

h1         {position:absolute; left:10px; margin:10px; font-
family:times, palatino, serif; font-weight:bold; font-style:italic;
font-size:27px; line-height:33px; color:#003366;}


#backblock     {position:absolute; z-index:10; left:50px; top:50px;
width:500; height:500px; border:1; bordercolor:#003333; background-
color:#003333;}

#clickButton    {position:absolute; z-index:1000; left:375px;
top:10px; width:100px; border-color:#003366; border-style:solid;
border:1px; width:100px; height:18px;}
#clickMenu         {position:absolute; z-index:1000; left:390px;
top:22px; width:100px; border-color:#003333; border-style:solid;
border:1px; width:100px; height:100px; visibility:hidden;}

#cframe         {position:absolute; z-index:40; left:20 px; top:20px;
width:500px; height:500px; border:1; bordercolor:#003366; background-
color:#003366;}
```

```css
#content     { position:absolute; z-index:80; left:4px; top:4 px;
width: 492px; height:492px; border:1; bordercolor:#FFFFFF; background-
color:#FFFFFF;}
#brand         {position:absolute; z-index:40; left:10px; top:10px;
width:248px; height:87px;}
#include     {padding:5px; position:absolute; z-index:40; left:10px;
top:100px;}
#ads           {position:absolute; top:675px; left:70px; background-
color:#FFFFCC; background-color:#FFFFFF; border-color:#FFFFFF; border-
style:solid; border:1px; width:475px; height:60px;}
#copyright     {position:absolute; z-index:90;left:10px; top:750px;}
#textnav     {position:absolute; z-index:90;left:10px; top:730px;}

//-->
</style>

<!--insert any javascript -->
<SCRIPT LANGUAGE="JavaScript">
    var visibleVar="null";
    function domhack(){
        if (navigator.appName == "Netscape") {
                    layerStyleRef="layer.";
                    layerRef="document.layers";
                    styleSwitch="";
                    visibleVar="show";
        }else{
                    layerStyleRef="layer.style.";
                    layerRef="document.all";
                    styleSwitch=".style";
                    visibleVar="visible";
            }
    }


    function showHideLayerSwitch(layerName){
            if
(eval(layerRef+'["'+layerName+'"]'+styleSwitch+'.visibility ==
visibleVar')){
                hideLayer(layerName);
            }else{
                showLayer(layerName);
            }
    }
```

```
        function showLayer(layerName){

eval(layerRef+'["'+layerName+'"]'+styleSwitch+'.visibility="visible"');
        }

        function hideLayer(layerName){

eval(layerRef+'["'+layerName+'"]'+styleSwitch+'.visibility="hidden"');
        }

</SCRIPT>

</head>

<body onLoad="domhack()">


<div id="backblock">
<div id="clickButton">
<a href="javascript:showHideLayerSwitch('clickMenu');">
<img src="../images/clicknav.gif" alt="[click here]" width="100"
height="12" border="0">
</a>
</div>
<div id="clickMenu">
<img src="../images/menu.gif" USEMAP="#click" alt="[click to go
somewhere cool.]" width="100" height="100" border="0">
</div>
    <div id="cframe">
        <div id="content">
        <!--don't forget the society logo. it has its own style-->
            <img id="brand" src="../images/brand.gif" alt="[Society
for Cognitive Dissonance]" width="248" height="87" border="0">

            <div id="include">
            <!--#include virtual="content.html" -->

            </div>

            </div>
        </div>
```

```
        </div>
</div>


<!--insert ads div here. we moved them down to give more visual
prominence to the organization logo.-->
<!--#include virtual="ads.htmlf" -->


<!--small text nav.-->
<!--#include virtual="textnav.htmlf" -->


<!--whoops! can't forget the copyright div.-->
<!--#include virtual="copyright.htmlf" -->


<!--imagemap for popdown menu-->
<map name="click
click">
                <area shape="rect" coords="-7, 79, 99, 100"
                    href="http://center-for-
cogdiss.org/pub/index.html">
                <area shape="rect" coords="-3, 58, 99, 79"
                    href="http://center-for-
cogdiss.org/co_info/index.html">
                <area shape="rect" coords="-2, 38, 100, 58"
                    href="http://center-for-
cogdiss.org/news/index.html">
                <area shape="rect" coords="-2, 16, 99, 39"
                    href="http://center-for-
cogdiss.org/meeting/index.html">
                <area shape="rect" coords="-2, -4, 100, 17"
                    href="http://center-for-cogdiss.org/index.html">
        </map>

</body>

</html>
```

The includes for each section follow.

copyright.htmlf   Since this is a sitewide resource, it makes sense to separate this out for easy inclusion and revision.

```
<div id="copyright" >
<p>Copyright &copy; 1998. Society for Cognitive Dissonance. For more
information, email us at <a href="mailto:webmaster@cog-
diss.org">webmaster@cog-diss.org</a>.
</p>
</div>
```

textnav.htmlf   This is the ubiquitous backup navigation area at the bottom of the page:

```
<div id="textnav">
<p>
<a href="http://center-for-
cogdiss.org/pub/index.html">publications</a> + 
<a href="http://center-for-
cogdiss.org/co_info/index.html">society</a> + 
<a href="http://center-for-
cogdiss.org/news/index.html">news</a> + 
<a href="http://center-for-
cogdiss.org/meeting/index.html">meetings</a> + 
<a href="http://center-for-
cogdiss.org/index.html">home</a> + 
</p>
</div>
```

ads.htmlf   As with the copyright statement and the text navigation device, ads are present across the site. It makes sense from both content production and ad production perspectives to separate them out for easier production:

```
<div id="ads">
<img src="../../../general/ad-littleban.gif" alt="[234x60 banner]"
width="234" height="60" border="1">
<img src="../../../general/ad-littleban.gif" alt="[234x60 banner]"
width="234" height="60" border="1">
</div>
```

The Source Code

The revised, round three code files are also available on the CD-ROM. They are:

- `index.html`
- `archive.html`
- `news_index.html`
- `news1.html`
- `news2.html`
- `arch1.html`
- `arch2.html`
- `article1.html`
- `article2.html`
- `pub_index.html`
- `meeting/index.html`
- `links.html`
- `schedule.html`
- `co_info_index.html`
- `award.html`
- `contact.html`

And the fragments are:

- `copyright.htmlf`
- `textnav.htmlf`
- `ad.htmlf`
- `list_plus_text.htmlf`
- `text_items.htmlf`
- `general_text.htmlf`
- `linked_items_in_list.htmlf`

Case Study #3: Escape-key.com

Escape-key.com is a directory of outdoor links targeted towards desk jockeys. It was started by two avid campers who held down day jobs in software programming. Looking around at their peers, they realized that there is a huge untapped market for people with discretionary income and little free time. Subsequently, Escape-key.com works on presenting outdoor activities in neat, digestible packages for the cubicle-bound itching to spend their weekends somewhere else.

I'm going to use Escape-key.com as a model for sites that are based on collections of other extra-Web resources. The idea behind these sites is typically to sell the organization of the information as the valuable part of the site. Topical directories are nothing to sneeze at from a strategy point of view: users often rely on them to find specialized information in a hurry, and return again and again if their first search was successful.

Escape-key.com, Round 1: Building the Site

Escape-key.com is run by a few people as part of a start-up venture hoping to get bought by a larger media company. In this case, Escape-key is run by two people: Kyle Cooper, who is responsible for all the editorial content, and Linda Jones, who does all the site production. Their first priority is building a site that causes as little work as possible for both of them. Kyle is going to want to modify the contents on the site—to add, delete, and copyedit material—while Linda is going to be concerned with how to let Kyle retain editorial control without breaking anything.

The solution is to compartmentalize the actual site components as much as possible, and to set up clear workflows between Kyle and Linda so they can each work in peace.

What Development Decisions Were Made

Since the site is fairly uncomplicated in its editorial scheme, the real concern is maintenance. In order to accomplish this, it's best to develop a production scheme that builds modularity and frequent maintenance into even the launch of the site. Linda and Kyle decided that the best strategy for this would be to hammer out the work flow between Kyle's editorial work and Linda's site maintenance, then build the site with that daily routine in mind.

The first step was to decide that Kyle would be responsible for getting content to Linda, and in return, she'd be responsible for doing all site production. Keeping that one condition in mind, Linda began to work on ways to design the site to accommodate her work schedule.

The first thing she worked on was the site's look. Some sites have intricate content nests—sidebars and related hyperlinks within articles, or frames carrying highly specific navigation systems peculiar to certain articles on certain days. These sites are wonders to behold, but they're also tremendously time-consuming to maintain. You have to either build and maintain a set of tools that permits you to perform these automatic functions, or you have to devote staff production time to assembling these pages.

Since this site is meant to change constantly, it's prudent to simply make the design as modular as possible so parts can be added, expanded, or deleted as necessary. Linda did this on escape-key.com by identifying three major types of information, and then making sure the three fit on the same page, but didn't interlock. Figure 18.4 shows an example.

So how can you balance the modular components with a comprehensive layout? In the case of escape-key.com, Linda relied on consistent, repeated colors to tie the parts together, and then reinforced the visual association by arranging them in a T-shape so there were strong vertical and horizontal associations. As a result, both the article and links list could expand to be as long as they'd like, but there would always be a corresponding lengthening of the other feature. If the article was longer than the links list, it would "hang" past the list; if the links list was longer than the article; it would be stretch out the bottom colored block.

This design and production compromise was necessary for a third step in the workflow: building high-end and low-end templates.

The Scope and Technical Requirements for the Site

Although style sheets would have permitted modularized production without compromising any of the appearances, the state of style sheet support and popular browser use are both contributing factors in an argument against using style sheets. However, in order to accommodate the widest possible audience with a layout that makes sense, one of two things has to happen: The developer needs to develop a site that won't be affected by style sheets and the lack thereof, or the developer needs to develop a site that can easily accommodate two separate levels of technical access.

FIGURE 18.4:

This is a typical page on escape-key.com. Notice that the information on the page is in three extremely separate chunks: the sitewide navigation at the top of the page, the links list on the right-hand side of the page, and the article on the left-hand side of the page.

In escape-key.com's case, Linda elected to do the latter. The primary reason for this was thinking ahead: style sheet implementation should become more robust over time, and the number of users upgrading their browsers to an HTML 4 or better browser will continue to grow over time. Style sheets allow the site to use basic DHTML elements to mix and match the already-agreed-upon modular components, and they allow for finer control of the layout.

Since there are only two distinct page layouts on the site, there was only the need to do two sets of high-end/low-end templates. The source code for each type of template is listed after this section. Below is a summary of key differences between the high-end and low-end templates:

- The high-end templates use style sheets and <DIV> tags to set up block-level containers and attach appearance attributes to them. The low-end templates rely on table cells with specific attributes attached as a way to set up stylized containers.

- Every item in the high-end template is modularized: The formats for the navigation, articles, links, copyright, and ads are all five separate includes, and the articles and link content are called into their formatting block-level containers via a second include (nested includes). The low-end template is much less modular: Although it calls the same content includes as the links and articles includes in the high-end format, the only formatting includes that the low-end template has are for advertising and copyright.

- The appearance in the high-end template is more finely controlled. The style sheets allow each item to be individually formatted, whereas table cells are linked together and therefore the appearance of one does often affect the other.

Figure 18.5 shows the original front page of escape-key.com.

How Site Templates Were Built

Because the chief draw of the site is the constantly updated content, Kyle and Linda had to agree on two things: how frequently content would be updated, and how much content each section would have. They settled on four discrete content items per section: one links list, and three separate feature articles. The articles would be updated once a month; the links would be updated once a week.

In order to access the material that is to be updated, Linda decided that the content would be enclosed in server-side includes. This way, she could easily swap new feature articles in or out simply by changing one line in the index file that referenced the files.

FIGURE 18.5:

Escape-key.com

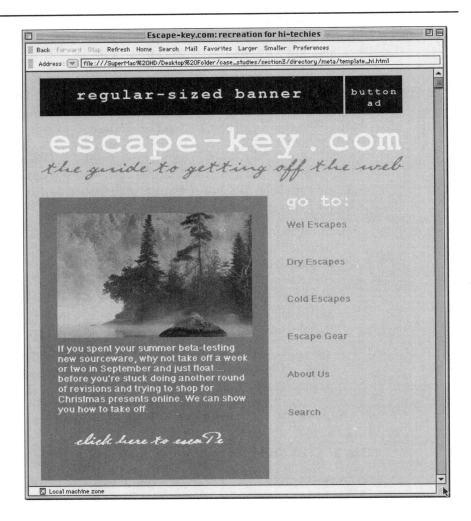

To simplify the include-swapping, Linda decreed that all content within the includes was to be formatted very simply, and any markup that controlled the appearance of text or images be coded in the "shell" template that called the includes. This way, she didn't have to worry about formatting disparities between the different content sections.

Here's how she built the original high-end template:

```
<html>

<head>
<title>Escape-key.com: recreation for hi-techies</title>

<!--insert scripts-->

<!--insert stylesheet-->
<style type="text/css">
#ads      {position:absolute; z-index:50; left:20px; top:10px;
width:560px; border:1px; border-style:solid; border-color:#FFCC99;}

#topbrand     {position:absolute; z-index:50; left:20px; top: 80px;
width:560px; border:1px; border-style:solid; border-color:#FFCC99;}

#article     {position:absolute; z-index:50; left:20px; top: 200px;
width:350px; height: 450px; background-color:#CC6666; border:1px;
border-style:solid; border-color:#CC6666;}

#wow     {position:absolute; z-index:60; left:25px; top:25px;
width:300px; height:200px; border:1px; bordercolor:#CC6666;}

#front_feature     {position:absolute; z-index:60; left:25px;
top:235px; width:300px; height:150px; border:1px; bordercolor:#CC6666;
font-family:helvetica, arial; font-weight:bold; font-size:14px;
color:#FFFFFF; line-height:16px;}

#frontlinks     {position:absolute; z-index:50; left:400px; top: 200px;
width:130px; height: 450px; font-family:helvetica, arial; font-
weight:bold; font-size:14px; color:#FFFFFF; line-height:16px;}

#copyright     {position:absolute; z-index:60; left:30; top:700;
width:535px; height:20px;  color:#999999; font-family:courier new,
courier; font-size:11px; line-height:12px;}
</style>

</head>

<body bgcolor="#FFCC99" link="#CC6666" vlink="#003333" text="#FFFFFF">
```

```
<!--this is the hi-tech version that users get when they access the
site with a 3.0 browser or below. -->
<!--this is the div where the ads go -->
<div id="ads">
<img src="../../../general/ad-banner.gif" alt="[468x60 banner]"
width="468" height="60" border="0">
<img src="../../../general/ad-button.gif" alt="[88x60 banner]"
width="88" height="60" border="0">
</div>

<!--this is the div where the logo goes -->
<div id="topbrand">
<!--insert new escape-key.com logo here -->
<img src="../images/brand-round1.gif" alt="[escape-key.com: the guide
to getting off the web.]" width="560" height="100" border="0">
</div>

<!--this div is brick-colored, the better to stand in contrast to the
mango-colored background.-->
<div id="article">
<!--this first child div is for the picture that makes people go oooh.-
->
<div id="wow">
<img src="../images/autumn.jpg" alt="[escape to the Rockies in time for
fall.]" width="300" height="200" border="0">
</div>
<!--this second child div is for the article that sells the idea of
actually disconnecting from a T1 to go someplace called "outside." -->
<div id="front_feature">
<p>
If you spent your summer beta-testing new sourceware, why not take off
a week or two in September and just float ... before you're stuck doing
another round of revisions and trying to shop for Christmas presents
online. We can show you how to take off.
</p>
<p> 
</p>
<p>
<a href="../outside_dry/index.html"><img src="../images/takeme.gif"
alt="[escape-key, take me away!]" width="300" height="24"
border="0"></a>
</p>
```

```
</div>
</div>

<div id="frontlinks">
<h1><font face="courier new, courier">go to:</font></h1>

<p><a href="../outside_wet/index.html">Wet Escapes</a></p>
<p> </p>
<p><a href="../outside_dry/index.html">Dry Escapes</a></p>
<p> </p>
<p><a href="../outside_cold/index.html">Cold Escapes</a></p>
<p> </p>
<p><a href="../outside_toys/index.html">Escape Gear</a></p>
<p> </p>
<p><a href="../site/aboutus.html">About Us</a></p>
<p> </p>
<p><a href="../site/search.html">Search</a></p>
<p> </p>
</div>

<!--this is the standard copyright disclaimer on every page -->
<div id="copyright">
Copyright &copy; 1998, escape-key.com. All rights reserved. To learn
more about us and our legal rights, <a href="mailto:webmaster@escape-
key.com">contact us</a>, or visit <a href="../site/aboutus.html">this
page</a>.
</div>

</body>


</html>
```

And here's the content template:

```
<html>

<head>
<title>Escape-key.com: recreation for hi-techies</title>

<!--insert scripts-->
<style type-"text/css">
<!--//
```

```
body      {background-color:#FFFFFF; color:#333333; font-
family:helvetica, arial, sans serif; font-size:10px;}

A:link    {font-family: helvetica, arial, sans serif; font-
weight:bold; color:#003333;}

A:visited     {position: absolute; font-family: helvetica, arial, sans
serif; color:#003366;}

h3              {font-family:courier new, courier; font-weight:bold;
font-size:18px; line-height:20px; color:#CC6666;}

h4              {font-family:courier new, courier; font-weight:bold;
font-size:14px; line-height:16px; color:#CC6666;}

#wow          {position:absolute; z-index:60; left:25px; top:15px;}

#ads      {position:absolute; z-index:50; left:20px; top:10px;
width:560px; border:1px; border-style:solid; border-color:#FFFFFF;}

#topbrand     {position:absolute; z-index:50; left:20px; top: 80px;
width:560px; border:1px; border-style:solid; border-color:#FFFFFF;}

#navtop    {position:absolute; z-index:80; left:20; top:180;
background-color:#CC6666; width:560; height:18; border:1px; border-
style:solid; border-color:#CC6666; font-family:helvetica, arial, sans-
serif; font-weight:bold;font-size:12px; color:#FFFFFF;}

#article      {position:absolute; left:19; top:211; z-index:90;
background-color:#FFCC99; width:365; height:100%; border-color:#FFCC99;
border:1px; font-family:helvetica, arial, sans-serif;font-size:12px;
color:#FFFFFF;}

#links     {position:absolute; left:390; top:217; z-index:90;
background-color:#FFFFFF; width:190; height:100%; border-color:#FFFFFF;
border:1px;}

#copyright      {position:absolute; z-index:60; left:20; top:900;
width:535px; height:20px; border-style:solid; border:1px;
bordercolor:#FFFFFF; background-color:#FFFFFF; color:#999999; font-
family:courier new, courier; font-size:11px; line-height:12px;}
```

```
//-->
</style>
<!--insert stylesheet-->

</head>

<body bgcolor="#FFFFFF" link="#CC6666" vlink="#003333" text="#333333">
<!--this is the hi-tech version that users get when they access the
site with a 4.0 browser or above. -->

<!--this is the div where the ads go -->
<div id="ads">
<img src="../../../general/ad-banner.gif" alt="[468x60 banner]"
width="468" height="60" border="0">
<img src="../../../general/ad-button.gif" alt="[88x60 banner]"
width="88" height="60" border="0">
</div>


<!--this is the div where the logo goes -->
<div id="topbrand">
<!--insert new escape-key.com logo here -->
<img src="../images/brick_brand.gif" alt="[escape-key.com]" width="560"
height="70" border="0">
</div>


<!--now we would get fancy with spacing between words, but no browser
consistently supports any margin properties, so we're stuck. -->
<div id="navtop">
<p>
 
<a href="../outside_wet/index.html"><span style="color:#FFFFFF">Wet
Escapes</span></a>
 
<a href="../outside_dry/index.html"><span style="color:#FFFFFF">Dry
Escapes</span></a>
 
<a href="../outside_cold/index.html"><span style="color:#FFFFFF">Cold
Escapes</span></a>
 
<a href="../outside_toys/index.html"><span style="color:#FFFFFF">Escape
Gear</span></a>
```

```
 
<a href="../site/aboutus.html"><span style="color:#FFFFFF">About
Us</span></a>
 
<a href="../site/search.html"><span
style="color:#FFFFFF">Search</span></a>
</p>
</div>

<!--here's the div for all the content.-->
<div id="article">
</div>

<!--here's the div for the links-->
<div id="links">

<h3>
     Related links
</h3>
<p>
So you've read some of our correspondents and you're jazzed to leave
the keyboard for the outdoors. Follow these links to research and plan
your trip. If you're looking for gear, visit any of our fine sponsors
listed on the site.
</p>
<div id="links">
     <h4>
          Rafting by Region
     </h4>
          <a href="http://www.qeed.com/ack/">Atlantic Coastal
Kayaker</a><br>
          <a href="Http://www.cyberwest.com">Cyberwest</a>
          <a
href="http://www.gorp.com/gorp/activity/paddling/pad_fw.htm">Far West
Paddling Guide</a><br>
          <A HREF="http://www.nps.gov/">PARKNET</A><br>
          <A HREF="http://www.fs.fed.us/">USDA Forest Service Home
Page</A><br>
     <h4>
          River and Ocean Conditions
     </h4>
```

```
        <a href=" http://orh-wc.orh.usace.army.mil/wc/whitewater.html
">US Army Corps of Engineers</a><br>
        <A HREF="http://info.er.usgs.gov/">USGS Home Page</A>

    <h4>
        Rafting Expeditions
    </h4>
        <a href="http://www.whitewaterconnection.com/">Whitewater
Connection</a><br>
        <a href="http://www.nocweb.com/">Nantahala Outdoor Center</a>
    <h4>
        Resources on the Web
    </h4>
        <a href="http://www.gorp.com/">Great Outdoors Recreation
Pages</a><br>
        <a href="http://www.sunshinedaydream.com/">Sunshine
Daydream</a><br>
        <A HREF="http://www.awa.org">American Whitewater
Affiliation</A>
    <h4>
        Rafting/padding gear
    </h4>
        <A HREF="http://www.dagger.com">Dagger</A><br>
        <A HREF="http://www.erols.com/dforsha/wavsport/">Wave Sport
Kayaks</A><br>
        <A HREF="http://www.wildsys.com/">Wilderness Systems
Kayaks</A><br>
        <A HREF="http://www.ecotravel.com/madriver/">Mad
River</A><br>
    <h4>
        Rafting/paddling instruction
    </h4>
        <a
href="gopher://ftp.std.com/11/nonprofits/canoe.kayak">David Reichert's
Paddling Pages</a><br>
        <a href="http://siolibrary.ucsd.edu/preston/kayak/">Preston's
Kayak Page</a><br>
        <a
href="http://www.princeton.edu/~rcurtis/rivplan.html">Planning a Safe
River Trip</a><br>
```

```
</div>

<div id="copyright">
Copyright &copy; 1998, escape-key.com. All rights reserved. To learn
more about us and our legal rights, <a href="mailto:webmaster@escape-
key.com">contact us</a>, or visit <a href="../site/aboutus.html">this
page</a>.
</div>

</body>
</html>
```

Here are the low-end templates, starting first with the index file, then moving to the content template.

This is the index file:

```
<html>

<head>
<title>Escape-key.com: recreation for hi-techies</title>

</head>

<body bgcolor="#FFCC99" link="#CC6666" vlink="#003333" text="#FFFFFF">
<!--this is the lo-tech version that users get when they access the
site with a 3.0 browser or below. -->
<table width="560" cellspacing="0" cellpadding="2" border="0">
<!--this row deals with the two ads we run-->
<tr valign="top" align="center">
<td><img src="../../../general/ad-banner.gif" alt="[468x60 banner]"
width="468" height="60" border="0">
</td>
<td><img src="../../../general/ad-button.gif" alt="[88x60 banner]"
width="88" height="60" border="0">
</td>
</tr>

<!--this row deals with the branding graphic -->
<tr valign="top" align="center">
<td colspan="2">
<img src="../images/brand-round1.gif" alt="[escape-key.com:  the guide
to getting off the web]" width="560" height="100" border="0">
```

```
</td>
</tr>
<!--a spacer row-->
<tr valign="middle" align="center">
<td colspan="2"><p> </p></td>
</tr>

<!--this row has two features: the story on the left, and the list of
links/nav on the right. -->
<tr valign="top" align="center">
<td bgcolor="#CC6666" rowspan="8">
     <table width="300" cellspacing="10" cellpadding="0" border="0">
     <tr>
     <td valign="top" align="center"><img src="../images/autumn.jpg"
alt="[escape to the Rockies in time for fall.]" width="300"
height="200" border="0">
     </td>
     </tr>
     <tr>
     <td valign="top" align="center">
     <p>
<font face="arial, helvetica">If you spent your summer beta-testing new
sourceware, why not take off a week or two in September and just float
... before you're stuck doing another round of revisions and trying to
shop for Christmas presents online. We can show you how to take
off.</font>
</p>
<p> 
</p>
<p>
<a href="../outside_dry/index.html"><img src="../images/takeme.gif"
alt="[escape-key, take me away!]" width="300" height="24"
border="0"></a>
</p>
     </td>
     </tr>
     </table>
</td>
<td>
<h1><font face="courier new, courier">go to:</font></h1>
</td>
</tr>
```

```
<!--i broke this up into several mini-rows so there would be more space
between the different items.-->
<tr valign="middle" align="center"><td><font face="arial,
helvetica"><p> </p><p><a
href="../outside_wet/index.html"><strong>Wet
Escapes</strong></a></p><p> </p></font></td></tr>
<tr valign="middle" align="center"><td><font face="arial,
helvetica"><p> </p><p><a
href="../outside_dry/index.html"><strong>Dry
Escapes</strong></a></p><p> </p></font></td></tr>
<tr valign="middle" align="center"><td><font face="arial,
helvetica"><p> </p><p><a
href="../outside_cold/index.html"><strong>Cold
Escapes</strong></a></p><p> </p></font></td></tr>
<tr valign="middle" align="center"><td><font face="arial,
helvetica"><p> </p><p><a
href="../outside_toys/index.html"><strong>Escape
Gear</strong></a></p><p> </p></font></td></tr>
<tr valign="middle" align="center"><td><font face="arial,
helvetica"><p> </p><p><a href="../site/aboutus.html"><strong>About
Us</strong></a></p><p> </p></font></td></tr>
<tr valign="middle" align="center"><td><font face="arial,
helvetica"><p> </p></font></td></tr>
<tr><td valign="middle" align="center"><font face="arial,
helvetica"><p><a
href="../site/search.html"><strong>Search</strong></a></p><p> </p>
</font></td></tr>
<!--a spacer row-->
<tr valign="middle" align="center">
<td colspan="2"><p> </p></td>
</tr>

<tr valign="top" align="left">
<td colspan="2"><font face="arial, helvetica">
Copyright &copy; 1998, escape-key.com. All rights reserved. To learn
more about us and our legal rights, <a href="mailto:webmaster@escape-
key.com">contact us</a>, or visit <a href="../site/aboutus.html">this
page</a>.</font>
</td>
</tr>

</table>
```

```
</body>

</html>
```

We've got another heavily tabled template that looks like this:

```
<html>

<head>
<title>Escape-key.com: recreation for hi-techies</title>

</head>

<body bgcolor="#FFFFFF" link="#CC6666" vlink="#003333" text="#333333">
<!--this is the lo-tech version that users get when they access the
site with a 3.0 browser or below. -->
<table width="560" cellspacing="0" cellpadding="2" border="0">
    <!--this row deals with the two ads we run-->
    <tr valign="top" align="center">
    <td colspan="2">
    <!--#include virtual="ads.htmlf" -->
    </td>
    </tr>

    <!--this row deals with the branding graphic -->
    <tr valign="top" align="center">
    <td colspan="2">
    <img src="../images/brick_brand.gif" alt="[escape-key.com]"
width="560" height="70" border="0">
    </td>
    </tr>
</table>
<!--rather than go to the hassle of matching up multiple table cells
and width, why not just make 3 tables? This is table #2 - the nav bar
table. The color in the table changes between brick and mango from page
to page, along with other elements, hence the screwy syntax.-->
<table bgcolor="#CC6666" width="560" cellspacing="10" cellpadding="2"
border="0">
    <tr>
    <td><a href="../outside_wet/index.html"><font face="helvetica,
arial"><strong><span style="color:#FFFFFF">Wet
Escapes</span></strong></font></a></td>
```

```
       <td><a href="../outside_dry/index.html"><font face="helvetica,
arial"><strong><span style="color:#FFFFFF">Dry
Escapes</span></strong></font></a></td>
       <td><a href="../outside_cold/index.html"><font face="helvetica,
arial"><strong><span style="color:#FFFFFF">Cold
Escapes</span></strong></font></a></td>
       <td><a href="../outside_toys/index.html"><font face="helvetica,
arial"><strong><span style="color:#FFFFFF">Escape
Gear</span></strong></font></a></td>
       <td><a href="../site/aboutus.html"><font face="helvetica,
arial"><strong><span style="color:#FFFFFF">About
Us</span></strong></font></a></td>
       <td><a href="../site/search.html"><font face="helvetica,
arial"><strong><span
style="color:#FFFFFF">Search</span></strong></font></a></td>
       </tr>
</table>

<!--and here's table #3, the one with all the content-->
<table width="560" cellspacing="0" cellpadding="10" border="0">
<tr>
<td width="65%" bgcolor="#FFCC99">
<!--#include virtual="article1.htmlf" -->
</td>
<td width="35%" bgcolor="#FFFFFF">
<h1><font face="courier new, courier">HOTLINKS</font></h1>

<h3><font face="courier new, courier">rafting trips</font></h3>

<h3><font face="courier new, courier">water conditions</font></h3>

<h3><font face="courier new, courier">paddling instructions</font></h3>

<h3><font face="courier new, courier">handy links</font></h3>

<h3><font face="courier new, courier">paddling gear</font></h3>

</td>
</tr>
<!--this row's a spacer-->
<tr>
<td colspan="2">
```

```
<p> </p>
</td>
</tr>
<tr>
<td colspan="2">
<!--#include virtual="copyright.htmlf" -->
</td>
</tr>
</table>
</body>

</html>
```

How the Templates Were Modified for Daily Production

This is the final set of templates for the site: First, we'll look at the high-end templates, then the low-end templates. Here's the HTML for the high-end index:

```
<html>

<head>
<title>Escape-key.com: recreation for hi-techies</title>

<!--insert scripts-->

<!--insert stylesheet-->
<style type="text/css">
#ads      {position:absolute; z-index:50; left:20px; top:10px;
width:560px; border:1px; border-style:solid; border-color:#FFCC99;}

#topbrand     {position:absolute; z-index:50; left:20px; top: 80px;
width:560px; border:1px; border-style:solid; border-color:#FFCC99;}

#article      {position:absolute; z-index:50; left:20px; top: 200px;
width:350px; height: 450px; background-color:#CC6666; border:1px;
border-style:solid; border-color:#CC6666;}

#wow      {position:absolute; z-index:60; left:25px; top:25px;
width:300px; height:200px; border:1px; bordercolor:#CC6666;}

#front_feature       {position:absolute; z-index:60; left:25px;
top:235px; width:300px; height:150px; border:1px; bordercolor:#CC6666;
```

```
font-family:helvetica, arial; font-weight:bold; font-size:14px;
color:#FFFFFF; line-height:16px;}

#frontlinks     {position:absolute; z-index:50; left:400px; top: 200px;
width:130px; height: 450px; font-family:helvetica, arial; font-
weight:bold; font-size:14px; color:#FFFFFF; line-height:16px;}

#copyright      {position:absolute; z-index:60; left:30; top:700;
width:535px; height:20px;  color:#999999; font-family:courier new,
courier; font-size:11px; line-height:12px;}
</style>

</head>

<body bgcolor="#FFCC99" link="#CC6666" vlink="#003333" text="#FFFFFF">
<!--this is the hi-tech version that users get when they access the
site with a 3.0 browser or below. -->
<!--this is the div where the ads go -->
<!--#include virtual="ads.htmlf -->

<!--this is the div where the logo goes -->
<div id="topbrand">
<!--insert new escape-key.com logo here -->
<img src="../images/brand-round1.gif" alt="[escape-key.com: the guide
to getting off the web.]" width="560" height="100" border="0">
</div>

<!--this div is brick-colored, the better to stand in contrast to the
mango-colored background.-->
<!--#include virtual="article.htmlf" -->

<!--#include virtual="frontlinks.htmlf" -->

<!--this is the standard copyright disclaimer on every page -->
<!--#include virtual="copyright.htmlf" -->

</body>


</html>
```

See how it's nothing but style sheets and container calls? That's par for the course in component-driven templates. Here are each of the includes, one by one.

ads.htmlf

```
<div id="ads">
<img src="../../../general/ad-banner.gif" alt="[468x60 banner]"
width="468" height="60" border="0">
<img src="../../../general/ad-button.gif" alt="[88x60 banner]"
width="88" height="60" border="0">
</div>
```

article.htmlf

```
<div id="article">
<!--this first child div is for the picture that makes people go oooh.-
->
<!--#include virtual="wow.htmlf" -->
<!--this second child div is for the article that sells the idea of
actually disconnecting from a T1 to go someplace called "outside." -->
<!--#include virtual="front_feature.htmlf" -->
</div>
```

NOTE   This is our first example of nested includes: The picture and the first article are also includes that are called within this one. The reason we called these separately is because "article" is a handy container, and we want the option of deleting or changing one component without mistakenly affecting another.

wow.htmlf

```
<div id="wow">
<img src="../images/autumn.jpg" alt="[escape to the Rockies in time for
fall.]" width="300" height="200" border="0">
</div>
```

front_feature.htmlf

```
<div id="front_feature">
<p>
If you spent your summer beta-testing new sourceware, why not take off
a week or two in September and just float ... before you're stuck doing
another round of revisions and trying to shop for Christmas presents
online. We can show you how to take off.
</p>
<p> 
</p>
<p>
<a href="../outside_dry/index.html"><img src="../images/takeme.gif"
alt="[escape-key, take me away!]" width="300" height="24"
border="0"></a>
</p>
</div>
```

frontlinks.htmlf

```
<div id="frontlinks">
<h1><font face="courier new, courier">go to:</font></h1>

<p><a href="../outside_wet/index.html">Wet Escapes</a></p>
<p> </p>
<p><a href="../outside_dry/index.html">Dry Escapes</a></p>
<p> </p>
<p><a href="../outside_cold/index.html">Cold Escapes</a></p>
<p> </p>
<p><a href="../outside_toys/index.html">Escape Gear</a></p>
<p> </p>
<p><a href="../site/aboutus.html">About Us</a></p>
<p> </p>
<p><a href="../site/search.html">Search</a></p>
<p> </p>
</div>
```

copyright.htmlf

```
<div id="copyright">
Copyright &copy; 1998, escape-key.com. All rights reserved. To learn
more about us and our legal rights, <a href="mailto:webmaster@escape-
key.com">contact us</a>, or visit <a href="../site/aboutus.html">this
page</a>.
</div>
```

If you take a look at the includes, you'll note that aside from the ID calls to the style sheet definitions, it's all simple, valid HTML.

Here's the HTML for the high-end content template:

```
<html>

<head>
<title>Escape-key.com: recreation for hi-techies</title>

<!--insert scripts-->
<style type-"text/css">
<!--//
body      {background-color:#FFFFFF; color:#333333; font-
family:helvetica, arial, sans serif; font-size:10px;}

A:link     {font-family: helvetica, arial, sans serif; font-
weight:bold; color:#003333;}

A:visited     {position: absolute; font-family: helvetica, arial, sans
serif; color:#003366;}

h3              {font-family:courier new, courier; font-weight:bold;
font-size:18px; line-height:20px; color:#CC6666;}

h4              {font-family:courier new, courier; font-weight:bold;
font-size:14px; line-height:16px; color:#CC6666;}

#wow          {position:absolute; z-index:60; left:25px; top:15px;}

#ads     {position:absolute; z-index:50; left:20px; top:10px;
width:560px; border:1px; border-style:solid; border-color:#FFFFFF;}
```

```css
#topbrand      {position:absolute; z-index:50; left:20px; top: 80px;
width:560px; border:1px; border-style:solid; border-color:#FFFFFF;}

#navtop      {position:absolute; z-index:80; left:20; top:180;
background-color:#CC6666; width:560; height:18; border:1px; border-
style:solid; border-color:#CC6666; font-family:helvetica, arial, sans-
serif; font-weight:bold;font-size:12px; color:#FFFFFF;}

#article1      {position:absolute; left:19; top:211; z-index:90;
background-color:#FFCC99; width:365; height:100%; border-color:#FFCC99;
border:1px; font-family:helvetica, arial, sans-serif;font-size:12px;
color:#FFFFFF;}

#links      {position:absolute; left:390; top:217; z-index:90;
background-color:#FFFFFF; width:190; height:100%; border-color:#FFFFFF;
border:1px;}

#copyright      {position:absolute; z-index:60; left:20; top:900;
width:535px; height:20px; border-style:solid; border:1px;
bordercolor:#FFFFFF; background-color:#FFFFFF; color:#999999; font-
family:courier new, courier; font-size:11px; line-height:12px;}

//-->
</style>
<!--insert stylesheet-->

</head>

<body bgcolor="#FFFFFF" link="#CC6666" vlink="#003333" text="#333333">
<!--this is the hi-tech version that users get when they access the
site with a 4.0 browser or above. -->

<!--this is the div where the ads go -->
<!--include virtual="ads.htmlf" -->

<!--this is the div where the logo goes -->
<div id="topbrand">
<!--insert new escape-key.com logo here -->
<img src="../images/brick_brand.gif" alt="[escape-key.com]" width="560"
height="70" border="0">
</div>
```

```
<!--now we would get fancy with spacing between words, but no browser
consistently supports any margin properties, so we're stuck. -->
<!--#include virtual="navtop.htmlf" -->

<!--here's the div for all the content.-->
<!--#include virtual="article1.htmlf" -->

<!--here's the div for the links-->
<!--#include virtual="links.htmlf" --"

<!--add copyright-->
<!--#include virtual="copyright.htmlf" -->

</body>
</html>
```

Again, we're using the same copyright and ads includes, so this is one way to economize the total code on the site. We're also relying on style sheets for placement and styling of the <div>s. The includes are actually the most interesting part of the template, again.

article1.htmlf

```
<div id="article1.htmlf">
<!--#include virtual="feature1.htmlf" -->
</div>
```

NOTE This is another case of embedded includes. Because there is more than one article on the front page of the sites, and the site developers want the option to switch between the three features, it makes more sense to change one variable in one include than it does to muck with the main template.

links.htmlf

```
<div id="links">
    <h4>
        Rafting by Region
    </h4>
        <a href="http://www.qeed.com/ack/">Atlantic Coastal
Kayaker</a><br>
```

```
          <a href="Http://www.cyberwest.com">Cyberwest</a>
          <a href="http://www.gorp.com/gorp/activity/paddling/
pad_fw.htm">Far West Paddling Guide</a><br>
          <A HREF="http://www.nps.gov/">PARKNET</A><br>
          <A HREF="http://www.fs.fed.us/">USDA Forest Service Home
Page</A><br>
     <h4>
          River and Ocean Conditions
     </h4>
          <a href=" http://orh-wc.orh.usace.army.mil/wc/whitewater.html
">US Army Corps of Engineers</a><br>
          <A HREF="http://info.er.usgs.gov/">USGS Home Page</A>


     <h4>
          Rafting Expeditions
     </h4>
          <a href="http://www.whitewaterconnection.com/">Whitewater
Connection</a><br>
          <a href="http://www.nocweb.com/">Nantahala Outdoor Center</a>
     <h4>
          Resources on the Web
     </h4>
          <a href="http://www.gorp.com/">Great Outdoors Recreation
Pages</a><br>
          <a href="http://www.sunshinedaydream.com/">Sunshine
Daydream</a><br>
          <A HREF="http://www.awa.org">American Whitewater
Affiliation</A>
     <h4>
          Rafting/padding gear
     </h4>
          <A HREF="http://www.dagger.com">Dagger</A><br>
          <A HREF="http://www.erols.com/dforsha/wavsport/">Wave Sport
Kayaks</A><br>
          <A HREF="http://www.wildsys.com/">Wilderness Systems
Kayaks</A><br>
          <A HREF="http://www.ecotravel.com/madriver/">Mad
River</A><br>
     <h4>
          Rafting/padding instruction
     </h4>
```

```
        <a href="gopher://ftp.std.com/11/nonprofits/canoe.kayak">
David Reichert's Paddling Pages</a><br>
        <a href="http://siolibrary.ucsd.edu/preston/kayak/">Preston's
Kayak Page</a><br>
        <a
href="http://www.princeton.edu/~rcurtis/rivplan.html">Planning a Safe
River Trip</a><br>

</div>
```

navtop.htmlf

```
<div id="navtop">
<p>
 
<a href="../outside_wet/index.html"><span style="color:#FFFFFF">Wet
Escapes</span></a>
 
<a href="../outside_dry/index.html"><span style="color:#FFFFFF">Dry
Escapes</span></a>
 
<a href="../outside_cold/index.html"><span style="color:#FFFFFF">Cold
Escapes</span></a>
 
<a href="../outside_toys/index.html"><span style="color:#FFFFFF">Escape
Gear</span></a>
 
<a href="../site/aboutus.html"><span style="color:#FFFFFF">About
Us</span></a>
 
<a href="../site/search.html"><span
style="color:#FFFFFF">Search</span></a>
</p>
</div>
```

Here are their low-tech counterparts—first the index page, then the content.

This is the index file:

```
<html>
```

```
<head>
<title>Escape-key.com: recreation for hi-techies</title>

<!--insert scripts-->

<!--insert stylesheet-->

</head>

<body bgcolor="#FFCC99" link="#CC6666" vlink="#003333" text="#FFFFFF">
<!--this is the lo-tech version that users get when they access the
site with a 3.0 browser or below. -->
<table width="560" cellspacing="0" cellpadding="2" border="0">
<!--this row deals with the two ads we run-->
<tr valign="top" align="center">
<td colspan="2">
<!--#include virtual="ads.htmlf" -->
</td>
</tr>

<!--this row deals with the branding graphic -->
<tr valign="top" align="center">
<td colspan="2">
<img src="../images/brand-round1.gif" alt="[escape-key.com:  the guide
to getting off the web]" width="560" height="100" border="0">
</td>
</tr>
<!--a spacer row-->
<tr valign="middle" align="center">
<td colspan="2"><p> </p></td>
</tr>

<!--this row has two features: the story on the left, and the list of
links/nav on the right. -->
<tr valign="top" align="center">
<td bgcolor="#CC6666" rowspan="8">
<!--#include virtual="article.htmlf" -->
</td>
<td>
<h1><font face="courier new, courier">go to:</font></h1>
</td>
</tr>
```

```
<!--i broke this up into several mini-rows so there would be more space
between the different items.-->
<tr valign="middle" align="center"><td><font face="arial,
helvetica"><p> </p><p><a href="../outside_wet/index.html"><strong>
Wet Escapes</strong></a></p><p> </p></font></td></tr>
<tr valign="middle" align="center"><td><font face="arial, helvetica">
<p> </p><p><a href="../outside_dry/index.html"><strong>Dry
Escapes</strong></a></p><p> </p></font></td></tr>
<tr valign="middle" align="center"><td><font face="arial, helvetica">
<p> </p><p><a href="../outside_cold/index.html"><strong>Cold
Escapes</strong></a></p><p> </p></font></td></tr>
<tr valign="middle" align="center"><td><font face="arial, helvetica">
<p> </p><p><a href="../outside_toys/index.html"><strong>Escape
Gear</strong></a></p><p> </p></font></td></tr>
<tr valign="middle" align="center"><td><font face="arial, helvetica">
<p> </p><p><a href="../site/aboutus.html"><strong>About
Us</strong></a></p><p> </p></font></td></tr>
<tr valign="middle" align="center"><td><font face="arial, helvetica">
<p> </p></font></td></tr>
<tr><td valign="middle" align="center"><font face="arial, helvetica">
<p><a href="../site/search.html"><strong>Search</strong></a></p>
<p> </p></font></td></tr>
<!--a spacer row-->
<tr valign="middle" align="center">
<td colspan="2"><p> </p></td>
</tr>


<tr valign="top" align="left">
<td colspan="2">
<!--#include virtual="copyright.html" -->
</td>
</tr>



</table>

</body>

</html>
```

The significant change is that there are three includes in this version, with no ill
effects. The table does an excellent job of keeping things in line.

Just notice that the hotlinks are tabled in this version, since our developers are using tables to control the layout.

And the content file looks like this:

```
<html>

<head>
<title>Escape-key.com: recreation for hi-techies</title>

</head>

<body bgcolor="#FFFFFF" link="#CC6666" vlink="#003333" text="#333333">
<!--this is the lo-tech version that users get when they access the
site with a 3.0 browser or below. -->
<table width="560" cellspacing="0" cellpadding="2" border="0">
    <!--this row deals with the two ads we run-->
    <tr valign="top" align="center">
    <td colspan="2">
    <!--#include virtual="ads.htmlf" -->
    </td>
    </tr>

    <!--this row deals with the branding graphic -->
    <tr valign="top" align="center">
    <td colspan="2">
    <img src="../images/brick_brand.gif" alt="[escape-key.com]"
width="560" height="70" border="0">
    </td>
    </tr>
</table>
<!--rather than go to the hassle of matching up multiple table cells
and width, why not just make 3 tables? This is table #2 - the nav bar
table. The color in the table changes between brick and mango from page
to page, along with other elements, hence the screwy syntax.-->
<table bgcolor="#CC6666" width="560" cellspacing="10" cellpadding="2"
border="0">
    <tr>
    <td><a href="../outside_wet/index.html"><font face="helvetica,
arial"><strong><span style="color:#FFFFFF">Wet Escapes</span></strong>
</font></a></td>
```

```
    <td><a href="../outside_dry/index.html"><font face="helvetica,
arial"><strong><span style="color:#FFFFFF">Dry Escapes</span></strong>
</font></a></td>
    <td><a href="../outside_cold/index.html"><font face="helvetica,
arial"><strong><span style="color:#FFFFFF">Cold
Escapes</span></strong></font></a></td>
    <td><a href="../outside_toys/index.html"><font face="helvetica,
arial"><strong><span style="color:#FFFFFF">Escape
Gear</span></strong></font></a></td>
    <td><a href="../site/aboutus.html"><font face="helvetica,
arial"><strong><span style="color:#FFFFFF">About
Us</span></strong></font></a></td>
    <td><a href="../site/search.html"><font face="helvetica,
arial"><strong><span
style="color:#FFFFFF">Search</span></strong></font></a></td>
    </tr>
</table>

<!--and here's table #3, the one with all the content-->
<table width="560" cellspacing="0" cellpadding="10" border="0">
<tr>
<td width="65%" bgcolor="#FFCC99">
<!--#include virtual="article1.htmlf" -->
</td>
<td width="35%" bgcolor="#FFFFFF">
<h1><font face="courier new, courier">HOTLINKS</font></h1>

<h3><font face="courier new, courier">rafting trips</font></h3>

<h3><font face="courier new, courier">water conditions</font></h3>

<h3><font face="courier new, courier">paddling instructions</font></h3>

<h3><font face="courier new, courier">handy links</font></h3>

<h3><font face="courier new, courier">paddling gear</font></h3>

</td>
</tr>
<!--this row's a spacer-->
<tr>
```

```
<td colspan="2">
<p> </p>
</td>
</tr>
<tr>
<td colspan="2">
<!--#include virtual="copyright.htmlf" -->
</td>
</tr>
</table>
</body>

</html>
```

The Source Code

This is the source code for the site, available on the CD-ROM. Remember that all the content is formatted as an include, so Linda can easily swap it in and out as Kyle directs her to.

- `Lo_index.html` (lo-tech)
- `hi_index.html` (hi-tech)
- `outside_cold_index.html` (lo-tech)
- `outside_cold_index.html` (hi-tech)
- `outside_cold_links.htmlf`
- `outside_cold_story1.htmlf`
- `outside_cold_story2.htmlf`
- `outside_cold_story3.htmlf`
- `outside_wet_index.html` (lo-tech)
- `outside_wet_index.html` (hi-tech)
- `outside_wet_links.htmlf`
- `outside_wet_story1.htmlf`
- `outside_wet_story2.htmlf`
- `outside_wet_story3.htmlf`

- `outside_dry_index.html` (lo-tech)
- `outside_dry_index.html` (hi-tech)
- `outside_dry_links.htmlf`
- `outside_dry_story1.htmlf`
- `outside_dry_story2.htmlf`
- `outside_dry_story3.htmlf`
- `outside_toys_index.html` (lo-tech)
- `outside_toys_index.html` (hi-tech)
- `outside_ toys_links.htmlf`
- `outside_ toys_story1.htmlf`
- `outside_ toys_story2.htmlf`
- `outside_ toys_story3.htmlf`
- `aboutus.html`
- `contact.html`
- `search.html`

And the fragments:

- `ads.htmlf`
- `article.htmlf`
- `wow.htmlf`
- `front_feature.htmlf`
- `frontlinks.htmlf`
- `copyright.htmlf`
- `article1.htmlf`
- `links.htmlf`
- `navtop.htmlf`

Escape-key.com, Round 2: Giving the Site a Facelift and Adding Leading-Edge Features

Now that the site is a successful brand name in their niche market, the Escape-key folks want to capitalize on their status by becoming a portal site. A portal site is one that acts as an Internet starting point for a targeted group of users; the goal of a portal site is to be the home page default for any browser. By rearranging the contents of Escape-key to highlight timely and new content, Escape-key.com is capitalizing on the trend to make sites accessible to task-oriented surfing.

Kyle (remember him from the last section? Content guy, wouldn't know HTML if it bit him?) is overjoyed because this is an excellent model for new and exciting editorial material. Linda—the nuts-and-bolts production diva—is a little less excited: She has to figure out how to smoothly move content from the front portal page to the inner-layer content pages and back. These two need to reassess their workflow/production issues in light of the site redesign and its altered content distribution.

What Development Decisions Were Made and How the Technical Requirements Affected Them

The most important development decisions were made nearly simultaneously with the technical decisions. The sharpest shift in the project workload is going to be in front door production. The best way to illustrate that is a before-and-after comparison.

Before: The front door had only one "moving part." The article and image on the front door were actually a teaser to an article featured on one of the subject directories inside, and so could share an include with one of the sections inside. The only front door production, therefore, was occasionally changing the include reference call.

After: The front door is acting as a "portal" to a limited network of websites indexed inside. In order to attract readers and let them know what features lay deeper in the site, there are now three separate moving parts: an article featured in the middle of the page layout, plus two columns of edited links and blurbs on the left and right.

Fortunately, the front door is the only part of the site undergoing substantial overhaul, so Kyle and Lisa don't have to worry about an increased workload on the content pages. Therefore, the two things they do need to worry about in escape-key.com version 2.0 are:

- How frequently will content be pulled from the site's inside pages for display on the front door?

- What production processes would make sharing content between the front door and the inside of the site easier?

The answer to number one is going to have to be hashed out before number two can be answered. Why? The frequency of updating content is going to shape the processes for updating said content.

In this case study, we're working on the premise that the content is updated daily. Now that we've established the frequency for updating content, let's take a look at the task in depth. The first thing we have to do is determine whether or not our developers need to reformat the content includes in order to accommodate the increased rotation in and out of various layouts.

Fortunately, the answer is no: The includes are nicely self-contained units, and can be swapped in and out with only a few lines of code changed here and there. The real issue is how to format those includes: the column width allocated for the links on a subject page is much wider than the column width on the front door.

The easiest answer: style sheets. You can either label each include with an ID and apply a different style definition to the ID depending on the page, or you can forsake styling in the include altogether and rely on browser parsing to add the style to the include content like this:

```
<div id="frontlink">
<!--#include virtual="raftlink.htmlf" -->
</div>
```

Once you've decided that you're going to use style sheets for everything, mixing and matching all those parts becomes easier for the front door. The real question is, how will these new include names affect your backend templates?

If we look at the way the site was assembled in the previous case study, in Chapter 10, you'll note that each directory had its own `links.htmlf` file, and that production was done by copying the template file into each topical directory and calling most of the includes locally. This worked well since there were several different file paths to signify the difference between the site's common includes like copyright and ads, and the subject-specific content includes.

Since the file path for the includes is still very local, it is all of five minutes' work to change the index file and the include name to reflect a topic-specific include.

So, to sum up the work it will take to build the new "portal" front door and rotate in existing content:

Design the new portal.   This is the toughest part of the entire process: How do you build a front page that presents enough information to the user to convince them that this is a useful resource without looking like a boring list of links? Kyle decided that the best way to do that was to present some of the content that lay on the internal pages as a "sneak preview" on the front page. The feature article would be the main visual attraction on the page, and the links lists would demonstrate related resources. In order to maintain some type of visual continuity with the rest of the site, Linda decided to use the same color schemes, and repeat the color-block visual trick that had worked so well on the inside pages. She also cleaned up the logo to give a better brand identity to the front page, since the philosophy behind portals is to provide a strong brand name with a specific organization of information, like Roget's for the thesaurus, or Yahoo! for the first Nnet portal site.

Rename the includes and include calls on existing index page templates. As we've already established, Linda's not going to radically restructure the subject page templates or the include structure she's set up, and she still has to find a way to rotate that distinct content into the front door. Therefore, each subject directory's `links.htmlf` file is getting renamed: `raftlinks.htmlf`, `snowlinks.htmlf`, and so on. The name changes will also be reflected in the `index.html` files for each section, so the content can remain as normal.

Test the new portal production.   After Linda has named and renamed files and checked her templates, it's time to see if her new page layout and include calls work. Every page that's affected needs to be tested. In this case, it's every top-level page on the site.

Launch the new site.   Linda needs to verify the pages she has to push out, then roll them out. Once she's done that, all she needs to do is set up a regular schedule for adding content, and another regular schedule for rotating the content on the front door. This schedule is actually Kyle's responsibility, since he's the one who will be coming up with an editorial calendar.

Devise the maintenance routine.   This should be pretty basic. The steps and frequencies are outlined below.

Step to Take	How Frequently You Should Perform It
Replace the lead articles on the front pages of the subject sites.	Once a week, possibly more. This entails formatting a new include, then calling it from the directory's `index.html` page.
Update the links includes for all the pages.	Once a week, possibly more. This entails checking the links in the existing includes, then adding or subtracting links.
Rotate contents on the front page.	Daily. All this means is putting in a new combination of include names.

How the Site Changed

The most significant overhauls are on the front page of the site. Let's summarize those first.

Moving to DHTML   There is no longer a low-bandwidth version of the page; because of the layout and positioning of the different page parts, a DHTML arrangement works best. The lower-browser version of the inside pages has been abandoned. With the increased rotation of content through the front door and on to the sites, it was easier to maintain one dynamically produced site.

Positioning Modification   The main article has been moved from the left-hand side of the page to the center. Here's the code in the template that sets up the article:

```
<!--this is the center content div. -->
<div id="center" style="position:absolute; z-index:50px; left:125px;
top:210px; width:350px; height:400px; border:1px; border-style:solid;
border-color:#CC6666; background-color:#CC6666;">
<img id="wow" src="../images/glacier.jpg" alt="Escape to Idyllic
Glacier Lake, Canada" width="300" height="200" border="0">
</div>
```

Rotating Links   The links list no longer leads immediately to the different navigation parts. Instead, different items within the links are rotated through, with the different headings for the links leading to the content sites.

Here is the code for each set of frequently rotating links:

```
<!--this is the left-hand content div-->
<div id="left" style="position:absolute; z-index:50; left:15; top:175;
width:100px; height:475px; border:5px; border-style:solid; border-
color:#CC6666; background-color:#FFFFFF;">
<!--include left-hand content include here.-->
</div>

<!--this is the right-hand content div-->
<div id="left" style="position:absolute; z-index:50px; left:485px;
top:175px; width:100px; height:475px; border:5px; border-style:solid;
border-color:#CC6666; background-color:#FFFFFF;">
<!--include right-hand content include here.-->
</div>
```

Here is the bottom code leading to the different sections:

```
<div id="navlast" style="position:absolute; z-index:60; left:30;
top:700; width:535px; height:20px; border-style:solid; border:1px;
bordercolor:#FFFFFF; background-color:#FFFFFF; color:#999999; font-
family:courier new, courier; font-size:11px; line-height:12px;">
<h6>go to: <a href="../outside_wet/index.html">Wet Escapes</a>
 </p>
<a href="../outside_dry/index.html">Dry Escapes</a>
 </p>
<a href="../outside_cold/index.html">Cold Escapes</a>
 </p>
<a href="../outside_toys/index.html">Escape Gear</a>
 </p>
<a href="../site/aboutus.html">About Us</a>
 </p>
<a href="../site/search.html">Search</a>
 
</h6>
</div>
```

Tweaking the Design   Finally, the logo has been streamlined to better "brand" the portal.

Figure 18.6 shows the final site.

FIGURE 18.6:

The revised
escape-key.com site

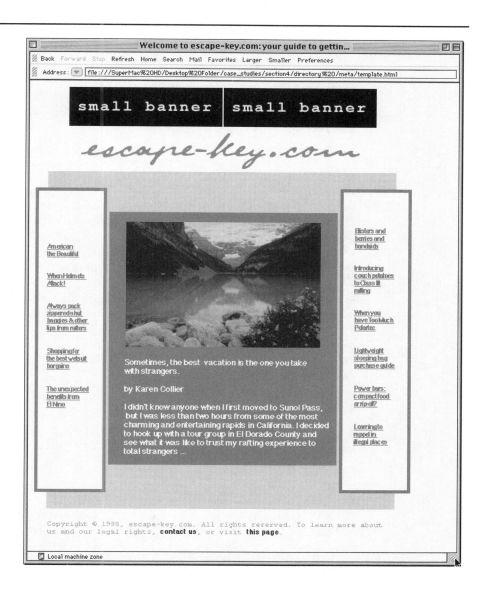

How Site Templates Were Built for Daily Production

Unlike the previous site design, Linda didn't have to figure out a way to make the
site gracefully degrade. Another different condition for this site upgrade: Everything about the site redesign was driven by Kyle's working editorial schedule, so

the entire front door was designed with daily production already firmly in place. Here, then, is the resulting template:

```
<html>

<head>
<title>Welcome to escape-key.com: your guide to getting off the
web</title>

<!--insert stylesheet-->
<style type-"text/css">
<!--//
body      {background-color:#FFFFFF; color:#333333; font-
family:helvetica, arial, sans serif; font-size:10px;}

A:link      {font-family: helvetica, arial, sans serif; font-
weight:bold; color:#003333; font-size:10px;}

A:visited      {position: absolute; font-family: helvetica, arial, sans
serif; color:#003366; font-size:10px;}

#wow           {position:absolute; z-index:60; left:25px; top:15px;}
//-->
</style>

<!--insert any scripty stuff-->

</head>

<body>

<!--this is the div where the ads go -->
<div id="ads" style="position:absolute; z-order:50; left:60; top:10;
width:475; border:1px; border-style:solid; border-color:#FFFFFF;">
<img src="../../../general/ad-littleban.gif" alt="[234x60]" width="234"
height="60" border="1">
<img src="../../../general/ad-littleban.gif" alt="[234x60]" width="234"
height="60" border="1">
</div>

<!--this is the div where the logo goes -->
```

```
<div id="topbrand" style="position:absolute; z-order:50; left:60px;
top: 80px; width:475px; border:1px; border-style:solid; border-
color:#FFFFFF;">
<!--insert new escape-key.com logo here -->
<img src="../images/brand_top.gif" alt="[escape-key.com]" width="470"
height="60" border="0">
</div>

<!--this is the mango-colored div in the background. Note that it has
no child divs. -->
<div id="mango" style="position: absolute; z-index:10; left:30px;
top:145px; width:535px; height:535px; border:1px; border-style:solid;
border-color:#FFCC99; background-color:#FFCC99;">
</div>

<!--this is the left-hand content div-->
<div id="left" style="position:absolute; z-index:50; left:15; top:175;
width:100px; height:475px; border:5px; border-style:solid; border-
color:#CC6666; background-color:#FFFFFF;">
<!--include left-hand content include here.-->
</div>

<!--this is the right-hand content div-->
<div id="left" style="position:absolute; z-index:50px; left:485px;
top:175px; width:100px; height:475px; border:5px; border-style:solid;
border-color:#CC6666; background-color:#FFFFFF;">
<!--include right-hand content include here.-->
</div>

<!--this is the center content div. -->
<div id="center" style="position:absolute; z-index:50px; left:125px;
top:210px; width:350px; height:400px; border:1px; border-style:solid;
border-color:#CC6666; background-color:#CC6666;">
<img id="wow" src="../images/glacier.jpg" alt="Escape to Idyllic
Glacier Lake, Canada" width="300" height="200" border="0">
<!--#include virtual="article_front.htmlf" -->
</div>

<!--this is the standard copyright disclaimer on every page -->
<div id="copyright" style="position:absolute; z-index:60; left:30;
top:800; width:535px; height:20px; border-style:solid; border:1px;
```

```
bordercolor:#FFFFFF; background-color:#FFFFFF; color:#999999; font-
family:courier new, courier; font-size:11px; line-height:12px;">
Copyright &copy; 1998, escape-key.com. All rights reserved. To learn
more about us and our legal rights, <a href="mailto:webmaster@escape-
key.com">contact us</a>, or visit <a href="../site/aboutus.html">this
page</a>.
</div>

</body>

</html>
```

Notice that the content all requires includes. Thanks to the style sheets on every
<div>, plus the document style sheet in the head, the content will simply render
according to the style assigned to the body. This way, Kyle can create a plain text
file and hand it off to Linda with a minimum of fuss.

The Source Code

The files for the revised site, available on the CD-ROM, consist of the following:

- `index.html`
- `outside_cold_index.html` (lo-tech)
- `outside_cold_index.html` (hi-tech)
- `outside_cold_links.htmlf`
- `outside_cold_story1.htmlf`
- `outside_cold_story2.htmlf`
- `outside_cold_story3.htmlf`
- `outside_wet_index.html` (lo-tech)
- `outside_wet_index.html` (hi-tech)
- `outside_wet_links.htmlf`
- `outside_wet_story1.htmlf`
- `outside_wet_story2.htmlf`
- `outside_wet_story3.htmlf`

- `outside_dry_index.html` (lo-tech)
- `outside_dry_index.html` (hi-tech)
- `outside_dry_links.htmlf`
- `outside_dry_story1.htmlf`
- `outside_dry_story2.htmlf`
- `outside_dry_story3.htmlf`
- `outside_toys_index.html` (lo-tech)
- `outside_toys_index.html` (hi-tech)
- `outside_ toys_links.htmlf`
- `outside_ toys_story1.htmlf`
- `outside_ toys_story2.htmlf`
- `outside_ toys_story3.htmlf`
- `aboutus.html`
- `contact.html`
- `search.html`

The sitewide fragment library consists of the following files:

- `Front_article.htmlf`
- `link_code.htmlf`
- `bottom_nav.htmlf`

Constants for Both Case Studies

Through the course of this chapter, you've seen two very different sites go through several stages of development. Even though the building philosophies behind each site changed from iteration to iteration, some things remained constant. The areas below cover two of those areas: the style guide and the QA process.

Style Guides

These tools act as reference guides for how the sitewide elements should look from page to page to page. Here, the style guides are broken down by site and by site version.

Society for Cognitive Dissonance

The details follow.

Color Guide   The body background is white (#FFFFFF) and the text is dark gray (#333333). There are two other colors used throughout the layout: a green used for headlines, horizontal and vertical rules, and visited links (#003333 or 0-51-51 in rgb), and a blue used for not-yet-visited links (#003366 or 0-51-102 in rgb).

Top-Level Headlines   These are all dark green (#003333 or 0-51-51), denoted with the H1 tag, and styled thusly:

```
font-family:times, palatino, serif; font-weight:bold;
font-style:italic; font-size:27px; line-height:33px.
```

Subheads   All subheads are listed in H2, and styled thusly:

```
font-family:times, palatino, serif; font-weight:bold;
font-style:italic; font-size:20px; line-height:23px.
```

Body Text   The body style is reflected in the body tag of the style sheet:

```
font-family:helvetica; arial; sans-serif; font-size:10px;
line-height:12px;
```

Items in a Series/Items in a List   There are two formats for these: unordered lists and definition lists. The archive entries are all definition lists. The unordered lists are saved for brief summaries on index pages. Neither list method has a specific style; they inherit the body text style. In text-heavy lists, the format is:

```
<p>
item<br>
item<br>
item<br>
</p>
```

Images   There is only one image on the site—the main logo. The image is composed in a browser-safe palette and dithered down to a 4 bits per pixel palette.

Escape-key.com

And now for Linda and Kyle's crowning achievement. The before-and-after sites (versions 1.0 and 2.0, that is) are shown together, if anything changed in those specific areas.

Color Guide, Version 1.0   There are two different page color schemes in this website. The front page has a peach-ish background (#FFCC99 or 255-204-153 in rgb) and a brick color (#CC6666 or 204-102-102 in rgb) that's used as a background color for sidebars, and as the primary link color. Expired links are dark green (#003333 or 0-51-51 in rgb) and body text is white (#FFFFFF).

Color Guide, Version 2.0   There are two different color schemes in the website. The front page has a white background (#FFFFFF), a peach background box on top of the white (#FFCC99), and brick-colored borders (#CC6666) around white sidebars. The links are the same brick color, and expired links are dark green. Body text is white, since it's only going to show up in the brick content area in the center of the page.

Top-Level Headlines   See the "Items in a Series" list.

Body Text   If the body text appears on the front page of the site, it is white and in sans-serif; if it appears in the content pages, it is dark-gray and sans-serif. Assuming the pages are from the lo-tech templates, the text is not modified or sized at all; it's just bracketed by <p></p> tags. In the high-tech versions, the format is:

```
P      {font-family: helvetica, arial, sans-serif;  font-size:12px;
line-height:13px;}
```

And the colors are modified independently.

Items in a Series/Items in a List   This is the list of links that characterizes every page. This is how they're formatted in the code for the low-tech version:

```
<h1><font face="courier new, courier">HEADLINE</font></h1>
<h3><font face="courier new, courier">item</font></h3>
<h3><font face="courier new, courier">item</font></h3>
```

The high-tech version has a style sheet for those h1 and h3 tags:

```
H1      {font-family: courier new, courier; font-weight:bold; font-size:
24 px; line-height:30 px; color:#333333;}
H3      {font-family: courier new, courier; font-weight:bold; font-size:
16 px; line-height:18 px; color:#333333;}
```

Images   There are two types of images on the site: the branding graphics on the page, and the graphics showing off the locations and activities the site is focused around. The branding graphics are all GIFs made in the browser-safe palette and dithered down to the smallest palette possible. The lovely scenery graphics are all mid-quality JPEGs, since they are all based on photographs and the GIF files would be huge and unwieldy.

QA Processes

You should never post a site without checking to see how it works. Here are the steps that our Web developers took in cleaning up these sites:

Validate the HTML.   This is easy to do, and can teach you a lot about "good" HTML coding practices. You can elect to validate a document one of two ways:

- Include a doc-type declaration at the top of your document. These declarations look like this:

```
<!DOCTYPE HTML PUBLIC "-//W3C//DTD HTML 4.0//EN"
"http://www.w3.org/TR/REC-html40/strict.dtd">
<!DOCTYPE HTML PUBLIC "-//W3C//DTD HTML 4.0 Transitional//EN"
"http://www.w3.org/TR/REC-html40/loose.dtd">
<!DOCTYPE HTML PUBLIC "-//W3C//DTD HTML 4.0 Frameset//EN"
"http://www.w3.org/TR/REC-html40/frameset.dtd">
```

  You only need to pick one. Then, enter the URL of the page you wish to validate at `http://validator.w3.org/`. Your page must be publicly accessible from a Web server—no checking pages that live only on your desktop or on a password-protected server.

- If you don't think this is a feasible step for your site, you can put an include like this into the bottom of all your files:

```
<div id="check"><a href="http://validator.w3.org/check/referer"
class="offsite">Check this page</a>
```

This sends a query to the validator at `http://validator.w3.org/`, querying a specific site.

Check the sites across different browsers. It never hurts to look at a site on at least four different browser/platform combinations:

1. Netscape 4.*x*/Mac
2. IE 4.*x*/Mac
3. Netscape 4.*x*/Windows
4. IE 4.*x*/Windows

Since the sites are also targeted for lower-end browsers, the sites were also checked against these browsers:

1. Netscape 3.*x*/Mac
2. IE 3.*x*/Mac
3. Netscape 3.*x*/Windows
4. IE 3.*x*/Windows

After you've checked to make sure the HTML is consistent from browser to browser, check to see how the site loads with the images off. Then, dump your browser cache and time how fast the page loads with and without images.

Once your site looks consistently lovely across all the different platforms, and loads relatively quickly, you're set to publish it.

Summary

These two case studies highlighted the steps taken as developers shepherded two very different sites through two very different development processes.

The first case study in this chapter followed the progress of a site that was built as a small, unsupported arm of a non-wired organization: at first, the site was a direct reflection of the paper-based contents of the department, but then it gradually gained an identity of its own. During the course of the case study, Jason also became more familiar with the serving aspect of site administration as he created several different versions of his site for audiences with varying levels of browser upgrades.

The second case study took a look at the complicated and persistent relationship between the work that goes in to putting out a regularly-updated site, the design of the site, and how each affects the other.

What you hopefully gained from each of these studies is the sense that building, upgrading, or maintaining a site should always be done with the methods the site developer uses to do the work being as important as the final product the user sees. If the site can't be assembled intelligently and efficiently, the overall quality of the end-product is affected.

So go ahead and make the argument to your boss: Making your job easier makes your site perform better in the long run.

PART III

Exploring the Cutting Edge

Adapting Your Site-Building Strategies to a Cutting-Edge Website

- Understanding knowledge management

- Applying knowledge management to your site

- Maximizing the potential of structural languages

As websites become increasingly more application oriented, the development process will become less focused on the means to publish the site and more focused on ways to produce the site while enhancing your company's overall information management.

Why? Because it's not going to be enough for websites to simply post information: A cutting-edge website will need to be able to offer its users the ability to manipulate information while keeping backend production overhead to a minimum. The easiest—and smartest—way to do this is to treat the content on your site as a commodity, and begin thinking of website production as an extremely hands-on form of knowledge management.

This doesn't mean that markup languages are going to go away: SGML, the granddaddy of all Web markup languages, is thriving, and there is currently little reason to believe that HTML will go away. In fact, with the growing support of metasyntactical structure languages like XML, markup languages will play a more useful role in presenting information.

They'll also help you handle that information for the widest possible dissemination, both across your website and throughout your organization.

What Is Knowledge Management, and How Does It Fit into Website Production?

Knowledge management sounds like one of those terms that people use to make their job sound more important than it really is, but the field is a burgeoning industry. Knowledge management, by definition, is the systematic effort to create, gather, distribute, and apply knowledge.

There are two critical things to take away from that definition: the four functions of knowledge management, and the word "knowledge." Let's tackle the last one first.

Knowledge is not synonymous with either information or data. A data point is one specific, isolated fact, like, "platypi lay eggs." This may be something you did or did not know before, but the point is, there's no context for the item. Information is a collection of related data; you could have the four data points: "platypi lay eggs"; "they live in Australia"; "most native Australian mammals do not carry their young to term internally"; "Australian mammals have been the most geographically isolated of all mammal species." With information, you have a fuller context of what each item of data is doing: It's building a factual picture for you within the boundaries of the information.

Continued on next page

Knowledge is the applied analysis of information. Using our information sample about the platypus and Australia, we could then make the assessment that Australia's early geographic separation isolated the mammals living there from other evolutionary patterns, and they developed their own reproductive methods.

Granted, this is a dramatic leap within the context of the example, but the lesson is clear: data is a singular fact or item; information is a collection of data; knowledge is the application of information.

Which brings us to the four functions of knowledge management:

Creating knowledge   This may be as simple as assessing information and hypothesizing about which conclusions the information lends itself to, or as difficult as building a sustained hypothesis through a series of experiments or written works.

Gathering knowledge   Knowledge isn't a plateau, but a necessary stage in processing information and using it as shrewdly as possible. By gathering different works of knowledge—a series of articles, for example—you can further refine your insights and hypotheses.

Distributing knowledge   The flip side of gathering knowledge is distributing it. Knowledge management is frequently a collaborative process, and so you need to have a means of disseminating your knowledge, as well as gathering it.

Applying knowledge   This is really the whole point to knowledge management. The other three steps are crucial, because without them, you can't apply knowledge. However, why would you bother unless you were able to do something with the results? Applying knowledge is a way of putting your money where your mouth is—you may take the research results you created or collected and build a new business strategy or product based on them.

This is all well and good, you're saying, but what does this have to do with website development?

Consider this: People have been using the Web for years to collect information and do their own knowledge management. This is why search engines and robots are so popular. So why shouldn't people who *build* the Web be able to appropriate the building technologies for their own knowledge management?

In a Web context, knowledge management frequently means subscribing to e-mail lists and surfing sites to stay abreast of the latest trends; that's developmental knowledge management. It also means documenting how a site works, keeping a template library for a team of developers, or building a script library.

Ideally, you're doing all of this so you can assess how to better do your current job, and how to create some interesting new opportunities for yourself or your team. As you read through the rest of the chapter, ask yourself how you can improve your knowledge creation and application for a less time-intensive Web-development regime.

Knowledge and Information Management

Managing knowledge comes first, then the abstract becomes concrete, and suddenly you find yourself managing information. And information is what the Web is all about, really. Or maybe partly. In any case, on a day-to-day basis, the typical Web developer is slinging information all over the place; distributing, storing, searching, and analyzing. The next four sections emphasize the considerations you should have in the back of your head when you're getting ready to integrate a new technology or retool your entire website production process.

Distributing Information

Current website production techniques often include building a template library and inserting template calls into assorted pages across the site. This is an efficient way to populate a specific chunk of code across a site, and it allows you to streamline your updates as well.

However, the templated include approach only works well for structural elements or boilerplated information, that is, items that are reliably the same from section to section. In addition, these boilerplated chunks are usually formatted in a way that doesn't allow easy re-appropriation into other formats, like a word processing document—unless you don't mind stripping out <H1> tags.

Templating is an excellent intra-site method of distributing simple, standard chunks of information. But an emerging issue is this: How do you distribute varied information in a format that allows it to be easily integrated into the site, without making the information useless?

Consider the following scenario. The same company report or magazine articles that your company's production team laid out in Quark Xpress need to be converted to HTML for widely accessible publication. When you throw in a complimentary ASCII e-mail service and a Pilot downloadable file or Pointcast Channel, you're faced with a mountain of file-conversion tasks. None of them have the same metalanguage for formatting. Someone is going to have to use their human judgement to pull out the same information and reformat it, over and over. Or, they're going to have to write some fairly sophisticated tools to do it for them.

One of the things a website is going to have to consider over the next two years or so is cross-medium appropriation of information and code. Perhaps it means producing or converting all your Web pages to XML or SGML (both browser-readable) so the content is easily sifted into a Word Document. It may mean dramatically simplifying formatting so the most information gets disseminated through the least conversion work.

The latter option is probably untenable, or else you wouldn't have this problem. You'd be happily publishing .txt files to anyone who accesses your data, regardless of method.

Therefore, one of the primary issues of effective information distribution—at least from a production standpoint—is how to efficiently produce a website from disparate sources (Word documents or Quark Xpress files) and then port it to other computer-mediated channels like Pointcast, e-mail, or a PDA. The current method of repeating oneself three times is three times as much work as necessary.

Storing Information

Hand-in-hand with the distribution issue, storing information in an easily accessible format is going to become more of an issue as people continue to blur the line between the Web and the real world. Although word processing programs like Microsoft Word allow an HTML-to-document conversion feature, and technologies like PDF allow you to format a document that can be downloaded and read, those still don't address the issues of storing information.

Those issues are, specifically:

- Storing information in a document-independent format. One of the obstacles I anticipate developers encountering when they try to port information from one format to another is an inability to retain formatting or hierarchical indications.

- Storing information in a compact format. If you're creating vast amounts of information, storing it is going to be an issue after a while. If much of an individual data file is comprised of specific formatting data, not only are you wasting space, you're obscuring your data for further reuse because you'll have to pull it out of one format and push it into another.

- Storing information in a perpetually accessible format. Aside from .txt files, any means of information storage is going to introduce the risk of obsolescence: What happens if you upgrade a software package or choose an entirely new software tool? Extracting salvageable data is both time-consuming and frustrating.

Searching for Information

Finding what you want on the Web won't be getting any easier. Not only are some sites producing hundreds of pages daily, but old sites are going down or re-arranging their pages without providing user redirection. Databases can't keep up.

I've already profiled ways to prevent you from contributing to the link-rot problem in the earlier chapter on backends, Chapter 8. This time, I want to focus on how to find information within your own site. Sometimes running a sitewide grep isn't going to cut it, especially when you have several specific queries you want to string together.

Searching for information may also be one of your more effective bug-zapping tools, especially as your site gets more complex and compartmentalized; finding out if the bug is a particular chunk of code or the result of a few separate components combining is slightly more difficult than simply reading an error log.

Analyzing Information

Intelligent agents are already creeping across the Web, with search engines offering customized interfaces, news sites offering customized front pages, and commerce sites offering a "personal" shopper who suggests related purchases based on your purchase history.

But what about using intelligent agents to construct these pages? Filling in Web page "shells" with specifically focused content chunks is already in practice across the Web at countless portal sites. The current technology relies on user cookies, databases, and a thin HTML layer to tie it all together. But is there any room for unexpected selections?

One site seems to think so: the archival site Alexa Internet (`http://www.alexa.com/`) positions itself as a navigation service focused on two user questions. Those questions—where have I been, and where might I like to go?—are answered via a data pool that looks at usage patterns within specific sites, and from site to site, and finds common threads. If you've uploaded any recent versions of Netscape 4.5, you may notice the browsing option in the right-hand corner of your browser. If you click on that button, you see all the Alexa-predicted choices for related sites.

Tying Knowledge Management to Everyday Web Development

Instead of looking for novel ways to retool everyday HTML, you should be assessing how you can use structural languages beyond HTML for keeping track of your site components as effortlessly as you keep track of your site content.

Use Structural Languages for Structure, Not Just Markup

One of the most overwhelming factors in information management is simply unstructured volume. So far, the focus on the information flood has been on users—faced with a glut of information, most users either shut down or begin applying aggressive filtering techniques to manage the flow of data.

So the user thinks they're exposed to too much information? How do they think you feel, having to produce all that? It's time to turn the tables and begin using structural languages as a way to impose a strict framework on the sea of files you've had to produce. Becoming a structural-language dictator has two benefits: It reduces the chance of platform-specific bugs and quirks, and it imposes order on creating, maintaining, and finding information within your site.

Web markup languages are currently engaging in a separation between content and appearance, and an increasing focus on a systemic organization of content through a structured vocabulary of markup language tags. Web developers and the people who employ them face a number of issues that tend to spawn new trends in Web development. In the structural language arena, that means an increased emphasis on a format that will either work well when ported from one software viewing app to the next, or not significantly harm the user's ability to view data.

Accept That Structural Languages Are Not Limited to Textual Data

From a user standpoint, data visualization is the love child of Quake and HTML. From a developer standpoint, data visualization is the love child of the CIA and Lucent. The result of years of research at Lucent's Bell Laboratories, data visualization is a way to render data as a visual schema, rather than a written explanation.

A primitive example of non-computer data visualization, for example, would be a diagram demonstrating the difference in scale between Godzilla and a human, as opposed to writing "Godzilla is more than five hundred times as tall as a human." For those more visual souls among us, Figure 19.1 illustrates this idea.

FIGURE 19.1:

This is an extremely primitive example of data visualization.

no real humans were harmed in the making of this graphic

The CIA initially used data visualization in the 1980s as a means for its analysts to visually assimilate the documents, pictures, and recordings they had. The goal was to organize complex, massive amounts of unstructured data into something where users could identify the complex interrelationships and deduce knowledge.

NOTE To the CIA and other members of the intelligence community, unstructured data is information that comes in a wide variety of formats—similar to the HTML, image, and multimedia files Web developers deal with daily.

A Web developer might use simple data visualization as a diagnostic tool. A chart could be color coded to display the date each file was last modified, or a directory tree could use different shapes to denote how much content is contained within each folder (see Figure 19.2).

FIGURE 19.2:

These are two examples of how data visualization might work for a Web developer: to demonstrate maintenance schedules for site files, or to demonstrate the relative sizes of different directories against each other.

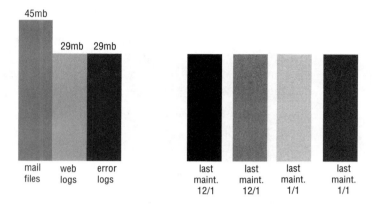

Another way to use data visualization would be to tag problem areas on the site. If the site is depicted as a pyramid, you could run queries against the site to search for specific strings of code that are sending error messages. Then, drill down on a glowing brick to find the code and fix it.

What's going to drive these data visualization tools? Very likely, proprietary software packages with pre-built functions. But in order to maximize any use data visualization has on your site, you'd need to encode all your information within a shell, so the data visualization tool knows to identify it, and as a tool for gluing together unstructured data, a structural language has yet to be beat.

Use Structural Languages to Make Unexpected Connections

Upon first glance, any structural language seems to exist solely to limit the number of ways in which you can present data. Some of the most visually compelling Web pages break the HTML rules for the sake of memorable data presentation—so why bother playing by the rules when you can design a visually attractive site with some clever hacks?

Because when used correctly, a structural language can provide a platform for creating unusual or insightful information connections. These information connections lead to knowledge creation—one of the knowledge management goals you want to apply to your site production over time.

Think of a structural language as being akin to a sonnet: You have exactly 14 lines, three verses of four lines apiece and a heroic couplet at the end. The number of syllables is prescribed, as is the rhyming scheme. But aside from the structural rules, you're free to write about anything you want—something poets have been doing with great success for years.

Your site is a sonnet of sorts: you have a prescribed set of syntactical rules, but how you sort your data within those parameters is your call. And after you're done organizing your site—writing your sonnet—it's time to show it to a critical audience and see how they interpret it.

For a poet, the audience may be a group of literary critics, but yours is a information brokerage.

Information brokers are people (or tools) that draw from a wide variety of information sources and use them to draw varied conclusions. Some information brokers specialize in collecting information for comparative use, like airline fare and schedules. Others may specialize in collecting information for a tightly categorized field like high-tech. Still others may look for information that fits previously-established patterns, like intelligence agents. And finally, information brokers may look at information and try to draw new contextual conclusions from it, to see if the addition or subtraction of a factor influences the final results. This rather abstract concept is illustrated by the Visual Thesaurus, shown in Figure 19.3. You have to see it in action, though, to truly appreciate it.

FIGURE 19.3:

The Visual Thesaurus (`http://www.plumbdesign.com/thesaurus/`) is an excellent example of a tool that lets you manipulate information choices for unexpected outcomes.

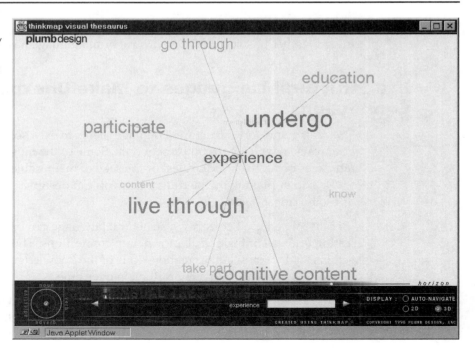

On the backend, you could use a set of simple scripts to rummage through your structural vocabulary and come up with new and unexpected connections. Or, you could use a set of scripts to find and publish specific pages for a user based on their past browsing history in your site. But these scripts will work a lot more effectively if you've got a strict set of parameters in which to work.

In other words, in order to add context to your content, you need to establish the parameters of that content. Structural languages offer an excellent point of reference, since they contain the informational metavocabulary that links all the information together.

And—because I can't leave a good metaphor alone—the low-maintenance results will be poetry to both your production staff and your users.

Moving Ahead Means Going Back to the Basics

Before you retrofit your entire site so you can visually analyze it or map the different types of information in a multimedia extravaganza, you should be warned. A lot of these future applications that demonstrate the synchronicity between structural languages and the information they hold are still very much in the planning stages.

In addition, a lot of the technologies mentioned, while being excellent ideas and good ways to make a lot of human-intensive work easier and more effective, have not yet adequately demonstrated an adequate return-on-investment. And don't forget that the technologies that drive widely adopted Web development tend to be quick, uncomplicated, and cheap: the gif89a set the tone for animated graphics on the Web because it was easy to build and the tools were available to everyone.

Until the tools for structural language optimization are as readily available as the shareware and open source that drive much of today's development, you're probably better off priming your site for information management by smartly implementing the existing structural language standards.

You can also start implementing knowledge management on an everyday level. The whole aim of knowledge management is to look for the shifts between patterns of information and try to figure out why these shifts appear; the answers often lead to new ideas or products. Start looking at the information patterns in your structural language to see what you can learn too.

Summary

This chapter highlighted the changing role structural languages will take in pushing your website production to the next level. We talked about structural languages as a tool for knowledge management, both for your final website product and for the behind-the-scenes code. We also talked about new diagnostic tools, like data visualization, and how information brokering may make generating your final site pages more intuitive.

The focus of all these future applications was on primarily text-based data, even if the results were visually oriented. For an alternate look at structural languages and how they apply to multimedia, read on.

CHAPTER
TWENTY

Exploring XML

- Understanding data structure

- Introducing XML

- Looking at possible implementations

- Overviewing XML tools

XML (Extensible Markup Language)has been hailed as the second coming for the Web. Like most divine phenomena, most of us get the big picture but are fuzzy on the details: XML is a big deal, but how is it going to work? More importantly, will it require you to convert your entire site?

This chapter takes some of the mystery out of XML. I outline what it is, how it assists in moving your site toward a data structure, and what is being done to customize it. Once you're done reading this chapter, you'll be able to see how XML can provide your site with extended functionality.

NOTE   This chapter provides you with an overview of XML and its capabilities. If you decide you'd like to learn more about XML, check out the soon-to-be-published *Mastering XML*, by Cheryl Kirk.

I'm also going to introduce a vital concept in this chapter: data structure. As different industries combine easy-to-build interfaces, readily accessible networks, and their own database systems, the demand to build intranets or websites that can let builders or users manipulate the contents of a site will increase. Mapping your site onto a data structure can ease the integration between old technologies, old website files, and third-party database systems. But before you can begin building the new supersite, you need to understand what a data structure is and how it provides an information model for site development.

Why XML Is Important

XML is important because it's a Web-based metalanguage with implications beyond the browser. Because XML is meant to provide developers with the means to develop specific data-organizing languages, it can be used in situations where the browser-plus-network configuration is flawed.

For example, XML will allow easier document transition between one format and another. If you've ever spent any time trying to replicate a formatted WordPerfect document in HTML, you can appreciate the need to come up with a file format that is equally functional for browsers, word processors, or graphics-layout programs. This is also known as media-independent publishing.

XML will also allow people and computers to exchange data without having to rely on a specific vendor. This increases the portability of data across networks and allows people who make their living manipulating and displaying data to access or distribute more material.

A third extra-Web use for XML is as the *lingua franca* for networked collaboration. Right now, the potential for a network to be used as a medium where several people can contribute data or authorship to a single project is greatly hampered. One obstacle is software—if people have different tools for accessing or contributing to the product, it will affect how work progresses. XML can preserve a lot of the work with little trouble and can be used as the conceptual backbone for building collaboration-specific tools.

But XML isn't meant to cue a great migration away from the Web; it's also giving Web developers the means to impose some order on the data flood around them and to integrate extra-Web activities into the Web. After all, why bother supporting Web technologies in your office unless you can use them to improve the ways you already do business?

XML can also be used to provide industry-dependent markup. The data structures specified and the terms defined in a DTD can be specific to a discipline. In the section titled "An Overview of XML Tools," we'll take a look at a number of applications, including three discipline-specific ones: MathML, CML, and BSML. These applications allow concepts and ideas that were previously difficult to depict in markup, like mathematical characters and molecular interactions, to be defined and invoked without using GIFs or other extra-textual methods.

Finally, XML will help poke holes in the barriers between desktop applications and Web-based data. This is not push media. Push media puts a network-connected document in a specific application on your desktop. XML works differently. It focuses on rendering an application according to its data structure, so the DTD that sets up the document in your local-network Web-formatted copy of a user manual will also render the same document reliably when you download it to your desktop and open it in a word processing document.

The remainder of this chapter will focus on integrating XML into websites and extending its powerful structural capabilities to everyday production.

Understanding Data Structure

Before you can appreciate why XML is such a big deal, it's necessary to explain the number one problem plaguing the Web as an informative medium: You can't find anything. Unlike a library, there is no central cataloguing system that imposes order on the items within.

In the world of computer programming, the idea of a card catalog for information has been adapted to meet programming parameters. Instead of writing a set of card catalog–like rules for handling information within a program, most programs rely on data structures. These data structures perform similar functions: they impose order and let you find ways to add or subtract data in an orderly manner.

So what is a data structure? A *data structure* is an abstract container for data. It's a handy way of thinking about how to group data and the first step toward imposing order on a big group of seemingly random items. It's primarily an interface for putting data in or taking it away. You tell data structures apart by their details; that is, by how you put data into or out of the structure. A data structure is the "big idea" model driving the way you organize data.

Since websites are moving from a text-library model of information cataloging to a more dynamic database-driven method, it makes sense to begin thinking of a site's organization and presentation in terms of data structures.

Envisioning your data structure is only a starting point; you also need to implement it. To do so, you use a markup scheme. A *markup scheme* is the definition of an internal structure. This differs from a markup language in that the scheme is the set of organizing principles for marking up a page, and the language is the nuts-and-bolts implementation. So when you're thinking of HTML, split it into two levels: the markup scheme would be the <h1>, <body>-driven hierarchical organization of data, and the markup language is the stylistic HTML you use to add appearance to the organization. Just shift your focus from the structure of a *page* to the structure of a *document*. The document may stretch out over several pages, so it's important to think of how you're organizing and rendering information from page to page.

Markup schemes describe data in *nodes, arcs,* and *internal methods*:

- Nodes contain data.

- Arcs connect nodes.

- Internal methods manipulate the nodes, like sorting them or deciding where they should go.

To make this a little less abstract, think of it this way: The content within a single Web page comprises a node. Hyperlinks connect different pages (nodes), and internal methods like server-side scripts and client-side scripts can change the order of nodes.

Now that you have an idea of the model programmers use when trying to figure out how to manipulate data, it's time to see how that model can be grafted onto Web development. The first step is to establish the vocabulary with which to build this model. That's where XML—which was created explicitly to provide a framework for data organization—comes into play.

Why XML Was Developed and What It Is

SGML, HTML, and XML are three distinct structural languages. HTML is actually a very abbreviated type of SGML, or Standard Generalized Markup Language. Figure 20.1 shows how the three languages are related.

FIGURE 20.1:

SGML, HTML, and XML are members of the same family tree.

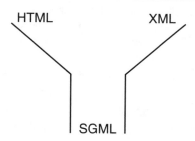

First Came SGML

SGML is a markup language. It predates HTML and is widely used in non-Web circles to create template-type markups. For example, in SGML, you can create a set of definitions, assign them to tags, then sprinkle the definitions throughout your document.

The beauty of SGML is threefold:

- It allows for highly complex and intelligent data-classification systems to be represented without much pain.

- It can adapt to additions or subtractions from that data-classification system.

- It is easy to maintain.

The drawbacks to SGML are equally weighty:

- SGML is a huge language, with many more unique tags than HTML.

- SGML is not nearly as flexible as HTML when it comes to linking.

- The rules that govern the behavior of SGML above data representation are complex and inconsistent.

- In order for an SGML organization structure to be understood, a DTD must be included.

- The limited back-and-forth linking and nonportability of SGML makes it less than ideal for markup of Web documents.

What Is a Document Type Definition (DTD)?

SGML is a powerful metalanguage because it can define data types and attributes that persist throughout a document. A persistent data type might be an unordered list, for example. But in order to do that, the SGML programmer needs to make sure those definitions hold throughout the file. To ensure that kind of consistency, programmers rely on something known as a *Document Type Definition* (*DTD*).

A DTD is a file that contains the formal definitions that describe the data markup of a document. It dictates what names will be used for different tags (also known as *elements*), how frequently elements can occur, and how various elements fit together. As a result, a DTD lets processors automatically parse a document and identify where every element goes and how it relates to other elements.

Setting up these elemental relationships is crucial if you want an application to be able to read and manipulate an SGML document and its data. A DTD that an SGML document uses can be useful if someone wants to print the document, display it electronically, index via a search engine, or break down the constituent parts into a database. Why? The DTD sets up the rules so any application that reads and recognizes SGML can reliably manipulate the document and the data.

SGML has DTDs because it is a language that can define new applications and meanings. As a result, there are a host of DTDs each geared toward specific applications and meanings.

Enter HTML

To address the problems inherent in SGML, developers created HTML. Focused on portable and consistent linking over several machines, HTML is a good way to physically render a document in several different physical locations. Unfortunately, the limited vocabulary of the language simply doesn't allow developers to establish or maintain consistent data structure representations. HTML allows you to map elements on a page, but how they're mapped has nothing to do with how they are cognitively related to each other. You can have four different blocks of text on a page, each enclosed in <p></p> tags, and there is no guarantee that there is any relationship between those blocks of text. In other words, you can sort books on labeled bookshelves, but there is no rule saying those books have to belong on the shelf where they're labeled.

So early Web developers faced a tricky dilemma: how could they build indexable documents, port them from one file format to another, preserve their topical organization independent of the file format, and still guarantee that users anywhere could read them? SGML has the data-organizing capacity, but its complex DTDs aren't very portable. HTML can guarantee semi-consistent end-user viewing, but it doesn't preserve a document's specific data structure.

NOTE   Because HTML does not have that application-definition ability, it only has one universal DTD.

Enter XML

Developed by the W3C with the specific purpose of quick client-side processing for any electronic publishing or data interchange, XML combines the discrete definitions found in SGML and the portability that makes HTML so useful.

NOTE   So think of HTML and XML as being different branches on the same SGML family tree. XML has inherited a lot of the same characteristics that make SGML a powerful data-depicting language.

XML is not really a development language. It's a *metalanguage* used to help develop other languages. XML provides a conceptual framework for organizing data into a coherent structure.

This conceptual framework is analogous to an outline. It provides a way for large-scale Web developers to set up an industry-specific language that reflects the vocabulary and data hierarchies established in the industry. For example, CML, the Chemical Markup Language, which I will cover in more detail later in the chapter, is an XML language specifically tailored to meet the data representation of different chemistry-related ideas and terms.

As shown in Figure 20.2, XML works by specifying three different parts of a language:

- The most basic part is an *entity*. An entity is a storage unit that contains parsed data. Parsed data contains the other two parts of an XML-specified language: character data and markup data.

- *Character data* describes the actual content of a document.

- *Markup data* describes the logical structure of a document, the way the document is stored, organized, and laid out.

FIGURE 20.2:

The three parts of an XML language

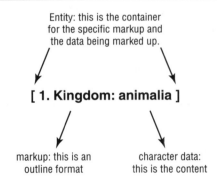

In the rest of this chapter, I'll focus on the various ways that XML can organize an outline and represent data within a structure.

XML and Document Type Definitions (DTDs)

XML can work with or without a DTD. However, in order for an XML-formatted document to be read without a DTD (a *DTDless file*), the document must be *well-formed*. This means that it sticks to a general set of basic rules about XML's basic structure, instead of creating and following a specific organization-driven set of rules.

Physical Structure and Logical Structure: What's the Difference?

The logical structure of a document is not the same thing as the physical structure of a document. A logical structure tells an XML processor and application how to organize the different parts of a document across different electronic media. The structure exists independently of a medium. You can write an outline:

I. Headline

   A. Topic 1

     1. Sub-topic 1

   B. Topic 2

The way the two topics are organized stays the same whether or not the outline appears in a word processor document or on a napkin you scribbled on during lunch.

Those organizing principles—Roman numerals first, then capital letters, then numbers—do not change, regardless of what physical media is used to "fix" content organized under the outlines.

Just as outlines provide a way to organize ideas on any type of surface that you can write on, and library card catalogs provide a way to organize books in any library space, XML provides a way to organize documents independently of how they'll appear.

A document marked up with XML is like an outline. You can make the outline show up in red text on a white computer screen, or you can print it out in black text on a yellow sheet of paper. No matter how the outline appears, the organization of the data within the outline will always be accurately reproduced.

To be a little more extreme: as long as you understand the order in which specific items within an outline are to be presented, you can write the outline in crayon on newsprint, or spell it out in seashells on a beach. The physical presentation does not affect the order of the items that are being presented.

To clarify: most HTML is neither well-formed nor valid, since it does not hew to the W3C's document type definition for the language. It can still be read by browsers, but there is no guarantee of how consistent the document appearance will be from site to site, nor is there any way to assign an organizational structure to the content within HTML tags.

XML written without a central document type definition may yield good-looking documents. However, those documents would not be valid or well-formed. Since the whole point to XML is to provide an organizational framework for information, why bother writing the documents without a DTD?

You don't have to custom-write a DTD every single time. But you do have to take care to make the document well-formed, or else it's completely unintelligible.

Any XML file that follows the rules listed below is well-formed:

- Any XML document that does not reference a DTD must open with a Standalone Document Declaration (SDD). An SDD is a one-line chunk of code that looks like this:

  ```
  <?XML version="1.0" standalone="yes"?>
  ```

- All the tags must be balanced. In other words, if you start a tag, close it. The only exception to this rule is an empty tag. For empty tags, which are analogous to HTML's `<IMG>` or `<HR>` tags, you have two choices: close the tag with a slash within the tag like this `<IMG/>`, or add a closing tag like this `<IMG></IMG>`.

- Any tag that has value-driven attributes must be written so the attribute is in quotes. For example, the tag `<IMG border=0>` features three parts: the tag definition IMG, the attribute `border`, and the attribute value 0. So to write a well-formed image tag, you'd rewrite this tag as `<IMG border="0"/>`.

- Elements can nest, but you cannot overlap nesting on any element. Because SGML and HTML already forbid this, remembering this rule is easy.

- No markup character can stand alone. You're already used to thinking about the < and > characters as markup characters, and know that for HTML-reading applications to render them properly as a piece of content, they have to be coded as < and >. But other XML markup characters include ' (apostrophes), " (quotation marks), and & (ampersands), so if you want to type the sentence:

  ```
  <caption>"The image at the right is titled 'A sample & an
  example',"</caption>
  ```

you would have to type it like this:

```
<caption>&quote; The image at the right is titled &apos;A sample
&amp; an example&apos;&quot;</caption>
```

Once you've mastered the art of the well-formed XML document, it's time to conquer valid XML documents. A valid XML document is a well-formed XML document with a bonus: it also has a DTD that defines the informational meaning and organizational roles each tag plays.

Any valid XML document begins with a two-line declaration:

```
<?XML version="1.0"?>
<!DOCTYPE advert SYSTEM "your_DTD_here.dtd">
```

The first line advises applications that the document adheres to the XML 1.0 spec, and the second line tells the application where the document's DTD lives.

To recap: an XML document can live without a DTD so long as it is *well-formed*. But for an XML document to be valid, it must also have a DTD.

The Document Object Model (DOM)

The Document Object Model (DOM) is a different specification than XML. The DOM provides developers with an interface for defining how data is accessed, added, or manipulated in a document. (See Chapter 11 for more information on the DOM.)

The important thing to know now is that the DOM works *with* XML so developers can write scripts that allow users to interact with data in a standard way. For example, a developer could write a script specifying that all elements in the data category <alphabet> are to be displayed in 18-point blue type. If a user clicks on a page displaying the <A> item from the <alphabet> category, the way item <A> is displayed is the same as items <B>, <C>, or <D>.

Another example is the onMouseOver property that can be attached to an anchor tag. Whenever a browser reads a tag like the following:

```
<A HREF="work/resume.html" onMouseOver="(window.status='Click here to
see what a smart website is'); return true">
```

it knows that the action onMouseOver is a standard action that can be taken on the object <A>.

So the DOM provides Web developers with a way to manipulate specific XML or HTML elements. It is both platform-neutral and language-neutral, which is perfect for the type of application programming typical to the Web. The DOM is fairly straightforward: It provides a standard set of objects that can be mapped to XML or HTML documents, rules for combining or manipulating these objects, and an interface for mere mortals to access and control how these objects work on a page.

As of this writing, both Netscape and Microsoft bundled proprietary DOMs into their 4.0 browser but promise to conform to the W3C specification when they release their 5.0 browsers. Once they adopt that, people can develop applications based on the DOM instead of a product-specific application programming interface. This will undo some of the browser-war, dual-development damage that developers have had to sustain for the last three years.

How XML Will Be Implemented across the Web

XML will be used to perform that all-important separation between content and appearance. It's the important first step in divorcing the way a document (and by extension, a website) is organized from the way it is marked up for appearance.

XML will be used in a few different ways. In addition to the data structure definition it permits, it will be used for two different types of data exchange:

- The first type of data exchange is one Web developers are most used to dealing with—data exchange between humans and machines.

- The second type of data exchange is the behind-the-Web communication between two different machines.

Because both types of data exchanges will appropriate a set of structural rules (the XML structure), they'll rely on a series of steps to implement XML documents via a website. An ideal setup would have a nonpublic data exchange where data is stored in data tables, a server that matches the data with the specifications set forth in the XML structures defined by the site, a final server that pulls the structured data with a corresponding set of formatting tags, and finally a client that reads the information and presents it to the human user.

How Browsers Read XML

Browsers that read XML can do so because they're equipped with a software bundle called an *XML processor*. A processor passes the XML data to the application (in this case, the browser) so the application can read and interpret the data for the user. Remember: XML is not a development language, it is a metalanguage that sets up structure.

How Netscape Navigator Handles XML

Netscape is responding to the XML standard with a two-pronged implementation. The most basic implementation is an XML processor that reads RDF; future releases of Netscape are supposed to include a generalized XML processor that recognizes any standard XML application.

The second component of Netscape's XML implementation is a desktop integration component, code-named Aurora. Aurora is a windowpane on a user's desktop that finds, manages, and displays files that relate to user-specified data types. The feature that makes Aurora an integration component, as opposed to Windows Explorer, is that it works across several different degrees of connectivity. So if you're working on a proposal, your Aurora window might pull up files from your desktop, the company intranet, and the Internet that all have data structure tags matching the ones specified in your report.

How Microsoft Internet Explorer Handles XML

Mercifully, both the browser-market giants are adopting W3C XML standards in their later browser versions. In fact, Microsoft is already slightly ahead of the game, having included a pair of XML processors in its summer 1997 release of Internet Explorer 4.0.

Why two different XML processors? One is a parser written in the programming language C++; this parser is bundled into the browser. The second processor is a Java-based package that Web builders can download and use in building applications. The Java processor functions as a validating processor, checking a document's DTD against files.

Both processors are nonspecific, meaning they aren't dependent on a specific implementation of XML (like RDF or CDF) to work well. But Microsoft does bundle in a host of Microsoft-specific tools to read and manipulate XML data. Among these tools are the XML Data Source Object, which helps bind XML to DHTML, and the XML Object Model (XML OM). The XML OM is not the same as the Document Object Model; instead, the XML OM works to expose HTML as objects based on a DOM. This way, developers can manipulate XML-defined objects in a browser.

NOTE   Microsoft doesn't plan on keeping XML-processing ability restricted to their browser. Bill Gates has already stated that he intends to incorporate XML support into Microsoft Office.

Using Software Tools to Write XML

Most of the big players in Web software have incorporated XML authoring tools in their Web authoring applications. These companies and applications are listed below:

Company	Application
Adobe	Framemaker and Framemaker+SGML will export and import XML documents.
Allaire	HomeSite 3.0 already supports CDF, an XML application. Full XML support will be incorporated in both HomeSite 4.0 and ColdFusion 4.0. Both HomeSite and ColdFusion support SMIL, or Synchronized Multimedia Integration Language, with tag packs. Allaire also has its own XML subset in the works.
ArborText	XML Styler, a free, Java-based XML editor has been on the market since January 1998. This styler will also be integrated into their print publishing tool, Adept.
Inso	The company provides a whole host of XML-driven editors, all of which are prefaced with Dyna-. They include DynaTag, DynaBase, DynaText, and DynaWeb.
Microsoft	The only public support Microsoft has shown for an XML editor is a statement that MS Office 2000, due out at the end of 1998, will support XML.
SoftQuad	HotMetal Pro is offering a feature called Live Data Base Pages; this feature will allow developers to drop and drag HTML on an interface and have it converted to XML. They've also developed a markup language: HMML, or HotMetal Markup Language.

Company	Application
Vignette	StoryServer 3.2 has tools that allow a developer to merge relational database items, multimedia, and XML-enabled webpages. It is worth noting that Vignette's offering falls under the heading of content-serving software rather than Web page editor, but since an ability to build and edit HTML/XML is a part of the software, it's included on this list.
WebMethods	The company has developed a Web Interface Definition Language (WIDL) that automates HTML-to-XML interactions.

Implementing XML on Servers

Because XML is meant to set up long-lived and persistent data structure libraries, it can be written in ways that allow for easy storage on servers. For example, you can write an XML document composed of different entities with each entity living in a different file, and the document will still reassemble when needed. You can also set aside a server that acts as an XML repository. In order to read and assemble XML entities in any format you will need server software that is capable of supporting XML.

As of this writing, a number of commercial server-software vendors supported XML, including Enigma's Insight 4.0, Hynet Technologies' Digital Library System, OpenMarket's Folio, and WebMethods' Web Automation Server. As the 5.0 browsers hit the market, the market for server software that supports XML will grow.

How XML Will Improve Interface Performance

If implemented according to the W3C standard, XML will solve many of the problems that plague website (not Web *page*, but web*site*) development. The over-arching problem in site development is that HTML doesn't allow a clear separation of data structure and data rendering.

In other words, HTML inextricably entwines interface and data organization. As a result, two elements of data interface—links to other documents, and stylistic rendering of a document—are often weakened by the fact that they are embedded in the same code that dictates the structure of the document. Therefore, if you wanted to rearrange the document structure to reflect additions or subtractions from your site, you also run the risk of affecting the style of the document and the intra-document links.

The key to reducing intra-site decay is to separate linking and styles from data structure. But since hypertext linking is an integral part of HTML, how do you separate linking from the document structure?

Easy: appropriate the XML linking scheme, known as *Extensible Linking Language* (*XLL*). This language allows you to treat linking as a functional object. You can separate link properties from the documents they appear in and maintain them separately.

NOTE   Various naming structures have been bandied about, but as of June 1998, it appears that the label XLL will persist and perhaps become the name of a new working group for XML linking. The XLL design work has already been subdivided into two components: XLink and XPointer, explained below.

Improving Hyperlinking via XLL

The XLL specification is designed to add functionality to linking, and to enhance a Web developer's ability to facilitate hyperlinking without high maintenance overhead. XLL was originally one specification, but it has since split off into two distinct specifications.

The first spec is *XLink* (*XML Linking Language*). This specification adds specific interface behavior to a hypertext link. Before XLink, if you wanted a description of the link to appear when a user passed the mouse over the link, or if you wanted a new window to pop up and load a document that had been referenced, you needed to either attach a target tag to the link (which launched a new window but gave developers no control over the window size, appearance, or name for future link-targeting) or use JavaScript to carefully control the linking behavior to a limited degree. XLink allows developers to define behavior for links by class, providing the mechanism for applying different sets of behaviors such as a secondary viewer window popping up on the first user mouseover of a hyperlink, and that window being a persistent feature of an article's hyperlinking.

The second part of the XLL split is called *XPointer* (*XML Pointing Language*). This refines the targeting capabilities of a hyperlink. Currently, if you want to send a reader to the middle of a document, you need to specify both the document and a target link within the document. (For example, `<A HREF="foo.html#endpoint">` tells the browser to load the file `foo.html` and then jump to the target called `endpoint`.) This works well if you only want to link to specific areas within your own site, but it doesn't work at all if you want to link to a specific (but unanchored) area of someone else's document.

Suppose you want to put a link on your site to someone else's directory page listing your site as their all-time favorite. If their directory file is 100k, and you're at the bottom, you've just provided your readers with a link to a wild goose chase. However, with XPointer, you can provide your link-jumpers with a specific address within the document, so the new page loads and displays right at the point you intended without depending on the kindness of strangers.

Extended linking behavior is only one facet of XLL and its specifications. Part of XLL still treats hypertext links as separate objects, therefore giving Web developers the ability to maintain links independently of the structural code that glues them into a document.

Extending Style Sheet Functionality via XSL

The other bugbear of Web interface building is that HTML leaves little room to cleanly separate an object's rendering attributes from the object itself. *Cascading Style Sheets* (*CSS*) are one effort to conquer this problem and make an excellent solution for any large-scale website that demands fine-tuned or frequent interface designs. For more information on how to implement CSS, see Chapter 6.

XML also recognizes the usefulness of developing standard styles and attaching those styles to specific named objects. Its style sheets specification, *Extensible Style Language* (*XSL*), takes CSS characteristics and runs.

XSL ultimately gives developers increased ability to program their site to self-modify its appearance. Remember how conditional HTML works: if the value of a variable is A, then B happens; if the value of the variable is C, then D happens. XSL allows you to link style characteristics to an object and then change those styles if the value of an object changes.

For example, you might write an XSL that says, "If an `<address>` starts with A, then make the text red; if not, make it black." If you attached that XSL to a database that backs a dynamic website, you've guaranteed the appearance of randomly accessed data without having to write complex subroutines anywhere in the data assembly and display scripts. The modularity XSL offers makes it just as easy as CSS if you want to change, add, or delete a set of styles from a site, yet it has data-handling abilities currently available only if you want to link CSS to JavaScript events and objects.

Creating Tools That Allow Customizable Applications over the Web

Remember to think of XML as a metalanguage. Think of it as the functional alphabet for writing data-handling sentences. These sentences are separate XML-based applications unto themselves. The remainder of the chapter focuses on areas where there is a demand for structured language definitions and transactions and then on some of the applications being spec'd out and built.

XML and E-Commerce

One of the chief barriers to smoothly implementing commerce over the World Wide Web has been the lack of standardization between different vendors and the lack of a common "alphabet" for data exchange between different catalogs and payment systems. This type of standardization is important if businesses are to make their customer–business and business–business transactions work uniformly.

Two ways to break down that barrier are to define the content that is to be exchanged between businesses and customers and to define the types of exchanges that take place between customers and businesses. This is where XML comes in: it allows businesses to define a common set of vocabulary terms and to write "sentences" that state the different types of transactions that take place.

CommerceNet, a 500-member nonprofit organization dedicated to Web commerce, is trying to define the data elements that compose different business transactions: things like price, tax, item inventory number, and so on. It is also trying to define information exchange. Because this exchange involves a transfer of data between two servers, using a common metadata scheme will allow these two servers to establish that they are talking about the same products or service transactions. CommerceNet has proposed *Common Business Language* (*CBL*) to describe product catalogs, server catalogs, business rules, and business terms.

CommerceNet hopes to eventually base all of its business protocols on CBL, which in turn is based on XML. Some of those specific business protocols are listed in the "Open Financial Exchange (OFX)" and "Open Trading Protocol (OTP)" sections below.

Although most of the press emphasis for XML has been on Web development, XML is also useful for facilitating use of the Web above and beyond development. Commerce applications are an example of how savvy Web development can foster informational transactions that do not take place within the World Wide Web.

XML and Software Application Development

The Web is a great place to find shareware, and it's a great place to display browser-hosted software. However, there isn't a good vocabulary for telling different servers and clients what sorts of characteristics the software package has. For example, does the software package rely on user-initiated action to start working, or does it start working on download? How do the different parts of the software work functionally? What platform was the code written for?

Some of the XML tools listed below focus on how to clearly label software so computer clients and users can run the software without trouble. This ultimately extends the functions that you can perform within a Web-like environment and provides yet another argument for using the Web as more than a point-and-click window.

An Overview of XML Tools

The remaining sections give brief overviews of different types of XML applications. They're meant to point out the extra-Web applications that a common development protocol can facilitate.

Bioinformatic Sequence Markup Language (BSML)

Biologists have been using the Internet to collaborate for years, but a frustrating aspect of working in an electronic medium is that there is no uniform protocol for creating and depicting graphics-based information.

A proposed panacea is *Bioinformatic Sequence Markup Language* (*BSML*), an XML-based protocol that defines and describes graphic objects used to represent different aspects of genetic biology.

BSML provides a specification outlining the vocabulary to be used when a developer wants to encode or display DNA, RNA, or protein sequences. DNA, RNA, and protein are three distinct types of molecules used in genetic expression; the order in which the molecules' parts are arranged is called the sequence.

The specification includes directions for depicting unique sequence features within a DNA, RNA, or protein sequence and directions on how to assign different graphics to different sequence features. Like a lot of other XML-driven tools, BSML also includes directions on how to store marked-up information and how to transmit that information so it can reliably be read on another machine.

NOTE   Not surprisingly, the organization that is spearheading the effort to read and map the human genome is also partially responsible for the BSML effort. The National Center for Genomic Research, which is part of the United States government's National Institutes of Health, gave the company TopoGEN funding via a small business research grant, which TopoGEN then used to begin developing BSML.

Channel Definition Format (CDF)

Channel Definition Format (*CDF*) is an XML application that acts as a recipe for push media. It allows Web developers to write a file that acts as a programming guide for pre-timed Web cruising.

Push media is a type of Web viewing that differs from the usual point-and-click. Although people using pushed websites (called *channels*) still have the option to click and follow a hypertext link, the delivery of the site is completely different. A 4.0 version of Netscape or Microsoft Internet Explorer allows users to display channels on their desktop in kiosk mode, meaning that the traditional button-and-scrollbar interface is replaced with a screen like a CD-ROM, and the Web channel content is sent from the server to the client over time, as opposed to the viewer actively requesting pages. The client requests are pre-set in the CDF, and sent to the server within the time settings that the file specifies.

From a user's perspective, push media is similar to PointCast. From a developer's perspective, the two are very different: PointCast requires a separate server, and it is developed using a different type of data representation language. The parts of a push media channel can be programmed using a combination of CSS, HTML, and scripting.

A CDF specifies the group of files that should be pushed to a client; it also tells how frequently new files or updates to old files should be pushed, and it sets up a regular schedule for pushing a Web channel package to a client.

One helpful analogy for a CDF is the American publication *TV Guide*. This publication lists what programs are on a specific network (like MTV) and what date and time new editions of the programs are going to be aired. CDFs do the same thing for Web files.

Chemical Markup Language (CML)

Chemistry, like biology, needs standard, consistent graphic protocols. The study of chemistry also relies heavily on graphic models to demonstrate different elements and theories in research, and also uses the Internet as a tool in conducting research.

Therefore, *Chemical Markup Language* (*CML*) was created as an object-based XML language meant to depict molecular and technical information within the chemistry discipline. CML combines XML and Java to depict graphical relationships between molecules and to show the technical characteristics associated with molecules and chemical reactions.

Like BSML, CML puts a lot of emphasis on transporting complex information models between two different machines and in making sure the methods for encoding the information are machine-independent so the data can be read virtually anywhere.

ColdFusion Markup Language (CFML)

One of the only XML proposals to be driven by a specific commercial product, *ColdFusion Markup Language* (*CFML*) is an XML-compliant system meant to work within Allaire's ColdFusion website assembly product.

CFML is a generalized markup language with tags that ColdFusion recognizes as it assembles separate CFML-written components into a cohesive Web page. The goal behind CFML is to build a system-specific vocabulary for building reusable Web parts and writing rules for assembling Web parts.

Unlike a lot of the XML specs mentioned here, CFML is a server-side-only assembly tool; it is not meant to represent data during a system-to-system data exchange. Think of CFML as being analogous to virtual includes: it's a tool with its own vocabulary, and it's only visible as such to the developer.

Encoded Archival Description Standard (EAD)

Electronically archiving information seems like a good idea but the practice can be challenging. Different methods of data recording can become obsolete over time and don't always transfer easily from one data reading mechanism to another. To address this problem, the United States Library of Congress has been working with other research institutions to develop the Encoded Archival Description Standard (EAD).

EAD works by providing archivists and indexers with a way to standardize common information management tools like inventories, indexes, guides, and registries. EAD was initially a set of SGML markup tags, so there was an EAD DTD that libraries and research institutions used to define and encode their archival material. The EAD DTD defined the terms to be used in building an archive metadata structure and specified ways to display documents conforming to the EAD DTD, including on-the-fly HTML translation. Then along came XML: as a result, the EAD Working Group is currently working on making the EAD DTD fully compliant with XML as well as SGML.

HTTP Distribution and Replication Protocol (DRP)

Not all XML applications focus on how to define data relationships. Some actually work on refining the protocols that machines use to talk to each other. HTTP *Distribution and Replication Protocol (DRP)* is aiming at improving the way data is distributed over HTTP.

NOTE For a refresher on HTTP, visit Chapter 5.

DRP aims at making data transfer more efficient and more reliable in several ways:

- It uses an RDF-based index to define the metadata driving a data exchange.

- It sets up unique content identifiers in the URI, thus giving each piece of data its own unique ID.

- It bundles in an index format to describe a group of files (think of this as the data equivalent of a folder display in Windows or on a Mac).

- It provides the HTTP with two new header fields. The first new header field is Content-ID, which offers a version number and therefore a built-in checkpoint for the most recent version of the information being transferred. The second new HTTP header is Differential-ID, which tells servers to obtain differential updates when needed.

Internet Content and Exchange (ICE)

Plenty of Web industry headlines bemoan the alphabet soup of standards proposals and ask, "Why can't we be friends?" One proposed standard is trying to answer that question.

Like the other specs we've discussed, *Internet Content and Exchange (ICE)* is a standard being developed to help companies exchange large, structured chunks of data. What makes ICE special is that it seeks to provide a common vocabulary for trading online assets like content, the metadata organizing content, or the applications that assemble content for the client.

ICE is a standard to look for; as Web sites become increasingly object-oriented and the backend becomes composed of lots of little parts and conditional assembly instructions, finding a way to download or exchange those parts is going to take high priority. The standard also bears watching because it is heavily backed by Microsoft and Vignette, both companies having an active interest in how data is organized and delivered via website.

Java Speech Markup Language (JSML)

The visually disabled rely on a suite of Web development tools to read Web pages aloud. These development tools read in a monotone that can make them difficult to understand.

Java Speech Markup Language (JSML) provides authors with the ability to annotate JSML-prepared text and thus add inflections, specific word pronunciations, special emphasis on words, and pauses in delivery. It also allows developers to control the rate that the data on a page is spoken and to control the pitch of a speaking voice. Clearly, JSML has applications in aural usability that parallel the use of color or spacing in visual information organization.

JSML is an iteration of a previous initiative, the Java Speech API. Whereas the API only provides a recommended production environment, JSML decided to adopt XML as its metalanguage, for the following reasons:

- APIs are generally not read by humans. Because JSML is built using XML as its metalanguage, both humans and machines can read and understand it.

- JSML can be used to write text anywhere, outside a specific development environment.

- JSML is easy for a speech synthesizer to parse.

Mathematical Markup Language (MathML)

One of the first proposed XML tools to be promoted from proposal to specification, *Mathematical Markup Language (MathML)* is meant to describe mathematical notation and the underlying organizational principles behind representing math via symbols.

At first glance, there may not seem to be much need for this because numbers and basic arithmetic symbols are all ASCII-specified. However, complex calculations often have symbols unique to the mathematical fields, and the way those calculations are represented often determines the sequence of steps used to illustrate why and how those calculations work. Before MathML, mathematicians and engineers who wanted to accurately depict their calculations had to resort to an odd combination of HTML and graphics.

MathML is a metalanguage, based on XML, that gives Web developers a way to accurately depict both mathematical notation and mathematical content. It provides tools for describing a math structure and for specifying how that structure is meant to be interpreted. This way, complex mathematical concepts can be represented and transferred from machine to machine, allowing the math to be read regardless of platform and regardless of how many times it's been transferred.

MathML is meant to be used mostly by machines as a tool for searching and indexing large collections of math data.Humans will read MathML-encoded data using software packages that render MathML into data humans can understand.

Open Buying on the Internet (OBI)

Open Buying on the Internet (*OBI*) is a protocol that outlines and specifies business-to-business transactions over a network. These are the types of transactions that you as a Web surfer might not see but may need to become fluent in if you're developing a corporate or financial Web system. One example of a business-to-business transaction is an automatic payment from your bank account to your student loan holder.

OBI is currently based on several already existing standards, including Secure Socket Layers (SSL) and HTML. Because OBI is backed by big names like Microsoft, Netscape, Oracle, Commerce One, and Open Market, it may be around for a while even though all documentation is vague about any XML implementation.

Open Financial Exchange (OFX)

A financial specification that predates XML, *Open Financial Exchange* (*OFX*) was based on part of SGML (XML's parent language) and developed to provide a *lingua franca* for the online transfer of financial data. OFX's chief backers are Microsoft, Intuit, and CheckFree; the three companies used OFX to integrate their banking and payment protocols.

OFX deviates sharply from XML in its syntax. XML requires closing tags for every opening tag, and OFX does not. However, most XML parsers should be able to read OFX without requiring an OFX DTD, and the people who develop OFX are reportedly thinking about restoring closing tags to make the protocol more closely XML-compliant.

Open Software Description Format (OSD)

Open Software Description Format (*OSD)* is aiming to become the jargon that varied software packages use to describe themselves to others. As more shareware and freeware proliferate on the Web and as users increasingly rely on the Web for trial versions of software to buy, clearly labeling software and its developmental dependencies will become important. Labeling that software with a set of common tags is the best idea.

Enter OSD. It sets up the vocabulary that describes software to itself and others. Components of OSD include software version number, the underlying structure that pulls the different components of a software package together, descriptions of those different software components, and platform-specific code for different operating systems. Having this type of information can make integrating a new software package on a local desktop less risky and more efficient for the user. And that's a powerful motivating factor for software developers who are aiming for the net market.

An extra bonus is that OSD can specify how software is delivered to the user's desktop. In an ideal world, that means that software upgrades, or specific platform installation, will be possible without redundant installations and extra files.

Open Trading Protocol (OTP)

One of the proposed business-based XML tools, *Open Trading Protocol* (*OTP*) is a proposal meant to facilitate consumer transactions on the Web. The idea behind OTP is to build a set of common tools that allows Web-based vendors to offer sales items, provide different payment methods, record and offer receipts, set product delivery into motion, and record transactions for future reference.

What this proposal translates into for Web developers is a vocabulary they can use to build the forms that act as the interface for online commerce and to define the under-form data transactions between machines. The idea behind OTP is to remove any proprietary features or platform-specific requirements from the interface people use to conduct any online buying. Removing such features and requirements will provide a crucial difference between Internet commerce systems built using OTP and closed software or online services systems that rely on a particular software package, like Quicken's bill paying service.

Not surprisingly, OTP is backed by a number of financial companies, including DigiCash, CyberCash, and MasterCard International.

Precision Graphics Markup Language (PGML)

Most of the graphics users see on the Web are actually small files called into and embedded into a HTML file. These files, usually GIFs, JPEGs, or PNGs, are separate ways of building an image out of really long strings of octet-value data. Each type of file extension represents a different way of encoding data.

Although embedding a GIF or JPEG into a document is painless, there are two problems with it from a data-development point of view. First, there is no way to embed the image file directly into the HTML file it is modifying, and second, there is no way to tag the image file to let a metadata structure know where it fits into the overall data scheme. Even if GIFs or JPEGs are wrapped in a `<div>` that can be used as a data label, they're not part of the file; and even if they were, there is currently no mechanism to separate the graphics-rendering data and interpret it within the page.

That's where *Precision Graphics Markup Language* (*PGML*) comes in. It is a vector graphics specification that provides Web developers with the tools to represent an image within a Web page and specify the behavior of that image. Vector graphics were chosen because they are composed of mathematical descriptions of the points, lines, curves, and angles that define a graphic. Those mathematical descriptions can tell a viewer how to best render that graphic for human viewing.

The same mathematical descriptions that allow a viewer to assemble a graphic also allow developers to look at the graphic as being composed of several discrete parts. Developers can then grab those different parts and attach motion, color change, or other dynamic effects to them.

PGML is the first specification for vector-based graphics. It uses XML to define those curves, lines, points, and angles that comprise a vector graphic; XML also allows developers using PGML to plot elaborate animations using the DOM and predefined PGML components.

In a nutshell, PGML is the first standard to allow developers to embed images into the very files that display them and to attach data-ready labels to those images, thus solving the biggest problems in treating images as part of a site's metadata structure.

Resource Description Framework (RDF)

Resource Description Framework (*RDF*) is a data modeling application that is created by using the XML structure and syntax. RDF focuses exclusively on data—how it is described, modeled, and accessed. RDF is basically a data language that talks about other data. In human terms, RDF is like using the letters of the alphabet to write an essay about the alphabet.

It is useful to have a data language about data because RDF can be used to impose order on an otherwise chaotic site. In more abstract terms, RDF is a tool for describing content and content relationships.

You'll be able to assign and maintain a sitewide data hierarchy so that both robots and humans can tell how every piece of data relates to every other piece of data on your site. You can create a content classification system that allows your site to be more accurately indexed by search engines; your users will be able to know exactly what they're looking at and how it fits into the scheme of the site at large. You can also set up a hierarchical site index by using RDF to define the types of data at each level in the hierarchy, or you can use RDF to create a site map composed of several uniquely typed nodes (see Figure 20.3).

FIGURE 20.3:

A site map created with RDF

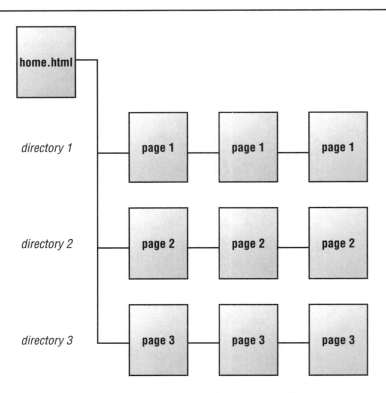

(note: these are all html files)

Ultimately, RDF should be able to influence the cross-platform, cross-everything ability of an application to work. Its goal is to provide a set of data properties that stay persistent under a wide variety of conditions.

Synchronized Multimedia Integration Language (SMIL)

Synchronized Multimedia Integration Language (*SMIL*, pronounced *smile*) recently graduated from proposal to W3C proposed recommendation, indicating that it is fast on its way to becoming a standard for Web developers struggling with porting multimedia to the Web.

Although the Web has been touted as the ideal medium in which to publish or experience multimedia enhancements to plain data, the reality is sharply different. A mishmash of conflicting graphics, motion, and sound standards, combined with a number of proprietary software tools and file extensions, mixed in with frequently slow bandwidth, have all combined to slow wide-scale distribution of multimedia as an integral component of a Web site.

SMIL aims to change that by providing two tools:

- An HTTP form that will tell client and server exactly what sort of data to expect and how to present it.

- An XML DTD to identify the different objects in a multimedia presentation and specify how those objects relate to each other.

The ultimate operating goal for SMIL is to integrate disparate multimedia objects like sound, images, and animation into a synchronized presentation. SMIL will provide developers with a way to mix and match some of those standards to reach a wider possible audience and to stop using one type of software to produce multimedia.

NOTE   For more information on SMIL, see Chapter 21.

Web Interface Definition Language (WIDL)

Web Interface Definition Language (*WIDL*) is currently a small XML tool implemented primarily by its authoring company, WebMethods. Billed by its developers as defining a universal schema for HTML documents based on the Document Object Model, WIDL is seeking to define the way Web server interactions can be accessed and manipulated.

WIDL aims to provide a way for developers who are working with a wide number of Web servers in different locations to integrate those servers into one workable protocol. It provides an XML-based metalanguage to develop an API that developers can use to refine their Web server programming and services.

If a Web developer lives in Raleigh, North Carolina and wants to run a maintenance script on an intranet based in San Jose, California, she currently has to telnet to the remote network and work there. WIDL hopes to provide an interface that allows her to treat the intranet in San Jose as a net-accessible interface. The input and output protocols are defined as objects in the XML metalanguage, and WIDL also provides a way to control those objects over standard Internet protocols like HTTP.

WIDL will permit developers to perform service-based programming like error repair and system maintenance, and it will also allow them to map a site as a series of functional objects that can be acted on with the service-based programming.

XML-Data

One of the first things people learn when they venture into the morass of specifications and data modeling for the World Wide Web is that there is data, and then there is information about data.

The former, actual data, is usually referred to as an *object*. Objects exist as discrete entities, although they may encompass child objects. You can think of the object as a pea pod and the child objects as peas. The pod is an object by itself, yet the peas within are also objects in their own right. The pod has a set of characteristics: it is flattish, long, and not too edible. The peas have a set of characteristics: they're round, small, and edible. Yet despite dissimilar characteristics, the pea and the pod are related. We call the relationship between the pea and the pod a *schema*.

XML-Data seeks to give Web developers the means to talk about peas and pea pods (objects and object schemata). There are two major categories of object schemata:

- The first is *syntactic schemata*, which describes objects with a vocabulary of defining terms, like XML.

- The second is *conceptual schemata*, which describes the relationships and concepts that tie objects together, like RDF.

The advantage to defining common schemata is that it provides a starting framework for moving large chunks of information over networks, thus helping build a context for clients to replicate the intended objects and relationships in whatever software tool they need to.

XML/Electronic Data Interchanger (XML/EDI)

Some of the data exchanges described in this chapter are highly industry-specific and address specific problems, but a larger issue still looms over the Web: How can developers create and maintain a data system that can move from network node to network node and be understood by all the participants?

For example, if six small subsidiary companies all have their own human resources departments and software packages, how would it be possible for the parent company to collect and compile the total data for the subsidiary companies' health insurance claims?

Electronic Data Interchange (*EDI*) provides a dictionary of standard message formats and their elements, and by defining those elements, provides the basis for a standard format that can be used to describe different types of data.

So if XML and EDI are combined, they'll work like the Rosetta Stone of paperwork, allowing things like loan applications, project reports, health care claims, and vehicle registration to move from machine to machine and system to system where they can be reliably formatted and read.

Summary

Right now, a lot of the promised XML tools seem like "vaporware." Critics of XML may counter that instead of developing *lingua francas* that address accurate information representation across several platforms, we're really creating proprietary languages and transferring the incompatibility problem from machines to networks.

But XML is still in its infancy as a Web standard, and it will provide a much-needed tool for helping map out and represent data within the website. XML also has a number of features going for it that make it a good language for building flexible products. Those features include:

Simplicty   The XML spec is all of forty pages long. It's easier to write in than HTML or SGML.

Extensibility   XML allows you to invent your own tags (via a DTD) and create data representations that you feel most accurately reflect your site's organizational scheme and content.

Efficiency XML is built to allow you to re-use fragments and definitions. Think of it as a sort of meta-include.

Non-propriety XML is a subset of SGML, an international standard. Therefore, nobody owns XML, so you won't have to worry about any upstart Web companies tacking on tags that only work with their product.

History Because XML is part of SGML, there are already a host of software tools out there that can author, read, or deliver XML-based products.

Already been tested XML can be read and rendered by browsers as-is. It's the discipline-specific XML applications that are still being integrated.

Non-nationalistic XML supports most of the world's alphabets and provides an area for specifying what language and ISO-standard alphabet your document is written in.

XML is a stepping stone for websites trying to move from a simulacra of paper to a truly hypertextual, data-organized presentation tool.

Think of learning XML as another round of learning how to read. Just like letters make up alphabets, individual tags make up DTDs. And just as you mix and match letters to make up words, you can mix and match tags to assign a specific meaning to a concept.

Eventually, XML will be as basic to the Web as ABC is to American schoolchildren. It's a building block for bigger, more extensible concepts.

CHAPTER
TWENTY-ONE

Future Looks, Future Sounds: Multimedia for the Cutting Edge

- Getting to know multimedia markup

- Understanding VRML, ASF, RTSP, and SMIL

- Putting SMIL to work

There's a line in a song somewhere that goes "everything old is new again." One of the most amusing applications of this might be in porting content to a networked collection of computers.

Originally, HTML was the glue that bound the Web together, the great leveler between different computers, different Web-viewing tools, and different skill levels. But competing browser models and increasingly complex methods of shuffling and presenting data have made HTML a really awkward way to present information. There are a host of server-side workarounds and extra files that most sites take for granted whenever they develop a suite of pages for their users.

But even if HTML was unevenly rendered across browsers and platforms, it was still more reliable than multimedia rendering on the Web. Until recently, audio and video presentations relied on proprietary formats, third-party browser extensions, and bandwidth-eating file sizes to present a few seconds of whiz-bang effects. Multimedia development was sharply limited.

Until now. The trend to watch out for as the century turns is a proliferation of languages that reduce multimedia files and presentations to a series of scripted attributes and events. Multimedia markup languages are emerging to pull Web content into a whole new direction, and their egalitarian syntax may just be the thing that snaps Web content back under one markup language umbrella.

Why Multimedia Markup Languages Will Matter

Until recently, the most daunting obstacle for including multimedia objects on the Web was finding a way to encode all the information in a lightweight file format. Now that software packages allow people to create lightweight multimedia packages, the focus has shifted from composing these files to controlling their playback on the Web.

Nowhere is the need for playback control more evident than in synchronizing multimedia across a client-server connection. Streaming audio and video are starts to controlling the pacing of events over time, instead of controlling pacing depending on how many different data packets the client is able to download at once.

Since the Web continues to move from a text/hypertext environment to a networked application environment, the demand for information to be presented in a more aggressive, broadcast-type style will increase. It will not be enough for users to enter queries or click on links; they will want to control extended action sequences and events.

In other words, it's like broadcast with the viewers directing segments of the action.

Therefore, streaming media and streaming data will increase in importance relative to a site's data presentation. The streaming audio and video formats courtesy of RealNetworks are a start, but they require separate servers, and the file formats are embedded in HTML pages. In order to dynamically produce and control streaming media, a hands-on markup language is necessary.

Familiarizing Yourself with the Coming Storm

The first type of markup language to control multimedia presentation is VRML, which is profiled briefly below. The three newcomers to the multimedia markup area are more accurately described as streaming media markup languages. They are RealNetwork's Real-Time Streaming Protocol (RTSP), Microsoft's Active Streaming Format (ASF), and the W3C's Synchronized Multimedia Integration Language (SMIL).

To learn more about each of the these four languages, keep reading.

VRML

Virtual Reality Markup Language (*VRML*) was the first markup language to pull the Web out of the text-only experience. Unlike the other languages profiled below, VRML regards websites as three-dimensional experiences, so it's necessary to think of a VRML-based site as a physically navigable experience instead of an abstract data tree. This is an interesting way to look at hyperlinked environments, but it may not be practical for wide-scale implementation. Still, since modeling environments is a part of overall digital culture—group games like Marathon proving that—it's important to explore the first attempted implementation on the Web.

VRML doesn't work on a standard browser; you have to download a separate VRML browser. For a list of browsers that read VRML 2, please see the sidebar.

VRML Browsers

A handful of companies publish VRML browsers to the Web. Here are two of the companies and thumbnail sketches of what they offer:

DimensionX   Liquid Reality is a Java-based VRML applet that runs on Windows 95/98 and NT, as well as Solaris and IRIX platforms. For more detailed information, and to download the applet, go to `http://www.dimensionx.com`.

Sony   Community Place is a VRML browser application or a plug-in, depending on what you prefer to install on your system. It comes bundled with full Java support, and is available for PCs running Windows 95/98 or NT. To learn more about the technical criteria for installing this app, plus links to product download, go to `http://vs.spiw.com/vs/downld2.html`.

Because there are now VRML browsers available for PCs, Macs, and Unix workstations, you will need to specify machine performance parameters in your VRML. Why? Because not all machines render graphics at equal speeds, nor are all machines equipped with 3-D acceleration, or a direct link to a T1.

Because VRML works with such a different model of what a user experience should be, it makes sense that the language is a little more complex than HTML. Consider this: VRML has to have a vocabulary that specifies an object's height, width, and depth—and where that object lies relative to other objects within a virtual space. It also has to provide a vocabulary for user-driven actions (behaviors) and for the details that will tell the individual objects and behaviors from each other.

Subsequently, you may want to use a modeling application—a software package that will let you create VRML objects (and a great list of them is here: `http://www.construct.net/tools/vrml/`)—to help you keep track of all your different VRML factors until you're comfortable enough with the basic VRML concepts to tweak the language on your own.

In the meantime, to get you started, here's a survey of some key VRML concepts:

Scenegraph   The blanket term for a VRML document, and the world that document encompasses. Scenegraphs are composed of separator nodes.

Nodes   Code constructions that describe the physical properties of individual objects within a scenegraph. Nodes are often grouped to economize on the code dictating physical descriptions and characteristics.

Separator node   A code construct that logically groups nodes together if they share common attributes. They're self-contained little groups, meaning that the individual elements within a separator node aren't aware of any elements outside their node. You can, however, set up a hierarchy of multiple separator nodes.

Avatar   A representation of a user in cyberspace. It's a tiny digital cipher for the user, relative to the "world" the user is currently exploring.

Spaces or worlds   The environments which house a VRML experience. They are similar to the worlds you enter whenever you fire up a copy of a computer game.

Polygon   The basic unit for composing VRML objects. Objects in video games, like characters or background, are made up of about 3,000 to 15,000 polygons; a VRML presentation targeted for a Pentium should have, at most, about 3,000 polygons.

Collision detection   If a polygon crashes in the forest, does anyone hear it? Only if collision detection—the ability to give objects a feel for "solidity" or gravity—is accounted for. Collision detection keeps avatars from running through walls, and makes sure they run into them instead. But reality checks aren't the only argument for collision detection: They also make your space perform better by reducing the number of objects the browser has to deal with as it steers your user through space. Making the browser work better is always a good thing.

Directional light   You're not going to know something's three-dimensional until you've seen it. A way of rendering an object and setting up a visual reference for the space is to dictate the illuminated area of an object; as an object approaches, recedes, or rotates, the reference for directional light is altered to reflect the actions.

Transform node   Changing that certain slant of light isn't enough to make an object move; you also have to provide Cartesian coordinates for the origin of the object so the browser can calculate how to modify position from an origin. It's a lot like figuring out how far you are from San Francisco by first determining what your base coordinates are (your desk in Washington, D.C.) comparing them to the coordinates in San Francisco, and calculating the difference necessary to move.

Texture map   A file that adds visual interest to the background of a VRML space. If directional light is analogous to switching on a light bulb, a texture map is the paint, wallpaper, and carpet for the room.

This basic vocabulary list should help you decipher the world of VRML. From a development perspective, VRML is an excellent tool for thinking about the Web in terms of a networked, 3-D space. It may not, however, be a practical investment of your time and resources yet.

VRML worlds are resource-intensive relative to the results they yield, and it's difficult to create cross-browser, cross-platform VRML. The directional light and texture maps are both byte-eating resources, and the results of a heavier VRML file are still only about as visually rewarding as a low-end computer game. Moreover, the additional 3-D considerations require a set of visual skills and programming skills you may not have on your Web development team. You'll have to weigh the possible benefits against the resource outlay.

So it may not be time yet to begin plotting the conversion of your file tree into a VRML labyrinth. But keep an eye on 3-D information modeling as a future model of Web development. To stay abreast of VRML, visit `http://vag.vrml.org/VRML2.0/FINAL/`.

Active Streaming Format

Microsoft's *Active Streaming Format* (*ASF*) is part of their NetShow multimedia package, so it's instantly attractive to anyone committed to developing for that suite of tools.

ASF works by breaking down the multimedia data package and storing it in a series of sequential packets. When an ASF data stream is sent from the server to the client, the individual data packets are queued and played in order. ASF allows you to prioritize the data within each data packet to optimize the packet size over limited bandwidth.

ASF bundles all of its multimedia elements—sound, video, text, and images—into one file. This is good for ensuring that you don't have any missing pieces or suddenly missing elements, but it limits the modularity of any multimedia presentation.

For more information on ASF and how it relates to current NetShow applications, visit `http://www.microsoft.com/mind/0997/netshow/netshow.htm`.

Real-Time Streaming Protocol

Real-Time Streaming Protocol (*RTSP*) is the brainchild of RealNetworks and Columbia University. The goal of the language is to provide a framework for synchronizing and streaming specific files so they can be delivered from server to client on a precise schedule.

RTSP deviates from standard HTTP data-reception models because it delivers and plays files only in a prescribed order. It's also similar to any Web-based multimedia application: RTSP comes with protocols for playing the streaming presentation, fast-forwarding, rewinding, and stopping.

And for the multimedia geek in all of us, RTSP also allows developers to have access to files for time-based seeking and manipulation. Finally, just in case one streaming outlet isn't enough for you, RTSP is designed to handle multicasting delivery of several disparate types of data streams, including ASF.

For more on RTSP, visit `http://www.real.com/rtsp/`.

Synchronized Multimedia Integration Language

Synchronized Multimedia Integration Language (*SMIL*, pronounced *smile*) is a markup language that proposes to attune different media within a Web page: images, text, audio, and video. SMIL is a big deal because it is being positioned as a Web-wide standard language, rather than as a proprietary corporate multimedia tool. Unlike ASF and RTSP, SMIL is not a streaming media language, but a way to carefully plot the trajectories of several disparate elements within a multimedia presentation. While this may seem like a drawback for performance, SMIL has a number of things going for it, especially the ease-of-use for development.

SMIL is another subset of XML, one that has a specific vocabulary geared toward coordinating different types of media events on a specific schedule. Like other XML-based documents, SMIL documents typically have both a head and a body area; the head carries a number of document-defining attributes like a DTD and a meta tag, but the real action goes on in the body.

SMIL Tags

The basic tags for coordinating SMIL include `channel`, `parallel`, `sequential` `timing`, `switch`, and `media-object`. These—and a few others—are covered below.

Channel   The channel element controls the position, size, and scaling of a media object, or multimedia file, within a specific window. For Web development purposes, the rendering window is the window object in the Document Object Model; any media objects that overlap the borders of the window object will be clipped.

The channel is the lynchpin of SMIL because it sets up the objects to be manipulated over time. To further increasing timing effectiveness, each object should have an `id` attribute; it acts as a reference point for coordinating a presentation.

The channel has an array of customizable elements, but it's important to include a default. The default syntax is:

```
"<layout type="text/smil-basic"></layout>"
```

The customizable elements are:

`id`   The unique identifier tag for each specific channel object.

`left`   The channel object's initial left coordinates. This is for layout purposes.

`top`   Also for layout purposes, this attribute sets the top coordinates.

`width`   This specifies the width of the channel object.

`height`   This specifies the height of the channel object.

`scale`   This is a worst-case-scenario tag: What happens if the height and width of the media object differ from the height and width attributes specified? There are a number of options you can set to ensure that your channel objects don't end up distorted as a result of clashing width tags:

`meet`   This is a simple proportional scaling.

`slice`   This is like cropping the object. Any overlap is clipped out of view.

`fill`   Scale the width and height of the object independently, just so everything fills the parameters set by the height and width values.

`hidden`   This clips the object to fit within visible parameters, and provides no way to view the overlap.

`auto`   This sets the default behavior for asynchronous height/width attributes. Typically, this will include scroll bars to allow users to see all of an object if it exceeds the visible space set by height and width.

`scroll`   If the dimensions of the object exceed the height and width set, the rendering software (e.g., a browser) provides scroll bars for the object so you can see all of it.

Parallel (par)   This element allows you to set up sophisticated timing routines for individual channel objects, and to coordinate multiple channel objects into one routine. It should have a discrete id, a value for the application to "hook" to for synchronization, values for the beginning and end of the synchronization cycle, and a channel element to specify the position, size, and scaling of a visual media object.

> sync   This specifies how to synchronize child objects in case of playback delays, especially if there is more than one type of child object (audio, video) and one of them gets delayed.
>
> endsync   This tag specifies when the parallel element ends. It can end when the first child channel object is finished with its schedule, or it can end when the last of its child objects ends.
>
> id   A handy tag for labeling a unique SMIL object. Remember that id tags are hooks for scripting actions later.
>
> dur   This tag sets the duration of the object's synchronization schedule.
>
> clock-val   This timing attribute has three possible sub-options: a full-clock value, which includes hours, minutes, and seconds; a partial-clock value, which includes minutes and seconds; and a timecount-val that sets the "ticks" for a specific coordinating timed cycle. The timecount can be set in hours, minutes, seconds, as long as the value for any of those is a 2-digit number between 00 and 59.

Sequential Timing (seq)   This tag sets the beginning and end time for a timing sequence. It can set a schedule, indicate a switch, or link an outside media object into a schedule. It has the same attributes as the parallel object (par), except for the endsync tag.

Switch   This option allows the SMIL author to specify a series of options for the users, with the end result being that one object is picked and displayed. A real-life example is having a user select an audio playback in a specific language, then playing the selected file.

Media Object Elements   This element allows you to include externally-linked multimedia files into a SMIL presentation. A media object has a mandatory src attribute—something that tells you where the linked file lives, much like an img tag, but the syntax for including audio, video, text, and image files is still undergoing modification.

Other Attributes You Should Know   This is neither a comprehensive list, nor a ratified one, since the specification wasn't ratified at press time. Nevertheless, here are some of the SMIL attributes you might see bundled into your SMIL files:

abstract   A tag to provide an encapsulated summary of the content. This is good for any page you want to search or have indexed.

begin   This sets the starting point for when a media object begins in relation to its parent container.

dur   This tag specifies exactly how long a media object is supposed to exist and behave.

end   This tag caps off the duration (dur) of a media tag.

repeat   This allows you to repeat a specific media object (like, say, a picture of a flying squirrel moving left-to-right across the screen) and to set the number of times the object can be repeated.

system-bitrate   This tag sets a parameter for the user's connection speed.

system-language   This sets the preferred language of the presentation—which will, in turn, provide a hook for the switch tag I was talking about.

system-screen-size   This dictates the optimal screen size for the SMIL file.

Using SMIL

Sounds great, you're thinking, but how does the browser know to read and recognize all of these events?

Well, right now it doesn't. But the language is specifying that the application playing the SMIL presentation have a clock measuring presentation time and advancing the speed of specific items as a result. To stay abreast of SMIL development and what Web-based software companies are endorsing it, visit the W3C site often at http://www.w3.org/TR/REC-smil/.

Writing SMIL

To give you a better idea of what a SMIL document would actually look like, here's an example of two different SMIL files. All comments are formatted like HTML comments, meaning they're bracketed: <!-- -- >.

The first file demonstrates a simple sequence file, with the img called in the body of the document formatted by a style sheet.

```
<smil>
<head>
<!-- note that stylesheets are denoted with "layout" tags -- >
<layout type="text/css">
#picture {position: absolute; top: 0; left: 0; width:500; height:500; _
visibility:visible; border:0; }
</layout>
</head>

<body>
 <seq>
<!-- note that every media type tag self-closes with a slash at the _
end -- >
<img id="picture" src="samplepic.gif" alt="[sample picture. More to _
come]" dur="10s" />
</seq>
</body>
</smil>
```

The second document demonstrates the switch in action; remember that you can set this to execute on a user's stated preference.

```
<smil>
<head>
<layout type="text/css">
#picture {position: absolute; top: 0; left: 0; width:500; height:500; _
visibility:visible; border:0; }
</layout>
</head>
<body>
<switch>
<img id="picture" src="samplepic_en.gif"  system-language="English" />
< img id="picture" src="samplepic_fr.gif" system-language="French"/>
< img id="picture" src="samplepic_cy.gif"  system-language="Cyrillic"/>
< img id="picture" src="samplepic_jp.gif" system-language="Japanese"/>
</switch>
</body>
</smil>
```

See how similar the syntax is? You should be able to pick up this new multi-media modeling system in no time at all.

Summary

Multimedia markup languages are the next direction for information rendering on the Web, and an elegant solution for bridging the gap between information storage and information presentation. Keep your eyes open for new languages, and begin playing with your code now to see how ably you can port it to a new way of presenting information.

CHAPTER

TWENTY-TWO

Supreme Organization through Version Control

- Appreciating the need for version control

- An introduction to CVS

- Arming yourself with version control

The previous chapters on setting up and maintaining a server environment all focused on the task of serving pages to the public. While this is indeed why you have a Web server, there's more to working on a backend than pushing files to the public.

A lot of people who are using content-delivery tools like OpenText and Vignette are already grappling with the next step in Web production: the collaborative workspace. While I'm going to discuss the collaborative workspace as a result of Web development in Chapter 23, here is where we look at how to make collaborative space on a server work toward improving your production processes.

More importantly, I'm going to discuss ways to make your production and serving process as thorough as possible, without being redundant. The answer: version control.

The Beauty of Version Control

For a lot of old-hand techies, version control and collaborative development is nothing new: people have been using version control tools like *Revision Control System (RCS)* to build software for years (for more on RCS, see the end of this chapter). The application of version control systems to Web development is a new step, however. This is a definite shift away from the "post in haste, revise in leisure" production model many sites were founded on, and toward a model where websites are treated as software applications within browsers.

If you've spent a lot of your time creating Web pages on your desktop and dropping them into a file tree (see Figure 22.1), you may have already been practicing a simple form of version control. A hierarchical production backend relies on human competence and agreed understanding of every folder's distinct function to maintain a form of version control from a file's first save to its live post.

Web development will probably continue to become increasingly compartmentalized, for two different reasons. First, the page elements themselves are compartmentalized; second, the skill levels required to build a professional-quality site are going to become increasingly specialized.

FIGURE 22.1:

This is a file tree that doubles as a version-control process. Specific files are added or moved as more people review them. Users can tell who's reviewed a file by how many sets of initials are displayed in the filename.

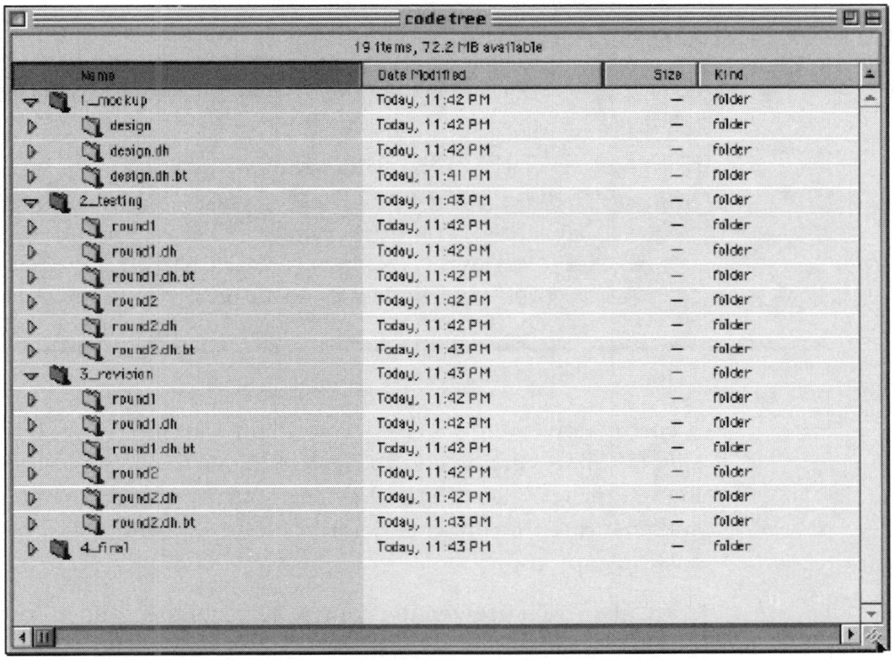

The increasing specialization is due to a number of reasons, but the primary one is user expectation. The audience for websites has shifted from people willing to take the time and effort to set up their computer and configure their software for optimum performance; today's Web audience expects a product that works for them as soon as they turn on the computer. If a user isn't getting the information or experience they want from your site, they won't be back.

The demand for high-performance multimedia and user-queried databases increases the overall complexity of the site structure and presentation. In order to execute each element in a complex product well, it often helps to have different people responsible for different facets of the product.

Needless to say, the potential for confusion and redundancy within teams looms large. Although collaborative workspaces are an efficient way to collect files that an entire group may use, unless the protocols for adding, modifying, or deleting a file are strictly defined and enforced, disaster can happen. *Disaster* is another word for a colleague inadvertently deleting your files on deadline.

The Death of DIY?

Before you get angry or nostalgic over the idea that the DIY website is dead: It's not. There will always be a niche for avocational sites, and for small, tightly focused professional sites.

But sites that are commercial properties—e.g., something developed for pay, for a client who wants to build or extend their business online—now require so many different skills to be well-developed that it makes sense to specialize. Consider this: Anyone can learn a software application like IIS or Flash, but unless you have the programming background or design training, you won't be able to use the product to its fullest advantage.

Fortunately, there's an easy way to prevent most disasters: *version control systems* (*VCS*). A version control system logs when a file has been revised, and how many times it's been revised. At its most primitive, it's handy for logging changes and ensuring that an amended file isn't inadvertently replaced with an older backup copy.

Ideally, you'll use version control systems to do the following:

Source control   This means keeping track of the code that fuels your project. In software development, base source code is used to create several different versions of a product (different operating systems, different platforms, etc.). In Web development, this source code could fuel several different versions of the same website.

Build systems   A *build* is a version of a product or file; substantial alterations of said file are considered a new build. If you're doing a backend overhaul of your site channel by channel, you may have several different builds of your site in the same system. Ideally, a good VCS lets you track what files are shared between builds, what files are local to specific builds, and how to find specifically-named files.

Bug tracking   One of the reasons a software product or website goes through so many builds is that the developers are trying to find and fix any and all bugs. An ideal VCS would let you record bug-zapping data, such as what build the bug emerged during; what the bug affects; what build the bug was finally eliminated from; and how the bug was eliminated.

Automated testing procedures   In order to maintain consistency from file to file, it helps if you're testing them all on the same set of criteria. Setting up and executing an automated testing procedure would save time while checking files for consistency.

Documentation   A VCS should also be a repository for all file-related documentation, on everything from technical specifications to build processes.

The key word in that last section was "ideally." Most VCSs work well in tracking source control, but don't quite do the rest yet.

A VCS performs an important administrative function for any collaborative working environment. By recording what was done to a file, you can streamline your production process and control the overall site development more closely.

Version Control System Profile: CVS

Concurrent Version Systems is an open-source VCS. You can use it for setting up and maintaining a file tree in a shared space, so your developers are all working from the same set of files, organized in the same ways.

Enabling multiple developers to handle the same files is a CVS-exclusive feature. CVS allows more than one person to check out the source code for a specific file. This may seem counterproductive, especially since the whole point to VCS is to make sure someone isn't inadvertently erasing all your work. But CVS comes with built-in controls for making sure that permanent file changes are committed only after all parties have a chance to see the updated files. One of those controls is file-locking. Someone can commit a file to CVS that's locked; any subsequent developer then knows that their work can have serious repercussions.

CVS is also a good tool for tracking changes introduced by an outside party. As a Web developer, there are two likely scenarios for this:

- You are working with a client or company team that's not on your network, and therefore must download all the source code from an FTP site. If you rely on independent contractors to fulfill specific website building tasks, you may not want a bunch of temporary employees mucking about your company filespace. But you can still track their work by streaming it through CVS.

- You rely on a commercial package for a vital site function (database, serving) and they send you continuous updates or new release models. The beauty of checking the new third-party code into CVS is that you can bundle any site modifications into a build that includes the new software. This prevents a lot of nasty surprises when you upgrade your server software and discover that half your site broke as a result.

The heart and soul of CVS is the *repository*. The repository stores a complete a copy of all of the files and directories that you've checked into CVS.

"So what?" you're asking. "My file tree on my Unix workstation does the same thing."

The key difference between a file tree on a machine and a file tree in CVS is that you don't open the file in the CVS repository and write to it directly. Instead, you check out the files into a *working directory*, modify the files there, then check the altered file back into the CVS repository. Even after you've checked a newer version of the file into the system, that's no guarantee that everyone else in the system is going to see the altered file. Therefore, you have to commit those changes.

Committing overwrites the old version of the file with your newer version and keeps track of what version number the file is. In other words, how many times has the file been revised? Tagging the files is insurance against having to re-create your work to track down specific modifications later; by simply going through versions of the same file, you can record what alterations were introduced when.

Therefore, the repository does more than store files: it also contains information that controls the behavior of CVS and its constituent files. This information is stored in a file called $CVSROOT/CVSROOT.

File Traffic in CVS: The Repository and the Working Directory

The repository can be an excellent example of a no-fuss collaborative workspace, but only if you know how to use it. Before you're hurled into your first CVS work experience, here's a rundown on how the repository works.

Let's look at how files are stored in the repository. This is important only because you may need to track down specific, locked files later and unlock them for development (locking and unlocking is covered below).

Files are stored in a directory tree, the structure of which will be familiar to everyone who has a copy in their working directory. Each directory and subdirectory also has a *history file*. These files are all-knowing, at least in the CVS world. History files contain enough information to reconstruct a specific file version based on its revisions, commit messages, and user who made the revisions and committed the files. These history files are also known as *RCS files*, since the RCS version control system was the first program to store history files in the specific format CVS uses.

> **NOTE**   There are some differences between a CVS RCS file and a standard-format RCS file. The most significant is in branch numbers. A *branch*, which I'll cover in more detail in a few pages, is a way to separate a line of revisions and development. Branch numbers log and define individual branches.

In addition to the history files, there's also a cvs directory in each repository directory. This directory contains more specific information about the files within the repository, including a file attributes listing. In some CVS applications, the history files go here too.

CVS also drops a cvs directory into all of the subdirectories that the working directory contains. This directory contains information files that CVS will log when a working directory file or file tree gets checked back into CVS. These files include:

Root   This file contains the current CVS root, so CVS will be able to pair working directory files with repository files.

Repository   This complements the root by telling CVS which directories in the repository correlate to the directories within the working directory. If that sounds confusing, think of the repository file as a card-catalog sticker on the spine of a library book. The sticker allows a librarian to move the book from its place in the Ancient History stacks at the branch office to its same place in the Ancient History stacks at the central library.

Entries   This lists all the files and directories currently living in the working directory. When CVS reads this, it can assess what files and directories have been added and deleted relative to the same file structure in the repository.

Sticky Tags

Not all administrative information about CVS files is restricted to the cvs directory. Sometimes a working copy file has extra data attached to it—branching will do this, for example, as will restricting file versions by a parameter like date. In this case, the data has to be applied to subsequent CVS commands in the working copy, so it's persistent. Or, in CVS parlance, *sticky*.

This sticky data is denoted by *sticky tags*. These tags are usually just a line of text used to indicate what branches, dates, or other options are meant to persist from file version to file version.

Branches

One of the beauties of revision control is that you can pick a chunk of code, create a separate line of development called a *branch*, and isolate that code for development via CVS without affecting the rest of the main trunk (repository).

Branches would be useful for refining specific features on a page, like client-side Java applets or JavaScript interface features. You can continue CVS development with updates and committals without holding up the rest of the team, especially if they're working on graphics, templates, or server-side scripting. After you're done working on the branch, you can reintegrate it back into the repository.

About That Locking and Unlocking Thing

One of the tenets to any RCS is that files within a given directory are not written over willy-nilly. In order to ensure that someone doesn't accidentally perform a directory-wide erase and commit process, there are two levels of file safeguarding.

The first, and most basic, is file permissions. History files are created to be read-only, so any and all changes that are made to the contents of a given directory are less likely to be erased and therefore can be reconstructed if necessary. The actual code files within a specific directory do have read-write permission, but only to specific groups. This allows you to determine, on a directory-by-directory basis, who can check files in and out.

The second method CVS uses to make sure that erasing all source code is more difficult than just hitting Delete is *file locking*. Also known as *reserved checkouts*, locking files is one way to make sure only one person can edit a file at a time.

NOTE   This is not the default method for CVS file traffic; the default is unreserved check-outs, where several developers can all simultaneously check out and modify a file without knowing that other people are working on the same file.

Setting up the locking option is a sysadmin job: They install a module that instructs CVS to lock the revision number until whoever checked out the file checks it back in again.

Examining the Drawbacks

Although locking a file seems like the best possible solution to any version control dilemma, it also has its drawbacks.

For example, if two different people want to edit two different sections of the same file, they can't. This means that your copyeditor can't scan your latest content for errors while the production team is checking links and pulling in template components. So overall production time slows down, which is not optimal for frequently published sites. Production time slows to a crawl when someone puts a lock on a file then forgets to remove it after they've checked their file back in.

This isn't to say that the locking option is useless: if you're working on files that don't merge well (like discrete graphics files), then you may want to lock them to prevent someone else from modifying them as you work.

Typically, CVS users strike a balance between a free-for-all in the file space and reserved (locked) checkouts. You can still monitor who's doing what to which files through any of the following options:

File status   You can determine whether or not a file is updatable or modifiable. The different CVS file status modes are:

- **Up-to-Date**   The working copy file is the same version as the repository copy.

- **Locally Modified**   A file in the working directory is altered, but not the repository copy.

- **Locally Added**   There's a new file in the working directory, but it hasn't been added to the repository yet.

- **Locally Deleted**   The exact opposite of Locally Added. A file that needs to be removed from the repository hasn't been yet.

- **Needs Checkout** The file you're working on has a newer, revised version in the repository. Note that you'd actually run a directory update to copy that latest file to your working directory; you wouldn't re-check out the file.

- **Unknown** If you've created a new file without adding it and then try to commit it to the repository, you'll get this message.

E-mail information Sometimes it helps to say it in e-mail. You can set CVS to e-mail messages to a working group notifying them when someone's committed a new revision of a file.

Watches You can tell CVS to check certain files to see who's working on them, and what time they began working. Note that watched files are checked out to workers as read-only, so if you want to revise and edit a watched file, you need to invoke the edit command, then commit your files.

Fear of Commitment?

Get over it. The reason CVS is so successful is that developers have to make a conscientious decision to add a modified file to the repository. The process is called *committing*: it writes a new file to a specific directory or overwrites an old file with a new version. Committing is how collaborators pass on their additions and revisions to a common workspace. No matter how many times you add, delete, or modify files in your working directory, it means nothing until you've passed on your work via committing.

Committing is also a good work habit, especially if more than one of your coworkers is going to be working on the same files as you. This way, you can work from the most recent file version, and pass your recent work back for your coworkers.

Getting CVS

Now that you have an idea what you can do in CVS, how do you get the software?

Since CVS is open-source software, it's available from a wide variety of places on the Web. Cyclic Software Company has an excellent source code repository on its site; they store CVS for a wide variety of operating systems, and they store multiple CVS builds so you can reinstall or upgrade your current version of the software. For downloads and instructions, go to http://download.cyclic.com/pub/.

RCS as an Alternative

The reason I focused on CVS is because the open-source developers have made it extremely easy for a Windows- and Web-based user group to migrate to a VCS. You can do command-line CVS, but there are a host of CVS tools out there that ensure you don't have to.

CVS may not be for everyone. For example, your site may already have RCS in place. If this is the case, you can begin plotting how to move your Web production process to that VCS.

In fact, RCS is what fuels most of CVS's work. RCS is a set of programs that keep track of individual file changes. This is different from CVS in that RCS treats every single file as an isolated individual, whereas CVS tries to append some group-related functionality. It's the difference between committing one file (RCS) and committing ten simultaneously (CVS).

RCS is widely regarded as a good version control tool, and is available from several different sites. The system does take some sysadmin savvy to set up, so beware installing it unsupervised. (Unless, of course, you happen to be a sysadmin.) To get RCS for Windows platforms, go to www.winsite.com, and search on RCS. It's available for Windows 3.x, 95, and NT. To get RCS for Unix go to http://www.cs.purdue.edu/homes/trinkle/RCS/.

Summary

This chapter introduced the idea of a version control system as a crucial part of your production environment. You should have an idea of the types of processes that go into building a version control system, and of the tools available to install your own revision control system.

A VCS is one component of a collaborative workspace, and a hands-on example of using a collaborative workspace to produce websites. For a discussion of collaborative workspaces as a side benefit of the World Wide Web, plus other "web dividends" that are filtering from the Web to everyday life, read on.

The Web Dividend: Intranets, Extranets, and the Web as a Killer App

- Understanding and developing intranets and extranets

- Making the Web tiny with PDAs

- Embracing push technology

- Bringing the Web out of cyberspace and into reality

Once upon a time, people who enthused about the potential for the Web to take over news, commerce, and personal organization were all shut down with this argument: It won't work because the Web isn't portable. You can't take it on a train. You need Internet access. People won't sacrifice the convenience of newspapers/handouts/daily planners for the Net.

That may have worked in 1994, but it's a dramatically diminished argument today. The Web has acted as a sort of evangelist for new technologies: showing people how easy it is to coordinate projects among people in geographically separate locations; providing a means to disseminate information quickly; providing a way to improve work through improved communication.

Most importantly, the Web has provided a low-cost implementation tool kit for people to develop new ways of moving information. Small, extremely client- or company-specific websites called extranets or intranets work because they're relatively cheap and easy to implement. Web-based Personal Digital Assistant (PDA) products work because they remove another barrier on the road to portable network connectivity.

Of course, none of these three technologies—intranets, extranets, or Web-based products for a PDA—would be so popular if they weren't easy to use.

This chapter is going to talk about the three technologies, and how to roll them into your Web development routines so you can extend the effectiveness of your Web-based technologies above and beyond your site. Because developing an intranet or an extranet has a different set of project considerations than developing a website, I'm going to focus on the ways you can use your Web-building and project management skills to create easy-to-use intranets and extranets. And because PDAs are gaining popularity as a way to organize a work day or keep reference materials close at hand, I'm going to talk about ways to port your company Web products to PDAs as well.

Then I'm going to move on to the subject of what the Web can do for you outside of the Web. That is, how the Web can allow you to use the networking and information tools for actual, non-Net-related work. It's time you started thinking of the Web in a different way.

The idea of using a network to pool work, share data, or collaborate is not new; local area networks (LANs) have been a part of corporate life since the late 1980s, and have mutated into intranets as the 1990s move on. But meshing Web technology with the seemingly utilitarian "corporate" Net has gotten surprisingly little interplay.

So start thinking of cutting-edge Web usability as the practice of pulling the Web into an everyday work world, instead of separating "the Internet" into something that can't be applied in everyday life.

Intranet Development

Intranet might seem to be one of those buzzwords that has no real-world analogue, but it is in fact, a real-world practical application. Intranets are websites that live behind company firewalls. Access is restricted to people who visit the intranet from behind a firewall, or via a user authorization, that is, company employees.

Before I get into the nitty gritty, you may appreciate a little history lesson.

From Push Craze to Intranet Frenzy

The first step toward integrating a user's "work" environment and the material available on the World Wide Web was a combination of three separate but closely-timed technologies. Each promised to deliver new and fresh information to a user's desktop, provided the user had the specific software running.

The first, PointCast, was a high-bandwidth, full-screen broadcast system. Although capable of running as a ticker on the bottom of a Windows machine desktop, it functioned best as an intelligent screensaver. The hullabaloo surrounding it was focused on the fact that it was the first medium to actively "push" Web content to the desktop; users specified what they wanted, and the content was downloaded to the desktop application on a scheduled basis.

The second, Marimba, was another specific software bundle. If PointCast aimed to be the CNN of the network medium, Marimba aimed to be Radio Free Europe. Users downloaded and installed software that could receive "transmissions" from Marimba's content-producing clients. The idea behind the company was that eventually, software and applications could be automatically modified via a well-timed broadcast when upgrades were available. Like PointCast, Marimba was aiming at the PC desktop.

The final debuting technologies were Java tickers and JavaScript windows, both of which were small extensions of a Web browser. Of the three approaches, this one perhaps had greatest mass appeal: Users were more likely to already have working Web browsers, and platforms beyond the PC were able to take advantage of them.

Continued on next page

The next step in integrating the Net with the desktop was browser compatibility with push media. The idea behind this effort was to integrate the Net's immediate information-gathering capabilities into the "working" area of the desktop.

This worked in two separate ways; you could make a Web page the wallpaper behind your desktop, or you could keep the kiosk-style application open and have new, timed downloads delivered to your desktop on a schedule. But like PointCast, push media is bandwidth-intensive, CPU-intensive, and works well as an intelligent screensaver.

Round one of integrating the Internet and the personal computer desktop was not an overwhelming success. Meanwhile, thousands of companies were looking at their external company websites and asking the question, "If we can organize our company information for an outside audience, why can't we organize our internal information with the same tools?"

Enter the company intranet. Once a creation of local networks and desktop-based windows, the intranet could now act as a central information repository and easy-to-navigate workspace.

If I were a power-mad control freak, I'd consider intranet development to be the perfect project: You have a captive audience and you get to decide what information they get to see. What power!

I usually manage to keep my dictatorial aspirations in check, and I still regard intranet development as the best of Web development worlds. Why is developing an intranet such a golden opportunity? Here are some of the reasons:

- **You can put all company-related information in one place**. This means that you can stop cluttering people's desks with a company newsletter and begin storing it in an archive online.

- **You can use it as an example of how your Web development ought to be done**. If your intranet is filled with valid HTML, well-designed navigation, and fast-loading pages, you can always point your new staffers at the intranet as an example of company quality standards.

- **You can use your intranet as a central tool to monitor company work processes**. If you're working on a project that spans several departments, the intranet is an excellent place to host all the project materials.

- **You can make your intranet the repository for all library and research materials**. A lot of professional journals now offer electronic subscriptions; you can also get sitewide licenses for Web-based information databases like

Knight-Ridder. By putting all these resources in one easily-accessible place, you're making it easier for people to find reference materials.

- **You can begin to eliminate paperwork, or implement better company organization**. One of the best examples of the latter is Razorfish's Mom project, which you can see on their website at `http://www.razorfish.com/template.cgi?casestudy=mom`. It's an intranet that allows employees to track their time and coordinate schedules.

- **You can use the intranet as a low-cost, self-guided orientation guide for new employees**. If your company is in the middle of a rapid expansion, or you're hiring people in the middle of a project crunch, you may not have the time to train everyone. By having training materials, company history, and other helpful material on your intranet, you're easing the hair-raising introduction you've offered your new hires.

Above all, an intranet is a way to use Web-based technology to achieve your business goals, whether or not they're related to the Internet. When developing an intranet, you'll be forced to examine several factors that can affect the way you do business. These include:

- **The types of communication that go on within the company**. How rigid are the boundaries between different departments, or between different organizational levels? You'll need to keep those boundaries in mind when you develop your intranet: If your company is strictly structured, you don't want a new employee forwarding jokes to the CEO just because he found the head honcho's e-mail address in the company phone book.

- **The types of information that comprise an organization's intellectual assets**. Does this include a library of published documents from the company? Does it include a well-defined protocol for producing a specific item?

- **The company culture**. This ties into the communication issue mentioned above. The perceived company culture will dictate exactly what functions the intranet performs. Some company intranets may simply be an online directory for information that's available in print, like the company newsletter. Then there are companies that are putting more of their work—project development, quality assurance, inventory tracking, timesheet registration—onto their intranet as a way to efficiently conduct a wide-ranging process. And then there are companies that encourage their employees to live online.

- **The groupings of information within the intranet**. There's a big difference between posting a lot of eye-crossing small print about health insurance coverage and putting up a series of Q&A pages that explicitly address questions like "I just broke my arm in a midnight skiing accident. How can I get it set in a local hospital and still get it covered by my HMO?"

The considerations listed above should help you focus your specific intranet mission. Like any other Web-based project, an intranet is best done if it is planned out instead of erected in response to a buzzword-happy client. The rest of this section will cover three different topics that will help you grow your own intranet:

- **The process for building an intranet**. This is a general step-by-step process for growing an intranet in your own company, or improving your already existing intranet.

- **The content considerations**. Before you post your entire HR department on the Web, what do you need to know?

- **Technical considerations**. Intranets may have a different set of technical criteria regarding bandwidth and browsers than does your public website. I give an overview.

Process Considerations

The following steps detail what you have to do to shepherd your intranet from someone's bright idea to much-loved company resource. When you're working on an internal project, there is the temptation to let different departments do things in their own specific manner. Resist this temptation.

1. Figure out what the driving idea behind your intranet is going to be. Sometimes this is referred to as "vision," or "the big picture." All this means is you need to nail down the reason you're putting up an intranet. Jump back a few pages to see some of the reasons.

2. Figure out how much work goes into initially launching the intranet, how much work goes into maintaining the intranet, and who's going to maintain what parts. It's no good to have a company intranet if half of the departments don't have the resources or time to contribute to it.

3. Settle on the policies for posting items on the intranet, and for accessing items on the intranet. If you plan on using the intranet as a place for inventory ordering, performance reviews, timesheets, or other administrative functions, you may want to restrict access in certain directories. Another

information policy you need to cover: Who gets to decide what gets posted and what does not? The final information consideration is what format is all your company data going to be posted in? Is there a boilerplate HTML template? Can people post links to word-processing documents?

4. One of the great advantages to having public file spaces is that anyone can read or write to them. One of the great disadvantages to having public file spaces is that anyone can read or write to them. If your intranet is going to be a document library, who is responsible for updating and filing documents? Will there be a feedback form so employees can add new information as it surfaces? The read and rights privileges of all the employees should be resolved before intranet development commences.

5. Determine who is going to staff the intranet, and how. Are you going to hire a few contractors to do the site, an outside firm to design and develop the infrastructure, or develop your intranet staff in-house?

6. Figure out how you're going to handle scaling the intranet operation. You will have more users as time goes by, and you will need to accommodate them. In addition, you will have more material to add, so you need to deal with increased volume or functionality as well.

7. Decide what applications you're going to have on your intranet. Will people be able to download licensed software? Will you have an approved shareware repository? Will people be executing applications over the intranet to do things like fill out their timesheets? Gauging your application use is absolutely necessary to setting up an intranet with enough power.

8. Hammer out a strategy for dealing with legacy documentation. This will be important because it will give you an idea for the scope of your project.

9. Solidify your technical strategy. You need to be able to account for increased traffic, net-based applications, and the extra security to keep outsiders from surfing around your company secrets.

10. Figure out what's going to fund your intranet. Like external websites, intranets cost money to develop and maintain. Your job is to find the money to keep the site going. Remember that an intranet should be its own argument for funding: In order to get the money, you're going to have to come up with a reasonable return on investment.

11. Sell the well planned intranet to the company executives, so you can get the time and resources necessary to launch it.

What Is the Difference between Developing an Intranet and Developing a Site?

There are two that come to mind immediately. The first is location: Even if your company has one central intranet, there is the issue of accessing it from outside the company walls. Do satellite offices have a way of accessing the intranet? You may need to set up some connection protocols with the MIS department to ensure that telecommuters and geographically different audiences are able to access the intranet—without opening the intranet to the public.

The second thing that comes to mind is also location—as in, where are things located within the intranet? Websites tend to be organized topically, and everything on a site usually has some sort of subject- or task-based connection to the rest of the site. An intranet may feature far more topics than a site, and those topics are much more diverse. Setting up a clear and complete navigation system on an intranet is mandatory.

Once you've completed all those tasks, you can actually get down to building your intranet. In order to build the initial product, you need to hammer out the content that you'll populate your intranet with.

Your intranet should be treated as a business product like any other. Define business goals for it—what it should do, and what you expect to get in return for your investment. Treat the intranet like you would any other product your company makes, or any other tool your company buys to do its work. And most importantly, think the intranet through before you begin coding.

Content Considerations

Before you go posting all 250 pages of insurance policy fine print on the company intranet, be sure you've pondered the following factors. This will prevent you from posting something that comes back to haunt you, and will help you to clearly define what you can post without adverse effects.

NOTE Be prepared to host 10 to 50 times as many files as your website holds. Why? The only items that make it to a website are those that are deemed publicly accessible. But for every 10-page website, there's 30 pages of documentation outlining the file structure, production process, and code quirks that build the site. Larger companies may have departments that exist solely to build internal tools; the data and documentation they produce is worth a website unto itself.

Legal Matters

Before you post your entire employee manual online, remember that there are possible legal concerns for any intranet content you post. An employee manual is typically a binding legal document, with the employee signing an agreement that they've read and understood the manual. The employee handbook is company property; it should not leave the building, and employees should have a signed record stating they've read and understood all versions of it.

When you put an electronic copy of the employee handbook online, you run a few risks:

- The employee will save a copy to disk and it will not be a recent copy. Therefore, they're not apprised of modifications to the handbook.

- It is very easy to e-mail a document file of the company handbook to anyone outside the company.

- It is difficult to control how the employee handbook is disseminated through the company.

This sounds surprisingly at odds with the free information ethos that defines the World Wide Web. But remember, this is not a publicly-accessible network; this is a company resource and as such is subject to company considerations.

Another legal consideration you might want to ponder: Exactly how much company information do you want fixed in a format that could come back to haunt you later? Think about all those nightmare subpoenas Microsoft got simply for e-mail. What if someone went after your company and requested the business plans and memos you had posted on the intranet?

This isn't to scare you away from posting information on your intranet: A well-informed company is one that allows employees to work more efficiently and more effectively. Just be aware of all possible legal repercussions before you post anything.

Proprietary Company Data

Remember that it is incredibly easy to copy files from a Web browser on to a local machine. In fact, that's how your Web browser reads files: It receives them from the server and a caches a local copy. If you have information that requires you to tightly control the distribution, do not put it on your intranet.

Another hazard of posting proprietary data on the intranet is the chance that disgruntled employees might erase it, hack it, or publish it to an audience you don't want to see. Last winter, an ex-employee at Pixar did precisely that, publishing the salary list for the entire company via e-mail.

Again, this is not to scare you away from posting company proposals and reports on your intranet: Just remember that information posted on any shared network, even one with sharp security, has legs and can walk away.

Intellectual Capital

Intellectual capital is data and data analysis that your company uses to do its job. It's usually proprietary, like a website's page counts or source code for a page-generating tool. Since intranets may lessen the degree of control you'll have over the distribution of intellectual capital, it's important to take steps to impress on your users exactly how they are to use the content on the intranets.

In order to preserve intellectual capital, most companies rely on documenting the stuff that comprises the capital—consulting tactics, research processes and results, or human contacts for business deals. The act of documenting may actually extend some legal protection if you take care to label all your documents with a copyright (Copyright ©1998, *your company*) and establish that they are company property.

Another legal tactic is to extend an employee noncompete agreement to cover intranet contents. Noncompete agreements typically prevent exiting employees from using intellectual capital (processes, contacts, research) for a direct rival: You can also argue that downloading and using the contents of the intranet for a competitor is covered.

Company Resources

Intranets exist as a central repository, and can be convenient storage places for licensed software and pre-release products. Before you put up the graphics layout program you just paid a few thousand for, you may want to determine exactly how much theft you're willing to tolerate.

Technical Considerations

Having a captive audience does not give you a license to make an unusable site. If anything, building a Web-based resource for a restricted audience should let you build a better interface, since you know exactly who your audience is and what they'll be accessing your site with. The following factors should remain in your mind as you consider design:

Organize your information.   This is actually more difficult than for an external site. You need to be able to organize information in a way that makes sense to the user if they're new to the company or the intranet, but allows seasoned employees to find and use data quickly. Ideally, there should be no more than one or two clicks between indexes or other navigational pages and the content they're organizing.

Navigation is key.   One of the dangers of building out a complex infrastructure like a company intranet is that it is easy to get lost, especially if the intranet is organized differently from department to department. If it is at all possible, try to impose a central navigation system and topical organization across the site. Users shouldn't need to know the company's org chart to use the site.

Feel free to restrict the technical parameters.   When you're developing a website, there's no telling what browser version/platform combination is going to hit your site. Fortunately, with an intranet, you have an opportunity to know exactly what computers and browsers will be accessing the site. If you're in MIS—or can appeal to someone who is—you can even control what browsers you will and won't support for intranet development. One company I worked at declared that it refused to support anyone who had installed a version 4 browser on their machines; another refused to permit its users to upgrade browser versions without express approval.

You don't have to be as extreme as this company, but the point is, you do enjoy an extraordinary amount of knowledge about your user base when developing an in-house site. So feel free to develop your intranet to cater to specific technologies, provided you have in-house support backing you up on the browsers you favor.

TIP

Try to combine your assets: Ask yourself if there are any tools you're using on your website that you can also use to perform your intranet tasks. For example, if you're using a CGI script that writes all data to a flat file and then parses and displays the results, you can copy the script to a separate /cgi-bin/ directory within the intranet and modify it to act as the basis for any user-input Web page, like a soon-to-be-former-employee exit interview Web page.

How Is the Intranet Going to Be Developed?

There are a few different development models for the company intranet. The first is to let every department develop and design its own section, then link them all together and let the users sort it out. The extreme opposite of that is to tightly control the intranet design, and have a single designer and file tree attached to the intranet project.

There are problems with both approaches. The each-department-is-an-island approach allows employees and departments to have access to and control over the information they're presenting, but the overall company intranet suffers from a lack of central organization. On the other hand, one tightly managed site can end up being less of an informative tool and more of a limited internal website.

A compromise between these two approaches is best for long-term development. Decide on a degree of centralization, and a set of common organizational elements, and let the project be. It's a good idea to have one central intranet for the company, especially if your company is spread out over several geographic locations or boasts a large population of telecommuters. It's also a good idea to have a central index area, and a template for formatting intranet content so users can use quick visual cues to find precisely what they need. Within these mild constraints, different departments should be able to write and publish everything they want to contribute to the intranet, and do so in a way that other departments can understand.

The advantage to developing an intranet is that your users come to the site knowing what the tool is supposed to do and knowing something about the organization behind the tool. Exploit employee knowledge and use it to add functionality to your site.

You may also want to investigate the feasibility of moving data between the public website and your workplace intranet, especially if you're in the business of analyzing moving information. At a conference I attended in Spring, 1998, I heard about one real-life challenge, illustrated by JavaSoft (`http://javasoft.com/`); they make their bug database public, so both the developers who work on the product internally and the bug-contributing public were able to read and write information to the database. The question the company faced was, how did they handle the bi-directional reading and writing between public and intranet sources, and how did they separate out the data that had to remain private? The answer was to set up a buffer server that parsed the intranet products before making them live.

If the intranet is just going to be a repository for documents, it doesn't have to be very technically complex. But if you're going to use it for collaborative working, or for checking files in and out, you're going to need applications that can carry messages, retain object-oriented hierarchies and attributes, or maintain file states for monitoring.

Extranet Development

So now that you've embraced intranet as part of your working vocabulary, it's time to learn about *extranets*. The key difference between intranets and extranets is where they live: Intranets are usually housed behind company firewalls so not everyone can get into them. Extranets may actually be on a "public" Web server that accepts queries from other clients, but you can only view the content via a username and password.

> **NOTE**
>
> The word *extranet* is probably a verbal shortcut for the phrase *extended intranet*. This still connotes the strictly functional client-company relationship that the mini-site is supposed to play.

Extranet access is set up on a sliding scale: Different users have different access privileges. This allows you to use the Web to do the following:

- Set up demonstrations that your sales, marketing, or other company traveling types can access no matter where they are. While canned demos are a handy failsafe measure, a robust Web-based demo is also impressive. Extranets let you set these demos up without worrying about your competition inadvertently finding them on the website.

- Post client sites. This is an excellent way to show a site in vitro, or in its natural environment.

- Act as a collaborative workspace between a company and its clients. If you're developing websites, you may want to set up an extranet to deposit central files from both parties.

Planning an extranet is similar to planning an intranet: It is a company business product and should be given the same time and strategizing effort as you would give to any other external Web products.

> **TIP**
>
> The difference between an *intranet* and an *extranet* is that an intranet is meant as a company's internal information tool, and an extranet is developed specifically as a tool for a company to use with a limited audience. The difference between a *website* and an *extranet* is that websites are meant to serve a broad and anonymous audience, while extranets are developed as task-oriented tools for a specific two-way interaction between the company and an outside party.

Extranets are powerful business tools because they allow you to find or present information quickly and securely. Thanks to the rise in groupware applications—software packages that allow you to pool information and act on it within a group of people—and the liberation from specific platforms that comes with Web browsing, extranets have grown into a niche of timely, accessible information. One example of an extranet might be a website's media kit. The media kit lists company-specific information like advertising rates, awards that the website has won, and the demographics of people who visit frequently. The kit is available to potential advertisers via a Web browser. But it may be available only via a specific URL not connected to the site, or via a username and password. Or you might set up an extranet that allows advertisers to see how many times their ad has been served, and where.

But for all the communication and collaboration potential that extranets offer, there are also drawbacks: The Web is great for initial platform freedom, but there are few tools for intelligently managing information on the Web. In addition, developing and supporting company-specific Web-based tools is expensive, especially with such a wide variation in browser performance. Finally, a company's bandwidth capacity may not be up to encouraging excessive traffic.

Extranet Design

Developing an extranet is different from developing a website, and it's different from developing an intranet. Look at it as the third leg in the networked-information triad. Each leg has something in common with the others:

- Intranets and websites share the interface and markup language that allows them to be easily accessed, information-organizing products.

- Intranets and extranets are both task-oriented information-organizing products.

- Extranets and websites are both open to a public audience.

We've already explored the overlap between intranet and website design, and the overlap between intranets and extranets. So it makes sense to look at extranet development as a hybrid process between intranets and websites. Here are some pointers to consider:

Interface counts.   Unlike an intranet, where both audience and technical levels are fairly well known, an extranet can be accessed by people from the outside world. Therefore, you lose control over all technical parameters. Play it safe, and use the same user interface criteria you would when designing a website.

Purpose counts.   Like an intranet, an extranet exists to perform explicit tasks. When designing your extranet, remember that it exists as a tool. Limit an extranet's scope and content to serve the purpose it's supposed to perform.

Design counts.   Since an extranet is publicly accessible, it is a good idea to design as though you're designing for the public. You may want to carry over some visual elements from your site just in case any users accidentally wander into the extranet. You may also want to maintain that visual continuity if your extranet is meant to act as a data-processing tool for your website; this way, the purpose of the extranet as a tool for interpreting the website is still clear.

The verdict on extranets is mixed: While they allow faster company-client communications and quicker turnaround on certain transactions like inventory or ordering, extranets are also expensive to maintain correctly. They require increased security, server space, and maintenance: If you're barely keeping up with your commercial website or intranet, you don't want to take on an extranet too.

Despite the drawbacks, extranets are a good way to make information mobile and accessible, so it's a good area to watch for future Web-specific applications and information architecture.

Personal Digital Assistants

A burgeoning area for Web development—or extra-Web development—is the personal assistant market. People have been using these to keep track of their lives via personal software like Microsoft Outlook or Lotus Notes. Now, with the rise of groupware, the exploding popularity of easy-to-develop software specifically for PDAs, and a markup language targeted toward bringing Web content to tiny screens, a new market has opened up for porting desktop functionality to PDAs. Websites, with their platform-independent clients, are an excellent way to dispense information for PDAs.

As a result, PDA users are able to do more with less machinery and less bandwidth.

Using the PDA as a Portable Intranet/Extranet Extension

Back in this chapter's introduction, I mentioned the old argument that the Internet wouldn't ever be portable. PDAs may be the finest refutation to that argument: It's possible to download news updates and documents and read them on a small handheld device.

For example, imagine that your company relies on a specific groupware package to coordinate meetings and set its weekly schedules. It would be easy to download the calendar file to your PDA and integrate that with your personal schedule entries. Similarly, you could download Microsoft Word documents for review at home, or keep track of corporate expenses while on the road. Or, your company could keep a database of business contacts and require you to download it to keep up with clients.

This isn't just vaporware or vague television commercial promises. PDA makers like Motorola and 3Com have been making deals with Oracle, Netscape, and Lotus to port applications to PDAs and store PDA-formatted data on existing systems. Look for increased integration of PDAs into corporate information structures beyond Silicon Valley through 1999.

Using the PDA as a Portable Website Extension

Of course, if you wanted to use your PDA to surf the Web on your way home from work, you can also do that.

Thanks to the ease-of-use for the PalmPilot SDK, a host of information resources and applications have been coded for the Pilot. You can download entire books, plot trips, or call up cocktails thanks to these home-grown resources. Code and command libraries are especially popular: These are useful if you're a traveling consultant and the machine you're debugging is far away from your trusty Perl manual.

HDML

The Pilot's SDK is specific to that one handheld device. Since I'm focusing on how to make your information more widely accessible to the Web at large, let's look at standards for developing Web-based resources. One proposed standard is *Handheld Device Markup Language* (*HDML*).

Created by Unwired Planet (`http://www.uplanet.com/`), HDML is designed to organize and display information on physically small displays. Because hand-held markup devices have physical constraints that personal computers do not— limited screen site, limited memory, and limited bandwidth—Web-based files need to be formatted so they are compact and still easy to read.

HDML tackles the problem of cramming a lot of information into a small space by breaking down information into a series of manipulatable objects called *cards*. A card is the basic building block for an HDML document. A user navigates through cards by moving forward or back, entering information, or changing paths if offered a choice. Cards are grouped in decks: a single HDML document is a deck, with individual cards accessed by anchors. For example, our hypothetical case study at `http://www.escape-key.com/rafting.hdml#kaweah` would access the card per-taining to the Kaweah River; `http://www.escape-key.com/rafting.hdml#klamath` refers to the Klamath River card. Both cards are part of one deck, or document.

This model allows you to break down information into easily displayed for-mats for the PDA's smaller screen, yet still repurpose the document for the Web.

HDML relies on a fairly simple syntax. It differs from HTML, however, because it also defines the navigation behavior through a deck of cards as a series of com-mands, as opposed to setting up a series of modular hyperlinks. HDML is very simi-lar to the Hypercard data presentations that used to be popular on Macintoshes: a document marked up with syntactic information, rendering information, and navi-gation behavior information.

This markup trend—dictating information navigation as well as its presenta-tion—is a good bet for diffusing out into the Web at large. Look for it in corporate applications first.

As for HDML, the proposal has been submitted to the W3C, but as of this writ-ing has not yet been approved. To view the proposal, go to: `http://www.w3.org/TR/NOTE-Submission-HDML-spec.html`.

Can the Web Be Its Own Killer App?

Although the previous sections have focused on ways to use Web-based technol-ogy to extend desktop-based applications into a networked space, the issue of how to extend the Web's capabilities is still valid. How can you put effective task-completing applications online?

There is still an argument to be made for using a network to push and update information. If you run a website with the primary purpose of publishing and updating news or software, you may want to look into techniques for pushing information to your users.

I touched on push technology briefly above; now it's time for the extended treatment. First, perhaps, a brief explanation of what *push* is. Most websites assume that an audience has to come to them in order to read information or download software. The user has to seek out the information, and they have to decide on the frequency with which they visit your site.

A push product sends information to interested users. It can be as low-tech as an e-mail newsletter that users can subscribe to, as mid-tech as a pop-up JavaScript window that lives in the corner of a desktop and updates content on a timed script, or it can be as high-tech as a push channel. These channels are trees of Web documents that are updated on a timed basis; both the document tree structure and the update schedule are defined by a Channel Definition Format (for more on CDFs see Chapter 20).

Push channels have their own set of usability considerations. Briefly, they are:

Bandwidth   A poorly written CDF can cause an entire website to be re-downloaded and displayed whenever an update is scheduled. Write both your files and your CDF to make the updates as lightweight as possible.

Design   If you're building a product that is meant to be specifically displayed on a version 4 browser, you're going to need to make sure it works across both browsers. You also need to make sure it degrades gracefully on lower-end browsers, either by automatically pushing users to an alternate URL, or by displaying a low-tech default page with links to the necessary technologies to view a push product.

Interface   A push product breaks out of the traditional browser and removes the navigational cues users are used to. You're not developing an interface that works on a browser; you're developing a closed interface experience much like a CD-ROM. Be sure to think of all of the functions you want the user to be able to perform, and how you can attach clear and unambiguous visual cues to connote the tasks and display the paths that the user has to take to in order to complete those tasks.

Cross-purposing the files and processes for production   A good push product should be able to extend the purpose of a website, and so should be able to benefit from the same content and production processes as the website production.

Pushing the Web Local

Although one of the growing obsessions in Web development will be smart use of bandwidth, the real action is going to be found someplace completely different: taking the best of Web-based technology and applying it to highly specific, smaller-scale ventures.

By "smaller-scale," I don't mean to denigrate the areas I'm about to cover. I mean that the emphasis on publishing a website to the world has shifted. Instead of posting one hundred pages of information to the presumed global audience, Web developers are shifting their skills to creating local products.

These local products can run the gamut from closed-feedback kiosk-style websites at a local store to a company intranet. Some of the emerging local-style Web development projects are outlined below.

Data Manipulation in Extra-Web Tasks

Push media tried to blend a Web surfer's computer desktop with the World Wide Web by introducing a browser that replaced the desktop. Although the push proponents had a point in trying to integrate network-accessing applications like a browser onto a self-contained computer application like a desktop, the push approach was the computer equivalent of coating a chocolate bar with peanut butter. Good idea, messy and inconvenient implementation.

What the desktop-driven world needed was the equivalent of chocolate-coated peanut butter. Since Reese's isn't getting into the software market, several existing companies have picked up the metaphor and begun working on ways to pull tasks off the desktop and into a networked environment.

One of the initial efforts to do this was the effort by mainstream software publishers to integrate their desktop apps into the browser via browser plug-ins. Both Microsoft and Lotus have published plug-ins that extend the browser's ability to handle documents or perform tasks within a browser, therefore allowing users to perform basic tasks on documents that didn't live within their desktops.

The next step is outfitting the browser with a way to read, recognize, and run simple, extensible applications without requiring the user to install software on their hard drive. As more people find that their work involves multiple computers, or several different physical locations with separate computers, the ability to use the browser to tap into their workplace will become increasingly important.

Moving Data within the Company   Netscape used to offer t-shirts to anyone who found a bug within its beta-version software. The campaign had several beneficial side effects: It reinforced the hacker chic of finding and diagnosing poorly-detected problems, built an interested body of users, and provided the company with a large pool of free labor.

More software companies have discovered that releasing beta versions of their products to the Web is a great way to build a customer base, and gather information about how their product really works. A website is more than a company marketing device for companies like these; it's also a data-gathering tool for both the customer base and the company.

The real question, then, is how do you move information about your customers off the Web server and on to the relevant people within your company?

There are several issues you'll need to consider before answering that question. First, how do the employees need the information formatted? Do these formatting needs change from department to department? For example, if you're running a bug submission database, a submitted entry could be passed to workers as an e-mail entry. This may be handy if you're aiming to provide your site users with instant responses, but how do you log the total information coming in to your site for further analysis?

The answer to the first question about information formatting may lie in your answer to the second question: Why are you collecting data from users? What site goals will the information help you attain? If you're using a bug registry to track where users are encountering bugs in your Web-based products, you're probably looking for trends in testing, like platform and user action. But the same bug registry could be used to track the demographics behind downloading too. Since it's doubtful that the same people who track demographics are also going to be doing iterative product revisions, it's pretty likely that each separate department will need different sections of user input formatted differently.

Enter the Web—or at least Web technology. You can plan your backend development so that one type of information moves from your Web server to your user in a one-to-one flow, and the user's returning information moves to a customizable database that can be accessed by a variety of users. Figure 23.1 illustrates how information flows.

The backend schematic for this sort of data flow would look like Figure 23.2.

FIGURE 23.1:

The gentle ebb and flow of information

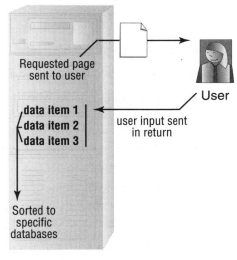

Requested page sent to user

User

data item 1
data item 2
data item 3

user input sent in return

Sorted to specific databases

Server

FIGURE 23.2:

Information schematic between the server and the client

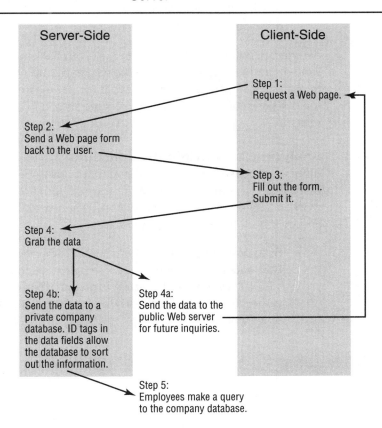

Server-Side

Client-Side

Step 1:
Request a Web page.

Step 2:
Send a Web page form back to the user.

Step 3:
Fill out the form.
Submit it.

Step 4:
Grab the data

Step 4b:
Send the data to a private company database. ID tags in the data fields allow the database to sort out the information.

Step 4a:
Send the data to the public Web server for future inquiries.

Step 5:
Employees make a query to the company database.

Here's how it works:

1. A user calls up your page with the express intent of registering a bug.

2. Your Web server sends back a form-driven page from the public Web server.

3. The user fills out the form and sends it in.

4. The CGI script that grabs the data from the form sends it to two places: the public Web server, where it can be logged in a flat-text file for site regurgitation; and a private company database, where hidden fields in the form help different company departments fit the specific chunk of user data into a larger analytical scheme.

5. Using a backend browser-based tool, different employees can pass query parameters to the company database and see what data corresponds to their queries.

6. If you're feeling especially generous, or you're trying to emphasize customer service, you could provide a one-way info dump between the company database and the public Web server. This would allow you to offer analyzed user comments and stats to your readers.

To recap: Before you begin setting up your backend so user-entered information can be sent to the employees on the backend, find out how your employees need to use that data. Then, figure out what format the data needs to be in. Finally, map the flow of data to your backend scheme so you know what additional security measures or databases you need to set up.

Analyzing Data within the Company Anyone who has ever struggled with filing an expense report will tell you that highly specialized paperwork may be helpful to the people who have to process it, but it confuses people who don't work with those forms on a daily basis. There are two sides to this phenomenon, and they both translate to the Web.

> **Side one** Specialized fields help the specialists collect, process, and analyze data quickly. Whether these fields are box #54 on a financial form, or `<INPUT type="text" name="iguana_diet">` on a Web form, the purpose is the same: to attach classifying labels to data that would not have a context otherwise.

Side two   Trying to sort data without understanding how the labels fit together often leads to one of two results. The data never gets submitted, or the data gets misclassified because the user doesn't clearly understand how to match information to a specialized category.

The answer   Leave all of the specialized data designations behind-the-scenes. Use XML applications to attach data tags that can be read selectively depending on the application a file is opened up in.

Controlling Data Remotely   As companies grow and more employees start their work day by logging into the office instead of walking into it, the need for workers to store their data in a reliable, consistent format will continue to grow.

There are actually reasons for data consistency that have nothing to do with sadistic, mission-statement-writin' managers. They are:

- Data consistency allows you to move information from one worker to another regardless of application and platform system. One of the reasons the Web took off so quickly was because the initial browsers allowed anyone using a Mac, PC, or Unix box to view content, or do simple file exchanges via Gopher or FTP. Take advantage of uniform networking protocols to break free.

- Data consistency allows you to reduce the steps you need to take when moving information from one medium, like a paper brochure, to another, like a website.

- Data consistency allows remote workers to have access to the same information-manipulation tools and results as onsite workers have.

- Data consistency guarantees that people in several different geographic locations don't have to be denied access to information or work-related materials to do their work, nor do they have to be limited by geographic locale.

As more employees request flexible work hours and different work environments, and as more companies rely on branch offices, translating the currency of any business into consistent data formats is going to be more useful.

The tools that made the World Wide Web so successful—limited data-processing tools combined with consistent data transfer protocols—can be harnessed for intranets and extranets.

Teaching, Learning, and Tutoring

The final role for the new-and-improved World Wide Web is actually a reprise of one of cyberspace's original visions: using the Web's technologies to facilitate learning.

This role has its roots in the hypermedia philosophy advanced by computer science pioneer Ted Nelson. Although hypermedia education had a strong association with earlier multimedia efforts like CD-ROMS, expanded electronic texts, and virtual reality, the basic premise has always been the same.

The underlying premise behind computer-mediated learning is basic, and translates well to Web-based technologies. The user accesses the lesson or knowledge base via a browsing interface. The interface has the following features:

- A consistent navigation guide that provides the user with a structured tool for accessing information. Ideally, the navigation guide allows the user to control the level of access, from novice to expert.

- A contents list that allows users to select what area, skill, or item of interest they wish to pursue within the application.

- A series of visual cues that tell the user when they have completed a specific task or acquired a specific skill. Conversely, there are also visual cues to indicate to the reader what missteps they have taken, and pointers to information on how to remedy those missteps.

- The user has the option to control their learning experience within the carefully designed interface by exploiting hypertext to move within the tutorial or educational project.

Although the Web does not readily lend itself to the self-contained atmosphere that most CD-ROMs offer, it can still provide a structured learning experience. And unlike CD-ROMs, Web pages don't demand intensive CPU resources or specific hardware.

By using JavaScript-controlled supplemental windows, timed events, or lightweight embedded applications, you can use the Web as an area to build a tutorial for users. One of the best examples of how to do this is the Web Review DOM tutorial at `http://www.webcoder.com/howto/15/index.html`. Another is the CNet browser playground at `http://builder.com/Programming/Playground/011398/index.html`. Both set apart their educational areas with clear, separate interfaces.

Summary

The Web has been around for a few years now, and it will be around for a while longer. It won't always be restricted to library-like repositories of data. It's time you widened your focus, and started considering how the tools developed for the Web can be extended to other functions, allowing you to accomplish any and all tasks as effectively and efficiently as possible.

The best and most persistent Web technologies may end up being those which facilitate tasks that people were doing long before the Web was a part of daily office life. This chapter outlined some of the possible applications of new technologies to old tasks—scheduling, inventory tracking, research—via Web-based methods like intranets and portable file formats.

If you want to veer into an area that's really on the edge of development trends, stop looking at ways to co-opt new technologies for Website presentation, and start looking at ways to co-opt Web technologies for everyday task execution. The Web has been good to office life so far—let's see if making that development track a two-way street will benefit the Web's toolbox as well.

CHAPTER

TWENTY-FOUR

Case Study #4: Moving from Mainstream Development to Leading-Edge Design

This last case study focuses on a site that changes dramatically when it has its first site overhaul. Before we can enjoy poking among the carnage and upheaval that a radical site overhaul can cause, we need to take a look at how the site was built, and what the developers were thinking as they built the site.

MediaDiet, Round 1: Building the Site

MediaDiet is the brainchild of a few friends who figured they could use the Web to showcase their writing and raise their visibility in editorial circles. Their goal is to publish one topical essay per month on six different topics, and to archive past issues for easy reference. They're anticipating a small audience, which is fortunate since they have a design and production staff of two, and they've wangled free server space from a friend.

I'm going to use MediaDiet as a model for any company that wants to maintain a separate publications section. Since content is what compels visitors to return, incorporating a small-scale, frequently updated content area into your site is a good way to showcase what your company has to offer in a user-friendly format.

Back in MediaDiet's world, there's a designer, David Gordon, who's going to use MediaDiet as an example in his portfolio. His emphasis is on developing a clean, consistent, and distinctive visual look, so he can point to MediaDiet in job interviews. David may be doing a lot of Photoshopping, but his partner, Michelle Edwards, wants to build a site that won't suck up too much production time.

The first thing they need to do is figure out how to translate his design into real-life code. Once Michelle's mocked up the designs, she's going to solidify the backend and set up a production and maintenance schedule that reduces the number of sleepless nights she'll spend each month.

What Development Decisions Were Made

Mediadiet.com is the type of *boutique* or thematic site that websites may launch as an auxiliary to their main site, or as an experiment to see how well their audience responds to a shift from one type of information-dispensing site like a tutorial site to a more editorial focus. As companies continue to woo Web surfers by expanding their sites from online brochures to actual information sources, content sites that have to be built quickly while maintaining a distinctive look and feel will be a more common task for Web developers.

Since establishing a visual identity was important for the site, the first step was to determine the scope of the site, so David could tell how many levels of navigation he wanted to include in the main site design.

To better understand the scope of the site, look at the sitemap depicted below.

Index (Top of Site)

archive/	current/	issues/	feedback/	info/	
index.html	index.html	9801/	9802/	index.html	index.html
		tv/	tv/		
		music/	music/		
		film/	film/		
		book/	book/		
		magazine/	magazine/		
		website/	website/		

Each directory has its own index.html file for that month.

As you can see, there is the top-level front page designed to suck people into the site, then five second-level directories: `archive`, `current`, `issues`, `feedback`, and `info`. Interestingly enough, the archive and current directories appear to only have one file in them. Why is that?

Let's start with the current directory. Rather than store an entire issue of Mediadiet .com in a directory and then move it whenever a new issue supplants it, it's easier to create a symbolic link between `/current/index.html` and the newest index page under the `/issues/` directory. If you look at the `issues` directory, it is where all the content files are stored: First, the files are grouped by issue date, then they are organized by topic. This way, the top-level page in each individual issue folder (`/9801/` or `/9802/`) can just point to `book/index.html`. This organization can readily be re-ordered if they wanted to group their files by topic—book, film, etc.—and cross-reference them by date instead. Since this site seems to be based on a publication model, it made more sense to organize the file tree that way as well, with the consistent topic directories like book and film drawing a parallel to the monthly columns you read in magazines.

The archive file is merely a listing pointing to past issues of Mediadiet.com; it doesn't serve as a storage area for the files.

So David and Michelle have a site that runs on the deep-and-narrow model: Three of the five directories only have one page, and the fourth is only a symlink to a recent file in the fifth directory. The smartest building strategy in this case is to do as little work as possible, since the majority of their reader eyeballs will be in the issues/ directories.

The only concern David and Michelle will have, in fact, is how to maintain a persistent navigation bar through nested directory levels without a lot of work. They solved this by taking the following steps:

- Decide that the primary navigation method is going to be a persistent frame at the bottom of the screen. This is excellent for people who are cruising through the whole site.

- Include a small text navigation bar at the bottom of the page for readers who happen on specific files or are approaching the site with an old browser. This small navigation bar is called as a virtual include at the bottom of the page.

When you look at the finished front door in Figure 24.1, you'll notice that the navigation only covers the five top-level directories. This is because the goal is to get readers to move down within a channel, instead of skipping from section to section and only visiting the top level of each. By addressing top-level navigation consistently, readers have a reliable returning point, but can narrow their surfing focus and stay in one channel longer.

The Scope and Technical Requirements for the Site

The production mandate for the site was to make a small content site have a look that would lend itself to easy association with the site name. In this case a little color and a distinctive font went a long way. The site is still really light on graphics—roughly 16K per page not counting ads—but it's definitely not boring.

Find a color combination that's browser-safe, usable, and unusual.
To find the two colors used repeatedly through Mediadiet.com, David surfed around a few "cool" site hubs, noted the color schemes, and then compiled a list of what they were and what they were not. Like publishing and fashion, certain color combinations go into vogue across the Net, and when David designed this site, it was a season for soft pastels and warm neutrals. So he went for slightly fluorescent colors; instead of looking at this site and thinking of the Pottery Barn, readers are going to be reminded of slurpees or other vaguely artificial colors.

FIGURE 24.1:

By addressing top-level navigation consistently, readers have a reliable returning point, but can narrow their surfing focus and stay in one channel longer.

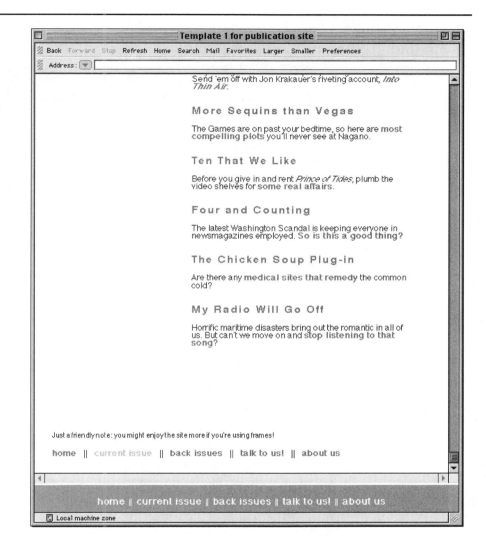

Send 'em off with Jon Krakauer's riveting account, *Into Thin Air.*

More Sequins than Vegas

The Games are on past your bedtime, so here are most compelling plots you'll never see at Nagano.

Ten That We Like

Before you give in and rent *Prince of Tides*, plumb the video shelves for some real affairs.

Four and Counting

The latest Washington Scandal is keeping everyone in newsmagazines employed. So is this a good thing?

The Chicken Soup Plug-in

Are there any medical sites that remedy the common cold?

My Radio Will Go Off

Horrific maritime disasters bring out the romantic in all of us. But can't we move on and stop listening to that song?

Just a friendly note: you might enjoy the site more if you're using frames!

home || current issue || back issues || talk to us! || about us

Find a font or some other distinctive visual trademark.   Some sites have wonderful little icons: The Disgruntled Housewife site (http://www .urbekah.com/housewife/index.html) uses little 1950s-style icons to denote each section (see Figure 24.2).

FIGURE 24.2:

The Disgruntled Housewife site relies on icons as a visual trademark and as a navigation tool.

In this case, since Michelle was trying to keep the site as lightweight as possible, she talked to David and they decided that the fonts used in headlines would do it instead. He used a font called Passtine to make the subheads in each page and balanced its ornate, near-illegibility with a simple, sans-serif head and content font.

Balance the noticeable visual elements with a consistent and easy-to-use layout.   Since David was working with such a non-subtle color palette and a funky font in the headlines, he deliberately made the rest of the site as minimal as possible, which made production grunt Michelle very happy. This has two results, both of which benefit you and your users: The site is ultimately more usable, and your novel site elements have more of a chance to stand out.

Repetition, repetition, repetition Now that David had distinctive elements, the key was to using them consistently. There is not a page on the site that doesn't have both the color scheme and the font—even the pages formatted for printing.

Next, Michelle thought ahead on usability. Frames are wonderful when used in moderation, but they do present a few usability issues. First and foremost is the issue of navigation and printing. Since MediaDiet does have a lot of content and some of it might be printed out for later reading, it's a good idea to offer readers a way to print the pages.

Their solution to this was to offer two article layouts: One was within the traditional frames structure, and the other was a no-frames option. In order to move between the two options, the no-frames option was formatted like this at the bottom of every article:

```
<a href="books/nc_index.html" target="top">Go to a printer-friendly
version</a>.
```

where the URL reflected the content page that would get loaded into the top of the page in the frames version, and the target would indicate a new frame. Since there is minimal text navigation at the bottom of the page, the reader can return to the rest of the site and the frames layout with no problem.

> **NOTE** A persistent bane of website development is the inability to print information easily. I'm not talking about technical difficulties in hooking up a printer to your computer or local network. I'm talking about being able to print Web pages without losing the last twenty letters on every line. If your layout isn't printer-friendly and it can't be simplified, offer a printer-friendly alternative. This is one of the tactics that makes ZDNet (www.zdnet.com/) one of the more consistently usable information resources.

If you brainstorm ahead on usability and the steps you'll have to take to ensure it, you'll be able to whack out the actual code in less time.

After Michelle had hashed out user considerations, she made all the site's graphics in one fell swoop. Since David had a page design in Photoshop or another graphics layout program, Michelle was able to make the graphics straight away.

Even if you don't have the page design in a layout program, the sooner you get all the graphics within the layout made, the better: You can set specifications for the size for heads and subheads, and use those when generating code.

When you're making your graphics, always make sure the file size is as small as possible. Remember that you can always opt for a smaller palette, or a JPEG if reducing the colors looks really gross. For a review of the step-by-step process you can use to reduce your graphics palette, visit Chapter 7.

Finally, Michelle and David considered degradation. Michelle and David had the wonderful advantage of having neither an audience, nor research to see what their target audience would be using to access the site. Keeping this in mind, they went for broke, using a strong HTML 4.0 bias in all their markup, and keeping the structure of the document simple for easy reading in case someone using Netscape 2.0 hits the site.

How Site Templates Were Built

This is the initial draft of the template. Michelle is going to work first on seeing if she can translate David's design into HTML, then work on optimizing the HTML. Since she hates re-doing work, she built her initial template with an eye toward daily production:

```
<html>
<head>
<title>Template 1 for publication site</title>
</head>

<--the nav bar stays the same size no matter what.-->
<frameset rows="*,40">
<!--by eliminating frame borders and spacing, you can create a really
seamless layout and economize on the amount of work you have to do for
persistent site elements.-->
    <frame name="content" src="nc_index.html"frameborder="0"
framespacing="0" border="0" resize="yes" scrolling="yes">
    <frame name="nav" src="nav.html" frameborder="0" framespacing="0"
border="0" resize="no" scrolling="no">
</frameset>

<!--alt for noframes visitors-->
```

```
<noframes>
<!--branding goes here. Remember that the top left corner of your site is
the best area for establishing the identity -->
<div id="brand">
<img src="../images/brand.gif" alt="[mediadiet.com - download me!]"
width="500" height="132" border="0">
</div>

<!--the rest of the layout is a grid: two ads on the left, then a slew of
headlines. Middle of the grid: special issue stuff. -->

<div id="ad">
<!--insert ad 1-->
<!--note: to accommodate sponsors, the ad is always in the same spot on
the screen. It's a good way to keep persistent elements persistent.-->
</div>

<div id="headlines">
<p>
<span id="headlinetext">
<!--insert headlines here-->
Can Guys in Suits Write About TeeVee?
</span>
<span class="slug1">
<br>
Who says that couch potatoes can't dress well? We review critics in
suits, this month in <a href="../9802/tv/index.html"
target="_content">television</a>.
</span>
</p>
<p>
<span id="headlinetext">
<!--insert headlines here-->
<br>
We're Not Worthy! We're Not Worthy!
</span>
<span class="slug1">
<br>
This month's <a href="../9802/magazine/index.html" target="_content">
glossy pages</a> decrees whether or not the media is worth its own
scrutiny.
</span>
```

```
</p>
<p>
<span id="headlinetext">
<!--insert headlines here-->
<br>
Clap If You Believe in Tori
</span>
<span class="slug1">
<br>
She communes with faeries and writes some strange lyrics, but <a
href="../9802/music/index.html" target="_content">her latest album</a>
rocks out.
</span>
</p>
<p>
<span id="headlinetext">
<!--insert headlines here-->
<br>
More Trenchant Stuff!
</span>
<span class="slug1">
<br>
Check out <a href="../issues/index.html">the latest issue</a> and see if
you don't agree with us.
</span>
</p>
</div>

<!--include nav here for people who are frames-impaired. also include
note telling them that they'd have a much better time looking at and
using the site if they were using frames. Provide a link to download. -->
<div id="frameoff">
<p>
<small>
Just a friendly note: you might enjoy the site more if you're using
frames!
</small>
</p>
<p>
<a href="index.html" target="_content">home</a>  ||  <a
href="issue/index.html" target="_content">current issue</a>
 ||  <a href="archive/index.html" target="_content">back
```

```
issues</a>  ||  <a href="feedback/index.html" target="
_content.html">talk to us!</a>  ||  <a href="info/index.html"
target="_content">about us</a>
</p>
</div>
</noframes>
</html>
```

The Style Sheet   As you look over the different pages, you may notice two
different things: Every piece of content is wrapped in a `<div>` tag or a `<span>` tag,
and each of these tags have `class="foo"` next to them, where `"foo"` is something
like "headline," "slug" or "brand." These `<div>` tags are block-level elements that
work within the Document Object Model, and allow us to attach a class to each section of the page. The class, in turn, refers to a specific style.

> **NOTE**   Keep in mind that `<span>` works only in NS4 and IE3. `<div>` works in all browsers.

The Javascript Ad Hovering   This script makes sure that the ad space
always occupies the same area on the page layout, no matter where the user has
scrolled on the page. This function sets the position for the pop-up cart. Basically,
it's saying, "measure the width of the display area within the browser, subtract
450 pixels from the right, and stick the cart div there. Be sure to place the card div
140 px from the top of the window too.

```
function moveLayers() {
        if (gotlayers) {
                if (NS4) {
                        screenWidth = window.innerWidth;
                        document.layers['searchKick'].left = _
screenWidth-450;
                        document.layers['searchKick'].top = 140;
                } else {
                        screenWidth = document.body.clientWidth + 18;
                        document.all['searchKick'].style.pixelLeft = _
screenWidth-450;
                        document.all['searchKick'].style.pixelTop = 140;
                }
        }
}
```

Figure 24.3 shows the MediaDiet site template.

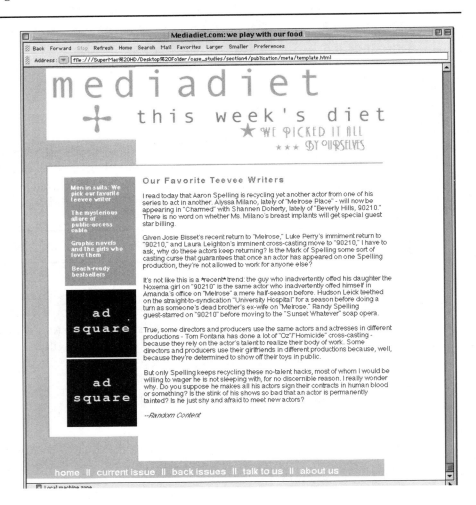

How the Templates Were Modified for Daily Production

This is the main document, the one that calls all the frames. Notice that it also offers a non-frames alternative:

```
<html>
<head>
<title>Template 1 for publication site</title>
```

```
</head>

#the nav bar stays the same size no matter what.-->
<frameset rows="*,40">
<!--by eliminating frame borders and spacing, you can create a really
seamless layout and economize on the amount of work you have to do for
persistent site elements.-->
    <frame name="content" src="nc_index.html" frameborder="0"
framespacing="0" border="0" resize="yes" scrolling="yes">
    <frame name="nav" src="nav.html" frameborder="0" framespacing="0"
border="0" resize="no" scrolling="no">
</frameset>

<!--alt for noframes visitors-->
<noframes>
<!--branding goes here. Remember that the top left corner of your site is
the best area for establishing the identity -->
<div id="brand">
<img src="../images/brand.gif" alt="[mediadiet.com - download me!]"
width="500" height="132" border="0">
</div>

<!--the rest of the layout is a grid: two ads on the left, then a slew of
headlines. Middle of the grid: special issue stuff. -->

<div id="ad">
<!--insert ad 1-->
<!--note: to accomodate sponsors, the ad is always in the same spot on
the screen. It's a good way to keep persistent elements persistent.-->
</div>

<div id="headlines">
<p>
<span id="headlinetext">
<!--insert headlines here-->
Can Guys in Suits Write About TeeVee?
</span>
<span class="slug1">
<br>
Who says that couch potatoes can't dress well? We review critics in
suits, this month in <a href="../9802/tv/index.html"
target="_content">television</a>.
```

```
</span>
</p>
<p>
<span id="headlinetext">
<!--insert headlines here-->
<br>
We're Not Worthy! We're Not Worthy!
</span>
<span class="slug1">
<br>
This month's <a href="../9802/magazine/index.html"
target="_content">glossy pages</a> decrees whether or not the media is
worth its own scrutiny.
</span>
</p>
<p>
<span id="headlinetext">
<!--insert headlines here-->
<br>
Clap If You Believe in Tori
</span>
<span class="slug1">
<br>
She communes with faeries and writes some strange lyrics, but <a
href="../9802/music/index.html" target="_content">her latest album</a>
rocks out.
</span>
</p>
<p>
<span id="headlinetext">
<!--insert headlines here-->
<br>
More Trenchant Stuff!
</span>
<span class="slug1">
<br>
Check out <a href="../issues/index.html">the latest issue</a> and see if
you don't agree with us.
</span>
</p>
</div>
```

```
<!--include nav here for people who are frames-impaired. also include
note telling them that they'd have a much better time looking at and
using the site if they were using frames. Provide a link to download. -->
<div id="frameoff">
<p>
<small>
Just a friendly note: you might enjoy the site more if you're using
frames!
</small>
</p>
<p>
<a href="index.html" target="_content">home</a>  ||  <a href=
"issue/index.html" target="_content">current issue</a>  ||  <a
href="archive/index.html" target="_content">back issues</a>
 ||  <a href="feedback/index.html" target="_content.html">
talk to us!</a>  ||  <a href="info/index.html" target=
"_content">about us</a>
</p>
</div>
</noframes>
</html>
```

And here are the files for each of the contents within the frame. This is the code
for the persistent nav bar:

```
<html>
<head>
<title>nav bar</title>

<style type="text/css">
body      {background-color:#99FF00; color:#FFFFFF; margin-left:10px;}
A:link     {font-family: helvetica, arial, sans serif; font-weight:
bold; color:#FFFFFF; font-size:14px; padding:10px;}
A:visited     {font-family: helvetica, arial, sans serif; color:
#0099CC; font-size:14px; padding:10px;}
#navbottom     {position:absolute; left:70px;}
</style>
</head>

<body>

<div id="navbottom">
```

```html
<a href="../index.html" target="content">home</a>  ||  <a
href="../issues/index.html" target="content">current issue</a>
 ||  <a href="../archive/index.html" target="content">back
issues</a>  ||  <a href="../feedback/index.html" target=
"content.html">talk to us!</a>  ||  <a href="../info/
index.html" target="content">about us</a>
</div>

</body>

</html>
```

Here's the code for an index page for the site:

```html
<html>
<head>
<title>content for publication index template</title>

<style type="text/css">
body      {background-color:#FFFFFF; color:#333333; font-family:
helvetica, arial, sans serif; font-size:12px;}
A:link      {font-family: helvetica, arial, sans serif; font-weight:
bold; color:#0099CC; font-size:12px;}
A:visited      {position: absolute; font-family: helvetica, arial, sans
serif; color:#99FF99; font-size:12px;}

#brand      {left:0px; top:25px; border:1; width:500;}
#pagebrand{}
#ad       {}
#dateline      {position: absolute; left:20px; top: 185px; width:500px;
border:1px; line-height:20px; color:#0099CC; font-family:helvetica,
arial, sans serif; letter-spacing:2px; font-size:20px;}

#headlines      {position: absolute; left:225px; top: 225px;
width:325px; border:1px;line-height:10px;}

h2      {color:#0099CC; font-family:helvetica, arial, sans serif;
letter-spacing:2px; font-size:15px; font-weight:bold;}

#slug      {color:#333333;font-family:helvetica, arial, sans serif;
font-size:8px; line-height:16px;}
```

```
#frameoff          {position:absolute; left:25px; top:800px; font-
family:helvetica, arial, sans serif; font-size:12 px; color:#333333;}
</style>


</head>

<body>

<!--branding goes here. Remember that the top left corner of your site
is the best area for establishing the identity -->
<div id="brand">
<img src="../images/brand.gif" alt="[mediadiet.com - download me!]"
width="500" height="132" border="0">
</div>

<!--the rest of the layout is a grid: two ads on the left, then a slew
of headlines. Middle of the grid: special issue stuff. -->

<div id="ad">
<!--insert ad 1-->
<!--note: to accomodate sponsors, the ad is always in the same spot on
the screen. It's a good way to keep persistent elements persistent.-->
</div>

<div id="headlines">
<p>
<span id="headlinetext">
<!--insert headlines here-->
Can Guys in Suits Write About TeeVee?
</span>
<span class="slug1">
<br>
Who says that couch potatoes can't dress well? We review critics in
suits, this month in <a href="../9802/tv/index.html" target="content">
television</a>.
</span>
</p>
<p>
<span id="headlinetext">
<!--insert headlines here-->
<br>
```

```
We're Not Worthy! We're Not Worthy!
</span>
<span class="slug1">
<br>
This month's <a href="../9802/magazine/index.html"
target="content">glossy pages</a> decrees whether or not the media is
worth its own scrutiny.
</span>
</p>
<p>
<span id="headlinetext">
<!--insert headlines here-->
<br>
Clap If You Believe in Tori
</span>
<span class="slug1">
<br>
She communes with faeries and writes some strange lyrics, but <a
href="../9802/music/index.html" target="content">her latest album</a>
rocks out.
</span>
</p>
<p>
<span id="headlinetext">
<!--insert headlines here-->
<br>
More Trenchant Stuff!
</span>
<span class="slug1">
<br>
Check out <a href="../issues/index.html" target="content">the latest
issue</a> and see if you don't agree with us.
</span>
</p>
</div>

<!--#an include goes here if the browser detects a low-end, no-frames
version of its software. -->
</body>
</html>
```

And here's the code for a sample index page:

```html
<html>
<head>
<title>content for publication index template</title>
<style type="text/css">
body      {background-color:#FFFFFF; color:#333333; font-family:
helvetica, arial, sans serif; font-size:12px;}
A:link      {font-family: helvetica, arial, sans serif; font-weight:
bold; color:#0099CC; font-size:12px;}
A:visited      {position: absolute; font-family: helvetica, arial, sans
serif; color:#99FF99; font-size:12px;}

#brand      {left:0px; top:25px; border:1; width:500;}
#ad      {}
#dateline      {position: absolute; left:20px; top: 185px; width:500px;
border:1px; line-height:20px; color:#0099CC; font-family:helvetica,
arial, sans serif; letter-spacing:2px; font-size:20px;}

#headlines      {position: absolute; left:225px; top: 225px;
width:325px; border:1px;line-height:10px;}

h2      {color:#0099CC; font-family:helvetica, arial, sans serif;
letter-spacing:2px; font-size:15px; font-weight:bold;}

#slug      {color:#333333;font-family:helvetica, arial, sans serif;
font-size:8px; line-height:16px;}

#frameoff      {position:absolute; left:25px; top:800px; font-
family:helvetica, arial, sans serif; font-size:12 px; color:#333333;}
</style>
</head>

<body bgcolor="#FFFFFF" text="#000000" link="#99FF99" vlink="#66CCCC">

<!--branding goes here. Remember that the top left corner of your site
is the best area for establishing the identity -->
<div id="brand">
<img src="../images/brand.gif" alt="[mediadiet.com - download me!]"
width="500" height="132" border="0">
</div>
<!--this the archive layout -->
<div id="dateline">
```

```
february: we ain't got no valentine. so what?
</div>
<div id="headlines">
<!--bigger headline-->
<h2>One Angry Mountain</h2>
<!--descriptive slug -->
<p>
So your significant other dumped you to go climb Everest? Send 'em off
with Jon Krakauer's riveting account, <cite><a href="../9802/book/
index.html" target="content">Into Thin Air.</a></cite>
<br>
</p>
<!--bigger headline-->
<h2>More Sequins than Vegas</h2>
<!--descriptive slug -->
<p>
The Games are on past your bedtime, so here are <a href="../9802/tv/
index.html" target="content">most compelling plots</a> you'll never see
at Nagano.
</p>
<!--bigger headline-->
<h2>Ten That We Like</h2>
<!--descriptive slug -->
<p>
Before you give in and rent <cite>Prince of Tides</cite>, plumb the
video shelves for <a href="../9802/film/index.html" target="content">
some real affairs</a>.
<br>
</p>
<!--bigger headline-->
<h2>Four and Counting</h2>
<!--descriptive slug -->
<p>
The latest Washington Scandal is keeping everyone in newsmagazines
employed. <a href="../9802/magazine/index.html" target="content">So is
this a good thing?</a>
<br>
</p>
<!--bigger headline-->
<h2>The Chicken Soup Plug-in</h2>
<!--descriptive slug -->
<p>
Are there any <a href="../9802/website/index.html" target="content">
medical sites that remedy</a> the common cold?
```

```
<br>
</p>
<!--bigger headline-->
<h2>My Radio Will Go Off</h2>
<!--descriptive slug -->
<p>
Horrific maritime disasters bring out the romantic in all of us. But
can't we move on and <a href="../9802/music/index.html"
target="content">stop listening to that song</a>?
<br>
</p>
</div>


<!--include nav here for people who are frames-impaired. also include
note telling them that they'd have a much better time looking at and
using the site if they were using frames. Provide a link to download. -
->
<div id="frameoff"><p>
<small>
Just a friendly note: you might enjoy the site more if you're using
frames!
</small>
</p>
<p>
<a href="../index.html" target="content">home</a>  ||  <a
href="../issues/index.html" target="content">current issue</a>
 ||  <a href="../archive/index.html" target="content">back
issues</a>  ||  <a href="../feedback/index.html" target=
"content.html">talk to us!</a>  ||  <a href="../info/
index.html" target="content">about us</a>
</p></div>


</body>
</html>
```

NOTE

Fast development tip: I've found that if you develop on a somewhat restrictive browser/platform combination, the tight parameters force you to build a solid product and it tests well across other browsers and platforms. Therefore, my current venue of choice is Internet Explorer 4 on a Mac—the somewhat limited stylesheet interpretation and equally novel scripting engine make it a perfect worst-case-scenario browser for testing JavaScript and style sheets.

The Source Code

The source code for the entire site is available on the CD-ROM that accompanies this book. Refer to the following filenames:

- `index.html`
- `archive_index.html`
- `current_index.html`
- `books_index.html`
- `music_index.html`
- `film_index.html`
- `teevee/index.html`
- `web_index.html`
- `magazine_index.html`
- `feedback_index.html`

MediaDiet, Round 2: Giving the Site a Facelift and Adding Leading-Edge Features

Now that MediaDiet's built a steady readership of 10,000 unique users a month, the editorial staff wants to increase the frequency of publication. This usually isn't a cause for alarm, but the backend of the site is built specifically to deal with monthly editions, not topic-specific divisions.

Michelle has a choice: re-organize the site and find a way to help readers think of MediaDiet as a subject-driven site instead of an edition-driven site, or find a way to cram four times the content into a predefined site structure. One of the features often found in CD-ROM presentations is the ability to flip seamlessly between pages in a narrative; the Web's hanging pauses between pages in a narrative are often annoying, and they ruin one of the primary objectives of usable media: The medium should not interfere with the message. The MediaDiet site is going from a monthly schedule to a weekly one, so David and Michelle are going to overhaul the `music/index.html`, `television/index.html`, `film/index.html`, `magazine/index.html`, `website/index.html`, and `book/index.html` to let readers flip from article to article within the month's publishing run.

What Development Decisions Were Made and How They Affected the Technical Implementations

There are two specific challenges here: How do you devise a production routine that works well within the site's current directory structure, and how do you find a way to cram four times as much content into the same site structure—or expand gracefully?

The answer for this site is a combination of server-side includes and JavaScript-driven DHTML. The includes contain text and nothing but text; this way, they can render neatly in a DHTML space, or within a printable file.

> **NOTE**   We're preserving the printable files for two reasons. First, they're one way of establishing permanent URLs for a specific article, in case another site wants to link to the file. Second, they're a courtesy to readers, and it takes next-to-no time to produce them.

The JavaScript-driven DHTML is a little more complex, since you will be relying on your users to have their scripting capabilities turned on in the browser. However, it is a good way to fit distinct chunks of information into the same space. You have four different articles, each of which fits in its own `<div>` container. Three of the four articles are invisible. However, you can use a mini-table of contents to click between the articles, thus making different layers visible or invisible.

In the case of Mediadiet.com, David and Michelle are going to keep the same directory structure and general issue model: Each issue index page acts as a table of contents (`issue/index.html`), and the links on the issue table of contents page lead to index pages within the issue's topical subdirectories. In order to handle the increased content, instead of building out four times as many subdirectories, they're going to use different HTML layers plus visibility attributes, to stuff all the new content into one file.

To help you visualize this, take a look at Figure 24.4: layers 1, 2, and 3 are all contained within a parent document. Yet by using the visibility attribute in style sheets, only one layer needs to be visible at a time. As a result, you can stuff a lot of discrete text passages into one document.

FIGURE 24.4:

Several separate layers can occupy the same area in one parent document. In this diagram, I've staggered the blocks representing the layers to show you how they appear "stacked" one on top of the other.

<div #1>

<div #2>

<div #3>

In the case of MediaDiet, you have four different content items, each of which fits in its own `<div>` container. Three of the four articles are invisible. However, you can use a mini-table of contents to click between the articles, thus making different layers visible or invisible.

The big tradeoff to this, of course, is that archiving the articles for easy display becomes more complicated. Since the production plan calls only for a new `<div>` to be made visible every day, archiving a discrete list of hide-and-seek files is out of the question.

This is where the printer-only file comes to the rescue. Even though we have abandoned frames, it is still good usability practice to include content without a lot of extraneous formatting, and so we're going to keep including a link to a print-only file at the bottom of each article `<div>`.

So part of daily production will be twofold: incorporating a content include in the carefully structured DHTML template, and building a separate file with the same content include in a generic text format. Since the printer-ready files are all unique files, they can be listed in an archive.

NOTE   There is a drawback to the printer-friendly page solution because it does not immediately divert traffic to the main MediaDiet site. The best way to get around this is simply to add the navigation `<div>` to the bottom of the page to drive traffic back to the main site.

To solve the similar archive problem—the listings do not showcase the individual weekly pages—the archive can be formatted as shown in Figure 24.5.

Now that Michelle and David have tackled how to stuff four times the content into an existing file structure, it's time to tackle production duties. Since there is a rise in the amount of material being published, it makes sense that there is a corresponding rise in the amount of work. However, it doesn't have to be four times the work to produce four times the content.

Clearly, the question is: how do you do more with less?

The answer: includes, includes, includes. It's far easier to set up a few boilerplate templates and stick a few malleable includes in them than it is to produce a number of discrete pages each week. Using the includes and DHTML solutions we've discussed above, let's take a look at the two types of workflow David and Michelle will deal with.

FIGURE 24.5:

The hierarchical links in the archive present the weekly issues, then the specific articles in each issue.

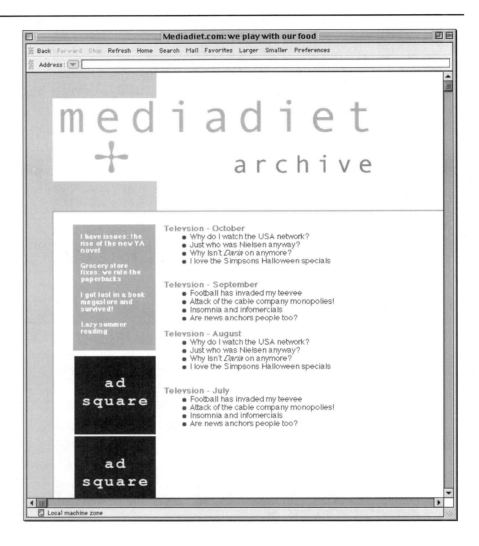

As you may have noticed from other case studies, work flow becomes more complex when you're moving a site from one iteration to the next. Since Mediadiet .com is moving to a more frequently-updated schedule, it's necessary to look at workflow in two different ways: as a set of renovation tasks, and as a set of regular production tasks.

Workflow #1: Setting Up the Site for the New and Improved Look and Feel   This is the prototyping and experimenting stage. Although integrating existing content into the new layout should be a concern, David and Michelle plan on designing and building the first rounds of this new site as if it were their first site. This way, they can assess how to build the parts independently and efficiently, and then match up their processes and parts without their existing website production routines.

> **Assess graphics**   Can you re-incorporate the same graphics into your new layout? Michelle wanted to do as little work as possible, so she decided the answer was going to be yes. By staggering the brand ID (the MediaDiet logo) and the section head, she was able to re-arrange two old elements to look newer and nicer.

> **Assess the color scheme**   Since the color combination still looks fresh and usable, David's sticking with it.

> **Hash out what types of pages you'll have**   Michelle knows from looking at the sitemap that there are three distinct types of content pages they'll be updating on a regular basis: the index pages (front door and issue pages), the content pages, and the archive.

> **Determine whether each page has a distinct layout, or if it's going to have smaller, topic-specific distinct formatting**   In this case, since the staff hasn't expanded while the content has, it's better to have one document "shell" and rely on different data organization to set the different types of content apart.

> **Design the new layout**   They already have a list of graphic elements, plus the functions for the pages, so they only need to figure out what you need from the new layout. In this case, it's a one-document layout that still manages to cram several types of information into the page without looking crowded. No problem, right?

> **Build the templates**   There is only one shell, so they can spend more time refining the data presentation and organization in the three content-heavy types of pages.

> **Test the templates and existing includes**   This is to determine whether or not Michelle and David are going to have to reformat their current content. The answer they want to hear is "no," since it's very likely that changing your formats will affect the production schedule and the editorial process.

Workflow #2: Migrating Old Material to a New Production Scheme

Since all we're doing is expanding the content, the most significant part of remaking the site will be in the ease of daily production. However, whenever you remake a site, it never hurts to figure out where the makeover begins, and what persistent existing material—like archives and index pages—it affects.

Decide where your cut-off point for old and new material is   Sometimes it's smarter to simply leave old material alone.

Determine if any of your new and improved template files have the same names or functions as your old files   For example, if you're used to assembling the front page by typing `<!--#include virtual="template .htmlf" -->` and you have an old version and a new version, you could have all sorts of formatting trouble. It's simply easier to rename your new files so they don't work retroactively in ways you didn't anticipate.

Determine if any of your content needs to be moved over   Since all of the content includes were formatted using extremely basic standard valid HTML, this isn't a problem. However, if you're trying to make the switch from a `<font color="#336600" size="6" face="courier">Headline </font>` type of markup to a valid style-sheet-driven markup, you may need to strip out your includes of any wayward formatting.

Workflow #3: Doing Weekly Production   This is the routine that you should devise only after you've gotten in touch with your inner slacker. The idea is to build out those templates and your existing chunks of content, plus all the new material, while doing as little new work as possible. To do this:

Break down your new template into modular parts   This will make it easier to modify separate parts if sections appear or disappear.

Identify the frequently-updated parts in each "model" (i.e. template) page   After you've itemized all the parts, determine how frequently they get updated. Here's the survey for Mediadiet.com:

Part	Tasks Involved
Topic article	Updating JavaScript variables to make the new article the visible one, adding the new include call to the template, formatting include so it fits in the template, changing links on mini-table of contents in the page, formatting the printer-friendly version of the article.

Part	Tasks Involved
Index page to site	Drop in new content links, add blurbs promoting new articles. Ideally, the only file you'll have to update is an include file.
Issue page	Rewrite blurbs to reflect the current week's contents. Remember that links to topical articles stay the same for the entire month.
Archive page	Because the month's articles are all accessible on topical pages or issue pages, there's no need to archive them until a new monthly issue comes out. When you do have to add new issues to the archive, it's a matter of adding the articles week by week.

Set up a routine for yourself   In this case, a weekly routine might include doing all article production first, then issue production, then archive production.

Now that we've taken a look at the meta-steps, let's get a little more specific about the production particulars in assembling the template for the new Mediadiet.com.

How the Site Changed

There were many particularly spectacular and dramatic changes when MediaDiet moved from one design to the next. Briefly, they included:

- Eliminating frames from the design. This is a good thing, since it makes bookmarking specific pages easier.

- Moving to a total DHTML format.

- Since the site overhaul was so complete, it's simpler to just look at the newly redesigned site.

How Site Templates Were Built

Let's start with specific skills, then move to larger site issues. The most dramatic change is the incorporation of DHTML, so let's start there:

1. Set up the styles for the four divs. Each div will be assigned to a corresponding week's content chunk.

```
#article1     {}
#article2     {}
```

```
#article3      {}
#article4      {}
```

These styles go in the style sheet at the head of your document, or within the style sheet document you're referencing for the entire site. Notice that #article1 is set to visible, and the rest are invisible.

2. Set up the style for the mini-table of contents.

```
#minitoc       {}
```

3. Format all five of your divs—the four content areas, plus the mini-table of contents. The source code for this is included in the companion CD-ROM.

4. Write your JavaScript. Here's the whole script:

```
<SCRIPT LANGUAGE="JavaScript">

    var totalLayersInLoop=4;
    var layerNumShowing=1;

    function domhack(){
    if (navigator.appName == "Netscape") {
                layerStyleRef="layer.";
                layerRef="document.layers";
                styleSwitch="";
    }else{
                layerStyleRef="layer.style.";
                layerRef="document.all";
                styleSwitch=".style";
        }
    }

    function showArticleNumber(number){
        var layerNumToShow=number;
        hideArticle(eval('"article' + layerNumShowing+'"'));
        showArticle(eval('"article' + layerNumToShow+'"'));
        layerNumShowing=layerNumToShow;
    }

    function showArticle(layerName){
```

```
            eval(layerRef+'["'+layerName+'"]'+styleSwitch+'.visibility=
"visible"');
    }

    function hideArticle(layerName){

eval(layerRef+'["'+layerName+'"]'+styleSwitch+'.visibility="hidden"');
    }

</SCRIPT>


<SCRIPT LANGUAGE="JavaScript">
//Define your variables. This line tells you how many article
containers there are.
    var totalLayersInLoop=4;
//This stipulates what article number ought to be visible when the user
loads the page.
//Since a new article div is going to be added weekly, you can just
change the variable
//to correspond with the most recent article, so the first week of the
month has a value
// of 1, the second week has a value of 2, etc.
    var layerNumShowing=1;

//This loads with the page, and we have to include it to make sure
//both Netscape and IE can handle the div manipulation, since
//they treat style application differently in their document object
models.
        function domhack(){
        if (navigator.appName == "Netscape") {
                layerStyleRef="layer.";
                layerRef="document.layers";
                styleSwitch="";
        }else{
                layerStyleRef="layer.style.";
                layerRef="document.all";
                styleSwitch=".style";
        }
    }
```

```
//This is function is a routine that says, "when you pass me
// the specific number for a layer, I'm going to show that layer and
// hide the others." The components in the function are:
     function showArticleNumber(number){

//This line takes the number that got passed in (number), and makes it
the global
//variable for the layer to be shown.
         var layerNumToShow=number;

//This calls the hideArticle function and passes it the number of the
article
//div that is currently live.
         hideArticle(eval('"article' + layerNumShowing+'"'));

//This calls the showArticle function and passes it that new variable
//we created a few lines back.
         showArticle(eval('"article' + layerNumToShow+'"'));
//This resets the old showing layer to the new layer we want to show.
         layerNumShowing=layerNumToShow;
     }

//This shows whatever layerName value gets passed to it. In this
//case, it's the layername (article+number) concatenated
//with a visibility style call.
     function showArticle(layerName){

eval(layerRef+'["'+layerName+'"]'+styleSwitch+'.visibility="visible"');
     }
//This hides whatever layerName value gets passed to it. In this
//case, it's the layername (article+number) concatenated
//with a visibility style call.
     function hideArticle(layerName){

eval(layerRef+'["'+layerName+'"]'+styleSwitch+'.visibility="hidden"');
     }

</SCRIPT>
```

Once you've followed those steps, it's time to focus on the HTML.

```
<html>

<head>
<title>Mediadiet.com: we play with our food</title>

<!--insert div-swapping script here-->
<!--/end div-swapping script-->

<!--insert stylesheet here-->
<style type="text/css">
body     {background-color:#FFFFFF; color:#333333; font-
family:helvetica, arial, sans serif; font-size:12px;}

A:link     {font-family: helvetica, arial, sans serif; font-
weight:bold; color:#0099CC; font-size:12px;}

A:visited     {position: absolute; font-family: helvetica, arial, sans
serif; color:#99FF99; font-size:12px;}

h2     {color:#0099CC; font-family:helvetica, arial, sans serif;
letter-spacing:2px; font-size:15px; font-weight:bold;}

#greenback     {position:absolute; left:0px; top:0px; width:200px;
z-index:10; height:800px; border-style:solid; border-color:#99FF99;
border:1px; background-color:#99FF99;}

#brand     {position:absolute; z-index:20; left:40px; top:40px;
border:1px; border-color:#FFFFFF; width:500; height:132;}

#subject_subhead     {position:absolute; z-index:100; left:72px;
top:452px; width:125px; height:255px; border:1px; border-color:#FFFFFF;
border-style:solid; background-color:#FFFFFF;}

#blueborder     {position:absolute; z-index:40; left:40px; top:220px;
border:1px; border-style:solid; border-color:#66CCCC; background-
color:#66CCCC; width:600px; height:502px;}

#canvas     {position:absolute; z-index:60; left:42px; top: 222px;
border:1px; border-style:solid; border-color:#FFFFFF; background-
color:#FFFFFF; width:600px; height:500px;}

#nav     {position:absolute; z-index:80; left:40px; top:769px;
background-color:#99FF99; width:600px; height:30px; margin:10px;}
```

```
#ads        {position:absolute; z-index:100; left:72px; top:452px;
width:125px; height:255px; border:1px; border-color:#FFFFFF; border-
style:solid; background-color:#FFFFFF;}

#copyright      {position:absolute; z-index:100; left:72px; top:790px;
width:125px; height:255px; border:1px; border-color:#FFFFFF; border-
style:solid; background-color:#FFFFFF;}

#article1     {position: absolute; z-index:100; left:210px; top:242px;
width:450px; height:480px; background-color:#FFFFFF; border-
color:#FFFFFF; border:1px border-style:solid; visibility:visible;}

#article2     {position: absolute; z-index:120; left:210px; top:242px;
width:450px; height:480px; background-color:#FFFFFF; border-
color:#FFFFFF; border:1px border-style:solid; visibility:hidden;}

#article3     {position: absolute; z-index:140; left:210px; top:242px;
width:450px; height:480px; background-color:#FFFFFF; border-
color:#FFFFFF; border:1px border-style:solid; visibility:hidden;}

#article4     {position: absolute; z-index:160; left:210px; top:242px;
width:450px; height:480px; background-color:#FFFFFF; border-
color:#FFFFFF; border:1px border-style:solid; visibility:hidden;}

#minitoc      {position:absolute; z-index:100; left:72px; top:242px;
width:125px; height:200px; border:1px; border-color:#66CCCC; border-
style:solid; background-color:#66CCCC; margin:10px;}
</style>
<!--/end stylesheet-->

<body onLoad="domhack()">

<!--this div deals with the big green block down the side of the page--
>
<div id="greenback">
</div>

<!--this div pulls in the mediadiet logo-->
<div id="brand">
<img src="../images/brand2.gif" width="500" height="132" border="0">
</div>
```

```
<!--this div pulls in the page title gfx -->
<div id="subject_subhead">
<img src="../images/issue_hed.gif" alt="[this week's diet]" width="450"
height="104" border="0">
</div>

<!--this div sets up the blue lines ringing the main content area-->
<!--note that in order to maintain the DOM set up the in the
javascript, we don't have a lot of child divs. instead, we use a lot of
z-index values to make sure things float where they're supposed to. -->
<div id="blueborder">
</div>
<!--keeping with the white/blue-no-child divs theme, here's a white div
to provide a backdrop for the articles.-->
<div id="canvas">
</div>

<!--mini-toc for switching between articles-->
<div id="minitoc">
<br>
<p><a href="javascript:showArticleNumber(1)"><span style="color:
#FFFFFF; font-family:helvetica, arial, sans-serif; font-weight:bold;
line-height:11px; font-size:10px">I have issues: the rise of the new YA
novel</SPAN></a></p>
<p><a href="javascript:showArticleNumber(2)"><span style="color:
#FFFFFF; font-family:helvetica, arial, sans-serif; font-weight:bold;
line-height:11px; font-size:10px">Grocery store fixes: we rate the
paperbacks</SPAN></a></p>
<p><a href="javascript:showArticleNumber(3)"><span style="color:
#FFFFFF; font-family:helvetica, arial, sans-serif; font-weight:bold;
line-height:11px; font-size:10px">I got lost in a book megastore and
survived! </SPAN></a></p>
<p><a href="javascript:showArticleNumber(4)"><span style="color
:#FFFFFF; font-family:helvetica, arial, sans-serif; font-weight:bold;
line-height:11px; font-size:10px">Lazy summer reading</SPAN></a></p>
</div>

<!--the div for ads-->
<div id="ads">
<img src="../../../general/ad-square.gif" alt="[125x125 banner]"
width="125" height="125" border="0">
<img src="../../../general/ad-square.gif" alt="[125x125 banner]"
width="125" height="125" border="0">
```

```
</div>

<!--article 1-->
<div id="article1">
<!--#include virtual="book/article1.htmlf" -->
<!--this is where content goes-->
<h2>Our Favorite Teevee Writers</h2>
<p>
I read today that Aaron Spelling is recycling yet another actor from
one of his series to act in another. Alyssa Milano, lately of "Melrose
Place" - will now be appearing in "Charmed" with Shannen Doherty,
lately of "Beverly Hills, 90210." There is no word on whether Ms.
Milano's breast implants will get special guest star billing.
</p>
<p>
Given Josie Bisset's recent return to "Melrose," Luke Perry's imminent
return to "90210," and Laura Leighton's imminent cross-casting move to
"90210," I have to ask, why do these actors keep returning? Is the Mark
of Spelling some sort of casting curse that guarantees that once an
actor has appeared on one Spelling production, they're not allowed to
work for anyone else?
</p>
<p>
It's not like this is a *recent* trend: the guy who inadvertently offed
his daughter the Noxzema girl on "90210" is the same actor who
inadvertently offed himself in Amanda's office on "Melrose" a mere
half-season before. Hudson Leick teethed on the straight-to-syndication
"University Hospital" for a season before doing a turn as someone's
dead brother's ex-wife on "Melrose." Randy Spelling guest-starred on
"90210" before moving to the "Sunset Whatever" soap opera.
</p>
<p>
True, some directors and producers use the same actors and actresses in
different productions - Tom Fontana has done a lot of "Oz"/"Homicide"
cross-casting - because they rely on the actor's talent to realize
their body of work. Some directors and producers use their girlfriends
in different productions because, well, because they're determined to
show off their toys in public.
</p>
<p>
```

But only Spelling keeps recycling these no-talent hacks, most of whom I would be willing to wager he is not sleeping with, for no discernible reason. I really wonder why. Do you suppose he makes all his actors sign their contracts in human blood or something? Is the stink of his shows so bad that an actor is permanently tainted? Is he just shy and afraid to meet new actors?
```
</p>
<p>
<cite> --Random Content</cite>
</p>
</div>

<!--article 2-->
<div id="article2">
<h2>The Mysterious Allure of Arty TV</h2>
<p>
```
Putting aside for a moment the irony of regional identity on television - which has done more to homogenize the nation than even a countrywide railway system or radio did - let's examine the wisdom behind putting big, Irish families on television.
```
</p><p>
```
It's a bad idea because television is pulling out the same myths that justified NINA: the Irish are all manic for the auld sod, and, even after a hundred years in the New World, retain the bezerker Celtic id that makes life so very interesting. This why the Irish on TV this fall are all cops: it's the logical career choice for a clan of people who used to paint themselves blue.
```
</p><p>
```
So why is television suddenly so interested in the Irish? To quote Robert Singer, executive producer of _Turks_, a show about the Irish clan Turk, all of whom are evidently employed by the Chicago police department, "people of ethnicity are interesting. They bring more to the emotional table."
```
</p><p>
```
Does this mean when _Turks_, _Costello_, _To Have and to Hold_, and _Trinity_ all go the way of the May Day peace accord, we can mine other ethnic groups for what they bring to the table?
```
</p><p>
```
Like, say, Haitians? There's a large Haitian population in this country. Surely they bring the same amount of cachet to the table that the Irish do. Imagine the possibilities for shows ...

```
</p><p>
_The Voodoo That You Do_: a large, close-knit Haitian family grapples
with working on an urban police force while re-examining tricky
metaphysical issues like involuntary servitude after death.
</p><p>
"We went with the Haitians because spiritual rituals are such a rich,
vital part of their culture. They bring more to the organized religion
table." explained John Doe.
</p><p>
Not likely. Any ethnic group originating south of the 40th parallel
goes beyond the pale - and I do mean that literally - of television's
ethnic experience.
</p>
<p>
<cite> --Random Content</cite>
</p>
</div>


<!--article 3-->
<div id="article3">
<h2>Graphic Novels & the Girls who love 'em</h2>
<p>
I read today that Aaron Spelling is recycling yet another actor from
one of his series to act in another. Alyssa Milano, lately of "Melrose
Place" - will now be appearing in "Charmed" with Shannen Doherty,
lately of "Beverly Hills, 90210." There is no word on whether Ms.
Milano's breast implants will get special guest star billing.
</p>
<p>
Given Josie Bisset's recent return to "Melrose," Luke Perry's immiment
return to "90210," and Laura Leighton's imminent cross-casting move to
"90210," I have to ask, why do these actors keep returning? Is the Mark
of Spelling some sort of casting curse that guarantees that once an
actor has appeared on one Spelling production, they're not allowed to
work for anyone else?
</p>
<p>
It's not like this is a *recent* trend: the guy who inadvertently offed
his daughter the Noxzema girl on "90210" is the same actor who
inadvertently offed himself in Amanda's office on "Melrose" a mere
```

half-season before. Hudson Leick teethed on the straight-to-syndication "University Hospital" for a season before doing a turn as someone's dead brother's ex-wife on "Melrose." Randy Spelling guest-starred on "90210" before moving to the "Sunset Whatever" soap opera.
```
</p>
<p>
```
True, some directors and producers use the same actors and actresses in different productions - Tom Fontana has done a lot of "Oz"/"Homicide" cross-casting - because they rely on the actor's talent to realize their body of work. Some directors and producers use their girlfriends in different productions because, well, because they're determined to show off their toys in public.
```
</p>
<p>
```
But only Spelling keeps recycling these no-talent hacks, most of whom I would be willing to wager he is not sleeping with, for no discernible reason. I really wonder why. Do you suppose he makes all his actors sign their contracts in human blood or something? Is the stink of his shows so bad that an actor is permanently tainted? Is he just shy and afraid to meet new actors?
```
</p>
<p>
<cite> --Random Content</cite>
</p>
</div>

<!--article 4-->
<div id="article4">
<h2>Beach-ready Bestsellers</h2>
<p>
```
Putting aside for a moment the irony of regional identity on television - which has done more to homogenize the nation than even a countrywide railway system or radio did - let's examine the wisdom behind putting big, Irish families on television.
```
</p><p>
```
It's a bad idea because television is pulling out the same myths that justified NINA: the Irish are all manic for the auld sod, and, even after a hundred years in the New World, retain the bezerker Celtic id that makes life so very interesting. This why the Irish on TV this fall are all cops: it's the logical career choice for a clan of people who used to paint themselves blue.

```
</p><p>
So why is television suddenly so interested in the Irish? To quote
Robert Singer, executive producer of _Turks_, a show about the Irish
clan Turk, all of whom are evidently employed by the Chicago police
department, "people of ethnicity are interesting. They bring more to
the emotional table."
</p><p>
Does this mean when _Turks_, _Costello_, _To Have and to Hold_, and
_Trinity_ all go the way of the May Day peace accord, we can mine other
ethnic groups for what they bring to the table?
</p><p>
Like, say, Haitians? There's a large Haitian population in this
country. Surely they bring the same amount of cachet to the table that
the Irish do. Imagine the possibilities for shows ...
</p><p>
_The Voodoo That You Do_: a large, close-knit Haitian family grapples
with working on an urban police force while re-examining tricky
metaphysical issues like involuntary servitude after death.
</p><p>
"We went with the Haitians because spiritual rituals are such a rich,
vital part of their culture. They bring more to the organized religion
table." explained John Doe.
</p><p>
Not likely. Any ethnic group originating south of the 40th parallel
goes beyond the pale - and I do mean that literally - of television's
ethnic experience.
</p>
<p>
<cite> --Random Content</cite>
</p>
</div>


<!--the div for navigation. -->
<div id="nav">
<!-- note that the styles are attached to the individual links and
whatnot. this is to get around the inheritance properties in cascading
stylesheets.-->
<br>
```

```
<a href="../issues/index.html"><span style="color:#FFFFFF; font-family:
helvetica, arial, sans-serif; font-weight:bold; line-height:18px; font-
size:16px">home</span></a>
<strong><span style="color:#FFFFFF; font-family:helvetica, arial,
sans-serif; font-weight:bold; line-height:18px; font-size:16px">
  ||  </span></strong>
<a href="../index.html"><span style="color:#FFFFFF; font-family:
helvetica, arial, sans-serif; font-weight:bold; line-height:18px; font-
size:16px">current issue</span></a>
<strong><span style="color:#FFFFFF; font-family:helvetica, arial,
sans-serif; font-weight:bold; line-height:18px; font-size:16px">
  ||  </span></strong>
<a href="../archive/index.html"><span style="color:#FFFFFF;
font-family:helvetica, arial, sans-serif; font-weight:bold;
line-height:18px; font-size:16px">back issues</span></a>
<strong><span style="color:#FFFFFF; font-family:helvetica, arial,
sans-serif; font-weight:bold; line-height:18px; font-size:16px">
  ||  </span></strong>
<a href="../feedback/index.html"><span style="color:#FFFFFF;
font-family:helvetica, arial, sans-serif; font-weight:bold;
line-height:18px; font-size:16px">talk to us</span></a>
<strong><span style="color:#FFFFFF; font-family:helvetica, arial,
sans-serif; font-weight:bold; line-height:18px; font-size:
16px">  ||  </span></strong>
<a href="../info/index.html"><span style="color:#FFFFFF; font-family:
helvetica, arial, sans-serif; font-weight:bold; line-height:18px;
font-size:16px">about us</span></a>
</div>

<!--the div for copyright and all that.-->
<div id="copyright">
Copyright &copy; 1998 Mediadiet. All rights reserved. For more
information, email us at <a
href="mailto:webmaster@mediadiet.com">webmaster@mediadiet.com</a>.
</div>
</body>

</html>
```

Now that you've seen the code for the template, Figure 24.6 shows how it looks.

FIGURE 24.6:

The MediaDiet, round 2 template

How the Templates Were Modified for Daily Production

The only thing that was changed in the templates was the excision of the body content; Michelle figured—wisely—that the fewer lines she had in an actual file, the easier it would be for her to double-check for errors. She decided to separate out the content as a series of includes; this way, she could simply re-use the same file over and over, and just call in new includes as needed.

Here's what her final formatting template looks like:

```html
<html>

<head>
<title>Mediadiet.com: we play with our food</title>

<!--insert div-swapping script here-->
<SCRIPT LANGUAGE="JavaScript">

    var totalLayersInLoop=4;
    var layerNumShowing=1;

        function domhack(){
        if (navigator.appName == "Netscape") {
                    layerStyleRef="layer.";
                    layerRef="document.layers";
                    styleSwitch="";
        }else{
                    layerStyleRef="layer.style.";
                    layerRef="document.all";
                    styleSwitch=".style";
            }
    }

    function showArticleNumber(number){
        var layerNumToShow=number;
        hideArticle(eval('"article' + layerNumShowing+'"'));
        showArticle(eval('"article' + layerNumToShow+'"'));
        layerNumShowing=layerNumToShow;
    }

    function showArticle(layerName){

eval(layerRef+'["'+layerName+'"]'+styleSwitch+'.visibility="visible"');
    }

    function hideArticle(layerName){

eval(layerRef+'["'+layerName+'"]'+styleSwitch+'.visibility="hidden"');
    }
```

```
</SCRIPT>

<!--/end div-swapping script-->

<!--insert stylesheet here-->
<style type="text/css">
body     {background-color:#FFFFFF; color:#333333; font-family:
helvetica, arial, sans serif; font-size:12px;}

A:link     {font-family: helvetica, arial, sans serif; font-weight:
bold; color:#0099CC; font-size:12px;}

A:visited     {position: absolute; font-family: helvetica, arial, sans
serif; color:#99FF99; font-size:12px;}

h2     {color:#0099CC; font-family:helvetica, arial, sans serif; letter-
spacing:2px; font-size:15px; font-weight:bold;}

#greenback     {position:absolute; left:0px; top:0px; width:200px;
z-index:10; height:800px; border-style:solid; border-color:#99FF99;
border:1px; background-color:#99FF99;}

#brand     {position:absolute; z-index:20; left:40px; top:40px;
border:1px; border-color:#FFFFFF; width:500; height:132;}

#subject_subhead     {position:absolute; z-index:100; left:72px;
top:452px; width:125px; height:255px; border:1px; border-color:#FFFFFF;
border-style:solid; background-color:#FFFFFF;}

#blueborder     {position:absolute; z-index:40; left:40px; top:220px;
border:1px; border-style:solid; border-color:#66CCCC; background-color:
#66CCCC; width:600px; height:502px;}

#canvas     {position:absolute; z-index:60; left:42px; top: 222px;
border:1px; border-style:solid; border-color:#FFFFFF; background-color:
#FFFFFF; width:600px; height:500px;}

#nav     {position:absolute; z-index:80; left:40px; top:769px;
background-color:#99FF99; width:600px; height:30px; margin:10px;}
```

```
#ads        {position:absolute; z-index:100; left:72px; top:452px;
width:125px; height:255px; border:1px; border-color:#FFFFFF;
border-style:solid; background-color:#FFFFFF;}

#copyright    {position:absolute; z-index:100; left:72px; top:790px;
width:125px; height:255px; border:1px; border-color:#FFFFFF;
border-style:solid; background-color:#FFFFFF;}

#article1     {position: absolute; z-index:100; left:210px; top:242px;
width:450px; height:480px; background-color:#FFFFFF; border-color:
#FFFFFF; border:1px border-style:solid; visibility:visible;}

#article2     {position: absolute; z-index:120; left:210px; top:242px;
width:450px; height:480px; background-color:#FFFFFF; border-color:
#FFFFFF; border:1px border-style:solid; visibility:hidden;}

#article3     {position: absolute; z-index:140; left:210px; top:242px;
width:450px; height:480px; background-color:#FFFFFF; border-color:
#FFFFFF; border:1px border-style:solid; visibility:hidden;}

#article4     {position: absolute; z-index:160; left:210px; top:242px;
width:450px; height:480px; background-color:#FFFFFF; border-color:
#FFFFFF; border:1px border-style:solid; visibility:hidden;}

#minitoc    {position:absolute; z-index:100; left:72px; top:242px;
width:125px; height:200px; border:1px; border-color:#66CCCC;
border-style:solid; background-color:#66CCCC; margin:10px;}
</style>
<!--/end stylesheet-->

<body onLoad="domhack()">

<!--this div deals with the big green block down the side of the page-->
<div id="greenback">
</div>

<!--this div pulls in the mediadiet logo-->
<div id="brand">
<img src="../images/brand2.gif" width="500" height="132" border="0">
</div>

<!--this div pulls in the page title gfx -->
```

```html
<div id="subject_subhead">
<img src="../images/issue_hed.gif" alt="[this week's diet]" width="450"
height="104" border="0">
</div>

<!--this div sets up the blue lines ringing the main content area-->
<!--note that in order to maintain the DOM set up the in the javascript,
we don't have a lot of child divs. instead, we use a lot of z-index
values to make sure things float where they're supposed to. -->
<div id="blueborder">
</div>
<!--keeping with the white/blue-no-child divs theme, here's a white div
to provide a backdrop for the articles.-->
<div id="canvas">
</div>

<!--mini-toc for switching between articles-->
<div id="minitoc">
<br>
<p><a href="javascript:showArticleNumber(1)"><span style="color:
#FFFFFF; font-family:helvetica, arial, sans-serif; font-weight:bold;
line-height:11px; font-size:10px">I have issues: the rise of the new YA
novel</a></p>
<p><a href="javascript:showArticleNumber(2)"><span style="color:
#FFFFFF; font-family:helvetica, arial, sans-serif; font-weight:bold;
line-height:11px; font-size:10px">Grocery store fixes: we rate the
paperbacks</a></p>
<p><a href="javascript:showArticleNumber(3)"><span style="color:
#FFFFFF; font-family:helvetica, arial, sans-serif; font-weight:bold;
line-height:11px; font-size:10px">I got lost in a book megastore and
survived!</a></p>
<p><a href="javascript:showArticleNumber(4)"><span style="color:
#FFFFFF; font-family:helvetica, arial, sans-serif; font-weight:bold;
line-height:11px; font-size:10px">Lazy summer reading</a></p>
</div>
<!--the div for ads-->
<div id="ads">
<!--#include virtual="ads.htmlf" -->
</div>

<!--article 1-->
<div id="article1">
```

```
<!--#include virtual="article1.htmlf" -->
</div>

<!--article 2-->
<div id="article2">
<!--#include virtual="article2.htmlf" -->
</div>

<!--article 3-->
<div id="article3">
<!--#include virtual="article3.htmlf" -->
</div>

<!--article 4-->
<div id="article4">
<!--#include virtual="article4.htmlf" -->
</div>


<!--the div for navigation. -->
<div id="nav">
<!-- note that the styles are attached to the individual links and
whatnot. this is to get around the inheritance properties in cascading
stylesheets.-->
<!--#include virtual="nav.htmlf" -->
</div>

<!--the div for copyright and all that.-->
<div id="copyright">
<!--#include copyright.htmlf" -->
</div>
</body>
```

Here's nav.htmlf, included at the top.

Nav.htmlf

```
<br>
<a href="../issues/index.html"><span style="color:#FFFFFF; font-
family:helvetica, arial, sans-serif; font-weight:bold; line-height:
18px; font-size:16px">home</span></a>
```

```
<strong><span style="color:#FFFFFF; font-family:helvetica, arial,
sans-serif; font-weight:bold; line-height:18px; font-size:16px">
  ||  </span></strong>
<a href="../index.html"><span style="color:#FFFFFF; font-family:
helvetica, arial, sans-serif; font-weight:bold; line-height:18px;
font-size:16px">current issue</span></a>
<strong><span style="color:#FFFFFF; font-family:helvetica, arial,
sans-serif; font-weight:bold; line-height:18px; font-size:
16px">  ||  </span></strong>
<a href="../archive/index.html"><span style="color:#FFFFFF;
font-family:helvetica, arial, sans-serif; font-weight:bold;
line-height:18px; font-size:16px">back issues</span></a>
<strong><span style="color:#FFFFFF; font-family:helvetica, arial,
sans-serif; font-weight:bold; line-height:18px; font-
size:16px">  ||  </span></strong>
<a href="../feedback/index.html"><span style="color:#FFFFFF;
font-family:helvetica, arial, sans-serif; font-weight:bold;
line-height:18px; font-size:16px">talk to us</span></a>
<strong><span style="color:#FFFFFF; font-family:helvetica, arial,
sans-serif; font-weight:bold; line-height:18px; font-size:
16px">  ||  </span></strong>
<a href="../info/index.html"><span style="color:#FFFFFF; font-family:
helvetica, arial, sans-serif; font-weight:bold; line-height:18px;
font-size:16px">about us</span></a>
```

copyright.htmlf

```
Copyright &copy; 1998 Mediadiet. All rights reserved. For more
information, email us at <a
href="mailto:webmaster@mediadiet.com">webmaster@mediadiet.com</a>.
```

ad.htmlf

```
<img src="../../../general/ad-square.gif" alt="[125x125 banner]"
width="125" height="125" border="0">
<img src="../../../general/ad-square.gif" alt="[125x125 banner]"
width="125" height="125" border="0">
```

The Source Code

The following files are available on the companion CD-ROM:

- Archive_index.html
- current_index.html
- books_index.html
- music_index.html
- film_index.html
- teevee_index.html
- web_index.html
- magazine_index.html
- feedback_index.html
- info_index.html

NOTE   `index.html` became `current_index.html` as part of the new site look.

The following files compose the fragment library:

- Nav.htmlf
- copyright.htmlf
- ad.htmlf
- content.htmlf

NOTE   The content include is a sample of the content you'd find on any of the index pages.

Constants for This Case Study

Through the course of this chapter, you've seen a site go through two dramatic development stages. Even though the building philosophies behind the site changed from iteration to iteration, some things remained constant. The areas below cover two of those areas: the style guide, and the QA process.

Style Guide

The MediaDiet Style Guide is something that David drew up to help Michelle meet his visual guidelines. Over the course of the project, it became a collaborative tool between the two of them, with Michelle adding more about code. The different versions of the style guide correspond to different version of the site.

Color Guide

Version 1.0   There are two different types of pages to style here: the content pages, and the navigation pages. The navigation frame in the bottom of the layout has a bright green background (#99FF00 or 153-255-0 in rgb) and white text and hyperlinks (#FFFFFF.) The content documents have a white background (#FFFFFF) and gray text (#333333); the hypertext links are turquoise (#0099CC or 0-153-204 in rgb) and expired links are light green (#99FF99 or 153-255-153 in rgb).

Version 2.0   The white background for text and gray body text is carried over from the 1.0 version of Mediadiet.com. The links within the body text are turquoise (#0099CC or 0-153-204 in rgb) and expired links are light green (#99FF99 or 153-255-153 in rgb); the links within the intra-document navigation are white (#FFFFFF), as are the navigation links. There are also two accent colors through the pages—a green bar in the same light green as the expired links (#99FF99), and a turquoise line that is also echoed in the intra-document navigation (#66CCCC or 102-204-204).

Top-Level Headlines   For both versions, all of these are graphics: the general size for these is 123 px. wide by 40 px. tall, and they're all dithered down to 4 bits per pixel. All graphics are made in colors from the browser-safe palette; the green is the same color as the links, but the blue is a lighter turquioise (#66CCCC or 153-204-204). All graphics also have descriptive ALT tags, and the height and width values are listed as well.

Subheads   For both versions, the text subheads in each page are also turquoise (#0099CC or 0-153-204 in rgb). They're denoted in the style sheet this way:

```
h2      {color:#0099CC; font-family:helvetica, arial, sans serif;
        letter-spacing:2px; font-size:15px; font-weight:bold;}
```

Body Text   The style for all body text should be:

```
font-family:helvetica, arial, sans serif; font-size:12px;
```

Items in a Series/Items in a List   This stayed the same for both versions. MediaDiet is a text-heavy site, but does have the occasional item in a series in its archive or issue section. Since these tend to also be text-heavy lists and organized by topic, the usual format is to list the items thusly:

```
<p>
item<br>
item<br>
item<br>
</p>
```

Images   All of the images stick to the browser-safe color palette. The images are dithered down to a 4 bits per pixel palette. All subsequent images should be as lightweight.

QA Processes

You should never post a site without checking to see how it works. Here are the steps Michelle and David took in cleaning up this site:

Validate the HTML   This is easy to do, and can teach you a lot about "good" HTML coding practices. You can elect to validate a document one of two ways:

- Include a doc-type declaration at the top of your document. These declarations look like this:

```
<!DOCTYPE HTML PUBLIC "-//W3C//DTD HTML 4.0//EN"
"http://www.w3.org/TR/REC-html40/strict.dtd">
<!DOCTYPE HTML PUBLIC "-//W3C//DTD HTML 4.0 Transitional//EN"
"http://www.w3.org/TR/REC-html40/loose.dtd">
<!DOCTYPE HTML PUBLIC "-//W3C//DTD HTML 4.0 Frameset//EN"
"http://www.w3.org/TR/REC-html40/frameset.dtd">
```

  You only need to pick one. Then, enter the URL of the page you wish to validate at `http://validator.w3.org/`. Your page must be publicly accessible from a web server—no checking pages that live only on your desktop or on a password-protected server.

- If you don't think this is a feasible step for your site, you can put an include like this into the bottom of all your files:

```
<div id="check"><a href="http://validator.w3.org/check/referer"
class="offsite">Check this page</a>
```

This sends a query to the validator at `http://validator.w3.org/`, querying a specific site.

Check the sites across different browsers   It never hurts to look at a site on at least four different browser/platform combinations:

- Netscape 4.*x*/Mac

- IE 4.*x*/Mac

- Netscape 4.*x*/Windows

- IE 4.*x*/Windows

Since we are also targeting the site for lower-end browsers, Michelle and David also checked the site against these browsers:

- Netscape 3.*x*/Mac

- IE 3.*x*/Mac

- Netscape 3.*x*/Windows

- IE 3.*x*/Windows

After you've checked to make sure the HTML is consistent from browser to browser, check to see how the site loads with the images off. Then, dump your browser cache and time how fast the page loads with and without images.

Once your site looks consistently lovely across all the different platforms, and loads relatively quickly, you're set to publish it.

Summary

This site didn't have to grapple with legacy users who were stuck on Netscape 2.0, nor did it have to deal with being under-appreciated in a big organization. However, it did have to deal with the tricky dilemma of how to increase its content and work frequency by a factor of four without tossing out the current infrastructure.

The solution Michelle and David came up with is perhaps the most creative use of DHTML: Use it to improve the way you do your work, and to improve the ease with which users can access the content. Don't be afraid of big change. Just be sure to plan ahead before you jump into a total site overhaul.

APPENDIX

A

Browser–HTML Compatibility

The following table breaks down common HTML tags by the earliest HTML standard, browser "brand," and browser version that support them.

An *X* in a column indicates that the tag is supported.

Tag	HTML 2.0	HTML 3.0	HTML 4.0	NS 2.0	NS 3.0	NS 4.0	MSIE 2.0	MSIE 3.0	MSIE 4.0	Opera 3.0	Lynx 2.7
Scripting Event Tags											
onblur			X	X	X	X		X	X	X	
onclick			X	X	X	X		X	X	X	
ondblclick			X			X			X		
onfocus			X	X	X	X		X	X	X	
onkeypress			X			X			X		
onkeydown			X			X			X		
onkeyup			X			X			X		
onmousedown			X			X			X		
onmouseup			X			X			X		
onmouseover			X	X	X	X		X	X	X	
onmousemove			X			X			X		
onmouseout			X		X	X			X	X	
onload			X	X	X	X		X	X		
onunload			X	X	X			X			
Style Sheet Tags											
Id		X				X			X		X
class		X				X		X	X		
DIV		X		X	X	X	X	X	X	X	X
DIV align		X		X	X	X	X	X	X	X	X
SPAN			X			X		X	X	X	
style			X			X		X	X		

Note: for a breakdown of style sheet attributes by browser, see Appendix C.

Tag	HTML 2.0	HTML 3.0	HTML 4.0	NS 2.0	NS 3.0	NS 4.0	MSIE 2.0	MSIE 3.0	MSIE 4.0	Opera 3.0	Lynx 2.7
Text Layout Tags											
BR	X	X	X	X	X	X	X	X	X	X	X
BR clear		X	X	X	X	X	X	X	X	X	
COLS								X	X	X	
GUTTER					X						
HR	X	X	X	X	X	X	X	X	X	X	X
HR align		X	X	X	X	X	X	X	X	X	X
HR color									X		
HR noshade		X	X	X	X	X	X	X	X	X	
HR size		X	X	X	X	X	X	X	X	X	
HR width		X	X	X	X	X	X	X	X	X	X
SPACER					X						
WIDTH					X						
Text Style and Formatting Tags											
ABBR			X								
ACRONYM			X						X		
ADDRESS	X	X	X	X	X	X	X	X	X	X	X
B	X	X	X	X	X	X	X	X	X	X	X
BASEFONT		X	X	X	X	X	X	X	X		
BASEFONT color		X						X	X		
BASEFONT face		X							X		
BASEFONT size		X		X	X	X	X	X	X		
BLINK				X	X	X					
BIG		X	X	X	X	X	X	X	X	X	
BLOCKQUOTE	X	X	X	X	X	X	X	X	X	X	X
CITE	X	X	X	X	X	X	X	X	X	X	X

Tag	HTML 2.0	HTML 3.0	HTML 4.0	NS 2.0	NS 3.0	NS 4.0	MSIE 2.0	MSIE 3.0	MSIE 4.0	Opera 3.0	Lynx 2.7
Text Style and Formatting Tags											
CENTER		X		X	X	X	X	X	X	X	X
CODE	X	X	X	X	X	X	X	X	X	X	X
DEL			X						X		
DFN		X		X				X			
EM	X	X	X	X	X	X	X	X	X	X	X
FONT		X	X	X	X	X	X	X	X	X	
FONT color		X		X	X	X	X	X	X	X	
FONT face			X	X	X	X	X		X	X	
FONT size		X		X	X	X	X	X	X	X	H1-H6X
I	X	X	X	X	X	X	X	X	X	X	X
INS			X						X		
LISTING	X	X	X	X	X	X	X	X	X	X	X
MARQUEE								X	X		
MARQUEE width									X		
MARQUEE height									X		
MARQUEE hspace									X		
MARQUEE vspace									X		
MARQUEE align							X	X	X		
MARQUEE behavior								X	X		
MARQUEE bgcolor								X	X		
MARQUEE direction									X		
PRE	X	X	X	X	X	X	X	X	X	X	X
Q			X						X		X

Tag	HTML 2.0	HTML 3.0	HTML 4.0	NS 2.0	NS 3.0	NS 4.0	MSIE 2.0	MSIE 3.0	MSIE 4.0	Opera 3.0	Lynx 2.7
				Text Style and Formatting Tags							
S			X		X	X		X	X	X	X
SAMP	X	X	X	X	X	X	X	X	X	X	
SMALL		X	X	X	X	X		X	X	X	
STRIKE		X	X		X	X		X	X	X	X
STRONG	X	X	X	X	X	X	X	X	X	X	X
SUB		X	X	X	X	X		X	X	X	
SUP		X	X	X	X	X		X	X	X	X
VAR		X	X		X	X	X	X	X	X	X
XMP	X	X	deprecated	X	X	X	X	X	X	X	X

User Interface Checklist

This appendix is a step-by-step checklist of all the questions you should be asking yourself as you go through your site's development process. You can use these questions to fine-tune your ideas for a new site, or to perform a diagnostic test on the site you're getting ready to revise and upgrade.

I. The User's Task: Broad Analysis

- Who is supposed to perform the task?
- What is the starting point?
- What is the action the task is supposed to accomplish?
- What is the ending point?

A. The User: More Detailed Analysis

- What are the characteristics of the people performing the tasks?
- What sort of pre-existing knowledge must the person performing the task have?
- What sort of knowledge is the performer supposed to acquire after performing the task?
- What kind of environment will the user be working in when they try to perform the task?
- Is your user motivated to use your site, or a site similar to yours?
- Does your user fully understand all the possible functions of a browser?
- Does your user use a website as part of a larger work/recreation environment?
- Does your user use a website as their primary work/recreation environment?
- What are your user's expectations of this website?

B. The Task: More Detailed Analysis

- Define and describe the starting point of your user's site visit.
- Does the user take a single action to complete their task, or is it a multistep operation?

- How does each step in a multistep process relate to the steps preceding and following it? Is there a clear relationship between each step?

- If the user task has more than one step, what is the ending point for every action? Is there a goal at the end of each step?

- Is there a clear signal indicating the step has been successfully completed?

- Does the user need to accumulate knowledge about the task from step to step?

- How will you reinforce that knowledge step to step?

- What are your criteria for a successfully completed task?

- Are these criteria clearly communicated to the user?

- Is it a motivational task? Does the task exist to motivate the user to explore the rest of the website?

- Is it an orientation task? Does it orient the user with the rest of the website?

- Is it a guidance task? Is the purpose of the task to provide instructional information to the user?

- Is it a reference task? Is the purpose of the task to provide specific topical responses to a query?

- What role does each task play relative to the user? Does it provide a way for the user to interact with the product? Or does it contribute to a user's broader understanding outside the product?

II. The Interface

- Is the dialogue that is aimed at the user clear and unambiguous?

- Are you speaking the user's language?

- Are the type of user tasks the site offers clearly outlined on the site's index page?

- Are the steps for each user task available throughout the task the user is completing?

- If the user enters the site on a non-index page, do you provide a clear marker to the site tasks?

- Is there a clear entry to the sequence of events the user needs to perform to complete a task?

- Is there a clear exit route for users during their execution of the sequence of events?

- Are there shortcuts? Are these shortcuts marked?

- Are user errors possible?

- If user errors are possible, do you provide informative error messages?

- Do you provide feedback for users who are making errors in the task?

- Do you allow users to retrace their route if they've made an error?

- Do you offer users a clear exit if they make an error?

- Do you offer users a chance to start over if they make an error?

- Have you evaluated ways to prevent user errors?

- Is each task visually and functionally discrete?

- What function does each task "module" perform?

- Is there a visual cue indicating to the reader when they have left or completed one task module and entered another?

- Is there a way to limit the number of options to a user in order to prevent cognitive overload or distraction from task completion?

- Are the functions available on the website functions people really do use, or functions the site builders could build?

- Are the user functions that are available readily apparent in the interface?

- Does the user always have a sense of being in control of their site interaction experience? Do they feel as though they are completing the tasks of their own volition?

III. Help and Troubleshooting

- Is a direct route to help available on every page of the website?

- Does the supporting documentation address specific user problems?

- Does the supporting documentation group possible problems by task?

- Does the supporting documentation describe the factors that led to a task failure for user recognition?

- Does the supporting documentation provide step-by-step tasks to address any user difficulties?

- Does the supporting documentation provide the user with a means of querying the site?

- Do you, the site planners, set aside time and personnel to provide users with direct feedback?

- Is there specific topical help available while the user is executing a complex task?

- Does the supporting documentation provide a time period for users to anticipate feedback?

- Is there an instructional angle to the supporting documentation?

- Is the supporting documentation linear, or can users answer specific queries on demand?

IV. Accessibility

- Are all units of measurement (distance, volume, time, currency, numerical systems, temperature, etc.) clearly labeled with reference to their origin?

- Is it necessary to provide conversion between two different systems of units, such as yen and U.S. dollars?

- Do your ALT tags for images clearly state what each image is, and what function it serves within the page?

- Do you use absolute font tags?

- Do you use ample white space?

- What is your color scheme like? Does it accommodate color-blind people?

- Does your HTML degrade for stripped-down, non-visual browsers?

- Do you separate all positioning and formatting from the text elements they affect?

- Do you provide keyboard shortcuts for links and imagemaps?

- Do you provide alternatives to drop-box style forms for mobility-impaired users?

- Do you tell your blind Web surfers what they are about to encounter?

- Do you provide alternatives to layouts that are strictly dependent on tables?

- Does your navigation scheme allow for clear and functional use by audio browsers?

- Do you provide an equally functional site for users with non-applet-supporting browsers?

- Do you provide transcripts and descriptions of any audio and video files on your site?

- If standard accessibility measures compromise the functional integrity and presentation of your site, do you provide a link to an alternate, access-abled analogue?

V. Usability Testing for Cutting-Edge Products

- What level of experience will a user have to have before using the new product?

- What level of technical expertise will the user have to have before using the new product?

- Are the technical requirements for optimal product use made clear to the user at the beginning of the product?

- Does the website provide users with advice/means to upgrade to optimal product performance?

- Is there a clear exit route for users who elect not to use the product?

- Does the interface contain a visual point of reference that calls on a user's prior knowledge and experience?

- Do you offer a means of returning to a familiar product from the cutting-edge one?

- Do you have a server-side way of serving a different site to people who don't meet the technical parameters for your new site?

- Do you have time built into your development cycle for recursive scheduling?

- Do you have persistent interface elements that you will not change over iterations and updates to the product?

- Do you provide a separate troubleshooting area for advanced or cutting-edge technologies?

APPENDIX

C

Style Sheets

You can read a million articles on how to apply style sheets, but they're not always useful when you're actually cranking out code. This appendix strips out everything but the basics for everyday site building.

A Brief Definition

Style sheets are a collection of definitions which dictate how the different objects within an HTML document will appear on rendering. The definitions have three parts:

1. The *selector*, which is the name or element being defined, for example:

   H3, .subhead

2. The *properties*, which are characteristics that an element can have, for example:

   font-family, text-align, z-index

3. The *values*, which attach specific traits to every property, for example:

   font-family: arial; text-align: left; z-index: 1

Thus the one specific style entry

```
.h2  {font-family arial, helvetica; font-weight: bold; font-size: 18
px; line-height: 20 px; font-color:#cc0000}
```

has the selector h2; the properties font-family, font-weight, font-size, line-height, and font-color; and the values arial, helvetica, bold, 18 px, 20 px, and #cc0000.

A Note about Syntax

As you may have read in Chapter 6, there are two different ways to attach a style to an object—by attaching it to a class, or an id. Please note that the syntax for each is different.

```
.headline    {font-family arial, helvetica; font-weight: bold; _
font-size: 18 px; line-height: 20 px; font-color:#cc0000}
```

is the class "headline."

```
#headline    {font-family arial, helvetica; font-weight: bold; _
font-size: 18 px; line-height: 20 px; font-color:#cc0000}
```

is a specific ID "headline." In this case "headline" might belong to a larger class of objects.

NOTE   Be sure to note that values always modify properties.

Incorporating Style Sheets

There are four ways to call style sheets within an HTML document. They're listed below.

1. Add the styles in the <HEAD> of your document, using this syntax:

    ```
    <STYLE type="text/css">
    <!-//
    insert your style here
    //->
    </STYLE>
    ```

    This is also known as the *global* style.

2. Inline the style in any HTML tag within the <BODY> of your document:

    ```
    <P style="font-family: arial; font-size: 10px; font color:#000000">
    <span style="font-family: courier new, courier; font-weight: bold;
    font-color:#006633">This style is "nested" inside another style</span>
    <div style="position:absolute; left: 10px; top: 10px; width: 300 px;
    height: 55 px; color: #FFFFCC">This produces a narrow yellow _
    container</div>
    ```

3. Link the style sheet from another internal document:

    ```
    <HEAD>
    <LINK rel="stylesheet" type="text/css" href="stylesheet.css">
    </HEAD>
    ```

4. Link the style sheet via an anchor tag:

    ```
    <HEAD>
    <STYLE type="text/css">
    <!-//
    @import url("stylesheet.css")
    //->
    </STYLE>
    </HEAD>
    ```

NOTE   This last option is highly quirky, and I recommend that you stick to the first or second options if you're doing a limited implementation of style sheets. If you're going to try using a site-wide style document, be sure that you test it thoroughly.

How Inheritance Works

The most specific style sheet takes precedence; specificity does not equal number of properties. Specificity is the location of the style relative to the object calling the style.

- Local overrides global.

- Global overrides linked.

- Linked overrides anchored.

- Inline style overrides ID (#styles in a global CSS) in the document.

- ID (#style) overrides class (.style) in a global CSS.

- Class (.style) overrides set HTML elements (h2).

Cross-Browser Compatibility

For this table, I stuck to the browsers that have a wider perceived scale of implementation for style sheets: Internet Explorer 4.x and Netscape 4.x. Your results are going to vary with the 3.x versions of either browser, and I recommend building an alternate page template if more than 40 percent of your audience skews to this demographic.

Type of Style Defined	Name of Property	Values per Property	Notes on Implementing
Background and Color	background-color	color values: hex or recognized color values	
	background-image	URL (address). Example: `background-image: url(foo.gif)`	
	color	color values: hex or recognized color values	
Boxes	border-color	color value	Default is the "color" value for any larger element where it is defined.
	border-style	dotted;dashed; ridge; groove; solid; souble; inset; outset	This is supported fully only on IE4 for Mac and works partially on NS4, both platforms, and IE4 for PC.

Continued on next page

Type of Style Defined	Name of Property	Values per Property	Notes on Implementing
Boxes	border-width (shorthand)	length; percentage; auto	
	border	This is the shorthand property. It is usually defined by the border-width, border-style, and color.	
	margin-top	length; percentage; auto	
	margin-left	length; percentage; auto	
	margin-right	length; percentage; auto	
	margin-bottom	length; percentage; auto	
	margin (shorthand)	length; percentage; auto	
	padding-top	length; percentage; auto	
	padding-left	length; percentage; auto	
	padding-right	length; percentage; auto	
	padding-bottom	length; percentage; auto	
	padding	length; percentage; auto	
Block-Level Elements	width	length; percentage; auto	
	height	length; percentage; auto	Support for the height property is tested as "reliable" almost everywhere, but usually works best if attached to something with a fixed height like an image. I've also found that putting a border on a block-level container enforces the height property.
	float	left; right	
	clear	none; left; right	

Continued on next page

Type of Style Defined	Name of Property	Values per Property	Notes on Implementing
Font Properties	font	ALL	This is the default tag, usually further defined with any of the properties listed below (shorthand property).
	font-family	You can specify font faces like arial, verdana, courier, or generic family tags: serif, sans-serif, cursive, fantasy, monospace.	IE4 for the Mac may not fully support the generic family tags.
	font-size	There are four to choose from: percentage (10%, etc.); relative size; absolute size; length—a number followed by a unit of measurement like pixel (px).	
	font-style	normal; italic	
	font-weight	Normal, bold, bolder, lighter (these two are used in relative styles). 100–900, in increments of 100.	
Postioning Properties	absolute, relative		
	left	length; percentage	
	top	length; percentage	
	z-index	number	As a rule of thumb, the higher the value, the closer to the "top" of the stack of layers.
	visibility	inherit; visible; hidden	
Text Properties	text-align	left; right; center; justify	
	text-decoration	underline; line-through	
	text-indent	length; percentage	
	text-transform	none; capitalize; uppercase; lowercase	

Tags That May Work in One Browser or the Other

Type of Style Defined	Name of Property	Values per Property	Notes on Implementing
Background and Color	background-attachment		Scroll (default); fixed. Works in IE4 only.
	background-position	either left,top coordinates like (0,0), or position tag like top/center/bottom or left/center/right	Works in IE4 only, but buggy in the PC version.
	background-repeat	There are three syntaxes: repeat, repeat x, repeat y (where x is the lowest # of times to repeat and y is the highest) or no-repeat.	Works fully in NS4, works in IE4 but buggy in both platforms.
Boxes	border-top-width	medium; thin; thick	Works in NS4 and IE4.
	border-left-width	medium; thin; thick	Works in NS4 and IE4.
	border-right-width	medium; thin; thick	Works in NS4 and IE4.
	border-bottom-width	medium; thin; thick	Works in NS4, although buggy, and IE4.
	border-top	default: not defined	Only works in IE4.
	border-left	default: not defined	Only works in IE4.
	border-right	default: not defined	Only works in IE4.
	border-bottom	default: not defined	Only works in IE4.
Font Properties	font-variant	normal; small-caps	Works only in IE4, and buggily.
Text Properties	letter-spacing	normal	Only supported in IE4.
	line-height	length; percentage	Works fully in IE4, buggy but fully in NS4; may be buggy on the Mac.
	word-spacing	length; percentage	Only works in IE4 for Mac.
	vertical-align	normal; baseline; sub; super; top; text-top; middle; bottom; text-bottom	Supported (partially) in IE4.

Unix Cheatsheet

These commands should let you move around files and directories in Unix, and accomplish a few key tasks for maintaining the backend of your website. The tasks are grouped by function.

File Manipulation

cp   This copies files. You can use this command to copy files within the same directory, or between directories. You can also rename files as you're copying them.

- To copy and rename a file in the same directory:

  `cp foo.html foo2.html`

- To copy a file to a different directory:

  `cp foo.html /file/path/here/`

- To copy and rename a file to a different directory:

  `cp foo.html /file/path/here/foo2.html`

cp -r   This copies groups of files, or directories. It works exactly like cp, except it also copies a directory and its file structures to a new location. The syntax is `cp -r foo/ foo/new/location/`.

mkdir   This makes a new directory. The syntax is `mkdir foonew`.

less   This displays a few lines of a text file. To move through the text, keep hitting Enter. To leave the file, type **q**. The syntax is `less foo.html`.

ln -s   This links an alias for a file to a real file. This is a great way to create a persistent URL while changing the file behind it. The syntax is `ln -s real_foo alias_foo`.

more   This displays a screenful of text at a time. To move through the text, keep hitting Enter. To leave the file, type **q**. The syntax is `more foo.html`.

mv   This overwrites one file with another. Like the `cp` command, you can use it within one directory, or among a few. The difference between copying a file and moving it is that copying a file leaves the original file intact and in the same location; moving the file replaces it.

- To move a file within the same directory:

    `mv foo1.html foo2.html.`

NOTE   `foo1.html` no longer exists.

- To move a file from one directory to another:

    `mv foo1.html /file/path/here/.`

NOTE   `foo1.html` now lives in `/file/path/here/`. It will have overwritten any same-named files in `/file/path/here/`.

---

rm   Remove a file. The syntax is `rm foo.html`.

rm -r   Remove a group of files or directories. The syntax is `rm -r foo/`.

File/Directory Information

cd   Change directories. To move down a level in the edit tree, you'd write **cd foo**, where `foo` is the name of the directory. To move up a level in the edit tree, you'd write **cd ../** which automatically bounces you back a level.

chmod   You can change file permissions with this command. Each file has three sets of capabilities: what the owner of the file can do, what the group that the owner belongs to can do, and what random system users can do. The capabilities themselves are basic: read, write, execute. The basic syntax is `chomd (option) foo.html`.

The options are set for the level of user (owner, group, user) and the capabilities (read, write, execute). You can either add or subtract a user's capabilities.

Examples:

```
chmod o+ rw - owner adds read and write permissions to owner only
chmod g + rw - owner adds read and write permissions to the group
chmod u + rw - owner adds read and write permissions for users
chmod g -x - owner removes a group's ability to run executable files
```

`chown`   You can change who owns a file. Usually this command is handy only if you have root on a system and can therefore decide who lives and dies. But you may need to change ownership of a file for someone if you're passing on a site directory. The syntax is `chown newowner foo`.

NOTE   If you wanted to change ownership for an entire website, you'd use the recursive option (-r), go to the head of the website file tree, and type **chown -r newowner ***.

`diff`   This allows you to compare two files. This little command comes in handy when you're trying to figure out what could have possibly happened to a file that's only slightly modified from an original; it's also handy for tracking data. The syntax is `diff file1 file2`.

`grep`   Use this to search and find patterns in one or several files. The syntax is `grep -option files`.

Examples:

`grep -c 'template' *.html`   finds all of the files that have `'template'` in them and prints out any matching lines.

`grep -l 'template'`   prints out the names of all files that have `'template'` in them.

`grep -n 'template'`   prints out the lines and line numbers that have `'template'` in them.

`ls`   This lists the contents of the directory you're in.

ls -a   This lists all files in a directory.

An ls -a of my home directory reveals:

```
computer:~> ls -a
.cshrc                  Bookmarks.html
book2(98)/              casestudies.rtf
.emacs
.login                  mail/
.netscape/              ssi docs
.netscape-cache/        stylesheet.rtf
```

ls -l   This lists the contents of the directory you're in, plus the permissions for the file and the last date the file was modified. For example, a quick ls -l of the same home directory as above:

```
computer:~> ls -l
rw-rw-rw-    1 lisa      staff       47557 Apr  1 19:08 Bookmarks.html
drwxrwxrwx  10 lisa      staff        1024 Apr  1 15:22 book(98)/
rw-rw-rw-    1 lisa      staff        5941 Apr  1 19:07 casestudies.rtf
drwx------   3 lisa      staff        1024 Aug 30  1997 mail/
rw-rw-rw-    1 lisa      staff       14056 Jan  6 16:33 ssi docs
rw-rw-rw-    1 lisa      staff       31479 Mar 30 23:13 stylesheet.rtf
```

tail -f   This prints the last ten lines of a file to your screen. The -f option tells the computer to keep printing those lines if the file should grow. You would use tail -f to spy on an access log or error log. It's a good diagnostic tool. The syntax is tail -f foo.log.

tar   This copies files to tape. Very handy if you want to roll things up and FTP them to a remote site. The syntax is tar foos. (Files are plural.)

APPENDIX

E

JavaScript Glossary

Alert A simple dialog box called via a JavaScript statement. A pop-up window called an alertbox is the result of using the `alert` command, and is a good way to debug scripts.

Array A list of variables stored together as a group:

```
Var months = new Array("January", 'February', "March")
```

Branching The process of using if-then statements to create different results, a.k.a. *branches* in the program's decision tree.

Document Object Model A standard that describes a hierarchy of objects, and their properties.

Feature An attribute that can be specified or altered via a features string. The features listed below are attached to the browser's *window* object.

> **height** The height of the browser window.
>
> **location** The area where you can type URLs.
>
> **menubar** The area storing the lists of functions an application can perform. Look at the top of your browser, where it says, File, Edit, View, and Go. That's the menubar.
>
> **resizable** An attribute dictating whether or not you can resize the browser window in question (similar to the noresize attribute for <FRAMESET> in HTML).
>
> **scrollbar** An attribute dictating whether or not you'll include scrollbars on a browser window (similar to the no scroll attribute for a <FRAMESET> in HTML).
>
> **status** The message bar at the bottom of a browser.
>
> **toolbar** The browser toolbar, home to the Back and Reload buttons, among others.
>
> **width** The width of the browser window.

Function A JavaScript routine that is written once, but can be executed repeatedly. There are two steps to using a function in JavaScript: the first is to name and write the actual code that comprises the function, and the second is to call the function.

To write a function:

```
function yearClock()
{
//set variables for seconds, hours, days, year
var sec = 60;
var min = 60;
var hour = 24;
var day = 365.25;

//do calculation
var sec_year = sec * min * hour *day
}
```

To call a function:

```
<a href="#" onClick="yearClock();">seconds per year</a>
```

Loop   A programming method to repeat actions until a specific result occurs.

> **For loop**   A looping statement that is set in motion if the variable for (foo) is set.
>
> **Nested loop**   A way to set multiple conditions to build a complex result.
>
> **While loop**   A looping statement that continues so long as the condition set forth in "while" is still relevant.

Method   The action an object can take. It is called `objectname.method`. For example:

```
window.alert('click me!');
```

`alert` is the method for the object window.

Object   A thing defined and acted upon. Objects are the discrete units that drive a JavaScript program.

onClick   An event handler that dictates an action to take place if the user clicks on a link. For example:

```
<A href="#" onClick="window.open('http://www.newsite.here/', _
'windowname');">Click here to read the new site</A>
```

onMouseOver   An event handler that dictates an action to take place if the user swipes their mouse over the object. For example:

```
<A HREF="build.html" onMouseOver="(window.status='learn to build a
site'); return true">
```

Property   The attribute of an object.

Statement   A discrete declaration in JavaScript.

- A statement can declare a *variable*: `var color = blue;`

- A statement can declare an *action*: `document.writeln(color);`

String   A group of characters between quotes.

Variable   A way to define and store data. In JavaScript, variable syntax is:

```
var FirstName = 'Lisa';
var age = 26;
```

APPENDIX

F

HTML Tags

Welcome to the HTML tags reference. Here you'll find the lowdown on each and every tag from the HTML 4 Document Type Definition. The information includes each tag's attributes, what other tags they can work with legally, style tips, and samples of HTML markup. The reference also includes Internet Explorer and Netscape Navigator extensions, which are marked with (IE) or (N) respectively.

TIP   The best source of up-to-date information about HTML is the World Wide Web Consortium site at `http://www.w3.org`. The current draft of the HTML 4 standard is available at `http://www.w3.org/TR/WD-html40-970708`.

To show how these tags relate to one another and to make them easier to remember, we've grouped them by type and function. Here's a quick overview of what you'll find in a typical tag description:

<TAG> (...</TAG>)   This is a formal HTML tag as it should be used in an HTML document. The large majority of tags come in pairs—for example, the boldface tags <B>...</B>, with an opening tag and a closing tag comprising the pair. Some tags are singletons, like the hard or horizontal rule tag <HR>, which does not require a closing tag. Any tag written as <TAG> (...</TAG>) means that the tag can be used correctly either as a singleton or as a pair. Underneath each tag name you'll find a brief, plain-English description of its purpose and capabilities.

Style Tip   Here we offer brief comments about how to use the tag properly, in accordance with good Web style. While Style Tips are suggestions, they represent our experience as Webmasters and Web citizens as well. We promise they won't lead you astray.

Attributes   Here you'll find a complete listing of all the attributes associated with each tag, their values, and a description of their effect on how the tag is rendered.

Parent Tags   This is a list of all the tags within which the present tag may be legally enclosed. This relationship derives from HTML syntax; while it's a little technical, it can affect the way a tag is rendered. It's included to indicate which tags may include the current tag, so as to keep you out of syntax trouble.

Content Tags   These are the opposite of parent tags; they represent those tags the current tag may contain legally. As with parent tags, this is a syntax thing. It's important to recognize that you shouldn't use any tag that does not appear in this list within the current tag.

Sample HTML   Real-life examples go further in showing how HTML is used than anything we can write or say. To that end we've included some sample markup for each and every tag, so you can see how all these tags work.

In the HTML 4 specification, several tags have become obsolete because they have been replaced by other markup; these tags will probably be phased out of HTML entirely in the next version. The majority of these tags have been *deprecated* (meaning that they are no longer recommended for use) in favor of style sheet rules. We have marked each of these tags or attributes as *[Deprecated]*. You may use these tags but we recommend that you look for other ways to achieve their effects, so you won't have to go back and remove them from your documents once they've been removed from the specification.

Finally, we have included style sheet tags in this reference. These use somewhat different conventions than standard HTML tags; we have noted those differences in that section.

That's the rundown. Let the tags begin!

Global Structure Tags

The global structure tags (also called document structure) help define the structure of HTML documents. They give each document as a whole an HTML label and divide it into head and body sections. These tags also provide a way to include information about a document's contents. This markup does not produce much visible output, but it's vital for the construction of a well-designed Web page.

<!DOCTYPE>

The <!DOCTYPE> tag is an SGML identifier, not an HTML tag. It defines which version of the HTML DTD should be used to interpret its tags. Every document should include <!DOCTYPE> as its first element. To create DTD-compliant documents, every HTML document must include a <!DOCTYPE> declaration.

Style Tip

Supplying a DTD declaration not only conforms to HTML standards but ensures compatibility with Web document tools such as validators, HTML editors, index tools, and even browsers.

Attributes

HTML PUBLIC "version name"

Defines the DTD to be used for this document. This is the only attribute for this tag.

> **NOTE**
>
> The "version name" must comply with a list of allowed names, known as *defined names*. You can find a list of defined names at `http://www.webtechs.com/html-tk/src/lib/catalog`.

Parent Tags

This tag must appear first in any HTML document, therefore it has no parents.

Content Tags

None.

Sample HTML

```
<!DOCTYPE HTML PUBLIC "-//W3C//DTD HTML 4.0//EN">
<HTML>
<HEAD>
<TITLE>Cogs of Chicago</TITLE>
</HEAD>
<BODY>
...
</BODY>
</HTML>
```

<ADDRESS>...</ADDRESS>

The ADDRESS tag pair is like a signature; it appears at the end of the Web page and contains contact, copyright, address, and other information.

Style Tip

Address information is an important component of any page because it gives you a place in your document to identify yourself and provide readers with other important document-specific information. Recommended information includes the date the page was last revised, an e-mail link to the person responsible for the page, and a copyright notice.

Attributes

None.

Parent Tags

<BLOCKQUOTE>, <BODY>, <BUTTON>, <CENTER>, <DD>, <DIV>, <FIELDSET>, <FORM>, <IFRAME>, <LI>, <NOFRAMES>, <NOSCRIPT>, <OBJECT>, <TD>, <TH>

Content Tags

<A>, <ACRONYM>, <APPLET>, <B>, <BASEFONT>, <BDO>, <BIG>, <BR>, <BUTTON>, <CITE>, <CODE>, <DFN>, <EM>, <FONT>, <I>, <IFRAME>, <IMG>, <INPUT>, <KBD>, <LABEL>, <MAP>, <OBJECT>, <P>, <Q>, <S>, <SAMP>, <SCRIPT>, <SELECT>, <SMALL>, <SPAN>, <STRIKE>, <STRONG>, <SUB>, <SUP>, <TEXTAREA>, <TT>, <U>, <VAR>

Sample HTML

```
<BODY>
<ADDRESS>
URL:http://www.mysite.com/home.html<BR>
Webmaster: <A HREF="mailto:bill@mysite.com">Bill "BBQ" Baker</A>
Revised: June 23, 1997
</ADDRESS>
</BODY>
```

<BODY>...</BODY>

The BODY tags block out an HTML document's body.

Style Tip

All of the content and HTML markup that will be displayed by a browser should be included within the BODY tags. While some browsers will display text placed outside of the BODY tags, others will not. Adding BODY tags before adding any body content helps eliminate forgotten tags.

Attributes

ALINK=(#RRGGBB|colorname)

Defines the color for any links in a document that are currently selected, or active. *#RRGGBB* is the RGB value defined by two-digit hex codes from 00 to FF (0–256). *Colorname* is a known color name. The standard 16 colors and their corresponding RGB values are shown in Table F.1.

BACKGROUND="URL"

Points to the location of the image that is to be used as the background of the document. Usually this image is tiled.

BGCOLOR=(#RRGGBB|colorname)

Specifies the background color for a document. (See Table F.1.)

TABLE F.1: Color Codes and the Colors They Represent

RGB Code	The Color It Represents
#000000	Black
#000080	Navy
#0000FF	Blue
#008000	Green
#008080	Teal
#00FF00	Lime
#00FFFF	Aqua
#800000	Maroon
#800080	Purple
#808000	Olive
#808080	Gray
#C0C0C0	Silver
#FF0000	Red
#FF00FF	Fuchsia
#FFFF00	Yellow
#FFFFFF	White

These color values are used by all color attributes.

BGPROPERTIES="URL"

Specifies the location of an image to use as a watermark. A *watermark* is an image that appears behind the other elements on the page and does not scroll.

LEFTMARGIN=number

Sets the left margin for the entire page.

LINK=(#RRGGBB|colorname)

Specifies the color of all hyperlinks within a document. (See Table F.1.)

TEXT=(#RRGGBB|colorname)

Specifies the color of all the regular text within a document. (See Table F.1.)

TOPMARGIN=number

Sets the top margin for the top of the page.

VLINK=(#RRGGBB|colorname)

Defines the color of all links within a document that have already been visited. (See Table F.1.)

Parent Tags

<HTML>, <NOFRAMES>

Content Tags

<A>, <ACRONYM>, <ADDRESS>, <APPLET>, <B>, <BASEFONT>, <BDO>, <BIG>, <BLOCKQUOTE>, <BR>, <BUTTON>, <CENTER>, <CITE>, <CODE>, <DFN>, <DIR>, <DIV>, <DL>, <EM>, <FIELDSET>, <FONT>, <FORM>, <H1>, <H2>, <H3>, <H4>, <H5>, <H6>, <HR>, <I>, <IFRAME>, <IMG>, <INPUT>, <ISINDEX>, <KBD>, <LABEL>, <MAP>, <MENU>, <NOFRAMES>, <NOSCRIPT>, <OBJECT>, <OL>, <P>, <PRE>, <Q>, <S>, <SAMP>, <SCRIPT>, <SELECT>, <SMALL>, <SPAN>, <STRIKE>, <STRONG>, <SUB>, <SUP>, <TABLE>, <TEXTAREA>, <TT>, <U>, <UL>, <VAR>

Sample HTML

```
<HTML>
<HEAD><TITLE>Insert the title of your document here.</TITLE>
</HEAD>
<BODY BGCOLOR="white" ALINK="teal" TEXT="navy">
Let's see, what goes here? The body of your document.
</BODY>
</HTML>
```

<DIV>(...</DIV>)

This tag defines divisions of an HTML document. <DIV> is a block-level element, and other block-level elements can be grouped with this tag.

Style Tip

When align attributes occur within tags grouped by the <DIV> tag, the grouped tags' alignment takes precedence over any alignment set in the <DIV> tag. <DIV> cannot be used to group elements within a paragraph since it will cause the paragraph to terminate. Use the <SPAN> tag to group within a paragraph without forcing termination. HTML defines <DIV ALIGN=CENTER> and <CENTER> as identical, but the <CENTER> tag is the preferred method of alignment.

Attributes

ALIGN=(LEFT|CENTER|RIGHT|JUSTIFY)

Defines the default horizontal alignment for the contents of the <DIV> tags.

STYLE="text"

Defines special style settings for the grouped elements. Refer to the <STYLE> tag for syntax of style markup.

Parent Tags

<BLOCKQUOTE>, <BODY>, <BUTTON>, <CENTER>, <DD>, <DIV>, <FIELDSET>, <FORM>, <IFRAME>, <LI>, <NOFRAMES>, <NOSCRIPT>, <OBJECT>, <TD>, <TH>

Content Tags

<A>, <ACRONYM>, <ADDRESS>, <APPLET>, <B>, <BASEFONT>, <BDO>, <BIG>, <BLOCKQUOTE>, <BR>, <BUTTON>, <CENTER>, <CITE>, <CODE>, <DFN>, <DIR>, <DIV>, <DL>, <EM>, <FIELDSET>, <FONT>, <FORM>, <H1>, <H2>, <H3>, <H4>, <H5>, <H6>, <HR>, <I>, <IFRAME>, <IMG>, <INPUT>, <ISINDEX>, <KBD>, <LABEL>, <MAP>, <MENU>, <NOFRAMES>, <NOSCRIPT>, <OBJECT>, <OL>, <P>, <PRE>, <Q>, <S>, <SAMP>, <SCRIPT>, <SELECT>, <SMALL>, <SPAN>, <STRIKE>, <STRONG>, <SUB>, <SUP>, <TABLE>, <TEXTAREA>, <TT>, <U>, <UL>, <VAR>

Sample HTML

```
<BODY>
<DIV>
<OL>
<LI>stop
<LI>drop
<LI>roll
</OL>
Section 1.
</DIV>
<DIV ALIGN=CENTER>
```

```
Section 2 centered.
</DIV>
</BODY>
```

<H*n*>...</H*n*>

The <H*n*> tags create a series of headings, numbered from 1 to 6 (H1 through H6). H1 is the topmost head level while H6 is the lowest level. Most browsers render headings in decreasing font sizes, although this can be overcome using either the <FONT> tag within the <H*n*> tag or with style sheets.

Style Tip

Headings should not be used for text formatting but rather to convey page and content organization. As a general rule, headings should be used in descending order.

Attributes

ALIGN=(LEFT|CENTER|RIGHT|JUSTIFY)

Specifies the alignment of the heading text.

Parent Tags

<BLOCKQUOTE>, <BODY>, <BUTTON>, <CENTER>, <DD>, <DIV>, <FIELDSET>, <FORM>, <IFRAME>, <LI>, <NOFRAMES>, <NOSCRIPT>, <OBJECT>, <TD>, <TH>

Content Tags

<A>, <ACRONYM>, <APPLET>, <B>, <BASEFONT>, <BDO>, <BIG>, <BR>, <BUTTON>, <CITE>, <CODE>, <DFN>, <EM>, <FONT>, <I>, <IFRAME>, <IMG>, <INPUT>, <KBD>, <LABEL>, <MAP>, <OBJECT>, <Q>, <S>, <SAMP>, <SCRIPT>, <SELECT>, <SMALL>, <SPAN>, <STRIKE>, <STRONG>, <SUB>, <SUP>, <TEXTAREA>, <TT>, <U>, <VAR>

Sample HTML

```
<BODY>
<H1>Heading 1</H1>
<H2>Heading 2</H2>
<H3>Heading 3</H3>
<H4>Heading 4</H4>
<H5>Heading 5</H5>
<H6>Heading 6</H6>
</BODY>
```

<HEAD>...</HEAD>

The document HEAD tags define the part of a Web page that contains the document's header information.

Style Tip

These header tags are another required tag pair and should be used in every Web page. Although the text included in <HEAD>...</HEAD> tags does not show up in the browser window, important information, such as the document's title, META tags, and base URL, is included here.

Attributes

Profile="URL"

Specifies the location of a meta profile or interpretation dictionary.

Parent Tags

<HTML>

Content Tags

<BASE>, <ISINDEX>, <LINK>, <META>, <SCRIPT>, <STYLE>, <TITLE>

Sample HTML

```
<HTML>
<HEAD>
<TITLE>Insert the title of your document here.</TITLE>
</HEAD>
</HTML>
```

<HTML>...</HTML>

The HTML tags define an HTML document. In other words, these tags surround all markup and text that comprise a Web document.

Style Tip

The <HTML> tag pair is required and should be used to begin and end every HTML document you create.

Attributes

VERSION="URL"

Specifies the location of a DTD that should be used to interpret the enclosed markup. This attribute performs the same function as the <!DOCTYPE> tag.

Parent Tags

There are no parent tags for <HTML>...</HTML>.

Content Tags

```
<BODY>, <FRAMESET>, <HEAD>
```

Sample HTML

```
<HTML>
<HEAD>
<TITLE>The Title of Your Document</TITLE>
</HEAD>
<BODY>
Everything else you wish to include in your Web page.
</BODY>
</HTML>
```

<META>

The META tag provides *meta* information—that is, information about information—for an entire document.

Style Tip

Meta information provides both search engines and users with a description of the content in your Web pages; it also provides keywords that a search engine can use for indexing content in its database. You can also use META tags to force the browser to automatically load a page after a certain amount of time has passed.

Attributes

NAME="text"

Specifies the name of the meta information contained within this particular META tag.

CONTENT="text"

Supplies a value for the named property.

HTTP-EQUIV="text"

Used to control some special meta information that is sent automatically by the Web server when a page is viewed. For example, this attribute can be used to force a browser to reload a page at a given interval of time.

Parent Tags

<HEAD>

Content Tags

None.

Sample HTML

```
<META HTTP-EQUIV="KEYWORDS" CONTENT="internet, vrml, books, networking,
intranets, windows nt, netware, html>
<META NAME="Copyright" CONTENT= "LANWrights, Inc.">
```

<SPAN>...</SPAN>

Similar to <DIV>, these tags group nonblock elements together. Their most common usage is to apply style to sections of text.

Style Tip

<SPAN>, unlike <DIV>, can be used within a paragraph since it is an inline division element. This means it does not prematurely terminate a paragraph.

Attributes

ALIGN=(LEFT|CENTER|RIGHT|JUSTIFY)

Specifies the horizontal alignment of the enclosed elements.

STYLE="text"

Used to define special style settings for the grouped elements. Refer to the <STYLE> tag for syntax of style markup.

Parent Tags

<A>, <ACRONYM>, <ADDRESS>, <APPLET>, <B>, <BDO>, <BIG>, <BLOCKQUOTE>, <BODY>, <BUTTON>, <CAPTION>, <CENTER>, <CITE>, <CODE>, <DD>, <DEL>, <DFN>, <DIV>, <DT>, <EM>, <FIELDSET>, <FONT>, <FORM>, <H1>, <H2>, <H3>, <H4>, <H5>, <H6>, <I>, <IFRAME>, <INS>, <KBD>, <LABEL>, <LEGEND>, <LI>, <NOFRAMES>, <NOSCRIPT>, <OBJECT>, <P>, <PRE>, <Q>, <S>, <SAMP>, <SMALL>, <SPAN>, <STRIKE>, <STRONG>, <SUB>, <SUP>, <TD>, <TH>, <TT>, <U>, <VAR>

Content Tags

<A>, <ACRONYM>, <APPLET>, <B>, <BASEFONT>, <BDO>, <BIG>, <BR>, <BUTTON>, <CITE>, <CODE>, <DFN>, <EM>, <FONT>, <I>, <IFRAME>, <IMG>, <INPUT>, <KBD>, <LABEL>, <MAP>, <OBJECT>, <Q>, <S>, <SAMP>, <SCRIPT>, <SELECT>, <SMALL>, <SPAN>, <STRIKE>, <STRONG>, <SUB>, <SUP>, <TEXTAREA>, <TT>, <U>, <VAR>

Sample HTML

```
<BODY>
<SPAN STYLE="margin-left: .3in"> This paragraph is styled to create a
.3 inch margin on the left.<SPAN>
...
</BODY>
```

<TITLE>...</TITLE>

The TITLE tags supply the title for the entire HTML document—this is the title that appears in the browser window title bar.

Style Tip

A good title should be less than 260 characters and is descriptive rather than general. Many search engines list pages by title, so it is often the first impression a user gets of your page. While "My Home Page" is concise and to the point, it doesn't tell a user much about your document. "Bill's BBQ Home Page" is still concise and gives the user a good idea of what to expect from the page.

Attributes

None.

Parent Tags

<HEAD>

Content Tags

None.

Sample HTML

```
<HEAD>
<TITLE>Bill's BBQ Home Page </TITLE>
</HEAD>
```

<!--...-->

The comment tag indicates a comment that is not seen by the browser.

Style Tip

Comment tags have many purposes, including to remind yourself why you used a certain tag construction, to leave messages for others who may also be working on the document, to identify authorship or revision dates, and to label sections of a document. A browser will not display commented text, but anyone looking at your HTML source will see it.

Attributes

None.

Parent Tags

All.

Content Tags

All.

Sample HTML

```
<!--The browser won't include this text in the displayed content.-->
```

Language Information Tags

Language information tags define the language to be used to interpret and display text. They also provide clues as to which direction the language runs (remember, some languages, like Arabic and Japanese, run right to left, not left to right).

<BDO>...</BDO>

The BDO (bi-directional algorithm) tags are used to define the language type and display direction of all enclosed text.

Style Tip

These tags should be used when displaying sections of text from languages other than the default.

Attributes

LANG=*language-code*

Defines the language to be used for the enclosed elements. The *language-code* values are determined by RFC 1766.

> **NOTE**
>
> You can retrieve a copy of RFC 1766 from `http://ds.internic.net/rfc/rfc1766.txt`. A list of the actual country codes is available at `http://www.sil.org/sgml/iso639a.html` or `ftp://ftp.ripe.net/iso3166-countrycodes`.

DIR=LTR|RTL

Used to define the direction of the language, left to right or right to left. This is a mandatory attribute.

Parent Tags

<A>, <ACRONYM>, <ADDRESS>, <APPLET>, <B>, <BDO>, <BIG>, <BLOCKQUOTE>, <BODY>, <BUTTON>, <CAPTION>, <CENTER>, <CITE>, <CODE>, <DD>, <DEL>, <DFN>, <DIV>, <DT>, <EM>, <FIELDSET>, <FONT>, <FORM>, <H1>, <H2>, <H3>, <H4>, <H5>, <H6>, <I>, <IFRAME>, <INS>, <KBD>, <LABEL>, <LEGEND>, <LI>, <NOFRAMES>, <NOSCRIPT>, <OBJECT>, <P>, <PRE>, <Q>, <S>, <SAMP>, <SMALL>, <SPAN>, <STRIKE>, <STRONG>, <SUB>, <SUP>, <TD>, <TH>, <TT>, <U>, <VAR>

Content Tags

<A>, <ACRONYM>, <APPLET>, <B>, <BASEFONT>, <BDO>, <BIG>, <BR>, <BUTTON>, <CITE>, <CODE>, <DFN>, <EM>, <FONT>, <I>, <IFRAME>, <IMG>, <INPUT>, <KBD>, <LABEL>, <MAP>, <OBJECT>, <Q>, <S>, <SAMP>, <SCRIPT>, <SELECT>, <SMALL>, <SPAN>, <STRIKE>, <STRONG>, <SUB>, <SUP>, <TEXTAREA>, <TT>, <U>, <VAR>

Sample HTML

```
<BODY>
<P>This is an English sentence.
<P><BDO LANG="FR" DIR="RTL">This is a French sentence.</BDO>
</BODY>
```

Text Tags

Text tags affect how text looks when displayed within your browser. Text tags are meant to reflect the content, or its place within the document. These tags differ from presentation tags, covered later, because presentation tags change text's appearance, but do not reflect its meaning or role within the document. Use text tags whenever possible, rather than presentation tags.

<ACRONYM>...</ACRONYM>

The ACRONYM tags mark the text they contain as an acronym.

Style Tip

Be sure to include the acronym's fully spelled-out version in the TITLE= attribute so users can learn what it stands for.

Attributes

TITLE="text"

Provides an acronym's expanded form, which appears in a highlighted box next to the acronym when a user runs his or her mouse over it.

Parent Tags

```
<A>, <ACRONYM>, <ADDRESS>, <APPLET>, <B>, <BDO>, <BIG>, <BLOCKQUOTE>,
<BODY>, <BUTTON>, <CAPTION>, <CENTER>, <CITE>, <CODE>, <DD>, <DEL>,
<DFN>, <DIV>, <DT>, <EM>, <FIELDSET>, <FONT>, <FORM>, <H1>, <H2>, <H3>,
<H4>, <H5>, <H6>, <I>, <IFRAME>, <INS>, <KBD>, <LABEL>, <LEGEND>, <LI>,
<NOFRAMES>, <NOSCRIPT>, <OBJECT>, <P>, <PRE>, <Q>, <S>, <SAMP>,
<SMALL>, <SPAN>, <STRIKE>, <STRONG>, <SUB>, <SUP>, <TD>, <TH>, <TT>,
<U>, <VAR>
```

Content Tags

<A>, <ACRONYM>, <APPLET>, <B>, <BASEFONT>, <BDO>, <BIG>, <BR>, <BUTTON>, <CITE>, <CODE>, <DFN>, <EM>, <FONT>, <I>, <IFRAME>, <IMG>, <INPUT>, <KBD>, <LABEL>, <MAP>, <OBJECT>, <Q>, <S>, <SAMP>, <SCRIPT>, <SELECT>, <SMALL>, <SPAN>, <STRIKE>, <STRONG>, <SUB>, <SUP>, <TEXTAREA>, <TT>, <U>, <VAR>

Sample HTML

```
<BODY>
<ACRONYM TITLE="Hypertext Markup Language> HTML </ACRONYM> is used to
create Web pages.
</BODY>
```

<BLOCKQUOTE>... </BLOCKQUOTE>

BLOCKQUOTE tags set off long quotations or citations from other sources.

Style Tip

BLOCKQUOTE tags are intended to set off longer passages. They indent all lines of enclosed text to the left. While multiple sets of BLOCKQUOTE tags can be used to create a series of indentations, this is a misuse of the tag. Use style sheet properties instead.

Attributes

CITE="text"

Provides additional information about the source of the quoted text.

Parent Tags

<BLOCKQUOTE>, <BODY>, <BUTTON>, <CENTER>, <DD>, <DIV>, <FIELDSET>, <FORM>, <IFRAME>, <LI>, <NOFRAMES>, <NOSCRIPT>, <OBJECT>, <TD>, <TH>

Content Tags

<A>, <ACRONYM>, <ADDRESS>, <APPLET>, <B>, <BASEFONT>, <BDO>, <BIG>, <BLOCKQUOTE>, <BR>, <BUTTON>, <CENTER>, <CITE>, <CODE>, <DFN>, <DIR>, <DIV>, <DL>, <EM>, <FIELDSET>, <FONT>, <FORM>, <H1>, <H2>, <H3>, <H4>, <H5>, <H6>, <HR>, <I>, <IFRAME>, <IMG>, <INPUT>, <ISINDEX>, <KBD>, <LABEL>, <MAP>, <MENU>, <NOFRAMES>, <NOSCRIPT>, <OBJECT>, <OL>, <P>, <PRE>, <Q>, <S>, <SAMP>, <SCRIPT>, <SELECT>, <SMALL>, <SPAN>, <STRIKE>, <STRONG>, <SUB>, <SUP>, <TABLE>, <TEXTAREA>, <TT>, <U>, <UL>, <VAR>

Sample HTML

```
<BLOCKQUOTE CITE="Julius Caesar">
Friends, Romans, Countryman, lend me your ears!
</BLOCKQUOTE>
```


The BR (line break) tag causes a line of text to break wherever the tag is placed.

Style Tip

The line break tag is best used to create short lines of text, as often seen in poetry. It guarantees a break in the text regardless of the size of the browser window.

Attributes

CLEAR=(LEFT|ALL|RIGHT|NONE)

Specifies how the text should flow in relation to any floating images it may follow. LEFT causes the text to be aligned directly under a left-floating image and to the left side of the screen. ALL positions the text after any floating images. RIGHT causes the text to be aligned directly under a right-floating image and to the right side of the screen. NONE, the default, allows the text to flow naturally based on the other elements on the page.

Parent Tags

```
<A>, <ACRONYM>, <ADDRESS>, <APPLET>, <B>, <BDO>, <BIG>, <BLOCKQUOTE>,
<BODY>, <BUTTON>, <CAPTION>, <CENTER>, <CITE>, <CODE>, <DD>, <DEL>,
<DFN>, <DIV>, <DT>, <EM>, <FIELDSET>, <FONT>, <FORM>, <H1>, <H2>, <H3>,
<H4>, <H5>, <H6>, <I>, <IFRAME>, <INS>, <KBD>, <LABEL>, <LEGEND>, <LI>,
<NOFRAMES>, <NOSCRIPT>, <OBJECT>, <P>, <PRE>, <Q>, <S>, <SAMP>, <SMALL>,
<SPAN>, <STRIKE>, <STRONG>, <SUB>, <SUP>, <TD>, <TH>, <TT>, <U>, <VAR>
```

Content Tags

None.

Sample HTML

```
This line will break here <BR>
and this text will be moved to the next line.
```

<CITE>...</CITE>

The CITE tags mark a citation or bibliographic reference.

Style Tip

Whenever you include other people's content within your Web pages, always be sure to give them proper credit enclosed in CITE tags.

Attributes

None.

Parent Tags

<A>, <ACRONYM>, <ADDRESS>, <APPLET>, <B>, <BDO>, <BIG>, <BLOCKQUOTE>, <BODY>, <BUTTON>, <CAPTION>, <CENTER>, <CITE>, <CODE>, <DD>, <DEL>, <DFN>, <DIV>, <DT>, <EM>, <FIELDSET>, <FONT>, <FORM>, <H1>, <H2>, <H3>, <H4>, <H5>, <H6>, <I>, <IFRAME>, <INS>, <KBD>, <LABEL>, <LEGEND>, <LI>, <NOFRAMES>, <NOSCRIPT>, <OBJECT>, <P>, <PRE>, <Q>, <S>, <SAMP>, <SMALL>, <SPAN>, <STRIKE>, <STRONG>, <SUB>, <SUP>, <TD>, <TH>, <TT>, <U>, <VAR>

Content Tags

<A>, <ACRONYM>, <APPLET>, <B>, <BASEFONT>, <BDO>, <BIG>, <BR>, <BUTTON>, <CITE>, <CODE>, <DFN>, <EM>, <FONT>, <I>, <IFRAME>, <IMG>, <INPUT>, <KBD>, <LABEL>, <MAP>, <OBJECT>, <Q>, <S>, <SAMP>, <SCRIPT>, <SELECT>, <SMALL>, <SPAN>, <STRIKE>, <STRONG>, <SUB>, <SUP>, <TEXTAREA>, <TT>, <U>, <VAR>

Sample HTML

```
<BODY>
All statistical references in this document are from <BR>
<CITE>Statistics Daily, Volume 3, Issue 2; March, 1994. </CITE>
</BODY>
```

<CODE>...</CODE>

The CODE tags are used to identify text that represents programming code. Code text is most often displayed in a monospaced font.

Style Tip

Any text that represents programming or computer code should be included within CODE tags so users recognize it as such. Also, the monospaced font will preserve code formatting, often an essential part of a program.

Attributes

None.

Parent Tags

<A>, <ACRONYM>, <ADDRESS>, <APPLET>, <B>, <BDO>, <BIG>, <BLOCKQUOTE>, <BODY>, <BUTTON>, <CAPTION>, <CENTER>, <CITE>, <CODE>, <DD>, <DEL>, <DFN>, <DIV>, <DT>, <EM>, <FIELDSET>, <FONT>, <FORM>, <H1>, <H2>, <H3>, <H4>, <H5>, <H6>, <I>, <IFRAME>, <INS>, <KBD>, <LABEL>, <LEGEND>, <LI>, <NOFRAMES>, <NOSCRIPT>, <OBJECT>, <P>, <PRE>, <Q>, <S>, <SAMP>, <SMALL>, <SPAN>, <STRIKE>, <STRONG>, <SUB>, <SUP>, <TD>, <TH>, <TT>, <U>, <VAR>

Content Tags

<A>, <ACRONYM>, <APPLET>, <B>, <BASEFONT>, <BDO>, <BIG>, <BR>, <BUTTON>, <CITE>, <CODE>, <DFN>, <EM>, <FONT>, <I>, <IFRAME>, <IMG>, <INPUT>, <KBD>, <LABEL>, <MAP>, <OBJECT>, <Q>, <S>, <SAMP>, <SCRIPT>, <SELECT>, <SMALL>, <SPAN>, <STRIKE>, <STRONG>, <SUB>, <SUP>, <TEXTAREA>, <TT>, <U>, <VAR>

Sample HTML

```
The following HTML markup must be included in every page: <BR>
<CODE>
<!DOCTYPE HTML PUBLIC &quot;-//IETF//DTD HTML 4.0//EN&quot;>
<HTML>
<HEAD>

<TITLE></TITLE>


</HEAD>
<BODY>

</BODY>
</HTML>
</CODE>
```

<DEL>...</DEL>

DEL (deletion) tags set off text that was included in previous versions of a document but has been deleted in the new version.

Style Tip

The DEL tags, and their companion INS (insertion) tags, are very useful tools for showing how a Web document has been revised over time. These are similar to the revision tools found in many word processors.

Attributes

CITE="url"

Provides a link to another Web document that contains information about why the text was deleted from the document.

DATETIME=YYYY-MM-DDThh:mm:ssTZD

Specifies when the enclosed text was deleted, using standard date and time notation. *YYYY* indicates the year, *MM* the two-digit month, and *DD* the two-digit day. *T* is the time indicator. *HH* stands for the two-digit hour (in military time), *mm* the two-digit minute, and *ss* the two-digit seconds. *TZD* is used to specify the time zone.

Parent Tags

```
<BODY>
```

Content Tags

```
<A>, <ACRONYM>, <APPLET>, <B>, <BASEFONT>, <BDO>, <BIG>, <BR>,
<BUTTON>, <CITE>, <CODE>, <DFN>, <EM>, <FONT>, <I>, <IFRAME>, <IMG>,
<INPUT>, <KBD>, <LABEL>, <MAP>, <OBJECT>, <Q>, <S>, <SAMP>, <SCRIPT>,
<SELECT>, <SMALL>, <SPAN>, <STRIKE>, <STRONG>, <SUB>, <SUP>,
<TEXTAREA>, <TT>, <U>, <VAR>
```

Sample HTML

```
<BODY>
<DEL CITE="changes.html" DATETIME=1994-09-21T23:10:15Z>
<H1>Introduction</H1>
...
</DEL>
<H1>New Introduction</H1>
...
</BODY>
```

<DFN>...</DFN>

The DFN (definition) tags are used to mark the first use of a term within a Web document.

Style Tip

If you are introducing new terminology for the first time in a Web document or series of documents, it is important to insure that users recognize the term as new, understand its meaning, and know that it will be used again in the document. Text enclosed within DFN tags is usually rendered in italics so it stands out to users.

Attributes

None.

Parent Tags

<A>, <ACRONYM>, <ADDRESS>, <APPLET>, <B>, <BDO>, <BIG>, <BLOCKQUOTE>, <BODY>, <BUTTON>, <CAPTION>, <CENTER>, <CITE>, <CODE>, <DD>, <DEL>, <DFN>, <DIV>, <DT>, <EM>, <FIELDSET>, <FONT>, <FORM>, <H1>, <H2>, <H3>, <H4>, <H5>, <H6>, <I>, <IFRAME>, <INS>, <KBD>, <LABEL>, <LEGEND>, <LI>, <NOFRAMES>, <NOSCRIPT>, <OBJECT>, <P>, <PRE>, <Q>, <S>, <SAMP>, <SMALL>, <SPAN>, <STRIKE>, <STRONG>, <SUB>, <SUP>, <TD>, <TH>, <TT>, <U>, <VAR>

Content Tags

<A>, <ACRONYM>, <APPLET>, <B>, <BASEFONT>, <BDO>, <BIG>, <BR>, <BUTTON>, <CITE>, <CODE>, <DFN>, <EM>, <FONT>, <I>, <IFRAME>, <IMG>, <INPUT>, <KBD>, <LABEL>, <MAP>, <OBJECT>, <Q>, <S>, <SAMP>, <SCRIPT>, <SELECT>, <SMALL>, <SPAN>, <STRIKE>, <STRONG>, <SUB>, <SUP>, <TEXTAREA>, <TT>, <U>, <VAR>

Sample HTML

<DFN>TCP/IP</DFN> stands for Transfer Control Protocol/Internet Protocol. TCP/IP is the universal translator for the Internet.

<EM>...</EM>

The EM (emphasis) tags indicate that the enclosed text has a special importance and should be noted by the reader.

Style Tip

As with all text-altering tags, do not overuse the EM tags, or their effectiveness will be reduced.

Attributes

None.

Parent Tags

<A>, <ACRONYM>, <ADDRESS>, <APPLET>, <B>, <BDO>, <BIG>, <BLOCKQUOTE>, <BODY>, <BUTTON>, <CAPTION>, <CENTER>, <CITE>, <CODE>, <DD>, <DEL>, <DFN>, <DIV>, <DT>, <EM>, <FIELDSET>, <FONT>, <FORM>, <H1>, <H2>, <H3>, <H4>, <H5>, <H6>, <I>, <IFRAME>, <INS>, <KBD>, <LABEL>, <LEGEND>, <LI>, <NOFRAMES>, <NOSCRIPT>, <OBJECT>, <P>, <PRE>, <Q>, <S>, <SAMP>, <SMALL>, <SPAN>, <STRIKE>, <STRONG>, <SUB>, <SUP>, <TD>, <TH>, <TT>, <U>, <VAR>

Content Tags

<A>, <ACRONYM>, <APPLET>, <B>, <BASEFONT>, <BDO>, <BIG>, <BR>, <BUTTON>, <CITE>, <CODE>, <DFN>, <EM>, <FONT>, <I>, <IFRAME>, <IMG>, <INPUT>, <KBD>, <LABEL>, <MAP>, <OBJECT>, <Q>, <S>, <SAMP>, <SCRIPT>, <SELECT>, <SMALL>, <SPAN>, <STRIKE>, <STRONG>, <SUB>, <SUP>, <TEXTAREA>, <TT>, <U>, <VAR>

Sample HTML

"I <EM>don't</EM> want to go to school today," the little boy said.

<INS>...</INS>

The INS (insertion) tags set off text that was not included in previous versions of a document but has been added in the new version.

Style Tip

The INS tags, and their companion DEL (deletion) tags, are very useful tools for showing how a Web document has been revised over time. These are similar to the revision tools found in many word processors.

Attributes

CITE="url"

Provides a link to another Web document that contains information about why the text was added to the document.

DATETIME=YYYY-MM-DDThh:mm:ssTZD

Specifies when the enclosed text was added, using standard date and time notation. *YYYY* indicates the year, *MM* the two-digit month, and *DD* the two-digit day. *T* is the time indicator. *HH* stands for the two-digit hour (in military time), *mm* the two-digit minute, and *ss* the two-digit seconds. *TZD* is used to specify the time zone.

Parent Tags

```
<BODY>
```

Content Tags

```
<A>, <ACRONYM>, <APPLET>, <B>, <BASEFONT>, <BDO>, <BIG>, <BR>, <BUTTON>,
<CITE>, <CODE>, <DFN>, <EM>, <FONT>, <I>, <IFRAME>, <IMG>, <INPUT>, <KBD>,
<LABEL>, <MAP>, <OBJECT>, <Q>, <S>, <SAMP>, <SCRIPT>, <SELECT>, <SMALL>,
<SPAN>, <STRIKE>, <STRONG>, <SUB>, <SUP>, <TEXTAREA>, <TT>, <U>, <VAR>
```

Sample HTML

```
<BODY>
<INS CITE="changes.html" DATETIME=1994-09-21T23:10:15Z>
<H1>Summary</H1>
...
</INS>
</BODY>
```

<KBD>...</KBD>

The KBD (keyboard text) tags are used around text to indicate that it should be typed in at a computer keyboard by the user.

Style Tip

KBD tags display text in a monospaced font, in the same way the CODE tags do.

Attributes

None.

Parent Tags

```
<A>, <ACRONYM>, <ADDRESS>, <APPLET>, <B>, <BDO>, <BIG>, <BLOCKQUOTE>,
<BODY>, <BUTTON>, <CAPTION>, <CENTER>, <CITE>, <CODE>, <DD>, <DEL>,
<DFN>, <DIV>, <DT>, <EM>, <FIELDSET>, <FONT>, <FORM>, <H1>, <H2>, <H3>,
<H4>, <H5>, <H6>, <I>, <IFRAME>, <INS>, <KBD>, <LABEL>, <LEGEND>, <LI>,
<NOFRAMES>, <NOSCRIPT>, <OBJECT>, <P>, <PRE>, <Q>, <S>, <SAMP>, <SMALL>,
<SPAN>, <STRIKE>, <STRONG>, <SUB>, <SUP>, <TD>, <TH>, <TT>, <U>, <VAR>
```

Content Tags

```
<A>, <ACRONYM>, <APPLET>, <B>, <BASEFONT>, <BDO>, <BIG>, <BR>, <BUTTON>,
<CITE>, <CODE>, <DFN>, <EM>, <FONT>, <I>, <IFRAME>, <IMG>, <INPUT>, <KBD>,
<LABEL>, <MAP>, <OBJECT>, <Q>, <S>, <SAMP>, <SCRIPT>, <SELECT>, <SMALL>,
<SPAN>, <STRIKE>, <STRONG>, <SUB>, <SUP>, <TEXTAREA>, <TT>, <U>, <VAR>
```

Sample HTML

```
<BODY>
When you get to the login prompt type in your <KBD>username</KBD> and
<KBD>password</KBD>
</BODY>
```

<P>(...</P>)

The P (paragraph) tags separate paragraphs of text within a Web document by inserting a line break and a blank line just before the P tag.

Style Tip

Paragraph markup can be used as either a singleton tag or a pair. Paragraphs are especially useful for applying style sheet rules to sections of text using the tag pair. Multiple instances of the singleton paragraph tag cannot be used to create large blocks of white space because most browsers will only display one blank line at a time, regardless of the number of paragraph tags.

Attributes

ALIGN=(LEFT|CENTER|RIGHT|JUSTIFY) *[Deprecated]*

Specifies the horizontal alignment of the enclosed elements.

Parent Tags

```
<ADDRESS>, <BLOCKQUOTE>, <BODY>, <BUTTON>, <CENTER>, <DD>, <DIV>,
<FIELDSET>, <FORM>, <IFRAME>, <LI>, <NOFRAMES>, <NOSCRIPT>, <OBJECT>,
<TD>, <TH>
```

Content Tags

```
<A>, <ACRONYM>, <APPLET>, <B>, <BASEFONT>, <BDO>, <BIG>, <BR>, <BUTTON>,
<CITE>, <CODE>, <DFN>, <EM>, <FONT>, <I>, <IFRAME>, <IMG>, <INPUT>,
<KBD>, <LABEL>, <MAP>, <OBJECT>, <Q>, <S>, <SAMP>, <SCRIPT>, <SELECT>,
<SMALL>, <SPAN>, <STRIKE>, <STRONG>, <SUB>, <SUP>, <TEXTAREA>, <TT>,
<U>, <VAR>
```

Sample HTML

```
<BODY>
This is the first paragraph of my document.<P>
This is the second paragraph of my document.
</BODY>
```

<PRE>...</PRE>

PRE (preformatted text) tags force the browser to display the enclosed text exactly as it appears in the HTML file.

Style Tip

Because preformatted text is displayed exactly as it is written in the HTML file, multiple spaces, hard returns, and character spacing will show up in the browser window. Use preformatted text to create large blocks of white space where multiple paragraph tags will not. The biggest drawback of preformatted text is that it is rendered in a monospaced font and is limited in the other HTML markup it can contain.

Attributes

WIDTH=number

Indicates the maximum number of characters that should appear on a line. Based on this number, the browser selects an appropriate font size and indentation.

Parent Tags

<BLOCKQUOTE>, <BODY>, <BUTTON>, <CENTER>, <DD>, <DIV>, <FIELDSET>, <FORM>, <IFRAME>, <LI>, <NOFRAMES>, <NOSCRIPT>, <OBJECT>, <TD>, <TH>

Content Tags

<A>, <ACRONYM>, <APPLET>, <B>, <BASEFONT>, <BDO>, <BIG>, <BR>, <BUTTON>, <CITE>, <CODE>, <DFN>, <EM>, <FONT>, <I>, <IFRAME>, <IMG>, <INPUT>, <KBD>, <LABEL>, <MAP>, <OBJECT>, <Q>, <S>, <SAMP>, <SCRIPT>, <SELECT>, <SMALL>, <SPAN>, <STRIKE>, <STRONG>, <SUB>, <SUP>, <TEXTAREA>, <TT>, <U>, <VAR>

Sample HTML

```
<BODY>
Class schedule:
<PRE>
Monday/Wednesday      Tuesday/Thursday
12:00  Chemistry      12:00  English
 1:30  Physics         1:30  Math
</PRE>
</BODY>
```

<Q>...</Q>

Q (quotation) tags enclose short quotations within a line of text.

Style Tip

Unlike BLOCKQUOTE tags, which set off large amounts of text from other text in the document, Q tags should be used to highlight bits of text that remain inline.

Attributes

CITE="text"

Provides additional information about the source of the quoted text.

Parent Tags

<A>, <ACRONYM>, <ADDRESS>, <APPLET>, <B>, <BDO>, <BIG>, <BLOCKQUOTE>, <BODY>, <BUTTON>, <CAPTION>, <CENTER>, <CITE>, <CODE>, <DD>, <DEL>, <DFN>, <DIV>, <DT>, <EM>, <FIELDSET>, <FONT>, <FORM>, <H1>, <H2>, <H3>, <H4>, <H5>, <H6>, <I>, <IFRAME>, <INS>, <KBD>, <LABEL>, <LEGEND>, <LI>, <NOFRAMES>, <NOSCRIPT>, <OBJECT>, <P>, <PRE>, <Q>, <S>, <SAMP>, <SMALL>, <SPAN>, <STRIKE>, <STRONG>, <SUB>, <SUP>, <TD>, <TH>, <TT>, <U>, <VAR>

Content Tags

<A>, <ACRONYM>, <APPLET>, <B>, <BASEFONT>, <BDO>, <BIG>, <BR>, <BUTTON>, <CITE>, <CODE>, <DFN>, <EM>, <FONT>, <I>, <IFRAME>, <IMG>, <INPUT>, <KBD>, <LABEL>, <MAP>, <OBJECT>, <Q>, <S>, <SAMP>, <SCRIPT>, <SELECT>, <SMALL>, <SPAN>, <STRIKE>, <STRONG>, <SUB>, <SUP>, <TEXTAREA>, <TT>, <U>, <VAR>

Sample HTML

```
<BODY>
Julius Caesar said <Q>Et Tu, Brute?</Q> when he was stabbed on the
steps of the Forum.
</BODY>
```

<SAMP>...</SAMP>

The SAMP (sample) tags are used to highlight text that represents output from a program or other literal text.

Style Tip

While the CODE tags are used to mark up the actual code for a program, use the SAMP tags to show what the output from the code should look like.

Attributes

None.

Parent Tags

<A>, <ACRONYM>, <ADDRESS>, <APPLET>, <B>, <BDO>, <BIG>, <BLOCKQUOTE>, <BODY>, <BUTTON>, <CAPTION>, <CENTER>, <CITE>, <CODE>, <DD>, <DEL>, <DFN>, <DIV>, <DT>, <EM>, <FIELDSET>, <FONT>, <FORM>, <H1>, <H2>, <H3>, <H4>, <H5>, <H6>, <I>, <IFRAME>, <INS>, <KBD>, <LABEL>, <LEGEND>, <LI>, <NOFRAMES>, <NOSCRIPT>, <OBJECT>, <P>, <PRE>, <Q>, <S>, <SAMP>, <SMALL>, <SPAN>, <STRIKE>, <STRONG>, <SUB>, <SUP>, <TD>, <TH>, <TT>, <U>, <VAR>

Content Tags

<A>, <ACRONYM>, <APPLET>, <B>, <BASEFONT>, <BDO>, <BIG>, <BR>, <BUTTON>, <CITE>, <CODE>, <DFN>, <EM>, <FONT>, <I>, <IFRAME>, <IMG>, <INPUT>, <KBD>, <LABEL>, <MAP>, <OBJECT>, <Q>, <S>, <SAMP>, <SCRIPT>, <SELECT>, <SMALL>, <SPAN>, <STRIKE>, <STRONG>, <SUB>, <SUP>, <TEXTAREA>, <TT>, <U>, <VAR>

Sample HTML

```
<BODY>
The output from my first program ever was:<BR>
<SAMP>Hello world!</SAMP>
</BODY>
```

<STRONG>...</STRONG>

STRONG tags indicate that the enclosed text is very important and should clearly stand out from the surrounding text. Strong text is usually formatted in boldface type.

Style Tip

This tag pair provides the strongest possible emphasis on text without changing its font size or separating it from the surrounding text. Be careful not to overuse these tags or your emphasized text will lose its effect.

Attributes

None.

Parent Tags

<A>, <ACRONYM>, <ADDRESS>, <APPLET>, <B>, <BDO>, <BIG>, <BLOCKQUOTE>, <BODY>, <BUTTON>, <CAPTION>, <CENTER>, <CITE>, <CODE>, <DD>, <DEL>, <DFN>, <DIV>, <DT>, <EM>, <FIELDSET>, <FONT>, <FORM>, <H1>, <H2>, <H3>, <H4>, <H5>, <H6>, <I>, <IFRAME>, <INS>, <KBD>, <LABEL>, <LEGEND>, <LI>, <NOFRAMES>, <NOSCRIPT>, <OBJECT>, <P>, <PRE>, <Q>, <S>, <SAMP>, <SMALL>, <SPAN>, <STRIKE>, <STRONG>, <SUB>, <SUP>, <TD>, <TH>, <TT>, <U>, <VAR>

Content Tags

<A>, <ACRONYM>, <APPLET>, <B>, <BASEFONT>, <BDO>, <BIG>, <BR>, <BUTTON>, <CITE>, <CODE>, <DFN>, <EM>, <FONT>, <I>, <IFRAME>, <IMG>, <INPUT>, <KBD>, <LABEL>, <MAP>, <OBJECT>, <Q>, <S>, <SAMP>, <SCRIPT>, <SELECT>, <SMALL>, <SPAN>, <STRIKE>, <STRONG>, <SUB>, <SUP>, <TEXTAREA>, <TT>, <U>, <VAR>

Sample HTML

```
<BODY>
"I <STRONG>really don't</STRONG> want to go to school today," the
little boy said.</BODY>
```

_{...}

The SUB (subscript) tags are used to mark text that should be displayed as subscript.

Style Tip

Although SUB tags can be nested within other SUB tags and SUP (superscript) tags, the final browser rendering is unpredictable and will vary from browser to browser.

Attributes

None.

Parent Tags

<A>, <ACRONYM>, <ADDRESS>, <APPLET>, <B>, <BDO>, <BIG>, <BLOCKQUOTE>, <BODY>, <BUTTON>, <CAPTION>, <CENTER>, <CITE>, <CODE>, <DD>, <DEL>, <DFN>, <DIV>, <DT>, <EM>, <FIELDSET>, <FONT>, <FORM>, <H1>, <H2>, <H3>, <H4>, <H5>, <H6>, <I>, <IFRAME>, <INS>, <KBD>, <LABEL>, <LEGEND>, <LI>, <NOFRAMES>, <NOSCRIPT>, <OBJECT>, <P>, <Q>, <S>, <SAMP>, <SMALL>, <SPAN>, <STRIKE>, <STRONG>, <SUB>, <SUP>, <TD>, <TH>, <TT>, <U>, <VAR>

Content Tags

<A>, <ACRONYM>, <APPLET>, <B>, <BASEFONT>, <BDO>, <BIG>, <BR>,
<BUTTON>, <CITE>, <CODE>, <DFN>, <EM>, <FONT>, <I>, <IFRAME>, <IMG>,
<INPUT>, <KBD>, <LABEL>, <MAP>, <OBJECT>, <Q>, <S>, <SAMP>, <SCRIPT>,
<SELECT>, <SMALL>, <SPAN>, <STRIKE>, <STRONG>, <SUB>, <SUP>,
<TEXTAREA>, <TT>, <U>, <VAR>

Sample HTML

```
<BODY>
CO<SUB>2</SUB> is a dangerous gas that can cause death if inhaled in
large quantities; in smaller quantities, it is used to carbonate soft
drinks!
</BODY>
```

^{...}

The SUP (superscript) tags are used to mark text that should be displayed as superscript.

Style Tip

Although SUP tags can be nested within other SUP tags and SUB (subscript) tags, the final browser rendering is unpredictable and will vary from browser to browser.

Attributes

None.

Parent Tags

<A>, <ACRONYM>, <ADDRESS>, <APPLET>, <B>, <BDO>, <BIG>, <BLOCKQUOTE>,
<BODY>, <BUTTON>, <CAPTION>, <CENTER>, <CITE>, <CODE>, <DD>, <DEL>,
<DFN>, <DIV>, <DT>, <EM>, <FIELDSET>, <FONT>, <FORM>, <H1>, <H2>, <H3>,
<H4>, <H5>, <H6>, <I>, <IFRAME>, <INS>, <KBD>, <LABEL>, <LEGEND>, <LI>,
<NOFRAMES>, <NOSCRIPT>, <OBJECT>, <P>, <Q>, <S>, <SAMP>, <SMALL>,
<SPAN>, <STRIKE>, <STRONG>, <SUB>, <SUP>, <TD>, <TH>, <TT>, <U>, <VAR>

Content Tags

<A>, <ACRONYM>, <APPLET>, <B>, <BASEFONT>, <BDO>, <BIG>, <BR>, <BUTTON>,
<CITE>, <CODE>, <DFN>, <EM>, <FONT>, <I>, <IFRAME>, <IMG>, <INPUT>, <KBD>,
<LABEL>, <MAP>, <OBJECT>, <Q>, <S>, <SAMP>, <SCRIPT>, <SELECT>, <SMALL>,
<SPAN>, <STRIKE>, <STRONG>, <SUB>, <SUP>, <TEXTAREA>, <TT>, <U>, <VAR>

Sample HTML

```
<BODY>
When I was little, my dad and I went to M<SUP>c</SUP>Dougall's House of
Pancakes every Saturday for breakfast.
</BODY>
```

<VAR>...</VAR>

VAR (variable) tags mark text that represents a placeholder for user-supplied text. Most browsers display variable text in italics.

Style Tip

When writing instructions that require users to supply their own information, use VAR tags to highlight where this information should be placed.

Attributes

None.

Parent Tags

<A>, <ACRONYM>, <ADDRESS>, <APPLET>, <B>, <BDO>, <BIG>, <BLOCKQUOTE>, <BODY>, <BUTTON>, <CAPTION>, <CENTER>, <CITE>, <CODE>, <DD>, <DEL>, <DFN>, <DIV>, <DT>, <EM>, <FIELDSET>, <FONT>, <FORM>, <H1>, <H2>, <H3>, <H4>, <H5>, <H6>, <I>, <IFRAME>, <INS>, <KBD>, <LABEL>, <LEGEND>, <LI>, <NOFRAMES>, <NOSCRIPT>, <OBJECT>, <P>, <PRE>, <Q>, <S>, <SAMP>, <SMALL>, <SPAN>, <STRIKE>, <STRONG>, <SUB>, <SUP>, <TD>, <TH>, <TT>, <U>, <VAR>

Content Tags

<A>, <ACRONYM>, <APPLET>, <B>, <BASEFONT>, <BDO>, <BIG>, <BR>, <BUTTON>, <CITE>, <CODE>, <DFN>, <EM>, <FONT>, <I>, <IFRAME>, <IMG>, <INPUT>, <KBD>, <LABEL>, <MAP>, <OBJECT>, <Q>, <S>, <SAMP>, <SCRIPT>, <SELECT>, <SMALL>, <SPAN>, <STRIKE>, <STRONG>, <SUB>, <SUP>, <TEXTAREA>, <TT>, <U>, <VAR>

Sample HTML

```
<BODY>
To change directories in DOS, type the following command:<BR>
<KBD>cd <VAR>dir</VAR></KBD>
</BODY>
```

List Tags

List tags define lists of elements that may be displayed as bulleted or numbered lists, glossary entries with definitions, and menu formats. All of these layouts are useful when organizing lists of items or elements to improve their readability.

<DD> (...</DD>)

The DD (definition description) tags mark the descriptive piece of a definition list.

Style Tip

Definition descriptions can be entire paragraphs used to define the definition term. Other markup, such as paragraphs and line breaks, can be used within <DD> markup.

Attributes

None.

Parent Tags

<DL>

Content Tags

<A>, <ACRONYM>, <ADDRESS>, <APPLET>, <B>, <BASEFONT>, <BDO>, <BIG>, <BLOCKQUOTE>, <BR>, <BUTTON>, <CENTER>, <CITE>, <CODE>, <DFN>, <DIR>, <DIV>, <DL>, <EM>, <FIELDSET>, <FONT>, <FORM>, <H1>, <H2>, <H3>, <H4>, <H5>, <H6>, <HR>, <I>, <IFRAME>, <IMG>, <INPUT>, <ISINDEX>, <KBD>, <LABEL>, <MAP>, <MENU>, <NOFRAMES>, <NOSCRIPT>, <OBJECT>, <OL>, <P>, <PRE>, <Q>, <S>, <SAMP>, <SCRIPT>, <SELECT>, <SMALL>, <SPAN>, <STRIKE>, <STRONG>, <SUB>, <SUP>, <TABLE>, <TEXTAREA>, <TT>, <U>, <UL>, <VAR>

Sample HTML

```
<BODY>
<DL>
<DT>SGML
<DD>Standardized General Markup Language
<DT>HTML
<DD>Hypertext Markup Language
</DL>
```

<DIR>...</DIR>

The DIR (directory list) tags render a plain list for short items, such as filenames. The items in the list must be labeled with the <LI> tag.

Style Tip

Directory lists are best for short groups of items that need to be set away from the text but not bulleted or numbered.

Attributes

None.

Parent Tags

<BLOCKQUOTE>, <BODY>, <BUTTON>, <CENTER>, <DD>, <DIV>, <FIELDSET>, <FORM>, <IFRAME>, <LI>, <NOFRAMES>, <NOSCRIPT>, <OBJECT>, <TD>, <TH>

Content Tags

<LI>

Sample HTML

```
<BODY>
Grocery List:
<DIR>
<LI>Pizza
<LI>Ice Cream
<LI>Dr. Pepper
</DIR>
</BODY>
```

<DL>...</DL>

DL (definition list) tags are used to mark glossary terms and their associated definitions.

Style Tip

Definition lists are not limited to terms and definitions. Use this list type for items with associated descriptions, such as article titles and related information. The definition description, marked by the <DD> tag, appears one line down, indented to the right of the definition term, marked by the <DT> tag.

Attributes

COMPACT

Indicates a list should be tightly spaced to make it more compact.

Parent Tags

`<BLOCKQUOTE>`, `<BODY>`, `<BUTTON>`, `<CENTER>`, `<DD>`, `<DIV>`, `<FIELDSET>`, `<FORM>`, `<IFRAME>`, `<LI>`, `<NOFRAMES>`, `<NOSCRIPT>`, `<OBJECT>`, `<TD>`, `<TH>`

Content Tags

`<DT>`, `<DD>`

Sample HTML

```
<BODY>
<DL>
<DT>SGML
<DD>Standardized General Markup Language
<DT>HTML
<DD>Hypertext Markup Language
</DL>
```

`<DT>`

The DT (definition term) tag marks the word actually being defined in a definition list.

Style Tip

Definition terms can be a single word or a string of words.

Attributes

None.

Parent Tags

`<DL>`

Content Tags

None.

Sample HTML

```
<BODY>
<DL>
<DT>SGML
<DD>Standardized General Markup Language
<DT>HTML
<DD>Hypertext Markup Language
</DL>
```

<LI>

The LI (list item) tag marks a list item in every type of list except the definition list.

Style Tip

Any element in a list, except in a definition list, must be preceded by an LI tag. While some Web browsers indent text in lists without the LI tag, this is not valid HTML. To guarantee that the list will appear indented as you intend, use the LI tag.

Attributes

TYPE=(DISC|SQUARE|CIRCLE) or (1|a|A|i|I)

When the <LI> element is used in an ordered list (<OL>), a number will appear before the list item. With the TYPE attribute, you can change the style of the number or letter that appears before the listed item. (See Table F.2.)

TABLE F.2: Numbering Systems

Use This	To Do This
1	Label the listed items with standard numbers (1, 2, 3, etc.). This is the default.
a	Provide a lowercase letter as the label (a, b, c, etc.)
A	Provide an uppercase letter as the label (A, B, C, etc.)
i	Provide a lowercase Roman numeral as the label (i, ii, iii, iv, etc.)
I	Provide an uppercase Roman numeral as the label (I, II, III, IV, etc.)

In an unordered list (<UL>), you can choose what type of bullet is displayed. (See Table F.3.)

TABLE F.3:   Types of Bullets

Use This	To Get This
DISC	A closed circular bullet
SQUARE	An open square bullet
CIRCLE	An open circular bullet

VALUE=number

Changes the counting order of the list.

Parent Tags

<DIR>, <MENU>, <OL>, <UL>

Content Tags

None.

Sample HTML

```
<BODY>
<OL>
<LI VALUE=2>List item 1, numbered 2
<LI>List item 2, numbered 3
<LI>List item 3, numbered 4
</OL>
</BODY>
```

<MENU>...</MENU>

The MENU tags are used for short lists of items or short paragraphs. You must use the <LI> tag within the menu list.

Style Tip

Menu lists and directory lists are interchangeable and are usually rendered the same by most major browsers.

Attributes

COMPACT

Indicates a list should be tightly spaced to make it more compact.

Parent Tags

<BLOCKQUOTE>, <BODY>, <BUTTON>, <CENTER>, <DD>, <DIV>, <FIELDSET>, <FORM>, <IFRAME>, <LI>, <NOFRAMES>, <NOSCRIPT>, <OBJECT>, <TD>, <TH>

Content Tags

<LI>

Sample HTML

```
<BODY>
For Dessert:
<MENU>
<LI>Chocolate cake
<LI>Ice cream
<LI>Cherry pie
</MENU>
</BODY>
```

<OL>...</OL>

The OL (ordered list) tags render a numbered list. Items in the list must be labeled with the <LI> tag.

Style Tip

Ordered list items always include a number before the item. The lists will always start with 1, and at this time there is no standard way to define the starting number as anything other than 1.

Attributes

TYPE= (1|a|A|i|I)

Changes the style of the number or letter that appears before the listed item. (See Table F.2.)

COMPACT

Indicates a list should be tightly spaced to make it more compact.

START="value"

Specifies where in the list to begin the numbering or lettering.

Parent Tags

```
<BLOCKQUOTE>, <BODY>, <BUTTON>, <CENTER>, <DD>, <DIV>, <FIELDSET>,
<FORM>, <IFRAME>, <LI>, <NOFRAMES>, <NOSCRIPT>, <OBJECT>, <TD>, <TH>
```

Content Tags

```
<LI>
```

Sample HTML

```
<BODY>
Things to do today:
<OL>
<LI>Wash the car
<LI>Grocery shopping
<LI>Clean house</OL>
</BODY>
```

<UL>...</UL>

The UL (unordered list) tags render a bulleted list.

Style Tip

Bulleted lists set items away from the surrounding text and include a bullet before each element. Use this list type when items should be grouped, and where order or rank is unimportant. Internet Explorer and Netscape Navigator currently support the TYPE attribute to change how bullets appear in a list. This attribute is not supported by many other browsers nor is it backward compatible with earlier browsers.

Attributes

COMPACT

Indicates a list should be tightly spaced to make it more compact.

TYPE=(DISC|SQUARE|CIRCLE)

Specifies the type of bullet used in the list. (See Table F.3.)

Parent Tags

```
<BLOCKQUOTE>, <BODY>, <BUTTON>, <CENTER>, <DD>, <DIV>, <FIELDSET>,
<FORM>, <IFRAME>, <LI>, <NOFRAMES>, <NOSCRIPT>, <OBJECT>, <TD>, <TH>
```

Content Tags

```
<LI>
```

Sample HTML

```
<BODY>
Cars I have owned:
<UL>
<LI>Saturn SL1
<LI>Ford Contour
<LI>Ford Probe
</UL>
</BODY>
```

Table Tags

Table tags are used to create HTML tables and their constituent elements: captions, rows, individual cells, and column and row groups. Tables allow you to add more organization to text by separating page content into rows and columns. Tables are more versatile than regular HTML because they provide more precision when placing text and images, both in relation to the page and to each other. Tables can also add interesting horizontal elements to HTML pages.

<CAPTION>...</CAPTION>

The CAPTION tags are used to attach a caption either before or after a table.

Style Tip

CAPTION tags help identify a table and its contents for users, but should be brief and to the point, like HTML document titles. Any text-level markup may appear within CAPTION tags.

Attributes

ALIGN=(LEFT|RIGHT|TOP|BOTTOM)

The default alignment for a caption is centered. With this attribute you can set the alignment to the left, right, top, or bottom.

Parent Tags

```
<TABLE>
```

Content Tags

```
<A>, <ACRONYM>, <APPLET>, <B>, <BASEFONT>, <BDO>, <BIG>, <BR>,
<BUTTON>, <CITE>, <CODE>, <DFN>, <EM>, <FONT>, <I>, <IFRAME>, <IMG>,
<INPUT>, <KBD>, <LABEL>, <MAP>, <OBJECT>, <Q>, <S>, <SAMP>, <SCRIPT>,
<SELECT>, <SMALL>, <SPAN>, <STRIKE>, <STRONG>, <SUB>, <SUP>,
<TEXTAREA>, <TT>, <U>, <VAR>
```

Sample HTML

```
<BODY>
<TABLE WIDTH="75%" ALIGN=CENTER>
<CAPTION>
This is a sample table
</CAPTION>
... table data ...
</TABLE>
</BODY>
```

<COL>

The COL (column) tag is used to set the properties for a column or a set of columns within a column group.

Style Tip

While the COLGROUP (column group) tag sets the properties for an entire group of columns, the COL tag can be used within a column group to provide specific information about one or more of the columns within the group.

Attributes

ALIGN=(LEFT|RIGHT|CENTER|JUSTIFY|CHAR)

Indicates how the text within the column's cells should be horizontally aligned. The CHAR value indicates that the text should be aligned to a specific character, as defined by the CHAR attribute (described next).

CHAR="text"

Identifies the character that text should be aligned with horizontally if the value of ALIGN is CHAR.

CHAROFF="number"

Specifies how many pixels the rest of the text in a line should be offset from the character defined by the value of the CHAR attribute.

SPAN="number"

Identifies how many columns the column tag properties apply to.

VALIGN= TOP|MIDDLE|BOTTOM|BASELINE

Specifies how the text within the column's cells should be vertically aligned.

WIDTH="number"

Specifies how wide each column controlled by the column tag should be.

Parent Tags

```
<COLGROUP>, <TABLE>
```

Content Tags

None.

Sample HTML

```
<TABLE>
<COLGROUP>
  <COL ALIGN=CENTER>
  <COL ALIGN=LEFT>
<COLGROUP>
  <COL ALIGN=RIGHT>
<TBODY>
  <TR>
  <TD>This is the first column in the group and is centered.</TD>
  <TD>This is the second column in the group and is left-aligned.</TD>
  <TD>This column is in a new group and is right-aligned.</TD>
  </TR>
</TABLE>
```

<COLGROUP>

The COLGROUP (column group) tag is used to set the properties for a group of columns.

Style Tip

Use the COLGROUP tag to identify general properties for a large group of columns, and then include the COL tag to set specific properties for individual columns or smaller groups of columns within the large group.

Attributes

ALIGN=(LEFT|RIGHT|CENTER|JUSTIFY|CHAR)

Indicates how the text within the column's cells should be horizontally aligned. The CHAR value indicates that the text should be aligned to a specific character, as defined by the CHAR attribute (described next).

CHAR="text"

Identifies the character that text should be aligned with horizontally if the value of ALIGN is CHAR.

CHAROFF="number"

Specifies how many pixels the rest of the text in a line should be offset from the character defined by the value of the CHAR attribute.

SPAN="number"

Identifies the number of columns to which the column tag properties apply.

VALIGN= TOP|MIDDLE|BOTTOM|BASELINE

Specifies how text within the columns' cells should be aligned vertically.

WIDTH="number"

Specifies how wide each column within the column group should be.

Parent Tags

<TABLE>

Content Tags

<COL>

Sample HTML

```
<TABLE>
<COLGROUP ALIGN=CENTER>
<COLGROUP SPAN=4 ALIGN=RIGHT>
<TBODY>
```

```
<TR>
<TD>This column is in the first group and is centered.</TD>
<TD>This column is in the second group and is right-aligned.</TD>
<TD>This column is in the second group and is right-aligned.</TD>
<TD>This column is in the second group and is right-aligned.</TD>
<TD>This column is in the second group and is right-aligned.</TD>
</TR>
</TABLE>
```

<TABLE>...</TABLE>

The TABLE tags create the table to which the following rows and cells belong.

Style Tip

The precise rendering of table markup varies from browser to browser. Always view complex tables using different browsers to make sure your content isn't confused or altered when another browser displays it differently. Also, text-only browsers do not support tables, and may make your content inaccessible to people who use them. Generally, text-only browsers present table information from left to right and top to bottom. Always check tables with nongraphical browsers.

Attributes

ALIGN=(LEFT|RIGHT|CENTER)

Assigns alignment to the table in relationship to the page. (See Table F.4.)

TABLE F.4:   Options for Alignment

Use This	To Do This
LEFT	Align the table to the left. (This is the default alignment.)
RIGHT	Align the table to the right. If there is any available space, the text will wrap along the left of the table.
CENTER	Place the table in the middle of the window.

BGCOLOR=colorname *[Deprecated]*

Provides the color of the background that is either a hexadecimal, red-green-blue color value, or a predefined color name. (See Table F.1.)

BORDER=number

Sets the table border. The default border size is 0; any other number creates a border equal to that number in pixels.

CELLPADDING=number

Specifies the amount of space (measured in pixels) between the sides of a cell and the text or graphics within the cell.

CELLSPACING=number

Sets the amount of space (measured in pixels) between the exterior of the table and the cells inside the table. In addition, it also sets the space that is between the cells themselves.

COLS=number

Defines the number of columns in a table.

FRAME=(VOID|ABOVE|BELOW|HSIDES|LHS|RHS|VSIDES|BOX|BORDER)

Specifies which sides of the outer border of the table should be displayed. (See Table F.5.)

T A B L E   F . 5 :   Options for Outside Borders

Use This	To Get This
VOID	No outside borders
ABOVE	A border on the top of the table
BELOW	A border on the bottom of the table
HSIDES	A border both on the top and bottom of the table
LHS	A border on the left side of the table
RHS	A border on the right side of the table
VSIDES	A border on both the left and right sides of the table
BOX	A complete border around all sides of the table
BORDER	A complete border around all sides of the table (This produces the same result as **BOX**.)

RULES=(NONE|GROUPS|ROWS|COLS|ALL)

Specifies which inner border lines of a table are displayed. (See Table F.6.)

TABLE F.6: Options for Inside Borders

Use This	To Get This
NONE	No interior borders
GROUPS	Horizontal borders between all table groups (THEAD, TBODY, TFOOT, and COLGROUP elements designate a group.)
ROWS	Horizontal borders between all table rows
COLS	Vertical borders between all table columns
ALL	Borders on all rows and columns

WIDTH=(pixels|"*n%*")

Determines the width of the table in pixels or as a percentage of the window. The *n* must end with the percent (%) sign and be contained within quotation marks to set a percentage.

Parent Tags

<BLOCKQUOTE>, <BODY>, <BUTTON>, <CENTER>, <DD>, <DIV>, <FIELDSET>, <FORM>, <IFRAME>, <LI>, <NOFRAMES>, <NOSCRIPT>, <OBJECT>, <TD>, <TH>

Content Tags

<CAPTION>, <COL>, <COLGROUP>, <TBODY>, <TFOOT>, <THEAD>

Sample HTML

```
<BODY>
<TABLE WIDTH="75%" ALIGN=CENTER>
... table data ...
</TABLE>
</BODY>
```

<TBODY> (...</TBODY>)

The TBODY (table body) tags are used to define the table body information and distinguish it from the rows of the table header or footer.

Style Tip

If the THEAD and TFOOT tags have not been used in a table, then the TBODY tag is optional. You can include more than one TBODY tag to create logical divisions within your document.

Attributes

None.

Parent Tags

<TABLE>

Content Tags

<TR>

Sample HTML

```
<BODY>
<TABLE WIDTH="75%" ALIGN=CENTER>
<CAPTION>
This is a sample table
</CAPTION>
<THEAD>
<TR> ... </TR>
<TBODY>
<TR> ... </TR>
</TABLE>
</BODY>
```

<TD>...</TD>

The TD (table cell) tags create individual cells within table rows.

Style Tip

As with TR (table row) tags, it is important to close each TD tag before beginning a new cell, or your table may not be displayed correctly. All browsers render empty cells a little differently, so test your table with a variety of browsers to see the different displays. Cell attributes and specifications override those previously defined by the row or table settings.

Attributes

ALIGN=(CENTER|LEFT|RIGHT)

Specifies the alignment. The default horizontal alignment of the text is centered.

AXIS="text"

Allows you to provide an abbreviated version of the cell's contents.

AXES="text"

Allows you to provide a list of keywords, separated by commas, that list a set of row and column headers related to the contents of the cell.

BGCOLOR=colorname *[Deprecated]*

Provides the color of the background that is either a hexadecimal, red-green-blue color value, or a predefined color name. (See Table F.1.)

CHAR="text"

Identifies the character that text should be aligned with horizontally if the value of ALIGN is CHAR.

CHAROFF="number"

Specifies how many pixels the rest of the text in a line should be offset from the character defined by the value of the CHAR attribute.

COLSPAN=number

Specifies how many columns the cell overlaps.

NOWRAP *[Deprecated]*

Shows that the contents of the cell are not to be wrapped; they will appear as a single line unless the <BR> tag is used.

ROWSPAN=number

Specifies how many rows the cell overlaps.

VALIGN=(TOP|MIDDLE|BOTTOM|BASELINE)

Designates the vertical alignment of text within a cell. The default text alignment is in the middle. (See Table F.7.)

TABLE F.7:   Options for Vertical Alignment in Tables

Use This	To Get This
TOP	Text aligned at the top of each cell
MIDDLE	Text aligned in the middle of each cell
BOTTOM	Text aligned at the bottom of each cell
BASELINE	Text in cells in adjoining rows aligned along a common baseline

WIDTH=number

Designates the width of the cell in pixels.

Parent Tags

<TR>

Content Tags

<A>, <ACRONYM>, <ADDRESS>, <APPLET>, <B>, <BASEFONT>, <BDO>, <BIG>, <BLOCKQUOTE>, <BR>, <BUTTON>, <CENTER>, <CITE>, <CODE>, <DFN>, <DIR>, <DIV>, <DL>, <EM>, <FIELDSET>, <FONT>, <FORM>, <H1>, <H2>, <H3>, <H4>, <H5>, <H6>, <HR>, <I>, <IFRAME>, <IMG>, <INPUT>, <ISINDEX>, <KBD>, <LABEL>, <MAP>, <MENU>, <NOFRAMES>, <NOSCRIPT>, <OBJECT>, <OL>, <P>, <PRE>, <Q>, <S>, <SAMP>, <SCRIPT>, <SELECT>, <SMALL>, <SPAN>, <STRIKE>, <STRONG>, <SUB>, <SUP>, <TABLE>, <TEXTAREA>, <TT>, <U>, <UL>, <VAR>

Sample HTML

```
<BODY>
<TABLE WIDTH="75%" ALIGN=CENTER>
<CAPTION>
This is a sample table
</CAPTION>
<TR>
<TH>Number</TH>
<TH>Color</TH>
</TR>
<TR>
<TD>One Fish</TD>
<TD>Red Fish</TD>
</TR>
<TR>
<TD>Two Fish</TD>
<TD>Blue Fish</TD>
</TR>
</TABLE>
</BODY>
```

<TFOOT>

The TFOOT (table footer) tag is used to define the table footer information and distinguish it from the rows of the table header or body text.

Style Tip

As with THEAD, you can include only one TFOOT section in any given table.

Attributes

None.

Parent Tags

```
<TABLE>
```

Content Tags

```
<TR>
```

Sample HTML

```
<BODY>
<TABLE WIDTH="75%" ALIGN=CENTER>
<CAPTION>
This is a sample table
</CAPTION>
<THEAD>
<TR> ... </TR>
<TBODY>
<TR> ... </TR>
<TFOOT>
<TR>... </TR>
</TABLE>
</BODY>
```

<TH>...</TH>

The TH (table head/column head) tags format column header information in a table.

Style Tip

Whereas a table caption provides information for an entire table, table row headers provide specific information related to data in each column. Use multiple table row headers within a single table to create logical divisions, and to group similar content.

Attributes

ALIGN=(CENTER|LEFT|RIGHT)

Specifies the alignment. The default horizontal alignment of the text is centered.

AXIS="text"

Allows you to provide an abbreviated version of the cell's contents.

AXES="text"

Allows you to provide a list of keywords, separated by commas, that list a set of row and column headers related to the contents of the cell.

BGCOLOR=colorname *[Deprecated]*

Provides the color of the background that is either a hexadecimal, red-green-blue color value, or a predefined color name. (See Table F.1.)

CHAR="text"

Identifies the character that text should be aligned with horizontally if the value of ALIGN is CHAR.

CHAROFF="number"

Specifies how many pixels the rest of the text in a line should be offset from the character defined by the value of the CHAR attribute.

COLSPAN=number

Specifies how many columns the row header overlaps.

NOWRAP *[Deprecated]*

Shows that the contents of the cell are not to be wrapped; they will appear as a single line unless the <BR> tag is used.

ROWSPAN=number

Specifies how many rows the row header overlaps.

VALIGN=(TOP|MIDDLE|BOTTOM|BASELINE)

Designates the vertical alignment of text within the header. The default text alignment is in the middle. (See Table F.7.)

WIDTH=number

Designates the width of the row header in pixels.

Parent Tags

<TR>

Content Tags

<A>, <ACRONYM>, <ADDRESS>, <APPLET>, <B>, <BASEFONT>, <BDO>, <BIG>,
<BLOCKQUOTE>, <BR>, <BUTTON>, <CENTER>, <CITE>, <CODE>, <DFN>, <DIR>,
<DIV>, <DL>, <EM>, <FIELDSET>, <FONT>, <FORM>, <H1>, <H2>, <H3>, <H4>,
<H5>, <H6>, <HR>, <I>, <IFRAME>, <IMG>, <INPUT>, <ISINDEX>, <KBD>,
<LABEL>, <MAP>, <MENU>, <NOFRAMES>, <NOSCRIPT>, <OBJECT>, <OL>, <P>,
<PRE>, <Q>, <S>, <SAMP>, <SCRIPT>, <SELECT>, <SMALL>, <SPAN>, <STRIKE>,
<STRONG>, <SUB>, <SUP>, <TABLE>, <TEXTAREA>, <TT>, <U>, <UL>, <VAR>

Sample HTML

```
<BODY>
<TABLE WIDTH="75%" ALIGN=CENTER>
<CAPTION>
This is a sample table
</CAPTION>
<TR>
<TH>Number</TH>
<TH>Color</TH>
</TR>
</TABLE>
</BODY>
```

<THEAD>...</THEAD>

The THEAD (table header) tags define the header of the table and distinguish it
from the rows in the footer or the main body text.

Style Tip

If you choose to use these tags in your tables, only one table header is allowed.

Attributes

None.

Parent Tags

<TABLE>

Content Tags

<TR>

Sample HTML

```
<BODY>
<TABLE WIDTH="75%" ALIGN=CENTER>
<CAPTION>
This is a sample table
</CAPTION>
<THEAD>
<TR> ... </TR>
</TABLE>
</BODY>
```

<TR>...</TR>

The TR tags create a row in the table.

Style Tip

Table rows are the first component you will create when building tables. Rows are then divided into cells. It's important to close one table row before you begin another or the table may not display properly.

Attributes

ALIGN=(CENTER|LEFT|RIGHT)

Determines how the text within a row should be aligned horizontally. The default alignment is centered.

BGCOLOR=colorname *[Deprecated]*

Provides the color of the background for the row that is either a hexadecimal, red-green-blue color value, or a predefined color name. (See Table F.1.)

CHAR="text"

Identifies the character that text should be aligned with horizontally if the value of ALIGN is CHAR.

CHAROFF="number"

Specifies how many pixels the rest of the text in a line should be offset from the character defined by the value of the CHAR attribute.

VALIGN=(TOP|MIDDLE|BOTTOM|BASELINE)

Designates the vertical alignment of text within the row's cells. The default text alignment is MIDDLE. (See Table F.7.)

Parent Tags

```
<TBODY>, <TFOOT>, <THEAD>
```

Content Tags

```
<TD>, <TH>
```

Sample HTML

```
<BODY>
<TABLE WIDTH="75%" ALIGN=CENTER>
<CAPTION>
This is a sample table
</CAPTION>
<TR>
<TH>Number</TH>
<TH>Color</TH>
</TR>
<TR>
</TR>
<TR>
</TR>
</TABLE>
</BODY>
```

Link Tags

Link tags provide a mechanism in HTML to create links to other Web resources. Hyperlinks, those underlined, clickable links found in most Web pages, are the most common type of link. However, links can be made to style sheets, to previous and next pages within a document, and to a base URL to which all documents within a collection are tied. Links make the Web hyper and enable Web designers to provide resources outside of their own domains.

<A>...</A>

The A (anchor) tags provide the essential hypertext link capabilities within HTML. They are used to create links to other resources and to name specified locations within a document.

Style Tip

Use hyperlinks liberally throughout your HTML pages to create links to related resources and to information on your own site as well as other sites. For long documents, use anchors within the document to help users navigate. The TITLE attribute is particularly useful to give users a sneak peek at a linked resource.

Attributes

ACCESSKEY="text"

Identifies a character to be used to create a keyboard shortcut to activate the link.

CHARSET="text"

Specifies what character set the linked Web resource uses. The default is ISO-8859-1.

COORDS="X1, Y1, X2, Y2, etc."

Provides the coordinates that define the shapes of a hot spot within a client-side imagemap. See the SHAPE attribute for details.

HREF="URL"

URL is the uniform resource locator, which specifies the location of a resource that is typically another HTML file. In addition, it can also specify other types of Internet resources such as files, Telnet, e-mail, FTP, or Gopher services.

NAME="text"

Marks a specific place within an HTML document.

REL="text"

Indicates the relationship between the current document and the document to which it is linked. Some common relations are REL="NEXT" to indicate that the link points to the next page in a sequence and REL="PREVIOUS" to indicate that the link points to the previous page in a sequence. REL="STYLESHEET" tells the browser that the linked document is a style sheet.

REV="text"

The opposite of the REL attribute. Defines the relationship between the linked document and the current document.

SHAPE=(RECT|CIRCLE|POLY|DEFAULT)

Specifies the shape of the region. (See Table F.8.)

TABINDEX="number"

Specifies the link's place in the tabbing order.

TARGET="window"

Specifies that the link should be loaded into the targeted frame or window. Use this attribute when the targeted frame or window is different from the frame or window in which the current document resides. The attribute can target a <FRAMESET> where a frame has been created and given a name using the <FRAME> element or an entire browser window. The targeted frame or window can be specified using the information shown in Table F.9.

TABLE F.8: Shapes That Can Be Used As Hot Spots in an Imagemap

Use This	To Get This
RECT	A rectangle, which is defined by the coordinates of its top left corner and its bottom right corner. For example, <AREA SHAPE=rect COORDS= "0,0,9,9"> defines a rectangle 10 by 10 pixels in size, starting in the top left corner of the image.
CIRCLE	A circle, which is defined by the coordinates of its center and radius. The coordinates of the circle's center are defined first, and then the radius, in pixels. For example, <AREA SHAPE=circle COORDS= "10,10,5"> defines a circle with a radius of five pixels at location (10,10) in the image.
POLY	A polygon, which is built from a list of coordinates, all connected in the order listed, with the last coordinate pair connected to the first. The POLY value allows you to build arbitrary figures with multiple sides. For example, <AREA SHAPE=POLY COORDS="10,50,15,20,20,50"> would specify a triangle, with edge locations (10,50), (15,20), and (20,50).
DEFAULT	The default URL is defined for those areas on an imagemap that are not otherwise linked with an <AREA> specification. It should be used only once within each imagemap.

Parent Tags

<ACRONYM>, <ADDRESS>, <APPLET>, <B>, <BDO>, <BIG>, <BLOCKQUOTE>, <BODY>, <CAPTION>, <CENTER>, <CITE>, <CODE>, <DD>, <DEL>, <DFN>, <DIV>, <DT>, <EM>, <FIELDSET>, <FONT>, <FORM>, <H1>, <H2>, <H3>, <H4>, <H5>, <H6>, <I>, <IFRAME>, <INS>, <KBD>, <LABEL>, <LEGEND>, <LI>, <NOFRAMES>, <NOSCRIPT>, <OBJECT>, <P>, <PRE>, <Q>, <S>, <SAMP>, <SMALL>, <SPAN>, <STRIKE>, <STRONG>, <SUB>, <SUP>, <TD>, <TH>, <TT>, <U>, <VAR>

TABLE F.9:   Options for Specifying Whether a Linked Document Will Appear in a Frame or a New Window

The Target	What It Does
window name	Identifies the name of the specific frame or window in which the document should be opened. The name must begin with an alphanumeric character to be valid.
_blank	Creates a new, unnamed window and loads the document into it.
_parent	Loads the linked file into the parent frame or window of the current frame or window. If the link is located in a window without a parent, then this will behave the same as specifying `_self`.
_self	Loads the linked file in the same window as the document containing the link. A link that specifies this target behaves the same as a link that does not specify a target.
_top	Overrides and erases the entire frame configuration and loads the document into the full body of the current window.

Content Tags

\<A>, \<ACRONYM>, \<APPLET>, \<B>, \<BASEFONT>, \<BDO>, \<BIG>, \
, \<BUTTON>, \<CITE>, \<CODE>, \<DFN>, \<EM>, \<FONT>, \<I>, \<IFRAME>, \<IMG>, \<INPUT>, \<KBD>, \<LABEL>, \<MAP>, \<OBJECT>, \<Q>, \<S>, \<SAMP>, \<SCRIPT>, \<SELECT>, \<SMALL>, \<SPAN>, \<STRIKE>, \<STRONG>, \<SUB>, \<SUP>, \<TEXTAREA>, \<TT>, \<U>, \<VAR>

Sample HTML

```
<A HREF="http://www.mysite.com/">A hyperlink to my site. </A>
<A HREF="#body5">A hyperlink to body paragraph 5 in the current
document.</A>
Body text
More body text
Even more body text
Some more body text
<A NAME="body5"></A>Paragraph 5 of my body text
```

\<BASE>

The BASE tag gives you an opportunity to define specific server and folder location information for the current document and others that are linked to it.

Style Tip

When you use relative addressing to link files that reside on the same server, a base URL provides the common file location information. Base URLs are not required but can be useful when managing large document collections.

Attributes

HREF="URL"

Defines the base URL.

TARGET="window"

Specifies that the link should be loaded into the targeted frame or window. Use this attribute when the targeted frame or window is different from the frame or window in which the current document resides. The attribute can target a <FRAMESET> where a frame has been created and given a name using the <FRAME> element or an entire browser window. The targeted frame or window can be specified using the information shown in Table F.9.

Parent Tags

<HEAD>

Content Tags

None.

Sample HTML

```
<BASE URL="http://www.mysite.com/webdocs/" TARGET=body>
```

<LINK>

The LINK tag provides the information that sets the relationship between the current document and other documents or URL resources.

Style Tip

LINK tags are best used for linking to externally referenced style sheets and other documents. Large document collections benefit from the use of LINK tags because they establish relationships among related documents, making them easier to rename and move as necessary.

Attributes

HREF="URL"

Works the same as the anchor tags (<A>...</A>). It supplies the address of the current link destination.

MEDIA=SCREEN|PRINT|PROJECTION|BRAILLE|SPEECH|ALL

Used to identify the presentation method for which the style sheet is best suited. Screen is the most common presentation method and the default, but style sheets can also be created specifically for print, projection, Braille, speech, or all types of media.

REL="text"

Indicates the source end of a link and identifies the link's type. REL="STYLESHEET" tells a browser that the linked document is a style sheet.

REV="text"

Defines the destination end of a link and its type.

TARGET="window"

Specifies that the link should be loaded into the targeted frame or window. Use this attribute when the targeted frame or window is different from the frame or window in which the current document resides. The attribute can target a <FRAMESET> where a frame has been created and given a name using the <FRAME> element or an entire browser window. The targeted frame or window can be specified using the information shown in Table F.9.

TYPE="text"

Specifies the specific style sheet language used to create the style rules. The type for Cascading Style Sheets (CSS1), the most common style sheet language, is text/css.

Parent Tags

<HEAD>

Content Tags

None.

Sample HTML

```
<LINK HREF="style/css/mystyle.css/" TYPE="text/css">
```

Inclusion Tags

Inclusion tags are used to incorporate non-HTML objects into a document. Such objects may be images, applets, imagemaps, programming controls, or even other HTML documents.

<APPLET>...</APPLET>

The APPLET tags are used to incorporate Java applets into HTML documents.

Style Tip

Java applets can add interactivity and a few bells and whistles to your pages. Remember that users with older browsers, or those who have turned Java off in newer browsers, will not be able to see your Java content nor use any Java-based controls. Always include alternate access to Java-based information for these users.

Attributes

ALIGN=(LEFT|RIGHT|TOP|MIDDLE|BOTTOM)

Defines the default horizontal alignment of the applet.

ALT="text"

If the applet cannot run, this alternate text will be displayed.

ARCHIVE="text"

A string of comma-delimited archive names that point to class files or other resources that are to be "preloaded."

CODE="URL"

Specifies the URL of a compiled subclass for an applet. The browser looks for the specific applet location within the server and file hierarchy defined in the CODE-BASE attribute.

CODEBASE="URL"

Defines the server and folder information for all of the applets within an HTML document (similar to the BASE tag).

HEIGHT=number

Sets the height of the applet's window.

HSPACE=number

Controls the horizontal blank space that appears around the applet.

NAME="text"

Points to the name of the applet.

OBJECT="text"

Defines the resource name which contains the applet in a serialized version.

VSPACE=number

Controls vertical blank space that appears around the applet.

WIDTH=(number|"%")

Sets the width of the applet's window.

Parent Tags

<A>, <ACRONYM>, <ADDRESS>, <APPLET>, <B>, <BDO>, <BIG>, <BLOCKQUOTE>, <BODY>, <BUTTON>, <CAPTION>, <CENTER>, <CITE>, <CODE>, <DD>, <DEL>, <DFN>, <DIV>, <DT>, <EM>, <FIELDSET>, <FONT>, <FORM>, <H1>, <H2>, <H3>, <H4>, <H5>, <H6>, <I>, <IFRAME>, <INS>, <KBD>, <LABEL>, <LEGEND>, <LI>, <NOFRAMES>, <NOSCRIPT>, <OBJECT>, <P>, <PRE>, <Q>, <S>, <SAMP>, <SMALL>, <SPAN>, <STRIKE>, <STRONG>, <SUB>, <SUP>, <TD>, <TH>, <TT>, <U>, <VAR>

Content Tags

<A>, <ACRONYM>, <APPLET>, <B>, <BASEFONT>, <BDO>, <BIG>, <BR>, <BUTTON>, <CITE>, <CODE>, <DFN>, <EM>, <FONT>, <I>, <IFRAME>, <IMG>, <INPUT>, <KBD>, <LABEL>, <MAP>, <OBJECT>, <PARAM>, <Q>, <S>, <SAMP>, <SCRIPT>, <SELECT>, <SMALL>, <SPAN>, <STRIKE>, <STRONG>, <SUB>, <SUP>, <TEXTAREA>, <TT>, <U>, <VAR>

Sample HTML

```
<APPLET CODEBASE="http://www.mysite.com/extras/applets/"
CODE="applet1.class" HEIGHT=50 WIDTH=100> </APPLET>
```

<AREA>

Image map areas can be rectangles, circles, polygons, or single pixels. It is usually best to avoid linking URLs to single pixels because it's difficult for users to locate the exact spot within the image. Numerous mapping applications are available that provide coordinates for areas within an image. Most common graphics programs also have mechanisms to determine the coordinates of any specific area.

Style Tip

Use this to drive image-based selections with buttons or labeled graphics. Remember to provide text alternatives for those users who've turned graphics support off in their browsers. (People do this for faster loading of pages, or to avoid seeing ads, or because they are visually impaired and can't see the images anyway.)

NOTE

Providing a phrase to describe each graphic makes your pages much friendlier to visually impaired visitors. Some Web browsers can even be configured to *speak* the text of a page, and they will speak out the phrase you've provided!

Attributes

ACCESSKEY="character"

Defines a hot-spot activation key, not case-sensitive.

ALT="text"

Furnishes an alternate string of text for text browsers to present the imagemap's URLs in a manner that is easier to read.

COORDS="X1, Y1, X2, Y2, etc."

Defines the coordinates of a shape within a clickable image. See the SHAPE coordinate for more information.

HREF="URL"

Links the hot spot on the imagemap to the appropriate Internet resource.

NOHREF

Indicates that the image area does not have an associated hyperlink.

SHAPE=(RECT|CIRCLE|POLY|DEFAULT)

Specifies the shape of the region. The possible region shapes are described in Table F.8.

TABINDEX=number

Defines the order of tab navigation for each hot spot. The value can be a positive or negative integer.

TARGET="window"

Specifies that the link should be loaded into the targeted frame or window. Use this attribute when the targeted frame or window is different from the frame or window in which the current document resides. The attribute can target a <FRAMESET> where a frame has been created and given a name using the <FRAME> element or an entire browser window. The targeted frame or window can be specified using the information shown in Table F.9.

Parent Tags

`<MAP>`

Content Tags

`None.`

Sample HTML

```
<BODY>
<IMG SRC="image.gif" HEIGHT=50 WIDTH=100 HSPACE=25 VSPACE=25
USEMAP="imagemap1" ALIGN=MIDDLE>
<MAP NAME="imagemap1">
<AREA SHAPE="RECT" COORDS= "0,0,25,50" HREF="home.html">
<AREA SHAPE="RECT" COORDS= "26,0,50,50" HREF="toc.html">
<AREA SHAPE="RECT" COORDS= "51,0,75,50" HREF="products.html">
<AREA SHAPE="RECT" COORDS= "76,0,100,50" HREF="contact.html">
</MAP>
</BODY>
```

`<IMG>`

The IMG (image) tag inserts an image into your document. The tag is a singleton and has many associated attributes you may use to control its placement.

Style Tip

Use images in your Web pages to add splashes of color as well as meaning to content. You should make your image files as small as possible, preferably 30K or less, and always remember to include descriptive alternative text for those users who surf with graphics turned off or with nongraphical browsers.

Attributes

ALT="text"

Provides an alternative text string that describes the image. Users with nongraphical browsers or browsers with graphics turned off will see text in place of the image. Internet Explorer 3 and Netscape Navigator 4 also display this text when the user points at a graphic.

ALIGN=(LEFT|RIGHT|TOP|MIDDLE|BOTTOM)

Specifies the alignment of the image in relation to the surrounding text. (See Table F.10.)

TABLE F.10: Options for Aligning Images

Use This	To Get This
LEFT	An image aligned to the left margin with the text displayed in the space to its right
RIGHT	An image aligned to the right margin with the text displayed in the space to its left
TOP	The top of the image and the top of the text aligned with each other
MIDDLE	The middle of the image and the baseline of the surrounding text aligned with each other
BOTTOM	The bottom of the image and the baseline of the surrounding text aligned with each other

BORDER=number

Indicates what size the border around the image should be. If the image is a hyperlink, the border will be rendered in the designated hyperlink color. If the image is not a hyperlink, the border is transparent (invisible).

HEIGHT=pixels

Used with WIDTH=, it specifies the image's height. If the image has different dimensions than those specified using the HEIGHT and WIDTH attributes, the image will be sized accordingly.

HSPACE=number

Used with VSPACE=, the horizontal space attribute assigns the blank space or margins that are created to the left and right of the image.

ISMAP

Indicates that the image is a server-side clickable map and has an associated CGI script for translating the image regions into Web resource addresses.

SRC="URL"

Specifies the location of the file you wish to incorporate into your Web page. This is a mandatory attribute.

USEMAP=map-name

Marks the image as a client-side imagemap and references the inline map information defined with the <MAP> tag that will translate the image areas into Web resource addresses.

VSPACE=number

Used with HSPACE=, the vertical space attribute assigns the blank space or margins that are displayed at the top and bottom of the image.

WIDTH=pixels

Used with HEIGHT=, it specifies the image's width. If the image has different dimensions than those specified using the HEIGHT and WIDTH attributes, the image will be sized accordingly.

Parent Tags

<A>, <ACRONYM>, <ADDRESS>, <APPLET>, <B>, <BDO>, <BIG>, <BLOCKQUOTE>, <BODY>, <BUTTON>, <CAPTION>, <CENTER>, <CITE>, <CODE>, <DD>, <DEL>, <DFN>, <DIV>, <DT>, <EM>, <FIELDSET>, <FONT>, <FORM>, <H1>, <H2>, <H3>, <H4>, <H5>, <H6>, <I>, <IFRAME>, <INS>, <KBD>, <LABEL>, <LEGEND>, <LI>, <NOFRAMES>, <NOSCRIPT>, <OBJECT>, <P>, <Q>, <S>, <SAMP>, <SMALL>, <SPAN>, <STRIKE>, <STRONG>, <SUB>, <SUP>, <TD>, <TH>, <TT>, <U>, <VAR>

Content Tags

None.

Sample HTML

```
<BODY>
<IMG SRC="image.gif" HEIGHT=50 WIDTH=100 HSPACE=25 VSPACE=25
USEMAP="imagemap1" ALIGN=MIDDLE>
</BODY>
```

<MAP>...</MAP>

The MAP tags work in conjunction with an image designated as a client-side imagemap to translate the image regions into associated URLs.

Style Tip

Client-side imagemaps save time and server resources because all map information resides within the HTML document itself. The client does not have to send a request to a CGI script stored on a server to get the URL associated with a specific region. You can include more than one map file per page, as long as each one has a unique identifier so it can be referenced by name. Users who view without images or with non-graphical browsers will not be able to see imagemaps at all. It's important to supply alternative navigation aids when using imagemaps.

Attribute

NAME="text"

Names the MAP so it can be referred to at a later time by the USEMAP tag.

Parent Tags

<A>, <ACRONYM>, <ADDRESS>, <APPLET>, <B>, <BDO>, <BIG>, <BLOCKQUOTE>,
<BODY>, <BUTTON>, <CAPTION>, <CENTER>, <CITE>, <CODE>, <DD>, <DEL>,
<DFN>, <DIV>, <DT>, <EM>, <FIELDSET>, <FONT>, <FORM>, <H1>, <H2>, <H3>,
<H4>, <H5>, <H6>, <I>, <IFRAME>, <INS>, <KBD>, <LABEL>, <LEGEND>, <LI>,
<NOFRAMES>, <NOSCRIPT>, <OBJECT>, <P>, <PRE>, <Q>, <S>, <SAMP>,
<SMALL>, <SPAN>, <STRIKE>, <STRONG>, <SUB>, <SUP>, <TD>, <TH>, <TT>,
<U>, <VAR>

Content Tags

<AREA>

Sample HTML

```
<BODY>
<IMG SRC="image.gif" HEIGHT=50 WIDTH=100 HSPACE=25 VSPACE=25
USEMAP="imagemap1" ALIGN=MIDDLE>
<MAP NAME="imagemap1">
... Map information ...
</MAP>
</BODY>
```

<OBJECT>...</OBJECT>

The OBJECT tags insert a non-HTTP object, such as an audio or video file, into an HTML document.

Style Tip

The OBJECT tags allow you to incorporate audio, video, and other multimedia files into your HTML pages. This allows you to go beyond plain text and graphics to make your pages more interactive and exciting. As with Java applets, some older browsers do not support this tag and their users will not be able to see any content you include in an embedded non-HTTP object. Always provide an alternative way for users to get at any information you present in this way.

Attributes

ALIGN=(baseline|center|left|middle|right|textbottom|textmiddle|texttop)

Sets the alignment of the object. The ALIGN value can be one of those shown in Table F.11.

BORDER=number

Specifies the width of the border in pixels.

CLASSID="URL"

Defines (with the associated URL) how the object should be implemented. The actual form the URL takes is based entirely on the object's type.

T A B L E   F. 1 1 :   Options for Aligning Objects

Use This	To Get This
BASELINE	The bottom of the object aligned with the baseline of the surrounding text
CENTER	The object centered between the left and right margins, with any following text beginning on the next line after the object
LEFT	The object aligned with the left margin, with any following text wrapped along the right side of the object
MIDDLE	The middle of the object aligned with the baseline of surrounding text
RIGHT	The object aligned with the right margin, with any following text wrapped along the left side of the object
TEXTBOTTOM	The bottom of the object aligned with the bottom of surrounding text
TEXTMIDDLE	The middle of the object aligned with the midpoint between the baseline and the x-height of the surrounding text
TEXTTOP	The top of the object aligned with the top of surrounding text

CODEBASE="URL"

Defines the server and folder information for all of the objects within an HTML document (similar to the BASE tag).

CODETYPE=codetype

Designates the Internet media type for code.

DATA="URL"

Defines the URL of the object's data source. The actual syntax of the URL is determined by the object's type.

DECLARE

Used to load an object without actually activating it. Use this attribute to reference and activate an object later in the page.

HEIGHT=number

Specifies the proposed height for the object in pixels. Some objects have the capability to violate this parameter.

HSPACE=number

Controls the horizontal blank space that appears around the applet.

NAME="URL"

Gives the object a name so it can be referenced by other objects and forms later on in the document.

SHAPES

Indicates to the browser that the object is an image, has been divided into shaped regions, and is being used for an imagemap.

STANDBY="message"

Provides a message that will display while the object is loading.

TYPE=type

Provides the object's Internet media type.

USEMAP="URL"

Specifies the imagemap file that will translate the clickable regions on an imagemap into the addresses of Web resources.

VSPACE=number

Controls the vertical blank space that appears around the applet.

WIDTH=number

Specifies the proposed width for the object in pixels. Some objects have the capability to violate this parameter.

Parent Tags

<A>, <ACRONYM>, <ADDRESS>, <APPLET>, <B>, <BDO>, <BIG>, <BLOCKQUOTE>, <BODY>, <BUTTON>, <CAPTION>, <CENTER>, <CITE>, <CODE>, <DD>, <DEL>, <DFN>, <DIV>, <DT>, <EM>, <FIELDSET>, <FONT>, <FORM>, <H1>, <H2>, <H3>, <H4>, <H5>, <H6>, <I>, <IFRAME>, <INS>, <KBD>, <LABEL>, <LEGEND>, <LI>, <NOFRAMES>, <NOSCRIPT>, <OBJECT>, <P>, <PRE>, <Q>, <S>, <SAMP>, <SMALL>, <SPAN>, <STRIKE>, <STRONG>, <SUB>, <SUP>, <TD>, <TH>, <TT>, <U>, <VAR>

Content Tags

<A>, <ACRONYM>, <ADDRESS>, <APPLET>, <B>, <BASEFONT>, <BDO>, <BIG>, <BLOCKQUOTE>, <BR>, <BUTTON>, <CENTER>, <CITE>, <CODE>, <DFN>, <DIR>, <DIV>, <DL>, <EM>, <FIELDSET>, <FONT>, <FORM>, <H1>, <H2>, <H3>, <H4>, <H5>, <H6>, <HR>, <I>, <IFRAME>, <IMG>, <INPUT>, <ISINDEX>, <KBD>, <LABEL>, <MAP>, <MENU>, <NOFRAMES>, <NOSCRIPT>, <OBJECT>, <OL>, <P>, <PARAM>, <PRE>, <Q>, <S>, <SAMP>, <SCRIPT>, <SELECT>, <SMALL>, <SPAN>, <STRIKE>, <STRONG>, <SUB>, <SUP>, <TABLE>, <TEXTAREA>, <TT>, <U>, <UL>, <VAR>

Sample HTML

```
<OBJECT CODEBASE="http://www.mysite.com/objects/audio/" TYPE=Audio/.avi
DATA="sound1.avi" STANDBY="Thank you for your patience while the audio
file loads.">
```

<PARAM>

This tag provides page-specific parameters for applets and non-HTTP objects such as scripts.

Style Tip

Because they are stored separately from HTML pages, a single Java applet and objects can be used by many different pages. Each use of the applet or object may be a little different, so the PARAM tag allows you to provide page-specific variables for the applet to use when it is called and run from the page. Reusing applets can save you time and programming costs.

Attributes

NAME="text"

Specifies the name of the parameter.

VALUE=number|"text"

Assigns a value to the named parameter. The value supplied here is not altered before it is passed to the applet unless it contains alphanumeric characters that must be replaced with character equivalents.

VALUETYPE=(DATA|REF|OBJECT)

Specifies how the value is interpreted. The type can be one of those shown in Table F.12.

TABLE F.12:   Options for Specifying the Type of Data

Use This	When
DATA	The value is data, which is the default value type.
REF	The value is a URL.
OBJECT	The value is the URL of an object that is in the same document.

TYPE=type

Specifies the Internet Media Type [MIMETYPE]. See `ftp://ftp.isi.edu/in-notes/iana/assignments/media-types/`.

Parent Tags

`<APPLET>, <OBJECT>`

Content Tags

None.

Sample HTML

```
<APPLET CODEBASE="http://www.mysite.com/extras/applets/"
CODE="applet1.class" HEIGHT=50 WIDTH=100>
<PARAM NAME="booktitle" VALUE="frontpage">
<PARAM NAME= "publisher" VALUE="sybex">
</APPLET>
```

Style Sheets

Style sheets do not contain HTML tags, but rather create style rules to modify the way HTML tags appear. Many deprecated HTML tags should be replaced with style sheet properties and values to give Web designers more control over their Web pages. But there is one HTML tag pair associated with style sheets—namely, the STYLE tags. In this section, we include standard tag information for the STYLE tags, and provide a complete rundown on all style sheet property families, their individual properties, and the values they take.

<STYLE>...</STYLE>

Use STYLE tags to include style sheet rules within the Web pages they affect.

Style Tip

Because style sheets are now part of the HTML specification, it's important to use them to replace deprecated STYLE tags.

Attributes

MEDIA=(SCREEN|PRINT|PROJECTION|BRAILLE|SPEECH|ALL)

Identifies what presentation method the style sheet is suited to support. Screen is the most common presentation method, and the default, but style sheets can be created specifically for print, projection, Braille, speech, or all types of media.

TYPE="text"

Specifies a specific style sheet language used to create the style rules. The type for Cascading Style Sheets (CSS1), the most common style sheet language, is text/css.

Parent Tags

<HEAD>

Content Tags

None.

Sample HTML

```
<HEAD>
<TITLE>Company Homepage</TITLE>
<STYLE>
BODY {background-color: navy;}
H1 {font: 24pt Verdana bold}
P {font: 12 Arial;
   text-align: right;
   }
</STYLE>
</HEAD>
```

Box Properties

The style sheet box properties are used with a box-model method of page layout to specify margin, border, height and width, and white space information for

HTML elements. Use box properties with text and image "boxes" to strictly control their placement in relation to each other and the page.

Style Tip

Always remember that style sheets are not backward compatible with older versions of HTML and older browsers. While the text affected by style sheets will still be displayed by the browser, your formatting will not apply. Since box properties control the margin and placement characteristics of text and image boxes, always check your pages using older browsers to insure that your content remains readable.

Properties and Values

margin-top: <length>|<percentage>|auto

Defines an element's top margin. (See Table F.13.)

margin-bottom: <length>|<percentage>|auto

Defines an element's bottom margin. (See Table F.13.)

margin-left: <length>|<percentage>|auto

Defines an element's left margin. (See Table F.13.)

TABLE F.13: Units of Measurement Recognized in the Use of Style Sheets

Units	What It Means
No units specified	The current font size
Em	The height of the the current font
Ex	The height of the letter x in the current font

NOTE Style sheet tags such as these define layout in style sheets. They are unlike other tags in that they are not surrounded by angle brackets, they usually include hyphenated words, and they are always followed by a colon. Convention has it that they are shown in lowercase, again unlike standard HTML tags, which are usually shown in uppercase.

margin-right: <length>|<percentage>|auto

Defines an element's right margin. (See Table F.13.)

margin: [<length>|<percentage>|auto]
Defines all of the margins for an element. (See Table F.13.)

padding-top: <length>|<percentage>
Specifies the amount of white space that should be included between the top border of an element and its contents. (See Table F.13.)

padding-bottom: <length>|<percentage>
Specifies the amount of white space that should be included between the bottom border of an element and its contents. (See Table F.13.)

padding-left: <length>|<percentage>
Specifies the amount of white space that should be included between the left border of an element and its contents. (See Table F.13.)

padding-right: <length>|<percentage>
Specifies the amount of white space that should be included between the right border of an element and its contents. (See Table F.13.)

padding: [<length>|<percentage>|auto]
Specifies the padding for all sides of an element. (See Table F.13.)

border-top-width: <length>|thin|medium|thick
Defines the thickness of an element's top border. (See Table F.13.)

border-bottom-width: <length>|thin|medium|thick
Defines the thickness of an element's bottom border. (See Table F.13.)

border-right-width: <length>|thin|medium|thick
Defines the thickness of an element's right border. (See Table F.13.)

border-left-width: <length>|thin|medium|thick
Defines the thickness of an element's top border. (See Table F.13.)

border-right-width: <length>|thin|medium|thick
Specifies the thickness of an element's left border. (See Table F.13.)

border-width: [<length>|thin|medium|thick]
Specifies the thickness of an element's borders. (See Table F.13.)

border-color: <color>
Specifies the color of an element's borders. (See Table F.1.)

border-style: none|dotted|dashed|solid|double|groove| ridge|inset|outset

Specifies the style of an element's borders.

border-top: <border-width>|<border-style>|<color>

Specifies the width, style, and color (see Table F.1) of an element's top border.

border-bottom: <border-width>|<border-style>|<color>

Specifies the width, style, and color (see Table F.1) of an element's bottom border.

border-left: <border-width>|<border-style>|<color>

Specifies the width, style, and color (see Table F.1) of an element's left border.

border-right: <border-width>|<border-style>|<color>

Specifies the width, style, and color (see Table F.1) of an element's right border.

border: <border-width>|<border-style>|<color>

Specifies the width, style, and color (see Table F.1) of an element's borders.

width: <length>|<percentage>|auto

Specifies the width of an element. (See Table F.13.)

height: <length>|<percentage>|auto

Specifies the height of an element. (See Table F.13.)

clear: none|left|right|both

Indicates whether or not other elements may be wrapped around the element as well as to which side.

float: left|right|none|both

Defines what direction text and other elements should be wrapped around an element.

Sample HTML

```
<STYLE>
P.body {margin: .75in;
        padding: 20%;
        border-width: thin;
        border-style: dashed;
        color: navy;
        }
</STYLE>
```

Classification Properties

The style sheet classification properties provide specifics about the display of white space, list numbers, and list bullets.

Style Tip

Always be sure to include alternate text, such as an asterisk (*), when substituting an image for a list marker. This allows those users with text-only browsers or images turned off to still see a marker of some type.

Properties and Values

display: block|inline|list-item|none

Defines how an element should be displayed. (See Table F.14.)

TABLE F.14:   Options for the Appearance of Elements

Use This	To Do This
block	Create a line break and space both before and after the element
inline	Remove all line breaks
list-item	Include a bullet with the item without using list markup
none	Disable any display already defined for the item

white-space: normal|pre|nowrap

Defines how an element's white space should be displayed. (See Table F.15.)

list-style-type: disc|circle|square|decimal|lower-roman|upper-roman|ower-alpha|upper-alpha|none

Identifies the type of bullet to be used with list items.

list-style-image: "URL"

Defines the URL for a graphic to be inserted instead of a standard bullet in a list.

TABLE F.15:   Options for the Appearance of White Space

Use This	To Do This
normal	Use the browser's standard display
pre	Interpret every space and hard return literally (like the PRE tag does)
nowrap	Prevent lines from being broken until a tag is inserted

list-style-position: inside|outside

Identifies how a list marker, such as a bullet, image, or number, is placed relative to the text in the list. (See Table F.16.)

TABLE F.16: Options for the Location of List Markers

Use This	To Do This
inside	Wrap text underneath the marker
outside	Indent all lines of text to the right of the marker

list-style: <list-style-type>|<list-style-position>|<list-style-image>

Specifies the style, position, and image source of a list's markers.

Sample HTML

```
<STYLE>
P.list {display: list-item;
        white-space: normal;
        list-style: url(bullet.gif) inside;
        }
</STYLE>
```

Font Properties

The font properties are used to specify information specific to the text font, such as face, color, and size.

Style Tip

Be careful when using a wide variety of font sizes as they may make your pages difficult to read.

Properties and Values

font-family: <family-name>|<generic family>

Identifies the specific font face that should be applied to the text display. Some examples of family names include Times, Helvetica, and Arial. The generic families are not specific font faces, but rather describe the type of font, i.e. serif, sans-serif, cursive, fantasy, or monospaced.

font-size: [xx-small|x-small|small|medium|large|x-large|xx-large]|<length>|<percentage>|[larger | smaller|<relative-size>]

Specifies the font size. (See Table F.13.)

font-style: normal|italic|oblique

Defines the style in which a font should be displayed.

font-variant: normal|small-caps

Identifies a font variant.

font-weight: normal|bold|100|200|300|400|500|600|700| 800|900| lighter|bolder

Defines the thickness of the text. Normal text is 400 while boldface text is 700.

line-height: normal|<number>|<length>|<percentage>

Defines the amount of space between lines of text. (See Table F.13.)

font: <font-weight>|<font-style>|<font-variant>| <font-size>|<line-height>|<font-family>

Combines all the modifiable aspects of text into one property.

Sample HTML

```
<STYLE>
P.byline {font-family: Helvetica sans-serif;
         font-size: large;
         font-weight: bold;
         font-variant: small-caps;
         line-height: 35%;
         }
</STYLE>
```

Text Properties

Text properties provide information about how text should be rendered, including color, spacing, case, decoration, and alignment specifics.

Style Tip

Be careful when using a variety of text colors because they can make your pages hard to read.

Properties and Values

color: <colorname|#RRGGBB>

Defines the text color. (See Table F.1.)

text-align: left|right|center|justify

Defines the alignment of the text.

text-indent: <length>|<percentage>

Specifies an indentation for the text. (See Table F.13.)

word-spacing: normal|<length>

Defines the amount of space that should be included between words. (See Table F.13.)

letter-spacing: normal|<length>

Defines the amount of space that should be included between letters. (See Table F.13.)

text-transform: capitalize|uppercase|lowercase|none

Defines how the enclosed text should be displayed regardless of how the text is typed.

text-decoration: none|underline|overline|line-through| blink

Specifies a decoration for the text.

vertical-align: base-line|sub|super|top|text-top|middle| bottom|text-bottom|<percentage>

Defines the text's vertical alignment.

Sample HTML

```
<STYLE>
P.article {color: navy:
         letter-spacing: 4px;
         word-spacing: 12px;
         text-transform: none;
         text-align: justify;
         }
</STYLE>
```

Background Properties

Use style sheet background properties to include backgrounds, and to define the placement and scrolling of background images.

Style Tip

Use different backgrounds to separate groups of text. You can also use the vertical or horizontal alignment properties to create a frame or color border for an entire page or a few sections of a page.

Properties and Values

background-color: transparent|<colorname>

Specifies the background color for an element. If the value is transparent, the background color of the element's parent will show through. (See Table F.1.)

background-image: none|<url>

Identifies the location of a background image using this notation: url(image.gif).

background-repeat: repeat|repeat-x|repeat-y|no-repeat

Defines how a background should be tiled. (See Table F.17.)

T A B L E   F . 1 7 :   Options for the Appearance of Background Images

Use This	To Do This
repeat	Tile the image in the standard way
repeat-x	Repeat the image in a single line horizontally
repeat-y	Repeat the image in a single line vertically
no-repeat	Include the image without repeating it

background-attachment: scroll|fixed

Specifies whether a background image should scroll with its element or remain fixed on the screen.

background-position: <percentage>|<length>|top|center|bottom

Identifies the position of an element relative to both its element and the browser window. (See Table F.13.)

Sample HTML

```
<STYLE>
P.body1 {background-image: url(topborder.gif);
        background-repeat: repeat-x;
        background-attachment: fixed;
        }
</STYLE>
```

Presentation Tags

Presentation tags govern how text is displayed within a browser, but without the content or contextual implications that come with text tags. Hard rules are also included with presentation tags to provide a graphical division within an HTML page without actually using an inline image that can take time to download. Half of these presentation tags have been deprecated in favor of style sheets.

\<B\>...\</B\>

The boldface tags render the enclosed text in boldface type.

Style Tip

Boldface adds emphasis to words and makes them stand out from the surrounding text.

Attributes

None.

Parent Tags

\<A\>, \<ACRONYM\>, \<ADDRESS\>, \<APPLET\>, \<B\>, \<BDO\>, \<BIG\>, \<BLOCKQUOTE\>, \<BODY\>, \<BUTTON\>, \<CAPTION\>, \<CENTER\>, \<CITE\>, \<CODE\>, \<DD\>, \<DEL\>, \<DFN\>, \<DIV\>, \<DT\>, \<EM\>, \<FIELDSET\>, \<FONT\>, \<FORM\>, \<H1\>, \<H2\>, \<H3\>, \<H4\>, \<H5\>, \<H6\>, \<I\>, \<IFRAME\>, \<INS\>, \<KBD\>, \<LABEL\>, \<LEGEND\>, \<LI\>, \<NOFRAMES\>, \<NOSCRIPT\>, \<OBJECT\>, \<P\>, \<PRE\>, \<Q\>, \<S\>, \<SAMP\>, \<SMALL\>, \<SPAN\>, \<STRIKE\>, \<STRONG\>, \<SUB\>, \<SUP\>, \<TD\>, \<TH\>, \<TT\>, \<U\>, \<VAR\>

Content Tags

<A>, <ACRONYM>, <APPLET>, <B>, <BASEFONT>, <BDO>, <BIG>, <BR>, <BUTTON>, <CITE>, <CODE>, <DFN>, <EM>, <FONT>, <I>, <IFRAME>, <IMG>, <INPUT>, <KBD>, <LABEL>, <MAP>, <OBJECT>, <Q>, <S>, <SAMP>, <SCRIPT>, <SELECT>, <SMALL>, <SPAN>, <STRIKE>, <STRONG>, <SUB>, <SUP>, <TEXTAREA>, <TT>, <U>, <VAR>

Sample HTML

I bet you're <B>really</B> tired of staring at HTML tags.

<BASEFONT>

[Deprecated] The BASEFONT tag sets the default font for any unformatted text.

Style Tip

Use BASEFONT to establish font style, including size and color, for the regular, unformatted text on a page. Users may choose to override or ignore font settings you specify in favor of their own—don't count on such settings to provide total font control.

Attributes

COLOR=colorname *[Deprecated]*

Assigns a color to the base font. (See Table F.1.)

NAME=name *[Deprecated]*

Allows you to give a name to your base font style.

SIZE="number" *[Deprecated]*

Defines the size of the base font using a number between 1 and 7. The default base font size is 3 and the largest is 7. The relative font size settings are determined according to this value all the way through the document.

Parent Tags

<A>, <ACRONYM>, <ADDRESS>, <APPLET>, <B>, <BDO>, <BIG>, <BLOCKQUOTE>, <BODY>, <BUTTON>, <CAPTION>, <CENTER>, <CITE>, <CODE>, <DD>, <DEL>, <DFN>, <DIV>, <DT>, <EM>, <FIELDSET>, <FONT>, <FORM>, <H1>, <H2>, <H3>, <H4>, <H5>, <H6>, <I>, <IFRAME>, <INS>, <KBD>, <LABEL>, <LEGEND>, <LI>, <NOFRAMES>, <NOSCRIPT>, <OBJECT>, <P>, <PRE>, <Q>, <S>, <SAMP>, <SMALL>, <SPAN>, <STRIKE>, <STRONG>, <SUB>, <SUP>, <TD>, <TH>, <TT>, <U>, <VAR>

Content Tags

None.

Sample HTML

```
<HEAD>
<BASEFONT SIZE=4 COLOR="navy">
</HEAD>
```

<BIG>...</BIG>

The BIG tags render the enclosed text one size bigger than the standard type size.

Style Tip

While many browsers support nesting <BIG> tags to increase text sizes correspondingly, this is not part of the actual HTML specification. Use <FONT SIZE=+n> where n is a number between 1 and 7, in place of the <BIG> tag.

Attributes

None.

Parent Tags

<A>, <ACRONYM>, <ADDRESS>, <APPLET>, <B>, <BDO>, <BIG>, <BLOCKQUOTE>, <BODY>, <BUTTON>, <CAPTION>, <CENTER>, <CITE>, <CODE>, <DD>, <DEL>, <DFN>, <DIV>, <DT>, <EM>, <FIELDSET>, <FONT>, <FORM>, <H1>, <H2>, <H3>, <H4>, <H5>, <H6>, <I>, <IFRAME>, <INS>, <KBD>, <LABEL>, <LEGEND>, <LI>, <NOFRAMES>, <NOSCRIPT>, <OBJECT>, <P>, <Q>, <S>, <SAMP>, <SMALL>, <SPAN>, <STRIKE>, <STRONG>, <SUB>, <SUP>, <TD>, <TH>, <TT>, <U>, <VAR>

Content Tags

<A>, <ACRONYM>, <APPLET>, <B>, <BASEFONT>, <BDO>, <BIG>, <BR>, <BUTTON>, <CITE>, <CODE>, <DFN>, <EM>, <FONT>, <I>, <IFRAME>, <IMG>, <INPUT>, <KBD>, <LABEL>, <MAP>, <OBJECT>, <Q>, <S>, <SAMP>, <SCRIPT>, <SELECT>, <SMALL>, <SPAN>, <STRIKE>, <STRONG>, <SUB>, <SUP>, <TEXTAREA>, <TT>, <U>, <VAR>

Sample HTML

```
I <BIG>know</BIG> I am.
```

<CENTER>...</CENTER>

[Deprecated] The CENTER tags center the text horizontally across the display window.

Style Tip

Centered text is especially nice for document and section titles because it sets them off from the remainder of the text that is usually left or double justified. Used centered text sparingly as it can be hard to read in large quantities.

Attributes

None.

Parent Tags

<BLOCKQUOTE>, <BODY>, <BUTTON>, <CENTER>, <DD>, <DIV>, <FIELDSET>, <FORM>, <IFRAME>, <LI>, <NOFRAMES>, <NOSCRIPT>, <OBJECT>, <TD>, <TH>

Content Tags

<A>, <ACRONYM>, <ADDRESS>, <APPLET>, <B>, <BASEFONT>, <BDO>, <BIG>, <BLOCKQUOTE>, <BR>, <BUTTON>, <CENTER>, <CITE>, <CODE>, <DFN>, <DIR>, <DIV>, <DL>, <EM>, <FIELDSET>, <FONT>, <FORM>, <H1>, <H2>, <H3>, <H4>, <H5>, <H6>, <HR>, <I>, <IFRAME>, <IMG>, <INPUT>, <ISINDEX>, <KBD>, <LABEL>, <MAP>, <MENU>, <NOFRAMES>, <NOSCRIPT>, <OBJECT>, <OL>, <P>, <PRE>, <Q>, <S>, <SAMP>, <SCRIPT>, <SELECT>, <SMALL>, <SPAN>, <STRIKE>, <STRONG>, <SUB>, <SUP>, <TABLE>, <TEXTAREA>, <TT>, <U>, <UL>, <VAR>

Sample HTML

```
<BODY>
<CENTER>
This is my title. It is centered.
</CENTER>
This is my body. It is not centered.
</BODY>
```

<FONT>...</FONT>

[Deprecated] The font tags allow you to designate the font, size, and color of the text within the tags.

Style Tip

While BASEFONT sets font size and color for an entire document, the FONT tag applies formatting only to text contained within the FONT tags. You can draw user attention to selected text by changing its size, color, or face. As with BASEFONT, keep in mind that this is a nonstandard tag and can be ignored by users. Also, be careful to choose sensible font combinations. No matter how useful or valuable your content is, bright yellow text on a white background is difficult to read and may cause users to leave your pages before they read a word.

Attributes

SIZE="number" *[Deprecated]*

Allows you to set font size between 1 and 7 where 7 is largest. If you put a plus or a minus sign before the number, the specified text will be that much bigger or smaller than the current size.

FACE="name [,name2[,name3]]" *[Deprecated]*

Specifies the font in which the text should be displayed. If you list several font face names separated by commas, the browser will try each one in turn if the first font is not available, until it finds one it can use. If none of the fonts you have specified is available, a default font is used.

COLOR=(#RRGGBB|colorname) *[Deprecated]*

Sets the font color. (See Table F.1.)

Parent Tags

<A>, <ACRONYM>, <ADDRESS>, <APPLET>, <B>, <BDO>, <BIG>, <BLOCKQUOTE>, <BODY>, <BUTTON>, <CAPTION>, <CENTER>, <CITE>, <CODE>, <DD>, <DEL>, <DFN>, <DIV>, <DT>, <EM>, <FIELDSET>, <FONT>, <FORM>, <H1>, <H2>, <H3>, <H4>, <H5>, <H6>, <I>, <IFRAME>, <INS>, <KBD>, <LABEL>, <LEGEND>, <LI>, <NOFRAMES>, <NOSCRIPT>, <OBJECT>, <P>, <Q>, <S>, <SAMP>, <SMALL>, <SPAN>, <STRIKE>, <STRONG>, <SUB>, <SUP>, <TD>, <TH>, <TT>, <U>, <VAR>

Content Tags

<A>, <ACRONYM>, <APPLET>, <B>, <BASEFONT>, <BDO>, <BIG>, <BR>, <BUTTON>, <CITE>, <CODE>, <DFN>, <EM>, <FONT>, <I>, <IFRAME>, <IMG>, <INPUT>, <KBD>, <LABEL>, <MAP>, <OBJECT>, <Q>, <S>, <SAMP>, <SCRIPT>, <SELECT>, <SMALL>, <SPAN>, <STRIKE>, <STRONG>, <SUB>, <SUP>, <TEXTAREA>, <TT>, <U>, <VAR>

Sample HTML

```
<BODY>
<FONT SIZE=+3 COLOR="teal" FACE="Times, Garamond, Arial">This font will
be three sizes larger than the default font, and displayed in teal
Times.</FONT>
</BODY>
```

<HR>

The horizontal rule tag inserts a plain line across the width of the page.

Style Tip

Horizontal rules are particularly useful to emphasize divisions and transitions in page content. Avoid overuse of this tag since too many rules can clutter up a page and distract readers' attention from the content.

Attributes

ALIGN=(LEFT|CENTER|RIGHT)

Lets you decide if you want the line left-aligned, right-aligned, or centered. The default is centered.

NOSHADE

Renders the rule without any 3D shading.

SIZE=number *[Deprecated]*

Allows you to set the height (thickness) of your rule in pixels. The smallest you can make the rule is 2, which is the default.

WIDTH=(number|"%") *[Deprecated]*

Allows you to specify the width of the rule. You can do this either in pixels or as a percentage of the window width. If you choose to do it as a percentage, you must end the number with the percent (%) sign. The default is 100%.

Parent Tags

<BLOCKQUOTE>, <BODY>, <BUTTON>, <CENTER>, <DD>, <DIV>, <FIELDSET>, <FORM>, <IFRAME>, <LI>, <NOFRAMES>, <NOSCRIPT>, <OBJECT>, <TD>, <TH>

Content Tags

None.

Sample HTML

```
<BODY>
This is the document title.
<HR>
Section 1
...
<HR>
Section 2
</BODY>
```

<I>...</I>

The I tags render the enclosed text in italics.

Style Tip

Large amounts of italics are difficult to read. Use this tag to make a brief point or to set the contained text apart from surrounding text.

Attributes

None.

Parent Tags

<A>, <ACRONYM>, <ADDRESS>, <APPLET>, <B>, <BDO>, <BIG>, <BLOCKQUOTE>, <BODY>, <BUTTON>, <CAPTION>, <CENTER>, <CITE>, <CODE>, <DD>, <DEL>, <DFN>, <DIV>, <DT>, <EM>, <FIELDSET>, <FONT>, <FORM>, <H1>, <H2>, <H3>, <H4>, <H5>, <H6>, <I>, <IFRAME>, <INS>, <KBD>, <LABEL>, <LEGEND>, <LI>, <NOFRAMES>, <NOSCRIPT>, <OBJECT>, <P>, <PRE>, <Q>, <S>, <SAMP>, <SMALL>, <SPAN>, <STRIKE>, <STRONG>, <SUB>, <SUP>, <TD>, <TH>, <TT>, <U>, <VAR>

Content Tags

<A>, <ACRONYM>, <APPLET>, <B>, <BASEFONT>, <BDO>, <BIG>, <BR>, <BUTTON>, <CITE>, <CODE>, <DFN>, <EM>, <FONT>, <I>, <IFRAME>, <IMG>, <INPUT>, <KBD>, <LABEL>, <MAP>, <OBJECT>, <Q>, <S>, <SAMP>, <SCRIPT>, <SELECT>, <SMALL>, <SPAN>, <STRIKE>, <STRONG>, <SUB>, <SUP>, <TEXTAREA>, <TT>, <U>, <VAR>

Sample HTML

```
Gee, it is <I>hot</I> in Texas.
```

<S>...</S>

[Deprecated] The S tags render the enclosed text in strikethrough format.

Style Tip

Strikethrough text usually represents a correction or text that has been removed. As with italics, large amounts of struck text can be difficult to read, so keep use of the S tag at a minimum.

Attributes

None.

Parent Tags

<A>, <ACRONYM>, <ADDRESS>, <APPLET>, <B>, <BDO>, <BIG>, <BLOCKQUOTE>, <BODY>, <BUTTON>, <CAPTION>, <CENTER>, <CITE>, <CODE>, <DD>, <DEL>, <DFN>, <DIV>, <DT>, <EM>, <FIELDSET>, <FONT>, <FORM>, <H1>, <H2>, <H3>, <H4>, <H5>, <H6>, <I>, <IFRAME>, <INS>, <KBD>, <LABEL>, <LEGEND>, <LI>, <NOFRAMES>, <NOSCRIPT>, <OBJECT>, <P>, <PRE>, <Q>, <S>, <SAMP>, <SMALL>, <SPAN>, <STRIKE>, <STRONG>, <SUB>, <SUP>, <TD>, <TH>, <TT>, <U>, <VAR>

Content Tags

<A>, <ACRONYM>, <APPLET>, <B>, <BASEFONT>, <BDO>, <BIG>, <BR>, <BUTTON>, <CITE>, <CODE>, <DFN>, <EM>, <FONT>, <I>, <IFRAME>, <IMG>, <INPUT>, <KBD>, <LABEL>, <MAP>, <OBJECT>, <Q>, <S>, <SAMP>, <SCRIPT>, <SELECT>, <SMALL>, <SPAN>, <STRIKE>, <STRONG>, <SUB>, <SUP>, <TEXTAREA>, <TT>, <U>, <VAR>

Sample HTML

```
When we went out to eat, <S>Donna</S> Amy ordered the steak.
```

<SMALL>...</SMALL>

SMALL tags render enclosed text one size smaller than the standard type size.

Style Tip

While many browsers support nesting <SMALL> tags to make text sizes increasingly smaller, this isn't part of the HTML specification. Use <FONT SIZE=-*n*> where *n* is a number between 1 and 7, instead of the <SMALL> tag.

Attributes

None.

Parent Tags

<A>, <ACRONYM>, <ADDRESS>, <APPLET>, <B>, <BDO>, <BIG>, <BLOCKQUOTE>, <BODY>, <BUTTON>, <CAPTION>, <CENTER>, <CITE>, <CODE>, <DD>, <DEL>, <DFN>, <DIV>, <DT>, <EM>, <FIELDSET>, <FONT>, <FORM>, <H1>, <H2>, <H3>, <H4>, <H5>, <H6>, <I>, <IFRAME>, <INS>, <KBD>, <LABEL>, <LEGEND>, <LI>, <NOFRAMES>, <NOSCRIPT>, <OBJECT>, <P>, <Q>, <S>, <SAMP>, <SMALL>, <SPAN>, <STRIKE>, <STRONG>, <SUB>, <SUP>, <TD>, <TH>, <TT>, <U>, <VAR>

Content Tags

<A>, <ACRONYM>, <APPLET>, <B>, <BASEFONT>, <BDO>, <BIG>, <BR>, <BUTTON>, <CITE>, <CODE>, <DFN>, <EM>, <FONT>, <I>, <IFRAME>, <IMG>, <INPUT>, <KBD>, <LABEL>, <MAP>, <OBJECT>, <Q>, <S>, <SAMP>, <SCRIPT>, <SELECT>, <SMALL>, <SPAN>, <STRIKE>, <STRONG>, <SUB>, <SUP>, <TEXTAREA>, <TT>, <U>, <VAR>

Sample HTML

```
That was the <SMALL>smallest</SMALL> monkey I've ever seen.
```

<STRIKE>...</STRIKE>

[Deprecated] The STRIKE tags render enclosed text in strikethrough format.

Style Tip

Strikethrough text usually represents a correction or text that has been removed. As with italics, large amounts of struck text can be difficult to read, so use STRIKE tags sparingly.

Attributes

None.

Parent Tags

<A>, <ACRONYM>, <ADDRESS>, <APPLET>, <B>, <BDO>, <BIG>, <BLOCKQUOTE>, <BODY>, <BUTTON>, <CAPTION>, <CENTER>, <CITE>, <CODE>, <DD>, <DEL>, <DFN>, <DIV>, <DT>, <EM>, <FIELDSET>, <FONT>, <FORM>, <H1>, <H2>, <H3>, <H4>, <H5>, <H6>, <I>, <IFRAME>, <INS>, <KBD>, <LABEL>, <LEGEND>, <LI>, <NOFRAMES>, <NOSCRIPT>, <OBJECT>, <P>, <PRE>, <Q>, <S>, <SAMP>, <SMALL>, <SPAN>, <STRIKE>, <STRONG>, <SUB>, <SUP>, <TD>, <TH>, <TT>, <U>, <VAR>

Content Tags

<A>, <ACRONYM>, <APPLET>, <B>, <BASEFONT>, <BDO>, <BIG>, <BR>, <BUTTON>, <CITE>, <CODE>, <DFN>, <EM>, <FONT>, <I>, <IFRAME>, <IMG>, <INPUT>, <KBD>, <LABEL>, <MAP>, <OBJECT>, <Q>, <S>, <SAMP>, <SCRIPT>, <SELECT>, <SMALL>, <SPAN>, <STRIKE>, <STRONG>, <SUB>, <SUP>, <TEXTAREA>, <TT>, <U>, <VAR>

Sample HTML

```
The cat <S>dog</S> ate my homework.
```

<TT>...</TT>

The TT (teletype text) tags render text in a monospaced font.

Style Tip

Teletype script logically represents typewriter style text. Physically it is displayed in the same way as code, keyboard, and sample text.

Attributes

None.

Parent Tags

<A>, <ACRONYM>, <ADDRESS>, <APPLET>, <B>, <BDO>, <BIG>, <BLOCKQUOTE>, <BODY>, <BUTTON>, <CAPTION>, <CENTER>, <CITE>, <CODE>, <DD>, <DEL>, <DFN>, <DIV>, <DT>, <EM>, <FIELDSET>, <FONT>, <FORM>, <H1>, <H2>, <H3>, <H4>, <H5>, <H6>, <I>, <IFRAME>, <INS>, <KBD>, <LABEL>, <LEGEND>, <LI>, <NOFRAMES>, <NOSCRIPT>, <OBJECT>, <P>, <PRE>, <Q>, <S>, <SAMP>, <SMALL>, <SPAN>, <STRIKE>, <STRONG>, <SUB>, <SUP>, <TD>, <TH>, <TT>, <U>, <VAR>

Content Tags

<A>, <ACRONYM>, <APPLET>, <B>, <BASEFONT>, <BDO>, <BIG>, <BR>, <BUTTON>, <CITE>, <CODE>, <DFN>, <EM>, <FONT>, <I>, <IFRAME>, <IMG>, <INPUT>, <KBD>, <LABEL>, <MAP>, <OBJECT>, <Q>, <S>, <SAMP>, <SCRIPT>, <SELECT>, <SMALL>, <SPAN>, <STRIKE>, <STRONG>, <SUB>, <SUP>, <TEXTAREA>, <TT>, <U>, <VAR>

Sample HTML

```
Type <TT>myfile.doc</TT> in the Find box.
```

<U>...</U>

[Deprecated] The U tags render underlined text.

Style Tip

Use underlined text judiciously as users may mistake it for the underlined hyperlinks they have become accustomed to clicking on.

Attributes

None.

Parent Tags

<A>, <ACRONYM>, <ADDRESS>, <APPLET>, <B>, <BDO>, <BIG>, <BLOCKQUOTE>, <BODY>, <BUTTON>, <CAPTION>, <CENTER>, <CITE>, <CODE>, <DD>, <DEL>, <DFN>, <DIV>, <DT>, <EM>, <FIELDSET>, <FONT>, <FORM>, <H1>, <H2>, <H3>, <H4>, <H5>, <H6>, <I>, <IFRAME>, <INS>, <KBD>, <LABEL>, <LEGEND>, <LI>, <NOFRAMES>, <NOSCRIPT>, <OBJECT>, <P>, <PRE>, <Q>, <S>, <SAMP>, <SMALL>, <SPAN>, <STRIKE>, <STRONG>, <SUB>, <SUP>, <TD>, <TH>, <TT>, <U>, <VAR>

Content Tags

<A>, <ACRONYM>, <APPLET>, <B>, <BASEFONT>, <BDO>, <BIG>, <BR>, <BUTTON>, <CITE>, <CODE>, <DFN>, <EM>, <FONT>, <I>, <IFRAME>, <IMG>, <INPUT>, <KBD>, <LABEL>, <MAP>, <OBJECT>, <Q>, <S>, <SAMP>, <SCRIPT>, <SELECT>, <SMALL>, <SPAN>, <STRIKE>, <STRONG>, <SUB>, <SUP>, <TEXTAREA>, <TT>, <U>, <VAR>

Sample HTML

By George, I think we're <U>underlined.</U>

Frame Tags

Frame tags create multipart display areas within a browser window. Each area, called a frame, can contain a separate document. This permits authors to create unique layouts with static navigation and logo areas. With properly attributed hyperlinks, actions in one frame can affect content displayed in another frame.

TIP	Creating good frames is complicated and takes practice. To learn all about frames from folks who've been there, visit these tutorials: `http://www.w3.org/TR/WD-html40/present/frames.html` and `http://home.netscape.com/assist/net_sites/frames.html`.

<FRAME>

This tag defines a single frame within a FRAMESET pair.

Style Tip

Frames are popular, but are not fully supported by all browsers. Therefore, it's good practice to create a nonframed version of a site, or to use NOFRAME tags to offer alternate unframed content to "frame-disadvantaged" users.

Attributes

FRAMEBORDER=(1|0)

Turns the 3D frame border on (1, the default) or off (0).

MARGINHEIGHT=(number|"%")

Defines the vertical margin within the frame in pixels.

MARGINWIDTH=(number|"%")

Defines the horizontal margin within the frame in pixels.

NAME="text"

Defines a name for the frame, used as a reference by the TARGET attribute.

NORESIZE

Prevents users from resizing the frame.

SCROLLING=(yes|no|auto)

Sets the scrolling abilities of the frame to yes (force display of scroll bar), no (never display scroll bar), or auto (default, display scroll bar if needed).

SRC="URL"

Specifies the URL of the file to be displayed within the frame.

Parent Tags

```
<FRAMESET>
```

Content Tags

None.

Sample HTML

```
<HTML>
<HEAD>
<TITLE>Sproket Sprinklers</TITLE>
</HEAD>
<FRAMESET COLS="30%,*, 10%">
```

```
<FRAME SCROLLING=YES SRC="nav_menu.htm">
<FRAME SRC="main.htm">
<FRAME SCROLLING=NO SRC="ss_logo.htm">
</FRAMESET>
</HTML>
```

<FRAMESET>...</FRAMESET>

These tags define the size and number of frames to be created.

Style Tip

Frames can be constructed in rows or columns with the appropriate attributes. A grid of frames can be established by including both ROWS and COLS attributes in the same FRAMESET tag. FRAMESET tag pairs can be nested to construct complicated shapes and arrangements of frames.

Attributes

COLS="col-widths|%|*"

Defines columns of frames in exact pixels, percentage (%), or a relative size (*).

ROWS="row-height|%|*"

Defines rows of frames in exact pixels, percentage (%), or a relative size (*).

Parent Tags

```
<FRAMESET>, <HTML>
```

Content Tags

```
<FRAME>, <FRAMESET>, <NOFRAMES>
```

Sample HTML

```
<HTML>
<HEAD>
<TITLE>Sproket Sprinklers</TITLE>
</HEAD>
<FRAMESET COLS="30%,*, 10%">
<FRAME SCROLLING=YES SRC="nav_menu.htm">
<FRAME SRC="main.htm">
<FRAME SCROLLING=NO SRC="ss_logo.htm">
</FRAMESET>
</HTML>
```

<IFRAME>...</IFRAME>

These tags define inline or floating frames. They operate in a manner similar to FRAMESET. Inline frames cannot be resized by the user.

Style Tip

Inline or floating frames offer intriguing design elements previously unavailable to Web authors. Considerable experimentation is required to master this tag. Content enclosed by IFRAME tags is used only when a browser does not support inline frames. Always include alternate versions of your content with this feature.

Attributes

ALIGN=(LEFT|CENTER|RIGHT|TOP|MIDDLE|BOTTOM)

This attribute specifies the alignment of the inline frame in relation to the surrounding text. (See Table F.10.)

FRAMEBORDER=(1|0)

Turns the 3D frame border on (1, the default) or off (0).

HEIGHT=(number|"%")

Specifies the pixel height of the frame.

MARGINHEIGHT=(number|"%")

Defines the vertical margin within the frame in pixels.

MARGINWIDTH=(number|"%")

Defines the horizontal margin within the frame in pixels.

NAME="text"

Defines a name for the frame, used as a reference by the TARGET attribute of the A tag.

SCROLLING=(yes|no|auto)

Sets the scrolling abilities of the frame to yes (force display of scroll bar), no (never display scroll bar), or auto (default, display scroll bar if needed).

SRC="URL"

Specifies the URL of the file to be displayed within the frame.

WIDTH=(number|"%")

Specifies the pixel width of the frame.

Parent Tags

<A>, <ACRONYM>, <ADDRESS>, <APPLET>, <B>, <BDO>, <BIG>, <BLOCKQUOTE>, <BODY>, <BUTTON>, <CAPTION>, <CENTER>, <CITE>, <CODE>, <DD>, <DEL>, <DFN>, <DIV>, <DT>, <EM>, <FIELDSET>, <FONT>, <FORM>, <H1>, <H2>, <H3>, <H4>, <H5>, <H6>, <I>, <IFRAME>, <INS>, <KBD>, <LABEL>, <LEGEND>, <LI>, <NOFRAMES>, <NOSCRIPT>, <OBJECT>, <P>, <PRE>, <Q>, <S>, <SAMP>, <SMALL>, <SPAN>, <STRIKE>, <STRONG>, <SUB>, <SUP>, <TD>, <TH>, <TT>, <U>, <VAR>

Content Tags

<A>, <ACRONYM>, <ADDRESS>, <APPLET>, <B>, <BASEFONT>, <BDO>, <BIG>, <BLOCKQUOTE>, <BR>, <BUTTON>, <CENTER>, <CITE>, <CODE>, <DFN>, <DIR>, <DIV>, <DL>, <EM>, <FIELDSET>, <FONT>, <FORM>, <H1>, <H2>, <H3>, <H4>, <H5>, <H6>, <HR>, <I>, <IFRAME>, <IMG>, <INPUT>, <ISINDEX>, <KBD>, <LABEL>, <MAP>, <MENU>, <NOFRAMES>, <NOSCRIPT>, <OBJECT>, <OL>, <P>, <PRE>, <Q>, <S>, <SAMP>, <SCRIPT>, <SELECT>, <SMALL>, <SPAN>, <STRIKE>, <STRONG>, <SUB>, <SUP>, <TABLE>, <TEXTAREA>, <TT>, <U>, <UL>, <VAR>

Sample HTML

```
<HTML>
<HEAD>
<TITLE>Inline Frames</TITLE>
</HEAD>
<IFRAME SCROLLING=NO SRC="float_main.htm">
Your browser does not support floating frames (IFRAME), click
<A HREF="http://www.domain.com/stuff/noif-nav.htm">
here to view the data without frames.</A>
</IFRAME>
</HTML>
```

<NOFRAMES>...</NOFRAMES>

These tags provide content to be used when a browser is unable to display frame-based information.

Style Tip

Frames are very popular, but are not fully supported by all browsers. It's good practice to create a nonframed version of your site, or to use NOFRAME tags to offer alternate content.

Attributes

None.

Parent Tags

<BLOCKQUOTE>, <BODY>, <BUTTON>, <CENTER>, <DD>, <DIV>, <FIELDSET>, <FORM>, <FRAMESET>, <IFRAME>, <LI>, <NOFRAMES>, <NOSCRIPT>, <OBJECT>, <TD>, <TH>

Content Tags

<A>, <ACRONYM>, <ADDRESS>, <APPLET>, <B>, <BASEFONT>, <BDO>, <BIG>, <BLOCKQUOTE>, <BODY>, <BR>, <BUTTON>, <CENTER>, <CITE>, <CODE>, <DFN>, <DIR>, <DIV>, <DL>, <EM>, <FIELDSET>, <FONT>, <FORM>, <H1>, <H2>, <H3>, <H4>, <H5>, <H6>, <HR>, <I>, <IFRAME>, <IMG>, <INPUT>, <ISINDEX>, <KBD>, <LABEL>, <MAP>, <MENU>, <NOFRAMES>, <NOSCRIPT>, <OBJECT>, <OL>, <P>, <PRE>, <Q>, <S>, <SAMP>, <SCRIPT>, <SELECT>, <SMALL>, <SPAN>, <STRIKE>, <STRONG>, <SUB>, <SUP>, <TABLE>, <TEXTAREA>, <TT>, <U>, <UL>, <VAR>

Sample HTML

```
<HTML>
<HEAD>
<TITLE>Sproket Sprinklers</TITLE>
</HEAD>
<FRAMESET COLS="30%,*, 10%">
<FRAME SCROLLING=YES SRC="nav_menu.htm">
<FRAME SRC="main.htm">
<FRAME SCROLLING=NO SRC="ss_logo.htm">
<NOFRAMES>
<EM>Your browser does not support frames.</EM>
</NOFRAMES>
</FRAMESET>
</HTML>
```

Form Tags

Use form tags to create HTML forms to solicit user feedback or add interactivity to Web pages. Form tags provide a variety of graphical and text items, as well as pick lists, that allow users to choose from different input options.

<BUTTON>...</BUTTON>

Use the BUTTON tags to create graphically interesting form input controls that provide more variety than standard submit and reset buttons.

Style Tip

If creating input objects that include images, use BUTTON tags instead of INPUT tags. Resulting images appear as raised buttons that depress when selected.

Attributes

DISABLED

Disables the button.

NAME="name"

Defines a name for the button.

TABINDEX="number"

Specifies the element's place in the tabbing order.

TYPE=(BUTTON|SUBMIT|RESET)

Defines the type of button. (See Table F.18.)

TABLE F.18: Options for the Function of Buttons

Use This	To Get This
BUTTON	A button that calls a script
SUBMIT	A button that sends the contents of the form to a specified URL. The button name and value are also sent.
RESET	A button that resets the contents of a form

VALUE="value"

Defines the button's value.

Parent Tags

<A>, <ACRONYM>, <ADDRESS>, <APPLET>, <B>, <BDO>, <BIG>, <BLOCKQUOTE>, <BODY>, <CAPTION>, <CENTER>, <CITE>, <CODE>, <DD>, <DEL>, <DFN>, <DIV>, <DT>, <EM>, <FIELDSET>, <FONT>, <FORM>, <H1>, <H2>, <H3>, <H4>, <H5>, <H6>, <I>, <IFRAME>, <INS>, <KBD>, <LABEL>, <LEGEND>, <LI>, <NOFRAMES>, <NOSCRIPT>, <OBJECT>, <P>, <PRE>, <Q>, <S>, <SAMP>, <SMALL>, <SPAN>, <STRIKE>, <STRONG>, <SUB>, <SUP>, <TD>, <TH>, <TT>, <U>, <VAR>

Content Tags

<A>, <ACRONYM>, <ADDRESS>, <APPLET>, <B>, <BASEFONT>, <BDO>, <BIG>, <BLOCKQUOTE>, <BR>, <BUTTON>, <CENTER>, <CITE>, <CODE>, <DFN>, <DIR>, <DIV>, <DL>, <EM>, <FIELDSET>, <FONT>, <FORM>, <H1>, <H2>, <H3>, <H4>, <H5>, <H6>, <HR>, <I>, <IFRAME>, <IMG>, <INPUT>, <ISINDEX>, <KBD>, <LABEL>, <MAP>, <MENU>, <NOFRAMES>, <NOSCRIPT>, <OBJECT>, <OL>, <P>, <PRE>, <Q>, <S>, <SAMP>, <SCRIPT>, <SELECT>, <SMALL>, <SPAN>, <STRIKE>, <STRONG>, <SUB>, <SUP>, <TABLE>, <TEXTAREA>, <TT>, <U>, <UL>, <VAR>

Sample HTML

```
<FORM METHOD=POST ACTION="http://www.mysite.com/bin/form">
...
<BUTTON TYPE=SUBMIT NAME="FORM1" VALUE="FORM1">
<IMG SRC="button.gif">
</BUTTON>
</FORM>
```

<FIELDSET>...</FIELDSET>

The FIELDSET tags are used to divide similar form controls into groups.

Style Tip

Always include LEGEND tags with FIELDSETs to help users understand the form and the data it is requesting.

Attributes

None.

Parent Tags

<BLOCKQUOTE>, <BODY>, <CENTER>, <DD>, <DIV>, <FIELDSET>, <FORM>, <IFRAME>, <LI>, <NOFRAMES>, <NOSCRIPT>, <OBJECT>, <TD>, <TH>

Content Tags

<A>, <ACRONYM>, <ADDRESS>, <APPLET>, <B>, <BASEFONT>, <BDO>, <BIG>, <BLOCKQUOTE>, <BR>, <BUTTON>, <CENTER>, <CITE>, <CODE>, <DFN>, <DIR>, <DIV>, <DL>, <EM>, <FIELDSET>, <FONT>, <FORM>, <H1>, <H2>, <H3>, <H4>, <H5>, <H6>, <HR>, <I>, <IFRAME>, <IMG>, <INPUT>, <ISINDEX>, <KBD>, <LABEL>, <LEGEND>, <MAP>, <MENU>, <NOFRAMES>, <NOSCRIPT>, <OBJECT>, <OL>, <P>, <PRE>, <Q>, <S>, <SAMP>, <SCRIPT>, <SELECT>, <SMALL>, <SPAN>, <STRIKE>, <STRONG>, <SUB>, <SUP>, <TABLE>, <TEXTAREA>, <TT>, <U>, <UL>, <VAR>

Sample HTML

```
<FORM METHOD=POST ACTION="http://www.mysite.com/bin/form">
<FIELDSET>
<INPUT TYPE=TEXT NAME="PET" VALUE="pet">
<INPUT TYPE=TEXT NAME="CAR" VALUE="car">
<INPUT TYPE=TEXT NAME="MUSIC" VALUE="music">
<BUTTON TYPE=SUBMIT NAME=ABOUT1 VALUE="about11">
<IMG SRC="button.gif">
</BUTTON>
</FIELDSET>
</FORM>
```

<FORM>...</FORM>

The FORM tags create the region on a page that holds the elements for soliciting user input.

Style Tip

Forms are the only built-in mechanism available in HTML to solicit feedback from and provide interactivity for users. Remember that a CGI script of some sort is usually needed to process the form's data, so you may need to enlist the assistance of a programmer to respond to data delivered via HTML forms.

Attributes

ACCEPT="Internet media type"

Defines a list of MIME types recognized by the server that processes the form.

ACCEPT-CHARSET="text"

Defines a list of character sets recognized by the server that processes the form.

ACTION="URL"

Specifies the location of a resource for the browser to execute once a form has been completed and submitted. This is generally some sort of CGI script that translates data into a usable format, and that may process it further to return more information to users.

METHOD=(GET|POST)

Lets the browser know how it should work with the resource identified by the ACTION attribute. If the value of METHOD is GET, the browser creates a query that includes the page URL, a question mark, and the values generated by the form. The browser then returns the query to the URL specified by ACTION for processing. The POST method returns the form data to the URL specified by ACTION as a block of data rather than a query string.

ENCTYPE="MIME type"

Specifies the type and format of the submitted form data. If the data is submitted using the POST method, this attribute is defined as a MIME type.

TARGET="window"

Specifies that the link should be loaded into the targeted frame or window. Use this attribute when the targeted frame or window is different from the frame or window in which the current document resides. The attribute can target a <FRAMESET> where a frame has been created and given a name using the <FRAME> element or an entire browser window. The targeted frame or window can be specified using the information shown in Table F.9.

Parent Tags

<BLOCKQUOTE>, <BODY>, <CENTER>, <DD>, <DIV>, <FIELDSET>, <IFRAME>, <LI>, <NOFRAMES>, <NOSCRIPT>, <OBJECT>, <TD>, <TH>

Content Tags

<A>, <ACRONYM>, <ADDRESS>, <APPLET>, <B>, <BASEFONT>, <BDO>, <BIG>, <BLOCKQUOTE>, <BR>, <BUTTON>, <CENTER>, <CITE>, <CODE>, <DFN>, <DIR>, <DIV>, <DL>, <EM>, <FIELDSET>, <FONT>, <FORM>, <H1>, <H2>, <H3>, <H4>, <H5>, <H6>, <HR>, <I>, <IFRAME>, <IMG>, <INPUT>, <ISINDEX>, <KBD>, <LABEL>, <MAP>, <MENU>, <NOFRAMES>, <NOSCRIPT>, <OBJECT>, <OL>, <P>, <PRE>, <Q>, <S>, <SAMP>, <SCRIPT>, <SELECT>, <SMALL>, <SPAN>, <STRIKE>, <STRONG>, <SUB>, <SUP>, <TABLE>, <TEXTAREA>, <TT>, <U>, <UL>, <VAR>

Sample HTML

```
<BODY>
<FORM ACTION="http://www.mysite.com/cgis/form1.pl" METHOD="POST">
... form data ...
</FORM>
```

<INPUT>

The INPUT tag defines type and appearance for input widgets.

Style Tip

The <INPUT> tag is a key element for any form because it supplies the mechanism through which users can provide you with data. Input widgets can take several different forms, from checkboxes, to radio buttons, to text fields. Think carefully about what kind of information you want to solicit from your readers, and match it with the appropriate input widget.

Attributes

ACCEPT="Internet media type"

Defines a list of MIME types recognized by the server that processes the form.

ALIGN=(LEFT|CENTER|RIGHT) *[Deprecated]*

Specifies how the widget will be aligned relative to the page.

CHECKED

Specifies that a checkbox or radio button should appear selected when the form is displayed by the browser.

DISABLED

Disables the input control.

NAME="text"

Names the input widget.

MAXLENGTH=number

Sets the maximum number of characters a user can enter into a text field.

READONLY

Prevents the user from altering the widget's contents.

SIZE="width|(width, height)"

Sets the width and height of a text input widget.

SRC="URL"

When TYPE=IMAGE is used, this attribute specifies the URL for the image.

TYPE=(TEXT|PASSWORD|CHECKBOX|RADIO|SUBMIT|RESET|FILE| HIDDEN|IMAGE|BUTTON)

Indicates which type of input widget to display. The default is text, and your options include those shown in Table F.19.

TABLE F.19:   Options for the Appearance of Input Boxes

Use This	To Do This
TEXT	Generate a text input field where MAXLENGTH limits how many characters a user can enter, and the field size is defined with the SIZE attribute.
PASSWORD	Create a text input field the same way the TYPE=TEXT attribute does, but any character entered by the user is replaced by a bullet or similar character.
CHECKBOX	Create a checkbox. When checked and a form is submitted, the browser automatically returns a value of **NAME=on**. If it is unchecked, no value is sent.
RADIO	Generate a radio button. Radio buttons are created in groups, each with the same name but with different values. When a form is returned, the name and value of the selected radio button is returned and the others ignored.
SUBMIT	Create the submit button that causes all of the form data to be returned to the URL specified by the ACTION attribute. You may have more than one submit button, but each should have a different name to differentiate between the data they are returning.
RESET	Create a reset button that restores the form to its original, clean state to allow users to begin entering data again.
FILE	Permit a user to upload a file from his or her computer to your server. This option is not yet widely implemented, however, and should be used sparingly.
HIDDEN	Generate form data that is necessary for the correct processing of the form but that you don't want users to see.
IMAGE	Create a submit button that uses the image specified by the SRC attribute.
BUTTON	Create a button that calls a script.

VALUE=value

For nontext field input elements, this attribute specifies the value that should be returned to the server when the form is submitted.

Parent Tags

<A>, <ACRONYM>, <ADDRESS>, <APPLET>, <B>, <BDO>, <BIG>, <BLOCKQUOTE>, <BODY>, <CAPTION>, <CENTER>, <CITE>, <CODE>, <DD>, <DEL>, <DFN>, <DIV>, <DT>, <EM>, <FIELDSET>, <FONT>, <FORM>, <H1>, <H2>, <H3>, <H4>, <H5>, <H6>, <I>, <IFRAME>, <INS>, <KBD>, <LABEL>, <LEGEND>, <LI>, <NOFRAMES>, <NOSCRIPT>, <OBJECT>, <P>, <PRE>, <Q>, <S>, <SAMP>, <SMALL>, <SPAN>, <STRIKE>, <STRONG>, <SUB>, <SUP>, <TD>, <TH>, <TT>, <U>, <VAR>

Content Tags

None.

Sample HTML

```
<BODY>
<FORM ACTION="http://www.mysite.com/cgi/form1.pl" METHOD="POST">
<INPUT TYPE=CHECKBOX NAME="ch1">Checkbox 1
<INPUT TYPE=CHECKBOX NAME="ch2" CHECKED>Checkbox 2
<INPUT TYPE=TEXT SIZE=25 MAXLENGTH=25 NAME="FNAME" VALUE="fname">First Name
<INPUT TYPE=TEXT SIZE=25 MAXLENGTH=25 NAME="LNAME" VALUE="lname">Last Name
<INPUT TYPE=SUBMIT VALUE="Send">
<INPUT TYPE=RESET VALUE="Clear">
</FORM>
```

<ISINDEX>

[Deprecated] The ISINDEX (document index) tag requires the user to input a single line of text, usually to perform a search of the site's documents.

Style Tip

Because site searches are miniforms anyway, the ISINDEX tag has been deprecated in favor of a standard form and the INPUT tag.

Attributes

PROMPT="text" *[Deprecated]*

This attribute's value specifies the text that will appear next to the search field box.

Parent Tags

<BLOCKQUOTE>, <BODY>, <CENTER>, <DD>, <DIV>, <FIELDSET>, <FORM>, <HEAD>, <IFRAME>, <LI>, <NOFRAMES>, <NOSCRIPT>, <OBJECT>, <TD>, <TH>

Content Tags

None.

Sample HTML

```
<ISINDEX ACTION="/cgis/search.pl" PROMPT="Enter a key word or search
string here to search our site."
```

<LABEL>...</LABEL>

Use LABEL tags to provide additional information about a form control, just like the TITLE attribute does for other HTML elements.

Style Tip

Use labels to provide specific information about how users should enter data into a form control.

Attributes

ACCESSKEY="text"

Identifies a character to be used to create a keyboard shortcut to activate the link.

DISABLED

Disables the input control.

FOR="text"

Specifically associates the label with a form control using the ID name provided in the control's markup.

TABINDEX=number

Specifies the link's place in the tabbing order.

Parent Tags

<A>, <ACRONYM>, <ADDRESS>, <APPLET>, <B>, <BDO>, <BIG>, <BLOCKQUOTE>, <BODY>, <CAPTION>, <CENTER>, <CITE>, <CODE>, <DD>, <DEL>, <DFN>, <DIV>, <DT>, <EM>, <FIELDSET>, <FONT>, <FORM>, <H1>, <H2>, <H3>, <H4>, <H5>, <H6>, <I>, <IFRAME>, <INS>, <KBD>, <LEGEND>, <LI>, <NOFRAMES>, <NOSCRIPT>, <OBJECT>, <P>, <PRE>, <Q>, <S>, <SAMP>, <SMALL>, <SPAN>, <STRIKE>, <STRONG>, <SUB>, <SUP>, <TD>, <TH>, <TT>, <U>, <VAR>

Content Tags

<A>, <ACRONYM>, <APPLET>, <B>, <BASEFONT>, <BDO>, <BIG>, <BR>, <BUTTON>, <CITE>, <CODE>, <DFN>, <EM>, <FONT>, <I>, <IFRAME>, <IMG>, <INPUT>, <KBD>, <LABEL>, <MAP>, <OBJECT>, <Q>, <S>, <SAMP>, <SCRIPT>, <SELECT>, <SMALL>, <SPAN>, <STRIKE>, <STRONG>, <SUB>, <SUP>, <TEXTAREA>, <TT>, <U>, <VAR>

Sample HTML

```
<FORM METHOD=POST ACTION="http://www.mysite.com/bin/form">
<FIELDSET>
<LABEL FOR="PET">Your Favorite Pet</LABEL>
<INPUT TYPE=TEXT NAME="PET" VALUE="pet" ID=PET>
<BUTTON TYPE=SUBMIT NAME=ABOUT1 VALUE="about11">
<IMG SRC="button.gif">
</BUTTON>
</FIELDSET>
</FORM>
```

<LEGEND>...</LEGEND>

LEGEND tags provide labels for field sets that explain their capabilities or contents.

Style Tip

Use legends to instruct users how to enter data into a form control.

Attributes

ALIGN=(LEFT|RIGHT|TOP|BOTTOM)

Sets the alignment of the legend with respect to the field set.

ACCESSKEY="text"

Identifies a character to be used to create a keyboard shortcut to bring the field set into focus.

Parent Tags

```
<FIELDSET>
```

Content Tags

```
<A>, <ACRONYM>, <APPLET>, <B>, <BASEFONT>, <BDO>, <BIG>, <BR>, <BUTTON>,
<CITE>, <CODE>, <DFN>, <EM>, <FONT>, <I>, <IFRAME>, <IMG>, <INPUT>, <KBD>,
<LABEL>, <MAP>, <OBJECT>, <Q>, <S>, <SAMP>, <SCRIPT>, <SELECT>, <SMALL>,
<SPAN>, <STRIKE>, <STRONG>, <SUB>, <SUP>, <TEXTAREA>, <TT>, <U>, <VAR>
```

Sample HTML

```
<FORM METHOD=POST ACTION="http://www.mysite.com/bin/form">
<FIELDSET>
<LEGEND ALIGN=CENTER>Tell Us About Yourself</LEGEND>
<INPUT TYPE=TEXT NAME="PET" VALUE="pet">
<INPUT TYPE=TEXT NAME="CAR" VALUE="car">
<INPUT TYPE=TEXT NAME="MUSIC" VALUE="music">
<BUTTON TYPE=SUBMIT NAME=ABOUT1 VALUE="about11">
<IMG SRC="button.gif">
</BUTTON>
</FIELDSET>
</FORM>
```

<OPTION>

The OPTION tag assigns a value or default to an input item in a selection menu.

Style Tip

Use the OPTION tag with a selection menu to provide a series of choices for users. Drop-down menus usually take up less space than radio or checkbox lists.

Attributes

DISABLED

Disables the input control.

SELECTED

Indicates that the option should be the default choice that appears in the menu window.

VALUE="text"

Sets the value for the individual option.

Parent Tags

<SELECT>

Content Tags

None.

Sample HTML

```
<BODY>
<FORM ACTION="http://www.mysite.com/cgis/form1.pl" METHOD="POST">
<SELECT NAME="dogs" MULTIPLE SIZE="2">
<OPTION VALUE="lab">Labrador
<OPTION VALUE="shep">German Shepherd
<OPTION VALUE="wiener">Dachshund
</SELECT>
<INPUT TYPE=SUBMIT VALUE="Send">
<INPUT TYPE=RESET VALUE="Clear">
</FORM>
```

<SELECT>...</SELECT>

The SELECT tags create a menu or scrolling list of input items.

Style Tip

This input widget creates a list of items users can choose from. This allows you to provide specific choices to match the data types you need. Using the MULTIPLE tag, users can select more than one option from a list, or you can restrict them to a single choice by default.

Attributes

DISABLED
Disables the input control.

MULTIPLE
Allows users to choose more than one item from the set of <OPTION> values supplied within the <SELECT>...</SELECT> tag pair.

NAME="text"
Associates a name with the list.

SIZE=number
Sets the number of choices visible within the drop-down menu.

TABINDEX=number
Specifies the control's place in the tabbing order.

Parent Tags
<A>, <ACRONYM>, <ADDRESS>, <APPLET>, <B>, <BDO>, <BIG>, <BLOCKQUOTE>, <BODY>, <CAPTION>, <CENTER>, <CITE>, <CODE>, <DD>, <DEL>, <DFN>, <DIV>, <DT>, <EM>, <FIELDSET>, <FONT>, <FORM>, <H1>, <H2>, <H3>, <H4>, <H5>, <H6>, <I>, <IFRAME>, <INS>, <KBD>, <LABEL>, <LEGEND>, <LI>, <NOFRAMES>, <NOSCRIPT>, <OBJECT>, <P>, <PRE>, <Q>, <S>, <SAMP>, <SMALL>, <SPAN>, <STRIKE>, <STRONG>, <SUB>, <SUP>, <TD>, <TH>, <TT>, <U>, <VAR>

Content Tags
<OPTION>

Sample HTML
```
<BODY>
<FORM ACTION="http://www.mysite.com/cgis/form1.pl" METHOD="POST">
<SELECT NAME="dogs" MULTIPLE SIZE="2">
... menu data ...
</SELECT>
<INPUT TYPE=SUBMIT VALUE="Send">
<INPUT TYPE=RESET VALUE="Clear">
</FORM>
```

\<TEXTAREA>...\</TEXTAREA>

The TEXTAREA tags create a text input box usually used for multiline text input.

Style Tip

Text areas in forms allow users to provide information that does not conform to strict input limitations. Open-ended comments and suggestions are best solicited using text areas.

Attributes

COLS=number

Specifies the width of the text box in columns. Convention limits this number to 72.

DISABLED

Disables the input control.

NAME="text"

Associates a name with the data entered in the text box for processing by an associated CGI script.

READONLY

Prevents the user from altering the text area's contents.

ROWS=number

Specifies the height of the text box in rows.

TABINDEX=number

Specifies the text area's place in the tabbing order.

Parent Tags

\<A>, \<ACRONYM>, \<ADDRESS>, \<APPLET>, \<B>, \<BDO>, \<BIG>, \<BLOCKQUOTE>, \<BODY>, \<CAPTION>, \<CENTER>, \<CITE>, \<CODE>, \<DD>, \<DEL>, \<DFN>, \<DIV>, \<DT>, \<EM>, \<FIELDSET>, \<FONT>, \<FORM>, \<H1>, \<H2>, \<H3>, \<H4>, \<H5>, \<H6>, \<I>, \<IFRAME>, \<INS>, \<KBD>, \<LABEL>, \<LEGEND>, \<LI>, \<NOFRAMES>, \<NOSCRIPT>, \<OBJECT>, \<P>, \<PRE>, \<Q>, \<S>, \<SAMP>, \<SMALL>, \<SPAN>, \<STRIKE>, \<STRONG>, \<SUB>, \<SUP>, \<TD>, \<TH>, \<TT>, \<U>, \<VAR>

Content Tags

None.

Sample HTML

```
<BODY>
<FORM ACTION="http://www.mysite.com/cgis/form1.pl" METHOD="POST">
<TEXTAREA NAME="comments" ROWS="10" COLS="60">
</TEXTAREA>
<INPUT TYPE=SUBMIT VALUE="Send">
<INPUT TYPE=RESET VALUE="Clear">
</FORM>
```

Script Tags

Script tags invoke inline programming scripts that execute on the client side within a Web document. These client-side scripts can be embedded directly into HTML or loaded from separate files. You will need to be adept in some specific programming language—such as C, JavaScript, VBScript, etc.—to benefit from these tags.

<NOSCRIPT>...</NOSCRIPT>

The NOSCRIPT tags define alternate content to use when the browser is unable to use the data defined by the SCRIPT tag.

Style Tip

Not all browsers support scripting or the specific scripting language used in a particular script; therefore, providing alternate content for these users is a good idea.

Attributes

None.

Parent Tags

<BLOCKQUOTE>, <BODY>, <BUTTON>, <CENTER>, <DD>, <DIV>, <FIELDSET>, <FORM>, <IFRAME>, <LI>, <NOFRAMES>, <NOSCRIPT>, <OBJECT>, <TD>, <TH>

Content Tags

<A>, <ACRONYM>, <ADDRESS>, <APPLET>, <B>, <BASEFONT>, <BDO>, <BIG>, <BLOCKQUOTE>, <BR>, <BUTTON>, <CENTER>, <CITE>, <CODE>, <DFN>, <DIR>, <DIV>, <DL>, <EM>, <FIELDSET>, <FONT>, <FORM>, <H1>, <H2>, <H3>, <H4>,

<H5>, <H6>, <HR>, <I>, <IFRAME>, <IMG>, <INPUT>, <ISINDEX>, <KBD>, <LABEL>, <MAP>, <MENU>, <NOFRAMES>, <NOSCRIPT>, <OBJECT>, <OL>, <P>, <PRE>, <Q>, <S>, <SAMP>, <SCRIPT>, <SELECT>, <SMALL>, <SPAN>, <STRIKE>, <STRONG>, <SUB>, <SUP>, <TABLE>, <TEXTAREA>, <TT>, <U>, <UL>, <VAR>

Sample HTML

```
<HEAD>
<SCRIPT LANGUAGE="VBScript">
{script statements and instructions}
</SCRIPT>
<NOSCRIPT>
Your browser does not support our script, please follow this <A
HREF="http://www.domain.com/special/noscript.htm">link to an alternate
form of the same content.</A>
</NOSCRIPT>
</HEAD>
```

<SCRIPT>...</SCRIPT>

The SCRIPT tag informs the browser that the text contained within the tags should be rendered as script instead of as content for the Web page.

Style Tip

Scripts provide an easy way to add interactivity to pages without accessing external applets or programs. Use scripts to display messages based on user URL choices, to create customized pages, and more. Keep in mind that not all browsers can execute scripts—always provide alternative content to match material contained within scripts.

NOTE Internet Explorer and Netscape Navigator allow developers to use scripts to create such effects as the highlighting of items as the mouse moves over them. Find out more at `http://www.w3.org/TR/WD-html40/interact/scripts.html`.

Attributes

TYPE="scripting language"

Defines the scripting language type for the script text enclosed by the tag pair. The value of scripting language must be an Internet Media Type (MIME); see `ftp://ftp.isi.edu/in-notes/iana/assignments/media-types`.

LANGUAGE="scripting language"

Specifies what scripting language the enclosed script was written in, such as JavaScript and VBScript.

SRC="URL"

Specifies the URL of an external script. If this attribute is used, all text enclosed by the tag pair is ignored.

Parent Tags

<A>, <ACRONYM>, <ADDRESS>, <APPLET>, <B>, <BDO>, <BIG>, <BLOCKQUOTE>, <BODY>, <BUTTON>, <CAPTION>, <CENTER>, <CITE>, <CODE>, <DD>, <DEL>, <DFN>, <DIV>, <DT>, <EM>, <FIELDSET>, <FONT>, <FORM>, <H1>, <H2>, <H3>, <H4>, <H5>, <H6>, <HEAD>, <I>, <IFRAME>, <INS>, <KBD>, <LABEL>, <LEGEND>, <LI>, <NOFRAMES>, <NOSCRIPT>, <OBJECT>, <P>, <PRE>, <Q>, <S>, <SAMP>, <SMALL>, <SPAN>, <STRIKE>, <STRONG>, <SUB>, <SUP>, <TD>, <TH>, <TT>, <U>, <VAR>

Content Tags

None.

Sample HTML

```
<HEAD>
<SCRIPT LANGUAGE="VBScript">
{script statements and instructions}
</SCRIPT>
</HEAD>
```

HTML Extensions

The HTML 4 DTD is not the only brand of HTML you can use in your Web documents. Rogue tags and attributes abound, including proprietary markup from Microsoft and Netscape. We've gathered a list of these extensions to provide you with the most extensive possible HTML coverage.

While most of this information should remain consistent, check with both vendors for the latest details on their proprietary HTML.

TIP

Get the scoop on developing sites to be viewed with Microsoft Internet Explorer and Netscape Navigator at `http://www.microsoft.com/sitebuilder` and `http:// developer.netscape.com`.

In the sections that follow, only those tags or extensions that do not appear in the HTML 4 DTD are listed. They are identified by (N) for Netscape and (IE) for Microsoft. If details are not provided, they did not differ from the 4 DTD, or they were not available.

<BGSOUND> (IE)

The BGSOUND (background sound) tag links a sound file of .WAV, .AU, or .MID/.MIDI to a document. The sound plays when the page is accessed.

Attributes

SRC=URL

Defines the URL of the sound file.

LOOP=number/INFINITE

Specifies how many times a sound will repeat or loop. If INFINITE is specified, it loops indefinitely.

<BLINK>...</BLINK> (N)

The BLINK tags cause enclosed text to blink on and off.

<Comment>...</Comment> (IE)

The COMMENT tags are the same as the <!-- ... --> tag.

<Iframe> (IE)

The IFRAME tag inserts a frame within a block of text so that you can insert a second HTML document there.

Attributes

NORESIZE (IE)

Prevents the user from resizing the frame.

<MARQUEE>...</MARQUEE> (IE)

The MARQUEE tags create a scrolling text marquee.

Attributes

ALIGN=(TOP|MIDDLE|BOTTOM)

Defines how text wraps around the marquee.

BEHAVIOR=(SCROLL|SLIDE|ALTERNATE)

Sets the scrolling behavior.

BGCOLOR=(#RRGGBB|colorname)

Sets the color of marquee text. (See Table F.1.)

DIRECTION=(LEFT|RIGHT)

Sets the direction of scrolling.

HEIGHT=number|"%"

Sets the height of the marquee in pixels or as a percentage.

WIDTH=number|"%"

Sets the width of the marquee in pixels or as a percentage.

HSPACE=number

Sets blank space in pixels to the left and right of the marquee.

VSPACE=number

Sets blank space in pixels above and below the marquee.

LOOP=number|INFINITE

Sets the number of times the message repeats.

SCROLLAMOUNT=number

Sets the number of pixels between repeated messages.

SCROLLDELAY=number

Sets the delay in number of milliseconds before the next display.

<MULTICOL>...</MULTICOL> (N)

The MULTICOL (multiple column) formatting tag creates a multiple column display of text.

Attributes

COLS=number

Defines the number of text columns.

GUTTER="gwidth"

Defines the space between columns. The default is 10 pixels.

WIDTH="colwidth"

Defines the width of the columns.

<NOBR>...</NOBR> (N, IE)

The NOBR (no break) tags turn off line breaking and render text without line breaks.

<NOEMBED>...</NOEMBED> (N)

The NOEMBED tags provide alternate content for browsers that do not support the plug-in required for an inline media type.

<SPACER>...</SPACER> (N)

The SPACER tags are used to control spacing by forcing white space around the enclosed elements.

Attributes

ALIGN=(LEFT|RIGHT|TOP|ABSMIDDLE|ABSBOTTOM|TEXTTOP|MIDDLE|BASELINE|BOTTOM)

Defines alignment of external text. Only applies when TYPE=BLOCK. Default is BOTTOM.

HEIGHT=number

Defines the height in pixels. Applies only when TYPE=BLOCK.

SIZE=number

When TYPE=HORIZONTAL, specifies the absolute width of blank space. When TYPE=VERTICAL, specifies the absolute height of blank space.

TYPE=(HORIZONTAL|VERTICAL|BLOCK)

Determines the action of the spacer—space between words (HORIZONTAL), space between lines of text (VERTICAL), or as an invisible image (BLOCK).

WIDTH=number

Defines the width in pixels. Applies only when TYPE=BLOCK.

<WBR> (N, IE)

The WBR (word break) tag inserts a line break in a block of <NOBR> text.

INDEX

Note to the Reader: Throughout this index **boldface** page numbers indicate primary discussions of a topic. *Italicized* page numbers indicate illustrations.

B

<B> tags, **1009–1010**
b.htmlf code, 458
backbone providers, 119
backends, **250**
  advertising effects on, **579**
  building, **270–271**
  commerce servers for, **279–282**
  commercial software for, **272–286**, *273*
  content management software for, **276–277**
  in development process, **82–83**
  expandability of, **266–267**
  file management in, **261–266**
  file structure in, **251–261**, *252*
  flexibility in, **250–251**
  maintaining, 12, **46–47**
  open source software for, **286–291**
  organization of, **100–102**
  personalization software for, **282–284**, *284*
  for QA processes, 318, **624**
  script languages for, **425–426**
  testing, **284–286**
  tools for, **268–270**, *269*
  upgrading, 14
  for workflow, **267–270**, *269*, *275*
BACKGROUND attribute, 936
background music, 613
background sound, **1040**
backgrounds
  color of, 191, 230, **935–937**
  images for, 936
  for movies, 543
  style sheets for, 914, **1008–1009**
  transparent, **237**, *237*
  variables for, 191
backslashes (\) for scripts, 486
backups
  by ISPs, 120
  for servers, 122
  for sound, 555
balanced elements in MediaDiet case study, 848
balanced tags in XML, 766

bandwidth
  in development process, **104**
  for multimedia, 536
  for push channels, 834
  for QA processes, **626**
  for streaming video, 547
  in usability, **315–316**
  in Web access, **116–118**
banner advertising, **567–568**
  effectiveness of, **573–575**, *574*
  HTML, **575**
  Java, **576**
  JavaScript, **575–576**
  Shockwave, 576
  specs for, **571–572**
Banner Server Software website, 586
bars (|) in scripts, 487
<BASE> tags, **986–987**
<BASEFONT> tags, **1010–1011**
BASELINE alignment option
  for objects, 996
  for tables, 977
Basic Server, 556
Basic Server Plus, 556
BBEdit HTML editor, 58
<BDO> tags, 945
begin attributes, 800
begindrag() function, 515, 517–518
BEHAVIOR attribute, 1041
BELOW option, 974
benchmarks, **76–79**, *77–78*
beta versions, 836
BGCOLOR attribute
  with <BODY>, 936
  with <MARQUEE>, 1041
  with <TABLE>, 973
  with <TD>, 977
  with <TH>, 980
  with <TR>, 982
BGPROPERTIES attribute, 936
<BGSOUND> tags, **1040**
bi-directional algorithm tags, 945
bibliographic references, **949**
<BIG> tags, **1011**

G

H

I

M

Q

R

S

T

U

W

From the Experts...

Who bring you Mark Minasi's #1 best-selling *Complete PC Upgrade & Maintenance Guide,* Sybex now presents...

The Complete Network Upgrade & Maintenance Guide	The Complete Website Upgrade & Maintenance Guide	The Complete PC Upgrade & Maintenance Guide, 9th edition
BY MARK MINASI, JIM BLANEY, CHRIS BRENTON	**BY LISA SCHMEISER**	**BY MARK MINASI**
The Ultimate Networking Reference—this book is a practical and comprehensive guide to implementing, upgrading, and maintaining networks, from small office LANs to enterprise-scale WANs and beyond.	Destined to be the industry's ultimate Website reference, this book is the most comprehensive and broad-reaching tome, created to help you turn an existing site into a long-lasting sophisticated, dynamic, effective tool.	After selling nearly <u>one million copies</u> of its previous editions, the 9th edition carries on the tradition with detailed troubleshooting for the latest motherboards, sound cards, video boards, CD-ROM drives, and all other multimedia devices.
ISBN: 0-7821-2259-0 1536 pp., $69.99	ISBN: 0-7821-2315-5 912 pp., $49.99	ISBN: 0-7821-2357-0 1600 pp., $59.99

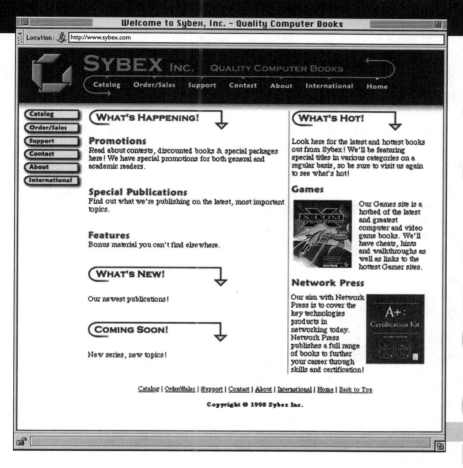

What's on the CD

The CD-ROM that comes with this book is packed with all the code mentioned throughout the book plus evaluation copies of these valuable utilities:

Adobe® After Effects®   This award-winning software allows you to add composites, animation, and visual effects to your site. (Windows and Mac)

Adobe® Premier®   Use Premier to produce broadcast-quality movies for video, multimedia, or the Web. (Windows and Mac)

Allaire HomeSite   This HTML editor allows you to create websites in a snap. (Windows)

The Apache server   This speedy, stable, and powerful Web server is considered tops in the field. (Windows, Linux, Irix, and Solaris)

Boutell MapEdit   Create both client-side and server-side clickable imagemaps with this graphical editor. (Windows and Mac)

Equilibrium DeBabelizer   This helpful tool eases conversion and management of digital images, animation, and video for delivery on the Web, in print, or in multimedia. (Windows and Mac)

Macromedia Dreamweaver   This tool combines the productivity of a visual HTML editor with flexibility and control over source code. (Windows and Mac)

Nico Mak WinZip   This is the indispensable archive utility for Windows. (Windows)

Ulead GIF Animator   Create animations for the Web with this easy, fast, and powerful utility. (Windows)